Signed, Sealed, and Delivered

Signed, Sealed, and Delivered

Highlights of the Miller Record

Edited by
Sarah Eby-Ebersole

Compiled by
Office of Planning and Budget

MERCER UNIVERSITY PRESS
Macon, Georgia

ISBN 0-86554-648-7
MUP/H484

Mercer University Press
6316 Peake Road
Macon, Georgia 31210-3960

10 9 8 7 6 5 4 3 2 1

∞The paper used in this publication meets the minimum requirementsof American National Standard for Information Sciences—Permanence of Paper for Printed Library Materials, ANSI Z39.48-1984.

Library of Congress Cataloging-in-Publication Data
Signed, sealed, and delivered: highlights of the Miller administration/ edited by Zell Miller.

p. cm.
Includes index.
ISBN 0-86554-648-7 (alk. paper)
1. Georgia—politics and government—1951– 2. Miller, Zell, 1932-. I. Miller, Zell, 1932–
F291.2.S5 1999
975.8'043—dc21 98-50767
CIP

Table of Contents

A Dedication

No governor has ever been blessed with a more loyal and effective staff. No governor ever had better agency heads. All of these hard-working men and women consistently made me look better than I was. To them this volume is lovingly and gratefully dedicated. The accomplishments between these covers are theirs more than mine. I may have *signed* it, but they *sealed* and *delivered* it.

Zell Miller
October 1998

A Special Thanks

I want to acknowledge and give a special thanks to Lieutenant Governor Pierre Howard and Speaker Tom Murphy, and to all the members of the Georgia General Assembly. What is between these covers would never have been accomplished without their support. As they have often heard me say, “Governors advocate; legislators legislate and appropriate.”

Zell Miller

The Governor with Tom Murphy

The Governor with Pierre Howard

Introduction

To the readers of *Signed Sealed and Delivered*:

On January 14, 1991, immediately after taking the oath of office as Georgia's 79th Governor, Zell Miller presented the goals of his administration to the citizens of Georgia. "We draw strength from our heritage, but we set our course for the horizon ahead," he said. "Our future prosperity depends not just on strong backs, but on strong minds. Georgia faces a choice: We can plow new ground, or we can let the weeds grow."

Governor Miller made it clear that he had chosen to plow new ground. The central purpose of his administration would be to prepare Georgia for the 21st century, and strengthening education was at the heart of that task. He wanted to create a culture of higher expectations in Georgia, so that students would not ask "whether" to go to college or technical school, but "where." He also wanted to make government leaner and more efficient, to preserve more of Georgia's natural environment, to make streets and neighborhoods safer, and to give Georgia's citizens a tax break every time they sat down to eat a meal.

He dedicated his administration to real Georgians—the farmer who planted his own crops and baled his own hay, the small businesswoman who stayed open late and called her customers by their first names, the entrepreneur who built a better mousetrap or microchip, the senior citizen who feared having to choose between eating and heating her house, the young family struggling to pay for daycare and save for college at the same time, and to every Georgian who worked and saved and sometimes came up a little short at the end of the month. It was these salt-of-the-earth citizens of the state whose lives Governor Miller wanted to touch in tangible ways that they could understand and appreciate.

Perhaps the proudest achievements of the Miller Administration occurred in education. They included national firsts like statewide voluntary prekindergarten for all four-year-olds whose parents wanted to enroll them, and the HOPE Scholarship Program for students at Georgia's colleges, universities and technical institutes. They included unprecedented amounts of technology for classrooms, labs and media centers, and unique partnerships between higher education and the business sector. Over eight years as Governor, Miller injected an additional $3.1 billion into education, increasing total education funding to $7,067,963,618. The entire state budget had not reached that milestone until Fiscal Year (FY) 1990—the year before he took office.

While the entire state budget increased 60.2 percent during the Miller Administration, the education budget skyrocketed by 78.4 percent. Education's portion of the budget soared to putting a more vigorous emphasis on education required a broad-based commitment. The state lottery was partially responsible for the large increase in state funding. From the time the first lottery funds were appropriated in FY 1994, until Miller left office in FY 1999, the lottery pumped $3.013 billion into education. Miller also increased state general funding at the same time.

Large spending increases without a plan or accountability do not necessarily translate into classroom improvement, which was Miller's first and paramount goal. But the Governor had a plan for education when he took office, and that plan was followed. Thus, the budget numbers were an indication of the high priority Miller placed on education and a reflection of the accomplishments outlined in this book.

With lottery funds, the Governor had two important goals—to launch a voluntary prekindergarten program for four-year-old children and to provide scholarships to students who maintained high grades. The lottery-funded prekindergarten program was successful beyond the Governor's dreams. By the time he left office in the 1998-99 school year, 61,000 children were being served by that program each year at an annual cost of almost $218 million. Prekindergarten was expected to make a major difference in future years by preparing children to perform at a higher level of achievement, the ultimate goal of education.

HOPE scholarships were unique to Georgia. No other state had such a far-reaching program. President Clinton liked the program so much he proposed a national scholarship program based on HOPE, which stood for Helping Outstanding Pupils Educationally. The scholarship provided financial assistance for college to students who graduated from a Georgia public or private high school with at least a B average. Those attending Georgia's public colleges or universities received free tuition and mandatory fees, plus

---

NOTE: The state fiscal year ran from July 1 to the following June 30, and was referred to by the year in which the latter half of it fell. For example, Fiscal Year (FY) 1991 began on July 1, 1990 and continued through June 30, 1991. Governor Miller took office on January 14, 1991, midway through FY 1991.57.05 percent of total state spending from 50.7 percent in the original FY 1991 budget.

a book allowance. Those attending private institutions in the state received a scholarship of $3,000 a year. If they kept up a B average, year by year, those benefits continued through all four years. Any Georgia high school graduate could enroll in a diploma program at a technical institute on a HOPE scholarship. HOPE offered a post-secondary education to many students who could not have afforded it previously. The $213 million budget for FY 1999 assisted approximately 160,000 students. By the end of the Miller Administration, some 331,000 Georgia students had gone to college or a technical school on a HOPE scholarship.

Funding prekindergarten and HOPE scholarships alone would have made the Georgia Lottery a treasure for education. But lottery funds were also sufficient enough to appropriate $625 million for technology and $581.5 million for school construction during the Miller years.

The technology expenditures would have a major impact on education during the Miller Administration and for years to follow. These funds provided computers, satellite dishes and other information technology for public school classrooms and media centers, colleges and universities, public libraries and technical institutes. They created training centers to give teachers the skills they needed to use technology to raise student achievement. They linked all of the libraries of Georgia's 34 public colleges and universities and made it possible for any student in the University System to use the resources of all libraries at all institutions. All public libraries and technical institutes were also linked to GALILEO, the University System's massive online library, and all public schools, colleges, universities, technical institutes and libraries provided with direct access to the Internet.

In addition to lottery-funded technology, the Governor used the funds from a telephone over-earnings case to establish a hard-wired communications network called the Georgia Statewide Academic and Medical System (GSAMS) that included over 400 sites by the end of his administration. This system allowed up to a dozen educational sites to be interactive simultaneously, and delivered medical care from experts at the Medical College of Georgia to rural hospitals around the state in a telemedicine program that the *New York Times* called the most sophisticated in the nation.

The most effective way to improve education was to put better teachers into the classrooms. The best way to do that was to increase teacher salaries at a faster pace than other states in order to attract more highly qualified teachers. Over the second term of his administration, Governor Miller pursued that goal by giving teachers in public schools, colleges and universities, and technical institutes a six percent pay raise each year for four straight years. He succeeded in making the average salary of Georgia's public school teachers competitive with the average national salary. Based on projections,

Georgia teachers moved to the top of the salary range throughout the entire South during the administration's final year. The challenge for the next Governor would be to keep them there.

In 1992, the average faculty salary at four-year institutions in the University System of Georgia ranked seventh among the states that comprised the Southern Regional Education Board. Miller wanted to move Georgia's average salary to number one among the SREB states, and the FY 1999 budget achieved that goal.

Governor Miller had another major goal for the University System—a larger building program to cope with the significant student enrollment increases Georgia's 34 public colleges and universities had experienced in prior decades. Many years prior, the state had implemented a regular annual program to meet the facility needs of its K-12 public schools, but higher education facilities had not kept pace with a rising enrollment. An appropriation of $206,925,000 for University System construction in the 1998 legislative session brought the total spending on new buildings for the system during the Miller Administration to more than $1 billion ($1,052,367,090).

A major reason for Miller's focus on education was to make sure that Georgia workers had the knowledge and training required for highly skilled jobs. Thus, Georgia's technical institutes were another important component of the educational delivery system. In a rapidly changing workplace, the type of technical training provided by the state was becoming more and more important. The Governor felt this area of education needed a significant boost, including increased operating money and expanded facilities to keep pace with a climbing enrollment and make technical education more accessible to all Georgians.

To fulfill those needs, the budget of the Department of Technical and Adult Education grew from $127 million to $271 million, an increase of 113 percent, and $215 million in capital improvements were made. To better serve students while holding administrative costs down, the Miller Administration opened 17 new satellite centers attached to existing technical institutes. By the time he left office, every Georgian had access to technical education within a reasonable driving distance.

The number of citizens who were illiterate or semi-literate handicapped Georgia's economic development efforts. Miller's first budget focused on this problem, and he continued to expand adult literacy initiatives in every successive budget, increasing the adult literacy budget by $10,962,190. One of the most important of his many adult literacy initiatives was to locate at least one full-time adult literacy teacher in every county of Georgia. Another 110 part-time adult literacy teachers further improved the delivery of community literacy services.

Beyond education, one of the highest priorities for Governor Miller was economic development, because he knew that a vibrant economy would provide a higher standard of living for all citizens. In searching for new approaches to a long-time priority, Miller wanted to involve the vast capabilities of the University System. A number of university system institutions had been engaged in economic development activities before Miller became Governor, but these efforts were lodged within the service missions of their parent institutions. Under the Miller Administration, economic development was incorporated into both the research and academic missions of the University System as well as its service mission.

The Georgia Research Alliance embraced all six of Georgia's major research universities—public and private—in a unique partnership with each other and with the private sector. Soon after its creation, Miller made state government a partner in this effort to spur high-quality, high-tech economic growth. The Alliance conducted practical applied research that would boost industry in the areas of telecommunications, biotechnology and environmental technology. Between FY 1993 and FY 1999, the Miller Administration invested over $200 million in the Research Alliance, which attracted more than $500 million in federal and private funds.

Governor Miller also called on higher education to improve the competitiveness of Georgia's traditional manufacturing industries. The state spent $44.4 million for the Traditional Industries Program to serve the research needs of three traditional manufacturing industries—pulp and paper, textile and apparel, and food processing. These funds were matched by the industries.

Economic development was also brought into the academic mission of the University System through the creation of ICAPP, the Intellectual Capital Partnership Program, which focused on workforce preparation, both for the immediate needs of specific private industry partners and for the state's broader, longer-term needs for college-educated workers.

Transportation was always a central ingredient of any strong economic development plan. Improved highways were fundamentally important to locating industry and business, and especially to boosting rural and small community economies. The Governor's Road Improvement Program (GRIP) was the state's tool for building a better transportation system. During the Miller Administration, the state allocated slightly more than one billion dollars to continue work on the 2,479-mile-long system. This funding allowed construction of about 560 miles-—23 percent of the entire GRIP program—based on the cost of construction at the close of the administration.

Another key element of economic development was strong trade and ports programs that not only promoted the export of Georgia products throughout the world, but also made Georgia a gateway to the world for the entire Southeast. The Miller Administration budgeted $221,314,000 for port construction, launched construction of a new, higher bridge to open the Brunswick Harbor to the tallest ships, presided over the deepening of the Savannah ship channel to 42 feet, and took the initial steps toward further deepening at both the Savannah and Brunswick ports. Targeted trade initiatives increased the export of Georgia products by 104 percent.

Two initiatives in 1998 would be important in any summary of economic development efforts during the 1990s. One was the new alliance between the Department of Industry, Trade and Tourism and the Department of Community Affairs to staff state development teams with a responsibility for promoting regional and rural development. The Atlanta metropolitan area had been the largest growth area in Georgia and one of the largest in the nation since World War II. More emphasis was needed to help the remaining areas of Georgia to share in the continuing growth. This new alliance between the Departments of Community Affairs and Industry, Trade and Tourism was designed to accomplish that goal by placing a team of state employees in each of 11 economic development regions outside Atlanta to coordinate state services in and for the region. A second initiative was a $35,350,000 program to upgrade and improve 28 general aviation airports in Georgia, so that businesses anywhere in the state would be within a 45-minute drive of a top-level general aviation airport with the capacity to handle corporate jets.

One of the most important initiatives of the Miller Administration had nothing to do with increased spending. Indeed, it had the opposite impact—reducing state spending for welfare. The administration abolished the old welfare entitlement system and replaced it with a new program called Temporary Assistance for Needy Families (TANF).

Even before TANF, however, Governor Miller was dealing with the problems of increasing welfare dependency. Under his leadership, Georgia became a national leader in implementing reforms like requiring teenage mothers to remain with their families to qualify for benefits, refusing additional benefits for children conceived while on welfare, requiring community service in exchange for benefits, shifting the focus of county welfare offices toward helping clients find jobs, and assisting at-risk and welfare families with child care. As a result of these efforts and an improving economy, welfare enrollment peaked at 143,489 families in August 1994, then began to decline. The decrease accelerated with the implementation of TANF on January 1, 1997, replacing the old welfare system with a new system that provided a maximum of four years of cash assistance while helping to prepare recipients to find jobs.

By the end of the Miller Administration, the average welfare caseload was projected at just over 85,100, a decrease of 41 percent in five years. This decrease of some 58,000 caseloads reduced actual cash payments by more than $100 million. A significant portion of the savings was used to provide transportation, child care, GED education, treatment for drug abuse and other services needed to help welfare recipients become productive citizens.

Governor Miller also slowed runaway Medicaid growth. In the 10 years before he took office, the Medicaid budget had increased 376 percent. It continued to increase at a more modest pace, but had climbed to more than $1.3 billion by July of 1995, so Miller decided to put on the brakes. Even as he expanded services to pregnant women and children, he flattened Medicaid budget growth through managed care and tougher fraud and abuse provisions. The cumulative increase in the Medicaid budget during his last three years in office totaled less than three percent.

The protection of environmentally sensitive land was another high priority for Governor Miller, and two of his initiatives dramatically expanded the natural land under state protection—Preservation 2000 and RiverCare 2000. Preservation 2000 was created to protect 100,000 acres of natural land for future generations to enjoy. That goal was met in 1996 with 105,602 acres at 56 different locations, procured with $65 million in state bond funds and $57 million in private and corporate donations of land and funds.

RiverCare 2000 was modeled on Preservation 2000. Launched in 1995, its goal was to protect and preserve the more than 70,250 miles of freshwater rivers and streams in Georgia, not only through land acquisition, but also through covenants with other landowners in these river corridors. Under Miller's leadership, a total of $45.8 million was committed to this program from state, federal and private funds, with nearly 10,000 acres purchased and other acreage under consideration when he left office. Of $20 million in bond funds for RiverCare in the FY 1999 budget, $15 million was earmarked for the Chattahoochee River corridor, which had been designated one of the most abused rivers in the nation.

One of the fastest-growing departments during the 1990s was Corrections, as Governor Miller opened a record number of prison beds. The prison expansion was triggered by the sentencing of more criminals to incarceration, by tougher laws requiring longer sentences and by compelling prisoners to serve out more of their terms before being paroled. The additional bed capacity also enabled Governor Miller, early in his administration, to end the practice of managing inmate population through the early release of criminals. During Miller's tenure, correctional spending increased by a total of $322.4 million, or 68 percent. The increase funded an expansion in prison capacity from 24,386 beds to 44,745 beds, setting a record of 20,621 beds opened during the Miller Administration. Miller left another 1,710 beds in the pipeline for future opening to increase the total bed capacity to 46,455.

Juvenile crime also became a serious problem in the early 1990s, and beginning in 1995, the Governor was forced to triple juvenile facilities from 1,457 beds to 4,081 beds.

When Governor Miller took office, the nation was in a recession. State revenues were slipping below the level of appropriations, and the reserves were empty. Miller refused to raise taxes. He cut expenditures by a total of $944 million and abolished about 5,000 state jobs over a period of three years, easing the state through the recession and preparing the way for prosperity. He used the budget cuts to prune low-priority programs and reorganize state government for greater efficiency, establishing a pattern of forcing government to set priorities and focus on achieving results that continued throughout his administration.

It was this disciplined approach to state finance that enabled the Miller Administration to achieve a remarkable array of accomplishments while simultaneously reducing taxes by $831 million through the three largest tax cuts in Georgia's history—two income tax cuts and the removal of the state sales tax from groceries. The second and largest of the three tax cuts, which abolished the four percent sales tax on groceries, was completed on October 1, 1998. This tax cut alone saved taxpayers more than $500 million a year. The third Miller tax cut, which was the second largest, increased the personal exemption on income taxes for both taxpayers and dependents to $2,700 (the prior exemption was $1,500 for taxpayers and $2,500 for dependents), and raised the deduction for citizens over age 65 from $700 to $1,300. The increase in the personal exemption impacted 5.2 million Georgians, and the increased deduction for the elderly affected 300,000 citizens.

As Georgia emerged from the recession of the early 1990s, its economy became one of the most active in the nation. With a million new citizens from 1990 through 1997, Georgia ranked fourth in numerical population growth and sixth in percentage growth. Many newcomers moved to Georgia because of the 630,000 new jobs created during the Miller Administration—an average of more than 2,000 new jobs a week. During the same time, 1990 through 1997, total personal income increased 59.3 percent, ranking Georgia sixth among all states in income growth. By the end of 1997, per capita income of Georgians had risen to 94 percent of the average American's income.

The end of an administration is a time to look back and sum up the accomplishments of an entire time in office. This book summarizes some of the accomplishments of Governor Zell Miller's administration, and offers a reflective look at the overall impact of eight great years for the people of Georgia.

I. Efficient and Effective Government

There is no such thing as "government money." There is only "taxpayers' money"... and I am convinced that we must be very deliberate about identifying the priorities that taxpayers want accomplished with their money, and then focus on doing those things as efficiently and effectively as possible.

Governor Zell Miller, December 10, 1996

Fiscal Management

I've always believed that government can be an agent of change to accomplish positive good for the benefit of the public, but that doesn't mean we have to have big government. The issue is not whether we have more government or less government. We need wise government that provides fundamental services to its citizens in the most efficient way possible and not in an indifferent, wasteful fashion.... We should be asking not only how much we spend, but also how sound are the purposes we are spending it for.

Governor Zell Miller, August 18, 1991

Financial strategy and planning in the face of recession

Fiscal Year (FY) 1991, the first to feel the hand of the new Governor, had begun on July 1, 1990, after an ominous end to FY 1990. The budget in FY 1990 had been $7.4 billion and had included a one percent increase in the sales tax which had provided an additional $687 million. However, even with that tax increase, when the fiscal year ended on June 30, 1990, the net treasury receipts fell short, totaling only $7.2 billion. The entire Revenue Shortfall Reserve of $194 million was used to help make up the difference between actual revenue collections and the FY 1990 budget. The remainder was covered by delaying some expenditures. The recession was upon the state and would greet Governor-elect Miller with the most difficult budget challenges any Georgia Governor had ever faced.

NOTE: The state fiscal year ran from July 1 to the following June 30, and was referred to by the year in which the latter half of it fell. For example, Fiscal Year (FY) 1991 began on July 1, 1990 and continued through June 30, 1991. Governor Miller took office on January 14, 1991, midway through FY 1991.

On August 21, 1990, then-Governor Joe Frank Harris had sent a memorandum to all department heads saying that his FY 1991 budget estimate would likely be short by $332 million. The plan was to cut budgets by $190 million and make up the rest by replacing cash appropriated for capital outlay projects with bond proceeds. The agencies were asked to submit voluntary budget cut proposals. The fact that a $200 million shortfall still occurred espite such precautions caused Governor Miller to press for revisions in the budget act, giving the Governor more authority to control expenditures during times of budget crisis.

Revenue growth rates changed dramatically from the FY 1990 budget through the FY 1991 supplemental budget, which was the first budget recommended by Governor Miller. The following captures these changes:

FY 1990 over FY 1989 without new sales tax increase: 5.9 percent

FY 1990 over FY 1989 including new sales tax increase: 16.7 percent

FY 1991 original over FY 1990 5.1 percent

FY 1991 revised (Governor Miller) over FY 1990 (Governor Harris) 0.25 percent

Zell Miller's first budget action as Governor-elect was to reduce the revenue estimate for FY 1991 and make expenditure cuts to balance the budget for the remainder of the year. He reduced the FY 1991 revenue estimate by $359 million, establishing a rate of revenue growth of 0.25 percent over the FY 1990 estimate, or practically a "no growth budget" for FY 1991 over FY 1990.

The Office of Planning and Budget had prepared recommendations for cuts in the fall of 1990, but Miller's cuts went beyond OPB's initial recommendation. On December 11, 1990, he sent a memorandum to all department heads announcing yet another one percent cut to what they had already submitted. The total reduction would be six percent for the common budget object classes, four percent for institutional budgets (prisons and hospitals), and three percent for "life-safety" institutions. In that same memo, Miller directed agency heads to reduce personnel costs by a minimum of two percent. This cut to personnel fit into his plan to downsize government as he had promised in his gubernatorial campaign. The net cut to expenditures was $175 million, with the difference made up with funds from the Midyear Adjustment Reserve plus other monies available from converting cash capital outlay projects to bonds.

During the same time that Governor-elect Miller was balancing the current year budget, he had to put together his first original budget. The FY 1992 budget he sent to the General Assembly was based on revenue growth projected to be 6.4 percent over his FY 1991 amended estimate ($7.426 to $7.9 billion), but only a 1.5 percent rate of growth over the original FY 1991 budget ($7.785 billion to $7.9 billion).

The recession continued during 1991 and was more drastic than either the Governor or the General Assembly had expected. By spring of 1991 it was clear that the revenues were not coming in at a sufficient rate to sustain the FY 1992 budget, which would begin July 1. The Governor took drastic action. State employees, both classified and unclassified, had been enjoying within-grade pay increases, a step increase given on their anniversary date until they reached a longevity period. The Governor had already vetoed language in the FY 1992 General Appropriations Act that would have allowed agencies to transfer funds into their personal services budget from other operating line items to pay for within-grade salary increases. He asked the State Merit System Board and the Office of Planning and Budget to withhold within-grade increases effective May 1, 1991. This was a precursor to other actions resulting in what would be one of the largest budget cuts the State of Georgia had ever made.

The recession was prolonged and a quick recovery was not in sight. On June 30, 1991, the state ended FY 1991 with net treasury receipts of $7,258,196,887 which was slightly less than one percent over the FY 1990 collections of $7,196,352,753. Revenues would have had to grow by almost nine percent to meet the FY 1992 budget as it had been passed during the 1991 legislative session. It was obvious from the actual FY 1991 revenue collection amount that the Governor's revenue estimate for the next fiscal year could not be reached without a major tax increase, and Governor Miller had already said that a tax increase was out of the question.

As a result, Governor Miller made a difficult decision. He would not just try to control agency expenditures voluntarily as had been done the year before. He had already called a special session for August 1991, as was usual every decade, for the purpose of reapportionment, or redrawing the boundary lines of congressional and state legislative districts to re-equalize them according to the 1990 census. He would broaden that legislative session to include the approval of an amended FY 1992 budget.

On July 10, 1991, Governor Miller issued a statement to the press that outlined bold and swift actions he would immediately take to begin to control expenditures even before the General Assembly gathered to approve his revised revenue estimate and expenditure reductions. He also set the stage for Georgia's largest budget reductions in modern times. He announced he would lower the revenue estimate for the fiscal year that had just begun by as much as $400 million. He also announced that a monthly furlough day would be required for each state employee, continuing indefinitely. However, the Fulton County Superior Court took this cost-containment tool away from the Governor almost immediately by issuing a restraining order on employee furloughs that was not appealed. Agencies were notified of this decision on July 25, 1991, and furloughs were never implemented.

Each agency was required to prepare a contingency plan to reduce its workforce by five percent. All hiring was frozen. Only the Office of Planning and Budget could grant an exception and only for the most critical positions. The start up of all new programs in the original FY 1992 budget was canceled, including the Governor's own new programs. Equipment and vehicle purchases were prohibited and travel restricted to only necessary trips.

In addition to these steps, the Governor sent a memorandum to all state agency heads on July 12, 1991, requiring them to put together a plan by July 19th to reduce the state funds in their budget by ten percent. This action gave the Governor flexibility and an array of options to use in preparing for the August 1991 special session. He made it clear that the actual budget cut would not be ten percent, which would have amounted to $790 million rather than the $400 million that he had announced two days before. He wanted the department heads to put together a list that represented the lower priorities of the department and included items that could be permanently removed from the agency. This information was used to compile a list of reductions that the Governor recommended for the amended FY 1992 budget.

After the Governor made his preliminary decisions on which programs to cut, he met with the leadership of the House and Senate before the special session was convened. He wanted to make sure the cuts would be acceptable and that the special session could be limited to two weeks as planned, without incurring additional expense when money was tight.

Noting that he had taken a scalpel to the budget, not a meat ax, the Governor pointed out that rather than across-the-board percentage-based cuts to budget categories, he had fine-tuned hundreds of individual budget items and even gone beyond budget items into individual operations and offices within state departments and agencies. Over 200 individual budget items were cut; another 200-plus were reduced. Programs that were inefficient, not producing results or had begun as pilots years before but never expanded, were cut. Service provision was evaluated statewide, and areas that had been receiving extra funding were brought back in line with the rest of the state. Administrative overhead was reduced, while basic services were preserved. The amended budget included more than a dozen calls for the reorganization or combination of functions across agency lines, resulting in administrative reorganization in the Departments of Corrections; Education; Natural Resources; Agriculture; and Industry, Trade and Tourism, as well as the Georgia Building Authority and the Board of Regents.

The Amended General Appropriations Act for FY 1992 (House Bill EX 1) was signed into law on August 21, 1991. The revenue estimate had been reduced by five percent or $385 million. The growth rate required to attain the new revenue estimate was now 3.5 percent as opposed to the original 6.4 percent. The budget cuts included 2,834 positions and a net reduction in expenditures of $414,737,703. It was the largest budget cut in Georgia history.

The special session budget included one particular Governor's recommendation freeing up $70 million in state funds that had been previously appropriated for debt service payments. The Governor recommended and the General Assembly approved using $70 million in motor fuel funds to replace general treasury funds that had been appropriated to pay debt service on bonds previously sold for construction and maintenance of roads and bridges. An additional $70 million in new bonds were approved to take the place of the motor fuel funds transferred from the Department of Transportation to the General Obligation Debt Sinking Fund. As a result, the Governor could cut $70 million in general funds from the General Obligation Debt Sinking Fund, and the Department of Transportation in turn would receive $70 million in bond proceeds, which could be matched with federal funds in the same manner as if it were motor fuel money. Although the process of selling the additional $70 million in bonds incurred a small net cost for the sale, this decision prevented major program cuts overall. The Governor reversed one-half of this financial move in the FY 1998 budget, when he recommended a $35 million addition to the General Obligation Debt Sinking Fund to replace a like amount of motor fuel funding that had been continually appropriated for debt service payment since the amended 1992 General Appropriations Act.

Soon after the special session ended, work began on the FY 1993 budget. However, the bad news continued regarding the economy. The recovery was slow, and more cuts would be needed to guarantee that the state would end FY 1992 in balance. The Governor had to take a strong hand in managing the state's money; there were no funds in the Revenue Shortfall Reserve. Even as he began work on the FY 1993 spending plan, Miller was also looking for places to cut even more from the special session budget.

On January 7, 1992, the Governor told the General Assembly that he was going to cut another $50 million from the revenue estimate he used for the special session amended budget, reducing the FY 1992 budget from $7,515 million to $7,465 million. Careful management by department heads had saved extra money, and delayed projects had generated enough surplus to balance the budget with this revised estimate without further job reductions. The Governor reminded the General Assembly that there were no reserves, and this extra cut would provide a cushion in the event the recession lingered. Later during the 1992 regular session, the Governor lowered the revenue estimate yet another $75 million because of further concerns about the recession. His final revenue estimate for FY 1992 was $7,390 million, exactly $510 million less than his original estimate of $7,900 million.

Never before had such a drastic reduction in expenditures been approved. The Governor's conservative fiscal policies and his ability to get the General Assembly's cooperation in adopting these budget cuts made it possible to keep vital services funded while dealing with a severe recession without increasing taxes.

The FY 1993 budget included a group of initiatives that the Governor called "Georgia Rebound." Georgia Rebound was designed to stimulate economic growth by improving education, preserving the environment, making streets safer, and providing investment in all parts of Georgia. The Governor chose a conservative revenue growth rate of 6.9 percent over the existing revenue sources to set the revenue estimate. The FY 1993 budget also included a revenue increase based on updating several user fees that the Williams Commission had suggested to capture the cost of providing the services. The growth of existing revenue sources was projected to generate $7,901 million and the fee increases would yield $273 million for a total FY 1993 estimate of $8,174 million.

In the 1993 session of the General Assembly the Governor recommended cutting the FY 1993 budget by $75 million as a precautionary measure. The recovery was slower than anyone thought it would be and again, the Governor was still without a Revenue Shortfall Reserve and could not risk ending the year with a close call. Budget Director Hank Huckaby sent out a memorandum on August 18, 1992, informing all agency heads that even though the state revenue collections had begun an upward trend, the national economic downturn was still not showing signs of quick recovery. Only $18 million in surplus was available for mid year adjustments, which was not even enough to take care of the student enrollment adjustment for public schools. Therefore, the Governor required each agency to propose a two percent reduction, except for the University System and the Department of Technical and Adult Education, whose reduction was limited to one percent. Not only did the agencies have to prepare a plan for the reduction, but they were also informed that they must absorb a rate increase in the employer health insurance rate of approximately two percent.

The revenue estimate for FY 1994 represented a 7.5 percent increase over the adjusted FY 1993 estimate ($8,714.5 million over $8,099 million). Governor Miller held firm with this estimate and was able to begin some important program improvements. The actual collections for FY 1994 provided funds to begin replenishing the Revenue Shortfall Reserve for the first time since Miller took office, and the year ended with $122 million in the this "rainy day" account. Governor Miller's cuts and fiscal management during those two turbulent years had finally paid off. He could safely say that his Georgia Rebound program was a catalyst in stimulating the recovery. It was important for the bond rating agencies to see Governor Miller's commitment to restoring the Revenue Shortfall Reserve and getting the state's financial house in order. Miller's tough stand against tax increases and his determination to give the taxpayers the most efficient and effective state government were instrumental not only in letting everyone know that he meant business and a new way of doing business was at hand, but also in enabling Georgia to maintain its high bond ratings.

Budget redirection: Fiscal Years 1997–1999

The recovery was in full steam by the time the Governor began to put his FY 1995 budget together in the latter part of 1993. His original revenue estimate was $9,396 million or a 7.8 percent increase over the FY 1994 estimate, and was later increased during the 1994 legislative session to $9,492 million, or 8.9 percent over the final estimate for FY 1994. Even so, he made it clear to department and agency heads that he had no intention of returning to business as usual. When their agency budget proposals, added together, represented a 31 percent increase in the state budget, he sent them back to the drawing board with instructions to limit their requests to those few new initiatives that were of utmost importance, and to search for existing money in their budgets to help fund them. "We can no longer continue to fund programs just because we have done so in the past," he told them. "Every program, those that are very old and those that are brand new, must be scrutinized and justified. Existing programs that cannot stand the scrutiny must be abolished or reduced in size, with the money reallocated to higher priorities. I am not talking about reducing costs through the sacrifice of services. I am talking about the opposite—providing more services at less cost; or delivering a needed service in a new and more efficient and effective manner."

The Governor's revenue estimate for FY 1995 accounted for a $100 million revenue loss from a tax cut. Not only would it the largest tax cut in Georgia history, but it also came on the heels of four years of tough stands on budget cuts and refusing to consider tax increases as a way out of the recession. At the end of FY 1995, the Revenue Shortfall Reserve and Midyear Adjustment Reserve were both full, and there was an additional $28 million of surplus besides. It had taken over four years to fill the reserves after they had been depleted at the end of FY 1990. The Governor was able to provide for one of the worst natural disasters in Georgia history, the 1994 flood, and to meet other program needs without budget cuts.

The FY 1996 budget, enacted during the 1995 General Assembly, was the first of Governor Miller's second term. Revenues were still holding strong and the 1996 Olympic Games would provide an additional boost. During the 1995 session the Governor made clear his commitment to education,

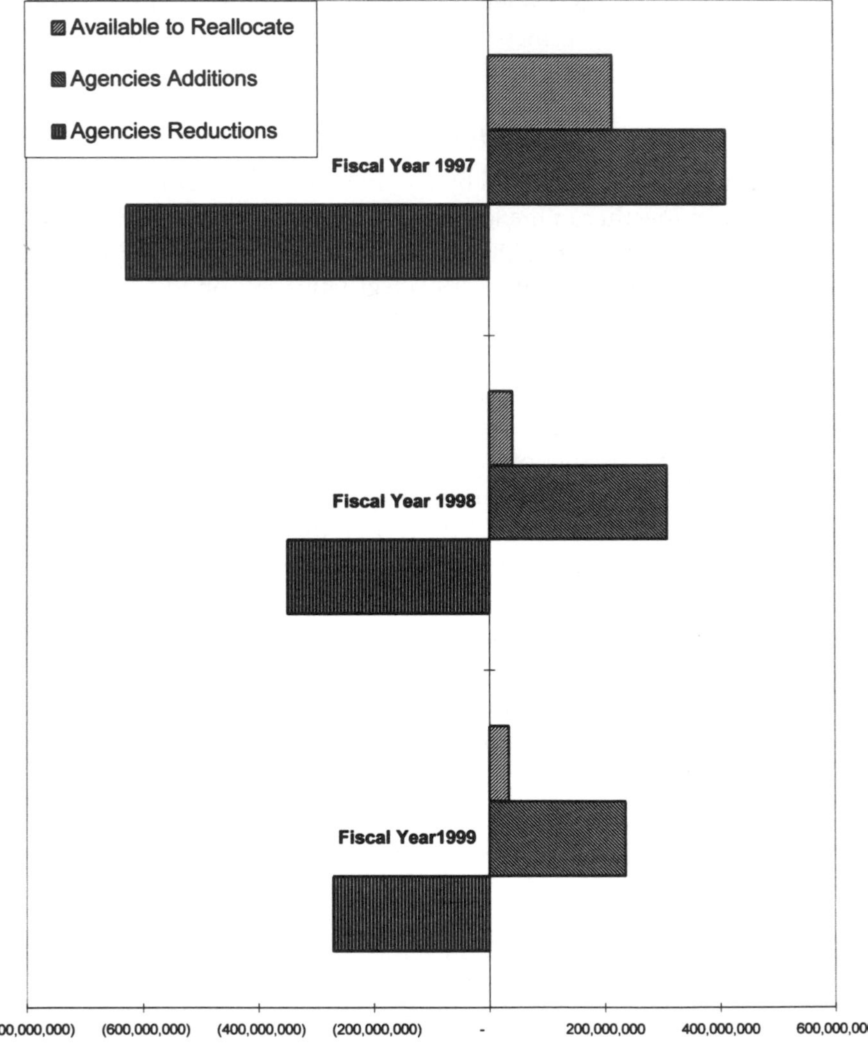

especially his promise to provide four consecutive six percent increases to make salaries for teachers and university faculty competitive in the South. The Governor's pay for performance plan for state employees was also ready to be implemented. However, the General Assembly had passed a tax cut in the 1995 session that Miller had had to veto because of constitutional problems, and Miller had promised to bring the legislature a tax cut proposal of his own to replace the ill-fated plan of 1995.

Immediately after the 1995 session, he promised to build a budget for FY 1997 that both fulfilled his pay raise commitment and included a tax cut, setting in motion the budget priorities and challenges for the remainder of his second term. He was advised that the economic recovery would begin to wane in FY 1996. That economic outlook combined with his commitment to a tax cut and to provide pay increases for teachers and university faculty, made it clear to Governor Miller that his FY 1997 budget could not be put together in the same way budgets had been compiled, not only during his past term but for the past several governors' administrations. After the FY 1996 budget was passed, Governor Miller began to set the stage for comprehensive reallocation of budget priorities.

A quick look at the total cost of implementing a tax cut of $100 million or more, addressing projected enrollment growth in Georgia's schools, providing another six percent salary increase for teachers and university faculty, opening new state prisons, and paying debt service for a minimum bond package showed that all of these things could not be funded without a change in the way the budget was put together. Even without a tax cut, early revenue projections indicated there would not be enough new money for the other priority items. Medicaid and the other health and social programs in the Department of Human Resources had not yet even been considered at this point. The Governor knew something had to be done quickly to change the way department heads approached their budget submission.

Miller decided that every agency would identify five percent of its budget to be offered up in reductions. Agencies were also allowed to identify how they would add back, or redirect, that same five percent if they were allowed to keep any of it. This was the essence of what the Governor called "budget redirection": to identify and cut or reduce lower priority items or programs in order to fund higher priorities, both within agencies and across agency lines. He pointed out to the department heads that his priorities for education, in particular the pay increase, and his resolve to balance the budget with a tax cut, would override almost all other priorities. Essentially, funds freed up by cutting lower priority programs, and from privatization and efficiency savings, would enable the Governor to balance his budget and at the same time provide a tax cut, fund education priorities, finance necessary construction and open new facilities. "This is about setting our priorities in an orderly fashion, and then 'squeezing down' state government so that it is tightly focused and efficient in achieving those priorities," he told his department heads.

The budget redirection process also had another feature. It limited agency requests for enhancements to an amount parallel to the anticipated rate of new revenue growth. Basically, Miller told agency heads that he only had a limited amount of new money to deal with and that they should be under the same constraint in requesting enhancements to their budgets. This milestone in state budgeting was instrumental not only in keeping agencies from wasting time developing and justifying unrealistic budget requests, but also in limiting debate on what new things needed to be considered.

Budget redirection took form in late May of 1995. The budget would be divided into four main sections: an adjusted base section; a redirection section divided into reductions and additions; a limited program enhancement section; and a capital outlay section that was unchanged. Traditionally, agencies' capital outlay requests were converted to bonds by the budget office, and agency heads already knew that all the state's capital outlay projects had to fit into the Governor's bond financing package.

To prepare for budget redirection, Governor Miller did something that had not been done in the prior 20 years. He gathered all the agency heads together and laid out the next year's budget strategy with them. The budget director, the state economist and the Governor met with all agency heads and made sure they understood what Miller's budget priorities were and how he would attain his goals. All agency heads left those meetings with a clear understanding that they would in some way participate in making the Governor's priorities balance with the fund availability after a major tax cut. Governor Miller emphasized three factors that were integral in his decision to move ahead with this budget redirection. One, he would not assume a continued high level of revenue growth. Two, he believed that the citizens wanted a better level of government services. Three, he believed that Georgia citizens did not think they were getting true value from their tax dollars, and thus were not willing to pay more to get the better level of service they expected.

Budget deferral: a new tool in controlling expenditures

In 1993, a section was added to the budget act that gave the Governor the authority to require state agencies to reserve such appropriations as specified by the Governor for budget reductions to be recommended to the General Assembly at its next regular session. Accordingly, as a prelude to budget redirection in FY 1997, Miller announced on June 30, 1995 that he would required the Office of Planning and Budget to give him a list of new programs that would be delayed until the 1996 General Assembly could act on the Governor's deferral plan. Many state agency heads received a letter from the budget director on June 30, 1995, reminding them of the Governor's upcoming redirection plan and including any of their expenditures that were to be deferred until the 1996 session of the General Assembly. It was the first time that this legal provision was used as a method to hold back on expenditures until the General Assembly could take official action. It was an historic and significant move.

The items deferred in the FY 1996 budget totaled $17,301,737. It is important to note that Miller included some of his own initiatives in the deferral list, including $1 million to add 25 new state troopers, which the General Assembly subsequently chose not to restore. The Governor's intent was to defer funding for any new jobs or initiatives that were designed to replace federal or privately funded programs.

Allotments for the first quarter's state funds for FY 1996 excluded all deferral items and these items were shown as recommended cuts in the Governor's supplemental budget for FY 1996. Even though the General Assembly did not cut most of the deferred items, especially the ones they had put into the budget, Miller's action established his firm control over the expenditure level for the next three years. This deferral action in FY 1996 also served as a clear message to department heads that the Governor would be aggressive in controlling expenditures and not allowing their expectations to override the tax cut plan that he had begun to put in place immediately after the 1995 session.

In FY 1997, his first year of budget redirection, the Governor's budget included $627 million in agency cuts from lower priorities, of which $412 million was added back to higher priorities within the same department, and the rest was freed up for Miller's statewide priorities such as the salary increase for teachers and the tax cut. Once the $627 million had been cut and the $412 million added back, the FY 1997 budget totaled $10,126 million, which was slightly less than the prior year's budget. Fund availability was projected at $10,804, with the difference available to fund Miller's priorities.

The Governor's first decision was to recommend a phased-in removal of the sales tax on groceries, a long-time personal goal which he had promoted since the late 1970s. It would be the largest tax cut in the history of the state, and at full implementation would take more than $500 million out of the annual revenue stream. The first phase would eliminate two of the four cents on the dollar as of October 1, 1996, removing $175 million from the revenue stream for FY 1997. The remaining two cents would be removed one at a time on October 1st of each of the following two years. The funds freed up through budget redirection allowed the Governor to lower his revenue estimate to account for the tax cut, without reducing the level of new funding available for high-priority items.

Two departmental budgets were critical in making this redirection system work in the first year: the Medicaid budget and the budget for the Department of Human Resources. Probably no other Governor made such a dramatic change in the Medicaid budget as Miller did for FY 1997. The reductions in Medicaid totaled $114.5 million while the additions amounted to $62.5 million for a net reduction of $52 million. Changes for the Department of Human Resources were equally dramatic with a total of $74 million in reductions and $31 million in additions for a net reduction of $43 million. Neither of these cuts involved reducing services. The medicaid savings resulted from a managed care initiative and from curbing fraud. The Human Resources savings resulted largely from declining welfare rolls.

Between these two agencies the Governor's budget recommendation made $95 million in existing funds available for other commitments, including $10 million for Medicaid to increase the amount of community services for the elderly and disabled. This was all done while the Governor was recommending a major tax cut and $310 million for a pay increase package.

The redirection process was well received by the General Assembly, who, despite making their usual changes, could not reverse its major impact. The tax cut and pay raise packages were politically popular, locking the members into accepting this major change in the budgeting process. The Governor made budget redirection easy to understand. There were no complicated formulas and no difficulty in seeing what was happening. The language of budget redirection was easy to understand and the General Assembly was prevented from side-stepping the issue of dealing with priorities. The Governor's budget redirection process had changed the budget culture for state government.

Governor Miller continued to use budget redirection for FY 1998 and FY 1999. In FY 1998, he cut $349 million from lower priorities, of which $308 million was returned to the agency of origin to be used for higher priorities. The FY 1999 budget cut $270 million from lower priorities, of which $236 million was returned to the agency it came from to be used for higher priorities.

Even though most redirected funds remained with the agency of origin in the second and third years, the continued use of budget redirection over three years dramatically transformed agency heads' budget expectations and strategy. A department head who did not receive a net reduction in the Governor's budget recommendation was considered a winner. Instead of competing with each other for new funding from revenue growth, agency heads ceded it to the Governor for statewide priorities. The continual evaluation and pruning demanded by budget redirection prompted agencies to cover routine cost increases internally, which preserved new funding for new initiatives.

Managing state debt: Attaining the highest credit ratings possible

Zell Miller was the first Governor to establish a debt management plan for the State of Georgia. He created the first Debt Management Advisory Committee by Executive Order on February 25, 1993, to develop a management plan for the effective use of debt financing to meet the state's capital needs. The first plan was drafted and approved in January 1994. The Executive Order also called for the committee to determine an affordable debt limit for the state and make a recommendation to the Governor and the General Assembly on a total amount of debt that should be authorized in the subsequent fiscal year. The goal was to ensure that the State of Georgia managed its resources to meet critical capital funding needs while maintaining its high credit ratings. At the time the Executive Order was executed, Georgia enjoyed a triple-A rating from both Moody's Investors Service and Fitch Investors Service. From Standard & Poor's , the state had a double-A rating, which was an overall excellent rating. However, Governor Miller wanted the highest rating possible from all crediting rating agencies, which would require a triple-A from Standard & Poor's. He left office with that significant achievement. Only seven other states besides Georgia were rated triple-A by all three rating agencies in 1998.

The debt management plan was one of several fiscally conservative steps taken by Governor Miller along the way to the highest possible bond ratings. Filling the reserves and making the necessary decisions to keep them filled was another key element in reaching a triple-A rating from all rating agencies.

The Governor also asked the Debt Management Advisory Committee to look at what the rating agencies used as factors in rating state and local government bond offerings. He wanted to see what Georgia needed to do to not only manage its capital investment within the constitutional limits, but also to manage it in such a way that the State of Georgia would rank among the highest rated states in the nation. The committee examined the state's debt burden as measured by ratios, and by the quality and strength of the state economic base, its fiscal management practices and its administrative characteristics. The debt management plan provided Governor Miller with a target level of capital improvements that could be financed with General Obligation bonds and with assurance that he was on sound financial ground. The use of a debt level management plan was another of the self-disciplined actions taken by Miller that was necessary for the state to be awarded the highest rating allowable.

On July 7, 1998, the State of Georgia sold $299 million of 20-year serial bonds at an average interest rate of 4.5502 percent, the lowest rate on any bond sale since the first General Obligation Bond issue was sold in 1974. The highest rate had been 11.74 percent on a $121 million bond issue in 1982. A July 1998 article in the *Bond Buyer* had referred to Maryland as the "cream of the crop" in terms of low interest rates for state bonds sales. However, Georgia's rate on July 7 was even lower than Maryland's sale of $250 million 15-year serial bonds the next day, July 8, for which the average interest rate was 4.5678 percent. Based on what actually happened in those bond sales, Georgia should have been referred to as the "Crème de la Crème" of the crop.

Results Based Budgeting: Time for accountability

Governor Miller implemented a new budget system in FY 1998 that was designed to promote a more efficient and effective state government that would be more accountable and responsive to the public for the tax dollars it spent. The new Results-Based Budgeting (RBB) process was phased in over a three-year period to give budget and program personnel in state agencies the knowledge they needed for successful implementation. For the first time ever, the Office of Planning and Budget, in partnership with the State Merit System Training Division, developed and provided RBB training to over 600 state budget and program personnel. This training enhanced the quality of two year's RBB submissions from the agencies and the information provided in the FY 1998 and FY 1999 budget documents.

In his last budget address on January 13, 1998, Governor Miller said, "As you look through this budget report, you will find something new. As we implemented budget redirection to focus our resources on priority programs that work, we have also begun what I call 'results based budgeting.' For every budgeted program, you will see in writing the results that state agencies are hoping to achieve. I believe that putting our expenditures and our anticipated results hand-in-hand will help us do a better job of meeting the needs of Georgia's citizens."

Governor Miller believed that the new system would link planning and evaluation to budget development and management. He wanted measured results to be used more systematically to assess progress made toward meeting state goals and objectives for each department or agency of state government. Through RBB, Miller wanted all activities of state government to be grouped into programs and subprograms. For each program, a purpose, goal, and desired result was developed for the fiscal year. This desired result would then be measured at the completion of the funding period and progress toward the program goal could be measured.

In 1996, Governor Miller directed state agencies to begin this budgeting process by identifying all of their programs and developing a program purpose and goals for each program. Additionally, the FY 1998 budget report provided financial summaries that indicated the total cost of each program.

Then in 1997, the Governor asked agencies to expand the previous year's information to include the desired results for each program. A reader of this new budget was able to review information that defined a program, set the purpose and goals of the program, identified the measurable results that the program intended to provide, and indicated the money that was appropriated and spent to achieve those results. Connecting program results with program expenditures enabled the Governor and the General Assembly to decide through public debate whether the state was investing its funds properly. The first baseline data for desired results would be included the FY 2000 budget submission, which would be the benchmark year for most programs. In a memorandum to all state agency heads in May 1996, Governor Miller wrote:

> Constantly focusing our attention not simply on how we spend our resources, but rather on what we achieve or accomplish will keep Georgia on the right track towards effectively addressing the most important needs of Georgia citizens. I think we can substantially implement this new concept as we develop the state budget over the next two years. Approaching this challenge with the same dedication with which you implemented budget redirection will carry the state and this administration a long way towards fulfilling the vision I have for a fiscally sound, effective and results-oriented state government.

Governor Miller saw Results-Based Budgeting as a method the state could use to require accountability for every tax dollar spent by every executive branch department. RBB provided an organized process of gathering information and documenting the state's efforts designed to show whether expenditures actually achieved stated goals and results.

The specific goals of Results-Based Budgeting included:

* Focusing the legislative process upon the policy implications of funds expended in state agency programs and services.
* Identifying similar programs across state agencies and assess total impact.
* Identifying successful and unsuccessful programs.
* Enabling programs to be evaluated and funded on the basis of achieving a specific desired result.
* Aiding policy makers in determining if it was in the best interest of the state to expend funds for particular purposes.
* Enhancing the ability of the Governor's Office of Planning and Budget to track funding in programs across organizational boundaries.

Governor Miller was strongly committed to an effective, efficient and results-driven state government. The implementation of Results-Based Budgeting provided the Governor and General Assembly with a system that gave them the ability to allocate resources based on results. This new budget process was well received in the General Assembly and gained national attention for its innovation. Both the quality of the budget documents and the specialized training of state agency personnel were recognized. Senator Guy Middleton said, "I have pushed strongly for...Results-Based Budgeting as a floor leader for the Governor. I think it is very important to set goals and objectives in our state: set standards of performance, measure those, and hold people accountable. We must run our state more like a well run private business with outcome based government so people know where they are going, and not just continue to build on programs we already have, but determine where we are headed. I think we will see a great deal more efficiency in government."

State Strategic Plan

In 1998, Governor Miller published the second State Strategic Plan for Georgia, describing a comprehensive vision for the future of the state and setting clear directions in six major policy areas. The Governor's Office of Planning and Budget coordinated the development of the plan, using broad-based involvement across state agencies to build consensus and fulfill statutory requirements.

The strategic plan provided a view of the Georgia of tomorrow, and identified the activities that were already underway to move the state toward that future, as well as the additional initiatives that should be undertaken. Ultimately, the plan focused on the results that were necessary to achieve the vision.

Governor Miller's vision for the future of Georgia was inspiring, yet realistic. The future of Georgia was described in concrete terms that all Georgians could understand and explain to others. For example, the Governor saw citizens, communities and local governments working together in new ways to discover local solutions to unique local problems. He wanted Georgians to see education as a lifetime experience that prepared individuals for the constantly changing conditions of a world community. Further, he envisioned a fair and effective judicial system that resulted in respect for the law and an end to the cycle of violence.

Other parts of the vision included a strong economy that competed successfully at the national and global levels, natural resources that were protected and developed in an ecologically sound manner, human services guided by principles of prudent use and individual responsibility, and evolving partnerships among private, public and nonprofit organizations. The Governor saw Georgia as a network of communities that were focused on results and that offered a skilled workforce and infrastructure unrivaled in the world.

Six major policy areas were addressed in the plan: education; crime and public safety; economic development; human services; the environment; and an efficient, effective, results-oriented state government. For each policy area, Governor Miller spelled out what needed to be done and the desired results, as well as the linkages between the overall state plan and the plans of individual state agencies and authorities. The 1998 State Strategic Plan was the first document to integrate strategic planning efforts of state agencies and authorities with overall state planning across the six policy areas.

Governor Miller believed that achieving a future of hope and prosperity for Georgia was not a matter of chance, but required planning, action and results. Through his ongoing commitment to strategic planning, he took the lead in visualizing where the state should go, spelling out what needed to be done to get there, and identifying how progress could be measured along the way.

The Governor's Commission on Effectiveness and Economy (The Williams Commission)

The task with which this commission is charged has dimensions that go beyond eliminating waste in state government.... The whole purpose of streamlining and restructuring our administrative overhead is to shift our focus to service delivery. The end result must be not just a slimmed-down state bureaucracy, but one that is more productive and effective in providing high-quality services to the people of Georgia.

Governor Zell Miller, January 25, 1991

Governor Miller's creation of the Commission on Effectiveness and Economy in Government immediately after taking office in 1991 capped two years of effort on his part to bring the managerial resources of Georgia's business community to bear on state government. During his last years as Lieutenant Governor, Zell Miller saw an ever-increasing fiscal crisis develop, with state reserves dangerously close to depletion. In January 1989, he had introduced Senate Resolution 140 to create a commission on efficiency and effectiveness. His intent then was the same as his intent in 1991—to fund essential programs of state government through economizing and increasing the efficiency of state government. The Georgia Senate adopted SR 140, but the House of Representatives did not. While campaigning for governor, Miller persisted in his call for such a commission. The group would be similar to a federal commission that saved millions of dollars for the federal government.

After his election as Governor, Zell Miller immediately went to work to address the fiscal crisis facing the state. Before his inauguration and the 1991 session of the General Assembly, Miller huddled with budget advisors to begin cutting the Georgia budget. Simultaneously, he appointed a commission of business executives to develop recommendations to economize and streamline state government. "My first and foremost responsibility as CEO of this State is to bring discipline to the state budget process and to set this State on a new course, to pave the way for economic recovery and growth," he explained on August 16, 1991, as he presented budget cuts to a special session of the General Assembly.

Why was Georgia in need of repair?

When Georgia Governor Carl Sanders began his administration in the early days of 1963, not even the most optimistic Georgian could have forecasted the economic growth that was beginning in the state and would continue for most of the next three decades. By the completion of Governor Sanders' term in January 1967, state government's revenues had grown by 51 percent. Under Governor Jimmy Carter (1971 to 1975), state revenues surged to an unprecedented rate of 57 percent.

The growth continued, although at a declining rate, through Governor Joe Frank Harris' tenure from 1983 to 1991. However, with the advent of the 1980s came change. First, the nationwide economic boom of the 80s was stimulated by federal tax cuts. The federal government then adjusted for declining revenues and a burgeoning deficit by shifting responsibility for running many government social, environmental and infrastructure programs on to state governments. Simultaneously, the states were required to assume an increased responsibility for funding the programs. State governments were being ordered to take on new responsibilities with even less funding than they had been given before.

Because a national economic boom camouflaged the shift, most states did not make provision for funding these additional responsibilities. The warnings of trouble for the states were largely drowned out. In Georgia, state government spent every dollar in sight during the 1980s, ignoring the increased demands resulting from a decrease in federal funding. As Governor Zell Miller said in an August 1991 press conference, Georgia engaged in a "hiring orgy" in the 1980s. Total state employment escalated 23 percent in just four years, from 91,000 in FY 1987 to 112,000 in FY 1991. During the 1980s, the state payroll increased from $56.8 million in 1980 to $151 million in 1990. Beyond payroll, other major recipients of state dollars were prisons, medical care, and debt financing. The Department of Corrections budget alone grew from $92 million in 1980 to $525 million in 1990, an increase of 471 percent.

When Georgia's dizzying economic growth began to slow in the late 1980s, declining state revenue growth collided with increasing state government spending, and the first cracks began to appear. By January 1989, Governor Harris' budget advisors began seriously lowering revenue estimates, which had been floating downward to an annual 8.3 percent between 1984 and 1990, and the state legislature saw its final year of swelled coffers.

By April 1989, state revenues dropped by another 2.2 percent, but the decline was not apparent due to revenue generated by an increase in the state sales tax from three to four percent. The illusion lasted until mid-1990, when the national and state economy began slowing rapidly, propelled by the Gulf War and a recession that was far deeper and longer lasting than any economist had predicted. A dramatic turn of events was in full swing. To keep the state afloat, Governor Harris spent its reserve funds.

Consequently, when Zell Miller was elected Governor, he inherited a state government composed of 258 agencies and a totally depleted "rainy day" reserve fund. While other cities and states faced with similar crises were trying to "tax everything that moved," Governor Miller made it clear that Georgia was not one of the tax raising states. Speaking to the Joint Senate and House Appropriation Committees in August 1991, he said, "We have two roads we can travel, two choices we can make. We can raise taxes, or we can cut expenditures and live within our means. I do not think – and I believe most of you agree with me – that it is right for the state to balance its budget on the backs of working people struggling with their own financial problems."

It was against this background of prosperity, rampant growth, shifting responsibility, and a surging economy stopped dead in its tracks by recession that the Governor's Commission on Effectiveness and Economy in Government went to work.

The Commission

Governor Zell Miller created the Governor's Commission on Effectiveness and Economy in Government with the first Executive Order of his administration on January 15, 1991. In the order's preamble, the Governor said state government aspired "to provide necessary services to all Georgians as effectively and economically as possible," and pointed out that "the last comprehensive study and recommendation in Georgia on this issue was conducted during the administration of Governor Jimmy Carter." He ordered that a commission composed of "Georgia's best and brightest business and academic leaders, working with state government and a diverse range of citizen leaders, engage in a process of study and recommendations that is comprehensive in scope."

The Governor appointed the commission's members and designated an executive committee from among the members to direct certain aspects of commission policy and secure resources. The commission's recommendations were subject to review and final approval of the Governor. He directed the commission to work in a spirit of cooperation with state government and ordered all state departments and agencies to provide all information and support needed by the commission to perform its study and make its recommendations. The Governor empowered the chairman to establish any advisory panels or other supporting entities as appropriate, and to assemble a staff of loaned and paid executives from inside and outside government to support the commission.

The commission was charged with applying "business sense" to state government. In some ways government was like a business. Many of the managerial principles applicable to business were also useful to state government, such as adequate span of control, clear chain of command, and accountability. However, the commission also had to keep in mind the many ways state government and the business sector differed. For example, while businesses' purpose was to make a profit, state agencies had multiple and complex purposes, none of which included making a profit. In addition, state agencies had to function in a more open, pluralistic, and political setting; businesses could act in an autocratic environment and embark on multi-year programs with no regard to phenomena like elections.

To lead the commission, Governor Miller tapped Virgil R. Williams, a successful business and community leader from Gwinnett County. Williams, a native Georgian and Georgia Tech graduate, had built and successfully managed a multitude of businesses in engineering, construction, industrial maintenance, and banking. Because of his hands-on leadership, the commission's lengthy name was soon abandoned in favor of the "Williams Commission." In addition to Chairman Williams, the commission was composed of 45 business and academic leaders from throughout Georgia. An additional 25 Georgians joined the effort as task force members. Over 100 state staff were loaned from all areas of state government, as were 16 private sector staff, and interns from Oglethorpe University, Georgia State University, and Georgia Institute of Technology.

The work of the commission covered all aspects of state government. To handle the enormity of this agenda, the commission was organized into 13 task forces: Administration/Support, Business Regulation, Corrections/Pardons & Parole, Economic Development, EDP/Telecommunications, Education, Human Services, Law Enforcement, Natural Resources and Environmental, Personnel, Privatization, Purchasing, and Transportation. In addition, to support the work of the commission, Chairman Williams established three advisory committees: Communications, Management, and Quality. The executive committee was given authorization and oversight of the 13 task force areas.

As part of the Executive Order, the Governor had also directed that the commission, "in the interest of economy in state government," be funded without direct appropriations from state government. Per the Governor's directive, the commission did not incur any direct cost to Georgia taxpayers. By the conclusion of the commission's work, 117 companies and institutions had contributed financial support, personnel or other resources to the commission.

The Williams Commission's study and recommendation process included reviews and analyses of government practices; comparative or "benchmark" research of other state and private entities to measure Georgia's performance against; site visits to state facilities; and regular task force meetings. One of the commission's goals was to be as open and inclusive in its process as possible. To that end the commission kept close coordination with department heads via an introductory meeting with the Governor and chairman and in-depth interviews with task forces. A questionnaire was sent to 74,000 state employees, generating approximately 8,500 responses. The survey solicited state employees' opinions on how to improve the quality of service of state government. The responses were analyzed in detail and influenced the commission's recommendations.

The commission also involved the General Assembly by holding one-on-one meetings between the chairman and Senate and House leaders, surveying all legislators, and maintaining ongoing communications with legislators via meetings and correspondence.

Recommendations and implementation

Due to the extensive recession of 1991, the commission was directed by the Governor to complete its charge within a year rather than the two and one-half years originally allocated. The commission responded to that charge and, after examining over 130 issues covering virtually every aspect of state government, produced more than 400 recommendations, large number of which were implemented. By the end of FY 1994, the Governor's leadership in implementing the recommendations had resulted in savings and revenue increases of more than $520 million, of which almost $470 million were of an ongoing, annual nature. Of these amounts, less than half resulted from the fee increases the commission had recommended to cover the costs of providing the associated services.

After 1994, it became progressively more difficult to isolate the subsequent financial impact of the Williams Commission's recommendations, as intervening time introduced different leadership, saw the adoption of new programs not contemplated at the time of the commission, and created changing conditions which required different solutions. However, total state government employment could be tracked, and the results were astonishing. After decades of huge expansions, Governor Miller stopped state government employment growth in its tracks. Although the Governor had been compelled to hire staff for the new prisons opened to accommodate his get-tough-on-crime policies, the number of full-time employees per state resident actually decreased. Excluding the employees of the Corrections and Juvenile Justice Departments (as well as those of technical institutes, because several institutes were shifted from local to the state operation during the Miller Administration), the total number of state employees decreased as well.

Consequently, the commission's impact was still being felt almost seven years after the conclusion of its work, and the state's citizenry would continue to reap the benefits for more years to come.

The immediate effect of the Williams Commission's recommendations was to reduce the cost of government, increase revenues, streamline operations, make operations more responsive and/or customer friendly, and generally put state government on a more businesslike footing. More fundamentally, the commission's recommendations changed the foundation for managing state government, so that it would continue to become progressively more businesslike over the foreseeable future.

Plan for management improvement: Based on an exhaustive review, the commission proposed an overall Plan for Management Improvement. Governor Miller directed the implementation of a number of this plan's features, which subsequently became cornerstones of his administration. An important one was reforming the budget process. Under Governor Miller's leadership, the Budgetary Accountability and Planning Act of 1993 was introduced and passed, resulting in comprehensive revision to the process by which agencies requested and received funds. This activity was tied to the performance of strategic planning, the identification of agency goals, desired results and performance measures, and the evaluation of agency performance.

The Williams Commission recommended modernizing personnel management through several fundamental proposals which were implemented over time. These included providing state managers with tools to better select the most qualified applicants for employment and downsizing operations where warranted. Before the 1996 legislative session, the Governor created a task force of top level private and public sector leaders to draft legislation restructuring the state's personnel management practices. This legislation eliminated the archaic civil service shackles of the previous half-century, and gave managers flexibility to utilize their workforces in the most effective and efficient manner. Georgia was the first governmental entity in the country to take this action, and it had dramatic effect. A pay-for-performance plan was also created to give managers the ability to retain good workers by rewarding good performers and withholding salary increases from poor performers.

The third commission recommendation to become a landmark of the Miller Administration was to privatize appropriate government functions. The recommendation defined the different types of privatization; objectively described the real potential benefits and possible pitfalls that could result from a privatization effort; and established a procedure for analyzing, and criteria for determining, whether an agency operation should be privatized. This recommendation set the stage for Governor Miller to direct agency heads to consider all agency operations as options for privatization and take appropriate steps when it appeared that privatizing would be beneficial. After an initial successful effort, agencies' progress slowed. Not willing to accept the loss of momentum in this crucial area, Governor Miller in 1995 established a privatization commission of private sector executives and agency heads, with an executive director and small staff. The privatization commission, with Governor Miller's outspoken backing, guided agencies in comprehensively reviewing all operations for privatization potential, identifying large numbers of potential projects, evaluating them, and proceeding in privatizing them.

The Williams Commission also recommended that delinquent taxes be collected and cash management be improved. Under the Governor's direction, the Department of Revenue moved aggressively in this area, offering a period of tax amnesty, and making changes that generated about $145 million increased revenue through calendar year 1993. Of that, more than $30 million was ongoing, expected to be generated every year to the benefit of Georgia's taxpayers.

In addition, the Governor created the Office of Treasury and Fiscal Services to manage state funds better. Among the commission's recommendations which this office implemented were using electronic master accounts, requiring state agencies use other electronic means to access and transfer funds, making Merit System health insurance payments, making Employee's Retirement System payments, and establishing a centralized cash management function for state government. Together, these recommendations enabled the state to leave funds in interest-bearing accounts for longer periods of time, and resulted in annual savings of about $3,000,000.

The commission proposed that state government embrace total quality management. As recommended by the commission, the Governor appointed a task force of ten agency heads to develop a framework for agencies to adopt quality management principles. When this group's work was complete, Governor Miller appointed a quality officer to advise agencies in adopting quality programs, to maintain contact with other large scale employers as to their practices, and to foster interagency communications.

Another commission recommendation was to better coordinate public-private economic development efforts, and Governor Miller wasted no time in taking several key steps to implement it. He reconstituted the Governor's Development Council to include key business leaders, and charged this new council with establishing a comprehensive strategic plan for economic development. The strategic plan and policies proposed by the Governor's Development Council formed the basis for many of the Governor's bold actions which moved Georgia forward in subsequent years. Once the council served its purpose, the Governor disbanded it and reorganized the Department of Industry, Trade and Tourism to institutionalize the council's recommendations.

The Williams Commission recommended that the Governor create a chief information officer position, and Miller responded by creating the Information Technology Policy Council and the Office of Information Technology Policy directed by a chief information officer. These actions also resulted in implementation of the commission's related recommendations to coordinate the state's data processing and telecommunications functions so the state could more aggressively take advantage of productivity enhancements made possible by improved technology.

At the time of the commission's work, state government was providing services to various groups of citizens at fees that were substantially less than what the services cost to provide. The citizens utilizing those services were benefiting from subsidies being paid by the general taxpaying public. The commission recommended that agencies raise their user fees to cover the costs of services, thus eliminating unfair subsidies and achieving equity. This apparent raising of the price of government went against the Governor's grain. However, when he realized that it would have the effect of lowering the price of government for the majority of citizens who did not use individual services, he moved forward to implement the commission's recommendations. By making user services pay for themselves, over $130 million was freed up annually that otherwise would have been used to subsidize services.

Other recommendations: Another of the Williams Commission recommendations was privatizing specific functions performed by state employees where cost beneficial. Data processing services in the Department of Administrative services were privatized, eliminating 79 positions in computer systems application programming and systems support. The department contracted for these services on an as-needed basis. The savings in salaries and fringe benefit costs, plus other savings by other agencies, totaled about $4.9 million annually. After the cost of contracting, net annual savings were projected to be about $1.9 million. The department also cut seven positions in state motor vehicle maintenance and contracted for these services. Annual salaries and fringe benefit costs were reduced by $256,159. Another 46 positions were cut when the department privatized printing services for state agencies, reducing associated costs by about $1.7 million annually. Other DOAS expenses were reduced by about $2.5 million annually, with an estimated $500,000 saved by other agencies annually. Annual savings for contracting were projected to be about $644,000.

In the Department of Human Resources, several functions were privatized in the Office of Child Support Recovery. The office contracted for the collection of accounts for which the office had previously had to go to court to collect. The net amount saved was about $10 million annually. The office also awarded a contract in 1994 to a private firm to locate absent parents whom the office had been unable to find within 75 days. Privatizing case processing of applications from all custodial parents who were not receiving welfare benefits through Temporary Assistance for Needy Families (TANF) enabled the office to reassign staff who had been processing these claims, and had the side benefit of enabling electronic transfers directly from noncustodial to custodial parents. This change greatly reduced accounting and payment processing costs and permitted staff to focus on collecting child support owed to parents who were receiving TANF benefits. The resulting reduction in welfare costs was large enough to bring the office increased reimbursement from the federal government. The increase in federal funding was sufficient to pay for the cost of the contract.

In its Mental Health, Mental Retardation and Substance Abuse Services Division, the Department of Human Resources established a regional board concept for operating programs, as authorized by the 1993 General Assembly. Nineteen regions were created, with consumers, family members, business leaders, advocates, community leaders and elected officials appointed to the regions' community service boards. Executive directors and staff were selected, planning meetings were held, and the process begun of decentralizing and privatizing service delivery. As a result, the number of state office positions was reduced from 164 to 91; competition was injected into the system through increased use of private providers; consumers and families were empowered to make choices; and local community decision-making was strengthened.

At the recommendation of the Williams Commission, the Employees' Retirement System obtained legislation and a one-time appropriation of

$2,880,000 to permit members of the new retirement system to count forfeited annual and sick leave as time worked for the purpose of calculating retirement benefits on the same basis as the old retirement system. This change improved job attendance by removing the incentive to make sure accummulated sick leave was used.

The commission recommended that the Department of Administrative Services mandate that all agencies use regular gasoline; implement laser printing of checks and on-line review of reports; implement a disaster recovery plan for the central data processing installation; and institute audio response technology. (Audio response technology was also implemented in the Department of Public Safety for driver's license inquiries, in the Office of Child Support Recovery for inquiries, and in several other areas.)

For the Department of Community Affairs, the commission recommended reorganizing or abolishing several functions and their associated positions for annual savings of just under $400,000. For the Department of Corrections, the commission recommended privatizing certain low security facilities, funding the expansion of county work camps instead of building more expensive state prisons, and continuing and expanding the use of inmate labor to construct projects for state agencies. Implementation of these recommendations resulted in annual savings of just under $20 million.

For the Department of Education, commission recommendations included changing the textbook replacement cycle from five years to seven. A committee appointed by the state superintendent recommended going to a six-year cycle, which was implemented in 1993 and resulted in annual savings of about $28 million. The commission also recommended substantial organizational changes, which resulted in the elimination of more than 200 positions in the central office and the consolidation of many regional offices. Automated data bases were recommended for public libraries. This electronic resource-sharing among libraries was implemented using the University System's PeachNet, which also provided public libraries with Internet connections and access to the University System's electronic library, GALILEO.

For the Georgia Building Authority, the commission recommended and the authority implemented expanded use of inmates for grounds maintenance activities where cost effective. Many other activities, including food service operations, were contracted out, and the New Georgia Railroad, a tourism venture that was operating at a loss, was sold.

For the Georgia Forestry Commission, recommendations included eliminating selected programs and reducing staff based on changing fire-fighting needs. The result was a reduction of 141 positions and almost $900,000 annual savings. The recommendations also urged the Forestry Commission to discontinue its seedling program and sell its seed orchards and nurseries.

The commission closed two nurseries and put the third on a self-sustaining basis, eliminating 28 positions and generating annual savings of more than $2.5 million.

For the Department of Human Resources, the Williams Commission recommended discontinuing the provision of rabies certificates and numbered tags to veterinarians free of charge. This action saved $50,000 a year. Another recommendation was converting food stamps from paper coupons to an electronic transfer system. This action was originally estimated to generate annual savings of almost $3.7 million through reduced manual processing cost and better control of fraud. In addition the department implemented an electronic eligibility system for welfare, food stamps and medical assistance.

In addition, the commission recommend that the Department of Human Resources be restructured. Governor Miller moved the care of juvenile offenders to a new Department of Juvenile Justice to better address the correction of teenage delinquency and lawlessness. The department also eliminated a middle layer of management and one entire division.

For the Department of Industry, Trade and Tourism, the Williams Commission recommendations included closing three visitor information centers with low usage rates at an estimated savings of $340,000 and elimination of 11 staff. The department submitted to the Office of Planning and Budget a proposal to close the three centers sited in 1991. However, the measure was defeated by the General Assembly. The commission also recommended that the grants to local visitor information centers be eliminated. Although the General Assembly was not willing to eliminate them entirely, the grants were decreased in FY 1994 at a savings of $72,000. The department privatized custodial and grounds-keeping functions at visitor information centers in 1994. Production of the state's visitor information guide was also privatized at a savings of over $200,000.

For the Department of Medical Assistance, the commission recommended a statewide physician access control program for Medicaid clients. The department implemented the Georgia Better Health Care program which required Medicaid clients to have a primary care provider for all health care needs and subsequent referrals. As of February 1998, approximately 618,000 Medicaid members were enrolled in the program and approximately 3,500 primary care providers were contracting with DMA to serve as case managers.

For the Department of Natural Resources, commission recommendations included reconfiguring field districts and reducing them in most instances. In March 1993, DNR's Region Two parks office was consolidated within the new wildlife division office located near Social Circle. Federal funds were used for 59 percent of the cost of constructing this facility, to which the division moved on April 1, 1993. State funds were reduced by $718,204 and 20 positions were eliminated. The department also made modest increases in the rental rates for lodge, cottage, campsite, picnic shelter and golf cart rentals, and historic site admissions over several years to make them more self-supporting.

The Georgia Environmental Protection Division began phasing in permit fees, designed to fund at least 80 percent of the state's environmental programs over time. In the summer of 1991, EPD began to charge the state's water systems a fee for testing, and gave them the option of having the testing done by the private sector instead. The 1992 General Assembly amended the state's Air Quality Control Act to provide for an air quality fee program. Two other programs approved by the General Assembly and signed into law by the Governor in early 1992 addressed the clean-up of scrap tires and abandoned hazardous waste sites. Both required fees, which were used to fund clean-up operations. Overall, the department experienced an increase in revenue for environmental programs of approximately $22.5 million dollars as of December 1993. Annual revenues were estimated to be at least $27.4 million thereafter. EPD reduced the number of its staff by 21 positions.

For the Department of Public Safety, commission recommendations included a revamping of the driver's licensing process. Although the department did not extend operating hours across the board as the commission recommended, it provided evening hours at high-volume sites. In addition, satellite offices were opened in shopping centers and grocery stores across the state to improve customer service.

The commission also recommended that the agencies attached to the Department of Public Safety be reorganized. The police and firefighter's academies were consolidated with the Public Safety Training Center, as were the training delivery functions of the Police Officer Standards and Training Council. This enabled more consistent and efficient delivery of training statewide and the overall reduction of required administrative resources.

For the Department of Revenue, recommendations besides those impacting cash management included reducing the compensation provided vendors for collecting sales tax in excess of reasonable costs incurred. By the end of calendar year 1993, this change had saved the state $92 million, and further annual savings of $42 million were anticipated. The internal tax processing system was also overhauled. Governor Miller took aggressive action to get this effort moving by appointing a private industry/state government/local government task force. The work of this task force and new departmental management culminated in the retention of a respected private consulting firm, which made comprehensive recommendations to reorganize the department and overhaul its antiquated computer systems.

Fees for motor vehicle tag registration and titles, and for prestige tags were increased to cover the cost of providing these services. By the end of calendar year 1993, the state had saved over $200 million, and more than $100 million was anticipated to accrue annually.

For the Department of Transportation, Williams Commission recommendations included computerizing all permanent weigh stations. The department piloted portable stations in FY 1994, but it was still implementing computerized permanent weigh stations in certain areas of the state in 1998. Legislation was introduced in 1992 to simplify the handling of fines charged truckers whose trailers were either overweight or over-large. Under the prior arrangement, the Georgia DOT collected the overweight fine revenues and shared them with local governments, and local governments collected the over-dimension fines and shared them with the DOT. Under the new law, each simply kept its own revenues.

The commission also recommended that the DOT automate gasoline distribution at selected locations and eliminate the associated staffing. The department began automating their sites in FY 1996, and also began to close sites that were determined to be unnecessary or obsolete. By 1994, the DOT had transferred responsibility for all of its highway sign production to Georgia Correctional Industries in the state prison system, and associated staff was eliminated. DOT facilities located within the same county were consolidated, and surplus property was sold/given to local government.

For the Workers' Compensation Board, Commission recommendations included replacing full-time staff court reporters with contract court reporters. The Board decreased full-time staff, saving $100,000 through December 1993. An estimated additional savings of $50,000 was anticipated through further reductions resulting from attrition/retirement.

The changes implemented as a result of the Williams Commission saved the state hundreds of millions of dollars, reduced staff, and streamlined government. As Governor Miller left office, the state's "rainy day" fund was full and the state enjoyed a healthy economy.

Commission Members

Virgil Williams, Chair
Ivan Allen, III
James Allen
Veronica Biggins
Charles Brown
Wally Bruce
William Clement, Jr.
Thomas Cousins
Salvador Diaz-Verson

Eleanor Main
James Mathis, Jr.
William McCoy
Robert McCullough
John McIntyre
Robert McMahan
E. R. Mitchell
Ben Porter
Hal Rainey

Anderson Dilworth
Thomas Dowden
John Duke
Douglas Dunn
William Gaston
Elsie Hand
Harold Hansen
Ronald Hogan
John Hunt
Douglas Ivester
Tobe Johnson
Wyckliffe Knox, Jr.
Clay Long
Wayne Reaves
Raymond Riddle
Edgar Roberts
David Roessner
Gloria Shatto
Jane Shivers
Lewis Shurbutt
John Stephens
Patrick Thomas
Richard Ussery
Thomas Wheeler, Jr.
Issac Willis
Patricia Willis

Executive Committee Members:
Virgil Williams, Chairman
Ronald Hogan
Douglas Ivester
William McCoy
Robert McCullough
John McIntyre
Patrick Thomas

Privatization Initiatives

Government cannot do everything; it cannot do all the things we used to think it could. We need to identify clearly the important responsibilities that government should rightfully undertake, and then deliver those vital services effectively and efficiently with a minimum burden on our taxpayers. Privatization offers us the opportunity to do that.

Governor Zell Miller, January 10, 1996

Governor Miller was committed to changing the culture of state government to make privatization of programs, facilities and services a viable option for managers to increase effectiveness and efficiency, and reduce costs. When this initiative began, privatization was seldom considered by agency managers as a potential alternative to performing functions and programs in house. To them privatization meant a loss of control, and lower costs meant poorer quality service.

Governor's Commission of Privatization of Governmental Services

Governor Miller changed that perception with the creation of a nine-member bipartisan Governor's Commission of Privatization of Governmental Services to spearhead the effort toward greater privatization. Once Miller made clear his intention to implement the commission's recommendations, agency managers increasingly came to regard privatization as a viable management tool that could yield cost savings, and generate revenues that could be used to improve the quality of services delivered or redirected to other programs. Soon department heads began to propose and implement privatization initiatives on their own.

Governor Miller also put in place tools to assist future governors and their administrations to identify and implement additional opportunities for privatization. These tools included a standard analytical framework to identify and evaluate candidates for privatization, and very detailed guides for dealing with private providers, from developing requests for proposals to developing performance-based contracts to providing strong contract administration.

Recommendations and implementation

During his administration, Governor Miller implemented a wide range of privatization projects throughout state government. Virtually every state department had at least one such project. These initiatives were projected to result in cost savings or increased revenues to the state in excess of $1.6 billion.

The Department of Veterans Service undertook two extensive and very successful privatization efforts. First, the department privatized the Georgia War Veterans Home at Milledgeville which cared for over 470 veterans. After reviewing operations and costs at the facility, the department contacted neighboring states to learn of their experiences with privatized veterans nursing homes. Based on an extensive review, the department initiated a competitive procurement that resulted in privatizing the Milledgeville facility on July 1, 1996.

The results of this privatization initiative were very impressive. First year savings approached $9 million and over a ten-year period were projected to exceed $106 million. As importantly, residents at the facility received new speech therapy and respiratory therapy services, and improvements in physical therapy, occupational therapy, food services and medication delivery. Quality indicators for residents as verified by independent reviews reflected significant improvement in all treatment and other areas as well. In short, the department achieved a substantial upgrading of its services at a lower cost. In fact, after privatization, the War Veterans Home in Milledgeville received the 1998 American Health Care Association Quality Award.

The department also privatized selected functions at the Georgia War Veterans Home at Augusta, a facility which served over 170 veterans and had been operated as a teaching facility under a contract with the Medical College of Georgia. Because of its tie to the Medical College, the department retained overall management of the home, but encouraged the staff to develop a proposal that would reduce costs to a level that approximated the Milledgeville privatized operation. In addition to continuing their already outsourced security, grounds keeping and laundry services, the home outsourced its physical, occupational and speech therapy services, food service and maintenance. These actions reduced the staff by 45 positions as of July 1, 1997, and were projected to save $919,000 annually. As a result, the Augusta facility's costs were brought into line with the privatized Milledgeville nursing home.

The Lake Lanier Islands Development Authority was originally established to promote economic development in the Lake Lanier region of the state. Initially, state appropriations provided the authority with capital funds for its development and operating funds to cover those ongoing costs which could not be fully defrayed by revenues. Over time, the authority brought a privately financed and operated resort hotel to the site, invested in substantial development, and operated another resort hotel, golf courses, a water park and various other concessions. The operations were well managed, and revenues grew to the point that the authority was financially able not only to cover all of its ongoing costs, but also to repay the state on an annual installment basis for bond funds received for additional development.

However, as the authority prospered, the business community in the area had also grown significantly and came to operate a number of facilities with which the authority directly competed. The question that arose was whether a state entity should compete directly with the private sector. The answer was no. As a result, a competitive procurement was initiated to lease the facilities in their entirety to a private company. The successful offeror agreed to pay the state $9 million up front, make annual payments exceeding $3 million over the term of the lease, and pay additional annual payments of 3.5 percent of annual gross revenues over $20 million. The overall benefits of this action were substantial. Over the 50-year term of the lease, revenues coming to the state were projected to be $340 million. In addition, the agreement relieved the state of any future obligation to commit bond proceeds to meet the capital maintenance and improvement needs of the facilities.

Stone Mountain Park presented a unique challenge. The Stone Mountain Memorial Association was responsible for preserving and protecting the mountain and surrounding natural area, for maintaining the park as a memorial to the Confederacy, and for providing public access to the park. At the same time, the park operated hotel and conference center facilities and various other amenities and attractions. A delicate balance was crafted to enable some of these responsibilities to be privatized. The Stone Mountain Memorial Association retained total responsibility for protection and preservation of the park's natural, historical and cultural resources, but leased out to a private company responsibility for the operation, maintenance and development of the hotel and conference center facilities and various other amenities and attractions. The general public's continued access to the park was assured under this initiative. The lessee was an active participant with the association in educating the public on environmental issues and projecting an appropriate historical perspective in its attractions, and paid the state rents estimated in excess of $1 billion over the term of the lease.

The Department of Corrections needed additional bed space to house inmates and chose to seek private investment and operation of the required facilities. State laws were amended to give the department the authority to contract with a private company for these services. Through two separate competitive procurements, the department contracted with one company for one prison and with a second company for two prisons. Under both contracts, the outside companies would finance, build and operate the new prison facilities in which the department would buy bed space on an inmate-day basis. The cost per inmate day under both contracts was less than the department's comparable costs.

The results were impressive. First, the state did not have to use its bonding capacity to finance the estimated $60 million construction cost for the three facilities. Second, the cost per inmate day established in each of the contracts was less than the department would have spent, generating estimated savings of approximately $4.9 million in the first year of full operation and almost $74 million over the full 20 year term of the contracts. Third, the state took no risk with these facilities in that its contracts were for only one year at a time, but the department maintained absolute control including the right to take over the prisons if conditions necessitated such action. Finally, these privately run prisons would provide the department with some basis on which to judge their own institutions' performance and adopt identified best practices internally.

The Department of Juvenile Justice expanded its privatization initiatives to include entire facilities. Its first privatization effort, the Irwin County Youth Development Center (YDC), offered the benefit of a much faster startup than would have been possible if staffed in house, and was also cost effective ($90.65 per day compared to state YDCs' cost per day that ranged between $93 and $111). Subsequently, the department successfully privatized the Pelham, McIntosh and Emanuel YDCs, the Paulding Regional Youth Development Center (RYDC), three wilderness treatment programs and the Augusta Girls Group Home through management contracts. Finally, the medical services for all RYDCs and several YDCs, as well as the management of several aftercare programs, were fully privatized. As a result, critically needed facilities and services were brought on line quickly and, in most instances, at a savings to the taxpayers of the state.

The Department of Natural Resources assessed all of its programs and functions, and identified a number of instances in which outsourcing was appropriate. The Environmental Protection Division (EPD) privatized the federally mandated Vehicle Emissions Inspection and Maintenance Program for the two million vehicles in the 13-county metro-Atlanta region. Through a competitive procurement, EPD awarded an eight-year management contract to a private firm, the cost of which was financed through emission test fees by motorists. Actual vehicle emission inspections were performed by several hundred private businesses which invested in the test equipment, facilities and training. EPD was responsible for managing the program, certifying the equipment and test stations, checking the quality of all the test data and test methods, and providing information to the public on how the program worked, why it was important, and how to go about getting tested.

In addition, EPD privatized most of the state SuperFund, which involved investigation and cleanup at contaminated sites where action was necessary to mitigate a present or future danger to human health and the environment. After deciding that state government should not compete with well-established private sector companies, EPD initiated a contract with four cleanup companies to assess and prepare the sites for cleanup, and to do the actual on-site work. Also, EPD privatized Georgia's scrap tire cleanup program. Utilizing a $1 fee collected and paid to EPD by retail dealers upon the sale of each new tire, EPD selected three contractors through a competitive bid process to clean up scrap tire piles which had the most potential for causing environmental or human health problems. This process enabled EPD to clean up over three million tires at a cost of about $4.3 million. The use of private contractors proved to be competitive and efficient, and resulted in good quality work done in a timely and cost-effective manner. In addition to privatization efforts by EPD, the department outsourced golf course maintenance at selected state parks on a pilot basis, and contracted with a private vendor to manage the new conference center at Georgia Veterans Memorial Park.

The North Georgia Mountains Authority was responsible for the Brasstown Valley Resort, which was located on state property and successfully operated by a private company under a management contract since it was built in 1995. In 1997, the authority also assumed responsibility for the lodge/conference center facilities at three state parks — Unicoi, Amicalola and Red Top Mountain. These facilities were all originally constructed with state funds and collectively generated an excess of revenues over expenditures. However, there were two concerns about their operations. First, available funding had been inadequate to maintain the facilities properly as they aged and the effects of deferred maintenance were projected to have a negative impact on future revenues. Additional investments were needed to enhance and expand those facilities if current customer usage was to be maintained and expanded over time, and the competition for such capital funding within state government suggested that prospects were not good. Second, the facilities competed directly with private sector operations which had grown up in the areas around them.

As a result, the authority developed and issued a request for proposals, and through a formal evaluation and selection process leased the lodge/conference facilities to a private company for 20 years with an option to renew for an additional 10 years. Under that lease agreement, the private company contracted to pay the authority $2 million up front; $600,000 per year; and additional annual payments of 3 percent of annual gross revenues over $7 million beginning in year three of the agreement. In addition, the company agreed to set aside 5 percent of its gross annual revenues to be used solely for rehabilitation and replacement purposes. Through that lease agreement, all future funding for improvements to those facilities will be the responsibility of the lessee, relieving the state of that financial commitment, but at the end of the lease term the improvements become the property of the authority.

The Department of Revenue was responsible for the administration of state tax laws and the collection of over $10 billion in state revenues each year. One of its functions was to identify delinquent taxpayers and collect unpaid taxes along with any associated penalties, fees and interest due. Over the years, a backlog developed of approximately 61,000 delinquent tax accounts with an estimated total liability of $282.4 million, some of which were still collectible and some of which were uncollectible. Through a competitive procurement, the department selected three well-qualified private collection agencies which assumed responsibility for collection of those accounts and were compensated from collection fees paid by the delinquent taxpayers. The department began assigning delinquent accounts to those firms in late spring, 1997.

The Department of Human Resources bid out commercial banking services for its major accounts and was able to obtain the best combination of service and price, saving the state $600,000 annually in banking fees. In addition, the department competitively bid responsibility for the Adoption Reunion Registry with savings of about $90,000 per year. The mental health assessment process which had been performed in house as part of the community care services program was also privatized. Although there were no cost savings, more clients were served with the same level of funding.

The Department of Administrative Services outsourced its Capitol Hill motor vehicle maintenance facility and contracted with a single vendor to provide a network of dealers and repair shops for use by some 1,200 state-owned vehicles. The purpose of this procurement was to assess the feasibility of extending such a contract to cover state-owned motor vehicles throughout state government. The department also privatized its rapid copy printing services early in the administration at a savings to the state, and in 1997 rebid the contract with a further savings of $250,000 per year.

The Department of Technical and Adult Education operated 32 technical institutes around the state. In reviewing the operations of those institutes, the department determined that certain functions that were common to most of those institutes had the potential to be performed more economically by outside vendors. As a result, the bookstores, custodial services, food service, grounds maintenance, on-campus security and other similar functions were reviewed on an institute-by-institute basis. Many of these functions were outsourced to private vendors at an estimated annual savings to the department of $807,000.

The Department of Transportation undertook a very unusual outsourcing project — its technologically advanced Automated Traffic Management System in Metropolitan Atlanta. Developed in preparation for the 1996 Olympics and financed by federal funds, this system was designed around state-of-the-art optical fiber communications, video transmission and computer control and processing facilities. It provided instantaneous information to the general public on the status of traffic on interstate highways through a distribution system that included television stations and Internet access. Because it was critical to maintain the system at a technologically current level, which would involve funding and expertise, the department elected to seek a private sector partner to assume the associated financial and technological upgrading responsibilities. A detailed request for proposals was developed and a highly qualified vendor selected, continuing this valuable service to the public while relieving the taxpayers of the associated costs. In another initiative, the department outsourced the maintenance of the rest areas on the interstate highways throughout the state, achieving annual cost savings of almost $220,000.

Commission Members

George Israel, chair
Rep. Bill Lee
Veronica Biggins
C. V. Nalley, III
Allen Franklin
Sen. Sonny Perdue
Julie Hunt
Willou Smith
Johnny Isakson

II. Education

I am committed to expanding the educational opportunities of all Georgians, from the moment they enter my prekindergarten program to when they enter one of our colleges, universities or technical schools on a HOPE scholarship.

- Governor Zell Miller, December 19, 1995

When Governor Zell Miller took office, Georgia was near the bottom in practically every educational category. More than 210,000 school-age Georgia children, or one of every five, were living in poverty. Only four states had worse records. More than 136,000 Georgians over age 25 had not completed fifth grade. Only 48 percent of Georgia high school graduates enrolled in a college or university. Georgia classroom teachers were paid $2,650 less than the average national annual teacher salary. Georgia was spending $3,879 per student on elementary and high school education, ranking it 27th among the states. But in 22 of the states that were spending less per pupil, students were scoring better than Georgia students on national tests. Fewer than half of Georgia's eighth graders were scoring "average or above" on mathematics aptitude tests. In Scholastic Aptitude Test (SAT) scores, Georgia ranked 49th of the 50 states. The average Georgia student was scoring 948 out of a possible 1600 points, compared to a national average score of 1008.

Miller's devotion to improving public education was supported by many of the state's educators, who saw Georgia as falling farther and farther behind its neighbors. In a column that appeared in newspapers across Georgia in February 1989, Charles K. Knapp, president of the University of Georgia, wrote "In an economy where currency is the power of ideas, it is imperative that we develop and nurture the intellectual capacities of our young people... It is time for the state to write the next chapter in its commitment to education - a chapter not for its history, but for its future."

Governor Miller recognized that every facet of Georgia's well-being was affected by the quality of education its citizens possessed. More education meant less crime, less poverty, and less welfare. More education meant more prosperity, more jobs, higher salaries, opportunities for more happiness and freedom, and more control over one's own destiny.

He believed that education was the best investment a state could make, but that investment must be targeted, focused, and understood by the taxpayer. The value of a quality education was sometimes difficult to explain because the tangible benefits often came years later. Governor Miller dedicated his administration to making quality education a normal topic of dinner table conversation in Georgia.

Some wondered whether money really mattered when it came to education. Governor Miller believed, and research supported, that money did matter – if it was used wisely to improve student instruction directly in the classroom. The Governor committed necessary financial resources to education in Georgia including prekindergarten, K-12 education, the University System of Georgia and the Department of Technical and Adult Education.

Education Spending in Georgia

We can no longer claim to have improved education simply because we have increased spending. We can no longer prove that our schools are good simply by pointing to the dollars per pupil that we appropriate.... Taxpaying citizens are looking for concrete results in the form of improved student performance. Student achievement is the bottom line.

Governor Zell Miller, November 13, 1995

When Governor Miller took office he was faced with serious financial constraints. The state was in a recession, and the reserve funds meant for such a situation were gone. However, within one year the Governor had education funding on a gradual upward path. In fact, the percentage of state funds devoted to education had never been higher than it was when Miller left office. In Fiscal Year (FY) 1999 – Miller's last – education funding comprised 57.05 percent of the state budget (including the Department of Education, the University System of Georgia, the Department of Technical and Adult Education, the Georgia Public Telecommunications Commission, and the Professional Standards Commission). That percentage had never been higher.

In 1985, the General Assembly passed the Quality Basic Education Act (QBE) without a dissenting vote. QBE was hailed as a significant improvement in the programs it authorized for children, kindergarten through twelfth grade, and in the way it funded them. More funding was concentrated in the lower grades, full-day kindergarten was begun, the local system investment in the QBE program was clarified, middle school programs were authorized and funded, state standards were required, and special cost items like laboratories were funded. Then-Lieutenant Governor Miller was instrumental in both the development and the implementation of QBE. He saw the state start in a positive new direction for education. But QBE alone was not enough to give Georgians the jump start they needed to significantly raise their expectations of the kind of education they needed and deserved. The culture of education needed to change to reflect higher expectations and a realistic chance for everyone to recognize the benefits of educational achievement. While improvements in K-12 and higher education were needed, they would not accomplish the higher expectations so necessary to lasting improvement.

The Georgia Lottery only added to education funding – Governor Miller kept his pledge to the citizens of Georgia to use the lottery only to enhance, never to supplant, funding for education. The constitutional amendment he pushed through the 1991 General Assembly and on to the 1992 ballot not only dedicated the lottery revenues to education, but also kept them out of the general revenue stream, requiring that they be separately accounted for and specifically identified in the budget document the Governor presented to the General Assembly.

As with the lottery, the Governor targeted public tax dollars for education to areas that were most likely to make lasting improvements. He methodically developed new funding initiatives that improved opportunities for every student in Georgia regardless of grade level, socioeconomic status, academic standing, or area of interest.

Education Appropriations As Percentage of State Budget

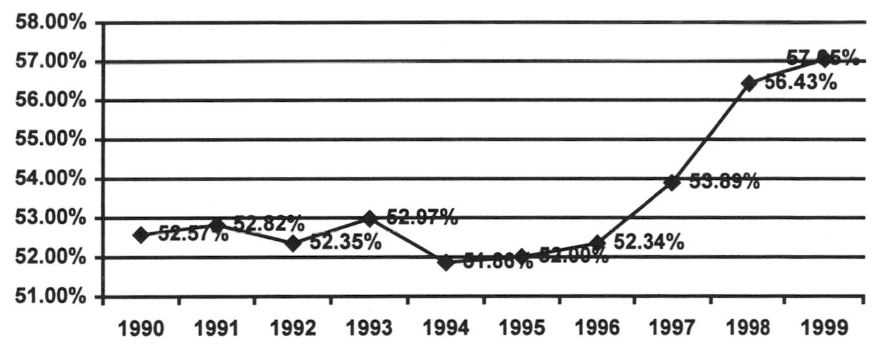

Lottery for Education Act

Governor Miller realized that a growing state like Georgia would have to spend millions of new dollars merely to provide the same level of services for new students coming into the system. Funding for educational improvements would be hard to find. New taxes were foreign to his political philosophy, so he proposed a state lottery for education as the answer to the funding problem. During his first two years in office, Governor Miller established the framework for the lottery, including how the lottery would operate and what

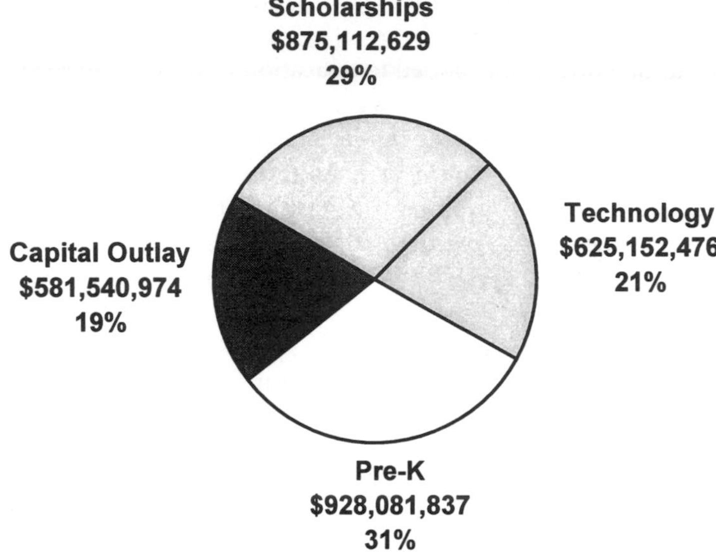

programs would be funded with its proceeds. In November 1992, voters approved a constitutional amendment allowing the lottery to be created, dedicating its proceeds to education and establishing a separate funding track for its revenues. By the time of the 1992 election, Governor Miller had already pushed the Georgia Lottery for Education Act through the 1992 session of the General Assembly, specifying that the lottery would fund prekindergarten, post-secondary financial assistance, and capital outlay for technology and special construction. By the time voters went to the polls, it was clear how the lottery would operate and what educational improvements it would fund.

The Georgia Lottery was the most successful start-up state lottery ever, with unprecedented ticket sales. The lottery began selling tickets on June 29, 1993. It met its first year sales goal of $465 million within five months, and ended the first year with total sales of over $1.1 billion.

The national average for sales during a lottery's first year was $68 per resident. Florida had beaten that record in 1988 with first-year per capita sales of $128. In Georgia, first-year sales were $165 per person, shattering the old national standard. This figure translated into a record $1.13 billion in sales and $360 million for Miller's three education programs. Even the most optimistic forecasters, including Miller himself, who had campaigned on an annual payout of $250 million, had never envisioned $360 million in new revenues for education.

The trend in record sales continued. Although most of 35 state lotteries begun prior to Georgia's experienced a drop in sales in their second year, the Georgia Lottery increased sales by $300 million, to $1.5 billion. By 1998, annual sales of more than $1.7 billion were being recorded. By the last budget of the Miller Administration for FY 1999, the lottery had provided a cumulative total of more than $3 billion for education.

Georgia Lottery President Rebecca Paul had a simple explanation. "You really can't go anywhere in Georgia without seeing what the lottery has done," Paul said. "You live in a neighborhood where children are in prekindergarten classes or on HOPE scholarships at colleges and technical institutes. You go to your child's school and see new computers bought by the lottery. So, when a Georgia parent goes into a convenience store and puts down a $20 bill for $18 worth of gas, they more than likely will take that extra $2 and buy lottery tickets to support these programs."

Governor Miller always envisioned lottery revenues as an enhancement for education. He was adamant that Georgia not repeat what he felt was the major mistake of other state lotteries, which dumped their millions into state general fund coffers where the lottery money was mixed and lost among other state revenues such as income and sales taxes, and user fees funding. "That man that's sitting there watching TV with a beer in his hand is already suspicious of any money he's sending to the Governor," Miller told *The Atlanta Journal-Constitution.* "He doesn't think it's being used very wisely. You've got to tell him in a very simple and direct way how it's going to help him and his family."

Miller made a firm commitment to protect both state general funds and lottery funds for education, and fought any effort to use lottery funds to supplant education revenue by diverting the money into the general fund where it could not be monitored and would ultimately supplant rather than supplement existing education funding. The constitutional amendment creating the lottery, which Miller pushed through the 1991 General Assembly, then campaigned for during the 1992 general election, not only dedicated Georgia's lottery revenues to education, but also required that they be accounted for separately from the normal funding stream and presented separately in the state budget. Unlike other states in which lottery funds replaced other education funding, Georgia's lottery was used only for new programs to enhance education.

Lottery revenues eliminated barriers to education through two new, innovative and nationally recognized programs: voluntary prekindergarten for four-year-olds and the HOPE Scholarship Program. The Georgia Lottery for Education Act specified that proceeds from lottery sales would be used for three educational purposes: financial assistance for Georgia students at the

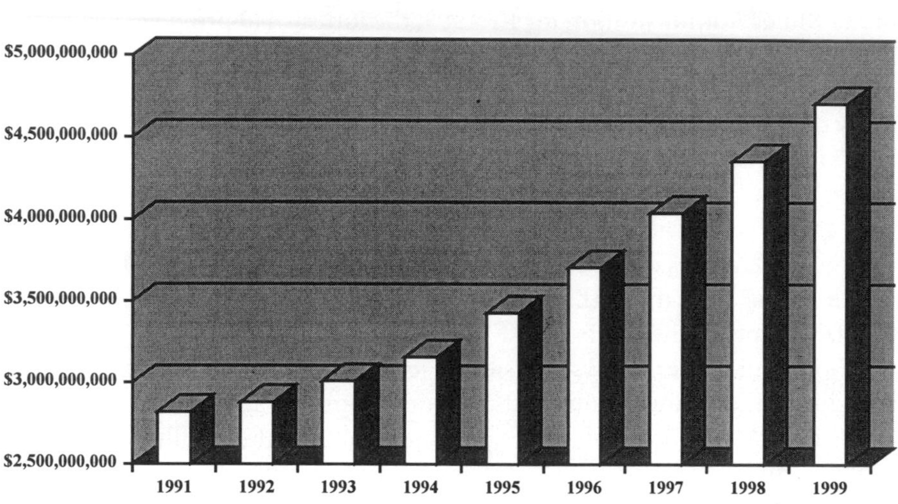

state's public and private colleges, universities and technical institutes; voluntary prekindergarten for four-year-olds, with services delivered by school systems, public and private non-profit providers and private for-profit providers, and capital outlay for educational technology and facilities. Technology funds provided instructional technology, including computer hardware and software, automation of media centers, satellite dishes, networking and Internet access for every public school, college, university, and technical institute in the state. Public libraries also received technology and Internet access. Funds were provided for construction in school systems that showed exceptional growth in student population, and for equipment to make Georgia's schools safer.

Enrollment and funding increases (K-12)

Public school enrollment increased by 210,529 full-time equivalent students, or 18.9 percent during the Miller Administration. The Governor provided the necessary resources each year to fund student enrollment increases under the Quality Basic Education funding formula. Even during the first two years of his administration when state revenue growth was virtually flat, Miller was dedicated to fully funding K-12 education. During years of stronger revenue growth, the Governor provided significant resources to enhance educational achievement in public schools, including operations increases and reduced class sizes. The Governor also invested financial resources in teachers by providing four consecutive years of six percent salary increases to attract and retain the best teachers for Georgia's children. State general funds for K-12 education increased by more than $1.89 billion, or 67.02 percent, during the Miller Administration.

University System of Georgia
Fall Quarter Headcount Enrollment Growth

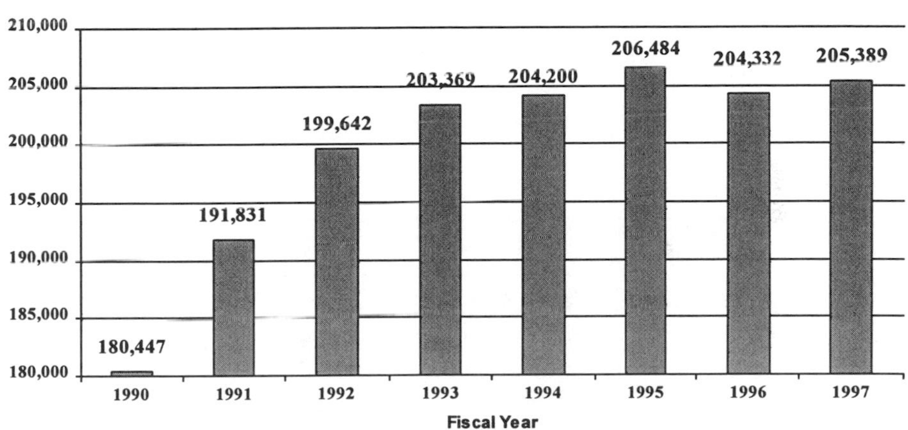

University System of Georgia Funding By Year

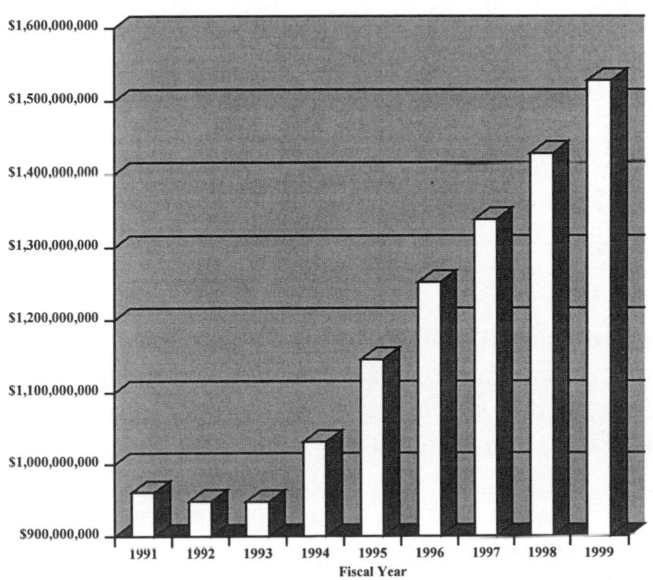

Enrollment and funding increases for the University System

More Georgians than ever before were taking advantage of higher education. The University System's fall quarter headcount enrollment increased by about 25,000 students (13.8 percent) during the Miller Administration. Enrollment at Georgia's postsecondary technical institutes also grew at a record pace. The University System enjoyed a 58.9 percent increase in total state general fund appropriations, not only for traditional programs, but also for new and innovative initiatives that propelled the system to the forefront of national higher education. *The Chronicle of Higher Education* praised Governor Miller for making "a strong financial investment in public higher education" and indicated that the rest of the country is "now very much aware of the innovation and progress of the University System."

K-12 Public Schools Enrollment Growth

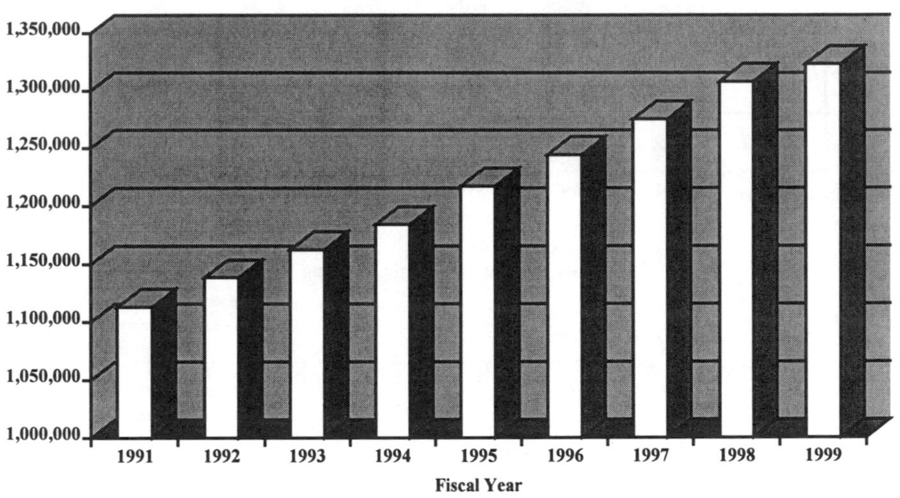

Georgia Voluntary Prekindergarten Program

Georgia has the most comprehensive, most extensive prekindergarten program in the United States, and we are the first state to make prekindergarten available to all parents who want their four-year-olds to attend.

Governor Zell Miller, April 25, 1997

"Georgia is in the midst of a massive education experiment to help reduce its high school dropout rate, teen pregnancy, and crime," reported the *Christian Science Monitor* on August 29, 1996. "Its target audience: four-year-olds." During his last State of the State address in January 1998, Governor Zell Miller told the state that he had grown up in a South that was ill housed, ill clad and ill nourished, "but it is not the South my grandchildren and great-grandchildren will grow up in." The Governor himself had contributed to changing Georgia for its children through the opportunities he provided for young children and preschool education.

Georgia entered the 1990s with an unacceptable school drop-out rate and an increasing teenage pregnancy problem. In 1992, after reviewing research indicating that students with strong preschool experiences were more successful in school, had higher self-esteem and were less likely to drop out of school, Governor Miller decided to make a significant preventive investment in the lives of Georgia's children. The Georgia Voluntary Prekindergarten Program was begun as a part of the solution.

The purposes of the prekindergarten program were to provide children with quality preschool experiences necessary for future school success and to provide resources and support for parents to ensure that success. The prekindergarten program provided children with a foundation of appropriate learning skills and activities that would enable them to be successful in school. They were provided with an appropriate learning environment to increase their cognitive skills while they were developing physically and emotionally.

Experts anticipated that this investment in children's lives would return larger dividends through decreased school drop-out rates, higher test scores, and increased participation in postsecondary education. Children who participated in the prekindergarten program would strive for higher academic achievement so they would be ready to accept the challenges of the twenty-first century. National studies also showed that society saved significant costs from an investment of this type in its youth. Research conducted by Florida State University's Center for Prevention and Early Intervention Policy documented that every dollar invested in quality preschool programs saved up to $7.16 in other costs to society.

A program of this magnitude had not been previously available in Georgia or anywhere in the nation. During the 1997-98 school year, approximately 70 percent of all eligible four-year-old children received preschool experiences in Georgia—60,000 served through the prekindergarten program and an additional 13,000 through enrollment with federally funded Head Start. The Georgia Voluntary Prekindergarten Program provided the largest preschool initiative, per capita, in the nation.

During the 1990 gubernatorial election in Georgia, Governor Miller proposed the creation of a state lottery for education. To ensure public support for the requisite constitutional amendment, he committed to the Georgia electorate that all funds would be used to supplement, not supplant, existing educational programs. He specifically supported the development of a preschool program. His efforts were bolstered by a study by the Carnegie Foundation for the Advancement of Teaching, which found that 40 percent of Georgia's kindergarten pupils were at risk, and a study that had tracked preschoolers to adulthood and discovered significant positive differences between them and their peers who had not attended preschool. He funded prekindergarten pilots with state general funds before the lottery began, to speed up its implementation statewide. After the voters of Georgia passed the constitutional amendment in November of 1992, he assigned senior staff in his Office of Planning and Budget, leaders of the Department of Education, and staff in the Department of Human Resources to plan the preschool initiative.

Unlike the development of other statewide initiatives, formative hands-on management came directly from the Governor, giving this program high priority in all policy deliberations. This high priority from Governor Miller was the driving force which enabled a program that was serving only hundreds children in its pilot stage to become the largest and most successful prekindergarten effort in the nation by the time Miller left office five years later. The success of the program was directly related to the personal involvement of Governor Miller.

The prekindergarten program began during the 1992-93 school year as a pilot program serving 750 at-risk four year old children and their families at 20 sites. These programs were school-based, center-based, and home-based programs, designed to meet individual community needs. Services were provided by 17 local school systems, one Head Start provider, one private non-profit provider and one private college. Three million dollars in state general funds paid for the program.

In 1993-94, the first lottery funds became available. Twelve of the original 20 pilots were expanded and 167 new sites began operation in more than 100 of Georgia's 159 counties. In its first year of lottery funding, the prekindergarten program continued its focus on at-risk children, and served more than 8,700 four-year-olds.

The next major prekindergarten milestone took place in September 1995 when the program was universally opened to all eligible four-year-old children, not just at-risk families. The program tripled its expansion efforts from 15,500 children in the 1994-95 school year to 44,000 slots during the 1995-96 school year. During this time, the private sector became an integral part of the program, which allowed the program to expand quickly without utilizing funds for capital outlay expenses on new buildings or expansion facilities. The formation of a public-private partnership of this magnitude was a first in Georgia and the nation.

The program continued to expand under the newly created Office of School Readiness from 57,000 children in 1996-97 to 60,000 children in the 1997-98 school year. Major improvements in program quality, implementation of learning goals and quality standards, simplified administrative requirements, and intense training for teachers were implemented during this two-year period.

By the time Miller left office, the infusion of more than $210 million annually for early childhood education had resulted in an unanticipated benefit. First and foremost, some 250,000 four-year-olds had enrolled in prekindergarten during the Miller Administration. In addition, because much of the funding was directed to private providers, quality in the child care industry in Georgia improved. By the 1997-98 school year, more than 925 private preschools were participating in the prekindergarten program—approximately 62 percent of the provider base. Since funding provided for equipment and materials for the four-year-old classrooms as well as salaries for certified teachers, much of the emphasis on quality early childhood education was trickling down to classes serving children age birth to three.

Prekindergarten Funding

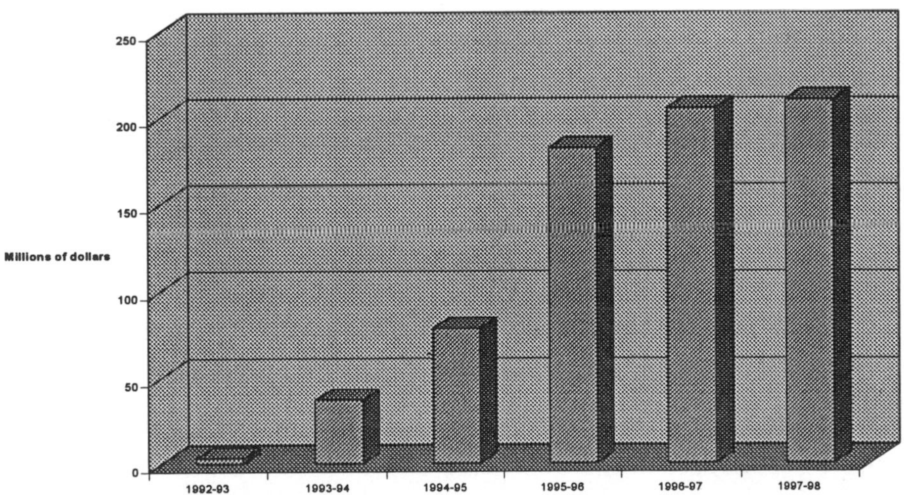

Unique program components

A national survey of public kindergarten teachers noted three primary essentials for school readiness: that children were physically healthy, rested and well nourished; that they were able to communicate needs, wants, and thoughts verbally; and that they were enthusiastic and curious in approaching new activities. The prekindergarten program provided children with experiences that fostered all these essentials.

An appropriate program for four-year-olds was not a watered down kindergarten program. Children learned through play and learning centers that were integral parts of prekindergarten classrooms. Prekindergarten programs reflected an understanding of how children learned by emphasizing active learning, consistent daily routines, and the use of positive behavioral management and assessment strategies. The school readiness goals of the prekindergarten program provided appropriate preschool experiences emphasizing growth in language and literacy, math concepts, science, arts, physical development, and personal and social competence.

By the close of the Miller Administration, the prekindergarten program was offered free statewide to all four-year-old children, regardless of parental income. To participate, children had to be four years of age on or before September 1 of the school year. The program provided a full 6.5 hour instructional day for children, five days a week, 180 days a year.

Choices for parents: Parents were given choices regarding their child's prekindergarten education. They had several school settings and curricula from which to choose, and, if income eligible, several different services that they might also qualify to receive.

A variety of organizations provided prekindergarten services—public/private elementary schools, public/private secondary schools, postsecondary vocational technical institutes, private and state colleges, private non-profit and for-profit child care learning centers, Department of Family and Children's Services offices, Head Start sites, hospitals, military bases, and YMCA/YWCAs. The public/private partnership enabled parents to choose the most appropriate classroom setting for their child.

Originally, all providers were trained in only one specific prekindergarten curriculum. As the program began to expand, it became readily apparent that additional curriculum options were needed to meet the varied requirements of a diverse prekindergarten population. Providers were allowed to choose from the following curricula: Bank Street, Creative Curriculum, High/Scope, High Reach Framework, Montessori, Scholastic Workshop, or a locally developed curriculum approved by the Office of School Readiness. Parents, after learning about each of these curricula, could choose a center that used the curriculum they felt would best meet the needs of their children.

Additional services were provided to children considered at-risk. Children could receive free/subsidized before and after school care if their parents participated in education or job training programs. Low-income children received free or reduced-price breakfasts, lunches and snacks. Also, transportation to and from the school was provided at no cost for income-eligible children.

Funding: To furnish optimal classroom environments, one-time start-up funding was provided to equip new prekindergarten classrooms. Providers were given a Basic Equipment, Supplies and Materials List to guide them as they purchased manipulatives, books, and supplies. Centers could also utilize funding to purchase computers or playground equipment with prior approval.

Funding, based on 20 children per classroom, was provided for salaries and benefits for lead teachers and teaching assistants, and for operating expenses. Each classroom was required to have a lead teacher and a teaching assistant. Providers were encouraged to employ teachers who were credentialed in early childhood education, and different levels of funding were provided based on types of teacher credentials. By the end of the Miller Administration 77 percent of lead teachers in the prekindergarten program were fully certified in early childhood education.

Quality standards for classrooms were established to ensure interactive learning opportunities that were age appropriate and met individual needs, to require appropriate scheduling practices and transitions to group practices, to promote interactions of children with materials/children/adults, and to enhance children's feelings of comfort, security and self-esteem. Learning goals for prekindergarten children were also developed. Intensive instruction was provided in the areas of language development, mathematical development, scientific development, creative development, physical development, and social/emotional development.

Health requirements and services: To ensure a healthy start, all children enrolled in the prekindergarten program had to have hearing, vision, and dental examination certificates on file within 90 days of starting the program. Evidence of age-appropriate immunizations had to be on file within 30 days of the start of the program. At the end of the school year, parents were provided with comprehensive information on all health and other documentation necessary for successful entry into kindergarten.

Parents as first teachers: Parents were encouraged to volunteer in the prekindergarten classroom and to participate in meetings, parent group activities, or workshops offered by providers or the Office of School Readiness. At least two individual conferences per year between the lead teacher and family had to be offered by providers and documented in each child's on-site file.

The prekindergarten program strongly encouraged parents to read to their children on a daily basis. To foster this habit at the beginning of each school year, children in the program were given a special edition of *The Little Engine That Could* with a personal message from Governor Miller discussing the timeless lesson of persistence.

Family support - resource coordination: Support services were a vital component of the prekindergarten program. On a voluntary basis, families were provided access to services that promoted stability and aided in the child's preparation for kindergarten. Resource coordinators were assigned to each at-risk student and were available to assist other families as requested.

The key focus of the resource coordinator was to involve parents in their child's educational development process. Parents were given opportunities to obtain needed health services for their child, attend informational seminars, attend child development seminars, etc. Individual parents were provided with community resource help as needed, such as GED information, employment counseling, access to literacy classes, assistance in obtaining Temporary Assistance for Needy Families (TANF) payments, access to substance abuse services, etc. Lastly, resource coordinators were responsible for helping families transition from prekindergarten into kindergarten through the Kindergarten Readiness Initiative.

Teacher training: To maintain quality teaching standards, various mandatory training options were available for all staff directly associated with the prekindergarten program. Lead teachers and teaching assistants were trained in the curriculum of their choice by curriculum representatives. Project directors and resource coordinators received customized training through the Office of School Readiness.

In addition, in-service training was available for lead teachers, teaching assistants, and project directors. Best Practices in-service training, developed by the Early Childhood Education Department at Georgia State University, was a collection of appropriate educational lessons and strategies for teachers and teaching assistants, who were encouraged to adapt the material to match their own personal teaching styles. This training was not linked to a specific curriculum, but pulled together math, science and language/literacy concepts from several curricula. Best Practices training was available at Georgia State University and was also disseminated through a variety of sources including an actual broadcast from a prekindergarten classroom via the Georgia Statewide Academic and Medical System (GSAMS). Multiple locations throughout the state received training simultaneously making the training more convenient and accessible for everyone.

Local coordinating councils: To assist in strengthening public/private partnerships, local coordinating councils were established in some counties. They included parents, representatives from public and private providers, health officials, educators, and representatives from business communities.

The purpose of the councils was to facilitate the sharing of resources and information. For example, local coordinating councils might provide forums for sharing instructional services, develop non-confidential waiting list information, update lists of community resources, or provide forums to discuss ideas and common problems.

Collaboration: Lottery funds were leveraged and combined with other fund sources to enhance and expand services to children and families. Before and after school programs were financed through a collaborative effort with the Department of Human Resources. Lottery funds were also combined with Head Start funds to provide full day prekindergarten opportunities for approximately 40 percent of Georgia's Head Start population. In addition, prekindergarten funds for family services were combined with other state funded initiatives such as Family Connection to hire full-time community resource workers. Lastly, federal at-risk dollars were blended to expand reading enhancement and literacy programs for prekindergarten families.

At-risk children: Special efforts were made to assist as many children from economically disadvantaged families as possible, since studies estimated that 40 percent of the population may be at-risk. These studies documented that disadvantaged children benefited educationally and socially from the opportunities provided in preschool programs. More than 30,000 children in the prekindergarten program were categorized as at-risk. Combined with a Head Start population of 13,000 children, Georgia reached an exceptionally high percentage of its four-year-old at-risk population. This high level of service to at-risk children was a critical component of the prekindergarten program. To qualify for at-risk prekindergarten services children/families had to be participants in at least one of a list of programs that included Food Stamps, SSI, Medicaid, Temporary Assistance to Needy Families (TANF), or free and reduced meal programs.

Office of School Readiness

In March 1996, the Office of School Readiness was created as a one-stop children's department incorporating prekindergarten, nutrition programs, childcare regulations and some early intervention services. The department's enabling legislation provided authority to:

* Administer programs and services necessary for the operation and management of voluntary prekindergarten;

* Administer programs and services necessary for the operation and management of preschool and child development programs, such as Even Start and child care regulation and food programs;

* Act as the agent of the federal government in administration of any federal funds granted to the state to aid in the furtherance of any functions of the office; and

* Assist local units of administration in Georgia to assure the proliferation of services under this chapter.

Since programs were administered at the local level, only a small state level staff was required. Consolidation of services streamlined the administration of each of the following programs at the state level:

Voluntary Prekindergarten Program (Age 4) - provided free preschool services to 61,000 four-year-old children by the end of the Miller Administration, helping develop school readiness skills necessary for future school success.

Child Care Services - licensed 925 private child care learning centers participating in the prekindergarten program at the end of the Miller Administration. The inclusion of authority to regulate private centers in the legislation creating the Office of School Readiness made a profound impact on the ability of the office to provide accurate and timely customer service to inquiries from parents, centers and the media.

United States Department of Agriculture (USDA) Child and Adult Care Food Program (CACFP) - provided nutritious meals to children and adults in structured care programs throughout the year. The program operated through providers approved by the Office of School Readiness to receive reimbursement for meals that met USDA guidelines.

USDA Summer Food Service Program (SFSP) - provided nutritious meals to children from needy areas during periods when public schools closed for summer vacation. This voluntary program operated through sponsors which administered sites approved by the Office of School Readiness to feed children free of charge. Children had to be 18 years or younger to participate.

Standards of Care Initiative (SOC) - was an integral component of Georgia's early care (ages 0-3) and preschool (age 4) services continuum. The SOC addressed brain development and early learning opportunities with very small children. The program recognized quality child care learning centers and awarded Center of Distinction Certificates to programs meeting stringent standards.

Georgia Head Start State Collaboration Project (CP) - was a federally-funded grant administered by the Office of School Readiness. The CP facilitated the involvement of Head Start in developing state plans and policies which affected preschool and other services to low-income children and their families. It was also responsible for creating collaborative partnerships with state programs which serve children and families. Head Start services were an integral component of Georgia's overall school readiness strategy.

Significant achievements

From 1993 through 1996, the Department of Early Childhood Education at Georgia State University conducted a longitudinal study comparing 315 at-risk children who participated in the prekindergarten program to a matched sample of children who did not participate in the program. At the completion of the kindergarten year, the prekindergarten children surpassed the children in the control group on teacher ratings of five different areas of development, promotion to first grade, and attendance. At the completion of the first grade, the prekindergarten children achieved higher scores on ten separate measures of academic development and achievement.

The 1993-96 study concluded that prekindergarten children scored more than three months (3.23 months) higher than their peers on general academic skills as measured by the Developmental Profile II, a widely used standardized test. Prekindergarten children scored higher than the national average on the Iowa Test of Basic Skills (ITBS):

National Average	50.00 percentile
Prekindergarten Average	55.00 percentile

On the Iowa Test of Basic Skills, the scores for the prekindergarten and control group of children were:

	Prekindergarten	Control
Math Problem Solving	56.39	49.84
Reading Comprehension	56.32	51.00

Prekindergarten children also had a higher level of school attendance as well as slightly more promotions and fewer retentions than the control group of children. The control group was absent over 26 percent more days than the prekindergarten children. The average number of days absent were 7.42 for the prekindergarten group compared to 9.38 for the control group.

Over 96 percent of the parents of prekindergarten children believed positive results from attending preschool were still evident in their children at the completion of the first grade. A parent survey found that the actual benefits exceeded parent expectations in the areas of developmental play, motor activities, and program enjoyment.

During the summer of 1996, the Council for School Performance in Georgia surveyed parents of children who had participated in the prekindergarten program and found that they overwhelmingly gave the program high marks in terms of quality and effectiveness. The parents indicated the prekindergarten program prepared their children for success in further schooling, helped their children develop social skills, and provided their children with a safe environment. Specifically, parents believed the program enhanced future academic achievement by improving children's vocabulary, counting and social skills.

In the fall of 1996, a new 12-year longitudinal study was initiated by the Office of School Readiness with the Applied Research Center at Georgia State University. The purpose of the study was to evaluate the long term impact of the Prekindergarten Program on children's academic achievement and attainment. The study tracked 4,000 children, both at-risk and non-at-risk. Methods for collecting this data included site visits, teacher and parent surveys, and review of school academic records.

The first year of the study focused on the service delivery aspects of the prekindergarten program. For the 1996-97 school year, across all measures of quality, findings suggested that services received by children and families were of high quality. Overall, findings revealed that most prekindergarten classrooms were fully equipped and prepared for prekindergarten children with various learning centers, equipment and materials. The majority of prekindergarten teachers seemed to be very satisfied with their students, and parents were overwhelmingly pleased with the program as a whole.

Second-year research for the 1997-98 school year addressed student readiness for kindergarten. The structure of the kindergarten classroom and teacher philosophies were also be measured. At year end, children were evaluated on the extent to which they had mastered skills for first grade, social readiness for first grade, frequency of recommendations for developmental first grade and the need for special education classes.

Year three longitudinal results for the 1998-99 school year tracked student performance, absenteeism, and grade placement. The effectiveness of specific curriculum related to at-risk and non-at-risk children was also analyzed, and the consistency of teacher beliefs and practices documented. Subsequent years of research would continue to study student, classroom, curriculum, teacher and parent issues.

Innovations in American Government Award: The prekindergarten program, already considered a success in Georgia, was recognized as the most comprehensive and unique preschool initiative in the nation, receiving the prestigious Innovations in American Government Award in November 1997. States from around the nation began to pattern new preschool initiatives on the successful Georgia model.

The Ford Foundation established the awards program to honor exemplary programs that addressed important social and economic initiatives that could be replicated. Administered by the John F. Kennedy School of Government at Harvard University, the program celebrated the capacity of federal, state and local governments to meet critical societal needs in a period of reduced resources and increased public skepticism about government. More than 1,500 applications were submitted annually for ten awards.

The *Atlanta Journal and Constitution* summarized the success of the prekindergarten program in a November 1997 editorial which said, "The words 'innovative' and 'Georgia' aren't usually found in the same sentence, but the state's acclaimed prekindergarten program is changing that. The pre-K program is often described as Miller's 'pet project,' but it may well end up being called his legacy."

Raising Standards and Achievement

I may be old-fashioned, but I believe that when it comes to education, children have to study, teachers have to inspire and parents have to care. As an old school teacher, I can tell you that when all that comes together, there's no stopping a child.

Governor Zell Miller, May 2, 1995

A former college history professor who returned to the classroom after his administration ended, Governor Zell Miller made education the priority of his administration. He set the tone in his inaugural address on January 14, 1991, when he said "The central purpose of the Miller Administration will be to prepare Georgia for the 21st century. Education is the most important part of that purpose. Without it, nothing else can save it. With it, nothing else can stop us." The Governor said he wanted to create in Georgia "a culture of higher expectations," in which the question was not "whether" to go to college or technical school, but "where." His goal was that two years of education beyond high school would become an expectation in Georgia. He succeeded by providing improvement tools throughout the spectrum of public education in Georgia.

Reading and after-school initiatives

Reading ability was always a primary concern of the Miller Administration because of the foundation it provided for all learning. The Governor was concerned that nationally normed reading scores for third, fifth and eighth grade students in Georgia were not increasing. In fact, the scores decreased slightly in the fifth and eighth grade reading between 1994 and 1997. To improve student performance in reading, Governor Miller earmarked $19 million to create two new reading initiatives, Reading 1st and Georgia's Reading Challenge.

The Reading 1st initiative began in 1996-97 with a two-school pilot at DeKalb County's Meadowview Elementary and Wilkes County's Washington-Wilkes Primary and Elementary Schools. In school year 1997-98 the project was expanded to include eight schools. Preliminary data showed students improving against each assessment measure as well as improving their scores on the Iowa Test of Basic Skills. The following assessment measures collected regarding these schools suggested that the Reading 1st program was making a difference.

Reading 1st Schools Preliminary Data - January 1998		
	January 1997	January 1998
Discipline referrals	2,591	1,296
Discipline referrals are down 49.98% as of January 20, 1998		
Special education referrals	172	104
Special education referrals are down 39.53% as of January 1998		
Library books checked out	99,250	107,097
Library books checked out increased 7.91% as of January 1998		
5,143 students involved in 8 schools		

In FY 1999, $9 million was provided to expand Reading 1st to 351 additional schools to improve the reading achievement of all students grades K-3.

Research and anecdotal evidence indicated that after-school hours were a volatile time for many of Georgia's school children. For example, most juvenile crime and teen pregnancies occurred during this time. One strategy that Georgia used to combat this problem was increasing the number of after-school programs. Beginning in FY 1998, grants totaling $2.6 million in state funds supported 26 after-school programs around the state. Governor Miller created Georgia's Reading Challenge to supplement that effort, earmarking $10 million for it in FY 1999.

The purpose of Georgia's Reading Challenge was to provide a quality after-school reading program for students in grades four through eight with opportunities to improve reading skills and enhance their interest in reading. The Georgia Department of Education offered competitive grant funding to public and private organizations for after-school reading programs. Certified teachers and support staff assessed students and provided individualized and small group instruction. Students were involved in meaningful, reading-related activities geared to their specific needs. State funding supported reading activities in existing after-school programs or established new ones. All Georgia's Reading Challenge programs were free of charge for those participating.

Elimination of general track diplomas

After listening to countless parents, teachers, school administrators, education organizations and concerned citizens, Governor Miller felt it important to have higher academic standards for all students so that they could leave school prepared for the future. The general track diploma, which no longer prepared students adequately for the requirements of either future education or work, was eliminated. Students were required to choose either vocational/technical or college preparatory curricula necessary to gain the proper skills needed to succeed. The number of courses in mathematics that students must take was increased. The Governor also reformed Georgia's student testing system, so that students took fewer but tougher and more comprehensive exams, and implemented a tougher test as a requirement for high school graduation.

At the same time as the general track diploma was abolished, Georgia's high schools and technical institutes developed a Tech Prep track, parallel to the college prep curriculum, to provide students with a planned program of study designed to prepare them for further study at a postsecondary technical institute. In addition to academic and applied classes, Tech Prep students were often give the opportunity to engage in job shadowing, internships, apprenticeships and other community-based learning experiences to help them define the careers they wanted to pursue. Students could also choose a dual program that combined college prep with Tech Prep, linking academic and theoretical concepts with the practical applications needed in a technological society. By the end of the Miller Administration, 385 Georgia high schools offered Tech Prep programs that were coordinated with the state's 33 public technical institutes and 14 colleges or universities throughout the state.

Georgia P-16 initiative

Prior to Georgia's P-16 Initiative, education agencies were essentially competing with each other for limited state resources. Governor Miller conceived of P-16, which symbolized a continuum from prekindergarten through four years of post-secondary education, as a strategy to change this competitive culture to a collaborative one. Through P-16, educational leaders learned that the success of each level of education depended upon excellence in the other levels. They looked for ways to build upon one another's resources and to work together to achieve common goals.

Governor Miller appointed 38 leaders from around the state to serve on Georgia's P-16 Council, which provided state-level coordination and leadership for the P-16 Initiative. The P-16 Council was composed of officials from the Governor's Office, the Department of Education, the University System of Georgia, the Department of Technical and Adult Education, the Office of School Readiness, representatives from the legislature, public schools, health and human service professionals, individuals from the private sector, community members and students.

The council held its first meeting on July 26, 1995. In charging the council with its responsibilities, Governor Miller stated, "My great hope for this council is that all three public education systems and the business community will come together and build upon their existing partnerships to create educational reform, which will ultimately improve student learning." The P-16 Council engaged in policy-setting discussions aimed at achieving educational reform throughout the state. The goals of the Georgia P-16 Initiative were:

* To improve student achievement from preschool through post-secondary education;
* To help students move smoothly from one educational system to another;
* To ensure that all students who entered post-secondary education were prepared to succeed;
* To increase access and success of all students in post-secondary education, especially from minority and low income groups; and
* To focus the co-reform of teacher education, advanced educator preparation programs, and the public schools toward practices that resulted in all children and youth meeting high academic standards.

The Georgia P-16 Council set the direction for educational change in Georgia. According to the Council, "The successful student is one who has met high standards and demonstrated achievement at each level, and is ready to advance to the next level – of work, of occupational training, of education – resulting in productive employment and responsible citizenship."

The Georgia P-16 Council worked with the Department of Education to link high school graduation requirements with the college admission requirements established by the Board of Regents. Additionally, the Georgia P-16 Council:

* Developed recommendations for strengthening post-secondary options available to students;
* Established standards of what students should know;
* Initiated efforts to improve teacher preparation and development programs; and
* Supported creation of a common student database to monitor progress of students as they advance through Georgia's public educational systems.

Governor Miller provided over $1 million in state funds to assist the Georgia P-16 Council and attract private and local match to support P-16 efforts. The Georgia P-16 Council received another $6 million in private funds through the end of the Miller Administration, including major gifts from the Woodruff Foundation, BellSouth Foundation and the Georgia Power Company. Private sector and philanthropic monies for the P-16 Initiative provided funding to support the efforts of 15 local P-16 Councils in piloting new directions and implementing grass-roots educational reform.

Mentoring programs

Mentoring was long known as an effective way to help students face challenges and build good decision making skills. When Governor Miller took office, the business community sponsored most of the mentoring programs in Georgia. While they were usually successful, there were not enough private resources being invested to make a significant difference to large numbers of students. The Governor decided to use a modest grant of state funds as an incentive for business to maintain and increase their investment.

The One-At-A-Time Middle School Mentoring program provided funds to local middle schools or nonprofit agencies for establishing new school-based mentoring programs or for continuing existing school-based mentoring programs, based on evidence of students' improvement in grades, attendance and conduct.

When Miller left office the program was in its fourth year of funding, targeting students at the middle school level who received one-to-one mentoring from an adult mentor. Volunteer mentors were carefully screened and went through an orientation and training program before working with students. Schools used mentoring models such as One-to-One Mentoring from United Way, A Mentoring Partnership for Our Children from Georgia Power Company, and Big Brothers/Big Sisters mentoring program.

Grants of up to $15,000 per school system were provided, and school systems and nonprofit organizations could work together to design and implement a mentoring program. An independent review committee read and rated applications, then submitted recommendations for approval by the State Board of Education.

The appropriation for the Mentoring Program was $500,000 annually beginning in FY 1996. In FY 1996, 90 sites were funded with grants ranging from $4,500 to $14,500. In FY 1997, 90 sites were again funded with grants ranging from $2,500 to $14,500. In FY 1998, 68 sites were funded with grants ranging from $5,000 to $14,000. In FY 1999, 72 sites were funded with grants ranging from $3,500 to $14,900. The number of students served grew significantly, increasing 56 percent from 1996 to 1998.

Summer school programs

A long summer vacation period had always been a part of the public education calendar. However, the summer break could have a negative effect on student learning. Studies documented that students typically returned to school each year having lost some of what they learned in the prior year. This was especially true of at-risk students. In 1990, no statewide program existed to offer at-risk students an opportunity to receive enrichment during the summer, resulting in the deterioration of academic skills and knowledge.

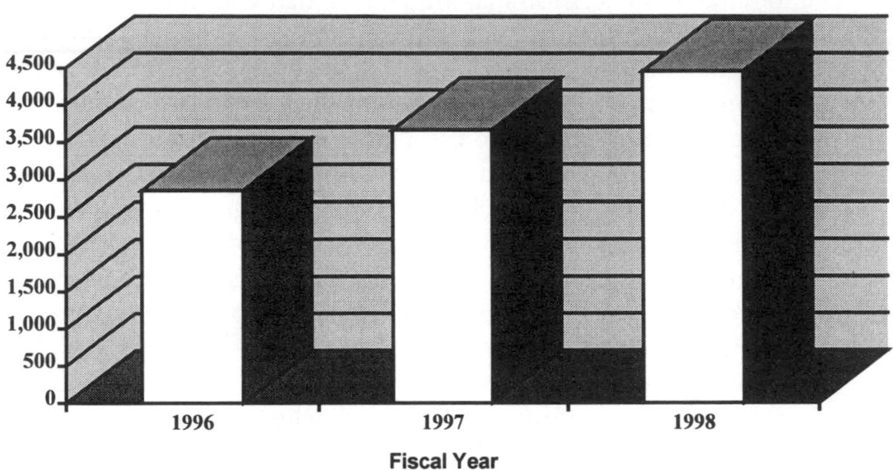

Governor Miller created the At-Risk Summer School Program and the High School Graduation Test Remedial Program to raise the academic expectation and performance of middle school and high school students in danger of failing academically.

The At-Risk Summer School Program provided funds for students in grades four to eight who were at risk as determined by their local school system. These students had been retained or had failed academic subjects. The program of studies included language arts, social studies, mathematics, and science. Participation was optional for local school systems and students. In the summer of 1997, the At-Risk Summer School Program served 20,275 students.

The Georgia High School Graduation Test (GHSGT) Summer Remedial Program provided grants to local systems for summer remedial programs for 11th grade students who had failed any part of the GHSGT. In the summer of 1996 (FY 1997), 4,494 students from 173 school systems attended summer remedial programs in one or more subjects. Program length ranged from five to 34 days, with some systems providing their program on the weekend while others used the early morning hours so as not to interfere with students' summer jobs. The appropriation for GHSGT Summer program was based on the number of 11th graders failing the various portions of the graduation test the previous year.

Governor Miller asked the Georgia Department of Education to evaluate both the At-Risk Summer School Program and the GHSGT Summer Remedial Program. The evaluations examined the data collected for summers 1995, 1996, and 1997 to determine if other data is needed to ascertain the effectiveness of the two summer remedial programs. Other questions asked were: What percentage of the target population was served? How much did the programs cost? What were their goals? Did the local school districts consider the goals to have been met? How did the programs notify parents of their existence?

Georgia High School Graduation Test Summer School, 1997

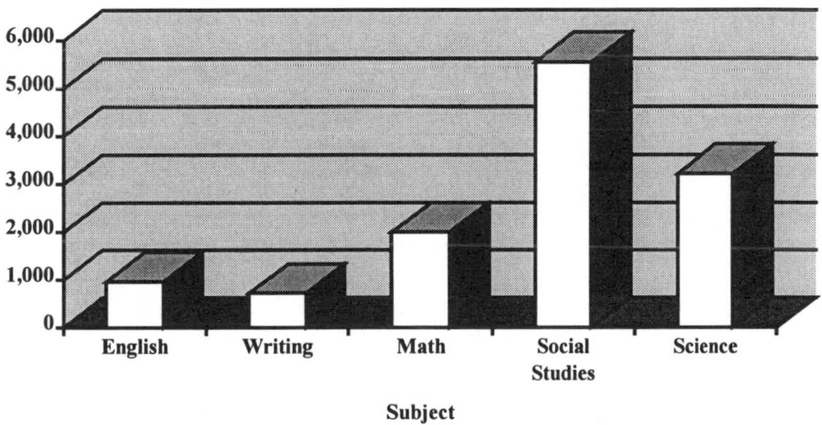

Youth Apprenticeship Program

Governor Miller entered office determined to change the low academic reputation of vocational education. Too often, vocational education programs offered unchallenging coursework for students identified as non-college bound. He developed the Youth Apprenticeship Program to address the critical need to provide a solid academic education, improve linkages between secondary and postsecondary technical institutes, and improve work-related learning options for these students. The Georgia Youth Apprenticeship Program offered students an opportunity to obtain an education that was both academically challenging and relevant to employment.

The program enabled a student to receive a high school diploma, a postsecondary certificate or degree, and certification of attainment of industry-recognized competencies. Employers and industry associations played a vital role in defining appropriate standards of performance, providing structured work-based learning, assessing student achievement, and awarding a credential that certified a student's mastery of skills. Upon completion, a student had an excellent opportunity to gain entry into a high-skill occupation.

The 1992 legislation creating the Youth Apprenticeship Program required that a comprehensive state system be in place by FY 1996. Governor Miller started the program in FY 1994 with $280,272 to fund 12 training sites, serving 44 students. In FY 1995, $2,000,000 funded 24 training sites, serving 280 students. These programs were pilots. In FY 1996, the first year of full-scale implementation, 51 sites served approximately 1,023 students. In FY 1997, 68 sites served approximately 1,480 students. In FY 1998, 67 sites served 1,830 students. During FY 1999, the program expanded further to over 100 sites.

Youth Apprenticeship Program

Fiscal Year	Implementation Sites	Students Served	Funding
1994	8	44	$280,272
1995	24	280	$2,000,000
1996	51	1023	$4,320,000
1997	68	1480	$4,320,000
1998	67	1830	$4,320,000
1999	100*		$4,320,000

* Projected number of sites

The state made a major commitment to this program, funding it at a level of $4.32 million from FY 1996 to FY 1999, the four years of full-scale operation under the Miller Administration. At the end of FY 1998, there were 67 Youth Apprenticeship sites involving 93 high schools, 75 technical institutes and colleges, over 600 companies, and the military. In each of the participating school systems, a position was funded for a Youth Apprenticeship coordinator to work with the students and business and industry.

The grants were over and beyond regular QBE funding and were intended to be used as start-up funding for program sites. Funding was for a maximum of three years per site, because the program sites were intended to become self-supporting.

Council for School Performance

Governor Miller always promoted quality and progress in education. To this end he established the Council of School Performance in 1993. The Governor and others appointed members of the governing board for the Council. Through a competitive bid process, the Applied Research Center of Georgia State University was awarded a contract to conduct the work of the Council. The Council for School Performance was legislatively mandated to provide the public with information about public schools and school systems and to evaluate Georgia's lottery-funded educational programs. Educators used the Council's findings to target school improvement efforts. Parents looked to the Council's reports to find out how well their child's school was serving its students and the community. Policy makers relied on the Council for guidance in the best use of public funds. As an independent entity, the Council stood in a unique position to provide accurate and impartial information regarding the state of education in Georgia.

According to Governor Miller, "The Council for School Performance, along with the Applied Research Center at Georgia State University, has done an outstanding job in keeping the public aware of school performance across the state. Their services include documenting the success of our state's lottery programs, especially HOPE and prekindergarten, and providing local school systems with data for further student achievement and advancement. Together, the Council for School Performance and the Applied Research Center continue to aid Georgia in her goal for excellence in education."

Helping Outstanding Pupils Educationally (HOPE)

The American Dream has always been that if you work hard and play by the rules, you can go places, you can be somebody. That's what the HOPE Scholarship Program is about.... It's about giving young students an incentive to study and work hard in school, by rewarding their achievement with a chance to get the education they need for the jobs of tomorrow.

Governor Zell Miller, June 1, 1994

Governor Miller realized that higher education was essential to his twin goals of an educated citizenry and a highly qualified workforce. Too many of Georgia's top high school graduates were choosing higher education institutions in other states, too many did not attend college at all, and too many were entering the workforce without the technical skills needed to get high paying jobs with bright futures. Conceived and named by Governor Zell Miller, the HOPE (Helping Outstanding Pupils Educationally) Scholarship Program put academic achievement on the minds of every family in Georgia. By the end of the Miller Administration, the HOPE Scholarship Program was fulfilling the Governor's commitment to provide Georgians with an opportunity to attend these great institutions. Five years, 331,000 students and $578 million in scholarships after it began, HOPE was inspiring Georgia students to study harder, record numbers were seeking educational opportunities beyond high school, and the burden of high college costs was lifted off the shoulders of thousands of Georgia families.

For the state itself, the HOPE Scholarship Program meant keeping the state's best and brightest students in Georgia colleges, attracting new jobs as corporate executives saw a more highly skilled workforce, and remaking

Georgia's national image as a state where education really mattered. HOPE "is the kind of thing you look at half in amazement and half in anger, and wonder why your own bonehead state didn't think of it," *The Philadelphia Inquirer* said in a editorial. "Not only does it solve the college expense problem for a lot of people, middle-class on down, but it gives students another reason to pay attention in school." Students were paying attention. A June 1998 analysis by the Georgia Council of School Performance concluded: "HOPE gives Georgia students more incentive to improve their academic performance, and more students are meeting the challenge."

Georgia's HOPE Scholarship Program was funded entirely by proceeds from the Georgia Lottery. Any student who enrolled in a degree program as an entering freshman at one of Georgia's 34 public colleges and universities, could become a HOPE scholar if that student was a legal resident of Georgia., was a 1993 or later graduate of an eligible high school, and had earned a B average, defined as a 3.0 cumulative grade point average on a 4.0 scale, or 80 percent grade average, meeting the college preparatory track requirements. If the student was on the technical curriculum track, the student had to have a 3.2 cumulative grade point average on a 4.0 scale, or 85 numeric grade average, meeting the curriculum requirements. The scholarship funded the cost of tuition, mandatory fees and a $150 per semester book allowance. Students had to maintain a B average year by year during college to remain eligible for HOPE. Full-time enrollment was not required.

If a student enrolled in a degree program as an entering freshman at one of Georgia's 35 HOPE-eligible private colleges and universities, the student could become a HOPE scholar if he or she was a legal resident of Georgia, was a 1996 or later graduate of an eligible high school, and had earned a B average, defined in the same way as public college students. Students at Georgia's private colleges received a $3,000 HOPE scholarship per academic year if they maintained a 3.0 grade point average. Full-time enrollment was required. In addition, all Georgia students at Georgia private colleges received a $1,000 tuition equalization grant, funded with general state revenues.

Students enrolled in diploma and certificate programs at any of Georgia's 33 public technical institutes also received tuition, mandatory fees and a $100 per quarter book allowance regardless of their high school graduation date or grade average. However, students enrolled in associate degree programs at technical institutes were treated the same as college students. They had to be a Georgia resident, a 1993 or later high school graduate and have completed high school with a B average, and they were required to maintain a 3.0 grade point average.

A student who graduated from high school before the HOPE program began in 1993, or who was not immediately eligible for a HOPE scholarship after high school graduation, could earn a HOPE scholarship with a cumulative 3.0 grade point average at the end of 45 quarter (30 semester) or 90 quarter (60 semester) hours of study.

HOPE also included a second-chance provision. Students who had failed to maintain a 3.0 cumulative grade point average after their freshman year could continue their sophomore year at their own expense. If such students had earned a 3.0 cumulative grade point average at the completion of the sophomore year (90 quarter or 60 semester hours attempted), they could receive a HOPE scholarship for their junior year. However, if they had not maintained that cumulative 3.0 grade point average at the end of their junior year, they would lose the scholarship and all opportunity to requalify.

Georgia residents who earned a General Education Diploma (GED) high school equivalency received a one-time $500 HOPE voucher, good for two years. This award could be used toward tuition, books and other educational costs at an eligible public or private college, university or technical institute.

Students who graduated from high school in the year 2000 and thereafter, were required to have earned a B average in their academic core-curriculum subjects of math, English language arts, social studies, science and foreign language.

History of HOPE

After a long and sometimes bitter campaign, Zell Miller was elected Georgia's 79th Governor in November 1990. "Zell Miller won the game of issues on a one-run single scored in the first inning," wrote Tom Baxter, a political columnist for *The Atlanta Journal-Constitution*, a week after the election. "The lottery may not be such a great reason for electing a Governor, but it's one more than his opponent gave, and last Tuesday, it was enough."

After his inauguration in January 1991, Miller quickly put a resolution before the General Assembly calling for a statewide referendum on an amendment to the Georgia Constitution to allow a lottery to be established. In 1990, as Lieutenant Governor, Miller had lost a fight to get a lottery referendum before the voters, when the House Industry Committee had killed his resolution by an 11-6 vote. Governor Joe Frank Harris was an outspoken opponent of the lottery, and House Speaker Tom Murphy said after the vote, "I just don't think people are that interested in it."

Once Miller was in the Governor's Mansion, however, the resolution to put the amendment before the voters passed the House on January 31, 1991, by a vote of 126-51, and was adopted by a 47-9 vote of the Georgia Senate. With the referendum vote set for November 1992, Miller hit the campaign trail again to sell his idea to Georgia voters.

"There were two groups of people who were opposed to the lottery," Miller told *The Columbus Ledger-Enquirer* in June 1998, as he recalled the 1992 referendum campaign. "About 33 percent opposed the lottery strictly for moral reasons, but there was another group, a pretty good-sized group, that did not believe a politician simply saying it would go for education. They had seen it frittered away in other states." That wasn't going to happen in Georgia. At a campaign rally in Athens on October 23, 1990, Miller had promised that if elected Governor, he would not let the General Assembly appropriate the lottery money. "The point is to make sure that the lottery money is not lost in the education bureaucracy or is not lost on the local level," he had said.

To get his message about a lottery's benefits and his promises to run it properly to voters, Miller immediately organized a 39-member commission called Georgians for Better Education, and named as chairman David Garrett, chief executive officer of Sunbelt Industrial Contractors. Bumper stickers supporting the lottery began appearing on automobiles reading "Georgia's Newest Cash Crop."

On September 22, 1992—six weeks before the crucial referendum vote—Miller held a series of press conferences in major cities across Georgia to formally announce his dream for a better future for all Georgians—Georgia's HOPE Scholarship Program. At the Atlanta kickoff at DeKalb College, Miller said, "The State of Georgia is going to reward academic achievement, not just with rhetoric and recognition, but with dollars. But the only way we can pay for the HOPE program, the only way we can make sure that we reward the hard work of our students, is to pass Amendment Number One this November, the amendment authorizing a lottery for education."

Quoting a study from the University of North Carolina, Miller said economic gains the South made during the 1980s would be wiped out without a massive effort to improve the skills of Georgia's workforce. He believed that the significance of college and technical institute education had grown to the point where it was absolutely critical to the state's future prosperity. "We are at a critical juncture in our state's history," Miller said. "It has never been more important for our students to get a college education, but it has never been harder for their families to pay for it. That's why I am offering HOPE."

At a lottery rally at Macon Technical Institute later that day, Miller said, "Sadly, too many of our families are realizing that their savings have left them too rich to qualify for most college aid, but too poor to actually pay the high cost of college. HOPE will catapult Georgia from the bottom 10 states to the top five in the nation in scholarship assistance we can give our children."

As the campaign for passage of the lottery progressed, Miller also argued that recruiting new jobs to Georgia would be impossible without a better-educated and skilled workforce. "Low-skill jobs are gone with the wind,"

Miller told *The Chronicle of Higher Education.* "Agriculture has changed, and the textile mills are all computerized. We were lucky in the 1980s, because people wanted to come here to get away from the problems elsewhere. But that won't happen anymore."

On November 3, 1992, the lottery amendment narrowly passed by a vote of 1, 146,340 to 1,050,674. A scant 52 percent of Georgians had supported it. A month after the election, Miller told a breakfast meeting of IBM executives that without HOPE, another generation of low and middle-income students would not have been able to afford education beyond high school. "By the year 2000," Miller said, "one year at a state college or university will cost 20 percent of the median family income. And one year at a private college will be half of median family income."

With the lottery approved, Miller quickly set about establishing a scholarship program modeled after the famous GI Bill. After serving three years in the United States Marine Corps, Miller had used the GI Bill to finance his own college education. Like the GI Bill, which required service in the U.S. armed forces, HOPE's most fundamental component was simple but iron-clad: students had to earn it. "Everybody wants dessert," Miller explained, "but few are willing to eat their spinach to get it." Many of the state's newspapers agreed. An editorial in *The Courier Herald* of Dublin was typical: "This program follows everything that is right about earning a college degree and becoming a member of society. Students are not handed money just for being students."

For administrative purposes, HOPE was placed in the Georgia Student Finance Commission, a state agency which had been helping students finance education beyond high school with a variety of student grants, loans and scholarships since 1965. In December 1992, the commission mailed letters to 100,000 Georgia high school seniors explaining HOPE's general operating guidelines. In addition, the Commission requested that all Georgia high schools provide a list of seniors who had maintained a B average during the first half of their senior year. Early in 1993, several drafts of proposed HOPE regulations were mailed to college and high school administrators for their comments and revisions.

To publicize the program, "HOPE Nights" were held across the state. More than 600 parents attended the first meeting in Macon. After listening to the presentation, Macon College President S. Aaron Hyatt told *The Macon Telegraph*, "There are a lot of families in our society with no way to support a child in college. This could be an excellent tool for parents. Say their child has a 2.9 (grade point average) going into their senior year, that child is going to get more encouragement at home." In addition to town meetings, an hour-long television special called "Dollars For Scholars: The HOPE Scholarship Program" was aired on stations across Georgia.

On September 1, 1993, Governor Miller personally awarded the first HOPE Scholarship to Matthew Miller (no relation) of Snellville to attend Gwinnett Technical Institute. HOPE had a modest beginning. When it was launched, it only covered the cost of tuition at Georgia's public colleges and universities, and only for the first two years of study. It also provided tuition for technical institute students who did not need to earn a B average to attend school. Private college students received a $500 grant which did not require a B average. In addition, the program had a family income cap of $66,000, an amount chosen to correspond with the federal income cap then in effect for EE Savings Bonds for college.

More than 42,800 students earned $21.4 million in HOPE scholarships that first year. Although enrollment at Georgia's public colleges and universities increased slightly, HOPE had a tremendous impact almost immediately within Georgia's technical institutes. "It's more successful than we realized it would be," said Alvin F. Anderson, president of Albany Tech. Anderson told *The Atlanta Journal-Constitution* that enrollment jumped 33.7 percent because of HOPE during the 1993-94 school year. "The average class size is now 37; previously, tops would be 19. We've got them in converted conference rooms. We've got them everywhere we can put them, and we're running classes from 8 a.m. to 10 p.m." East of Albany at Altamaha Tech in Jesup, enrollment mushroomed 71 percent because of HOPE. Eddy Dixon, vice president for student services at Macon Technical Institute, where enrollment increased 26.4 percent, told *The Macon Telegraph* that HOPE "basically provides a no-excuse plan for people who need to pursue some sort of educational training."

HOPE also helped sell the lottery to a skeptical public, which had narrowly approved the statewide referendum. "One doesn't have to agree with Georgia's lottery to admit that it is pouring money into education to fill needs that would have been literally ages coming, if at all," said a March 14, 1994 editorial in *The Times* of Gainesville. The *Calhoun Times* said, "There is one reason, and one only, to support the Georgia lottery and that is what it can do for education... Miller is trying to vault Georgia's education stature from the dunce's seat of the nation to the head of the class. He probably can't do it, but he should be given an 'E' for effort and an 'A' for sticking to the task." Mamie Pipkins, superintendent of the Echols County School System, echoed the sentiments of many Georgians when she told *The Valdosta Times* in January 1994: "We do not necessarily endorse the lottery. But it is good as long as it keeps giving benefits to the children."

The University of Georgia Alumni Association magazine *The Record* said in its September edition, "Zell Miller's political gamble has proved to be a bonanza for education." The magazine quoted Dwight Douglas, UGA's vice president for student affairs: "The scope of this program is unprecedented, and it sends a terrific signal that the people of Georgia value education and its importance to our future." The Macon *Telegraph* on May 16, 1994 interviewed Bettye Amica, a Northeast High School counselor, who said, "A lot of our good students are staying in-state because of HOPE. Out of 62 students, about 60 are staying in state."

Even the state's editorial cartoonists had fun with HOPE. An editorial cartoon appeared in *The Courier-Herald* of Dublin in May 1994 under the headline "How the HOPE Scholarship program got its name." The cartoon shows a child dropping off his report card with his father, who is holding a list of college costs. The parent is saying: "Oh, I hope it's a B.....I hope it's a B....I hope it's a B...I hope, I hope, I hope!"

Overlooked in the accolades showered on HOPE that first year was a little known facet of the program. Miller had recognized early on that something had to be done about adult illiteracy if Georgia's economy was to improve and the cycle of poverty that gripped successive generations of Georgians was to end. In some Georgia counties, four out of 10 adults had not graduated from high school. Many could not do the simplest of tasks—read a prescription bottle or fill out a job application.

Georgia's First Lady Shirley Miller was leading the fight against illiteracy. She recalled that when she and Miller sat down to talk about education before he announced his candidacy for Governor, adult illiteracy stuck out as a problem of immense proportions.

"We discovered that more than 592,000 adults in our workforce were functionally illiterate, which cost Georgia employers $2.1 billion each year in lost time, poor productivity and reduced profits," she said

Miller added a provision to the HOPE regulations that adults who earned their General Education Diploma (GED) would receive a one-time $500 HOPE voucher that could be used over the next two years to pay for tuition, books and other education costs at a Georgia college or technical institute. At the dedication of Chattooga County's Adult Continuing Education Services Center (ACES) in September 1994, Miller said, "More than ever before, what you earn depends on what you learn. Never has such a high level of literacy been demanded to get a good job."

From 1993 until the end of the Miller Administration, more than 100,000 Georgians earned their GED and received a $500 HOPE voucher to continue their education. The vouchers were valid for two years. By the end of 1998, nearly 20,000 of those vouchers had been cashed in at the state's colleges and technical institutes.

The Atlanta Journal-Constitution on January 12, 1994, profiled Bill Kaiser of Decatur High School. Kaiser had a college offer from Duke

University in North Carolina, but his single mom could not afford the cost of an out-of-state education. "Today, Kaiser is a premed student at the University of Georgia and his mother, a school teacher who didn't buy Governor Zell Miller's promises about the Georgia Lottery, is a believer in legalized gambling," the newspaper reported.

Joan Hollingsworth, principal of the Bradwell Institute in Hinesville, told *The Savannah Morning News* that 119 of her students qualified for HOPE Scholarships in 1994. "Our kids have benefitted more from the HOPE scholarships than from anything I've seen in 36 years," she said.

Miller also began faxing a series of campaign-style press releases to newspapers across Georgia touting what HOPE had done for their readers. "Not a single red cent of tax money is being used to provide these scholarships," Miller said in a release sent to *The Donalsonville News*. "And with my new proposals, even more students from Seminole County will be able to take advantage of the HOPE Scholarship program."

To *The Madison County Journal*, Miller wrote, "Just think of it, not only will these (changes) ease the financial burden on (Georgia) families, but it will give virtually every child in Georgia the opportunity to compete for tomorrow's jobs."

Pam Galloway, a guidance counselor at Central High School in Macon, told *The Macon Telegraph* that HOPE was a "godsend" for middle class students who may not have outstanding grades or the ability to win an athletic scholarship. "This is the group that would be going into the military or doing something else," Galloway said. "This is something for students who fall into this category, so now they can consider higher education."

Neighboring states were also beginning to take notice of HOPE, in particular because Georgia student enrollment in out-of-state colleges was falling. "Their program in Georgia has been innovative and it has worked," Democratic State Representative Doug Jennings warned the South Carolina House Judiciary Committee in late January 1994. Jennings told his colleagues that college tuition in South Carolina is "a struggle for the average middle-class family."

Randall Dahl, director of admissions at the University of Alabama, told The Birmingham News, "Since the HOPE scholarships, we've seen the number of applicants and admitted students (from Georgia) drop off markedly, perhaps by as much as 33 percent."

Auburn University president William Muse, noting that 12 percent of the school's undergraduate students were from Georgia, said HOPE "is a concern to us because we have over the years attracted a fair number of students from Georgia."

Auburn magazine, a publication of the Auburn University Alumni Association, said improvements such as prekindergarten and HOPE "have already proved an enticement to industry, business, and even such international events as the Olympics, as scores of companies have relocated to the state (Georgia) to take advantage of its increasingly well educated workers. "In short, educationally, Georgia is in the best of times," the magazine said. "It is a shining example of how an educational partnership between a state and its citizens can work to the benefit of both."

At Furman University in Greenville, S.C., 26 percent of the 1993-94 freshman class were Georgia residents. A year later, Georgia freshman enrollment dropped to 17 percent. In response, Furman hired a fulltime marketing person in Atlanta, and began offering HOPE-eligible Georgia applicants a $3,000 grant to offset the HOPE Scholarship. "The HOPE program is such a huge financial benefit that we had to do something," Benny Walker, Furman vice president for enrollment, told *The Wall Street Journal.*

Expanding and fine-tuning HOPE

As the 1994 General Assembly opened in January, Governor Miller unveiled an ambitious program to expand HOPE for FY 1995, which would begin following July 1. He proposed that HOPE pay for four years of a college or university education instead of just two, that the family income cap be raised from $66,000 to $100,000, and that in addition to full tuition, HOPE pay mandatory fees and provide a book allowance of $100 per quarter at public colleges, universities and technical institutes. The HOPE grant for students at private colleges would double, from $500 to $1,000, and students who had graduated from high school before 1993 or did not have a B average would be able to earn a HOPE Scholarship by attaining a cumulative 3.0 grade point average during their first two years (90 quarter or 60 semester hours) of study.

HOPE for Teachers: The following year, the Governor proposed another expansion to promote quality teachers for Georgia's classrooms. Zell Miller was first and foremost a teacher. "To me, this is the most noble of professions," he explained. "I grew up in a time and place where teachers were revered and were considered among the most important people in the community." As he visited schools across Georgia, Miller was bothered by the almost total lack of interest by the top students in pursuing a teaching career. He was also deeply concerned about the inability of Georgia's 180 school systems to fill positions with qualified teachers. More than 25,000 new students were pouring into Georgia's schools each year, and the pipeline of new teachers from Georgia colleges and universities was not keeping up. He knew that the key to improving Georgia education was finding and keeping the best classroom teachers possible. "No child learns to read in the Governor's office or in the chambers of the General Assembly," he said repeatedly in speeches across Georgia. "No child learns to multiply or divide in the offices of the State Department of Education or their local superintendent. If we want to improve education, we must change what happens in the classrooms of Georgia where our children learn."

To improve the quality of Georgia's teachers, Governor Miller proposed two special HOPE scholarships, funded through the lottery. The HOPE Teacher Scholarship provided cancelable loans ($10,000 maximum) to individuals seeking advanced education degrees in critical shortage fields of study such as math, science, foreign language and special education. Recipients agreed to teach in their critical shortage field of study at a Georgia public school (prekindergarten through 12th grade) for one academic year for each $2,500 awarded, with a maximum of four years to repay.

The PROMISE Teacher Scholarship provided cancelable loans ($6,000 maximum) to high-achieving undergraduate students (juniors and seniors with a minimum 3.6 grade point average) who aspired to be teachers in Georgia public schools. Recipients agree to teach in their field in a Georgia public school (prekindergarten through 12th grade) one academic year for each $1,500 awarded, with a maximum of four years to repay.

To publicize both programs, Governor Miller mailed a letter to every teacher and high school principal in Georgia on March 31, 1995. "Teachers are our children's most valuable resource," Miller wrote, "and I hope that you will be able to take advantage of this exciting new program." In addition, a live call-in public television program aired on May 3, 1995 on PeachStar, GPTV1. Both scholarship programs debuted on July 1, 1995.

Ten days later on July 11, 1995, Governor Miller hosted a milestone ceremony for Georgia's HOPE Scholarship Program. To a gathering of reporters, educators, parents and students, Miller introduced Amy Bradley of Stockbridge as Georgia's 100,000th HOPE Scholar. Bradley was an art education major at the State University of West Georgia.

"Thousands of parents all over Georgia have been urging their kids to do well in school, and scrimping and saving along the way in hopes of finding a way to send them to college or a technical institute," Miller told his audience. He said 100,000 HOPE Scholars meant "thousands and thousands of families in every corner of the state are receiving financial assistance.....that is both the promise and the fulfillment of HOPE."

Fine-tuning based on experience: Other changes in HOPE took place during FY 1996. Governor Miller completely removed the family income cap from the HOPE program, and instituted a new policy that gave students a second chance to earn HOPE if they lost the scholarships after their freshman year because their grade point average was not above a 3.0. While the family cap provision got little notice—it affected only five percent of Georgia families—the second chance program raised some eyebrows, particularly because Miller at first had been against it.

The issue was first publicly raised in September 1994 by *The Chronicle of Higher Education*, a national education publication based in Washington, which began its HOPE article by noting: "Georgia attracted the attention of educators across the country last year when it started the most generous state student-aid program in the nation. But after the program's first year, it appears that more than half of those who received the awards failed to meet the academic requirements to keep receiving the grants." The story said that 50 to 55 percent of HOPE recipients lost their scholarships because they did not have a 3.0 grade point average at the conclusion of their freshman year.

Two months later, on the eve of the 1995 General Assembly in January, Miller conceded that, "too many of the HOPE freshmen are failing to keep their B average. I want to reward hard work, I want to reward persistence, I want to reward good grades. If you made all Cs your freshman year you would have to make all As your sophomore year." Miller said he would give students "a second chance, but it's not going to be easy; it's going to be tough. That's what it's supposed to be."

With one controversy settled, two more popped up. First, some educators and legislators complained that HOPE scholars at private colleges were getting a free ride because they did not have to have a B average. Senator Guy Middleton, D-Dahlonega, said many newspapers printed a list of HOPE Scholarship recipients each year. "They (readers) see listed the people who qualify, and they know that some of these people are not particularly good students, and they are then calling their representatives and senators. It's an area really that's confusing the public a little bit. At some point, we're going to have to deal with it."

In January 1996, Miller dealt with it. He proposed that beginning with the 1996-97 academic year, Georgia students attending private colleges would also have to earn a B average in high school in order to qualify for HOPE, and then maintain that B average in college, just like students at public colleges and universities. In return, they would receive a $3,000 HOPE Scholarship. "This change will provide parity between public and private colleges, both in the academic requirements of the HOPE program and in the financial assistance it provides," Miller said.

Legislators supported the change. State Senator Richard Marable, chairman of the Senate Education Committee, summed up the opinion of most of his colleagues when he told his committee, "It's amazing what people can do when they have a little motivation."

Many of the Georgia's private colleges objected to Miller's proposal, insisting that achieving a B average at a private college was more difficult than at a public institution. However, their argument was diluted when *The Associated Press* reported that 45 percent of the in-state students attending Georgia's 32 private colleges in 1996 completed their freshman year with a B average.

The second change Miller proposed was that Georgia high school students, beginning with the class of 2000, would have their B average calculated on only academic core curriculum courses: math, science, English, social studies and foreign language. Miller proposed this change after newspapers across Georgia reported that more than 1,500 HOPE Scholars at public universities and colleges had to enroll in remedial math and English courses during their freshman year. He felt that if high school students were encouraged to work harder and do well in the more difficult courses, they would enter college better-prepared and less likely to lose their HOPE scholarships.

The Council for School Performance supported Miller's proposal with a report, released on January 24, 1996, that said 44 percent of the 1994-95 HOPE freshman at Georgia's public colleges, about 7,200 students, had earned a B average in high school by taking what Miller had called "easy, nonacademic courses." Eighty percent of those students subsequently failed to maintain a B average during their freshman year and lost their HOPE benefits. Without the scholarship, many transferred to colleges closer to home, or dropped out.

Most of Georgia's newspapers supported this *change. The Atlanta Journal-Constitution* said in an editorial. "Merit scholarships, like good jobs and worthwhile accomplishments in the real workaday world, shouldn't be to easy to attain. Giving students a false sense that merit is the same as mediocrity is cheating them and us."

The White House announces America's Hope

On June 5, 1996, speaking at Princeton University's commencement and 250th anniversary celebration, President Bill Clinton told graduates that a national Hope scholarship modeled after Georgia's program would be the centerpiece of his education platform in the coming election year. Sitting in the audience was his good friend Governor Zell Miller.

"More than ever before in the history of the United States," Clinton said, "education is the fault line, the great Continental Divide between those who will prosper and those who will not in the new economy... My proposal today builds mostly on the enormously successful HOPE scholarships in Georgia, which guaranteed any student in the state of Georgia free college as long as they had a "B" average. In recognition of Georgia's leadership, I have decided to call this proposal America's Hope Scholarship."

With President Clinton's praise, HOPE began receiving even more national attention. A month after Clinton's Princeton address, *USA Today* on July 29th profiled Melissa Bugbee, a straight A student at Oconee County High School who scored a perfect 1600 on her SAT and was accepted at Stanford, Duke and Harvard Universities. She chose The University of Georgia and a HOPE scholarship. "It (UGA and HOPE) was the best deal," she said. "I didn't want to pay $30,000 (a year) for an undergraduate degree."

In August, Miller found himself on the cover of *Lotto World* magazine. Inside, under a headline "High Marks for the Georgia Lottery," the article began, "If you've ever spent a dollar on a Georgia Lottery ticket, you probably didn't know you were educating a deserving young person. But because of a program developed by Governor Zell Miller, America's 'Education Governor', you're contributing to the higher education of Georgia high school students."

The Baltimore Sun reported on November 21, 1996, "About 77 percent of Georgia students with Bs or better now stay in the state (Georgia) for college, more than twice as many as did before the program. Governor Zell Miller has championed the scholarship as a core part of his economic development plans, as most college graduates tend to settle near their campuses."

That same day, *The Washington Post* discussed Maryland's plan to copy Georgia's program, and interviewed Dr. Stephen R. Portch, chancellor of the University System of Georgia on HOPE. "I think the HOPE program is in the process of changing the face of society in Georgia," Portch said. "It is raising aspirations and achievement. What you learn around the country is for many poor kids, they don't aspire to higher education because they think it's unreachable."

The next day, *The Washington (D.C.) Times* called HOPE "a peachy-keen idea" that was "not only an incentive to low-income residents,"but also forestalled "the exodus of bright students overall."

In October, a new Georgia Legislative Poll conducted by Beth Schapiro & Associates found overwhelming approval of the HOPE Scholarship. Five hundred adults were asked: "Do you think providing HOPE Scholarships to students with a B average or better is a good use of Georgia Lottery proceeds?" Ninety percent answered "Yes."

HOPE's impact

The first comprehensive analysis of Georgia's HOPE Scholarship Program was released on February 3, 1997, by the Council for School Performance. The Council, established by the legislature in 1993 at the request of Governor Miller to monitor public education, said a survey of all 311 public Georgia high schools found HOPE was having a tremendous impact on academic achievement. The study found that between the 1994-95 and 1995-96 academic years the Georgia high school students scoring at or above the national average on the SAT had increased from 31 percent to 33 percent. The high school dropout rate had declined from 8.6 percent to 8 percent. Nearly 11 percent of Georgia high school students scored in the top 25 percent in math on the SAT, up from 9.4 percent. Only 23.3 percent of high school graduates did not meet Board of Regents standards, requiring them to take remedial classes in the state's public colleges and universities, down from 27 percent.

That evening, President Clinton delivered his annual State of the Union address. Proposing a $51 billion package of education initiatives, including America's Hope Scholarship, Clinton repeated the praise he had given Georgia's HOPE program at Princeton University the previous summer. "We must make the 13th and 14th years of education - at least two years of college - just as universal in America as a high school education is today, and we must open the doors of college to all," Clinton told a national television audience. "To do that, I propose America's HOPE Scholarship, based on Georgia's pioneering program."

Governor Miller, in Washington attending a National Governors' Association meeting, was a Clinton guest in the Capitol gallery and later spent the night at the White House. The next morning, Clinton and Miller boarded Air Force One for a trip to Augusta State University and a roundtable discussion of education. Clinton's proposal of the past evening was bombarded with criticism, despite his plea to Americans that "politics must stop at the schoolhouse door."

The Augusta Chronicle ran an editorial which said, "We join in welcoming the President and hope he learns a lot, makes new friends, has a good time and will return some day. Taxpayers, however, be forewarned: Don't swallow his HOPE elixir." But Miller defended the President. "We believe you're right when you say the fight for our future must be waged and won in our classrooms," he said.

In a February 6, 1997 article in *The Christian Science Monitor* entitled "Why Georgia Grants Give Students HOPE," University of Georgia President Charles Knapp said HOPE has "begun to transform Georgia into a state with an education culture."

The Red & Black, student newspaper at The University of Georgia, said, "Congratulations are in order for Governor Zell Miller, whose HOPE scholarship plan was cited by Clinton as inspiration for creating a similar scholarship program nationwide. It's nice to see Georgia in the spotlight as a guideline for something positive for a change."

On February 10, *The Washington Post* said of HOPE: "Educators say it is having a wide impact. College enrollment in Georgia is surging, and analysts say the program is attracting more lower-income students to seek an education after high school."

Shortly after *The Washington Post* story appeared, United Negro College Fund released a new study that said black enrollment in Georgia public colleges was growing more than twice as fast as the national average. Black enrollment in Georgia's public colleges grew from 21,824 students in 1985 to 43,609 in 1996—a 99.8 percent increase. Nationwide, black college enrollment increased 40 percent over that same period. HOPE "really opened up doors for students that could not formerly afford to go to school," Joseph Silver, a University System of Georgia vice chancellor, told *The Atlanta Journal-Constitution* following release of the study. "Now if a student does what he or she is supposed to do, they'll see that they can get it and go to college."

Once they graduated, good-paying jobs would be available, according to a new report by the U.S. Bureau of Labor Statistics. The report said between 1990 and 1995, Georgia had added more high-tech jobs than any state except Texas. By the following year, Georgia had moved into first place, adding more high-tech jobs than any other state in the nation from 1990 to 1996.

HOPE for home schoolers

In his final change to the HOPE Scholarship Program, Governor Miller addressed the question of how to qualify home-school students for HOPE. Home schoolers had no school transcripts showing a B average, and were thus ineligible for HOPE. The issue was first raised in December 1996 by *The Rome News Tribune*, which pointed out that "there is no reason in a financial sense to deny their (home school) children access to those scholarships for no other reason than they attended a non-traditional school."

The issue was put into human terms by *The Associated Press*, which on March 24, 1997 profiled John Fuchko III, a 19-year-old student at Kennesaw State University. Fuchko had scored an impressive 1270 on his SAT and had a perfect 4.0 average after his freshman year. Yet he was ineligible for HOPE because he had been schooled by his parents at home. "They're (HOPE officials) are basically saying, 'We're going to punish you because you chose to pursue your education differently,'" Fuchko said.

Miller asked the Georgia Student Finance Commission, which administered HOPE, to adopt a policy. On November 18, the commission enacted a pilot program that allowed home-school students who maintained a B average during their first year in college to receive a HOPE scholarship retroactively for their freshman year. For the remainder of their college career, they would be on the same footing as all other HOPE scholars and would have to maintain at least a 3.0 grade point average to keep their benefits.

"Georgia's HOPE Scholarship Program is about expanding educational opportunities to all Georgia children," said commission board chairman Richard Maddux. "Home school students who meet our academic criteria should be able to earn a HOPE Scholarship, just like students in our public high schools."

In September, the State Board of Regents adopted a policy that home schoolers and others who attended non-accredited high schools must take SAT II tests in math, English writing, American history and social studies, and one of the biology, chemistry or physics tests to enroll in one of Georgia's public colleges and universities. For the 1997 fall term, 11 home school students were admitted to the state's public colleges and universities, and 92 home schoolers entered private colleges and universities.

Grade inflation?

The question of whether HOPE promoted grade inflation had simmered under the surface since the scholarship program was launched. *The Chronicle of Higher Education* said yes. The headline of a 1997 article said applicants to the University of Georgia "have better credentials, but grade grubbing and grade inflation are growing." The publication quoted UGA Professor Will Holmes as admitting, to participating "in some pretty wholesale grade inflation" to help students remain eligible for HOPE Scholarships.

The article did praise the program. "Many public colleges in Georgia are admitting more students with good grades and test scores," *The Chronicle* said. "HOPE is also credited with helping to increase the number of black students on public campuses, which has doubled—to about 44,000—over the past decade. With outcomes like that, the public's attachment to the scholarships has only grown." But the article also accused many Georgia high school teachers of inflating grades. "In a lot of Georgia high schools, a B is for breathing," Arnold Fleischmann, a UGA associate professor of political science, told *The Chronicle.*

Eight months later, however, the Council on School Performance released a study demonstrating that SAT scores had steadily risen over the prior four years for students who had barely made the B average required to receive HOPE benefits, indicating that making a B average in Georgia's high schools was getting harder, not easier. The study said had grade inflation increased, more marginal students with lower SAT scores would be qualifying for HOPE scholarships. "If grade inflation had occurred in those borderline students, you would have figured their SAT scores would be declining," Gary Henry, head of Georgia State University's Applied Research Center which performed the study for the Council, told *The Athens Banner- Herald.* "We find the opposite results... There has been grade inflation in Georgia throughout the last 10 years," Henry said. "There has been grade inflation in every other (southern) state. What we find peculiar is the grade inflation has slowed since HOPE."

The study also found that recipients of Georgia's HOPE Scholarship were more likely to stay in college, have higher college grade point averages and earn more credit hours than students who did not receive the scholarship.

HOPE after five years

The first lottery ticket had been sold on June 29, 1993. As its fifth anniversary approached, newspapers across the state returned to the opponents of the lottery who fought Governor Miller's proposal. Typical were Tom Black and Mary Sue Polleys in Columbus. Both told *The Columbus Ledger-Enquirer* that they still opposed the lottery, but praised Governor Miller's steadfast resolve to keep the proceeds channeled toward education. "As far as I'm concerned, the real positive is that the promise has been kept for the proceeds to be used for education," Black, who chaired the Columbus Lottery Defeat Committee in 1992, said.

Polleys, who had become chair of the Muscogee County school board, still felt the lottery "causes some who are economically disadvantaged to become even poorer... I think state leaders have done a good job using it for extras in education, and not letting it become replacement money as has happened in so many states," she said. "The governor promised he would and that's what he has done."

Whereas the lottery squeaked by with a 52 percent vote in 1992, five years later it had widespread approval, according to a June 1998 poll by *The Atlanta Journal-Constitution.* The poll found 75 percent of Georgia voters would vote to continue the lottery, with weekly churchgoers, the biggest opponents of the lottery five years ago, now favoring it by nearly a 2-to-1 margin.

Governing magazine in its January 1998 edition said many state lotteries were "shams," with state officials "playing a shell game, using lottery money to supplant general revenue funds for education, while the legislature reassigns those dollars to Medicaid, corrections and social services." The magazine said the lone exception was the State of Georgia.

"Is it possible for a state to create a lottery law that does guarantee extra money to a favored cause? Apparently, yes. Georgia seems to have done it," the magazine said, quoting figures that showed state funding for education in Georgia had climbed from 52 percent of the state budget to 54 percent in the prior three years. Excluding the lottery money for education, state tax dollars earmarked for education had increased from \$4.7 billion to \$5.6 billion.

HOPE's statewide approval rating was better than 90 percent, in no small part due to studies and reports that said HOPE had done far more than even

Governor Miller promised. A 1998 study by the Council on School Performance concluded HOPE "has encouraged the development of local business by providing a better skilled and equipped workforce. It has promoted educational values within the community (and) upgraded the human capital of workers in the community, which has resulted in a higher standard of living."

A good portion of the training for that "better skilled and equipped workforce" took place within Georgia's 33 public technical institutes, the study said. When HOPE was created, 64,100 Georgians were enrolled in HOPE-eligible programs at technical institutes across Georgia. During the 1997-98 academic year, the enrollment was more than 97,500 students, and the Georgia State study noted that HOPE had "a particularly strong impact on increasing the accessibility of technical education to groups that were previously under represented at technical institutes, particularly females and minorities."

Moreover, schools across Georgia were reporting that students were earning better grades, and a higher percentage of Georgia students were enrolling in state colleges and universities. According to a June article in *The Augusta Chronicle*, the "average high school grade point average was 3.24 on a 4.0 scale and the average SAT score was 1147 out a possible 1600 for incoming freshman in the fall of 1992, the year before the HOPE Scholarship started. Last fall (1997), the average GPA was 3.45 and the SAT was 1174."

At both the University of Georgia and the Georgia Institute of Technology, 98 percent of the incoming freshmen during the 1997-98 academic year were HOPE Scholars. At Spelman College, 100 percent of the freshmen were HOPE recipients.

HOPE had also catapulted Georgia into a number one national ranking, something Zell Miller had long dreamed about. A study by the National Association of State Student Grant and Aid Programs (NASSGAP) found as a result of HOPE, Georgia distributed more than twice as much academic-based financial aid to students seeking postsecondary education than any other state. After almost eight years of effort by Miller, Georgia was finally ranked first among the 50 states in an education category. The Top Ten NASSGAP rankings were:

State	Academic-Based Student Financial Aid	Principal Program
Georgia	$183.7 million	HOPE Scholarship Program
Florida	75.2 million	Florida Undergraduate Scholars Fund
Ohio	41.9 million	Ohio Academic Scholarships
North Carolina	28.8 million	Principal Fellows Program

Illinois	26.1 million	Merit Recognition Scholarships
Virginia	21 million	Virginia Scholars Program
Missouri	13 million	Higher Education Academic Scholars
Colorado	11.2 million	Undergraduate Merit Scholars
Louisiana	9.5 million	Louisiana Honors Scholarships
New Jersey	8.6 million	Garden State Scholars Program

Georgia was also ranked number one in another category. The study found that 76.6 percent of Georgia undergraduate college and university students were receiving some type of financial aid during the 1996-97 academic year. In second place was Vermont (50.5 percent); followed by New Jersey (48.1), New York (47.1), Ohio (44.5), Pennsylvania (39.3), Illinois (37.1), Maine (35.7), New Mexico (35.3) and Colorado (34.8).

The number one rankings sparked a number of complimentary editorials in Georgia newspapers. The *Warner-Robins Daily Sun* said, "As Governor Zell Miller stated just last week, 'The message that HOPE sends to Georgia students is clear: if you work hard in school, you'll be rewarded for it.' Isn't that the American dream?"

"This is good news for everyone, regardless of their stance on the lottery," *The Americus Times* said. "It keeps people employed in the state's educational institutions and it stimulates the local economy when students come to our communities to live, work and spend money, and when their families come to visit. Students who are in school are less likely to get into trouble, as in getting arrested or pregnant... The HOPE Scholarship has made and is making dreams come true in Georgia - you can bet on it."

HOPE even began to influence where people in states surrounding Georgia chose to live. The *Wall Street Journal*, under the headline "Chasing HOPE Scholarship Plan is Sparking Migration Into Georgia," reported that while HOPE was created "to jump-start the state's education system, (it) is having another, less-expected effect. It is shifting where people live in the Southeast." The newspaper told the story of Jim Gaines, whose employer transferred him from Atlanta to Chattanooga. Instead of locating in Tennessee, Gaines moved his family to Graysville, Georgia—just a 20 minute drive from downtown Chattanooga. "We're folks who live paycheck to paycheck," his wife Robin told the newspaper. "The whole package is so good, you'd be crazy not to take advantage of it."

The Atlanta Journal-Constitution reported on the same trend. Dr. Robert Becker, director of the Strom Thurmond Institute at Clemson University in South Carolina, told the newspaper that people with school-age children were settling on the Georgia side of the Savannah River in the Augusta area. "But I think the real effect of the HOPE scholarship upon Georgia is more than the incremental change in property values," he added. "It's the impression of Georgia as a forward-thinking state that has drawn in brighter kids around the region and nation."

The Journal-Constitution found the same pattern in Chattanooga. It quoted Tennessee Senate Majority Leader Ward Crutchfield (D, Chattanooga), "It's not a mass exodus (of Tennesseans to Georgia), but unless we do something, there's so much money going into Georgia that it's hurting us." Patsy Reynolds, the University of Tennessee-Chattanooga admissions director, put it more simply: "We're banging our Bibles here, but we're spending our money there (in Georgia)."

Tennessee was not the only state looking for a HOPE scholarship program. More than 36 states and Puerto Rico asked for information about the program. Florida's new "Bright Futures" scholarship program was directly modeled after HOPE. Kentucky Governor Paul Patton proposed spending $10 million in 1999-2000 to begin a merit scholarship program like HOPE. In Alabama, the 1998 Democratic nominee for Governor proposed establishing a lottery to fund a HOPE program. In addition, staff members from the Georgia Student Finance Commission were invited to address legislative committees in Maryland, North Carolina and Connecticut.

Officials of each of these states saw a scholarship program that after just five short years had revitalized public education in Georgia. Education statistics for Georgia from 1993 to 1998 painted an awesome picture of achievement. Some 331,000 Georgia students earned HOPE Scholarships valued at nearly $615 million. The high school dropout rate was down to 6.7 percent. Georgia had the third largest one-year gain in teacher salaries in the nation last year. Per pupil expenditures had risen 55 percent in the past five years, or more than $2,000 per pupil. The HOPE Teacher and PROMISE Teacher Scholarship programs awarded more than $22 million in scholarships to 5,257 Georgia teachers and students. High school graduates enrolling in college increased by eight percent from 1988 to 1996. The number of Georgia high school students completing 18 or more courses in academic subjects increased by six percent. The percentage of Georgians 25 years of age or older who had earned a bachelor's degree increased by 2.8 points between 1990 and 1996.

But after all the accolades, all the accomplishments and all the awards, the story of HOPE was really about Georgia's children, whom Governor Miller considered the future of Georgia. One of those children, Misty Denise Smith of Gainesville, addressed an audience gathered at Columbia University in New York on April 8, 1998, to honor Governor Miller with the Thomas H. Kean Award for special contributions to education. Smith was a HOPE Scholarship recipient at Gainesville College.

She told her listeners that her father and mother had carefully planned for three daughters' education. "My father had a good job with a good income and was able to save for the future. But fate had another plan. When my twin sister and I were 12 and my oldest sister was 16, our dad was diagnosed with cancer and two years later he died. As you would expect, before his death all the family savings, including the three savings accounts for his three daughters' education, were spent in an attempt to save his life." Misty's mother had an eighth grade education and worked on an assembly line. College was in danger of becoming only a dream.

"I can honestly say that without Governor Zell Miller's vision of a scholarship program for all Georgians called HOPE," Misty said, "My twin sister and I could not have attended college." She concluded, "I think this would be an appropriate time for me on behalf of all those Georgia students that have benefitted from Governor Zell Miller's monumental vision, to thank him for giving us hope."

Other scholarships

The Law Enforcement Personnel Dependents Grant (LEPD) was created by Governor Miller to assist children of a law enforcement officer, fire officer, or prison guard in Georgia who had been permanently disabled or killed in the line of duty, to attend an eligible private or public college, or public technical institute in the State of Georgia. Students had to be full-time, enrolled in an undergraduate program, and maintain satisfactory academic progress. Recipients could receive up to $8,000 for four years of undergraduate study, i.e., $2,000 per academic year. In FY 1998, a total of 38 students were served by this program, and awards totaled $68,665.

Georgia Military Scholarships were provided to assist outstanding students at Georgia Military College, (GMC) and North Georgia College and State University who intended to pursue a military career. The goal was to strengthen Georgia's National Guard with young people who had a high-quality military education. Given the small number of military schools in Georgia, Governor Miller began this scholarship program to provide access to students across the state. The Georgia Military College Scholarship was entirely lottery funded. Recipients had to be enrolled as a full-time undergraduate at GMC and have had at least a 2.5 high school GPA. Students who received scholarships were obligated to serve in the Georgia Army National Guard for two years after graduation. In FY 1998, 64 students were awarded GMC scholarships totaling $554,694.

Law Enforcement Personnel Dependents (LEPD) Grant Awards

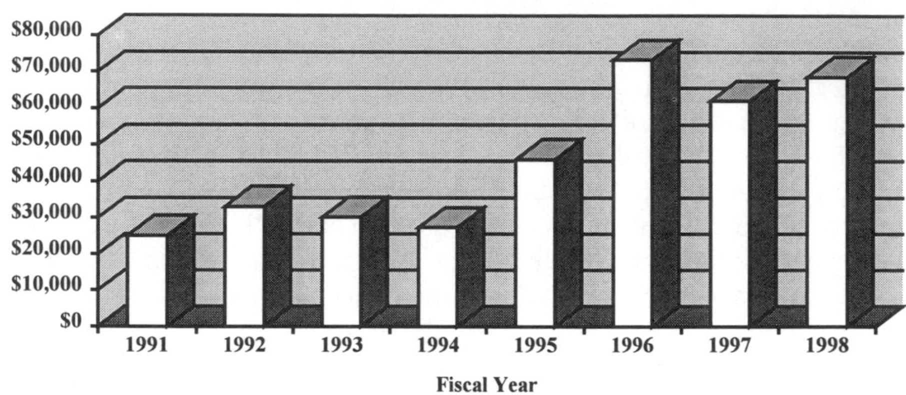

Georgia Military College State Service Scholarship Awards

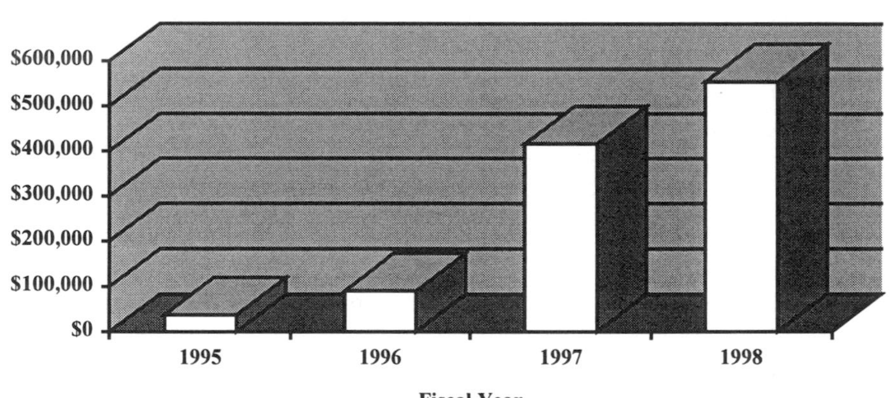

Other Programs to Increase Access to Higher Education

Anyone in American can aspire to be a doctor, a teacher, a governor, even the President but the only way you can actually get any of these important jobs is if you have the opportunity to acquire the education and skills you need.

Governor Zell Miller, April 30, 1997

Tuition equalization grants

Governor Miller always promoted state support for private colleges and universities. He would point out that for every student educated in a Georgia private college, the state saved 75 percent of the cost of public college tuition for that student. As a young state senator in 1962, he introduced legislation that would later be the basis for the tuition equalization grant (TEG). TEGs actually became law in 1973. The TEG was state-funded support for Georgia students enrolled at private Georgia colleges and universities, and for certain residents who lived near the state's border and attended out-of-state four-year public colleges for programs that were not available closer at a Georgia college.

TEGs were provided to students in most states across the nation. Some states awarded private college grants that were restricted to students with a demonstrated financial need. Other states, like Georgia, provided grants that were non-need-based and available to all students. There were a few states that offered both restricted and non-restricted grants. Typically, TEGs awarded to need-based students remained constant from FY 1991 through FY 1994. These grants ranged from approximately $1,200 to $2,900 in states such as Florida, Kentucky, North Carolina, South Carolina and Texas. For grants that were not need-based, the awards fluctuated over time. Grants in Alabama, Florida, North Carolina and Virginia ranged from $750 to $1,500.

In 1991, Georgia's tuition equalization grant was $925 per student per academic year, which was not sufficient to maintain healthy competition between public and private institutions of higher education. Even though Governor Miller succeeded in raising the TEG to $1,000 in 1992, the inception of HOPE for the public colleges would have exacerbated the situation had he not included private colleges in the HOPE Scholarship Program in 1993. Originally, HOPE included a what was called a second-tier TEG of $500 per year in addition to the $1,000 TEG provided from state general funds. For the 1994-1995 school year, this HOPE/TEG was raised to $1,000 and again in 1995-96 to $1,500 on top of the traditional $1,000 TEG. For the first three years of the HOPE/TEG grant, its recipients did not have to maintain a certain GPA to renew the grant each year, as the students at public colleges did in the regular HOPE Scholarship Program.

Beginning with the 1996-97 school year, however, the HOPE/TEG was discontinued. All new students entering private colleges from that point on received the traditional $1,000 TEG, and those who maintained a B average received a HOPE scholarship of $3,000 in addition, double what the HOPE/TEG had been. This change provided parity between students at public and private institutions in both the requirements for HOPE eligibility and value of the assistance. Those students who were already receiving the $1,500 HOPE/TEG when the 1996-97 school year began, continued to receive it through their graduation or until spring term 1999, when it was phased out completely. A total of 49,489 students received the HOPE/TEG grant at private colleges from 1993 to 1998. Governor Miller wanted Georgia students to have the option of attending a public or private institution in the state. This HOPE scholarship along with the TEG grant offered young students this choice by reducing the cost differential between public and private institutions and creating an incentive for students to work hard in school.

Georgia Tuition Equalization Grant Awards

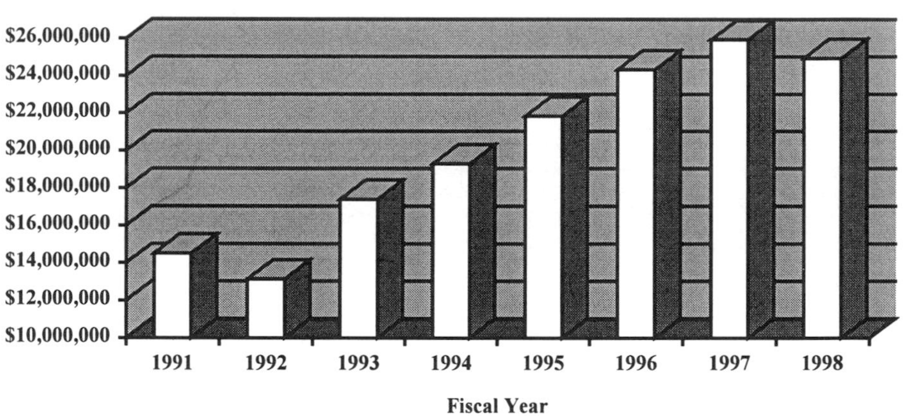

Postsecondary Options

Governor Miller believed that increasing access to quality postsecondary education had to begin in high school. High school should create the expectation that students would attend a postsecondary institution. In 1991, few opportunities existed for students to develop this attitude, so the Governor sponsored three initiatives to provide incentives for students to develop the skills needed to be successful after high school. In 1991, the only way a student could get a jump on a postsecondary education while still in high school was through a "joint enrollment" program. Certain high schools would make arrangements with nearby colleges to have college courses taught at the high school, with the students' families paying the tuition.

Governor Miller created the Postsecondary Options (PSO) program to give all 11th and 12th grade students in Georgia public schools access to the benefits of such a program. Eligible students could take college and technical school courses free of charge and earn both high school and postsecondary credits while still in high school. Students who lived 25 miles or more from a public institution could enroll in PSO courses at private post-secondary institutions. Lottery funds paid for tuition, books and fees.

At that time, 20 states, including Georgia, offered statewide programs that allowed high school students to take college courses for credit. Of those 20 state programs, 11, including Georgia's, were considered comprehensive programs in which students could earn both high school and college credit, with few restrictions on eligible courses and most of the associated costs paid by the state.

According to the Council for School Performance, the available data showed that participation in PSO was related to student performance. Schools with higher PSO enrollments tended to have above average student performance as measured by SAT scores and the percentage of students passing the state graduation exams. In schools with the highest PSO enrollment (upper quartile), 42 percent of the students scored at or above the national median on the SAT. In schools with no PSO enrollment, only 29 percent of students attained that level. Almost 88 percent of students in schools with the highest number of students enrolled in PSO passed the state graduation test in writing, compared to 81 percent in schools without PSO.

The PSO program grew considerably after its inception in 1993; enrollment increased by 180 percent over the remainder of the Miller Administration. Data concerning the number of credit hours earned also mirrored this increase. PSO's growth showed that high school students throughout Georgia were capable of higher levels of achievement and that providing greater access to higher education pays off.

Postsecondary Options

Fiscal Year	Number of High School Students	Number of Quarter Credit Hours Earned	Funding
1994	2,406	19,240	$545,855
1995	3,933	34,305	$1,128,214
1996	4,904	42,744*	$1,313,015
1997	6,015	51,183	$1,925,693
1998	7,797	78,019	$3,061,000
TOTAL	**25,005**	**225,491**	**$7,973,777**

* Estimated

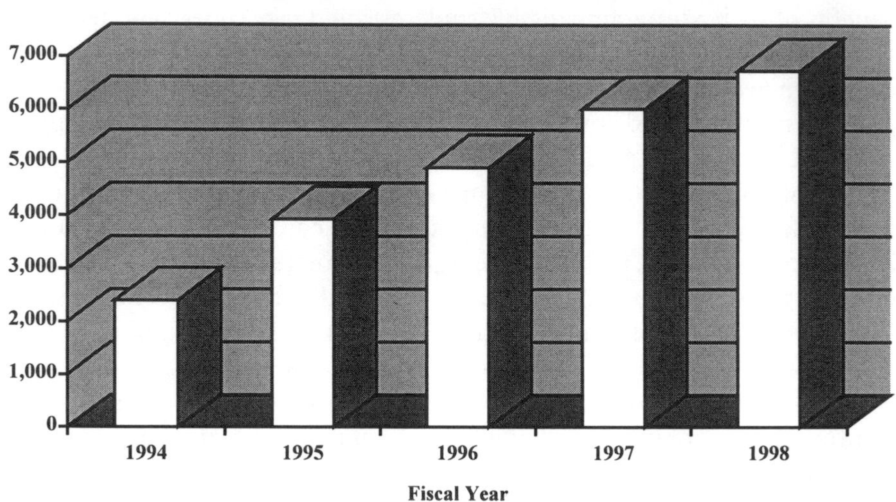

Postsecondary Readiness Enrichment Program

Governor Miller never believed that academic achievement was only for a few. He often said that he wanted all Georgians to be concerned with which educational path to take after high school, not whether to take one. When the P-16 Council developed the Postsecondary Readiness Enrichment Program (PREP) initiative, Governor Miller supported it enthusiastically.

PREP was a year-round academic support and outreach program created by the University System of Georgia in cooperation with the Departments of Education and Technical and Adult Education. PREP provided exposure to the campuses of public colleges, universities and technical institutes and was designed to help students and their parents make timely, informed decisions that would prepare young people for their higher education and career goals. It was launched as a pilot program in 1996 at four University System institutions.

The Board of Regents launched its "PREP it Up!" communications campaign in spring 1997, which was developed with private sector support and targeted seventh and eighth grade students. This video and broadcast campaign sought to increase students' awareness of the new admission requirements which would go into effect for University System institutions in 2001. The new standards increased the number of high school college preparatory curriculum (CPC) units required for admission to all public institutions from 15 to 16, with the additional unit being in mathematics. Students would be required to present a transcript that included four units of English, four of mathematics, three of science, three of social science and two of foreign language. A new formula called the Freshman Index, which was a combination of an applicant's SAT or ACT (American College Test) score and high school GPA would be used to help determine a student's readiness for college work. The campaign targeted successive classes of seventh graders, increasing their awareness of the new challenges they faced.

PREP's primary and critical goal was to help students in at-risk situations get on the right track for admission into the state's public colleges, universities and technical schools, broadening the choices they would have after graduating from high school. The program provided year-round academic readiness and enrichment programs through after-school activities with college students and faculty that included leadership development, tutoring and mentoring. PREP also held Saturday morning academies in which students were invited to visit colleges to take part in some classes and talk with college students and faculty.

Students who had been involved with the academic program during the year were invited to attend two-week summer camps on a college campus. They typically took classes in math, science, humanities or the arts in the mornings, then participated in recreational activities like tennis, golf and swimming in the afternoons. An overnight stay in a campus dormitory was another exciting part of this summer program.

By 1998, PREP programs were offered by 25 University System institutions at approximately 208 middle schools throughout Georgia. The 25 University System institutions were grouped, with two to four of them working together to enhance the efficiency and effectiveness of the program. Approximately 20 technical institutes were also involved in the collaborative sites.

PREP funding came largely from private partners like BellSouth, Georgia Power Company and the Woodruff Foundation, and state grants. State appropriations for FY 1999 totaled $1.6 million and a typical grant to a PREP program was approximately $135,000.

Middle school personnel and PREP coordinators selected students, using criteria of at-risk situations as established by the Department of Education. Academic potential was also a criterion used in the selection process. All PREP students were required to do community service projects; they were involved in over 120 different projects in 1998. PREP gave these students a wonderful opportunity and it was important for them to learn about giving back to the community. This feature proved to be a great success in the community.

In its first year, 6,189 seventh and eighth graders enrolled in PREP. Outreach to this initial class was designed to continue through grade 12, with successive classes of seventh graders added each year through 2002. Thirteen-thousand students had been served by the program by 1998, with 2,500 students enrolled in the summer program. According to the Board of Regents, PREP had the potential to touch 72,000 students through its various programs and services by the year 2001.

Advanced Placement exams

The Advanced Placement (AP) program was an integral part of Governor Miller's overall reform of Georgia's education. The AP program was designed to provide college credit and appropriate placement to secondary school students who successfully mastered college-level course work as demonstrated by a passing score on an exam. The Miller Administration provided funding to cover the cost of the exam for Georgia students, which led to extraordinary growth in the number of students enrolled in AP courses. From school year 1991-92 to 1994-95, the number of AP exams taken by public school students increased by 121 percent. The state paid the Advanced Placement examination fees for all Georgia public school students from 1992 to 1995, and again in FY 1999.

According to research conducted by The College Board, AP programs motivated students to undertake more challenging course work in both high

Advanced Placement Exams
Students Tested

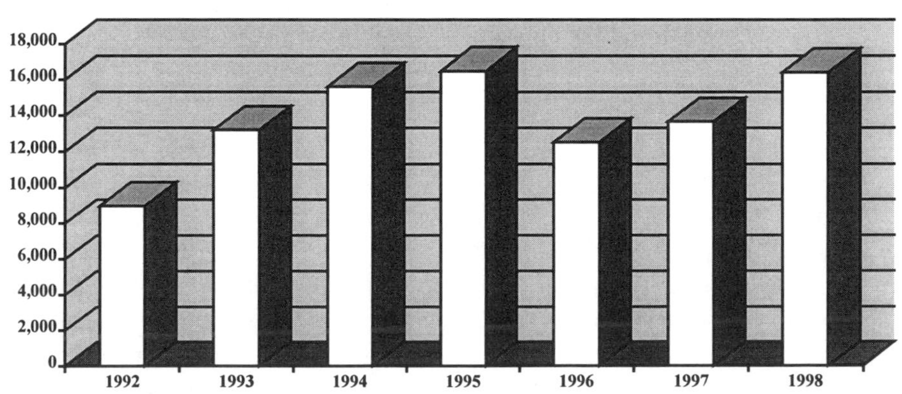

school and college. AP students were more likely than non-AP students to persist in college and go on to graduate school. The examination also enhanced the quality of high school curriculum and improved the articulation of both high school and college curricula.

The phenomenal growth of Georgia's AP program caught the attention of numerous states and educational leaders from around the nation who looked at Georgia as an exceptional model. Georgia became one of the top ten states in the nation for AP exam participation. Especially significant was the increase in the participation of racial minorities and female students who were given an opportunity to take challenging academic courses in preparation for postsecondary education.

Preliminary Scholastic Aptitude Test (PSAT)

The Preliminary Scholastic Aptitude Test (PSAT) was published by the College Board as a 10th or 11th grade practice instrument for students taking the Scholastic Aptitude Test, (SAT). Most colleges, community colleges and technical schools required SAT scores for admission. It was the Governor's intention for students to complete the PSAT exam as an evaluation of where they stood in relation to the SAT exam.

Administration of the PSAT was at the choice of both the local school system and the student from 1992 to 1997. Students paid their own registration fees until several Georgia school systems began to use local revenues to fund the PSAT for system-enrolled students. In 1997, the State Board of Education voted to fund PSAT for all 10th grade students in Georgia's public schools who wished to take the test, ensuring that all 10th graders had equal opportunity to practice taking high-stakes assessments and no one was excluded because of inability to pay. In addition to giving students an early opportunity to test their performance strengths and weaknesses on formalized, high-stakes tests, the statewide testing program provided educators with test performance results through individual student scores, school and district scores, and PSAT Summary of Answers item analysis. Thus, both students and educators could see what needed to be done to prepare students for an improved performance on the critical SAT, which could determine the path of the students' post-secondary careers.

In fall 1997, the first year of PSAT funding for 10th grade students in all Georgia public schools, 60,865 of 95,000 eligible students chose to take the test. Statistics from 1997 data in Georgia showed that PSAT-takers subsequently scored an average of 126 points higher on their SAT verbal and math scores than students who chose not to take the PSAT. The PSAT 10th grade results were distributed to individual students, Georgia high schools, and school districts. The State Department of Education conducted statewide workshops for science, math, social studies and English teachers, counselors, local school and central office administrators. Workshops focused on instructional improvement through analysis and instructional planning from the PSAT Summary of Answers information. Improving student SAT performance through the use of PSAT information and developing instructional improvement strategies were among the purposes of these workshops. Professional development activities reached approximately 16,000 teachers and administrators in every Georgia school system and high school between February and May 1998. Improvement efforts were directed to all Georgia high school students.

The PSAT offered an early indication of student performance with a two-year opportunity for instructional intervention, if needed. It also provided vital career/college guidance and planning information. Based on preliminary local system information, over 70,000 Georgia public school 10th graders were expected to choose to take the PSAT in October 1998.

Intellectual Capital Partnership Program

In 1990, Georgia already had in place one of the nation's best programs for helping industry train new workers. Called Quick Start, it was a major asset in luring new manufacturing jobs to Georgia. It was especially effective in labor-intensive industries. However, there was no similar effort to attract and retain intellectually intensive industry.

Several key institutions in the University System of Georgia had been conducting economic development activities around the state for a number of years, but they were lodged exclusively in the service functions of these institutions and did not address workforce education. Recognizing that intellectual capital would be the business capital of the 21st century, the Miller Administration began a systemwide initiative, coordinated from the Chancellor's office of the Board of Regents, that incorporated economic development into the academic mission of higher education.

ICAPP, the Intellectual Capital Partnership Program, was launched in 1996 in response to the specific need of a specific company for information technology employees. This first project resulted in a $100 million expansion of Total System Services in Columbus, creating 1,500 new jobs for knowledge workers over several years. According to the *Wall Street Journal*, it was the largest single investment announced in the Southeast during 1996. The company chose Columbus because ICAPP offered it the opportunity to be a partner in a computer programming education program at Columbus State University designed to produce 400 graduates a year.

The Total System Services project was the beginning of ICAPP Advantage, which continued to attract, create and preserve high-skill, high-wage jobs by leveraging the resources of the University System to meet the needs of individual companies for college-educated knowledge workers. Companies could specify the disciplines to be taught, then recruit and select participants to be sponsored and educated in those skills. After successfully completing the ICAPP education program, participants were assured a well-paying job with growth potential. ICAPP Advantage developed into an effective tool to recruit and cultivate high-tech knowledge-based companies.

ICAPP rapidly expanded to include three additional programs. ICAPP Needs Assessment surveyed Georgia's private-sector CEOs and personnel directors, and worked with the State Labor Department to develop a long-term statewide picture of changing and emerging needs and patterns for college-educated employees. Its ongoing research kept system institutions apprised of the abilities business valued in employees, and enabled the University System to anticipate jobs market trends and be ready with education programs that addressed changing needs for educated workers with particular skills.

ICAPP Access was created to promote private-sector access to the University System and match the resources of the system with the needs of for-profit, non-profit and government organizations. An information clearinghouse of the system's faculty expertise, centers, institutes and programs of excellence, it also maintained a bibliography of economic development studies conducted for local communities within the prior decade.

ICAPP Regional recognized that each of Georgia's dozen economic regions had unique economic development goals and needs, and tailored the resources of the University System to respond to those unique needs.

The Miller Administration invested $12 million in ICAPP, which the Governor viewed as a complement to the Georgia Research Alliance, enabling the state to offer both the cutting-edge research and the highly skilled workforce it needed to grow a technology-based economy.

Improving Teacher Quality

Teachers are the architects who guide and shape the building of young lives, with a special emphasis on creating a strong foundation for lifelong learning. Teachers are the key ingredient to improving education.... If we're to build a first-class education system in Georgia, we must have at least a fighting chance to attract and hold good teachers.

Governor Zell Miller, January 9, 1995

Research confirmed that the quality of the teacher had a significant influence on the academic success of students. In 1990, the quality of Georgia's teachers was less than its potential. The teacher training and certification processes were unwieldy, average pay was well below the national average, and almost no programs were in place to challenge teachers to improve their performance. During his administration, Governor Miller demonstrated a strong commitment to teacher salary increases, teacher scholarships, and performance-based awards.

Teacher salaries (K-12)

Governor Miller came into office promising to increase those educational resources that would have the most dramatic impact on student learning. He decided to enable Georgia to compete nationally for the best teachers and keep them in Georgia's classrooms. During his eight years in office, he made several difficult decisions to free up the funds required to increase teacher pay on the state salary schedule. He increased the state portion of teachers' salaries by 33 percent in an effort to raise the salaries of public school teachers in Georgia to the national average, helping to recruit and retain the most qualified teachers in the classroom.

In 1996 the average salary of Georgia public school teachers trailed the average salaries both for the nation and for Virginia in the Southeast. With Governor Miller's leadership, Georgia's average was expected to surpass Virginia's and almost equal the national average in 1999.

Average Teacher Salaries

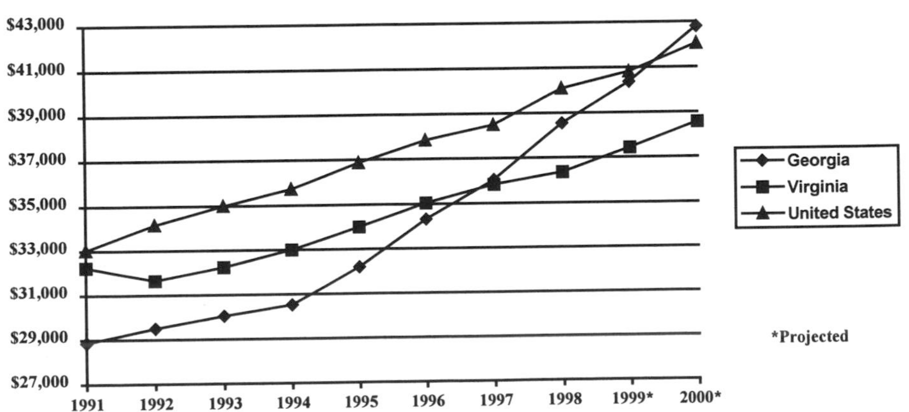

According to the American Federation of Teachers (AFT), Georgia outpaced all other states in raising the average salary of its public school teachers during the Miller Administration. From school year 1994-95 to school year 1996-97, the national average teacher salary increased by 4.5 percent. Over the same time period, Georgia's average teacher salary increased by 10.8 percent.

According to the AFT, when teacher salaries were adjusted for cost of living, the national ranking of Georgia's average teacher salary went from 26th (no cost-of-living adjustment) to 18th.

Faculty salaries (University System of Georgia)

Governor Miller increased the merit-based salary of all University System of Georgia faculty by 29 percent over a five year time span, from school year 1994-95 to 1998-99, enabling Georgia institutions of higher education to compete nationally for the best researchers and instructors.

In school year 1997-98, Georgia ranked second among Southern Regional Education Board (SREB) states in faculty salaries, up from seventh in school year 1991-92. The salary increase for school year 1998-99 was expected to move Georgia into first place among SREB states. In school year 1994-95, Georgia's average faculty salaries significantly trailed the national average, and the state averages of Virginia and North Carolina in the SREB region. With Governor Miller's commitment to faculty salaries, Georgia passed Virginia in school year 1998-99 and was poised to pass the national average in school year 1999-2000.

Governor Miller's long-term commitment to the University System enabled Georgia to continue its competitiveness with peer systems in the southeastern states, such as Virginia and North Carolina, and around the U.S. He believed in promoting faculty productivity and requiring excellence of Georgia's teachers, and his commitment to improving salaries enabled institutions to continue to attract and retain the highest caliber of faculty and staff.

Colleges in the University System of Georgia praised the performance-based salary increases, which enabled them to recruit new faculty and hold tenured professors who were an inspiration to their colleagues and students and added strength to the University System as a whole. Improved salaries created faculty development opportunities and the ability to retain outstanding employees, even when they were recruited for better pay at other institutions across the U.S. From FY 1993 to FY 1997, the average salary of full-time faculty members at four-year institutions in the University System increased by 20.5 percent from $43,666 to $52,637.

Governor Miller's commitment to higher education also resulted in an increase in endowed chairs and eminent scholars, giving Georgia institutions

Average Teacher Salary Rankings of Southeastern States
Adjusted by the AFT Interstate Cost-of Living Index
School Year 1996-97

State	Average Salary	Cost of Living Index	Salary Adjustment	Adjusted Salary	Adjusted Ranking	Original Ranking	National Ranking After Adjustment	National Ranking Before Adjustment
Georgia	**35,679**	**92.8**	**2,762**	**38,441**	**1**	**2**	**18**	**26**
Tennessee	34,267	89.9	3,833	**38,100**	2	3	19	27
Kentucky	33,802	88.7	4,297	**38,099**	3	5	20	29
West VA	33,258	88.6	4,267	**37,525**	4	6	21	32
Virginia	36,116	97.2	1,056	**37,172**	5	1	23	23
Alabama	32,470	89.4	3,850	**36,320**	6	8	26	37
Florida	33,885	93.7	2,271	**36,156**	7	4	28	28
South Carolina	32,659	90.8	3,295	**35,954**	8	7	30	36
Arkansas	30,987	87.8	4,297	**35,284**	9	10	34	44
North Carolina	31,167	91.5	2,899	**34,066**	10	9	39	43
Mississippi	27,662	88.1	3,751	**31,413**	11	12	45	50
Louisiana	28,347	90.7	2,899	**31,246**	12	11	47	48
National Avg.	38,436	100.0		**38,436**				

Source: American Federation of Teachers Survey & Analysis of Salary Trends 1997.

Trends in the Average Teacher Salary Among Southeastern States			
State	**1994-95 Average Salary**	**1996-97 Average Salary**	**Percent Change**
Virginia	33,995	36,116	6.2
Georgia	**32,198**	**35,679**	**10.8**
Tennessee	32,477	34,267	5.5
Florida	32,600	33,885	3.9
Kentucky	32,434	33,802	4.2
West Virginia	31,944	33,258	4.1
South Carolina	30,279	32,659	7.9
Alabama	31,112	32,470	4.4
North Carolina	30,768	31,167	0.8
Arkansas	29,359	30,987	5.5
Louisiana	26,461	28,347	7.1
Mississippi	26,801	27,662	3.2
National Avg.	36,796	38,436	4.5
Source: American Federation of Teachers Survey & Analysis of Salary Trends 1997			

University System of Georgia Regional Salary Comparisons

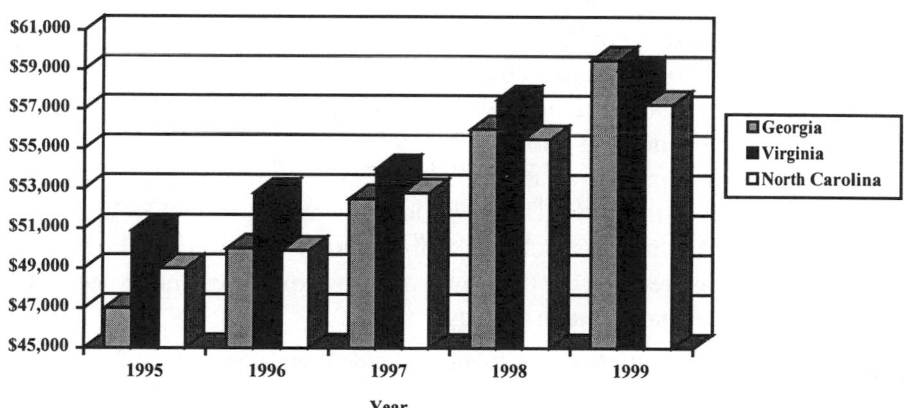

excellent and distinguished professors who were experts in their fields. As a result, Georgia gained a leading edge in teaching and could give the best chance in higher education to aspiring students.

Pay-for-Performance

In 1990, Georgia's schools and teachers had few incentives to improve their performance and the academic achievement of their students. Excellent teachers received the same pay as mediocre teachers on the state salary schedule. School faculties that pulled together to achieve improved student achievement, greater parental involvement, more efficient use of resources, or a lower dropout rate rarely had a tangible reward for their efforts.

In 1991, Governor Miller convened a group of educators and business leaders to explore the creation of a merit-pay plan to reward outstanding teachers and attract more highly qualified people to the profession. The group wrestled with merit pay issues for several months before concluding that merit pay would create more problems in the profession than it solved.

Still determined to find a way to reward success in education, Governor Miller created the Pay-for-Performance program in 1992 as an incentive for individual schools to pursue excellence through collaboration among faculty and administrators at the school level. Each school year, faculty and administrators could set performance goals for their school relating to academic achievement, parental involvement, educational programming, and resource development. An independent panel of educators decided whether the performance goals were exemplary and whether the goals had been met by the end of the year. Schools meeting 80 percent of the goals receive a PfP award of $2,000 per certified staff member with no strings attached. The school staff decided how the money was allocated.

Pay-for-Performance was a school-based merit program that rewarded schools rather than individuals. The program was open to all K-12 public schools in Georgia, not just schools whose students scored well on tests. Schools were measured against their own prior performance and expected to do better than they had done in the past.

Pay for Performance Participants and Recipients

School year for implementing plan	Number of schools that applied	Number of schools that participated	Number of schools that received awards	% of schools that applied and received awards
1993-94	67	18	10	15%
1994-95	100	45	19	19%
1995-96	100	37	29	29%
1996-97	228	91	59	26%
1997-98	210	99	53-63*	25%-30%

*Figures not final at time of publication

Schools that Received PfP Awards

School	System	FY 1995	FY 1996	FY 1997	FY 1998
Capitol View Elem	Atlanta				$64,000
Harper-Archer HS	Atlanta				$148,000
Miles Elem	Atlanta		$52,000		
Mitchell Elem	Atlanta			$62,000	
E. Rivers Elem	Atlanta				$92,000
South Atlanta HS	Atlanta		$180,000		
Sutton Middle	Atlanta		$124,000		$128,000
Sylvan Middle	Atlanta				$138,000
Thomasville Heights El	Atlanta				$98,000
West Fulton MS	Atlanta		$126,000	$132,000	$134,000
Woodson Elem	Atlanta				$78,000
Northside Elem	Baldwin				$68,000
Banks County Primary	Banks				$62,000
Banks County Elem	Banks		$52,000		
County Line Elem	Barrow				$70,000
Mission Road Elem	Bartow				$102,000
Appling MS	Bibb		$94,000		$92,000
McEvoy MS	Bibb			$142,000	
Bleckley County MS	Bleckley				$86,000
Buford Elem	Buford				$110,000
Southeast Bulloch HS	Bulloch		$90,000		
Jackson Primary	Butts				$104,000
Cartersville Primary	Cartersville				$130,000
Alps Road Elem	Clarke		$74,000		$80,000
Baker Elem	Cobb		$128,000		
Clarkdale Elem	Cobb			$78,000	
Davis Elem	Cobb		$102,000		$104,000
Ford Elem	Cobb		$168,000		
Griffin MS	Cobb			$150,000	
Kincaid Elem	Cobb		$112,000		
LaBelle Elem	Cobb	$102,000			
Mabry MS	Cobb		$146,000		
Sedalia Park Elem	Cobb	$80,000		$86,000	
Shallowford Falls Elem	Cobb	$94,000			
Simpson MS	Cobb			$126,000	
Sprayberry HS	Cobb	$244,000			
Tritt Elem	Cobb	$116,000			
Columbia MS	Columbia			$106,000	

N. Columbia Elem	Columbia			$60,000	$62,000
Johnson Elem	Decatur				$68,000
Avondale Elem	DeKalb		$130,000		
Hooper Alexander Elem	DeKalb			$114,000	
McNair Junior High	DeKalb		$150,000		
Midvale Elem	DeKalb			$78,000	
Murphey Candler Elem	DeKalb				$72,000
Pine Ridge Elem	Dekalb			$104,000	$124,000
Rainbow Elem	DeKalb			$100,000	
Sexton Woods Center	DeKalb				$68,000
Terry Mill Elem	DeKalb				$104,000
Tilson Elem	DeKalb				$90,000
Woodridge Elem	DeKalb				$100,000
Woodward Elem	DeKalb				$108,000
Douglas County HS	Douglas				$214,000
Adrian Elem	Emanuel				$28,000
Fayetteville Elem	Fayette				$80,000
Pepperell MS	Floyd				$114,000
Mashburn Elem	Forsyth				$68,000
Midway Elem	Forsyth				$104,000
Camp Creek MS	Fulton			$168,000	
Chattahoochee HS	Fulton				$374,000
Crabapple Crossing El	Fulton			$144,000	
Dolvin Elem	Fulton			$166,000	
Haynes Bridge MS	Fulton			$230,000	
Independence HS	Fulton				$64,000
Milton HS	Fulton				$310,000
Roswell HS	Fulton			$268,000	
Sandy Springs MS	Fulton			$132,000	
Tri-Cities HS	Fulton				$288,000
Arcado Elem	Gwinnett				$114,000
Jackson Elem	Gwinnett				$190,000
Lilburn Elem	Gwinnett				$154,000
Peachtree Elem	Gwinnett				$168,000
Pinckneyville MS	Gwinnett			$142,000	
Fairview Elem	Habersham			$40,000	
West Hall MS	Hall				$154,000
North Jackson Elem	Jackson				$44,000
Lee County Primary	Lee	$108,000			
Lowndes County HS	Lowndes				$264,000
Morgan Co. Elem.	Morgan			$88,000	
Morgan Co. Middle	Morgan			$106,000	
Arnold MS	Muscogee				$110,000

Eastway Elem	Muscogee			$86,000	
Edgewood Elem	Muscogee	$58,000	$58,000	$60,000	$64,000
Kendrick HS	Muscogee				$172,000
Livingston Elem	Newton			$90,000	
Abney Elem	Paulding				$86,000
Rabun Gap School	Rabun				$42,000
Glenn Hills HS	Richmond				$146,000
Salem HS	Rockdale				$168,000
East Central Elem	Rome		$66,000	$74,000	
Elm Street Elem	Rome	$56,000	$54,000	$56,000	$60,000
Rome MS	Rome	$114,000	$112,000	$112,000	$108,000
Social Circle Elem	Social Circle	$76,000			
Stewart County Elem	Stewart				$58,000
Chattanooga Vally Elem	Walker				$90,000
Odum Elem	Wayne				$48,000
Westside MS	Whitfield				$80,000
Cohutta Elem	Whitfield				$48,000
TOTAL		**$1,048,000**	**$2,018,000**	**$3,300,000**	**$6,696,000**

To earn a PfP award, a school had to prepare an application and be approved to participate, implement the approved plan over the course of a school year, and demonstrate that approved objectives were achieved. The entire process typically took two years, with the plan prepared and approved prior to the school year in which it was to be carried out, and the results evaluated and awards given after the school year had concluded.

After the initial implementation of the PfP program in school year 1993-94, the number of schools submitting and executing exemplary PfP plans and subsequently receiving awards grew considerably. For school year 1993-94, 67 schools submitted PfP plans and 10 schools received awards totaling $1,048,000. For school year 1994-95, 100 schools submitted plans and 19 schools received awards totaling $2,018,000. For school year 1995-96, 100 schools submitted plans and 29 schools received awards totaling $3,300,000. For school year 1996-97, 228 schools submitted plans and 59 schools received awards totaling $6,696,000. For school year 1997-98, 202 schools submitted PfP plans and 99 were approved to participate. In March 1998, 262 schools submitted plans and 155 were approved for implementation during school year 1998-99.

From its inception until the Miller Administration ended, funding for the PfP program increased by 568 percent, and the number of schools receiving awards increased by 490 percent.

National Board certification

One of Governor Miller's main goals was to improve student learning by strengthening the teaching profession. Until the National Board for Professional Standards was created in 1990, the teaching profession did not define the knowledge, skills and accomplishments that added up to excellence in the classroom. In contrast, physicians, architects and other professionals worked under clear and objective standards for accomplished practice and had to demonstrate their accomplishments on challenging sets of assessments. The National Board for Professional Teaching Standards identified teachers who met high and rigorous standards and communicated what accomplished teaching looked like. The standards were developed by committees of teachers and other experts and then reviewed extensively before being approved by the board of directors.

To obtain National Board certification, teachers had to successfully complete a two-step process. The teachers first submitted a school-site portfolio showing evidence of their teaching practice through student work, videotapes of classroom interaction, and written commentaries reflecting what they did and how they thought about it. Second, the teachers demonstrated their knowledge of content and teaching strategies by providing written

National Board Certified Teachers

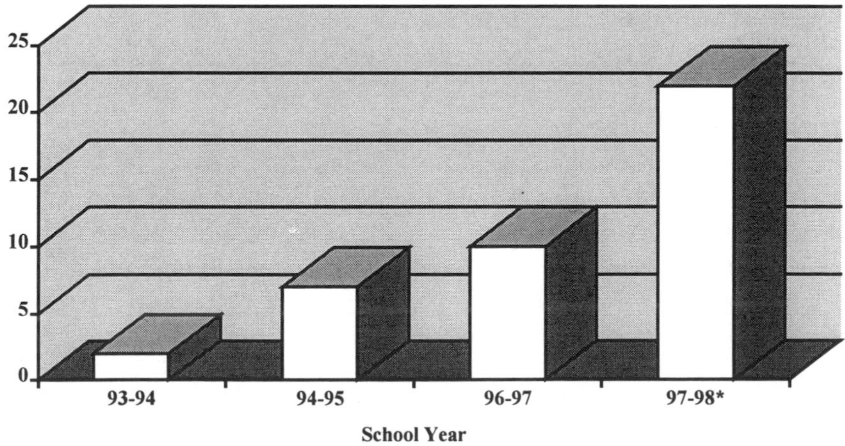

*Georgia teachers currently going through the National Board Certification proc

responses to prompts like journal articles and samples of student work. A certificate awarded by the National Board attested that a teacher had been judged by his or her peers to be one who met high and rigorous professional standards. He or she demonstrated the ability, in a variety of settings, to make sound professional judgments about students' best interests and to act effectively on those judgments.

In an effort to promote the establishment of high standards for what accomplished Georgia teachers should know, Governor Miller developed a plan to pay the participation fee and to award a five percent salary supplement for teachers who successfully completed the rigorous certification process. From school year 1993-94 until school year 1997-98, 19 Georgia teachers successfully completed the National Board certification process. During school year 1997-98, 22 additional teachers were aspiring to meet the rigorous standards of this worthwhile process.

Professional Standards Commission: Teacher certification

In 1990, teacher certification was so bogged down in red tape that it was the number one source of complaints to members of the General Assembly. As a unit of the Georgia Department of Education, it was a low priority for the State Board of Education. The relationship between teacher certification and the colleges of education was often strained, because the colleges felt that the certification process was dictating college curriculum. The average time it took to get an initial certificate after all preparation was achieved and all applications were properly submitted was one month.

Teacher shortages and educational quality became major issues in the mid to late 1980s. Many school systems were finding it difficult to place qualified teachers in Georgia's classrooms, and more and more students were receiving inadequate instruction in the fundamentals. This problem was compounded by the fact that teacher shortages could be localized in specific subject areas or grade levels. Many Georgia parents became concerned and questioned the rigid certification requirements imposed on potential teachers who had education and expertise in academic subjects, but whose formal training had not included traditional teacher education programs. Many potentially qualified applicants became discouraged and simply walked away. Parents were also concerned about the quality of the new teachers who did enter the classroom. They questioned whether the teacher education programs were producing qualified candidates prepared for the changing student population. Complicating these problems were teacher burnout, school population increases, and instances of teachers being forced to teach subjects in which they were not proficient.

Governor Miller wanted to ensure that Georgia's schools were filled with qualified, competent teachers, and at the same time open the classroom door to the thousands of qualified professionals who had the passion to teach but were dissuaded by requirements that made it difficult to enter the profession in non-traditional ways. In 1991, he removed the certification process from the Department of Education and established it as an independent agency called the Georgia Professional Standards Commission, which was attached to the Office of the Governor. In his charge to the new commission, Governor Miller emphasized flexibility, simplicity and practicality.

More specifically, the commission was charged with creating new certification requirements guaranteeing that teachers were competent and prepared to enter the classroom upon graduation from teacher education programs. The commission was also charged with providing flexibility in recognizing the qualifications of those who aspired to teach but whose bachelor's degrees were not in education. He pointed out that even though he had taught at four colleges and universities, he could not get a certificate to teach in a Georgia high school.

The Professional Standards Commission was responsible for creating and implementing standards and procedures for certifying and recertifying education personnel as qualified to practice in the public schools of Georgia and for approving teacher education programs offered at Georgia's teaching colleges. The commission was also charged with the maintenance of professional standards and was authorized to revoke or deny a certificate for good cause after an investigation.

During the 1998 session of the Georgia General Assembly, Governor Miller persuaded the legislature to transfer the authority of the Professional Practice Commission to the Professional Standards Commission in an effort to streamline the investigation of alleged teacher misconduct. This move gave the Professional Standards Commission the responsibility for enforcing the Professional Teaching Practices Act along with adopting a code of professional ethics for educators. The intent of the law was to protect the health, safety and general welfare of students and educators within the state, and to assure the citizens of Georgia that the education profession was accountable for acts of unprofessional conduct.

The Professional Standards Commission simplified certification procedures by cutting the application turn-around time in half, from an average of one month to two weeks. It provided more flexibility in the certification process by allowing potential teachers whose educational background was not in education to enter the classroom much more easily. Of the 116,359 certificates issued between FY 1992 and FY 1998, 5,496 were by way of the alternative certification process and 302 were special permits issued to individuals who possessed special skills needed in a particular area.

Provisional Teaching Certificates

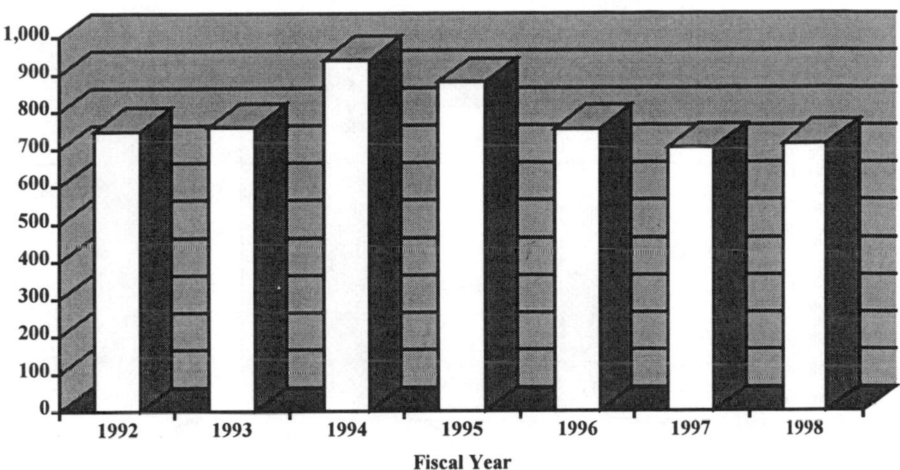

By the end of the Miller administration, the commission's accreditation standards mirrored those of the National Council for Accreditation of Teacher Education (NCATE). Educator preparation programs were strengthened to provide greater flexibility by changing old "course-by-course" requirements to competency based requirements which had to be met prior to graduation.

PROMISE scholarships

One of Governor Miller's goals during his administration was to recruit and train the best teachers for students in Georgia. HOPE became one way to achieve this goal by providing scholarships that encouraged bright college students to become teachers. The PROMISE Teacher Scholarship Program, a component of the HOPE Scholarship Program, provided forgivable loans to high-achieving students who aspired to be teachers in Georgia public schools. This program began in 1995 with the first awards in 1996. Students could receive up to $6,000 in financial assistance, and in return they committed themselves to teach in Georgia's public schools for up to four years—one year for each $1,500 in scholarship assistance they had received.

The maximum award for a full-time student was $3,000 a year for the junior and senior years of college. Part-time student taking fewer than six hours could receive a maximum award of $1,500 per academic year. This forgivable loan could be used for tuition and any other educational expenses at

PROMISE Teacher Scholarship Awards

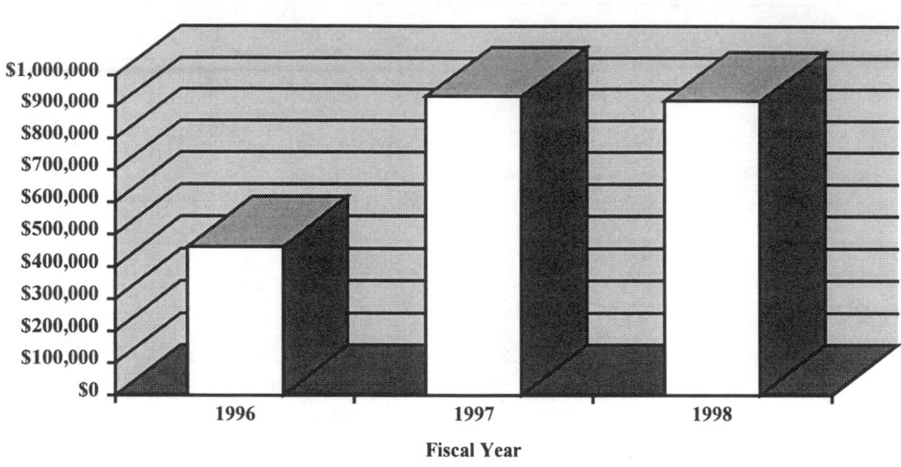

HOPE Teacher Scholarship Awards

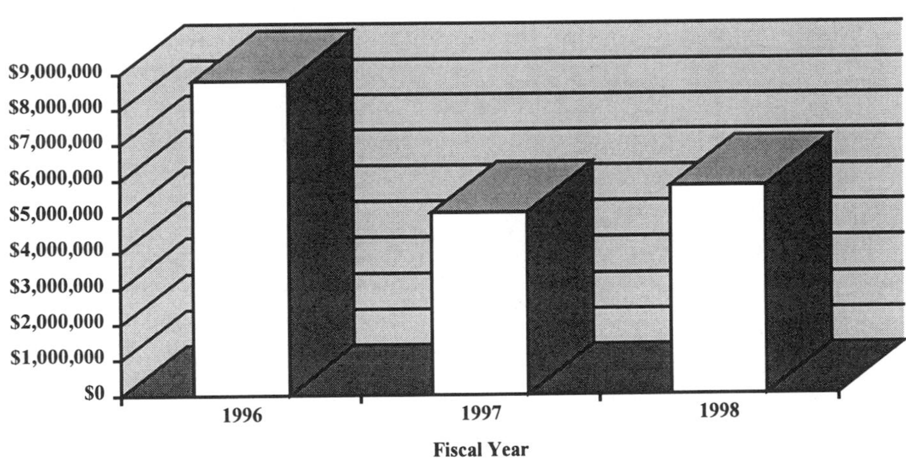

any eligible public or private college or university in Georgia. These benefits were in addition to the financial assistance available through other components of the HOPE Scholarship Program.

To be eligible for a PROMISE Scholarship, a student had to have earned a maximum overall GPA of 3.6 based on a 4.0 scale, be academically classified as a junior, and be accepted for enrollment in an approved teacher education program in Georgia leading to initial certification. Recipients were required to teach in a Georgia public school at the preschool, elementary, middle, or secondary level for one academic year for each $1,500 awarded through the scholarship. Anyone unable to complete the program or meet the teaching obligation, had to repay any outstanding loan amounts plus interest to the State of Georgia. Recipients had to fulfill their service obligation before they became eligible for the HOPE Teacher Scholarship for graduate study in a critical shortage field. An average of 300 PROMISE Scholarships were awarded each year during the Miller Administration.

Teacher scholarships

The HOPE Teacher Scholarship Program provided forgivable loans of up to $10,000 to teachers seeking advanced education degrees in fields of study which suffered from critical teacher shortages. This program, like the PROMISE scholarship, started in 1995 with the first awards in 1996.

The purpose of the HOPE Teacher Scholarship was to steer more teachers into teaching fields that had a shortage of trained professionals and to improve the quality of instruction in these fields. Recipients were obliged to teach in their field of study in a Georgia public school one academic year for each $2,500 awarded through the scholarship. This scholarship was designed to provide Georgia with an increasing number of highly qualified teachers in areas where they were needed most.

The HOPE Teacher Scholarship Program attracted teachers who wanted to earn a master's or specialist's degree, teachers with advanced degrees who wanted to change their field, Georgians with a bachelor's degree who were not teaching or who had not taught, and educators seeking to complete approved programs in fields in which degree programs are not generally offered, e.g., gifted and preschool handicapped education

Recipients had to be legal residents of Georgia and be admitted to a graduate school and an advanced degree teacher education program leading to certification in a critical shortage field. Students received $75 per quarter hour or $200 per semester hour, and the maximum award for each recipient was based on the number of credit hours necessary to complete the program of study. Scholarship funds could be used toward tuition and fees, or any other part of the student's cost of attendance.

Recipients of the HOPE teacher scholarship were granted a grace period of one year after completing their approved program. After the grace period, recipients were obligated to teach in their critical shortage field of study in a Georgia public school at the preschool, elementary, middle, or secondary level one academic year for each $2,500 awarded, with a maximum of four years to repay. If the teaching/service obligation could not be met, any outstanding loan amount plus interest had to be repaid to the State of Georgia.

Approximately 1,500 scholarships were available each academic year and were awarded on a first-come, first-served basis.

Governor's Teaching Fellows

Governor Miller established the Governor's Teaching Fellows (GTF) program to provide Georgia's college and university faculty with expanded opportunities to develop important teaching skills and to address the pressing need for faculty members to learn how to use emerging technology in the classroom. The GTF program was jointly sponsored through the Institute of Higher Education and the Office of Instructional Support and Development at the University of Georgia. Faculty members from both public and private colleges and universities around the state were invited to participate. The program accepted up to two participants from each public or private higher education institution in Georgia each year. Data suggested that participants in the program increased their use of Georgia's distance learning technology after participation. By the end of the Miller Administration, 37 colleges and universities, including a dozen private institutions, had sent faculty members to participate in the program.

GTF offered its participants three options: an Academic Year Symposia Program, a Summer Symposia Program, and an Academic Year in Residence Program. The Academic Year Symposia program allowed participants to attend three-day symposia, while engaging in instructional improvement projects on their home campus. Participants received a stipend of $250 for each day of full participation. The Summer Symposia Program invited participants to attend a two-week symposium at the University of Georgia, where they received a combination of structured instructional and faculty development. Participants in this program received $2,500 for full participation in the ten-day symposium. The Academic Year in Residence Program allowed faculty members to study for an entire year at The University of Georgia to enhance their skills. Participants received up to $15,000 for their year of study.

In addition to improving teaching skills and the application of new instructional technology in the classroom, GTF also increased the level of communication among the state's scholars in higher education.

Opportunity for Local Innovation

No child was ever educated in the Governor's Office or the Georgia Department of Education or even in the county school offices. Children are educated in schools and communities, not in bureaucracies, and it is from the teachers, parents and business leaders in Georgia's local communities that education change must spring.

Governor Zell Miller, October 20, 1991

In 1990, the culture of education in Georgia was marked by a "top-down" mentality. In order to assure that all students had at least a minimum opportunity to achieve, the state had developed extensive sets of rules and regulations. While the purpose was laudable, the effect was to limit local initiative and restrict the local community's feeling of ownership of its schools. Governor Miller instituted several initiatives that were designed to return ownership to the community, allow local initiative to flourish, and provide resources to address many of the most difficult challenges to local schools.

Elected school boards

Throughout his career in public office, Governor Miller promoted opportunities for citizens to influence education policy through their local school officials. He viewed his role and the role of other state-level education officials not as being the final arbiters who had all the answers, but as the support structure for parents and teachers who worked in the schools daily and had the practical knowledge of what worked.

Prior to 1994, local school board members in 34 school districts across the state were not directly elected by district residents, blurring the line of accountability for educational performance. In a majority of these districts, a grand jury selected the school board and in the remaining few the city council selected the school board. Critics of this policy argued that it created an unnecessary barrier between voters and their local school boards, the policy making and governing bodies for education at the local level.

Also prior to 1994, 109 local superintendents were elected, despite the fact that they were not accountable to the voters, but charged with executing the policies of the local school boards, most of whom had not been elected. Critics of this arrangement argued that while school boards should be elected to provide for accountability to the residents of their districts in the setting of school policy, superintendents should be appointed by local school boards, giving them more independence to manage and lead without having to attend to special interest politics.

Governor Miller believed that elected local school boards and appointed superintendents would provide the best governing structure, empowering parents and teachers to influence the setting of education policy while removing political considerations from the day-to-day administration of that policy. He drafted a constitutional amendment requiring these structural changes. At the time, according to the National School Board Association data for 1991, 97.14 percent of the nation's school boards were elected, 2.84 percent were appointed, and 0.02 percent were selected using a combination of elections and appointments. With the passage of this constitutional amendment, Georgia joined the rest of the nation in ensuring that its citizens had a voice in education policy.

Charter schools

Although a strong supporter of Quality Basic Education, Governor Miller knew that no education law could be perfect. As QBE was implemented, it became obvious that schools seeking to break the mold would have a difficult time. Such schools had to get approval from both the State Board of Education and their local school boards for each innovation they wanted to implement. This approach forced schools to think piecemeal about school reform rather than to think creatively about how different elements could work together to increase student achievement. Board members at both the state and local levels valued uniformity more than diversity, and the governance in Georgia education was top down.

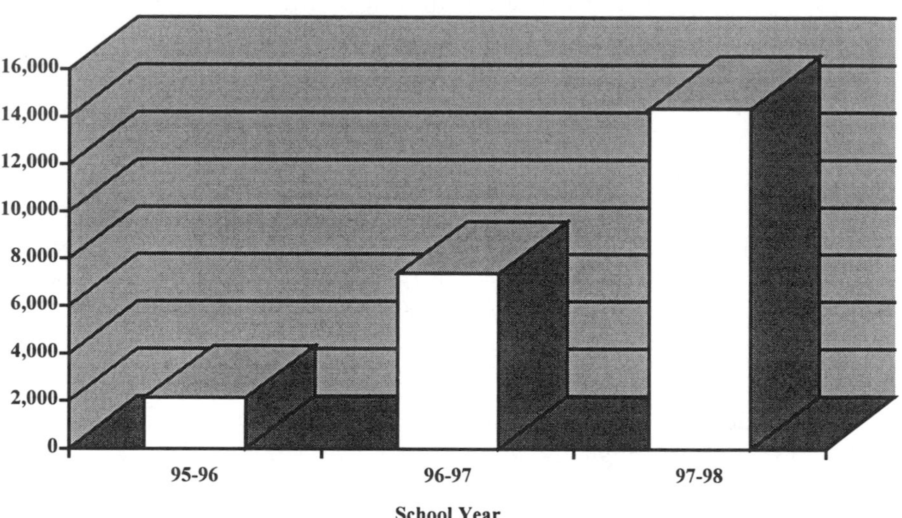

Governor Miller came into office believing the role of the state was not to dictate and enforce rules and regulations, but to be a support structure for schools. It was obvious that the innovators in Georgia schools needed new and better tools to improve student achievement and to lead the education establishment to new ways of thinking about schools.

The concept of charter schools was still in its formative stages when Miller took office. Minnesota enacted the first charter school law in 1991. Georgia was one of six states to enact charter school legislation in 1993, and Governor Miller used the Minnesota law as a guide. The next southern state to enact charter school legislation was Louisiana in 1995, so Georgia was a charter school pioneer nationally and in the South.

Charter Schools as of 1998

System	School	Charter Expiration Date
Bartow	Adairsville Elementary	June 30, 2002
	Cloverleaf Elementary	Jan 31, 2002
	Emerson Elementary	June 30, 2003
	Kingston Elementary	June 30, 2002
	Mission Road Elementary	June 30, 2002
	Pine Log Elementary	June 30, 2002
	Taylorsville Elementary	June 30, 2002
	White Elementary	June 30, 2002
Cartersville	Cartersville Elementary	June 30, 2001
	Cartersville High	June 30, 2001
	Cartersville Middle	June 30, 2001
	Cartersville Primary	June 30, 2001
Chatham	Charles Ellis Montesorri	June 30, 2003
	Mercer Middle	June 30, 2003
	Savannah Arts Academy	June 30, 2001
Cobb	Addison Elementary	June 30, 2003
	Bryant Elementary	June 30, 2001
	Eastvalley Elementary	June 30, 2001
	Green Acres Elementary	June 30, 2002
	Mt. Bethel Elementary	June 30, 2002
	Sedalia Park Elementary	June 30, 2001
	Walton High	June 30, 2003
DeKalb	Druid Hills High	June 30, 2002
	Rainbow Elementary	June 30, 2003
Griffin-Spalding	Third Ward Elementary	Jan 31, 2002
Trion City	Trion Middle	June 30, 2003

Charter schools were independent public schools, freed from both state and local bureaucratic regulations and micromanagement to design and deliver programs tailored toward educational excellence and the needs of their communities. They were held accountable not for compliance with reams of rules, but for how well they educated children in a safe and responsible environment. They promoted choice for parents, students, and teachers; autonomy for school-level decision-makers; and accountability for explicit academic objectives. They became laboratories for education, and provided models for school reform.

In Georgia, 21 charter schools were formed under the original charter school law during the Miller Administration. Another five schools had written their charters according to the guidelines of the original law and were awaiting approval from their local boards and the State Board of Education as Miller left office. By this time, the number of students enrolled in charter

Next Generation Schools Funding

School Year	Grant Sites	State Funds	Local Funds	Total Funds
1993-1994	Bibb County	$142,500	$386,838	$529,338
	Calhoun City	$142,500	$233,730	$376,230
	Carrolton City	$142,500	$1,699,982	$1,842,482
	Cartersville City	$142,500	$250,125	$392,625
	Clarke County	$142,500	$245,866	$388,366
	Dalton City	$142,500	$213,415	$355,915
	Emanuel County	$142,500	$207,227	$349,727
	Gwinnett County	$142,500	$530,000	$672,500
	Habersham County	$142,500	$332,526	$475,025
	Paulding County	$142,500	$360,106	$502,606
	Rockdale County	$142,500	$380,260	$522,760
	Savannah-Chatham County	$142,500	$140,804	$283,304
	Ware County	$142,500	$354,062	$496,562
1994-1995	Coweta County	$85,000	$86,686	$171,686
	Decatur City	$85,000	$85,396	$170,396
	DeKalb County-Druid hills	$85,000	$218,580	$303,580
	Floyd County	$85,000	$220,000	$305,000
	Gainesville City	$85,000	$218,868	$303,868
	Glynn County	$85,000	$147,300	$232,300
	Grady County	$85,000	$121,828	206,828
	Houston County	$85,000	$220,000	$305,000
	Irwin County	$85,000	$420,000	$505,000
	Jackson County	$85,000	$85,000	$170,000
	Jenkins County	$85,000	$95,007	$180,007
1995-1996	Bibb County	$80,000	$151,754	$231,754
	Carrollton City	$80,000	$1,371,250	$1,451,250
	Clarke County	$80,000	$60,000	$140,000
	Decatur City	$80,000	$42,625	$122,625
	DeKalb County-Druid Hills	$80,000	$154,400	$234,400
	Emanuel County	$80,000	$65,018	$145,018
	Gainesville City	$80,000	$194,284	$274,284
	Glynn County	$80,000	$161,350	$241,350
	Grady County	$80,000	$70,700	$150,700
	Irwin County	$80,000	$447,500	$527500
	Jefferson County	$80,000	$55,299	$135,299
	Muscogee County	$80,000	$64,998	$144,998
1996-1997	Carrollton City	$50,000	$498,415	$548,415
	Clarke County	$50,000	$128,879	$178,879
	Decatur City	$50,000	$116,009	$166,009
	DeKalb County	$50,000	$132,000	$182,000
	Emanuel County	$50,000	$200,000	$250,000
	Grady County	$50,000	$215,586	$265,586
	Habersham County	$50,000	$37,500	$87,500

schools had increased 574 percent since school year 1995-96, the first year charter schools operated in the state. In that school year, 2,130 students were enrolled in charter schools; in school year 1996-97, the number more than tripled to 7,379; and in school year 1997-98, the number of students enrolled in charter schools had almost doubled to 14,365.

	Jefferson County	$50,000	$65,891	$115,891
	Muscogee County	$50,000	$144,111	$194,111
	Savannah-Chatham County	$50,000	$388,496	$438,496
1997-1998	Bremen City	$45,450	*	$45,450
	Carroll County	$45,450	*	$45,450
	Coweta County	$45,450	*	$45,450
	Decatur County	$45,450	*	$45,450
	DeKalb County	$45,450	*	$45,450
	Emanuel County	$45,450	*	$45,450
	Grady County	$45,450	*	$45,450
	Habersham County	$45,450	*	$45,450
	Morgan County	$45,450	*	$45,450
	Muscogee County	$45,450	*	$45,450
	Randolph County	$45,450	*	$45,450
1998-1999	Bremen City	$20,000	*	$20,000
	Carroll County	$42,500	*	$42,500
	Clarke County	$42,500	*	$42,500
	Coweta County	$42,500	*	$42,500
	Decatur county	$42,500	*	$42,500
	DeKalb County	$42,500	*	$42,500
	Dougherty County	$20,000	*	$20,000
	Emanuel County	$42,500	*	$42,500
	Georgia School for the Deaf	$20,000	*	$20,000
	Grady County	$42,500	*	$42,500
	Gwinnett County	$20,000	*	$20,000
	Habersham County	$42,500	*	$42,500
	Morgan County	$20,000	*	$20,000
	Murray County	$20,000	*	$20,000
	Muscogee County	$20,000	*	$20,000
	White County	$20,000	*	$20,000

*Data not available at time of publication

Although charter school participation rose steadily in Georgia, by 1997 it was obvious that the original law could be improved. In the 1998 General Assembly, Representative Kathy Ashe of Atlanta and Senator Clay Land of Columbus proposed a charter school reform bill which the Governor signed into law. The revisions allowed private individuals, private organizations, and state or local public entities (excluding home study programs, sectarian or religious schools, private for-profit schools, and private educational institutions not established by the State of Georgia) to establish charter schools. These charter schools then became public schools governed by local boards under the terms specified in the charter.

Next Generation Schools

The Next Generation School Project was a collaborative effort between government, the business community and individual schools to enable the schools to prepare students for success in the 21st century. This school improvement process was based on nine field-tested criteria: establishing a community collaborative; emphasizing world class performance standards;

Cross Roads Sites

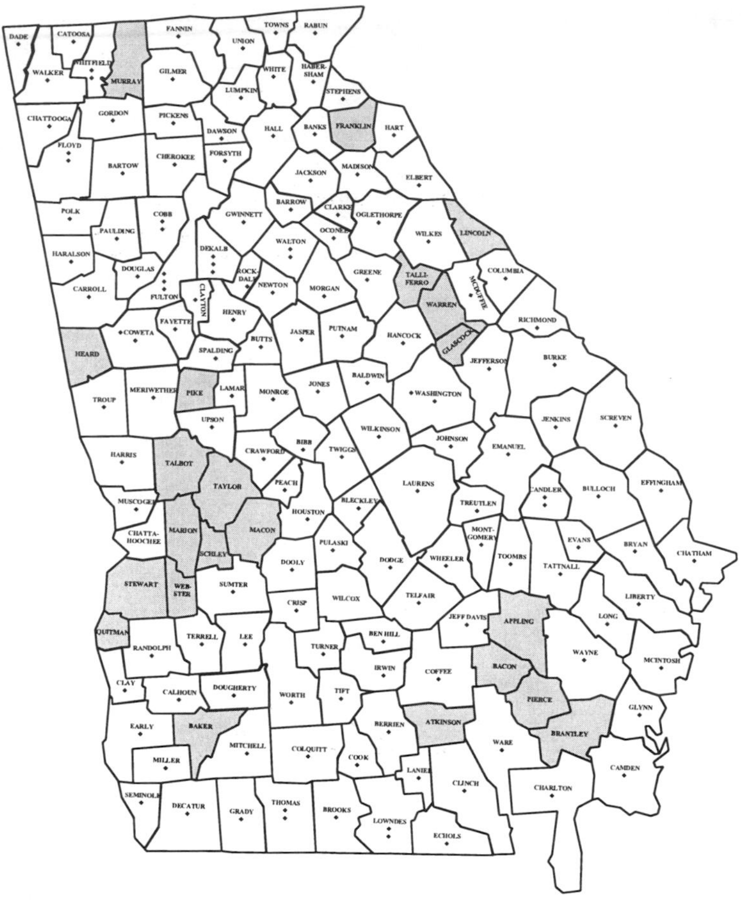

◆ designates the counties served by a CrossRoads site. There are 124 sites across Georgia, serving 154 school systems. Several rural systems share sites. For example, Terrell and Calhoun counties share a CrossRoads site. In addtion some counties, like DeKalb county, have more than one site. Counties which are not served by a site are highlighted in gray.

personalizing instruction and emphasizing continuous progress; emphasizing vocational skills; reorganizing the learning environment; using telecommunications and computing technology as tools; attending to at-risk children and youth and their families; adopting continuous improvement and evaluation processes; and providing continuous staff development.

Governor Miller was a proponent of the project and approved over $5 million in state funding after it began in 1993. More than $3 million in private funds was raised to match the state funds. In addition, grant sites were

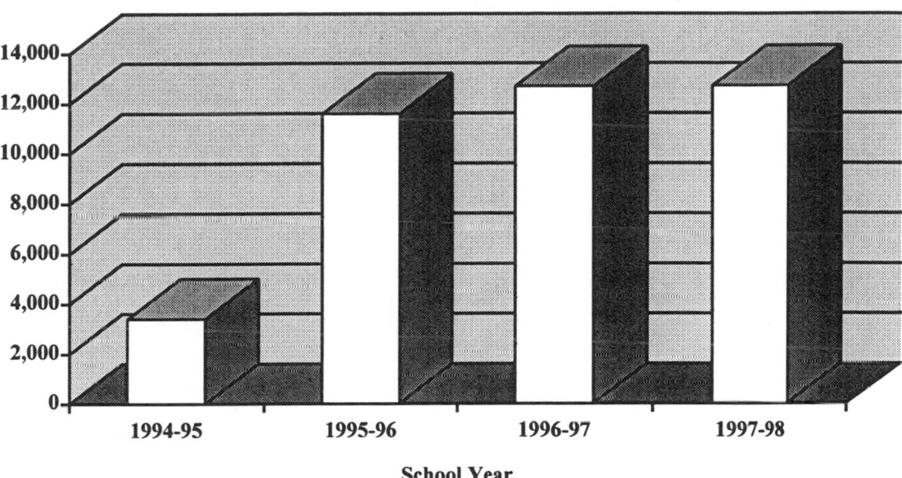

required to match half of their grant with locally raised funds, and they usually far exceeded this requirement.

Alternative schools

Governor Miller created the CrossRoads alternative school program to turn at-risk kids around by providing a safe and nurturing alternative learning environment, with the opportunities and support services needed for success in school and the community. Prior to the creation of the CrossRoads program, options for dealing with chronically disruptive students were limited to punishing the student with little regard to the student's long term academic and social development. Often disruptive students were expelled from school, which merely threw them back into the environment that had played a role in creating the disruptive behavior in the first place, without much consideration for how that action would induce the student to improve when reintroduced to the classroom.

The purpose of the CrossRoads program was threefold: To provide chronically disruptive students (including adjudicated) in grades 6-12 with the social services, individualized instruction and transitions to other programs they needed to become successful students and good citizens in the school and community; to make the public schools safer and more secure by removing chronically disruptive students in grades 6-12 from the public classroom; and to enable students to complete requirements for their high school diplomas.

School systems or consortia of school systems could apply for annual grants to operate CrossRoads programs. These grants were in addition to regular Quality Basic Education formula funding. The program began in school year 1994-95, serving 3,405 students. In school year 1995-96, it served 11,587. In school year 1996-97, it served 12,675. In school year 1997-98, it served approximately 12,703 students.

The Governor initiated a three-year comprehensive evaluation of the CrossRoads program. Phase I of the evaluation was designed to ascertain, among other things, student demographic and discipline data, services received by students, academic performance of students, and reasons why students entered and exited the program. Phase II was designed to determine the impact of the program on students and its cost effectiveness.

Technology Improvements

The computer can be a very effective teaching tool. It engages students, one-on-one in interactive learning. It never forgets a key point. It never gets tired of working the same concept over and over if a student's having trouble... But it is not enough just to buy the computers. Our teachers must also know how to make the best possible use of this educational tool.

Governor Zell Miller, July 1, 1993

In 1990, the business community and the rest of the job market were engaged in a rapid transition from a labor-intensive to a technology-intensive workforce. That transition continued and accelerated during the 90s. However, in 1990, very few Georgia students had the opportunity to use the technology tools that were to be so important to their success in the working world. The educational system was stuck in an outdated model in which information was controlled and available in only limited ways. Teachers knew very little about how to use technology to improve learning and prepare students for the new world of work. Technology was not applied to the needs of handicapped students or to the challenge of improving school safety. Discussion was only beginning on technology's value to the goal of providing a seamless educational system for all Georgians.

Prior to the passage of the statewide lottery in 1992, Georgia had not established a method of supporting classroom technology. In fact, technology-related expenditures before the lottery included vocational equipment and television technology, with no funding for computer-related technology. That changed in the early years of the Miller Administration. Georgia used funds allocated from utility rate overpayments to establish a Universal Services Fund to provide a statewide hard-wired distance learning and telemedicine network, then used lottery funds to provide technology and training for classroom instruction, as well as satellite dishes and a state-of-the-art production center for educational programming.

Technology for learning

Policy makers and educators knew that a 19th century education system could not adequately prepare students to live, learn and work in the new digital world and global economy. In 1992-93, before the availability of lottery funding, less than 12 percent of Georgia classrooms had computers and only 15 percent had distance learning capabilities. By 1997-98, after five years of lottery funding, 44.9 percent of Georgia classrooms had computers and distance learning capability was available to 78.9 percent of all classrooms and 100 percent of all schools.

Governor Miller was committed to placing cutting-edge technology in Georgia's classrooms and schools. Under his leadership, Georgia appropriated over $625 million for education technology in the last five years of his administration. Over $340 million in lottery funds were appropriated to make sure every single public school, college, university and technical institute had a satellite dishes, and to make computers and other instructional technology available in Georgia's classrooms, school media centers and public libraries. Approximately $126 million in lottery funds provided classroom computers. Lottery proceeds were expended every year to provide the necessary tools and technology training to ensure Georgia's students are ready for the technology demands of the 21st century. Miller's goal was to make the students of his administration as proficient in using computers as the students of his generation had been in using textbooks, rulers, pens and paper.

During the Miller Administration, the Internet rapidly emerged as a powerful learning tool for students and teachers, providing even the most remote locations with access to vast amounts of information and knowledge not available any other way. By the time Miller left office, the University System of Georgia had begun to offer college degrees entirely by distance learning and computers. Access was also readily available throughout the state to the University System's electronic library called GALILEO (Georgia Library Learning Online), which had recorded over 11 million "hits" or instances of access by the middle of 1998 and had become a national model.

The Governor wanted to provide a system that enhanced the quality of teaching at Georgia's public colleges and universities by expanding research, student learning, and services. When GALILEO first came on-line in September of 1995, it included only three databases and had recorded 317,000 "hits" as of December 1995. By 1998, GALILEO included over 135 databases (public and licensed) that indexed thousands of periodicals and 15 full text reference databases, and provided access to over 2,000 journals in

Department of Education
Lottery Funding for Computers in the Classroom
Fiscal Year 1994 to Fiscal Year 1998

SYSTEM NAME	FY 1994	FY 1995	FY 1996*	FY 1997	FY 1998	SYSTEM TOTAL
APPLING CO.	$107,000	$96,000	$0	$66,440	$91,415	$360,855
ATKINSON CO.	$53,500	$45,000	$0	$53,000	$53,000	$204,500
BACON CO.	$71,000	$64,159	$0	$53,000	$54,338	$242,497
BAKER CO.	$18,000	$15,000	$0	$53,000	$53,000	$139,000
BALDWIN CO.	$142,500	$144,589	$0	$122,440	$167,796	$577,325
BANKS CO.	$71,000	$78,207	$0	$53,000	$53,000	$255,207
BARROW CO.	$178,500	$156,632	$0	$134,760	$195,253	$665,145
BARTOW CO.	$249,500	$226,422	$0	$188,660	$277,351	$941,933
BEN HILL CO.	$71,000	$60,000	$0	$70,800	$96,225	$298,025
BERRIEN CO.	$107,000	$66,063	$0	$56,620	$79,487	$309,170
BIBB CO.	$724,500	$627,260	$0	$486,140	$662,004	$2,499,904
BLECKLEY CO.	$53,500	$49,716	$0	$53,000	$59,120	$215,336
BRANTLEY CO.	$79,884	$75,000	$0	$54,520	$77,508	$286,912
BROOKS CO.	$71,000	$83,648	$0	$53,380	$73,660	$281,688
BRYAN CO.	$107,000	$105,000	$0	$97,960	$135,089	$445,049
BULLOCH CO.	$249,500	$231,219	$0	$163,080	$227,466	$871,265
BURKE CO.	$133,500	$90,000	$0	$94,620	$132,313	$450,433
BUTTS CO.	$71,000	$60,000	$0	$58,340	$82,592	$271,932
CALHOUN CO.	$53,000	$70,434	$0	$53,000	$53,000	$229,434
CAMDEN CO.	$142,500	$188,287	$0	$166,460	$241,895	$739,142
CANDLER CO.	$53,500	$58,977	$0	$53,000	$53,000	$218,477
CARROLL CO.	$329,500	$309,819	$0	$209,400	$293,430	$1,142,149
CATOOSA CO.	$214,000	$199,503	$0	$166,460	$235,546	$815,509
CHARLTON CO.	$71,500	$79,663	$0	$53,000	$53,000	$257,163
CHATHAM CO.	$828,500	$716,870	$0	$702,260	$964,449	$3,212,079
CHATTAHOOCHEE CO.	$18,000	$31,714	$0	$53,000	$53,000	$155,714
CHATTOOGA CO.	$125,000	$163,072	$0	$57,540	$77,398	$423,010
CHEROKEE CO.	$438,116	$413,534	$0	$413,420	$599,283	$1,864,353
CLARKE CO.	$339,000	$280,371	$0	$214,120	$293,980	$1,127,471
CLAY CO.	$18,000	$18,410	$0	$53,000	$53,000	$142,410
CLAYTON CO.	$783,116	$715,259	$0	$795,420	$1,123,477	$3,417,272
CLINCH CO.	$35,500	$30,000	$0	$53,000	$53,000	$171,500
COBB CO.	$1,568,116	$1,321,936	$0	$1,629,100	$2,324,434	$6,843,586
COFFEE CO.	$161,000	$158,161	$0	$137,120	$191,653	$647,934
COLQUITT CO.	$259,116	$253,181	$0	$156,760	$217,022	$886,079
COLUMBIA CO.	$356,000	$319,284	$0	$340,920	$478,184	$1,494,388
COOK CO.	$89,000	$75,000	$0	$56,460	$76,463	$296,923
COWETA CO.	$303,000	$305,636	$0	$264,880	$381,409	$1,254,925
CRAWFORD CO.	$53,000	$45,000	$0	$53,000	$53,000	$204,000
CRISP CO.	$98,000	$100,891	$0	$86,720	$119,340	$404,951
DADE CO.	$71,000	$96,769	$0	$53,000	$65,194	$285,963
DAWSON CO.	$71,000	$88,961	$0	$53,000	$58,461	$271,422

DECATUR CO.	$160,500	$140,514	$0	$113,800	$157,434	$572,248
DEKALB CO.	$1,947,116	$1,723,062	$0	$1,690,960	$2,388,694	$7,749,832
DODGE CO.	$71,000	$69,850	$0	$65,780	$92,789	$299,419
DOOLY CO.	$71,000	$78,578	$0	$53,000	$53,000	$255,578
DOUGHERTY CO.	$543,000	$435,968	$0	$351,360	$479,531	$1,809,859
DOUGLAS CO.	$374,000	$320,901	$0	$304,220	$428,656	$1,427,777
EARLY CO.	$53,000	$45,000	$0	$53,000	$72,835	$223,835
ECHOLS CO.	$35,500	$49,196	$0	$53,000	$53,000	$190,696
EFFINGHAM CO.	$125,000	$113,761	$0	$138,740	$199,816	$577,317
ELBERT CO.	$107,000	$92,485	$0	$75,900	$103,536	$378,921
EMANUEL CO.	$143,000	$204,305	$0	$94,880	$131,681	$573,866
EVANS CO.	$53,500	$57,764	$0	$53,000	$53,000	$217,264
FANNIN CO.	$89,000	$78,814	$0	$60,200	$81,823	$309,837
FAYETTE CO.	$320,500	$278,868	$0	$331,040	$474,171	$1,404,579
FLOYD CO.	$284,500	$306,082	$0	$191,900	$271,882	$1,054,364
FORSYTH CO.	$231,500	$210,000	$0	$206,100	$314,841	$962,441
FRANKLIN CO.	$89,000	$82,697	$0	$66,320	$91,827	$329,844
FULTON CO.	$960,500	$848,538	$0	$1,097,080	$1,610,786	$4,516,904
GILMER CO.	$89,000	$83,567	$0	$60,420	$87,182	$320,169
GLASCOCK CO.	$35,500	$45,000	$0	$53,000	$53,000	$186,500
GLYNN CO.	$258,000	$248,586	$0	$224,520	$310,663	$1,041,769
GORDON CO.	$142,500	$142,363	$0	$100,720	$146,303	$531,886
GRADY CO.	$125,000	$135,000	$0	$89,660	$124,947	$474,607
GREENE CO.	$106,500	$81,029	$0	$53,000	$63,518	$304,047
GWINNETT CO.	$1,166,116	$1,069,677	$0	$1,674,040	$2,415,684	$6,325,517
HABERSHAM CO.	$187,616	$194,888	$0	$106,020	$148,309	$636,833
HALL CO.	$428,000	$397,499	$0	$332,580	$479,201	$1,637,280
HANCOCK CO.	$71,000	$64,491	$0	$53,000	$53,000	$241,491
HARALSON CO.	$107,500	$131,236	$0	$62,180	$88,886	$389,802
HARRIS CO.	$89,000	$82,312	$0	$66,300	$97,544	$335,156
HART CO.	$125,000	$107,894	$0	$66,660	$95,675	$395,229
HEARD CO.	$89,000	$115,303	$0	$53,000	$53,000	$310,303
HENRY CO.	$321,000	$305,008	$0	$315,200	$472,852	$1,414,060
HOUSTON CO.	$480,500	$396,943	$0	$371,120	$525,101	$1,773,664
IRWIN CO.	$53,000	$58,262	$0	$53,000	$53,000	$217,262
JACKSON CO.	$125,000	$116,726	$0	$85,340	$124,754	$451,820
JASPER CO.	$53,000	$69,762	$0	$53,000	$53,000	$228,762
JEFF DAVIS CO.	$71,000	$70,105	$0	$53,000	$72,066	$266,171
JEFFERSON CO.	$106,500	$110,694	$0	$73,140	$98,946	$389,280
JENKINS CO.	$71,000	$65,266	$0	$53,000	$53,000	$242,266
JOHNSON CO.	$71,000	$60,000	$0	$53,000	$53,000	$237,000
JONES CO.	$71,000	$79,115	$0	$84,960	$118,543	$353,618
LAMAR CO.	$53,000	$63,830	$0	$53,000	$69,042	$238,872
LANIER CO.	$53,000	$52,993	$0	$53,000	$53,000	$211,993
LAURENS CO.	$151,000	$135,521	$0	$98,360	$136,491	$521,372
LEE CO.	$89,000	$111,746	$0	$95,080	$135,391	$431,217
LIBERTY CO.	$178,000	$150,000	$0	$211,380	$297,113	$836,493
LINCOLN CO.	$35,500	$73,739	$0	$53,000	$53,000	$215,239
LONG CO.	$53,000	$63,518	$0	$53,000	$53,000	$222,518
LOWNDES CO.	$169,500	$183,536	$0	$161,980	$225,734	$740,750
LUMPKIN CO.	$79,884	$98,812	$0	$56,880	$80,806	$316,382

MACON CO.	$124,500	$131,011	$0	$53,000	$66,871	$375,382
MADISON CO.	$107,000	$122,604	$0	$85,760	$118,460	$433,824
MARION CO.	$35,500	$30,000	$0	$53,000	$53,000	$171,500
MCDUFFIE CO.	$107,000	$103,218	$0	$85,620	$119,697	$415,535
MCINTOSH CO.	$53,000	$51,140	$0	$53,000	$53,000	$210,140
MERIWETHER CO.	$160,500	$149,826	$0	$78,720	$109,115	$498,161
MILLER CO.	$53,000	$61,702	$0	$53,000	$53,000	$220,702
MITCHELL CO.	$53,500	$56,594	$0	$57,380	$78,662	$246,136
MONROE CO.	$53,000	$72,577	$0	$68,980	$96,198	$290,755
MONTGOMERY CO.	$53,000	$60,015	$0	$53,000	$53,000	$219,015
MORGAN CO.	$71,000	$78,404	$0	$53,000	$74,127	$276,531
MURRAY CO.	$124,500	$130,173	$0	$116,620	$165,927	$537,220
MUSCOGEE CO.	$909,616	$748,770	$0	$639,240	$888,508	$3,186,134
NEWTON CO.	$196,500	$187,927	$0	$177,280	$257,370	$819,077
OCONEE CO.	$89,000	$82,681	$0	$90,440	$128,630	$390,751
OGLETHORPE CO.	$53,000	$53,334	$0	$53,000	$53,733	$213,067
PAULDING CO.	$249,500	$232,190	$0	$222,360	$330,700	$1,034,750
PEACH CO.	$106,500	$101,388	$0	$88,480	$123,133	$419,501
PICKENS CO.	$71,000	$73,809	$0	$63,940	$92,707	$301,456
PIERCE CO.	$71,500	$106,555	$0	$60,000	$83,637	$321,692
PIKE CO.	$53,000	$60,000	$0	$53,000	$64,755	$230,755
POLK CO.	$195,500	$165,000	$0	$132,780	$183,875	$677,155
PULASKI CO.	$53,000	$45,000	$0	$53,000	$53,000	$204,000
PUTNAM CO.	$53,000	$45,000	$0	$53,000	$68,163	$219,163
QUITMAN CO.	$18,000	$23,819	$0	$53,000	$53,000	$147,819
RABUN CO.	$71,500	$84,410	$0	$53,000	$53,000	$261,910
RANDOLPH CO.	$53,000	$62,206	$0	$53,000	$53,000	$221,206
RICHMOND CO.	$1,043,500	$898,029	$0	$707,220	$979,318	$3,628,067
ROCKDALE CO.	$284,500	$256,552	$0	$245,460	$352,523	$1,139,035
SCHLEY CO.	$18,000	$15,000	$0	$53,000	$53,000	$139,000
SCREVEN CO.	$61,884	$69,670	$0	$63,180	$86,056	$280,790
SEMINOLE CO.	$53,500	$49,735	$0	$53,000	$53,000	$209,235
SPALDING CO.	$348,000	$257,465	$0	$204,620	$282,326	$1,092,411
STEPHENS CO.	$107,000	$100,658	$0	$83,320	$112,963	$403,941
STEWART CO.	$53,000	$57,030	$0	$53,000	$53,000	$216,030
SUMTER CO.	$53,500	$123,307	$0	$112,840	$154,273	$443,920
TALBOT CO.	$35,500	$49,642	$0	$53,000	$53,000	$191,142
TALIAFERRO CO.	$18,000	$20,248	$0	$53,000	$53,000	$144,248
TATTNALL CO.	$71,500	$113,294	$0	$62,860	$90,041	$337,695
TAYLOR CO.	$53,000	$55,544	$0	$53,000	$53,000	$214,544
TELFAIR CO.	$71,000	$63,318	$0	$53,000	$56,509	$243,827
TERRELL CO.	$71,000	$80,947	$0	$53,000	$54,008	$258,955
THOMAS CO.	$89,116	$82,685	$0	$100,580	$140,778	$413,159
TIFT CO.	$178,000	$169,915	$0	$147,080	$202,729	$697,724
TOOMBS CO.	$71,000	$87,622	$0	$53,000	$69,427	$281,049
TOWNS CO.	$35,500	$47,280	$0	$53,000	$53,000	$188,780
TREUTLEN CO.	$53,500	$45,000	$0	$53,000	$53,000	$204,500
TROUP CO.	$257,420	$298,668	$0	$218,460	$300,988	$1,075,536
TURNER CO.	$89,000	$76,856	$0	$53,000	$53,706	$272,562
TWIGGS CO.	$89,000	$75,000	$0	$53,000	$53,000	$270,000
UNION CO.	$106,000	$97,756	$0	$53,000	$68,163	$324,919

UPSON CO.	$107,000	$60,000	$0	$99,000	$133,742	$399,742
WALKER CO.	$321,500	$256,797	$0	$171,200	$232,358	$981,855
WALTON CO.	$160,000	$165,006	$0	$157,600	$222,766	$705,372
WARE CO.	$250,000	$231,861	$0	$127,860	$174,887	$784,608
WARREN CO.	$53,000	$45,000	$0	$53,000	$53,000	$204,000
WASHINGTON CO.	$107,000	$93,357	$0	$73,860	$106,120	$380,337
WAYNE CO.	$142,500	$120,000	$0	$97,100	$135,611	$495,211
WEBSTER CO.	$18,000	$19,693	$0	$53,000	$53,000	$143,693
WHEELER CO.	$53,500	$45,000	$0	$53,000	$53,000	$204,500
WHITE CO.	$71,000	$76,741	$0	$53,580	$76,656	$277,977
WHITFIELD CO.	$320,000	$283,663	$0	$208,020	$290,791	$1,102,474
WILCOX CO.	$71,500	$45,000	$0	$53,000	$53,000	$222,500
WILKES CO.	$71,000	$78,344	$0	$53,000	$53,211	$255,555
WILKINSON CO.	$71,000	$69,201	$0	$53,000	$53,000	$246,201
WORTH CO.	$89,000	$105,132	$0	$92,160	$125,469	$411,761
AMERICUS CITY	$88,500		$0			
ATLANTA CITY	$1,965,000	$1,618,086	$0	$1,182,820	$1,622,604	$6,388,510
BREMEN CITY	$53,000	$74,023	$0	$53,000	$53,000	$233,023
BUFORD CITY	$53,000	$57,376	$0	$53,000	$53,000	$216,376
CALHOUN CITY	$71,000	$72,646	$0	$53,000	$56,619	$253,265
CARROLLTON CITY	$53,000	$67,193	$0	$70,980	$96,390	$287,563
CARTERSVILLE CITY	$71,000	$71,851	$0	$60,840	$83,609	$287,300
CHICKAMAUGA CITY	$53,000	$50,578	$0	$53,000	$53,000	$209,578
COMMERCE CITY	$53,000	$66,553	$0	$53,000	$53,000	$225,553
DALTON CITY	$152,000	$120,000	$0	$86,000	$123,600	$481,600
DECATUR CITY	$161,000	$146,454	$0	$53,040	$76,326	$436,820
DUBLIN CITY	$124,500	$116,423	$0	$76,260	$102,409	$419,592
GAINESVILLE CITY	$89,000	$88,841	$0	$61,240	$89,354	$328,435
JEFFERSON CITY	$53,000	$55,569	$0	$53,000	$53,000	$214,569
LAGRANGE CITY	$45,580		$0			
MARIETTA CITY	$160,500	$165,725	$0	$121,800	$170,434	$618,459
PELHAM CITY	$53,000	$51,000	$0	$53,000	$53,000	$210,000
ROME CITY	$179,000	$165,787	$0	$93,520	$131,983	$570,290
SOCIAL CIRCLE CITY	$53,000	$56,419	$0	$53,000	$53,000	$215,419
THOMASVILLE CITY	$124,500	$112,703	$0	$70,660	$94,438	$402,301
TRION CITY	$53,000	$49,478	$0	$53,000	$53,000	$208,478
VALDOSTA CITY	$143,000	$144,606	$0	$148,940	$201,190	$637,736
VIDALIA CITY	$71,000	$60,000	$0	$53,000	$67,888	$251,888
STATE TOTAL	**$32,379,696**	**$30,032,131**	**$0**	**$27,111,320**	**$36,853,819**	**$126,242,886**

* No funding authorized for FY 1996

full text. It also included an encyclopedia, business directory and government publications. Links were also provided to Georgia law and many state agency homepages.

GALILEO recorded its 10.7 millionth keyword search in June of 1998. By this time the 34 University System institutions, seven system resident centers, the Governor's Office, three legislative research offices, 168 public libraries, 33 public technical institutes, nine Department of Education technology training centers, 180 K-12 school systems, and 44 private higher educational institutions subscribed to the system. GALILEO, which received an award from the Smithsonian Institute for its "visionary use of information technology in the field of education and academia," helped put the University System of Georgia ahead of the nation's higher education systems in the use of information technology.

GALILEO also entered a partnership with the Jimmy Carter Presidential Library to digitize President Carter's Presidential Daily Diary. As monthly pages of the diary were made available, links to photographs of events from the time were implemented. An additional feature was a multi-media web presence with video and audio clips of events such as the Camp David Accord. Dr. Donald B. Schewe, director of the Carter Library, believed the new partnership with GALILEO would greatly expand the library's ability to provide high quality and timely teaching materials, especially to the classroom teacher.

The Governor also fully supported the next phase of this great initiative—GALILEO II, or the Interconnected Library System. GALILEO II allowed students and faculty to utilize the collections of all University System libraries as if they were one library, by providing computer access to each library's materials, a convenient and responsive system of book request and delivery, and open, systemwide checkout privileges. The addition of a single integrated library automation system to GALILEO would make on-line access even easier for patrons and staff.

GALILEO II would integrate in one system a web-based integrated union catalog of all book collections of the University System (over six million volumes, of which 60 percent of the titles were unique), a circulation system with self-service options, fund accounting, cataloging, and check-in and control functions. Users would have the ability to visit any library within the system and check out materials using their own identification cards, and each library would easily be able to validate that the user was a legitimate patron of the University System. In addition, librarians would able to gather data on the growth and use of the collections to guide future decision-making and cooperative collection development.

The GALILEO electronic database made a common set of information available to all students at public colleges and technical institutes, as well as residents throughout the state through schools and local libraries. The databases were originally available at 56 library system regional headquarters plus other branch locations around the state. Thanks to Governor Miller's Internet Connectivity initiative, 101 additional counties were connected to GALILEO during Fiscal Year 1998. This initiative gave the citizens of Georgia access to the Internet and a wide variety of information resources at 168 public libraries around Georgia.

The Miller Administration also made Georgia one of the earliest states to have statewide systematic Internet connections for education, providing local dial-in access for every one of its K-12 schools, public technical institutes, public colleges and universities, 168 public libraries, 44 private academic institutions, and the U.S. Navy's aircraft carrier USS Carl Vinson. As he began his final year in office, the Governor asked the state legislature to approve funds to begin creating a "virtual" technical institute with web-based instruction that would allow students to interact with teachers and classmates from their computers at home or at work.

Lottery-Funded Technology and Equipment*

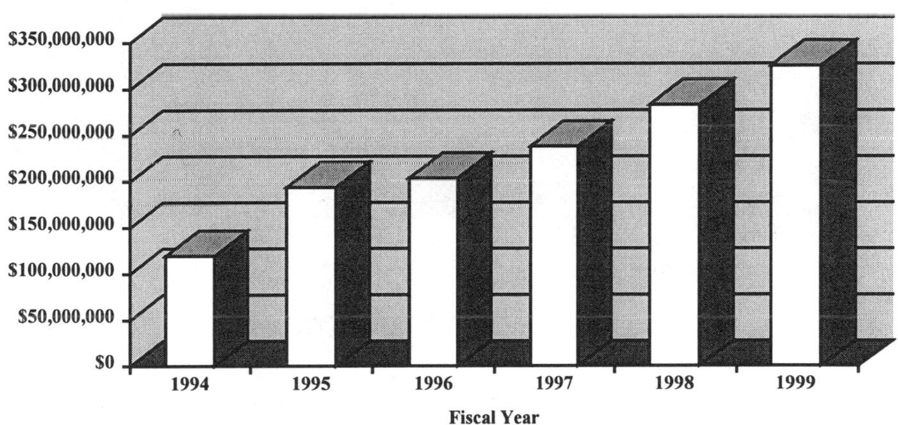

*This data is cumulative; cumulative means all years prior plus current y

Technology training

Governor Miller developed Technology Training Centers for Georgia educators to improve their expertise with technology and to assist them in integrating technology into their classrooms. The training was tuition free, and by 1998 more than 120,000 Georgia teachers had made use of this opportunity. Georgia's framework for INtegrating TECHnology, "In Tech," in the classroom was recognized as a model design consisting of three professional development modules: classroom, technical, and administrative. This program encouraged teachers, technology specialists and administrative personnel to become empowered educators through the use of modern technologies.

By the end of his term, Governor Miller had funded 11 centers, most operating under a partnership between the Department of Education and the University System of Georgia or Regional Educational Service Agencies (RESAs). To further expand accessibility to centers, the Governor chose two new sites for the 1998-99 school year, one each in Savannah and Carrollton.

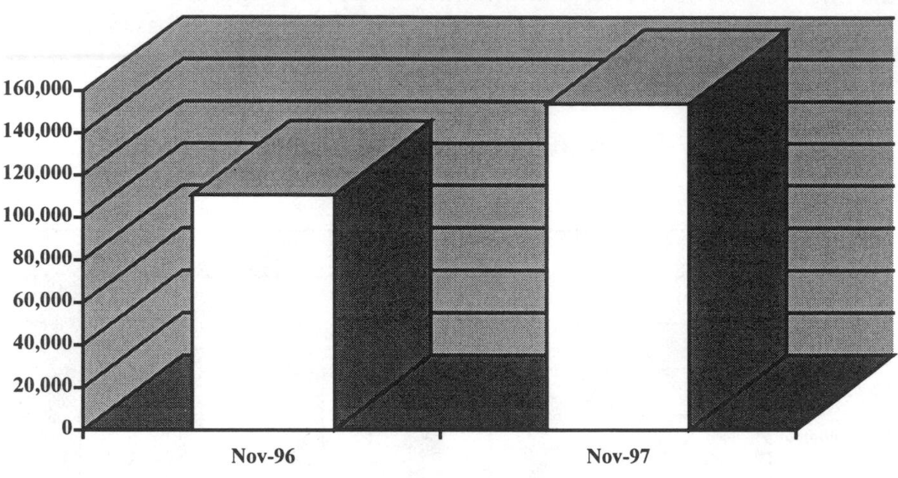

Technology Training Centers in Georgia

Training Center	Location
Albany State University	Albany
Armstrong State University	Savannah
Columbus State University	Columbus
First District RESA	Statesboro
Floyd College	Rome
Fort Discovery	Augusta
Georgia College & State University	Macon
Heart of Georgia RESA	Eastman
Kennesaw State University	Kennesaw
Pioneer RESA	Cleveland
University of Georgia	Athens/Lawrenceville
Valdosta State University	Valdosta
West Georgia	Carrollton

Safe schools grants

Before the Miller Administration, no systematic approach existed to provide local schools with safety equipment to deter violence on school campuses. Numerous tragedies involving violence in public schools across the nation painfully reminded Americans of the importance of school safety issues. Many parents in Georgia wondered how safe their children were in public schools. For educators, the issue was even larger than the physical safety of students and faculty, because the fear of violence on school campuses and the breakdown of discipline could have a dramatic impact on

K-12 Educators Trained by Technology Training Centers*

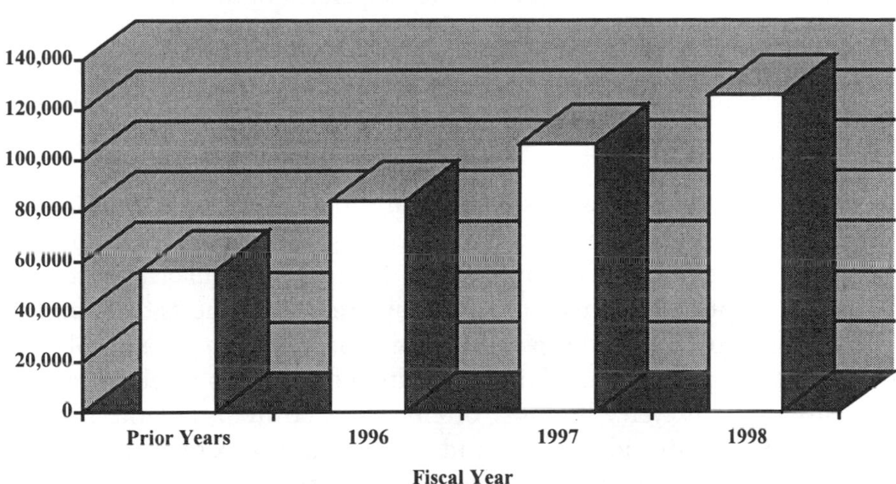

*This data is cumulative; cumulative means all years prior plus current year.

teaching and learning. In a 1995 Centers for Disease Control and Prevention national survey, for example, one in 20 students nationwide reported that they had skipped at least one day of school in the prior month because they felt unsafe at school or traveling to or from school. Additionally, the National Association of Secondary School Principals reported that 63 percent of students said they would learn more if they felt safer in school.

As school violence began to receive national attention, Governor Miller was already putting into place a six-point program to address violence in and around schools in Georgia. This program: (1) urged schools to develop a safe school plan, and offered "Safe Schools" grants to purchase video cameras, metal detectors, radios, or other security devices for school buildings, property and buses to protect students and school personnel; (2) created violence-free safety zones around school sites, where crimes were punished more severely; (3) increased the penalties for handgun assaults on teachers and students, and for possessing a weapon in a school safety zone; (4) provided state funding to local systems for alternative programs for disruptive students; (5) banned handgun possession by those under age 18, with certain exceptions, and made it a felony for any adult to furnish a juvenile with a weapon; and (6) prosecuted in superior court all 13 to 17 year old juvenile offenders who committed violent adult offenses, and made those offenders serve adult sentences in a special facility operated by the Department of Corrections in Eastman, Georgia.

According to statistics self-reported from Georgia public school systems to the Council for School Performance, a total of 23,861 incidents of violence occurred in school year 1996-97 in Georgia public school grades 5-12, including 423 firearm offenses. Overall, 2.96 percent of the 806,000 students in these grades were involved in serious acts of violence. Many schools had virtually no incidence of violence, but in one south Georgia elementary school, 52 percent of the students were reportedly involved in violent behavior.

To address the problem of school violence, Governor Miller recommended to the 1994 General Assembly that $20 million in lottery money be used to provide security equipment for schools. Georgia schools soon bristled with walkie-talkies, hand-held metal detectors, surveillance cameras in hallways and pocket alarms for secretaries. Funding requests from middle and high schools received top priority, but some elementary schools that submitted proposals demonstrating security needs also received money. Security cameras were the most often-requested item, but the list also included fencing, outside lighting and intercom call-back buttons for classroom teachers to contact the principal's office quickly when emergencies arose. During the Miller Administration, the Safe Schools Grant program allowed local schools to purchase $24 million safety equipment.

Assistive technology

Technological advances enabled students with disabilities to participate more fully in educational programs. Assistive devices included such items as communication devices for students with limited speech, adaptive computer technology for children with physical impairments, and listening devices for the hearing impaired. The Georgia Project for Assistive Technology (GPAT) provided essential training to educational personnel in using assistive technology to teach students with disabilities. GPAT staff also provided technical assistance to local school districts in assessing student assistive devices and loaned assistive technology to local school providers and their students to use on a trial basis.

Equipment, Technology, and Construction Trust Fund

In 1990, the University System was receiving only limited funds for technology and laboratory equipment through the funding formula for equipment replacement. Institutions, especially research universities, did not have reliable access to new equipment and had to conduct research with obsolete equipment or without the proper equipment. Obviously, the situation had an adverse effect on the quality of instruction and the ability of the University System to attract research funding.

Governor Miller recognized the importance of providing colleges and universities with the lab equipment and technology they needed to provide the most advanced and modern instructional services possible to students. As part of his FY 1994 budget, the Governor established the Equipment, Technology and Construction Trust Fund (ETACT) using funds from the lottery. ETACT matched private contributions, dollar for dollar, for the purchase of needed equipment at the 34 University System institutions. Funds were used to purchase advanced equipment for classrooms and high technology research equipment, and to build and equip technology related facilities, enabling students and faculty to work with equipment that represented the latest technological advancements. In addition to providing equipment, ETACT also gave Georgia's public institutions a tool to leverage private fund-raising, resulting in an increase in private donations to the state's public institutions. During his administration, Governor Miller provided over $114 million in lottery funds for ETACT.

Equipment, Technology and Construction Trust Fund
Fiscal Years 1994 to 1999

Fiscal Year	Lottery Funds	Private Match Funds	Total Impact
1994	17,483,329	17,483,329	34,966,658
1995	19,321,347	19,321,347	38,642,694
1996	18,000,000	18,000,000	36,000,000
1997	29,204,964	29,204,964	58,409,928
1998	15,000,000	15,000,000	30,000,000
1999	15,000,000	15,000,000	30,000,000
TOTAL	**$114,009,640**	**$114,009,640**	**$228,019,280**

ETACT played an integral part in the modernization of institutions throughout the University System. The following examples illustrate how institutions used ETACT funds to create high technology classrooms and research facilities:

Georgia State University (The CHARA Array) - $3,738,430 in ETACT funds and $3,629,895 in private funds: This facility consisted of five telescopes spread over the grounds of the Mt. Wilson Observatory. Georgia State faculty and students used this facility to embark on astronomy research programs previously unavailable to any scientists in the world.

Valdosta State University (Atomic Emission Spectrometer) - $101,174 in ETACT funds and $101,174 in private funds: This instrument could detect approximately 65 elements simultaneously at very low limits (parts per billion). The instrument would be a cornerstone for teaching and research activities in biology, chemistry, geology and nursing.

University of Georgia (Computational Science Research) - $188,939 in ETACT funds and $420,000 in private funds: The new computer system would enable researchers in physics, chemistry, mathematics, and computer sciences to model complex problems on a computer – often more cost effective than actual laboratory and theoretical research.

These are only three of the many projects made possible by the Equipment, Technology and Construction Trust Fund. All University System institutions, including smaller two-year institutions, benefited from the ETACT during the Miller Administration.

Distance learning

The Miller Administration put Georgia on the forefront of using technology in education with the Georgia Statewide Academic and Medical System (GSAMS). GSAMS was a partnership begun with BellSouth using $50 million from a telephone over-earnings case. During the Miller years, it became a worldwide leader in providing distance learning, telemedicine, and other programs and services, giving Georgia what the New York Times called "the most sophisticated telemedicine and distance learning network in the nation."

GSAMS allowed students to attend class in an environment equipped with cameras, monitors, microphones, speakers, and related electronic technology, which enabled them to interact with teachers and students in other GSAMS classrooms throughout Georgia and the world. By the end of the Miller Administration, GSAMS provided two-way interactive audio and video capabilities to over 400 participating sites in the state. These sites, ranging from elementary schools to rural hospitals, held over 65,000 conferences from GSAMS' inception in 1992 until 1998.

In 1998, GSAMS distance learning was serving over 257,000 students at 124 sites within the 34 member institutions of the University System of Georgia, over 228,000 students at 33 postsecondary technical institutes, and over 131,500 students at 170 K-12 schools. Distance learning via GSAMS was also available at correctional facilities; facilities for juvenile offenders; educational resources such as Zoo Atlanta and the Georgia Music Hall of Fame; and state agencies such as the Department of Revenue and the State Merit System. In addition, GSAMS provided telemedicine, allowing rural patients to be diagnosed by specialists at the Medical College of Georgia or other full-service hospitals without leaving their communities.

In August 1997, with the Georgia Public Telecommunication Commission's move to a new facility adjacent to the new Georgia Center for Advanced Telecommunications Technology (GCATT), Georgia owned the most technologically advanced public television and radio facility in the nation. The new facility was the first public broadcasting facility in the nation with digital technology capabilities. Georgia Public Television (GPTV) used its state of the art digital broadcasting facility, paid for with lottery funds, to produce and distribute high quality educational programming via the PeachStar satellite network. Every public school, technical institute, college, university and library in the state was equipped with a satellite dish in the 1993-94 school year, allowing GPTV to broadcast directly to the classroom. Georgia was the first state to do this, and also became one of the first states to own a transponder on a Telstar satellite to transmit programming. By the end of the Miller Administration, students in 26 states around the nation were using PeachStar's programming.

Within the University System of Georgia, the number of institutions offering distance learning courses doubled from 11 to 22 between fall 1994 and fall 1997. The total number of courses offered through distance learning technology grew even more, from 82 to 208, an increase of 154 percent. For the same period, enrollment in distance learning courses increased by over 179 percent from 1,270 to 3,544 students. Total quarter credit hours generated through distance learning also increased by over 195 percent, from 5,703 to 16,846.

By 1998, the Department of Corrections had 17 GSAMS sites that provided 12,196 hours of instruction to Georgia's inmate population. Four additional sites were approved for FY 1999 to increase instruction time to over 14,500 hours. The department, by changing to part-time teachers, conducting classes at night and using GSAMS, increased enrollment in General Education Diploma (GED) program classes from 5,170 in FY 1997 to 7,103 in FY 1998, an increase of 37 percent. The number of GED tests administered in state prisons increased by 68 percent from FY 1997 (1,900) to FY 1998 (3,204).

Under Governor Miller, Georgia emerged as the national leader in dollars spent for instructional programming for distance learning, and number one in the number of students and educational institutions served through satellite-based instruction. PeachStar Education Services became a leading national provider of instructional programming in mathematics, science and foreign language. Through partnerships with University System institutions, GPTC also offered a variety of college credit programming via satellite that led to Associate of Arts degrees.

PeachStar received the "Golden Camera Award" given by the International Film and Video Festival in the category of Children's Programming for the Elementary Spanish series *SALSA. Irasshai*, the high school credit Japanese Language and Culture series won a Certificate of Excellence in the Education 9 – 12 category in 1996, and nationally renowned Japanese language instructor Tim Cook, received an Emmy for his work in the series.

Infrastructure Improvements

We must not overlook our physical facilities. We have thousands of kids in makeshift mobile homes instead of classrooms, and the roof of the University System is leaking, because we have a lot of older buildings that have not been given the needed renovation and repair.

Governor Zell Miller, January 14, 1992

In communities across Georgia, overcrowded or dilapidated facilities were affecting the quality of education available to students. When Governor Miller first took office, he quickly recognized the significant infrastructure needs of the state's public schools, colleges, and universities. He was faced with overcrowding in the state's public schools, and aging and deteriorating facilities at University System colleges and universities. Throughout his two-term administration, the Governor was committed to providing high quality facilities for Georgia's public school, college, and university students.

School construction (K-12)

As Georgia grew, so did the need for more educational facilities to house the ever-larger population of school-aged children. Governor Miller wanted every student to enter the 21st century in adequate, safe public school facilities that supported the educational programs planned by the local school systems. The Miller Administration approved over $268 million in lottery funds to support "fast growing systems" in the state and over $1.2 billion in total funds for all systems throughout the state. From 1991 through 1998, the

K-12 School Construction Funding

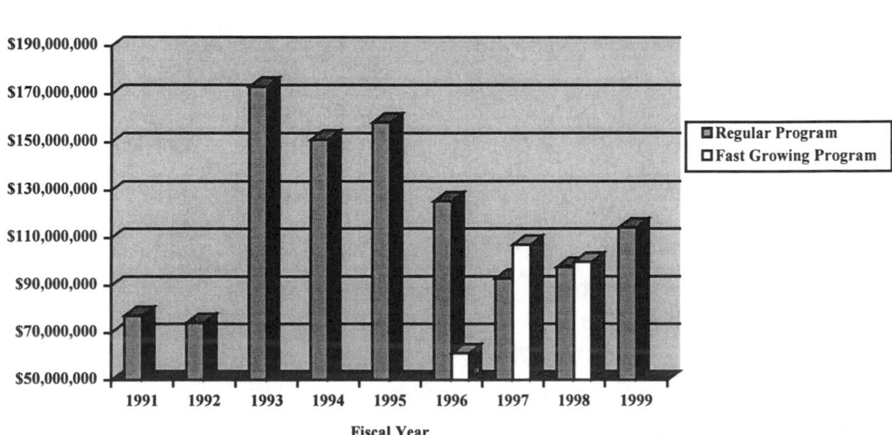

Department of Education
Regular Capital Outlay Funding
Fiscal Year 1991 to Fiscal Year 1999

SYSTEM NAME	FY 1991	FY 1992	FY 1993	FY 1994	FY 1995	FY 1996	FY 1997	FY 1998	FY 1999	SYS TOTAL
APPLING CO.			$3,853,143	$296,947						$4,150,090
ATKINSON CO.										$0
BACON CO.	$529,837		$331,668							$861,505
BAKER CO.								$1,213,785		$1,213,785
BALDWIN CO.			$1,940,280	$2,517,480	$1,488,937	$1,984,083				$7,930,780
BANKS CO.								$3,836,160		$3,836,160
BARROW CO.									$751,501	$751,501
BARTOW CO.			$3,528,668			$717,810	$6,037,720			$10,284,198
BEN HILL CO.			$5,544,450	$4,212,378	$1,928,362					$11,685,190
BERRIEN CO.	$2,816,126		$866,627	$601,616						$4,256,260
BIBB CO.		$2,101,897	$3,122,629	$1,560,771		$1,724,969			$3,078,064	$11,588,330
BLECKLEY CO.						$2,546,523				$2,546,523
BRANTLEY CO.				$389,743						$389,743
BROOKS CO.	$2,151,363				$3,365,964		$224,775			$5,742,102
BRYAN CO.	$2,381,616		$2,955,405	$1,176,921						$6,513,942
BULLOCH CO.		$1,122,737		$1,510,044	$2,011,986	$6,275,722		$11,296,193		$22,216,682
BURKE CO.	$1,143,421		$1,862,636							$3,006,057
BUTTS CO.									$4,606,888	$4,606,888
CALHOUN CO.			$263,452				$718,744			$982,196
CAMDEN CO.			$256,900	$2,517,480						$2,774,380
CANDLER CO.	$1,448,250			$1,124,915						$2,573,165
CARROLL CO.	$3,171,092				$1,113,348	$163,724	$4,400,095			$8,848,259
CATOOSA CO.	$727,362		$2,260,880	$2,133,452						$5,121,694
CHARLTON CO.				$209,790	$78,408		$2,751,246			$3,039,444
CHATHAM CO.		$5,254,740	$8,000,845	$7,095,828		$5,062,315				$25,413,728
CHATTAHOOCHEE			$340,112	$76,230				$502,505	$351,196	$1,270,043
CHATTOOGA CO.		$229,770			$119,790					$349,560
CHEROKEE CO.				$1,936,276	$4,891,104				$2,492,895	$9,320,275
CLARKE CO.		$380,698	$493,668	$685,000	$5,905,588					$7,464,954
CLAY CO.						$1,582,416				$1,582,416
CLAYTON CO.				$2,064,805	$3,452,544	$2,708,372	$1,053,441	$1,613,231	$4,109,587	$15,001,980
CLINCH CO.			$168,720							$168,720
COBB CO.		$3,877,300	$4,277,400	$4,443,100	$3,690,800	$7,219,200	$7,301,922	$6,031,352	$3,943,674	$40,784,748

COFFEE CO.		$9,664,143							$2,672,250	$12,336,393
COLQUITT CO.			$2,092,425	$863,739	$2,905,494					$5,861,658
COLUMBIA CO.	$843,381			$7,296,196						$8,139,577
COOK CO.				$5,183,922						$5,183,922
COWETA CO.				$5,758,735		$436,987		$3,372,699		$9,568,421
CRAWFORD CO.	$2,452,524		$1,074,638							$3,527,162
CRISP CO.	$6,399,345		$2,715,299	$1,412,725						$10,527,369
DADE CO.										$0
DAWSON CO.			$84,284	$12,947		$186,426	$3,986,010			$4,269,667
DECATUR CO.	$1,644,761		$1,894,689							$3,539,450
DEKALB CO.			$6,924,600		$3,124,872	$3,632,128			$20,818,390	$34,499,990
DODGE CO.		$268,117	$286,824							$554,941
DOOLY CO.			$1,197,763	$196,020	$141,134					$1,534,917
DOUGHERTY CO.		$935,908		$994,486	$1,285,084	$1,215,826	$796,257	$718,533	$644,471	$6,590,565
DOUGLAS CO.		$900,305	$953,525	$919,700		$2,398,070		$1,559,261	$1,814,863	$8,545,724
EARLY CO.		$4,571,424		$407,592	$2,513,284		$88,209			$7,580,509
ECHOLS CO.		$161,820		$927,043	$557,465					$1,646,328
EFFINGHAM CO.										$0
ELBERT CO.									$2,427,570	$2,427,570
EMANUEL CO.			$3,599,745	$3,605,535	$3,357,691					$10,562,971
EVANS CO.		$260,520		$2,932,688		$1,322,825				$4,516,033
FANNIN CO.	$3,600,140		$1,196,387	$1,390,363			$261,688			$6,448,578
FAYETTE CO.					$4,745,283				$1,422,507	$6,167,790
FLOYD CO.		$797,252	$572,227	$1,702,296				$2,832,165		$5,903,940
FORSYTH CO.	$953,461		$2,949,647				$4,400,096			$8,303,204
FRANKLIN CO.	$1,499,756		$1,067,445							$2,567,201
FULTON CO.		$3,076,706	$3,076,706	$3,351,905	$4,867,128	$5,860,518	$4,434,290	$4,800,953	$4,015,636	$33,483,842
GILMER CO.				$5,758,737						$5,758,737
GLASCOCK CO.				$1,926,638						$1,926,638
GLYNN CO.		$1,906,092				$2,695,685			$2,521,976	$7,123,753
GORDON CO.	$1,738,065		$1,540,287							$3,278,352
GRADY CO.		$107,329	$556,842		$339,768	$289,055	$1,521,144	$62,008		$2,876,146
GREENE CO.							$3,986,510			$3,986,510
GWINNETT CO.		$4,683,477	$5,284,023	$5,440,400	$4,593,600	$6,937,800	$3,945,795	$7,010,604	$5,841,540	$43,737,239
HABERSHAM CO.		$3,117,629								$3,117,629
HALL CO.		$4,665,730			$928,540	$1,432,580	$1,016,048		$1,506,413	$9,549,311
HANCOCK CO.										$0
HARALSON CO.		$171,000	$143,600	$138,900		$4,054,283				$4,507,783
HARRIS CO.							$6,044,215			$6,044,215
HART CO.										$0
HEARD CO.			$246,154	$227,958			$75,763			$549,875
HENRY CO.			$6,783,709					$3,933,565	$1,421,137	$12,138,411
HOUSTON CO.	$5,758,736		$2,206,818	$1,004,837	$2,853,144	$2,159,573	$2,050,457			$16,033,565
IRWIN CO.			$4,733,761							$4,733,761
JACKSON CO.								$215,141		$215,141
JASPER CO.			$755,101					$762,192	$1,468,319	$2,985,612
JEFF DAVIS CO.			$430,893		$4,484,262	$595,909				$5,511,064
JEFFERSON CO.		$808,048		$5,447,784		$503,678				$6,759,510
JENKINS CO.	$1,527,317		$2,357,984							$3,885,301
JOHNSON CO.	$3,227,849	$110,405								$3,338,254
JONES CO.										$0

LAMAR CO.										$0
LANIER CO.				$1,362,891						$1,362,891
LAURENS CO.		$1,551,883		$713,806		$1,927,384				$4,193,073
LEE CO.										$0
LIBERTY CO.				$4,573,422					$4,917,078	$9,490,500
LINCOLN CO.				$50,000	$65,000				$131,868	$246,868
LONG CO.					$3,391,093	$322,724				$3,713,817
LOWNDES CO.		$2,012,464	$1,991,335					$3,236,760		$7,240,559
LUMPKIN CO.					$2,157,840			$3,671,325		$5,829,165
MACON CO.			$232,554		$4,825,392	$4,406,675				$9,464,621
MADISON CO.			$2,449,548							$2,449,548
MARION CO.		$352,564	$158,543			$1,661,537				$2,172,644
MCDUFFIE CO.	$1,838,160		$3,146,033							$4,984,193
MCINTOSH CO.										$0
MERIWETHER CO.								$3,758,238		$3,758,238
MILLER CO.										$0
MITCHELL CO.				$3,093,449	$2,857,140					$5,950,589
MONROE CO.	$2,287,854			$3,755,707						$6,043,561
MONTGOMERY CO.					$2,369,447					$2,369,447
MORGAN CO.							$900,266			$900,266
MURRAY CO.					$2,789,208	$2,445,552	$4,328,445			$9,563,205
MUSCOGEE CO.		$1,161,236	$1,305,343		$6,137,323	$4,240,135	$2,823,129	$9,311,561	$3,634,717	$28,613,444
NEWTON CO.				$3,558,038	$646,153			$4,450,545		$8,654,736
OCONEE CO.				$1,906,092		$132,586				$2,038,678
OGLETHORPE CO.		$153,100			$145,433	$2,225,864				$2,524,397
PAULDING CO.	$1,967,365	$1,137,204	$113,262							$3,217,831
PEACH CO.		$188,811								$188,811
PICKENS CO.						$5,449,771		$801,099		$6,250,870
PIERCE CO.			$1,224,945	$2,910,070	$3,030,655					$7,165,670
PIKE CO.						$239,400			$3,074,922	$3,314,322
POLK CO.			$324,398	$1,303,915					$3,772,006	$5,400,319
PULASKI CO.						$677,872				$677,872
PUTNAM CO.			$459,288		$5,250,744					$5,710,032
QUITMAN CO.					$142,931	$1,319,985				$1,462,916
RABUN CO.		$158,994							$1,952,056	$2,111,050
RANDOLPH CO.	$1,965,917				$84,865	$816,318				$2,867,100
RICHMOND CO.			$4,899,096		$7,641,797	$929,081			$2,994,003	$16,463,977
ROCKDALE CO.							$1,304,290			$1,304,290
SCHLEY CO.					$1,338,304					$1,338,304
SCREVEN CO.					$3,088,109	$3,351,981				$6,440,090
SEMINOLE CO.		$299,700		$6,213,905	$1,421,470	$267,789	$101,697			$8,304,561
SPALDING CO.	$2,449,548		$2,482,164	$2,155,398			$436,563	$10,219,798	$1,278,696	$19,022,167
STEPHENS CO.			$860,472	$708,624						$1,569,096
STEWART CO.										$0
SUMTER CO.						$515,116	$5,316,870			$5,831,986
TALBOT CO.	$1,901,087		$194,184							$2,095,271
TALIAFERRO CO.										$0
TATTNALL CO.		$5,267,227								$5,267,227
TAYLOR CO.		$253,080								$253,080
TELFAIR CO.		$801,420				$398,474				$1,199,894
TERRELL CO.	$853,329		$104,834							$958,163

THOMAS CO.	$941,928		$3,233,432							$4,175,360
TIFT CO.			$5,630,614	$3,281,116	$1,346,064	$3,181,697	$9,870,120			$23,309,611
TOOMBS CO.										$0
TOWNS CO.		$15,400	$13,800	$17,100	$14,200	$1,035,891				$1,096,391
TREUTLEN CO.			$1,146,136	$2,233,509						$3,379,645
TROUP CO.					$7,552,440	$5,533,159				$13,085,599
TURNER CO.			$2,248,354	$3,711,902						$5,960,256
TWIGGS CO.										$0
UNION CO.	$2,958,887									$2,958,887
UPSON CO.			$8,106,885	$3,796,200	$1,475,067					$13,378,152
WALKER CO.	$3,613,200		$2,243,124	$175,942			$5,167,005	$6,475,674		$17,674,945
WALTON CO.	$818,215		$199,800					$4,612,383		$5,630,398
WARE CO.			$10,099,890	$3,250,080	$4,821,574					$18,171,544
WARREN CO.			$465,268							$465,268
WASHINGTON CO.			$156,994	$1,200,018		$350,980	$5,032,300			$6,740,292
WAYNE CO.			$1,066,349						$9,116,239	$10,182,588
WEBSTER CO.										$0
WHEELER CO.			$3,685,010							$3,685,010
WHITE CO.					$4,868,627					$4,868,627
WHITFIELD CO.			$1,350,890			$1,635,476			$2,913,084	$5,899,450
WILCOX CO.			$4,007,394		$141,725	$390,691				$4,539,810
WILKES CO.										$0
WILKINSON CO.			$1,334,605							$1,334,605
WORTH CO.	$4,388,807		$4,571,919	$1,351,464	$2,253,744					$12,565,934
AMERICUS CITY	$831,997									
ATLANTA CITY			$2,059,325		$17,104,261	$17,385,358				$36,548,944
BREMEN CITY		$65,430			$137,010					$202,440
BUFORD CITY								$676,059		$676,059
CALHOUN CITY		$124,400	$129,300	$129,800	$102,300		$266,669			$752,469
CARROLLTON CITY	$259,471									$259,471
CARTERSVILLE CITY							$315,734			$315,734
CHICKAMAUGA CITY		$31,968				$280,399				$312,367
COMMERCE CITY			$21,637		$207,999		$110,425			$340,061
DALTON CITY		$191,100	$161,277			$331,404			$6,364,629	$7,048,410
DECATUR CITY		$227,191	$14,400					$139,315	$196,614	$577,520
DUBLIN CITY	$3,633,099		$1,968,870							$5,601,969
GAINESVILLE CITY			$239,923	$230,344	$132,033	$135,384	$122,694	$144,691	$73,181	$1,078,250
JEFFERSON CITY		$206,583					$1,013,583			$1,220,166
MARIETTA CITY		$919,080	$240,760	$243,000	$223,500			$577,205	$257,143	$2,460,688
PELHAM CITY			$2,545,570			$159,840				$2,705,410
ROME CITY		$6,890,103								$6,890,103
SOCIAL CIRCLE CITY		$130,774	$65,926	$59,700					$5,478,556	$5,734,956
THOMASVILLE CITY	$1,305,493		$1,448,779	$1,010,793	$35,964					$3,801,029
TRION CITY					$5,660,914					$5,660,914
VALDOSTA CITY		$1,315,294	$20,011	$3,834,961						$5,170,266
VIDALIA CITY				$3,001,833						$3,001,833
STATE TOTAL	$76,027,759	$72,628,053	$173,205,000	$151,270,000	$158,203,906	$125,455,000	$92,204,215	$97,835,000	$112,063,669	$1,058,060,605

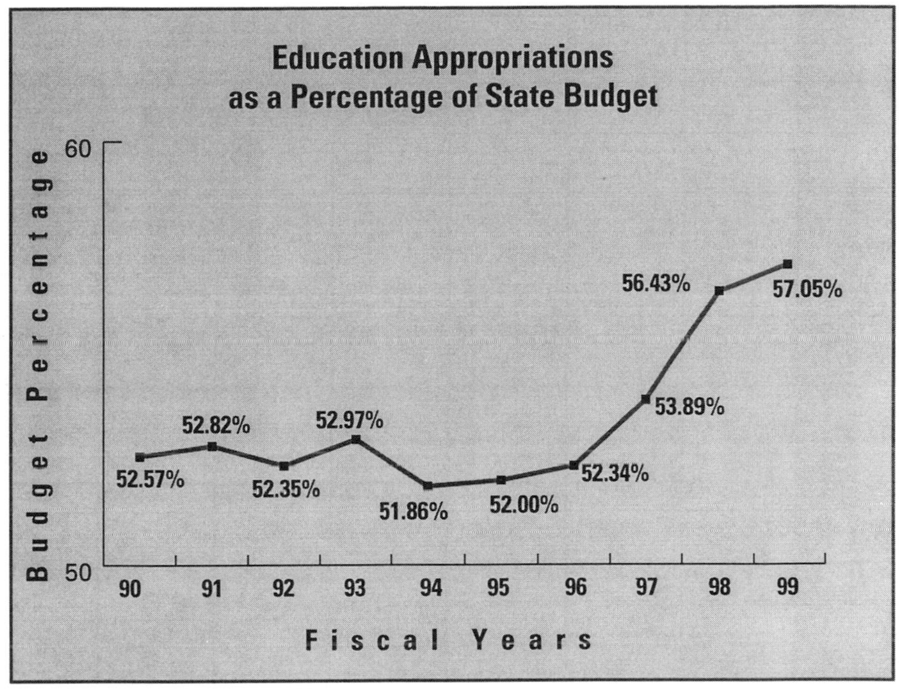
Education Appropriations
as a Percentage of State Budget
Budget Percentage
60
50
52.57%
52.82%
52.35%
52.97%
51.86%
52.00%
52.34%
53.89%
56.43%
57.05%
90
91
92
93
94
95
96
97
98
99
Fiscal Years

New School Construction Projects Approved

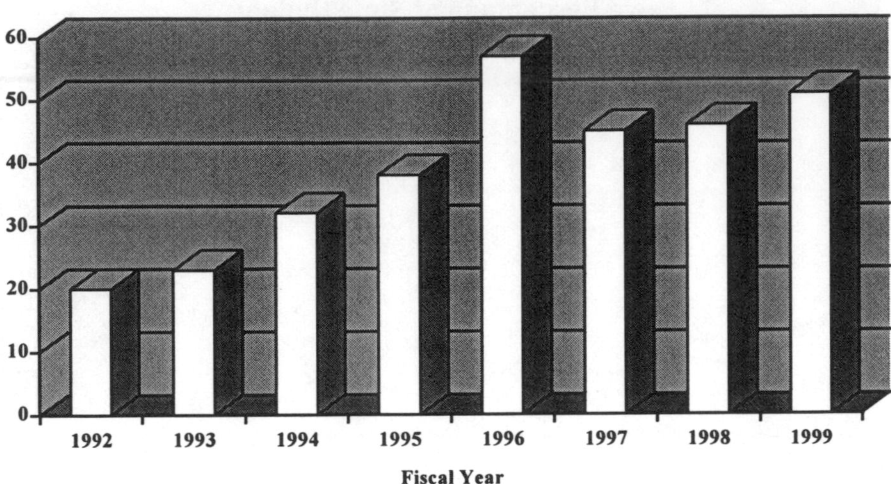

Governor approved funding to support the construction of approximately 312 new public schools.

University System construction

The University System of Georgia not only had a significant number of aging buildings in need of renovation, but also experienced a 13.8 percent increase in student enrollment during the Miller Administration. By 1998, Georgia had one of the largest public systems in the nation, with over 205,000 students in degree programs. This rapid enrollment growth required Georgia to expand dormitory space, build parking decks, expand libraries, add classrooms and modernize student activity centers throughout the University System. To meet this demand, Governor Miller launched the largest University System construction program in Georgia's history, authorizing over $1 billion dollars for capital projects This funding provided at least one project at each institution. An additional $15,495,000 was spent on other projects related to the University System of Georgia, including Georgia Military College, the Skidaway Institute of Oceanography and Rock Eagle.

Major repair and rehabilitation in the University System

Governor Miller recognized the need for new facilities, but also understood the need to protect the state's investment in the college and university facilities it already owned. He authorized over $298 million in major repair and rehabilitation (MRR) funding during his administration. These funds permitted educational institutions to make repairs and renovate existing

University System of Georgia Capital Outlay Projects

Fiscal Year 1991 to Fiscal Year 1999

Year	University System Projects	Project Amount	
1991	DeKalb College - Library	$10,000,000	
	Georgia Southern University - Continuing Education Center	23,500,000	
	Georgia Southern University - Land Acquisition	1,500,000	
	Georgia Tech - Dormitory Design	1,000,000	
	University of Georgia - Law School	2,500,000	
	Valdosta State College - Acquisition of Brookwood Hall	900,000	
1992	Georgia Tech - Olympic Dormitory	24,000,000	*
	Kennesaw State University - Bookstore Expansion	1,250,000	*
	Kennesaw State University - Parking Facility	3,500,000	*
	University of Georgia - Performing and Visual Arts	750,000	
	University of Georgia - Student Parking Deck	4,500,000	
	University of Georgia - Student Physical Activity Center	34,000,000	*
1993	Armstrong Atlantic State - Physical Education Building	7,065,800	
	Darton College - Community Classroom Building	7,333,600	
	Fort Valley State College - Classroom Building	5,438,400	
	Gainesville College - Academic Building Addition	2,451,400	
	Georgia College and State University - Classroom Building	12,493,900	
	Georgia Southern University - Academic Building	17,922,000	
	Georgia Southern University - Dormitory	12,000,000	*
	Georgia Southern University - Intramural Building	8,000,000	*
	Georgia State University - Business Administration Building	8,945,000	
	Georgia Tech - Manufacturing Related Complex	16,304,900	
	Georgia Tech - Olympic Village Land Acquisition	3,500,000	
	Gordon College - Fine Arts Building	4,614,400	

	Kennesaw State University - Science and Health Building	15,213,100	
	Macon State College – Classroom Building	6,519,900	
	North Georgia College - Classroom Addition	5,150,000	
	South Georgia College - Renovate Thrash Hall	1,184,500	
	University of Georgia - Performing and Visual Arts Center	18,990,000	
	Valdosta State University - Brookwood Plaza	8,806,500	
	West Georgia College - Education Center Addition	4,346,600	
	Albany State College - Flood Recovery	13,000,000	
1994	Georgia State University - Parking Deck	5,000,000	*
	Georgia State University - Science Building	2,000,000	
	Georgia Tech - Olympic Dormitory	113,000,000	*
	Georgia Tech - Olympic Village Land Acquisition	4,200,000	
	Georgia Tech - Parking Deck	6,600,000	*
	Gordon College - Dormitory	2,400,000	*
	Medical College of Georgia - Children's Medical Center	4,105,000	
	Middle Georgia College - Physical Education Facility	300,000	
	Southern Tech - Indoor Recreational Facility	2,500,000	*
	University of Georgia - Animal Facility	31,150,000	
	University of Georgia - Biocontainment Center	8,000,000	
	University of Georgia - Infrastructure Upgrade	2,500,000	
1995	Abraham Baldwin Agricultural College - Infrastructure	1,325,000	
	Albany State University - Design of Health Building	540,000	
	Albany State University - Renovation of Health Building	325,000	
	Armstrong Atlantic State - Classroom/Law Enforcement	325,000	
	Atlanta Metropolitan College - Land Acquisition	250,000	
	Augusta College - Design of Science Building	625,000	
	DeKalb College (North) - Design of Classroom/Office	655,000	
	Fort Valley State College - Small Ruminant Building	332,090	
	Georgia Southern University - Classroom Building	3,000,000	
	Georgia Southern University - Design of Education Building	630,000	

	Georgia Tech – Olympic Village Construction	8,500,000	*
	Kennesaw State College - Design of Classroom/Office	565,000	
	Medical College of Georgia - Children's Medical Center	42,385,000	
	South Georgia College - Industrial Technology Building	300,000	
	University of Georgia - Livestock Facility (Tifton)	500,000	
	Albany State College - Flood Recovery	3,639,611	
	Albany State College - Flood Recovery	7,650,000	
	Albany State College - Physical Education Building	13,460,000	
	Armstrong Atlantic State - Classroom Building	8,645,000	
	Augusta College - Science Building	15,015,000	
	Brunswick College - Academic Building	2,210,000	
	Dalton College - Humanities Building	6,360,000	
	DeKalb College - North Campus Classroom Building	15,670,000	
	Dublin Campus - Planning and Design	100,000	
	Floyd College - Classroom/Student Center	4,855,000	
	Georgia College and State - Old Governor's Mansion	300,000	
	Georgia Southern State University - Education Building	15,160,000	
	Georgia State University - Student Center	12,000,000	*
	Georgia Tech - Design Business Center	335,000	
1996	Georgia Tech - Olympic Village Construction	18,435,000	
	Georgia Tech/Macon College -Design Complex	1,600,000	
	Kennesaw State University - Classroom/Office Building	13,660,000	
	Kennesaw State University - Student Center Addition	8,000,000	*
	North Georgia College - Price Memorial Hall	3,045,000	
	Savannah State University - Athletic Recreation Center	11,800,000	
	South Georgia College - Drainage Improvements	1,725,000	
	Southern Tech - Academic Building	13,435,000	
	Southern Tech - Design of Dormitory	855,000	*
	University of Georgia - Agricultural Experiment Station	1,500,000	
	University of Georgia - Animal Science Complex	2,590,000	

	University of Georgia - Brooks Hall	2,500,000	
	University of Georgia - Veterinary Diagnostic Lab	300,000	
	Valdosta State University - Science Building	22,885,000	
1997	Albany State University - Flood Recovery	2,000,000	
	Atlanta Metropolitan College - Student Center	5,815,000	
	Augusta State University - Central Utility Plant	4,975,000	
	Clayton State College - Maintenance Addition	655,000	
	Clayton State College - Music Education Building	4,305,000	
	Columbus College - Physical Education Building	13,305,000	
	Darton College – Science and Math Building Renovation	4,965,000	
	DeKalb College – Renovate Building "C"	1,100,000	
	East Georgia College - Learning Resources Center	4,900,000	
	Georgia College and State - Renovate Herty Hall	4,800,000	
	Georgia Southern University - Continuing Education Facility	3,100,000	
	Georgia Southern University - Purchase of Facilities	3,240,000	
	Georgia Southwestern - Land Acquisition	400,000	
	Georgia Tech - Manufacturing Related Complex	27,260,000	
	Kennesaw State University - School of Nursing Renovation	3,380,000	
	Macon College - Health/Student Services Building	8,755,000	
	Medical College of Georgia - Dugas Building Renovation	4,585,000	
	Middle Georgia College - Walker Hall	7,885,000	
	Savannah State University - Renovate Payne Hall	1,750,000	
	University of Georgia - Athens Veterinary Building	6,000,000	
	University of Georgia - Bull Evaluation Construction	250,000	
	University of Georgia - Food Science Renovations	1,900,000	
	University of Georgia - Industry Interface Building	300,000	
	University of Georgia - Library Ventilation Building	4,200,000	
	University of Georgia - Parking Deck	10,000,000	*
	University System - New Research Facilities	2,200,000	
	Valdosta State University - Special Education Building	3,300,000	

	Waycross College - Students Services Building	6,060,000	
1998	Augusta State University - Classroom Planning and Design	1,280,000	
	East Georgia College - Physical Education Building Design	120,000	
	Georgia College and State - Old Governor's Mansion	359,000	
	Georgia State - School of Public Policy Renovation	8,000,000	
	Georgia Tech - Wood Products Lab	413,100	
	Middle Georgia College - Track Construction	105,000	
	South Georgia College - Technical Facilities Renovation	2,400,000	
	University of Georgia - Animal Science Building	4,900,000	
	Abraham Baldwin Agricultural College - Renovate Engineering	3,220,000	
	Armstrong Atlantic - Science Building	28,000,000	
	Augusta State University - Classroom Replacement	18,195,000	
	Clayton College and State - Learning Center Design	930,000	
	Clayton College and State - Lecture Hall Renovation	1,675,000	
	Columbus State - Commerce Facility Design	800,000	
	Dalton College - Library Addition	4,950,000	
	DeKalb College - Learning Resource Center	8,685,000	
	Floyd College - Planning of Cartersville Campus	50,000	
	Fort Valley State - Health Building	18,930,000	
	Gainesville College - Science Building	8,850,000	
	Georgia College - Old Governor's Mansion	25,000	
	Georgia Southern University - Ceramics/Sculpture Building	1,600,000	
1999	Georgia Southern University - Purchase Modular Facilities	2,000,000	
	Georgia Southwestern - Crawford Wheatley Hall Renovation	2,600,000	
	Georgia State University - Classroom Building	29,075,000	
	Georgia Tech - Environmental Sciences Design	1,340,000	
	Georgia Tech - Parking Deck	10,000,000	*
	Georgia Tech - Technology Research Facility	200,000	
	Gordon College - Instructional Complex Design	600,000	
	Kennesaw State University - Commercial Arts Classroom	4,700,000	

	Medical College of Georgia - Utilities Upgrade	4,000,000	
	Middle Georgia College - Dillard Science Hall	4,100,000	
	North Georgia College - Health/Natural Science Design	765,000	
	Savannah State University - Drew Griffith Building	4,100,000	
	Southern Polytechnic - Architecture Expansion	515,000	
	Southern Polytechnic - Plant Operations Building	1,600,000	
	State University of West Georgia - Arts and Science Center	19,350,000	
	University of Georgia - Facility	240,000	
	University of Georgia - Student Learning Center Design	1,710,000	
	University of Georgia/DeKalb College - Gwinnett Center	880,000	
	Valdosta State University - Odum Library	14,250,000	
	Valdosta State University - Student Recreation Center	9,750,000	*
	TOTAL - University System	**$1,103,068,801**	

* Denotes Payback Project: projects funded through the use of General Obligation Bonds but repaid with revenue generated by the project.

Year	**Other Projects**	**Project Amount**	
1994	Georgia Military College - Academic Building	$2,585,000	
	Georgia Military College - Renovate Sibley Cone Library	610,000	
	Skidaway Institute of Oceanography - Residence	250,000	
1996	Georgia Military College - Old Capital Building	3,500,000	
1997	Georgia Military College - Old Capital Building	1,000,000	
	Georgia Military College - Old Capital Renovations	4,500,000	
	Rock Eagle - Water and Sewer Improvements	1,200,000	
	Skidaway Institute - Oceanographic Vessel	1,700,000	
1998	Georgia Military College - Facility Construction	150,000	
	TOTAL - Other Projects	**$15,495,000**	

buildings. In addition to providing the money, Governor Miller increased the formula that provided funding for MRR from 0.75 percent to one percent of the total replacement value of University System buildings. The increase illustrated the Governor's commitment to maintaining and protecting higher education facilities.

University System of Georgia
Major Repair and Rehabilitation Funding
Fiscal Year 1991 to Fiscal Year 1999

Fiscal Year	Funding	Percent Increase	Funding Percentage[1]
1991	$22,762,500	5.5	0.75
1992	$24,066,757	5.7	0.75
1993	$25,206,426	4.7	0.75
1994	$27,756,534	10.1	0.75
1995	$32,144,360	15.8	0.75
1996	$35,490,135	10.4	0.75
1997	$41,924,444	18.1	0.75
1998	$41,124,444	-1.9	0.99
1999	$47,785,712	16.2	0.95
TOTAL	**$298,261,312**		

[1]Funding as a percentage of replacement value of total facility inventory.

University System of Georgia

As Georgia's Governor I have sought to establish a culture of higher expectations. I want the question to be not "whether" to go to college, but "where."

Governor Zell Miller, November 19, 1996

In less than a decade, Governor Zell Miller profoundly impacted the quality and status of higher education in Georgia by ensuring that Georgians have no financial excuse for not enhancing their lives through educational attainment. Combined, Miller's education legacies significantly raised the aspirations and achievements of Georgians, improved the quality of their lives, and fueled the state's economic engine.

A youngster growing up and coming of age in Georgia during the 90s, had the opportunity to attend free public prekindergarten, learn in technology-filled classrooms, qualify for a HOPE scholarship to attend college or a technical institute, send electronic mail through PeachNet, research a paper on GALILEO, and get a job through ICAPP.

During his 1990 gubernatorial campaign, then-Lieutenant Governor Miller said that he had "two simple but ambitious goals: first, to forge a new alliance between the Governor, the General Assembly, the higher education community, and the business community, and second, to make the University System of Georgia one of the standards by which other public universities measure themselves." Under the Miller Administration, the University System of Georgia moved to national prominence on a variety of fronts, from groundbreaking initiatives that linked higher education programs to the needs of business and industry, to collaborative partnerships that strengthened the ties between all levels and systems of education in the state, to the innovative, award-winning use of educational technology.

The Georgia Lottery generated more than $3.1 billion for specific education programs between its inception in 1993 and the end of the Miller Administration. One of the three programs funded by the lottery, the HOPE Scholarship Program, became the envy of the nation. "HOPE scholarships are unique. No other state has such a program," Governor Miller wrote in the introduction to the Fiscal Year (FY) 1999 budget, his last. "President Clinton likes the program so much he has proposed a national scholarship program based on HOPE." Clinton had come to Georgia in 1997 to salute the program and tell the national press of his desire to replicate it.

HOPE helped to raise the bar for aspiring University System of Georgia students, who understood that hard work in the classroom would earn them financial support for college. In Georgia, academic excellence equivalent to a B average or better throughout high school gave students free tuition and mandatory fees plus a book allowance at any one of the state's 34 public colleges and universities that accepted them. Students who chose to join the teaching ranks could benefit from additional financial support.

Like many of the programs and initiatives that Governor Miller brought to fruition, HOPE was focused on long-term return. He clearly understood that education was a sown seed that would reap harvests for generations to come. He looked forward to a Georgia where lives would be improved more through educational pursuits than through the sweat of the brow and the harvests of the fields.

Funding higher education

When Governor Zell Miller took office in January 1991, he inherited a dismal outlook for higher education in Georgia. In August of that year, Miller summoned the state's legislators to Atlanta for a special session to cut the FY 1992 budget, resulting in a $79 million cut for the University System of Georgia. All state agencies had been asked to develop two contingencies: a five percent reduction in the agency's workforce and a 10 percent reduction in spending.

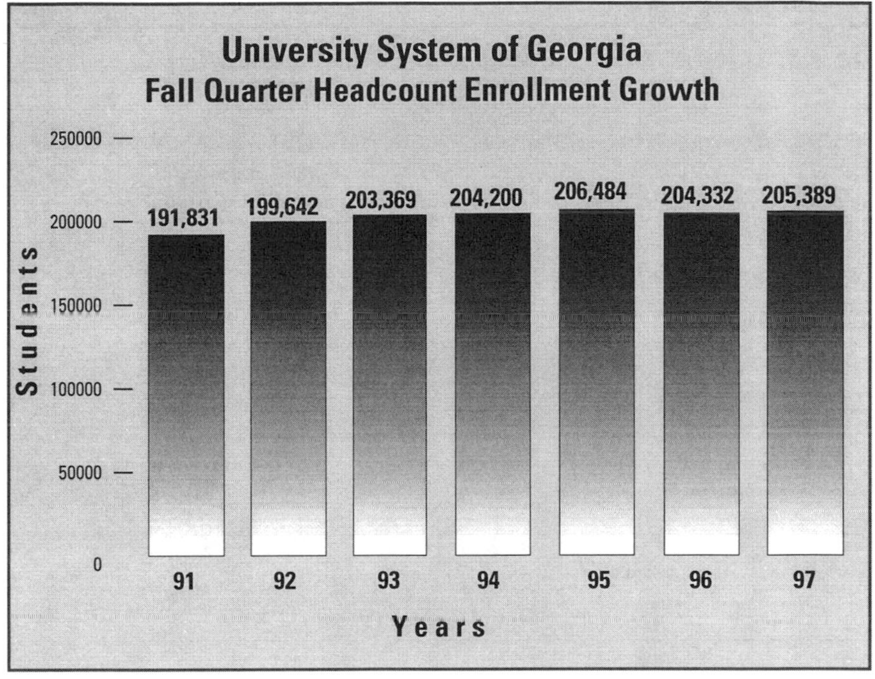
University System of Georgia
Fall Quarter Headcount Enrollment Growth
250000
200000
150000
100000
50000
0
Students
191,831
199,642
203,369
204,200
206,484
204,332
205,389
91
92
93
94
95
96
97
Years

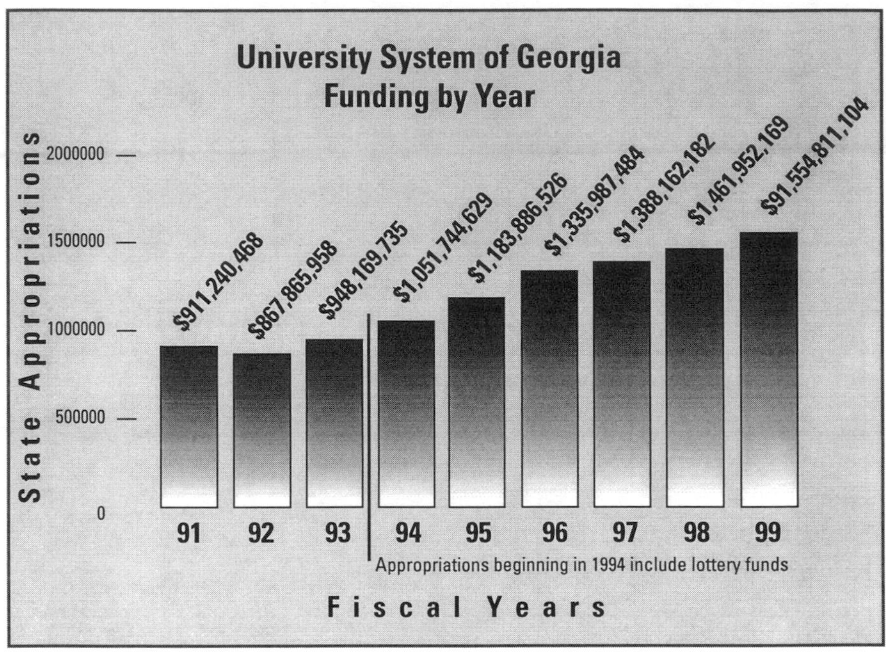

Four months later, Miller had his arms around the state budget and was ready to move ahead with educational improvements. According to a November 21, 1991 article in the *Chronicle of Higher Education*, Miller had been disturbed by a report from Illinois State University researchers on state appropriations for higher education, which cited Georgia as one of 13 states in which financial support had decreased during the past two years. Indeed, education appropriations as a percentage of the state's budget had hovered in the 52 percent range in FY 1990 before Miller took office, and dropped from 52.8 percent to 52.3 percent between FY 1991 and FY 1992. At the same time, the University System recorded major enrollment increases. In the fall of 1991, total enrollment was 191,831; in fall of 1992, enrollment increased to 199,642; and in fall 1993, enrollment reached 203,319.

Miller informed the Board of Regents that he would use the power of his office to shield higher education from such deep cuts in the future. He announced that the education portion of his Georgia Rebound proposal for FY 1993 would include a three percent raise for the University System's faculty and staff, and $140 million in bonds to finance capital improvements within the University System, of which $122 million was later approved by the General Assembly. Charles B. Knapp, then president of The University of the Georgia, said, "In my five years as president, this is the most encouraging thing I have heard from state government."

While funding for the University System continued to be relatively static during FY 1992 and FY 1993, funding levels jumped in Fiscal Year 1994 and continued to increase during the remainder of Miller's time in office. The University System received a significant share of the nearly 79 percent increase in education spending during the Miller Administration. Specifically, it meant a 59 percent increase in the University System's total state general fund appropriations since Miller took office in 1991.

That increased funding provided for operating budget increases, special funding initiatives, new buildings and facility repairs, increased formula funding to accommodate student growth, and a number of other critical needs integral to enhancing a rising university system. Faculty salary increases were an especially important goal for both Miller and University System Chancellor Stephen Portch. Both of them knew that good compensation packages were a strong incentive for attracting and retaining the best and brightest educators, and that eminent faculty were critical to improving the system and making it a national leader.

HOPE

"My goal as Governor has been to create a culture of higher expectations in Georgia," Governor Miller said. "I want the question for our students to be not 'whether' to go to college or technical school, but 'where' to go." To achieve that goal, Miller established the nation's most far-reaching scholarship program since the GI Bill in the form of HOPE, which stood for Helping Outstanding Pupils Educationally. Implemented in 1993, HOPE was Miller's brainchild. By the end of his administration, it had provided financial assistance to some 331,000 students at Georgia's colleges, universities and technical institutes. In addition, HOPE provided incentives for students who received a General Education Diploma (GED) to continue their education at a college or technical institute.

When he proposed a lottery in his 1990 gubernatorial campaign, Zell Miller was adamant that the lottery proceeds be used exclusively for new educational programs. "I've worked too hard for the lottery for someone to take that money away," Miller said while flipping hamburgers during a campaign visit to Allen's in Athens, where he had worked to put himself through The University of Georgia. After taking office in January 1991, he ensured that lottery reserves were used to augment rather than replace general appropriations for education.

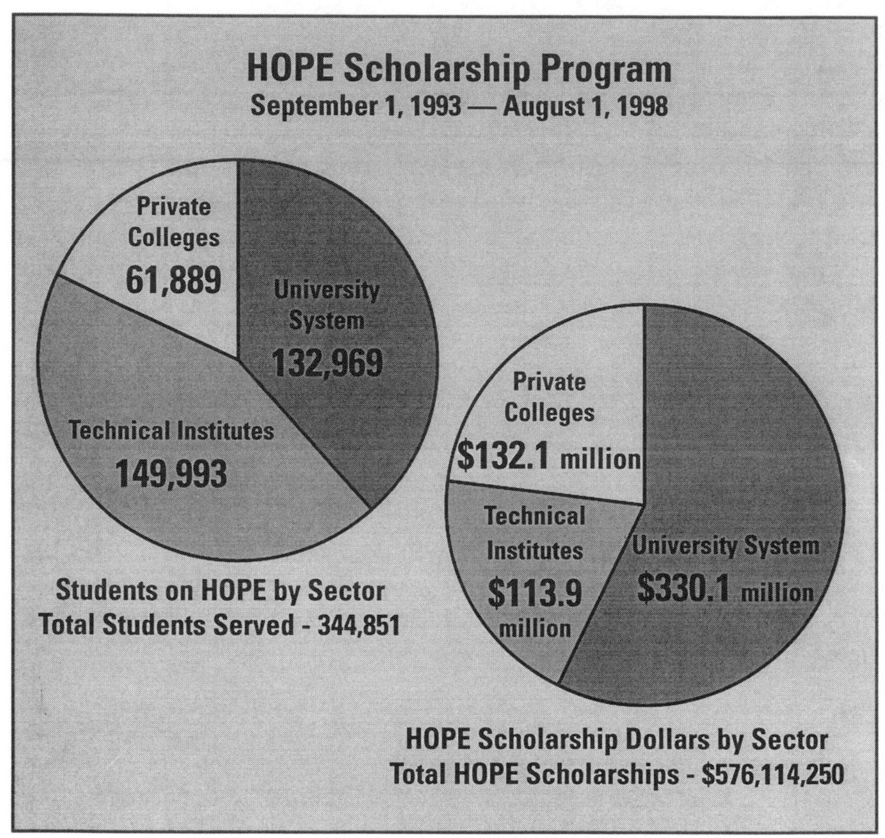

HOPE was designed to serve several critical functions: prevent high-school dropouts, motivate higher student performance, keep outstanding students in the state to attend colleges and universities, and provide higher education access to those who might have been excluded in the past. The program opened the door to students who never thought they would be able to afford a college education. Often referred to as Georgia's GI Bill, HOPE took over where Pell and/or other federal grants stopped, rewarding academic excellence in the University System by covering costs for tuition and mandatory student fees and providing book allowances for Georgia students who had maintained a B average in high school and continued it through college. By the end of the Miller Administration, it had singularly distributed more than twice as much academic-based financial aid to post-secondary students as any other state in the United States.

As Miller prepared to leave office at the end of 1998, nearly $615 million had been provided to eligible recipients, including some $360 million within the University System of Georgia. More than 144,000 students attended the state's public colleges and universities as a result of that funding.

After successfully launching the HOPE Scholarship Program, Miller expanded his scholarship initiative to attract Georgia's best students into teaching and steer experienced teachers toward fields where the state was experiencing shortages. He created the HOPE Teacher Scholarship Program to provide forgivable loans to those who pursued advanced education degrees in critical shortage fields of study. In return for each $2,500 awarded through the scholarship program, the recipient was required to teach in their field of study for one full academic year in a Georgia public school. To encourage bright young students to consider teaching, Miller created HOPE PROMISE, which provided forgivable loans to high-achieving students, beginning with their junior year. Eligible students could receive up to $3,000 in PROMISE assistance in each of their junior and senior years, a maximum of $6,000. In return, they made a commitment to teach in Georgia's public schools for one year for each $1,500 they received.

Miller knew the promise that HOPE held for young Georgians. Its validation was captured in the comments of one of its first recipients, quoted in a November 1993 article in the *Chronicle of Higher Education*: "Actually, when I heard about the program, I was in disbelief," he said. "But when I heard the legislature had passed it, it was a dream come true." The student, Michael Hair, was then a freshman at Georgia Southern University in Statesboro. He said that he would not have been able to attend the university without the financial support that HOPE provided.

Four years later, Jennifer Heidmann, a graduating advertising major at the University of Georgia, said that she was proud to have retained her HOPE scholarship for four years, placing her in the first graduating class of HOPE scholars. "I do consider having the HOPE a distinction," she said. "A lot of my friends and family were against the lottery being passed. Now they feel differently."

Paul Dunn, a Georgia Tech electrical engineering student from Woodstock, also was among the first class of graduating HOPE recipients. "It was hard," Dunn said in a June 1997 *Atlanta Journal-Constitution* article. "I'd say on a scale of 1-10, keeping my grades up for HOPE was a 9." Yet the 1997 graduate saw the benefits of the program, as he prepared for a job already secured in Atlanta. "There are a lot of people here at Tech and at other schools who benefited from HOPE who are now going to be out there working," Dunn said. "So maybe the state will get some compensation for its investment."

Salary increases

A teacher who was the son of teachers, Zell Miller appreciated the contributions educators made to society, and understood the importance of

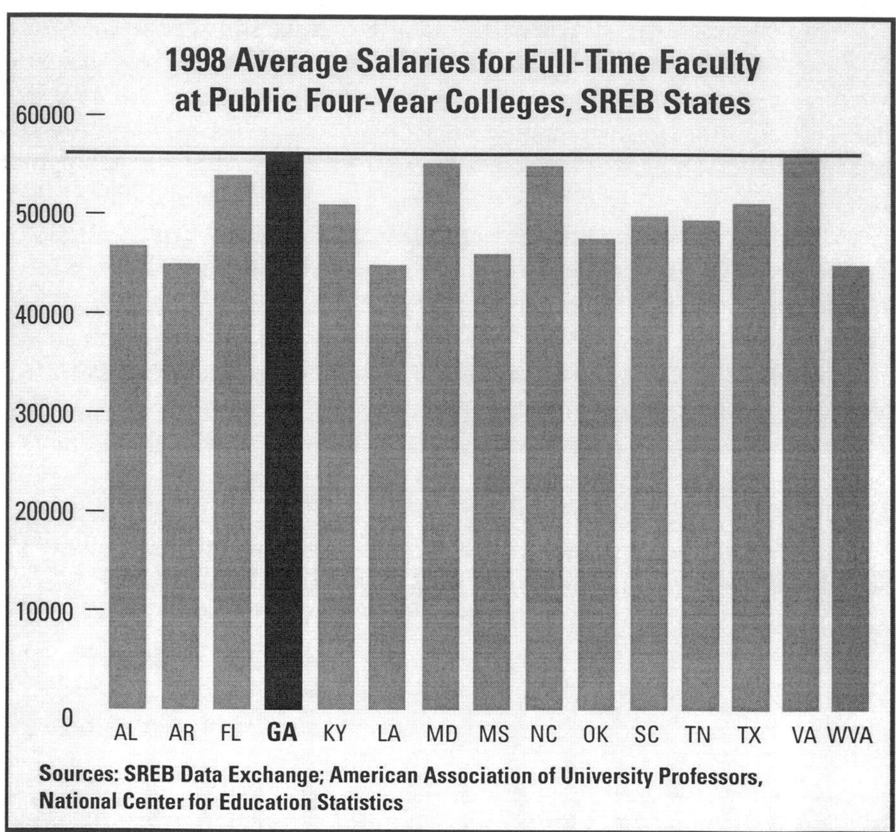

competitive salaries in recruiting excellent teachers. During the 1980s, average faculty salaries in the University System had fallen from first to seventh among states served by the Southern Regional Board of Education, creating difficulties in attracting and retaining the best and most-qualified academic personnel. The Governor believed that quality faculty were the key to excellence in higher education, and set a goal of returning the state to the top of the SREB region. "Faculty salaries are an investment in every field our faculty members teach, and their contributions to our state and nation add up each time a course is completed or a degree is earned," he said.

In his inaugural address for his second term as Governor, he pledged to seek six percent salary increases for University System of Georgia faculty and teachers in public schools and state technical institutes in each year of his second term. Miller made the salary increases an unyielding budget requisite, and convinced the General Assembly to implement the four consecutive raises he had promised.

The effort was unmatched in higher education circles, and caught national attention. "Places like Georgia... can afford to buy the best faculty in America, and they're doing it," the *New York Times* reported in a January 10, 1996, article, titled "Raising Standards Enhances Appeal of State Universities." In his FY 1999 budget statement, Miller wrote: "The results have been gratifying... For our University System faculty, our goal was to move their salaries to number one among the institutions that comprise the Southern Regional Education Board. That goal will be reached in FY 1999. In contrast, the average pay of University System faculty members at four-year institutions ranked only seventh among SREB states in 1992."

Education technology

Education, technology and student success were tightly interwoven in the emerging global society. In Georgia, educational technology became as integral to the classrooms of the state's colleges, universities, technical institutes and K-12 schools as blackboards and chalk. From classroom computers to satellite dishes and Internet connections at every public educational facility in the state, Miller spent more than $625 million in lottery revenues on technology initiatives across the various educational sectors in Georgia from 1993 through 1998.

For higher education, Governor Miller's goal was to build a model that was well-equipped to educate its students for a world where technology was integral to nearly every profession. Under Miller's leadership, Georgia launched the world's largest distance learning and education technology networks. He allocated nearly $150 million for five Special Funding Initiatives that helped propel the system into the Information Age. Just as importantly, Miller also has supported investment in the necessary training and staff required to put today's leading technology to efficient use on the college and university campuses.

GALILEO: GALILEO (Georgia Library Learning Online) was a statewide electronic library that provided universal access to on-line databases, information services and the University System's library resources. In addition to being the vehicle for GALILEO, the University System's PeachNet computer network provided access to Internet features such as electronic mail and the World Wide Web at all system and off-campus resident center libraries.

GALILEO connected the 34 colleges and universities of the University System of Georgia, as well as the 33 public technical institutes, all 180 K-12 school systems, and all 168 public libraries. In fact, GALILEO made Georgia one of the first states in the country to link all of its public universities and colleges to the Internet on a systemwide basis. In addition, GALILEO fostered informational equity, giving rural Waycross College, located near the South

Georgia coast, access to the full library holdings of The University of Georgia, hundreds of miles away in Athens.

Databases, which provided citations, abstracts and full-text in the humanities, social sciences, general sciences, and business and management, were available through GALILEO starting on September 20, 1995, only 150 days after Governor Miller pushed the initiative's $8.8 million in initial funding through the General Assembly. Additional databases, such as abstracts covering 29 U.S. newspapers and dissertation abstracts, became available online in early 1996. In all, Governor Miller infused close to $22 million into GALILEO after it came on line in fall 1995 as one of the first major initiatives of then new University System Chancellor Stephen Portch.

In the first three months of 1998 alone, GALILEO recorded 1.2 million log-ons, more than the 1.1 million logged during its entire first full year of operation in 1996. The steady increase in volume reflected the increasing statewide use of this landmark technology initiative.

GSAMS: The Georgia Statewide Academic and Medical System (GSAMS) linked students all over Georgia through high-technology, distance learning classrooms. GSAMS was the world's largest public two-way video network and was actively utilized by the 34 colleges and universities of the University System, as well as additional educational partners. As of June 1998, 124 of the 400-plus GSAMS sites were operable within the University System. The number of college-level academic courses offered via GSAMS increased by 350 percent between 1994 and 1997, with 338 courses offered by 18 institutions in 1997. GSAMS classrooms boasted state-of-the art camera equipment, monitors, microphones, speakers and other electronic technology that enabled multiple sites to be interactive simultaneously. The technology increased student access to a broad array of highly qualified faculty, while reducing the need for wasteful duplication of high-demand academic programs.

GSAMS also allowed the Medical College of Georgia to extend its allied health care programs to other system colleges around the state, and encouraged a consortium of colleges and universities to coalesce their resources to deliver high-quality foreign language programs. It allowed the programs of the state's only public liberal arts university in Milledgeville to be extended to students at a satellite campus in Dublin. In short, GSAMS mitigated distance and closed educational gaps in the state.

Connecting Teachers and Technology: A third initiative, which received close to $34 million from Governor Miller and the General Assembly, was called Connecting Teachers and Technology. It helped University System faculty integrate instructional and distance learning technologies into their teaching by training them to use the emerging technologies effectively. A major goal of the initiative was to increase the number of courses which integrated technology into the instructional process.

Miller also recognized the rapid-fire manner in which technology had exploded into educational instruction, and the need to have skilled personnel available on the state's campus with expertise in how to use it. The Governor supported the placement of campus instructional technology support staff at each of the 34 University System campuses. In addition, this initiative included a Faculty Development Institute, an intensive workshop for 60 University System faculty members representing all of the campuses, for which participants were competitively selected.

Connecting Students and Services: This initiative provided round-the-clock access to the information students needed to move through the University System's institutions and into successful careers. Connecting Students and Services gave students computer access to accurate and timely information about required college preparation courses, admissions and transfer information, and career information. Between its approval in FY 1996 and Miller's last budget for FY 1999, Connecting Students and Services received nearly $10 million in state funds. Those funds paid for the installation of Banner software to provide World Wide Web access for students to view course catalogs, class schedules and grades, and registration and academic advising information. In addition, some system campuses took advantage of Banner's voice response technology to implement "register-by-phone" services.

Through another element in this technology-focused initiative, college-bound high-school students were provided with "no-charge" access to the Georgia Career Information System, which offered assistance in selecting career and educational paths. High-school guidance counselors were also provided with the same no-charge access to facilitate on-line advising and counseling of college-bound students.

In his FY 1999 budget, Governor Miller allocated $2 million to support the University System's goal of placing credit and non-credit academic programs at the fingertips of Georgians via computer access. Primarily focused on increasing delivery of the system's programs to busy professionals, the two-year desktop learning pilot included eight University System schools representing research, regional, four- and two-year institutions. The University System's Office of Information and Instructional Technology worked with participating colleges and universities to create a prototype statewide distance learning system that was based on common instructional management and delivery software applications. The pilot would be assessed to determine the feasibility for broad-based expansion of on-line instruction within the University System.

Equipment, Technology and Construction Trust Fund: In FY 1994, Governor Miller used lottery revenues to create the Equipment, Technology and Construction Trust Fund (ETACT). ETACT provided matching funds for University System institutions to address equipment, technology and construction needs. ETACT funds were used to leverage matching funds from other sources, significantly expanding the University System's ability to address its equipment and technology needs. From FY 1994 through FY 1999, ETACT funneled more than $114 million in lottery revenues to University System institutions, which raised another $114 million-plus in matching private funds, generating more than $228 million in all. These funds provided for the purchase of equipment, the installation of technology infrastructure, and the renovation and construction of facilities which exposed students to technology. The projects added to the technology infrastructure of the University System, and increased its ability to prepare students for the work world.

Capital improvements

One of Governor Miller's greatest legacies to the University System of Georgia was the unprecedented funding he provided for its facility needs during his eight years in office. Beginning with his FY 1993 budget, his second in office, Miller made University System construction a major priority. In November of 1991, he announced the FY 1993 budget he would present during the 1992 legislative session would include $140 million in bonds for University System capital improvements. The proposed construction was part of his Georgia Rebound initiative, and was designed to meet pressing facility needs while simultaneously providing the short-term construction jobs that would help the state recover from the recession. The final FY 93 budget contained $122 million for University System capital outlay. That precedent set the stage for a much-needed pattern of support for the University System, which managed 55 percent of the state's real estate.

Six years later, Miller recommended $185 million in new construction funds for the University System in his FY 1998 amended budget, a record level of funding for non-payback capital outlay projects for the Board of Regents. It also contributed to yet another record. During his two terms, Miller allocated the University System over $1 billion in capital funding, a phenomenal level of support for public higher education's capital needs. Every single one of the University System's 34 colleges and universities received at least one building.

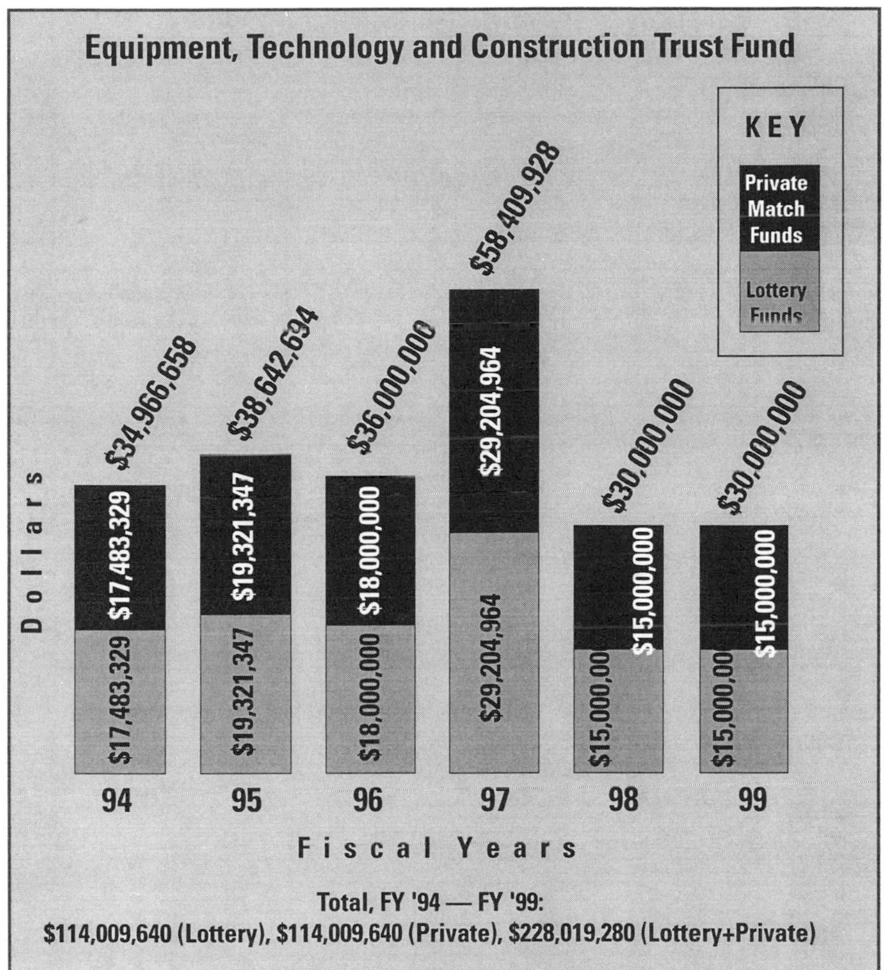

Equipment, Technology and Construction Trust Fund
KEY
Private Match Funds
Lottery Funds
Dollars
$34,966,658
$17,483,329
$17,483,329
$38,642,694
$19,321,347
$19,321,347
$36,000,000
$18,000,000
$18,000,000
$58,409,928
$29,204,964
$29,204,964
$30,000,000
$15,000,000
$15,000,000
$30,000,000
$15,000,000
$15,000,000
94
95
96
97
98
99
Fiscal Years
Total, FY '94 — FY '99:
$114,009,640 (Lottery), $114,009,640 (Private), $228,019,280 (Lottery+Private)

Capital Projects Funded during the Miller Administration

1991 Session

Georgia Institute of Technology	Undergraduate Residence Hall & Graduate Living Center	$24,000,000
University of Georgia	Student Physical Activity Center	$34,000,000
University of Georgia	Student Parking Deck	$4,500,000
University of Georgia	Performing & Visual Arts Center	$750,000
Kennesaw State University	Bookstore Expansion	$1,250,000
Kennesaw State University	Parking Facility	$3,500,000
Total	**6 projects**	**$68,000,000**

1992 Session

Georgia Institute of Technology	Manufacturing Related Disciplines Complex	$16,304,900
Georgia Institute of Technology	Land Acquisition for Olympic Dorms	$3,500,000
Georgia State University	Restoration of former Administration Building	$8,943,000
University of Georgia	Performing & Visual Arts Center	$18,990,000
Georgia Southern University	Academic Building	$17,922,000
Georgia Southern University	Intramural & Physical Education Center	$8,000,000
Georgia Southern University	Student Resident Center	$12,000,000
Armstrong Atlantic State U.	Physical Ed. Building addition	$7,065,800
Fort Valley State University	Computer Tech & Math Classroom Building	$5,440,000
Georgia College & State U.	General Classroom Building	$12,493,000
Kennesaw State University	Science & Allied Health Building	$15,213,000
North Georgia College & State U.	Classroom Building & Science Building addition	$5,150,000
Valdosta State University	Purchase & renovate Brookwood Plaza	$8,806,500
State University of West Ga.	Education Center addition	$4,346,000
Darton College	Allied Health, Community Service & Classroom Building	$7,333,600
Gainesville College	Academic Center addition	$2,451,400
Gordon College	Fine Arts Classroom Building and Theater	$4,614,400
Macon State College	General Classroom Building	$6,519,900
South Georgia College	Renovate Thrash Hall	$1,184,000
Total	**19 projects**	**$166,280,000**

1993 Session

University of Georgia	Comprehensive Agriculture Lab. & Poultry Facilities	$31,150,000
University of Georgia	Biocontainment Research Center	$8,000,000
Medical College of Georgia	Children's Medical Center	$40,960,000
Georgia Institute of Technology	Parking Deck	$6,600,000
Georgia State University	Parking Deck	$5,000,000
Gordon College	Dormitory	$2,400,145
Southern Polytechnic State U.	Indoor Recreation Facility	$2,500,000
Georgia Institute of Technology	Eighth Street Apartments	$19,894,506
Georgia Institute of Technology	Center Street Apartments	$8,451,273
Georgia Institute of Technology	University Apartments	$55,000,000
Georgia Institute of Technology	Hemphill Ave. Apartments	$9,189,753
Georgia Institute of Technology	Sixth Street Apartments	$10,703,174
Georgia Institute of Technology	Fourth Street Apartments	$3,246,294
Georgia Institute of Technology	Housing renovations and updating	$16,261,000
Total	**14 projects**	**$219,356,145**

1994 Session

Olympic Village land		$4,200,000
University of Georgia	infrastructure improvements	$2,500,000
Skidaway Institute of Ocean.	Dormitory	$250,000
Abraham Baldwin Agr. College	Hot water distribution system	$1,325,000
Albany State University	Design funds	
Augusta State University	Design funds	
Kennesaw State University	Design funds	
Georgia Southern University	Design funds	
DeKalb College	Design funds	
Armstrong Atlantic State U.	Design funds	
Subtotal: design funds		$3,125,000
South Georgia College	Building renovation	$300,000
Georgia Southern University	Building	$3,000,000
University of Georgia	Coastal Plains Bull Testing facility	$500,000
Fort Valley State University	Goat research facility	$332,000
Total	**14 projects**	**$15,532,090**

<u>1995 Session</u>

Albany State University	Flood recovery projects (lottery)	$13,000,000
Medical College of Georgia	Children's Medical Center (increase from 1993 session)	$1,425,000
Georgia Institute of Technology	Olympic Dormitory Projects	$8,500,000
Albany State University	Health & Physical Education Bldg. (planning & design)	$540,000
Albany State University	Flood recovery (lottery)	$3,639,611
	Flood recovery (FEMA)	$7,960,389
University of Georgia	Food Safety Laboratory - Griffin (lottery)	$7,000,000
Albany State College	Health and Physical Education facility (FEMA)	$13,460,000
Augusta State University (b)	Science Building	$15,015,000
Kennesaw State University ©	Academic Building	$13,660,000
Georgia Southern University (d)	College of Education	$15,160,000
DeKalb College (e)	Academic Building - North Campus	$15,670,000
Armstrong Atlantic State U. (f)	Academic Building & Law Enforcement Training Center	$8,645,000
Cost overruns in b-f above, Comprehensive Livestock facilities, biocontainment research center at University of Georgia; and Georgia Southern Continuing Education Center		$18,935,000
Georgia State University	Student Center (payback)	$12,000,000
Kennesaw State University	Student Center (payback)	$8,000,000
	Dublin Center planning	$100,000
Southern Polytechnic State U.	Dormitory (payback)	$1,600,000
Total	**16 projects**	**$142,889,611***

*Does not include FEMA dollars for Albany State University

<u>1996 Session</u>

Albany State University	Flood recovery projects	$7,650,000
Dalton College	Humanities Building	$6,360,000
Southern Polytechnic State U.	Academic Bldg.	$13,435,000
Savannah State University	Recreation Complex	$11,800,000
Floyd College	Student Center	$4,855,000
Valdosta State University	Science Building	$22,885,000
University of Georgia	Animal Science Complex	$2,590,000
University of Georgia	Brooks Hall	$2,500,000
North Georgia College & State U.	Price Hall renovation	$3,045,000
Coastal Georgia Com. College	Academic Bldg. renovation	$2,210,000
South Georgia College	Drainage system	$1,725,000
Georgia Southern University	Purchase of leased facilities	$1,725,000
University of Georgia	Center for Research on Environment & Milk Yield - Tifton (lottery)	$1,500,000
Total	**13 projects**	**$82,310,000**

<u>1997 Session</u>

Institution	Project	Amount
Macon State College	Student Services Building/ Health Education classrooms	$8,755,000
Georgia Institute of Technology	Manufacturing Related Disciplines Complex, Phase II	$27,260,000
Waycross College	Student Services and Physical Education Building	$6,060,000
Clayton College & State U.	Music Education Bldg.	$4,305,000
Middle Georgia College	Classroom Bldg. renovations & addition/Dublin Center addition	$7,885,000
Columbus State University	Physical Education facility	$13,305,000
Atlanta Metropolitan College	Student Center	$5,815,000
Albany State University	Flood Recovery	$2,000,000
Augusta State University	Central Utility Plant, phase II	$4,975,000
DeKalb College	Building C renovations	$1,100,000
Georgia College & State U.	Herty Hall renovations	$4,800,000
Savannah State University	Payne Hall renovations	$1,750,000
University of Georgia	Rock Eagle sewage and water systems improvements	$1,200,000
Clayton College & State U.	Maintenance Bldg. addition	$655,000
Darton College	Science/Math Building renovations	$4,965,000
Kennesaw State University	Old Science Building renovations for Nursing School	$3,380,000
Medical College of Georgia	Dugas Building renovations for Pediatrics Lab.	$4,585,000
Skidaway Institute of Ocean.	Purchase oceanographic vessel	$1,700,000
University of Georgia	Library ventilation system retrofit	$4,200,000
Valdosta State University	Special Education, Speech/Language Pathology Building	$3,300,000
University of Georgia	North Campus Parking Deck (payback)	$10,000,000
University of Georgia	Multi-purpose & Storage Facility at Bull Evaluation Center	$250,000
University of Georgia	Food Science & Technology Bldg. renovations (TIP)	$1,900,000
University of Georgia	Industry Interface Building (Gov. Traditional Industries)	$300,000
East Georgia College	Learning Resource Center Classrooms	$4,900,000
Georgia Southern University	Continuing Ed. & Cooperative Extension Service addition	$3,100,000
Georgia Southwestern State U.	Land acquisition	$400,000
Georgia State University	Public Policy Building	$8,000,000
Georgia College & State Univ.	Old Governor's Mansion renovations	$359,000
Total	**29 projects**	**$141,204,000**

<u>1998 Session</u>		
Augusta State University	Classroom Replacement I	$18,195,000
Georgia State University	Classroom Building	$29,075,000
Armstrong Atlantic State U.	Science Building	$28,000,000
Gainesville College	Science Building	$8,850,000
State University of West Georgia	Arts & Science Instructional Center	$19,350,000
Valdosta State University	Odum Library addition	$14,250,000
DeKalb College	Learning Resource Center	$8,685,000
Fort Valley State University	Health & Physical Education Building	$18,930,000
Southern Polytechnic State U.	School of Architecture Building expansion (plan & design)	$515,000
Gordon College	Instructional Complex (plan & design)	$600,000
Georgia Tech	Environmental Sciences & Technology Bldg. (plan & design)	$1,340,000
North Georgia College & State U.	Health and Natural Science Bldg. (plan & design)	$765,000
University of Georgia	Student Learning Center (plan & design)	$1,710,000
DeKalb College/Univ. of Ga.	Gwinnett Center - Phase I (plan & design)	$880,000
Clayton College & State U.	Learning Center (plan & design)	$930,000
Columbus State University	Technology & Commerce Center (plan & design)	$800,000
Georgia Southern University	Ceramics/Sculpture II Building	$1,600,000
Kennesaw State University	Visual & Commercial Arts Classroom and Office Bldg.	$4,700,000
Medical College of Georgia	Utility Upgrade - Hospital	$4,000,000
Middle Georgia College	Dillard Science Hall addition	$4,100,000
Savannah State University	Drew-Griffith Science Building renovation	$4,100,000
Abraham Baldwin Agr. College	Old Agricultural Engineering Building renovation and addition	$3,220,000
Clayton College & State U.	Multimedia Information Center Lecture Hall renovation	$1,675,000
Dalton College	Library Building renovation and addition	$4,950,000
Georgia Southwestern State U.	Crawford Wheatley Hall renovation	$2,600,000
Southern Polytechnic State U.	Plant Operations Building	$1,600,000
University of Georgia	Animal Science Arena	$4,900,000
University of Georgia	Public Service Building (plan)	$21,360
Floyd College	Bartow Center (plan)	$50,000
Georgia Southern University	Purchase Modular Facilities	$2,000,000
Georgia Institute of Technology	Multi-level Parking Structure (payback)	$10,000,000
Valdosta State University	Student Recreation Center (payback)	$9,750,000
Total	**32 projects**	**$212,143,360**
Grand Total	**143 projects**	**$1,047,715,206**

Economic development

Zell Miller understood the contribution of higher education to economic development and the state's quality of life. To underscore that recognition, he expanded the involvement of the University System of Georgia in the state's economic development efforts, leveraging the intellectual capital of the 34 public institutions to meet workforce needs. Miller's goal was an enhanced partnership between higher education and industry. At his request, the Georgia legislature appropriated $4.5 million in FY 1997 to launch the Board of Regents' Intellectual Capital Partnership Program (ICAPP). During his administration, ICAPP received nearly $12 million in funding.

ICAPP was aimed at supporting Georgia's economic development by providing the resources of the University System to attract and help create new industry, support the growth of existing business and industry, and prepare Georgia's workforce to meet the present and emerging needs of business and industry. While certain units of the University System had long played support roles in Georgia's economic development effort, ICAPP linked and leveraged the assets of the entire University System to have greater impact in attracting high-quality jobs and investments to Georgia.

ICAPP had three components, the most prominent of which provided classrooms, technology, and teachers to accelerate workforce education in response to critical demands. Workforce development analyses were conducted under ICAPP Needs Assessments to monitor supply and demand trends. ICAPP Access developed products to enable greater accessibility to the University System's expertise. ICAPP was a critical factor in the state's cultivation of a $100 million investment by Total System Services in Columbus, by developing a program to expedite the education of 1,200 computer systems analysts, resulting in the company's decision to stay in Georgia.

The value of linking higher education to economic development was demonstrated by the fact that Georgia's 1998 college graduates were hired at salaries that ranged from eight to 15 percent more than the prior year's graduates. In addition to salary increases, college graduates also benefited from a job market increasingly oriented to those who held baccalaureate degrees or higher.

P-16 Council

With a goal of preparing students to respond to the challenges of a 21st century society and workplace, the Board of Regents engaged in a vigorous effort to raise the bar of expectations and enhance the academic preparation of students entering the University System. The number of under-prepared entering freshmen in need of remedial and developmental coursework was so staggering that it prompted University System officials to devise strategies to reverse the trend.

The Board of Regents' Policy Direction on Admissions—viewed as perhaps one of the most far-reaching policy initiatives ever tackled by this 16-member body—set very clear expectations for future students. The new admissions policies, phased in at system institutions during the latter part of the 90s, were expected to enhance student success, retention and graduation rates. The ultimate goal was to raise the educational attainment level of Georgia's citizens, preparing them to be viable contributors to an increasingly competitive marketplace. But the University System recognized that standards could not be raised in a vacuum and partnerships were essential for Georgia to achieve a truly competitive and superior educational system.

That partnership came through a vehicle known as Georgia's P-16 Council, which involved officials from the University System, the Department of Education, the Department of Technical and Adult Education and the Office of School Readiness in policy-setting discussions aimed at coordinated educational reform throughout all levels of education. Launched in 1995 as the brainchild of Governor Zell Miller, the statewide P-16 Council was aimed at coordinating the implementation of policies and procedures among the participating state agencies to enhance student success. An overarching goal was to ensure students' successful movement from one educational level to the next, beginning with pre-kindergarten and moving through to college, university or a technical institute to the world of work.

"My great hope for this council is that all three public education systems and the business community will come together and build upon their existing partnerships to create educational reform, which will ultimately improve student learning," explained the Governor. His ulterior motive was that the council, composed of 38 educational and civic leaders, would alleviate some of the turf battles and competition that had traditionally marked the relationships of the educational players in Georgia. His goal was to change the competitive culture to a collaborative one.

The Governor provided over $1 million in state funds to assist the council's work, which leveraged more than $7 million in private funds from corporations and major foundations during his administration.

After the statewide council was launched in the summer of 1995, numerous local P-16 Councils were established around the state to implement grassroots educational reform efforts. Among its various activities, the P-16 Council worked extensively with the Department of Education to link high-school graduation requirements with the new admissions requirements established by the Board of Regents. The Council also researched the viability of proficiency-based admissions standards for entering colleges, universities, technical institutes and the world of work.

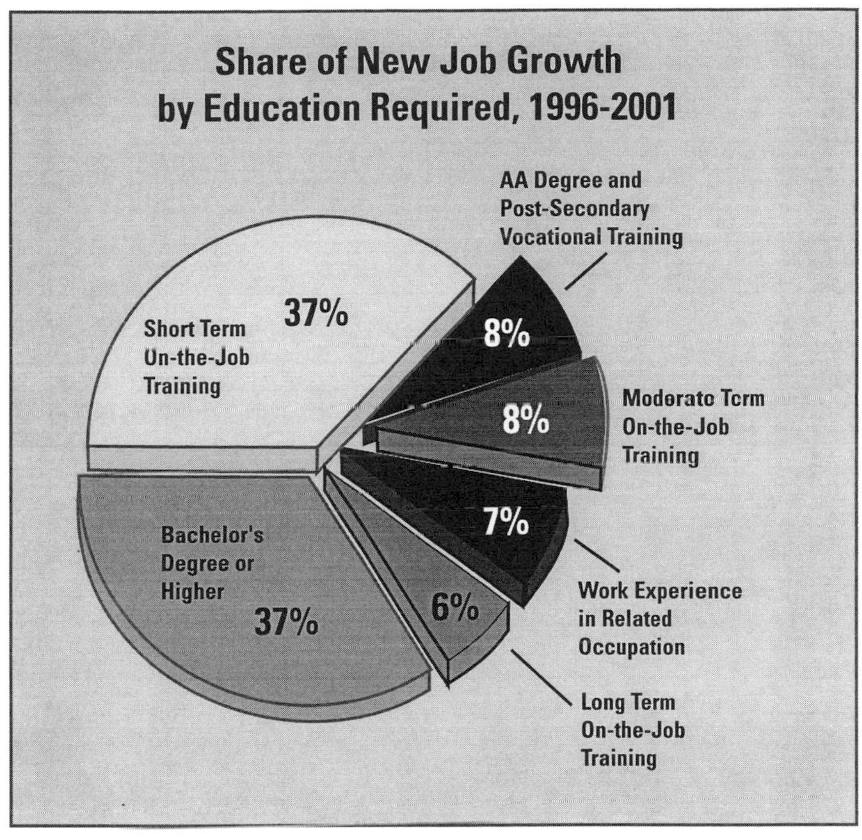
Share of New Job Growth
by Education Required, 1996-2001
AA Degree and
Post-Secondary
Vocational Training
Short Term
On-the-Job
Training
37%
8%
8%
Moderate Term
On-the-Job
Training
7%
Bachelor's
Degree or
Higher
37%
6%
Work Experience
in Related
Occupation
Long Term
On-the-Job
Training

III. Human Services

Government can never take the place of parents in raising children. Government can never take the place of families and churches and synagogues in teaching values. Government can never take the place of people in our communities working together and looking out for each other. Government programs by themselves can never do the job. But what I believe government must do is provide opportunities and encouragement for families and communities to strengthen and renew the ties that bind.

Governor Zell Miller, April 24, 1994

Welfare Reform and Self-Sufficiency

It's a tough approach, but it is also a hopeful approach. We are saying to those on welfare, "We have faith that you can do it. You can work and be self-sufficient just like the rest of us. We are going to help you do that. We are going to grant you that opportunity. We re going to smooth the path from welfare to work. But we are going to insist that you be like the woman in Proverbs who rises while it is not yet light, works and eats not the bread of idleness."

Governor Zell Miller, January 7, 1997

Throughout his administration, Governor Zell Miller pressed for the reform of a welfare system he felt did not serve either its recipients or the taxpayers of Georgia well. Raised by his widowed mother during the Depression, he knew poverty firsthand. However, he also saw firsthand the determination and hard-work with which his mother supported her family, and he was concerned that government assistance not cheapen the efforts of those who struggled valiantly to take responsibility for supporting themselves and their families. His efforts to craft a welfare program that simultaneously provided opportunity and required responsibility put Georgia on the leading edge of welfare reform around the nation.

As the result of a multitude of successful welfare reform efforts, Governor Miller's emphasis on employment as the ultimate goal of a welfare recipient, and an improved economy, the welfare rolls plunged dramatically during the Miller Administration. From 1994 to 1998, welfare caseloads dropped over 40 percent, from 142,867 to a projected caseload of 85,117 for Fiscal Year (FY) 1999. By the end of FY 1998 in June of 1998, the welfare rolls had dropped to their lowest levels since 1969. This unprecedented decrease in caseload was especially significant considering Georgia's remarkable population growth over the last two decades. While the state's population continued to increase, the number of welfare recipients in FY 1999 as a percent of the population was at its lowest level since the 1970s.

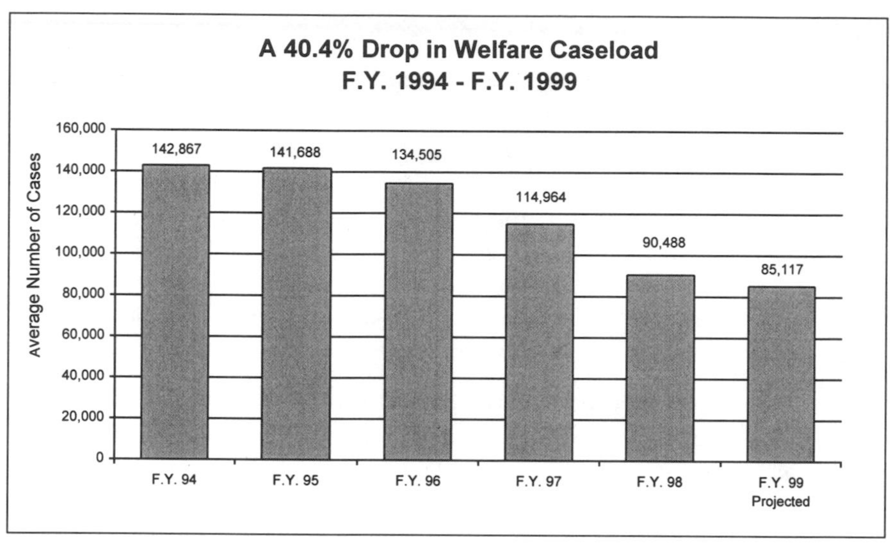

Early welfare reform efforts (1993)

Under Governor Miller's leadership, Georgia was one of the first states to adopt comprehensive welfare reform, long before any action was considered at the federal level. In 1993, the Governor spearheaded legislation that created sweeping changes in Georgia's welfare system. The goal was to break the cycle of dependence on public assistance by enforcing parental responsibility and assisting families to become independent. Key elements of the changes in welfare policy included:

Family cap: The Governor felt a strong message concerning personal responsibility needed to be sent to persons who had additional children while on welfare. Under the family cap, a parent who received welfare benefits for 24 months (after December 31, 1993) received no additional cash benefits if she had a child while on welfare. Only Medicaid coverage was provided the additional child or children. Family cap provisions were made even more restrictive when Georgia reformed welfare again in 1997. By May 1998, the family cap affected 11,193 women who had additional children while on welfare.

Teenage mothers residency requirement: Governor Miller believed that a key step in helping unmarried teenagers avoid welfare dependency was requiring young mothers to live in their parents' home to receive the help and guidance they needed to become effective parents themselves. Beginning

January 1, 1994, in order to receive welfare for themselves and their child, most unmarried teenage mothers had to live with a parent, legal guardian or another adult relative or in a supportive living program supervised by an adult. Exemptions to this requirement were allowed if needed to protect the mother and child from abusive living situations. By June of 1998, only 521 unmarried teenage mothers had refused to comply with this requirement.

Employment requirement (work for welfare): Those able but unwilling to work were not tolerated under the new requirements emphasized by Governor Miller. Able-bodied welfare recipients with no children under age 14, who quit or refused to take a suitable full-time job paying at least minimum wage were sanctioned by a reduction in cash benefits. Children, however, continued to receive assistance. Exemptions included recipients who took care of ill or disabled household members, those who were in school or in job training programs full-time, and those who had no transportation to their job.

This program also required able-bodied recipients 18 years or older and non-custodial parents who were at least two months behind in paying child support for children on welfare to work for 20 hours per month. The jobs, in government or nonprofit agencies, were identified by local coordinating councils. The program applied to recipients who had received cash assistance for 24 of the last 36 months and began as pilots in 10 counties including Bibb, Cook, Crisp, Dooly, Irwin, Jenkins, Lowndes, Walker, Wayne and White. Recipients who failed to participate as required were sanctioned by a reduction in cash assistance. Exemptions included parents caring for a child under five years old, those enrolled in the PEACH program (described below) or already working 20 hours per month, and those who did not have transportation.

The Work for Welfare requirements resulted in 668 recipients being sanctioned and having their benefits reduced by June 1998.

To help support recipients faced with these new changes, Governor Miller fully funded the PEACH (Positive Employment and Community Help) program statewide. PEACH was Georgia's job training and education program geared to prepare welfare recipients for work. When Governor Miller came into office, state-funded PEACH programs were only available in 16 counties. By the end of 1995, the Governor had expanded PEACH to all 159 counties. (The PEACH program later evolved into the WorkFirst and TANF programs.)

WorkFirst (1994)

In his 1993 State of the State Address, Governor Miller directed the Department of Human Resources (DHR) to "offer opportunity and incentives for people to take responsibility for their own lives, not encourage them to surrender... to a faceless bureaucracy, where the check just shows up automatically in the mailbox each month." The Department of Human Resources responded to the call with WorkFirst. Started as a pilot, WorkFirst changed the focus of Georgia's welfare program from cash assistance to education, job training and employment.

In January 1996, Georgia's WorkFirst program was implemented statewide. WorkFirst, a new welfare-to-work program, shifted the emphasis from establishing applicants' benefit eligibility to putting them to work. Finding a job became the number one goal for every person who walked into a DHR Division of Family and Children Services office intending to apply for welfare, food stamps or Medicaid. Waiting rooms in these county welfare offices became job search centers and support services such as childcare for clients assumed a larger role in the caseworkers' daily activities.

This shift in emphasis was extremely successful, and as Governor Miller noted in his State of the State Address on January 14, 1997, "Our WorkFirst Program has already reduced our welfare rolls by 20,000 families over the past four years, saving taxpayers $52 million."

TANF: Temporary Assistance for Needy Families (1997)

"We are going to stop the decades-old practice of simply putting checks in the mail, month after month, year after year, in some cases generation after generation," announced Governor Miller in his State of the State Address on January 14, 1997. "Cash assistance in Georgia will be limited to a total of four years... Instead, we are going to focus on two things: One, helping people to get the skills for the jobs they need to become self-sufficient and support their families. And two, pregnancy prevention, especially among teenagers."

After significant national debate and discussion, the federal Personal Responsibility and Work Opportunity Act was passed in 1996. The changes made to welfare as a result of this Act were dramatic. Welfare was no longer an entitlement, and the old Aid to Families with Dependent Children (AFDC) was renamed Temporary Assistance for Needy Families (TANF) to reflect a change in philosophy. All states were required to propose welfare plans that incorporated federal requirements under TANF legislation. Fortunately, Georgia was in an excellent position to implement federal reform as a result of legislation in 1993 and WorkFirst in 1994.

Georgia's TANF program, implemented on January 1, 1997, built on the successes and momentum of the state's reform efforts during the previous five years. Under TANF, welfare was no longer an entitlement but a program that provided temporary cash assistance while moving people into employment. The new federal law allowed states wide latitude to design programs to meet their own needs and to have rules that were more stringent than federal requirements. For example, federal rules limited welfare recipients to 60 months of assistance over a person's lifetime. Georgia's rules limited assistance to 48 months. The program emphasized a central focus on work; meeting the needs of children first; linking benefits to personal responsibility; and reducing teen pregnancy.

Georgia's TANF program continued the focus of previous welfare reforms. The new effort required more personal responsibility and stressed the need for self-sufficiency and parental responsibility. The program was designed to continue toward the ultimate goal of employment for those willing to help themselves. While assisting those who will assist themselves, the new program also increased penalties for those not willing to work, go to school or live within the law. "Our plan strikes a proper balance between fairness and toughness," the Governor explained. "The citizens of Georgia are willing to help those who want to help themselves, but they will not tolerate those who refuse to work and those who are unwilling to obey the law or accept their parental responsibilities."

Education and training: The plan's most important aspect was its emphasis on education and training as the long-term solutions for ending the cycle of poverty that traps so many on welfare. County offices provided job specific training to fill open positions, waiting rooms had job search information, and businesses were enlisted to help hire and train welfare recipients in return for training subsidies and tax credits. The program also required teen mothers receiving assistance to stay in school, adult recipients to ensure their minor children attended school, and parents to participate in parent-teacher conferences.

Strengthening the family cap: Family cap provisions already in place were strengthened so that families receiving assistance for 10 or more months received no increase in cash assistance for the birth of additional children. This time limit was reduced from the existing limit of 24 months.

Work participation rates: Federal TANF law required states to meet annual work participation rates or risk sanctions to their federal funding for TANF. Specific numerical targets were established for parents or caretakers receiving assistance under the program who were required to engage in work. The percent of families that had to participate in work activities and the number of hours they had to work per week rose each federal fiscal year from 1997 to 2002. For example, at least 25 percent of parents or caretakers had to be involved in a work activity at least 20 hours per week in FY 1997. This number rose to a 30 percent participation rate at 20 hours per week in FY 1998. By FY 2002 at least 50 percent of adults or caregivers had to work at least 30 hours per week. In 1997, Georgia far exceeded the work participation requirement, posting a rate of 34 percent compared to the requirement of 25 percent.

Making teen mothers live with their parents: Georgia was one of a handful of states that would not allow minors with children of their own to leave their parent's home if they received TANF. This requirement allowed children to receive the help they needed to be more effective parents and provided them with a greater possibility of finishing high school.

Support services: Childcare and transportation services were priorities for TANF recipients to ensure these potential barriers to success did not interfere with a client's progress toward education, training and self-sufficiency. The next section presents a more detailed discussion of childcare funding during the Miller Administration.

Sanctions: Persons who failed to cooperate in establishing paternity or obtaining child support were denied assistance or had their benefits terminated. In addition, those found guilty of drug felonies or serious violent crimes had their assistance terminated forever. For failure to comply with mandatory work requirements, the Governor's "Two Strikes and You're Off" policy led to a 25 percent reduction in benefits for the first offense and termination of assistance for the second offense. To ensure fairness and consistency in potential sanctions, Governor Miller agreed to the creation of a board composed of public officials and private citizens to review decisions to terminate welfare benefits.

Collaboratives: At Governor Miller's direction, state departments formed extraordinary collaborative working arrangements to help put TANF recipients to work. The Departments of Human Resources (DHR), Labor (DOL) and Technical and Adult Education (DTAE) came together to help develop a job-ready workforce from former TANF clients. DHR provided case management services, DTAE was the primary resource for training, and DOL took the lead in job development and job placement.

The Georgia Public Policy Foundation, based in Atlanta, had the following to say about Georgia's plan: "Georgia will seize the opportunity to send the clear message to everyone that welfare recipients must do everything in their power to get and keep a job, that a job is good for individuals, their families and the community, and that Georgians want all of their state's children to be raised in solid, stable and nurturing homes."

Child care

A lack of affordable child care contributed to welfare dependency. In fact, in a society with an increasing number of single-parent households, lack of child care could be the single greatest obstacle preventing a parent from getting off welfare. As part of his welfare reform efforts, Governor Miller significantly increased child care resources available to welfare recipients training to enter the workforce. Child care was also available for employed persons who had recently left the welfare rolls but needed help with their child care needs to ensure they maintained successful employment. In addition, child care was available to low-income families who were at risk of going on welfare for the first time and who needed help with child care to maintain their jobs and remain self-sufficient. TANF clients who lost their cash benefits when they got a job continued to receive transitional benefits including Medicaid and child care assistance for up to 12 months.

During the Miller Administration, Georgia's commitment to help families achieve and maintain self-sufficiency through the provision of child care reached unprecedented levels. Total funding increased by 675 percent and state funding by 237 percent, from $15.9 million in FY 1990 to $142.3 ($53.5 million state funds) in FY 1999. The funds in the FY 1999 budget would support 81,625 children in state-funded child care programs.

Electronic benefits transfer

In 1995, under Governor Miller's leadership, Georgia became one of the very first states to develop and use an electronic benefits transfer (EBT) system. Georgia took the initiative in this effort, primarily because of the central

A 675% Increase in Georgia's Child Care Appropriations

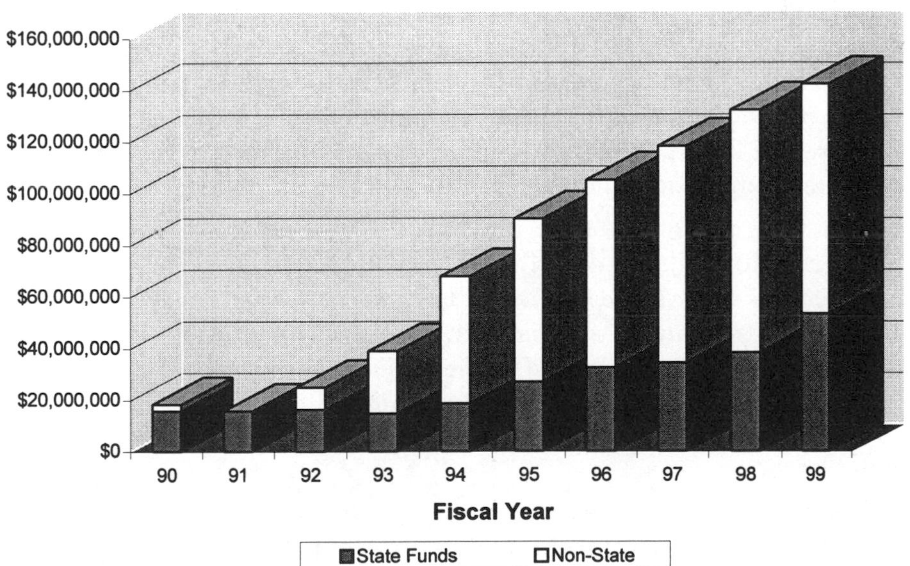

location of Atlanta and its proximity to the federal regional offices. The EBT system dramatically changed the way government benefits like welfare checks and food stamps were issued, spent, and redeemed. Prior to the EBT system, these government benefits were issued in the form of paper checks and vouchers and sent through the mail every month. While it was the only method available at the time, this process was extremely inefficient and costly. Postage costs were always a factor as well as the potential for fraud and abuse. The EBT system took advantage of the latest information technology to deliver welfare benefits to recipients electronically. Recipients could have access to their benefits much like accessing bank accounts through ATMs.

While Georgia's EBT began as a pilot project and only went statewide in 1998, even the early benefits of the system were extensive. EBT was a winning project for all parties involved – welfare recipients, taxpayers, government, retailers, and banks. This new system reduced costs and wastes associated with many human services, especially welfare programs such as TANF and food stamps. The electronic processing of food stamp benefits, for example, eliminated both the cost of producing and mailing paper food coupons, and the illegal trafficking of those coupons. In fact, the savings to taxpayers from EBT were estimated at $2 million per year in Georgia.

Welfare recipients also benefited because of the ease in which EBT could be used as well as the security offered by the system. EBT reduced crime associated with the postal delivery and cashing of welfare checks and coupons. Providing benefits electronically also supported the goals of Georgia's welfare system by increasing self-sufficiency for clients by moving them into a banking environment. Retailers and banks also benefited from EBT because they no longer had to handle food stamps or cash welfare checks. In fact, there was a 12 percent increase in food sales associated with the use of EBT in Georgia.

Overall, EBT was a great success in Georgia. It improved government services by reducing waste and fraud and better serving the citizens of Georgia.

Protecting Children From Abuse and Neglect

Family violence is one of the factors that has brought nearly 17,000 foster children into state custody.... As a short-term response, foster care is absolutely essential, and we are deeply grateful for the families who provide it. But it should not end up being any human being's entire childhood.

Governor Zell Miller, January 14, 1997

Foster care

During the 90s government found itself needing to step in with greater frequency to take custody of more and more children due to parents' inability or unwillingness to care for their children. This situation was made even more difficult by the fact that an increasing number of these children had significant emotional and behavioral problems. Foster care was a state program that provided temporary substitute homes for children whose families could not care for them. The care might last a few days or several years. In any given month of the Miller Administration, about 11,000 Georgia children were in family foster care and about 1,100 more were in institutions, group homes and hospitals.

During Governor Miller's Administration, state funding for foster care services increased every year, and by substantial amounts. Over $18.7 million in new state funds was appropriated during the Miller Administration to increase state resources for foster care and to help families who take in foster children. These funding increases and renewed emphasis on helping children under difficult circumstances did not go unnoticed at the national level. In 1996, the Division of Family and Children Services was named State Agency of the Year by the National Foster Parent Association. The association cited the division's outstanding partnership with foster parents as the reason for the award.

Most of the increased funding under Governor Miller was directed to providing more foster care placements, increasing the per diem rate for family foster care, and raising the reimbursement rate for institutional foster care. Specifically, the family foster care per diem was raised from $10.00 to $11.10, and the institutional foster care reimbursement rate was more than doubled, from 29 percent to 60 percent of the cost of care, during Governor Miller's terms of office. The family foster care annual allowance for school clothing was also doubled from $50 to $100, and a $100 annual clothing allowance was established for all preschool age children.

First Placement, Best Placement: One of the biggest challenges in foster care was preventing multiple placements. Children who endured these arduous circumstances were often characterized as "failing their way through the system" before they finally landed in a placement that was appropriate and successful.

At the Governor's direction, DHR created a new approach called "First Placement, Best Placement" that helped ensure children were placed in the most suitable foster care environment the first time they came into the system rather than failing their way through. Funding was put in place in FY 1999 to operate several pilot projects to test the effectiveness of the system, with $2.5 million appropriated to assess 2,250 children coming into the foster care system to determine the most appropriate type of living arrangements for these children, and to fund temporary placements for them while they were undergoing assessment.

Institutional foster care: Other enhancements made by Governor Miller during FY 1999 were also significant. Over $4 million was appropriated to provide much needed and more appropriate structured settings in institutional foster care facilities for 750 children who were then in family foster care settings. Governor Miller also recommended more stringent screening of potential foster parents along with more training to help them cope with behavioral and other problems their foster children may have.

Independent living services: Although the state had devoted considerable resources and effort to help children who needed foster care services, these efforts were often not enough to ensure the children grew into adults who led successful lives. New independent living services were established under Governor Miller's direction to help foster children over the age of 16 adapt to everyday life once they were out of foster care. This program taught older foster children the skills they needed to manage on their own. Skills were taught in five concentration areas: education, health, individual/peer counseling, employment and daily living.

The independent living program targeted foster children leaving the foster care system and entering college. Although tuition and fees could be obtained through sources such as HOPE and PELL grants, these sources did not cover room and board. Consequently, funds were set aside to pay room and board and post-secondary education expenses such as tutoring, training and student fees. In FY 1998, over $337,000 was spent on an average of 30 children per month for room and board, plus an additional $176,000 for other post-secondary education expenses.

Family and Children Electronic Tracking System (FACETS): Substantial state resources were also invested during Governor Miller's terms of office on the Family and Children Electronic Tracking System (FACETS), a new computerized tracking system to monitor each child in foster care, adoptive and child protective services, as well as adults in protective services, to ensure that they received the appropriate and best care possible. Prior to the creation of this system, the state had no computerized, systematic method of tracking persons being served, their history, their problems and their needs. For example, case workers responsible for foster children who moved frequently among different foster families, had difficulty reviewing case files and making well-informed decisions concerning the most appropriate placements and services for these children.

By tracking clients accurately and in a timely manner, the state expected to avoid incurring higher medical and placement costs associated with residential care. Over $69 million was appropriated for the new system, including $33 million in state funds. FACETS was expected to be fully operational statewide by January 2000.

Adoption: Finding families for children

The state always had an interest in finding permanent adoptive homes for children in state custody. However, under Governor Miller's direction, the state took several actions, symbolic as well as tangible, that showed his commitment to children needing a permanent and stable environment. One of the most dramatic and effective actions was to create a State Office of Adoptions. As the Governor declared in his 1997 State of the State Address, "Too many children are stuck in foster care for too long. And too many of them end up being 'aged out' of the foster care system as teenagers. They are left to navigate life completely on their own with no home or family, and many of them end up in shelters for the homeless… that's why we've created a separate Office of Adoptions within the Department of Human Resources." This move strongly emphasized the critical need to unite children with loving families in a single home rather than constantly moving them among multiple foster homes.

Governor Miller also enhanced adoption services by establishing a statewide system of Adoption Intake Coordinators to implement a uniform method for tracking prospective adoptive parents. In FY 1997, $219,752 was appropriated for six coordinators. These coordinators were charged with linking adoptive children with prospective families as soon as possible.

The State Office of Adoptions also increased the role of licensed private agencies in arranging special needs adoptions and privatized other adoption functions whenever cost effective. Many of the children in state custody were considered to have special needs that made it more difficult to find adoptive homes. During FY 1998 and FY 1999 alone, Governor Miller proposed nearly $5.7 million in new funding to increase contracts with private adoption agencies who were charged with finding homes for special needs children, recruiting more adoptive parents, and providing post-adoptive services for children.

Steps were also taken to increase the adoption supplement to 100 percent of the foster care per diem rate, so that adoptive parents receive the same reimbursement to offset the cost of child care as foster parents. Having a different reimbursement rate acted as a financial disincentive to foster parents who might consider adopting the children in their care. The *Atlanta Constitution* praised the Governor's action saying, "Miller is on the right track with his new proposals."

DHR took a unique step to promote and publicize adoptions by holding adoption galas throughout the state to bring together foster children and potential adoptive parents in an informal setting. With only enough funds to support one gala in FY 1998, DHR requested funding for FY 1999 to hold adoption galas in each of the state's 12 DFCS regions. However, Governor

Miller believed strongly enough in the effectiveness of these events that he saw to it funds were appropriated to hold galas in every region in both 1998 and 1999.

The state's increased emphasis on adopting children in its custody resulted in a continual increase in adoptions. Between FY 1991 and FY 1997, the number of adoptions rose from 441 to 749, an increase of 70 percent. Adoptions in FY 1998 exceeded 900.

Making "deadbeat parents" support their children

Noting that "Georgia must look after our most important asset, our children," Governor Miller moved aggressively during his terms in office to force absent parents to live up to their legal and moral obligations by paying child support, thus shifting the burden of supporting dependent children from the taxpayer to the responsible parent. Since Governor Miller took office in 1991 through 1998, nearly $1.7 billion in child support payments was collected for Georgia's children.

The state's Child Support Enforcement Program was established in 1973 to provide assistance to a custodial parent or caretaker caring for a child and needing help with collecting regular child support from a non-custodial parent. Although parents and caregivers who used the state to help collect child support were not necessarily on welfare, nevertheless lack of adequate child

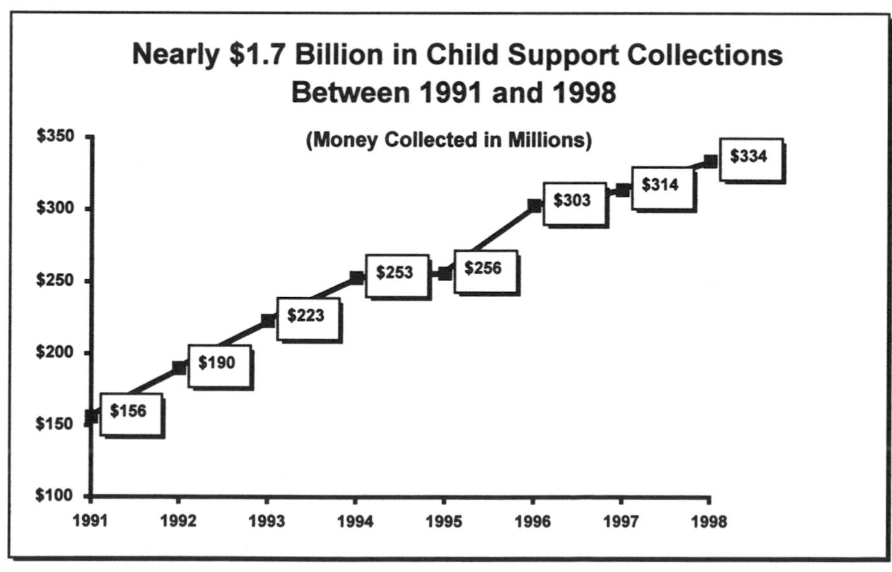

support was a major reason why women were on welfare. By increasing both the number of non-custodial parents required to pay child support and the amount of child support collected, the state helped more families become self-sufficient and avoid welfare dependency. Child support went directly to the custodial parent or to the state and federal governments to offset welfare payments.

Governor Miller took a number of tough actions that helped to more than double the amount of child support payments collected between fiscal years 1991 and 1998.

Privatizing collections: Georgia was one of the first states to begin privatizing child support collections by contracting with a collection agency to handle difficult non-welfare cases in several judicial circuits. Privatization initiatives were emphasized and undertaken during the Miller Administration to locate non-custodial parents and collect their child support. Governor Miller's recommendations for FY 1999 included funding to privatize the processing of applications from all custodial parents who were not receiving welfare benefits and needed help to collect child support payments from non-custodial parents. Existing state employees at the local level who had been responsible for processing payments were given new responsibilities to enhance customer service and collection enforcement.

Reporting new hires: In 1993, Governor Miller signed legislation requiring employers who had seven or more employees in the State of Georgia to report all new hires and rehires on a weekly basis to the Georgia state support registry within DHR. Georgia was the ninth state to pass legislation requiring W-4 reporting to help cross-reference employment records with the state's list of delinquent parents. Through this system, parents who were delinquent in their child support payments could be located and brought into compliance with the law.

Intercepting lottery prize money: When Governor Miller proposed the 1992 law that created the Georgia Lottery, he included a section that authorized withholding prize money from people who were delinquent in their child support payments. The law applied to lottery winners of prizes that amount to $5,000 or more. On September 13, 1993, Governor Miller announced the first intercept of lottery prize money to pay delinquent child support: "I'm pleased to see lottery winnings going back to the children who need support. Making sure that absentee parents pay their court-ordered child support is key to the financial independence of single-parent families. I wanted the lottery law to reinforce that effort, and as you can see, it does."

"Ten Most Wanted" posters: Continuing his push for more active enforcement of child support laws in 1994, Governor Miller put the pictures of Georgia's most wanted "deadbeat" parents on posters which were distributed throughout Georgia to district attorneys and law enforcement personnel. Parents chosen for the posters were seriously in arrears on their payments, had failed to keep the courts informed of their whereabouts, and when last heard from were financially capable of making their payments. Of the 40 mothers and fathers portrayed on these posters in 1994 and 1995, 20 were apprehended and over $191,000 in child support payments were recovered. The Georgia Office of Child Support Enforcement now utilizes the Internet to post pictures of delinquent parents and locate them, and updates its web page every six months with new referrals from all parts of Georgia.

Suspending licenses of "deadbeat parents": In 1995, Governor Miller signed into law bills that suspended the driver's, occupational and professional licenses of any parent who was more than 60 days late paying child support. Recreational licenses were added to this provision in 1997. "Denying your child support is reprehensible," he explained, "and in Georgia, if you do not pay your child support, we will cripple your ability to function in your daily life until you do right by your children."

Child support as a condition of parole: In October 1995, Governor Miller asked the Georgia Board of Pardons and Paroles to make child support payments a condition of parole. If a parolee fails to abide by the plan, they may be returned to prison as a violation of their parole.

Establishing paternity: Legislation was passed in 1997 allowing DHR to establish both the legitimacy and paternity of a child. DHR could order genetic tests on its own in cases in which paternity had not been established.

Seizing bank accounts: Because bank accounts of child support debtors could be identified and seized to satisfy judgments and liens created by the operation of law, Governor Miller sponsored legislation in 1997 to establish a bank match registry that was coordinated through the Department of Administrative Services (DOAS). The registry enabled DHR to obtain financial records, match them with corresponding accounts and seize the accounts. The legislation also allowed DHR to collect owed payments by filing liens against real property and personal property of parents who fell behind in child support payments.

Early Childhood Development

Parents are their children's first teachers, and we want to help parents get their little ones off to a good start.... As an educator, I can tell you that the research proves what good teachers have known for a long time—that what happens to children in the first few years of life makes a big difference.

Governor Zell Miller, October 10, 1998

Ensuring children "Thrive by Five"

In 1997, Governor Miller introduced "Thrive by Five" – an umbrella initiative which included a variety of programs and services that promoted and enhanced early childhood development. The intent of "Thrive by Five" was to emphasize the importance of the first years of life—from birth through age 4—in brain development; to increase the awareness of parents/caregivers as to the importance of nurturing and stimulating their infants; and to link common programs for greater effectiveness, results accountability and better use of resources. "What we are coming to realize is that if we nurture and stimulate our children starting at birth, and provide them with safe environments where they can explore and develop during their early years," the Governor said, "we will have fewer problems to deal with as they grow older... My goal is that our youngest children will be healthy, have stable, self-sufficient families and start school ready to learn."

The goal of Thrive by Five was not to create new programs, but to coordinate the many existing programs. State government and local communities were providing literally hundreds of programs for infants, young parents, new parents and parents-to-be, from Children 1st, which began at birth, all the way up to the Governor's award-winning prekindergarten program for four-year-olds. The FY 1999 budget provided over $46 million in state funds ($113 million total funds) to further support the Thrive by Five goals by expanding health care access to all children; increasing child care resources; expanding Family Connection statewide; expanding the pre-K program; and providing information on brain development to parents of all newborns at birth.

Children 1st

In 1997, Governor Miller won approval of $2.4 million for a major statewide expansion of the newborn screening and early intervention program, Children 1st, that he started during his first term in 1992. Children 1st identified children from birth to age three with conditions that placed them at risk for poor health and/or development outcomes due to biological and/or environmental factors. Approximately, two-thirds could be identified as at-risk from information on their birth certificates; others were referred by doctors, nurses and hospitals.

Children 1st then assisted families in linking their children to a primary health care provider where they would receive periodic comprehensive health assessments, developmental monitoring, referral to appropriate support services and service coordination. Program staff stayed in touch until the fourth birthday to make sure the child got regular checkups, appropriate health care, therapy, family support and other services needed so the child could stay well or overcome problems.

Children 1st worked in partnership with hospitals, doctors, public and private clinics, social services agencies and parents. The program linked children with providers in the private sector whenever possible. At the end of the Miller Administration, half of the children identified by the program were served by private providers; those remaining were served by public health departments.

In 1994, Children 1st received the Association of State and Territorial Health Officers Vision Award for "achieving excellence through innovation" and was cited by the U.S. Public Health Service in its *Models that Work: 1995 Compendium of Innovative Primary Health Care Programs for Underserved and Vulnerable Populations.*

First in the nation in vaccinating children

Speaking to the Georgia Immunization Coalition Conference in February 1997, First Lady Shirley Miller stated that there was absolutely no excuse for any child in Georgia not to be vaccinated. "Many of us in this room remember an era when childhood diseases decimated entire classrooms," she said. "Today, thanks to medical research, those fears are mostly memories. Today, we can immunize our children with preventive vaccines."

A 1997 study by the Centers for Disease Control and Prevention indicated that Georgia led the nation in immunizing its children. In fact, Georgia was so effective in getting children immunized by their second birthday that at least six other states were following Georgia's strategy. Georgia's immunization strategy was based on the development of a new computer program that reported the immunization rates by county for children seen in public health departments. The state was then able to identify those counties which needed to pay more attention to reminding parents about appointments and bringing children's shots up to date during clinic visits. Immunization levels for two-year-olds who came to public health clinics increased from 68 percent in 1991 to 89 percent in 1997.

Another initiative, the Vaccines for Children program begun in 1994, provided free vaccines to private and public providers for children up to age 19 whose vaccinations were not covered by insurance. More than 900 physicians, clinics, and hospitals were enrolled in the program. Georgia was one of the first states in the nation to implement this federally sponsored program.

Babies Can't Wait

In FY 1991, Governor Miller began aggressively funding the Babies Can't Wait program which served infants and toddlers ages birth to three who had disabilities or significant developmental delays. Once the children were identified, the Babies Can't Wait program provided comprehensive case management and early intervention services such as therapy, special instruction and assistive technology. In addition, the Babies Can't Wait program incorporated family support services such as respite care and environmental modifications.

Georgia was one of the first states to implement a program of this type and, under Governor Miller's leadership, the program reached full implementation. By FY 1999, the budget for the Babies Can't Wait program had grown from $1.5 million in state funds to over $11 million in state funds, a 633 percent increase in funding.

By identifying and providing these services for children at an early age, the program prevented more costly treatment in subsequent years. In addition, it helped in preparing the child for school. More than 7,000 children received services through the Babies Can't Wait program during the Miller Administration.

Governor's classical music initiative for newborns

One of Governor Miller's more original initiatives which garnered worldwide media attention was his proposal to provide every newborn baby in Georgia with a cassette or compact disc of classical music. Research showed that reading and talking with an infant and having that infant listen to soothing music helped develop brain connections, especially the ones related to math. After chairing a conference in Atlanta on brain development in the fall of 1997, the Governor was firmly convinced of the need to publicize the important message that an infant's brain needed early and frequent stimulation. In his FY 1999 budget speech, the Governor proposed that each child born in Georgia between July 1998 and June 1999 (an estimated 100,000 newborns) be given a copy of recorded classical music as they left the hospital.

Immediately after he made his proposal, hospital associations, recording companies, educators, and people throughout the music industry contacted him, wanting to know more about his initiative and how they could help. The press quickly picked up the story and the Governor spent many hours over the weeks following his speech talking with local, national and international media about his proposal.

Sony Music Entertainment, through its manufacturing plant in Carrollton, Georgia, agreed to produce and distribute 100,000 CDs and cassettes at no cost to the state. The musical selections were picked by representatives from Sony, Tony-award-winning tenor Michael Maguire, and Governor Miller. The Georgia Alliance of Community Hospitals and the

Georgia Hospital Association stepped forward to work with their member hospitals to ensure that every newborn received the music.

"It really works!" wrote the Governor in a message to parents on the tape cover. "Einstein knew it. So did Galileo. They knew that there was a direct relationship between music and math. What many studies have shown since, is that the connection begins in infancy and can be increased by a baby hearing soothing music on a regular basis. A six-month-old infant can tell whether the music is harmonious or not. Microscopic connections in the brain responsible for learning and remembering are enhanced through listening. That, my dear parent, is why Sony Music and I wanted you to have this recording. Play it often. I hope both you and your baby enjoy it— and that your little one will get off to a smart start."

Beginning July 1, 1998, every baby born in Georgia received the CD or cassette, "Build Your Baby's Brain Through the Power of Music." No other state had ever done an initiative of this kind. In fact, the CD and cassette were so popular that Sony established a 1-800 number for interested parties who wanted to purchase it.

As a companion to the music, the Governor also proposed that each newborn be given a copy of the book, *The Little Engine That Could*, as they left the hospital. The book was a special edition printed exclusively for the State of

Georgia with a forwarding message from the Governor regarding the impact of reading on brain development.

Combined, the book and tape were intended to increase awareness in parents and others of how important the interaction between a child and a caregiver was in that child's brain development. National and even international media coverage, as well as broad public interest, helped promote the concept of infant brain development far beyond the small amount of resources initially targeted for this initiative.

Family Connection and the Georgia Policy Council for Children and Families

The ultimate in creativity is not to invent something entirely new, but to take what you have and make it do something more. That is our goal—to take what resources and programs we already have for children and make them do something more.

Governor Zell Miller, December 11, 1991

Family Connection

Under Governor Miller, the state adopted a bold new vision to improve services for children and families. In the beginning of his first term, Governor Miller asked state agencies to work together to form a collaborative partnership with local communities to integrate services for children and families at risk. The state agencies involved were the Departments of Education, Juvenile Justice, Human Resources, Medical Assistance and the Office of Planning and Budget; the collaborative partnership was the Family Connection. As a result, the patchwork delivery system stitched together over time began to be replaced by a more responsive and flexible service delivery system designed and guided by communities and families.

Funded initially by a $5 million grant from the Joseph B. Whitehead Foundation, the Family Connection began with five pilot communities. Based on the success of these pilots, the Governor recommended and the General Assembly approved state funding to expand the program, gradually adding more communities. By FY 1999, funds were appropriated to expand the program statewide.

Georgia Policy Council for Children and Families

In 1993, the Governor created the Policy Council for Children and Families by Executive Order. The Council was composed of business, government, advocacy, and political leaders, and it was charged to assess the conditions of Georgia's children and families and the system established to

<u>Twenty-Six Benchmarks</u>

Healthy Children
- *Increase the percentage of babies born healthy.*
- *Increase the percentage of children appropriately immunized by age two.*
- *Reduce the percentage of children who have untreated vision, hearing or other health problems at school entry.*
- *Reduce the teenage homicide rate.*
- *Increase the percentage of youths who do not use alcohol, tobacco or illegal drugs.*
- *Reduce the pregnancy rate among school-age girls.*

Children Ready for School
- *Increase the percentage of low-income students in Head Start or prekindergarten.*
- *Increase the percentage of kindergarten students who attended preschool or child care.*
- *Increase the percentage of kindergarten students passing the Georgia Kindergarten Assessment Program.*
- *Reduce the percentage of students who are two or more years overage in the third grade.*

Children Succeeding in School
- *Reduce the percentage of students who are absent ten or more days from school annually.*
- *Increase the percentage of students performing above state standards on curriculum-based tests at fifth and eleventh grades.*
- *Increase the percentage of students scoring above the national median on normal achievement tests at the eighth grade.*
- *Increase the percentage of students who graduate from high school on time.*
- *Increase parental involvement.*

Strong Families
- *Increase the percentage of stable new families.*
- *Reduce the percentage of teenage mothers with repeat births.*
- *Reduce the incidence of confirmed child abuse or neglect.*
- *Increase the percentage of children in foster care who are placed in a permanent home.*
- *Reduce the percentage of youths arrested.*

Self-Sufficient Families
- *Reduce the percentage of children living in poverty.*
- *Reduce the percentage of female-headed families with children living in poverty.*
- *Increase the percentage of welfare recipients leaving public assistance due to employment.*
- *Increase the rate of growth in employment.*
- *Reduce the unemployment rate.*

serve them and to provide recommendations for improvement. To encourage and promote innovative efforts, the Council's initial report called for results accountability; community-based planning and decision-making; a focus on prevention; family-centered service strategies; government streamlining; and creative financing efforts.

Because of the long-range commitment required to achieve these goals, the Governor decided that new forms of governance were needed at both the state and local levels. His proposal, which was adopted by the General

Assembly in 1995 as Senate Bill 256, created a state-level governance mechanism, the Georgia Policy Council for Children and Families, attached to the Governor's Office of Planning and Budget. The legislation authorized the Council to designate community partnerships that are legally recognized to govern activities at the local level. Viewed as the second phase of Family Connection, these partnerships offered local communities greater flexibility in the design and implementation of services for children and families, in exchange for greater accountability for the outcomes. Twelve Family Connection communities had become community partnerships by the end of the Governor's second term.

The Policy Council also identified five targeted result areas to improve the well being of children and families: healthy children; children ready for school; children succeeding in school; strong families; and self-sufficient families. Additionally, the Council adopted 26 benchmarks that measured progress toward these results. Throughout Georgia, local Family Connection collaboratives decided which result areas to focus on and tailored their benchmarks to meet their communities' particular profile. By focusing on common results desired by the community, each collaborative could link programs to insure greater effectiveness and wiser use of resources.

Health Care and Medicaid

One of Publius Syrus' maxims is "Good health and good sense are two of life's greatest blessings." Unfortunately we have not always exercised the two of them in conjunction with each other.

Governor Zell Miller, February 2, 1991

Expanding Medicaid coverage

When Governor Miller took office, Georgia had one of the worst infant mortality rates in the nation due, in part, to the fact that a significant number of births were to women who had not received adequate prenatal care. In addition, low-income, uninsured families often did not get treatment for their children's health problems until a crisis arose.

Governor Miller believed that tremendous long-term human and financial costs resulted when Georgia's tiniest citizens lacked health care. During his two terms in office, he was instrumental in expanding access to health care services for the low-income and uninsured pregnant women and children who made up many of Georgia's neediest citizens. His actions represented a significant investment in ensuring that pregnant women received adequate and comprehensive prenatal care and that Georgia's children were healthy and ready to learn when they began school.

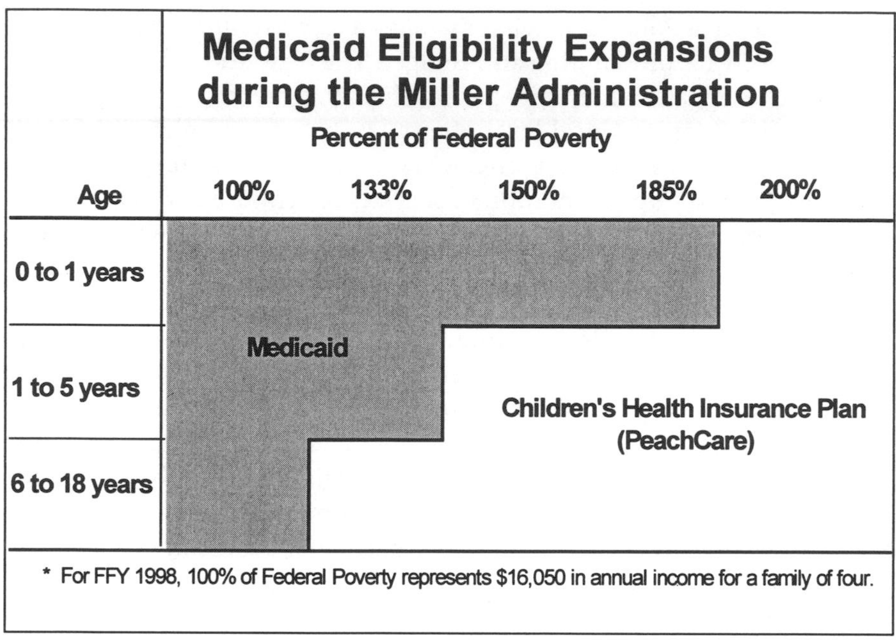

Under Governor Miller's leadership, the Department of Medical Assistance (the state agency that administered Georgia's Medicaid program for low-income and disabled citizens) expanded the eligibility criteria for Medicaid three times. Over $31.5 million in state and Indigent Care Trust Funds ($82 million in total funds) were appropriated to fund these expansions which covered more pregnant women and children. Overall, these expansions covered more than 55,000 pregnant women and children up to age 19 who previously had no access to or means to pay for medical care.

When Governor Miller took office, Medicaid was covering pregnant women and infants with family income levels up to 100 percent of the federal poverty level. The Governor's first expansion provided an additional $2.1 million in state funds ($5.6 million total funds) in the FY 1993 budget to raise the income ceiling for Medicaid benefits to pregnant women and infants from 100 percent to 150 percent of the federal poverty level.

In FY 1994, he used $19.1 million in Indigent Care Trust Funds ($49.2 million total funds) to expand Medicaid benefits to include all children under age 19 in families with incomes up to 100 percent of the federal poverty level. Previously Medicaid had not covered school-aged children. Another $10.3 million in Indigent Care Trust Funds ($27.4 million total funds) in FY 1994 was used to raise the income ceiling again for pregnant women and infants, this time from 150 to 185 percent of the federal poverty level.

Children's Health Insurance Program

Even with three Medicaid expansions, it was estimated in 1997 that 18 percent of Georgia's two million children were uninsured. Of those two million children, roughly 927,000 were covered by private insurance and 704,000 were covered by Medicaid – leaving an estimated 369,000 children with no medical coverage at all. Many of these children were uninsured because their parents' employers either did not offer dependent coverage, or the coverage that was offered was too expensive for the family to afford. Other families were self-employed or not employed at all. In fact, some of these uninsured children were eligible for Medicaid, but for whatever reason had not enrolled.

Typically, uninsured children only received health care when they needed immediate medical attention, such as in emergency situations. They did not receive preventive care and they did not have a doctor that they could go to on a regular basis. Uninsured children typically received care in more costly hospital emergency rooms or in public health departments.

Governor Miller was concerned about these uninsured children and the impact their neglected health would have on their ability to learn. He was also concerned that unchecked health problems could become more costly and more serious in the future. In July 1997, Congress authorized a new title, Title XXI, of the Social Security Act, which became more popularly known as the Children's Health Insurance Program (CHIP). The new program provided states with matching funds to develop health insurance programs for uninsured children up to 200 percent of the federal poverty level.

Governor Miller seized the opportunity and was instrumental in creating Georgia's new program, called PeachCare for Kids, to cover uninsured children. An estimated 113,000 uninsured children up to age 19 in families with incomes up to 200 percent of the federal poverty level – just over $32,000 for a family of four at the time – were provided with health coverage. In addition, the new PeachCare for Kids program, through extensive marketing and outreach efforts, was expected to help identify some of the estimated 140,000 children eligible for Medicaid but not enrolled.

Georgia's CHIP program was authorized by Senate Bill 410, which was passed almost unanimously by the General Assembly in 1998, following what many called an unprecedented bipartisan compromise. Although PeachCare for Kids was administered by the state Department of Medical Assistance, it was a separate program, not an expansion of Medicaid. Along with passage of the bill, $20 million in new state funding ($78 million total funds) was appropriated in the FY 1999 budget. This level of funding was unprecedented and represented one of the largest investments ever made at one time for children's health care.

PeachCare paid for preventive services and acute medical care, as well as vision and dental care. In keeping with the theme of personal responsibility and family self-sufficiency, families with children age 6 years and older were charged a monthly premium toward the cost of coverage. These nominal premiums were $7.50 per month for one child and $15 for households with more than one child, regardless of how many children were in the family.

Between the Medicaid expansions and the new PeachCare program, Governor Miller substantially increased the number of Georgia citizens – primarily children – having access to health care. Between these two programs, all children in families with incomes up to 200 percent of the federal poverty level had health care coverage as a result of the Governor's efforts.

Containing runaway Medicaid costs

Throughout the 1980s and early 90s, the Medicaid program experienced unchecked growth that approached 10 to 15 percent annually. This exponential growth outpaced state general revenue growth. As a result, the budget for the Medicaid program increased from four percent of the FY 1980 state appropriation to 12.6 percent of the FY 1996 state appropriation.

Beginning in FY 1997 and for the next three years, Governor Miller implemented aggressive cost containment strategies that significantly reduced Medicaid growth to almost two percent, the lowest rate of growth for

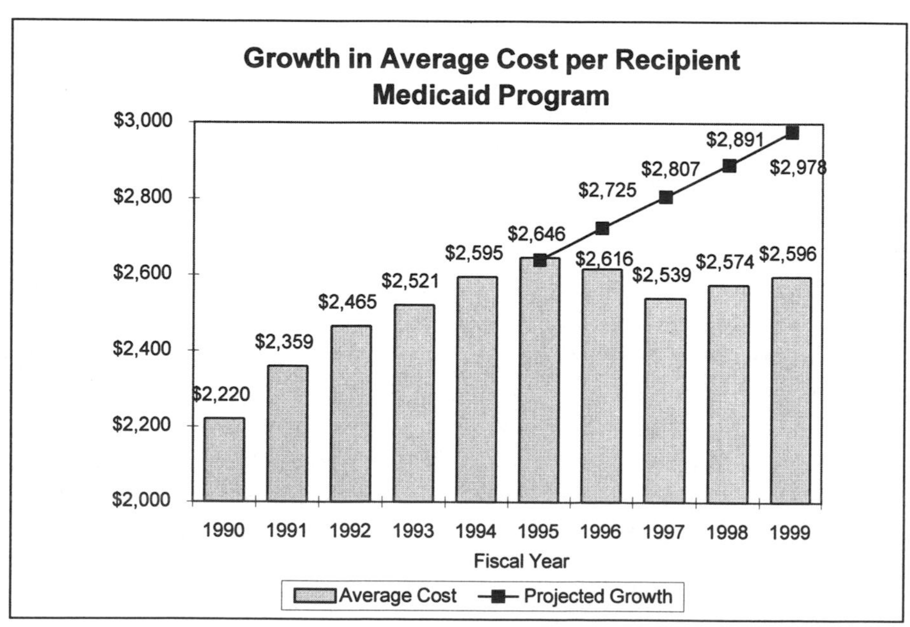

Medicaid in two decades. These strategies included innovative provider rate restructuring, managed care, and fraud and abuse initiatives. The following graph highlights the startling impact of Governor Miller's cost containment strategies by projecting average Medicaid expenditures per recipient had growth remained unchecked, and comparing it to actual growth.

Managed care: Governor Miller was instrumental in developing managed care programs for Medicaid eligible individuals. During his administration, the Department of Medical Assistance expanded enrollment in the Georgia Better Health Care program, and the Governor established the first ever voluntary HMO program for Georgia's Medicaid recipients. Both of these managed care programs provided Medicaid recipients with a "medical home" or single point of access for health care services. In many instances, this "medical home" represented the first time that these Medicaid recipients were assigned a primary care provider responsible for coordinating their health care services.

A 1997 survey conducted by Georgia State University for the Department of Medical Assistance revealed that the expansion of the Georgia Better Health Care program was coupled with significant declines in emergency room utilization and increases in access to health care for GBHC participants. As a result of the declines in emergency room use and inappropriate utilization of other services in both the GBHC and HMO programs, the Department of Medical Assistance saved over $28 million in state funds in the last two fiscal years of the Miller Administration.

Under Governor Miller's leadership, the Georgia Better Health Care program was started as a pilot program in seven counties in 1993. This program linked Medicaid recipients to primary care providers, who were reimbursed $3 per Medicaid recipient to coordinate the recipient's health care needs. By the end of the Miller Administration, the program had expanded statewide with almost 3,700 primary care providers delivering and managing the care for approximately 527,000 Medicaid recipients.

In 1996, Governor Miller was instrumental in creating the first voluntary Health Maintenance Organization (HMO) program in Georgia. The voluntary HMO program began as a pilot program in five metro Atlanta counties, and by 1998 it had been expanded to include the Augusta, Macon, and Savannah areas. Under the HMO program, the department contracted with private HMOs to provide a comprehensive array of health care services to Medicaid recipients who chose to enroll. As of June 1998, the program served approximately 40,000 Medicaid recipients each month.

Fraud and abuse initiatives: Prior to Governor Miller's taking office, there were many instances of people defrauding the state's Medicaid program – falsifying claims, billing for services that were never provided, using a recipient's Medicaid number illegally. The potential fraud and abuse schemes were endless and on the rise. The perception was that fraud and abuse were easy to do, because the Department of Medical Assistance processed over 35 million claims per year and no one would ever catch or notice the falsified claims. In addition, the department did not have the resources to investigate suspicious claims.

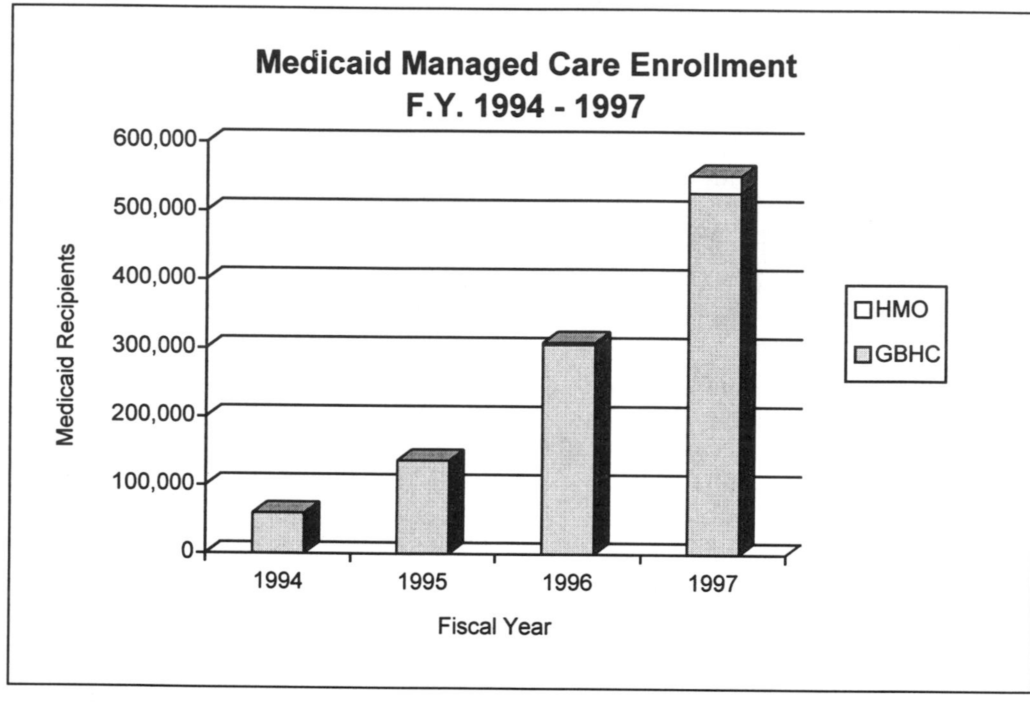

Medicaid fraud was a major problem, not just in Georgia, but throughout the United States. In 1996, the U.S. General Accounting Office estimated that fraud and abuse accounted for approximately 10 percent of all health care expenditures annually. Applied to the Georgia Medicaid program, this measure meant that as much as $355 million might be lost to waste, fraud and abuse every year.

Governor Miller recognized that every dollar defrauded from the Medicaid program was a dollar out of the taxpayer's pocket. He also recognized that fraud hurt the people who truly needed the health care. Every dollar defrauded from the system was one less dollar that helped a child get a checkup, a pregnant woman get prenatal care, a disabled person get a wheelchair, or an elderly person find a bed in the nursing home. Because of the magnitude of this problem, the state, under Governor Miller's leadership, took action to combat Medicaid fraud with a number of highly successful initiatives. Most of these initiatives centered on setting up whole new fraud units devoted specifically to combating fraud and abuse.

Prior to 1995, the state's fraud and abuse efforts consisted of a staff of 10 employees within the Department of Medical Assistance, with limited federal funding available to support their investigations. However, a provision in the federal Omnibus Budget Reconciliation Act of 1993 required all states to have a State Medicaid Fraud Control Unit (SMFCU) in operation by January 1, 1995. Federal matching funds were provided at a rate of 90 percent (10 percent state) for the first three years of operation and 75 percent (25 percent state) thereafter. The federal law also required that the unit be established within the state's Attorney General's Office or a state investigative agency such as the Georgia Bureau of Investigation.

Governor Miller seized this opportunity and created the State Health Care Fraud Control Unit by Executive Order in January 1995, which put together an outstanding record on behalf of Georgia taxpayers during the rest of the Miller Administration. Through June 30, 1998, the unit won 90 fraud convictions and recovered over $23 million in Medicaid funds. The Unit had an annual operating budget of over $3 million and included a staff of 37 attorneys, investigators, and analysts from the Georgia Bureau of Investigation, the Department of Audits and the Georgia Department of Law. The State Health Care Fraud Unit worked with the Department of Medical Assistance to identify and pursue potential fraud and abuse cases. The unit estimated that for every dollar spent combating fraud and abuse, approximately eight dollars were returned to the state treasury. This return on investment did not take into account the deterrent or "sentinel effect" of having a fraud and abuse unit in operation.

Governor Miller further targeted Medicaid fraud and abuse through the Medicaid Fraud and Forfeiture Act, which was passed by the General Assembly in 1997. Prior to passage of this law, prosecutors in state superior courts were often unable to recover property and funds in Medicaid fraud cases, because Georgia law did not allow for the seizure of assets, even after conviction. To recover the funds lost to fraud and abuse, authorities had to pursue civil actions, and by then most criminals had either spent or hidden what they had stolen. The Medicaid Fraud and Forfeiture Act attacked this problem head-on, authorizing the state to seize and hold the property of a person suspected of Medicaid fraud before that person was convicted. After conviction, the defrauded funds would be there for recovery.

In FY 1999, Governor Miller established a second Medicaid Fraud and Abuse Unit within the Department of Medical Assistance itself. The focus of this unit was proactive prevention by detecting fraudulent claims before they were paid and reducing the opportunities to "game" the reimbursement due to loopholes in program policy. Composed of 50 new staff, the unit continually monitored Medicaid services for abusive billing practices and conducted random on-site visits of Medicaid providers to ensure compliance with Medicaid rules and regulations. The unit also developed policy and reimbursement recommendations to limit opportunities for fraud and abuse.

The combination of two fraud units, one preventive in the Department of Medical Assistance and the other investigative in the GBI, quickly proved their worth. The following are examples of the types of cases prosecuted in Georgia:

A physician pled guilty to Medicaid fraud and was sentenced to ten years in prison. She was ordered to pay $200,000 in restitution and to surrender her medical license. This particular physician had billed Medicaid for nearly $500,000 for medical services never provided to Medicaid recipients – routinely billing for office visits for 50 to 130 recipients a day when 15 or 20 people had actually been seen. Investigators also found that the physician was prescribing narcotics without any documented medical necessity.

The owners of a non-emergency transportation (NET) company billed Medicaid for trips they never took, vastly overstated the mileage of trips they did take, and billed for stretcher services when they didn't use a stretcher. They were sentenced to eight years in prison and seven years probation each, and were ordered to pay more than $1 million in restitution. Ironically, one of the owners was president of the NET association and represented them in attempts to fight the crackdown on NET providers.

The three people who ran the "Youth Believing and Achieving Development Center" pled guilty on October 1, 1996 to Medicaid fraud, and admitted they had stolen $100,000 in Medicaid funds by saying they were helping kids with "psychological counseling services." What they were really doing was getting those children's Medicaid numbers and using them to cheat the government. Because of their scheme, children who never received psychological counseling ended up with falsified medical records indicating that they had psychological problems.

A pharmacist submitted claims for drugs that were never dispensed, and dispensed drugs illegally to people without prescriptions for them. The pharmacist was convicted in 1996 in federal court of mail fraud, Medicaid fraud and illegal distribution of controlled substances. The pharmacist was sentenced to five years in prison on each of the fraud counts, and three years for the drug charges as well as more than $1 million in fines.

Mental Health, Mental Retardation and Substance Abuse Services

When I became Governor, community-based services for severely emotionally disturbed children were available in only two counties. With the FY 1999 budget, service for severely emotionally disturbed children will be available in every county of the state. When I became Governor, less than half of the state had any community-based services for chronically mentally ill adults. With the FY 1999 budget, CMI services will, for the first time, be available statewide. As a result of these expanding community-based services, admission to our state mental hospitals has declined by 28 percent.

Governor Zell Miller, January 13, 1998

Under Governor Miller, Georgia made tremendous strides and improvements in mental health, mental retardation and substance abuse (MHMRSA) services. Prior to his administration, the state relied primarily on hospital care. Adequate community services were available in only a few areas of the state.

Until 1965, Central State Hospital, established as the State Asylum in Milledgeville in 1842, and Gracewood State School and Hospital, established in 1921 in Augusta, served the state as the main providers of public mental health and mental retardation services. In 1959, an investigative series was published by the *Atlanta Journal and Constitution* documenting overcrowding and poor care at Central State Hospital. This investigation led to major reforms in Georgia's mental health and mental retardation services.

By 1963, the state had begun comprehensive planning for both mental health and mental retardation services. The plan called for developing 33 community mental health centers to serve people in their home communities, and a modern state hospital system to provide intermediate and long-term care closer to home. The Georgia Mental Health Institute opened in 1965, and the Georgia Retardation Center opened in 1969. Between 1968 and 1972, construction of the regional hospitals was completed and development of community mental health and mental retardation centers was begun. The hospital system consisted of eight regional psychiatric hospitals and two mental retardation institutions.

During the 1970s, the state took advantage of federal funding to staff and operate the community mental health centers, build approximately 130 day service centers for the mentally retarded, and establish community alcohol and drug treatment programs.

In the 1980s, Georgia reached a crossroads. Because of serious overcrowding in state psychiatric hospitals, the state faced the decision of either expanding state hospitals or greatly increasing access to community services.

To address this issue, the Department of Human Resources developed a strategic plan for expanding community services that included:

* Clearly defining a single target population of those most in need;

* Identifying the critical services that were essential to this population, such as crisis intervention, residential options, day treatment and case management;

* Determining the level of these services needed in each service area of the state;

* Funding all critical services in a given service area at the same time, for maximum impact;

* Phasing in services statewide according to a multi-year plan.

Reform of the system: House Bill 100

In 1992, the Georgia General Assembly created a State Commission on Mental Health, Mental Retardation and Substance Abuse Service Delivery to study gaps and shortcomings in the 150 year-old system and to make recommendations for improvement. The commission brought together consumers, families, advocates, providers, and public and community leaders throughout the state. The group focused on the issues of accessibility, accountability, equity, integration, consumer empowerment, and privatization, and recommended that a new system:

* Be consumer and family driven;
* Provide more consumer choice;
* Move decision-making and accountability closer to the local level;
* Maximize tax dollars;
* Separate planning, contracting and monitoring from service delivery;
* Provide a single point of entry.

House Bill 100, one of the most sweeping health care reform proposals to be introduced for decades, passed the General Assembly in March 1993 and was signed into law by Governor Miller on April 27. The law created the framework for a new system as recommended by the commission. The key to the new system was 13 regional governing boards, to plan and coordinate mental health, mental retardation and substance abuse (MHMRSA) services on a regional basis. They assessed the needs in their regions and allocated all public funds, both community and hospital, based on regional plans to meet those needs. The county commissioners of each region appointed the members and at least half had to be consumers and family members.

House Bill 100 also created new community service boards to operate public MHMRSA services under contract with the regional boards. As with the regional boards, county commissioners appointed the members and at

Distribution of Funding for MHMRSA Services by Expenditure F.Y. 1990 vs. F.Y. 1999

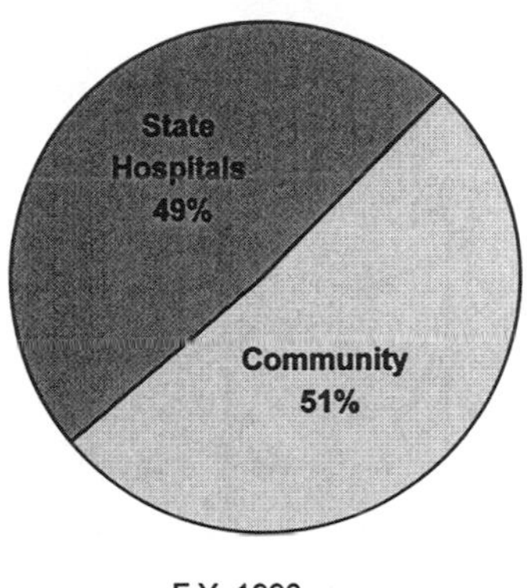

F.Y. 1990

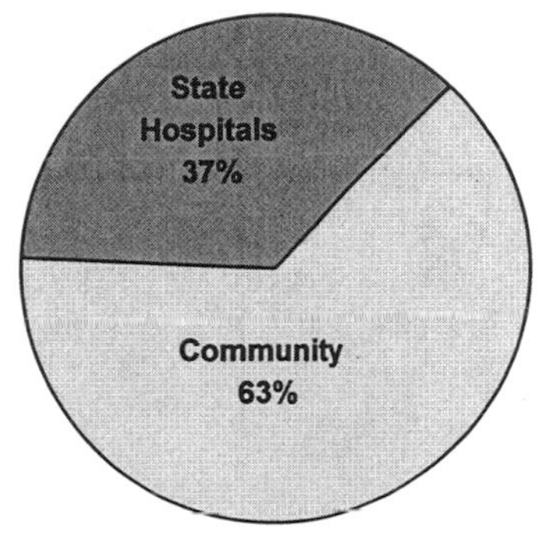

F.Y. 1999

least half were consumers and family members. The state was responsible for setting policy guidelines and priorities, statewide planning, broad oversight and evaluation, and allocation of state and federal resources. The regions had latitude and flexibility in choosing local approaches to achieve mutually established goals.

In 1995, a task force was appointed to recommend a methodology for allocating hospital resources consistent with the mandates of H.B. 100. The formula recommended by the task force primarily addressed services for adult mentally ill and substance abuse clients. As a result, from FY 1995 through FY 1998, the state made tremendous strides in shifting resources and workload away from state hospitals to community programs. The state hospital facility system experienced a 15.2 percent decrease in the total number of days of care, and a 30 percent decrease in the total number of admissions. The cost centers that were a part of the allocation formula had a 27.8 percent decrease. All regions of the state reduced their use of state hospital care. The regional average decreased by 28.9 percent, which represented 12,771 days of care per region.

The implementation of the hospital reallocation formula provided a formalized means for redirecting resources from hospitals to community services which was a key component of the Governor's redirection budget strategy. In FY 1997 and FY 1998, close to $30 million was transferred from hospital services to community services. These funds were used to expand services for the chronically mentally ill and for substance abusers. Community funding for FY 1998 was 17 percent higher than FY 1996.

Governor Miller Expanded Services Statewide for the Chronically Mentally Ill (CMI)

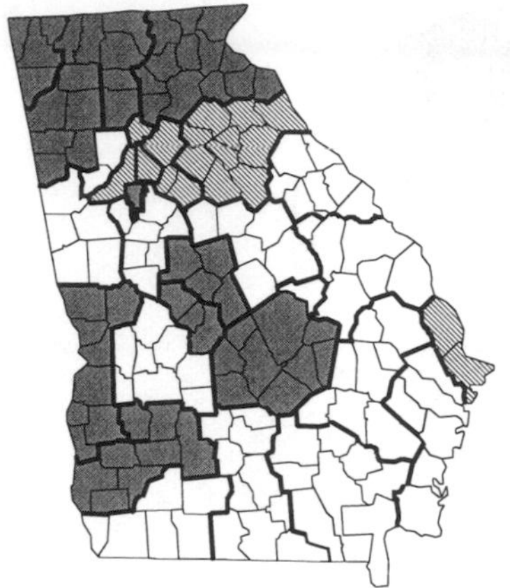

Fully Funded

Partially Funded

No Funding

Funding for CMI Services before Governor Miller took Office

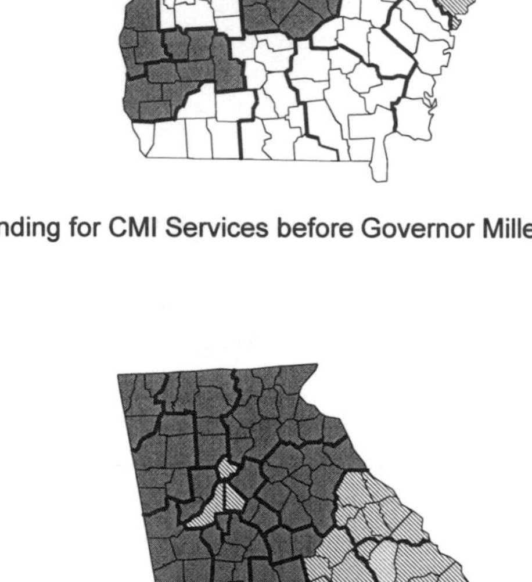

Funding for CMI Services when Governor Miller left Office

As a result of the decline in hospital utilization, the Governor recommended and the General Assembly approved the closure of the Georgia Mental Health Institute (GMHI) in Atlanta. Services provided by GMHI were relocated to Georgia Regional Hospital in Atlanta, freeing up $6.2 million to be redirected to fund community services for the chronically mentally ill, and $2 million for community substance abuse treatment for pregnant and post partum women.

Services for chronically mentally ill adults

If critical services were available in the community to treat seriously mentally ill individuals earlier in the course of their illness and at times of crisis, institutionalization could be avoided. The family and other social support systems could be kept intact and strengthened.

When Governor Miller took office, community-based services for chronically mentally ill (CMI) adults were funded in 13 of 28 service areas. When he left office, services were available in all areas of the state at a cost of $54 million in state funds. Of this amount, $32.6 million was added during the Governor's administration.

CMI was the primary beneficiary of the hospital reallocation formula. A total of $15.6 million was redirected to CMI target services in FY 1997 and FY 1998. If CMI services were not available, there would be an increased use of state psychiatric facilities, more mentally ill adults would be held in local jails and the number of homeless mentally ill would increase. As a result of the expansion of CMI services, in FY 1998, one of the state's eight psychiatric hospitals was closed and the funds redirected to services for the mentally ill and pregnant substance abusers.

Services for severely emotionally disturbed children

Most of the needs of emotionally disturbed children could be met in their own communities. However, prior to FY 1989, the only available community mental health services for youth in Georgia were limited outpatient services and two group homes. The lack of community-based mental health services for children in Georgia resulted in over-reliance on hospitals and out-of-community residential treatment.

When Governor Miller took office, funding for community services for severely emotionally disturbed (SED) children was available only in Richmond and DeKalb Counties. During the Governor's term, $31.8 million in new funding was appropriated for these services. The FY 1999 appropriation completed funding statewide. In 1998, 32,000 children were served in community programs.

If SED services had not been available, these children would have ended up in more costly hospital treatment or would have received no services at all. In FY 1997, 50 percent of the short-term child and adolescent beds at regional mental health hospitals were closed as a result of more SED services being available. These services include expanded outpatient services, in-home crisis intervention, after school/weekend day treatment, respite care, therapeutic foster care, and therapeutic group homes.

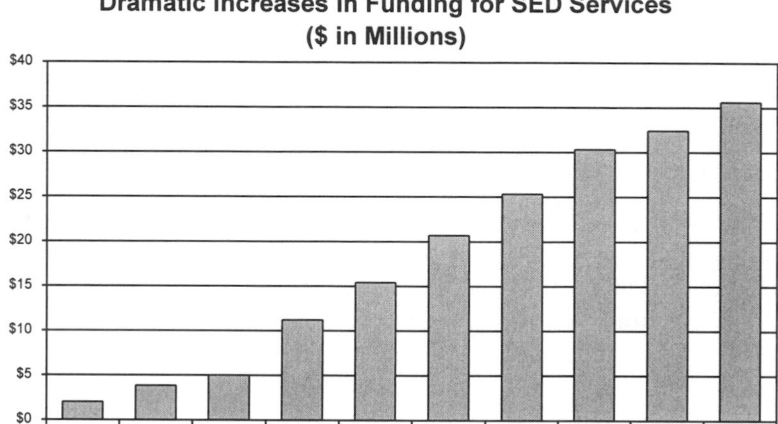

Expansion of community-based services for the mentally retarded

Community-based services for the mentally retarded increased significantly during the Miller Administration. The number of slots funded under Medicaid waivers rose from 146 to 3,017, an increase of over 2000 percent. By the end of the Governor's second term, funding had increased from $8.8 million to over $100 million in state and federal funds. Two events significantly impacted this increase. First, the passage of H.B. 100 made services much more responsive to family and consumer needs and preferences. Second, the Governor's budget redirection plan provided the impetus to move funds from outdated service models to more effective and cost-efficient services.

The state's implementation of the Medicaid Home and Community-Based Services Waiver Program represented a major initiative to decrease the use of institutions and increase the likelihood of mentally retarded individuals remaining at home or in an alternative community setting. Institutions had consistently been shown to be less effective than community settings in promoting growth and independence among those with mental retardation. Even individuals with severe or profound mental retardation showed significant improvement in behavior when placed in the community.

The closure of state institutions generated substantial savings which could then be used to expand community services to serve a greater number

Governor Miller Expanded Community Services Statewide for Severely Emotionally Disturbed (SED) Children and Adolescents

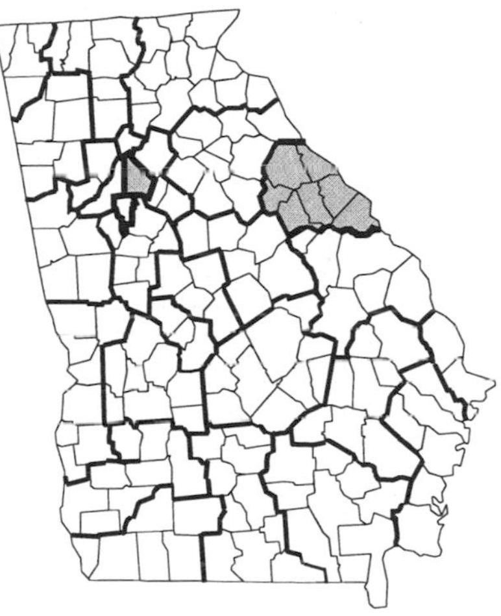

Fully Funded

No Funding

Funding for SED Community Services before Governor Miller took Office

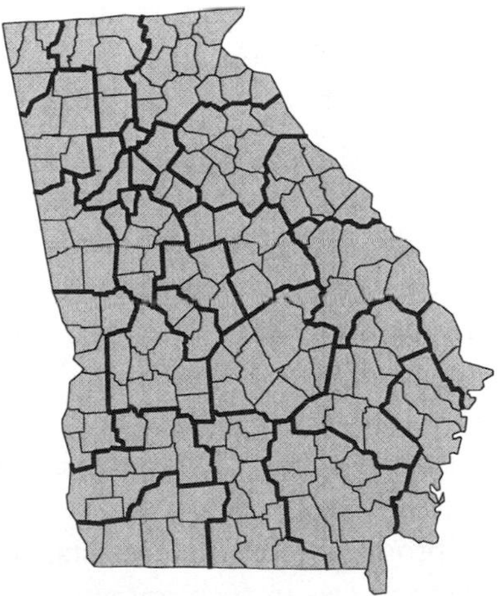

Statewide Funding of SED Services when Governor Miller left Office

Expansion of Waiver Slots for Persons with Mental Retardation

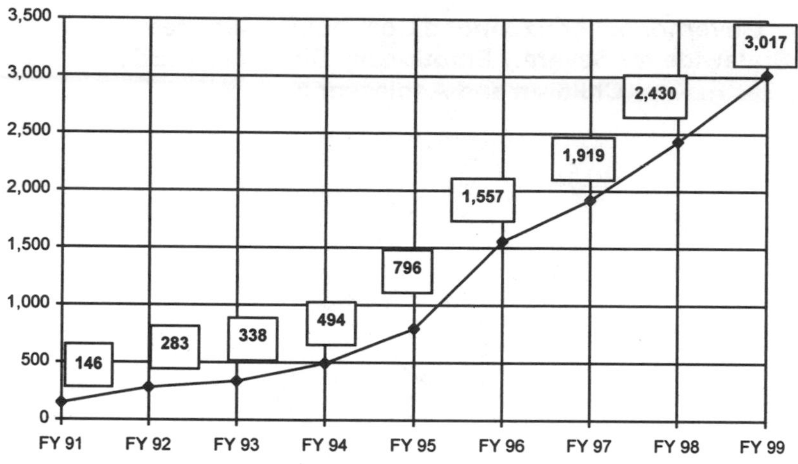

of clients. Rivers Crossing, a 37-bed facility in Athens, was the first mental retardation facility to be closed in Georgia. However, between FY 1994 and FY 1999, various MR units in other state facilities closed 147 beds.

In FY 1998, the Governor recommended and the General Assembly approved the closure of Brook Run in Atlanta and the redirection of $15 million to place the 326 residents of this institution in community-based services. As a result of the cost savings from closing Brook Run, an additional 284 people with mental retardation who were on waiting lists or graduating from special education classes were able to receive community services.

Substance abuse treatment

A significant number of welfare recipients were single mothers and were unable to participate in competitive employment because of substance abuse problems. Substance abuse was also a significant contributor to child abuse and neglect, and to the need to remove children from parental custody and place them in foster care. Babies born with complications due to prenatal exposure to alcohol and other drugs were a significant and costly health problem.

In 1995, a pilot program to provide substance abuse services for pregnant and postpartum women was implemented in Cobb, DeKalb, and Muscogee Counties and in 1998, the program was expanded to Sumter, Dougherty and Mitchell Counties. In addition to treatment, the participants received child care, prenatal care, job training and job placement services. For FY 1999, as recommended by the Governor, $8 million in state and federal funds were appropriated to expand this program statewide.

Hospital funds were also reallocated to expand community substance abuse treatment. As a result, during 1996, the alcohol and drug unit at GMHI was closed and funds were redirected to community services in the four regions served by GMHI.

Supported employment

Supported employment helped citizens with disabilities to hold paying jobs in an environment where they were integrated with co-workers who had no disabilities. The program included a wide variety of job-related supports to maintain successful employment, including job coaches and adaptations to the workplace. Some outcomes of supported employment were higher personal income, reduced dependency on government supports, and greater personal fulfillment.

In FY 1990, approximately 1,000 individuals with disabilities were employed in Georgia companies through supported employment. By 1998, that number was close to 4,000. In FY 1999, based on Governor Miller's recommendation, supported employment was redirected from total state funding to Medicaid waiver slots. As a result, 540 additional clients were placed in supported employment.

In response to demands from families and clients, more regional boards began to contract specifically for job-related outcomes such as independent employment, supported employment and vocational training. Changing financing for supported employment to use Medicaid waiver slots supported an initiative by the regional boards called *20 to Work By 2000* which established the goal of moving at least 20 percent of the clients enrolled in community day treatment programs into independent employment by the year 2000 – an increase of 2,400 slots.

Trends

The reform of the MHMRSA service delivery system accelerated the use of community services. As consumers were served closer to home in community placements, the need for hospital beds decreased and the hospital system began to shrink. Plans were developed and implemented at various hospitals to consolidate the administrative and patient support services and make them more efficient. In addition, some of the state hospitals that remained open began to undertake new or additional roles in providing services to clients, reaching out beyond their walls to set up assertive community treatment teams to help people avoid repeated hospitalizations.

Limited funding, the expectations of quality performance, and "doing more with less" caused the development of new and creative ways of supporting people in the community. Trends included the development and use of natural, and sometimes paid, community supports such as families, friends, churches and other community organizations.

Regional boards, as required by H.B. 100, brought more providers into the system to increase consumer choice. They began purchasing services tailored to individuals with special needs; and, as a result, consumers and families were more likely to get the help they needed to reduce the number of crises and avoid hospitalizations.

As members of regional and community service boards, clients and their families had a real voice in planning the service delivery system. Clients chose "jobs" as their top priority. This call for job-related services was expected to increase, and was reflected in the regional boards' *20 to Work by 2000* initiative. Due to improvements in technology and the public's increased awareness of their skills, people with disabilities were increasingly able to choose from a greater variety of jobs and have a much greater chance of self-sufficiency.

Community Services and Quality Care for Older Georgians

It's not easy being a senior citizen in a society that worships youth. All around us are messages implying that to qualify for first-class citizenship, you must be young and beautiful. Youth and beauty sell everything from soap to suitcases. But when it comes right down to it, the only way to keep from aging is to die young.

Governor Zell Miller, October 24, 1991

When Governor Miller assumed office in 1991, the elderly population in Georgia had grown nearly 80 percent from 1970 and was projected to grow at least another 40 percent by the year 2010. In addition, projections for Georgia showed that the age 65-plus population would grow at nearly twice the rate as the under-age-65 population. Of even greater significance, the age 85-plus population was projected to grow at nearly three times the rate as the under-age-65 population.

Governor Miller recognized that this substantial growth in Georgia's elderly population would have significant financial and social impact. The frail health of an aging population, as well as the financial and emotional pressures on family caregivers, had forced many older Georgians to turn to government for health care and financial assistance. At the same time, much of the burden for caring for older Georgians kept shifting from the federal government to the states.

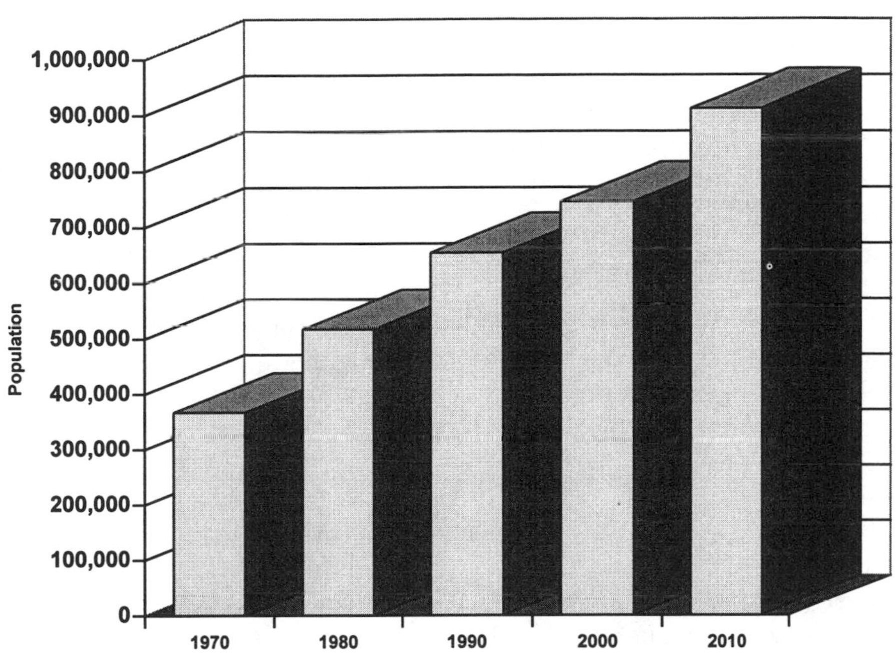

Despite all these factors, the options and services available to older Georgians consisted primarily of nursing home placements. Often, these placements were not only costly, but also removed an elderly person from his or her home and community, which could be a very emotional experience if the person was not truly ready for a nursing home. As a result, the Governor took action to strengthen and expand services that could be used as alternatives to nursing home placement. At the same time, Miller made sure that the nursing homes in Georgia provided quality care to protect those citizens that needed nursing home care. During the Miller Administration, funding for services for the elderly increased by more than 80 percent.

Community Care Services Program

The Community Care Services Program (CCSP) provided services that offered maximum independence and dignity for the elderly, especially the most vulnerable. CCSP was developed based on the fact that confinement in a nursing home could be avoided for some elderly people if they had some services provided in their own homes. Consequently, the goal of CCSP was to help people remain in their homes and communities for as long as possible, thereby preventing premature or even unnecessary placement in costly nursing homes. These efforts included such services as home health care, training for family caregivers, respite care, and home-delivered meals. Community services for the elderly generally fell into two categories – Medicaid and Non-medicaid.

Services Offered Through the Community Care Services Program

- Outreach
- Assessment
- Case Management
- Home Health Services
- Adult Day Care
- Alternative Living Services
- Respite Care
- Personal Support Services
- Home Delivered Meals
- Emergency Respite Care
- Transportation
- Alzheimer's Program

Medicaid community care services for the elderly: Medicaid served senior citizens who met specific income and health-related criteria. Under Governor Miller's leadership, funding for the Medicaid Community Care for the Elderly program increased by $34.6 million or 123 percent, from $28 million in FY 1990 to $62.8 million in FY 1999. The number of clients served by the program increased by 6,325 clients or 72 percent, from 8,829 in FY 1990 to an estimated minimum of 15,154 clients in FY 1999.

The community care program resulted in substantial savings in Medicaid funds, since the program's cost averaged about 21 percent of the Medicaid cost to stay in a nursing home. In fact, by using community services instead of nursing home care, an average of $11,127 per person served was saved.

Non-Medicaid community care services for the elderly: Non-Medicaid community services did not have income-based eligibility criteria, but were targeted to the most economically and socially needy individuals. Under Governor Miller's leadership, total funding for non-Medicaid community care for the elderly increased by $11.7 million or 41 percent, from $28.9 million in FY 1990 to $40.6 million in FY 1999. The number of clients served by the program increased by 8,394 or 25 percent, from 32,648 in FY 1990 to an estimated 41,042 clients in FY 1999.

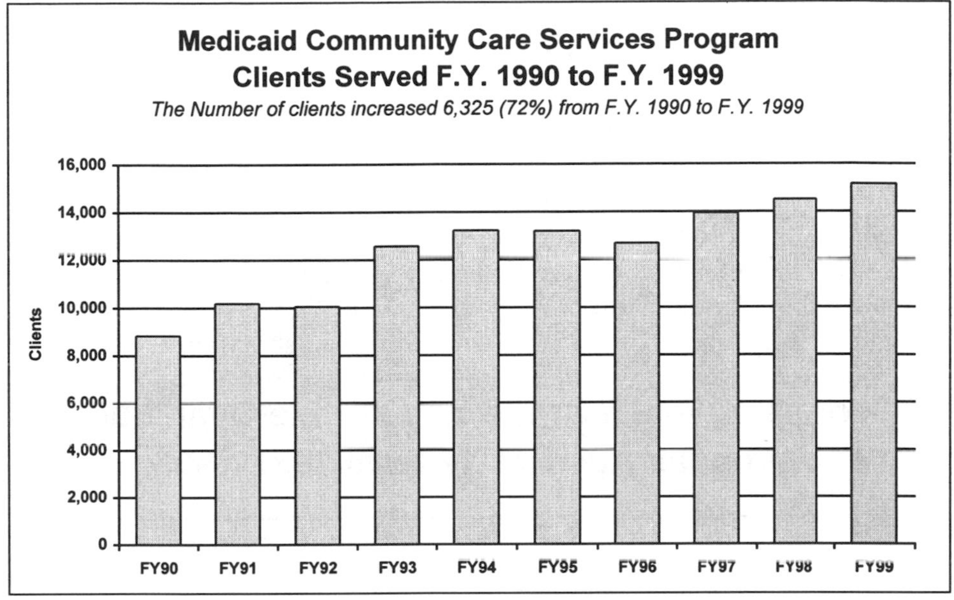

Juvenile Crime Solutions

Back when our juvenile justice system was first created, a juvenile delinquent was a youngster who stole hubcaps, shoplifted, ran away from home, or painted graffiti on public property. Our system did not envision the problems we see today—teenagers shooting people and committing rapes; young hoodlums running gangs and terrorizing neighborhoods, and showing little or no remorse when they're caught.

Governor Zell Miller, October 25, 1993

Beginning in the late 1980s, there was a rapid rise in the incidence of juvenile crime, both nationally and in Georgia. Juvenile offenses increased both in the sheer number of acts committed and in the severity of these acts. The Miller Administration was faced with responding to this growing problem, and did so with a proactive, multi-faceted approach.

The Governor's first and most dramatic step in attacking juvenile crime was the creation of a separate department to handle the state's efforts in managing this unwanted trend. Prior to the Miller Administration, there had been only a Division of Children and Youth Services within the Department of Human Resources devoted to this effort. This division ran a few facilities and some community programs for juvenile offenders with a budget of less than

$75 million—far short of the funding and resources needed to adequately address the problem.

In 1992, the Governor separated the division from the Department of Human Resources and created the new Department of Children and Youth Services. This agency was renamed the Department of Juvenile Justice in 1997. These actions, along with additional financial resources, gave the new department the true ability to be used as a major tool in the state's juvenile crime prevention efforts. The mission of the department under Governor Miller was to "protect the youth of Georgia and the public by providing safe and secure detention and incarceration and effective community supervision based on the risks and needs of the youth, and in all cases provide effective programs, including education, that lead youth to law abiding behavior."

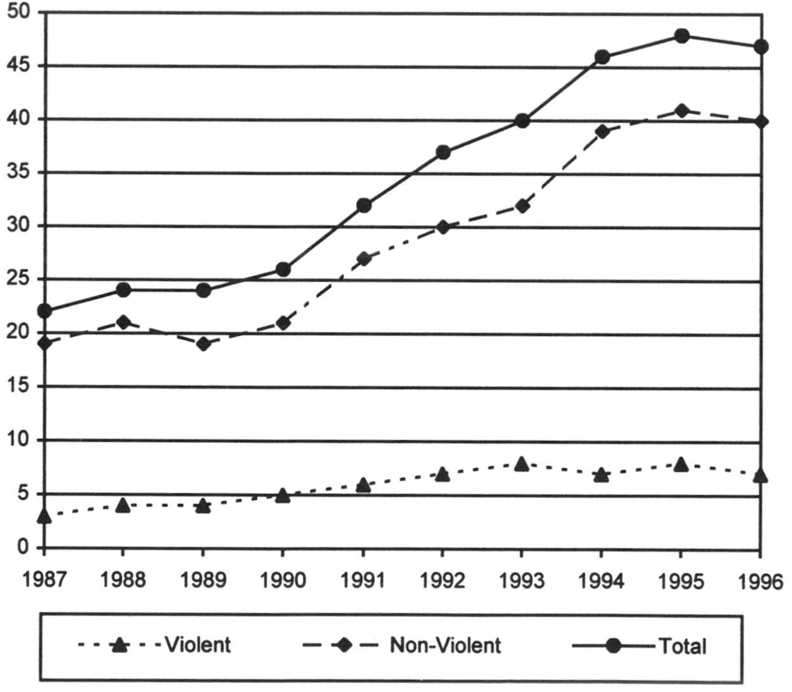

The School Safety and Juvenile Justice Reform Act of 1994

The Miller Administration responded to the rapid growth in juvenile crime during the 1990s with a "tough love" approach. Even though the young offenders knew they were being punished for what they had done wrong, emphasis was also placed on rehabilitation and not exclusively on punishment. Still, there was much concern and public outcry about the increasing juvenile crime rate. This interest culminated in Miller's proposing the School Safety and Juvenile Justice Reform Act of 1994, commonly known as Senate Bill 440, which the General Assembly passed.

This legislation included three major provisions, which focused on rehabilitation as well as the firm reforms needed due to the increase in the violent nature of juvenile crime. The first provided that the most violent acts by juveniles required the alternative of punishment as an adult. This change in the law gave prosecutors the option of trying juveniles as adults when they committed one of "seven deadly sins": murder; voluntary manslaughter; rape; aggravated sodomy; aggravated child molestation; aggravated sexual battery; or armed robbery if committed with a firearm.

Senate Bill 440 also gave judges the option of sentencing a juvenile offender to 90 days at a youth development campus or YDC. Previously, the most severe option a judge could give a juvenile was commitment to the department, which did not always ensure a stay in a YDC. Through this initiative, Governor Miller gave the juvenile judicial system an option it hadn't had in the past. Judges could guarantee that an offender would spend some time behind bars. It also gave judges a tool to teach youths a lesson. In some cases, judges just wanted a juvenile to experience the consequence of their actions by spending time in a YDC, but they did not necessarily want the youth to stay there long term. Judges began using this alternative extensively, and the Governor responded by re-opening many closed YDC beds and authorizing new construction to handle the tremendous growth this option created.

Through Senate Bill 440, the Governor also expanded the maximum amount of time a youth could spend in the custody of the department as a designated felon from 18 months to five years. A designated felon was a chronic or violent offender. In the past, the department only had a year and a half to work with these youth before they lost all ability to control their rehabilitation. Now, the state had authority to oversee and monitor youths for a much longer time.

Juvenile justice strategies and services

Policy changes in the Miller Administration concentrated not only on much needed, broad approaches like the ones mentioned above, but also focused on creating a continuum of services to handle the diverse population of juvenile criminals. Under Governor Miller, new programs were created and existing programs expanded at unprecedented levels. These programs had to accommodate a wide variety of children, from those who had committed minor truancies to those youth with far worse problems.

To handle this rapid expansion, the Miller Administration increased state funding for serving the juvenile justice population by over 200 percent since the department's creation. Funding increased from $71.3 million in state funds in FY 1992 to $216 million in FY 1999. Over half of the FY 1999 budget was dedicated to long-term placements in YDCs. The youths that benefit from these services were in need of secure rehabilitative detention ranging from 90 days to five years. Another quarter of the budget went for short-term placements in regional youth detention centers or RYDCs, where juveniles were detained for periods of a few days or weeks from the time of their arrest until their dispositions were heard in front of a judge. The final quarter of the budget was spent on community programs where juvenile offenders were rehabilitated in a community-based setting such as a wilderness program or attention home. Overall, the number of juveniles needing secured detention and rehabilitation increased dramatically from 29,000 in FY 1992 to over 55,000 in FY 1998, an increase of 89 percent.

F.Y. 1999 Budget Breakdown for the Department of Juvenile Justice

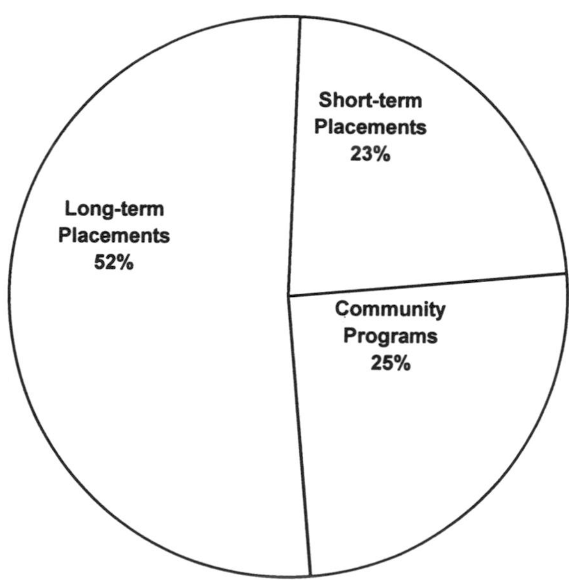

Regional Youth Detention Centers: Governor Miller helped to expand the network of facilities that temporarily housed juveniles in a secure environment. These institutions had a mission to protect the public from future actions by the juvenile delinquents. In many instances, when a juvenile was picked up by law enforcement authorities, the first institution they saw was a regional youth detention center or RYDC. At these facilities, an intake officer decided where the juvenile should stay until that child saw a juvenile judge.

By the end of the Miller Administration, over twenty RYDCs were located throughout the state, each serving a group of counties known as a catchment area. One of these facilities, opened in 1998, was the state-of-the-art Metro RYDC, a 300-bed secure facility serving all of metropolitan Atlanta. Expansion plans by the Miller Administration were slated to provide more than 1,500 short-term beds by the end of FY 2001, a dramatic increase from the 669 in FY 1992.

Youth Development Campuses: The youth development campuses or YDCs housed juveniles in a secure setting and provided services with the goal of rehabilitation to give youths who deserved it a second chance. Given the discipline and stability that these facilities provided, the Miller Administration envisioned a new short, intense program also located in YDCs. This program, known as the 90-day program, was developed for those youth whose major problems were a lack of personal discipline along with no history of respect for the world around them. Senate Bill 440 created the 90-day sentence to a YDC as an option for judges. The Miller Administration implemented it as the state's first juvenile delinquent boot camp program.

Both the boot camp program and the extension of the maximum amount of time a youth could stay in the state's custody as a designated felon were new planks in the continuum of sanctions for juvenile offenders available to juvenile judges. However, the impact of Senate Bill 440 took its toll on state resources. The Miller Administration had no choice but to respond with a period of rapid bed expansion. In 1992, there were only 742 beds available for long-term rehabilitation of youth. The Miller expansion plan called for over 3,000 rehabilitative beds by FY 2001.

Many of the youths housed in YDCs were also in dire need of special treatment for a variety of problems: sex offenses, alcohol and drug abuse, violent behavior, and other mental health problems. The Miller Administration not only provided bed space, but also funded an expansion of the treatment programs needed for these youths.

The capital construction committed to juvenile corrections by the Miller Administration was unprecedented. Between YDCs and RYDCs, Governor Miller invested over $100 million in capital outlay for new facilities. Facility openings, future institutional construction, and major expansions occurred statewide to respond to the need.

Privatization in the expansion of YDCs was a major tool used by the Governor during this growth. The Miller Administration authorized the department to contract out the operation of any new YDCs created by the

Facility	Number of Beds	Year Opened
Clayton RYDC	50	1991
Eastman YDC	100	1993*
Davisboro YDC	100	1994
Irwin YDC	316	1995
Chatham RYDC	100	1996
Wrightsville YDC	500	1996
Marietta RYDC	50	1997
Pelham YDC	120	1997
Emanuel YDC	168	1998
McIntosh YDC	168	1998
Metro RYDC	300	1998
Paulding RYDC	125	1998
Sumter YDC	150	2000 (Scheduled)
Gainesville RYDC	75	2000 (Scheduled)
Muscogee YDC	150	2001 (Scheduled)
South Central RYDC	75	2001 (Scheduled)
New 100-bed RYDC	100	2001 (Scheduled)

*An expansion of 300 beds is scheduled to open in 1999.

demand for bed space. One of the initial larger facilities, Irwin YDC, was opened as a privatized 316-bed institution. This opening was follow by the issuance of contracts for the operation of Pelham, McIntosh and Emanuel YDCs. Privatization of these facilities saved money for the state, and at the same time allowed these institutions to open more quickly.

Under Governor Miller, the need for additional bed space was also addressed through a unique working partnership with the Department of Corrections, in which over 1,000 beds were added to the juvenile justice system with minimal construction. First, Corrections, working in conjunction with the Department of Juvenile Justice, constructed the 100-bed Eastman Youth Development Facility or YDF. The term "facility" in YDF instead of "campus" as in YDC meant the institution was operated and staffed by Corrections, but would house juveniles. After the demand for bed space increased due to Senate Bill 440, Eastman was expanded and operations were transferred completely to the Department of Juvenile Justice.

In addition to the Eastman YDF, the Department of Corrections also operated two other facilities for Juvenile Justice: Wrightsville and Davisboro YDFs. Both institutions housed adult inmates prior to their use as juvenile institutions. Over 1,000 adult inmates were reassigned to other prisons to accommodate the transfer. Eventually, the operations of Wrightsville YDF were handed over to Juvenile Justice and the facility became Wrightsville YDC. Davisboro YDF was converted back to an adult institution, once enough juvenile facilities had been constructed to keep up with demand.

Community-based rehabilitative programs: Hard beds were not the only weapons the Miller Administration used in the fight against juvenile crime. The Governor saw a need to expand services available to juveniles who committed crimes of a less serious nature that did not demand secure detention in a state facility, but demanded a sanction with an emphasis on rehabilitation. These services would come through community-based rehabilitative programs.

Governor Miller increased funding for prevention-focused, community-based programs by almost 100 percent since the creation of the new department, from $28.6 million in FY 1993 to over $55 million in the FY 1999 budget. More programs were developed for youths who could not return home, but did not need secure detention. Special residential treatment services were also expanded for juvenile offenders who were severely emotionally disturbed. A new male group home was started in Albany, as well as two new separate privatized wilderness programs for boys.

Another initiative by the Miller Administration, a privatized group home for girls, was created in FY 1996. It was the first female state group home. Because it was so successful, a second female group home was funded in FY 1999. The Governor also oversaw the privatization of the attention and contract homes which house children who cannot be immediately returned to their family setting.

The U.S. Department of Justice

In 1997, the United States Department of Justice Civil Rights Division undertook an audit of the state's RYDCs and YDCs based on complaints of overcrowding and unsafe conditions. A final report released in February 1998 noted that improvements were still needed in Georgia's juvenile justice system. The report cited a lack of adequate mental health care, overcrowded conditions, abusive disciplinary practices, and inadequate educational and medical care in certain areas.

The Miller Administration worked with the Civil Rights Division in a cooperative effort to improve the state's juvenile justice system. This cooperative effort ensured that the federal rights of juveniles were protected while still preserving the state's basic policy choices regarding juvenile justice. The final product was a Memorandum of Agreement (MOA) signed by Governor Miller and Attorney General Janet Reno on March 18, 1998 in the Governor's Office. The MOA was a milestone and one of the most unique agreements in the nation. It allowed Georgia to determine its own philosophy in dealing with juvenile justice, a philosophy based on tough love and discipline. The agreement also allowed for an independent, yet state-sponsored monitoring of compliance with the MOA. In contrast, some juvenile justice systems in other states were under a federal takeover or a federal court monitor. The agreement built on steps already undertaken by Georgia. It also established a framework under which the state developed its own solutions to the problems identified in the investigation with input from the Justice Department. The MOA required the state to develop plans relating to specific areas of concern, often with the assistance of outside experts.

As a result, the state made a commitment to invest an additional $44 million in programs and services, including 238 new positions, in the juvenile justice system, along with an additional $21 million in bonds for capital outlay during the period from FY 1999 to FY 2001. This additional funding covered a 25-person, quick-response Quality Assurance unit to systematically audit all state and regional facilities; an additional 35 special education teachers, school materials, and classroom space; a new $1.5 million vocational program; over 120 additional juvenile correctional officers; an increase in medical and dental services for all detained juveniles; more than 380 slots which local judges can use as alternatives to the short-term detention centers currently available; and a mental health services package of counselors and psychiatrists.

Despite the challenges of an escalating juvenile crime rate, Governor Miller always remained committed to rehabilitating Georgia's youthful offenders. To him, those juveniles were part of the future of the state. In some instances, they needed punishment *and* they needed to be taught the lessons of life. These lessons would be valuable tools for them in the future, because, as Governor Miller noted, these children "deserve a second chance."

Award-Winning Videos for At-Risk Youth

Multiple Choice

In 1994, the General Assembly of the State of Georgia passed historic legislation aimed at reducing the alarming rise in juvenile violence and crime. The new law, known as the Juvenile Justice Reform Act, designated seven violent crimes for which juveniles would be tried and sentenced as adults. To communicate the terms of this new legislation to the public, the Governor's Children and Youth Coordinating Council produced a video called *Multiple Choice.*

Written and directed by ImageMaster Productions, which contributed over $40,000 in pro-bono services, the video was aimed at middle and high school students. It featured footage from a Youth Development Campus, a boot camp, a women's correctional facility in Atlanta and a men's correctional facility in Alto. It stressed the importance of personal responsibility and emphasized that youth would be held accountable for their personal choices. Instead of grown-ups telling kids what not to do, the video featured teen hosts talking straight to their peers.

After seeing clips of the video, WATL-TV in Atlanta accepted it for airing during prime time, to be followed by a live discussion program on juvenile crime and violence. After airing on commercial television, *Multiple Choice* aired numerous times on Georgia Public Television (GPTV). It was distributed via the state's PeachStar satellite network to the middle and high schools of the state, and over 5,500 VHS copies were distributed free of charge to youth organizations.

Reports came back from educators that classrooms full of teenagers, known for short attention spans, were watching the film in stunned silence. In 1997, *Multiple Choice* was nominated for Emmy awards for editing, youth program, and director, and went on to win the Emmys for youth program and director.

Ultimate Choice

Multiple Choice demonstrated television's effectiveness in reaching teenagers, so video was the medium of choice when another serious teen issue needed to be addressed. As part of Governor Zell Miller's attack on Georgia's high rate of teen pregnancy, the Children and Youth Coordinating Council again contracted with ImageMaster to produce a video, this time on the hardships and challenges of being a teen parent.

The title, *Ultimate Choice*, continued the theme of personal responsibility, as once again teens shared their stories and encouraged their peers not to make the same bad choices they had made. Teens told their peers that choosing to become sexually active could bring them consequences that would last a lifetime.

Ultimate Choice aired on television on April 1, 1997. In a first in state history, eight Georgia television stations aired the program simultaneously under the sponsorship of Promina Health System. Following its statewide commercial airing, it was also shown numerous times on Georgia Public Television, and sent to every middle and high school in the state by satellite. ImageMaster Productions handled the duplication and distribution of over 6,500 copies statewide virtually at cost, a donation that exceeded $1.5 million. *Ultimate Choice* won Emmy awards in 1998 for best youth program and best editor.

Driving Ambition

Prompted by the gruesome deaths of several Georgia teenagers in highway crashes, the Georgia General Assembly passed stringent new rules for teen drivers in 1997. House Bill 681 instituted a graduated driver's license and strengthened penalties for such offenses as DUI and reckless driving. Again, Georgia teens were being called to accept responsibility for their actions. The changes in the law were significant and the Children and Youth Coordinating Council was one of the state agencies Governor Miller asked to spread the word to the state's teenagers.

In a video entitled *Driving Ambition*, families shared their grief and their loss at the death of their teenager in a vehicle crash. The message was clear. Too many Georgia teens were dying and being severely injured on the road, many because of carelessness and speeding. The law enforcement perspective was equally clear. Georgia would no longer tolerate irresponsible and reckless behavior from teens behind the wheel.

Once again, with WSB-TV in the lead, television stations around the state aired the video simultaneously. The ratings indicated that over a half-million people watched. *Driving Ambition* won Emmy awards for photography and graphic arts.

Over 5,500 youth organizations, including juvenile courts, boys and girls clubs, YMCAs, churches, scout groups, and PTAs used these three videos for youth. In addition, the videos were available free of charge from all public libraries and Blockbuster Entertainment stores around the state. The videos were also translated into Spanish and were adapted for the hearing impaired. Information about the videos was available at the CYCC web site at www.ganet.org/cycc.

The Parenting Principle

A fourth video entitled *The Parenting Principle*, outlining the critical role a parent played in the development of well-adjusted children, became available in December of 1998. A strong call to responsibility for parents, its premise was that children are the future and how they are raised often determines whether they will contribute to or be a burden on society.

Through these four videos, the Governor's Children and Youth Coordinating Council established a reputation of excellence utilizing a medium and formula that produced results. Georgia set a standard that other states wanted to emulate, and over 200 requests for the videos were received from other states during the Miller Administration.

Honoring Georgia's War Veterans

We remember their loyalty, patriotism and courage in the face of danger. We pay tribute to their commitment to liberty and justice, and their devotion to their country. And we thank them for the gift of their services to us.

Governor Miller, October 28, 1993

Nursing home privatization

The Georgia War Veterans' Home in Milledgeville was one of two state-operated nursing homes that provided skilled nursing care, domiciliary care and related health services to sick and disabled Georgia veterans. Prior to FY 1997, Georgia was the only state in the Southeast with veteran nursing homes operated completely by the state. The cost of operating the Milledgeville nursing home had climbed nearly 48 percent from $12.2 million in FY 1990 to $18 million in FY 1996, raising cause for concern.

In one of his first privatization efforts, Governor Miller privatized the operation of the Georgia War Veterans' Home in Milledgeville in FY 1997, and it proved extremely successful. During the first year of privatization, the state saved nearly $7 million in operating costs while continuing to provide high quality care for Georgia veterans. The state was projected to save an estimated $28 million through FY 2000.

History of Nursing Home Costs and Projected Savings
Georgia War Veterans' Home – Milledgeville

Fiscal Year	State Run Cost	Cost Under Privatization	Savings
1990	$12,218,225	--	--
1991	$14,725,014	--	--
1992	$14,217,069	--	--
1993	$15,255,296	--	--
1994	$16,284,745	--	--
1995	$17,386,621	--	--
1996	$18,072,234	--	--
1997	$20,654,364	$14,009,003	$6,645,361
1998	$22,619,364	$14,134,310	$8,485,054
1999	$23,584,364	$14,314,840	$9,269,524
2000	$24,549,364	$14,500,932	$10,048,432

Note: The privatization of the facility was effective in F.Y. 1997 on October 1, 1996.

After the facility was privatized, residents of the home reported improvements in the quality of care in terms of increased staff attention. In addition, residents began receiving new speech therapy and respiratory services, and experienced improvements in physical therapy, occupational therapy, food services and medication delivery. Quality indicators for residents showed an overall improvement in many other areas as well. Through Governor Miller's privatization efforts, the Department achieved a substantial upgrading of its services to nursing home residents at a much lower cost. In 1998, the War Veterans Home in Milledgeville received the American Health Care Association Quality Award for quality improvement.

Privatization efforts also took place at the Georgia War Veterans Nursing Home in Augusta. This facility served over 170 veterans and was operated as a teaching facility under a contract with the Medical College of Georgia. The association gave the Augusta nursing home access to technology and expertise that was not readily available to other nursing facilities, enabling it to become a leader in teaching nursing and providing quality patient care.

Beginning in 1995, the Georgia War Veterans' Nursing Home in Augusta outsourced security, grounds keeping and laundry services in an effort to reduce costs. The facility also saved the state over $500,000 by reducing and reorganizing staff in nursing, social work, and physician services. To make these reductions without affecting patient care, the management team made a conscience effort not to eliminate any front-line nursing positions. Instead, the reduction was attained mostly through attrition and reorganization of managers. In addition, dietary services were outsourced to Morrison Health Care in April 1998, saving approximately $100,000 annually.

From 1995 to 1998, the Georgia War Veterans' Nursing Home in Augusta has saved a total of over $600,000 through reorganization and outsourcing. The facility became a good example of public and private enterprise meeting the needs of veterans efficiently and effectively.

Memorials in honor of Georgia veterans

Governor Miller, himself a United States Marine Corps veteran, always recognized and valued the great sacrifices made by Georgia veterans to protect the freedom of people around the world. In appreciation and respect, monuments were erected during the Miller Administration at the Floyd Veterans Memorial Building in Atlanta to honor veterans of World War I, World War II, the Korean War, and the Persian Gulf War.

Georgia Korean War Memorial, dedicated November 11, 1993: The memorial consisted of a bronze plaque attached to a tablet of Georgia granite that stood approximately five feet eight inches tall. Inscribed on the monument were the names of the 740 Georgians who were killed during the Korean War.

Georgia Persian Gulf War Memorial, dedicated March 10, 1993: This memorial was dedicated to the Georgia military personnel who either were deployed or were mobilized during the Persian Gulf War. Inscribed on the monument were the names of the 13 Georgians killed in action and the two Georgians who were taken prisoners of war. Also engraved on the monument were the designations of the Georgia active, reserve and national guard units that participated in the crisis.

Georgia World War II Monument, dedicated December 7, 1995: The monument contained a chronology of World War II events and quotes from

President Franklin Roosevelt and World War II Generals George Marshall, Dwight Eisenhower and Douglas MacArthur. The monument also listed the names of 6,781 Georgians who died outside the United States during the war.

Georgia World War I Memorial, dedicated April 6, 1998: The monument listed the 1,937 Georgians who were killed in the war. It also contained a map showing how the war unfolded, plus quotes from President Woodrow Wilson and General John J. Pershing, and poems associated with the war.

In October 1993, the Governor presided over a ceremony adding the names of the 1,584 Georgians killed in the Vietnam War to the state's Vietnam Memorial, which is also located at the Floyd Veterans Memorial Building in Atlanta.

Georgia War Veterans Cemetery in Milledgeville

In FY 1998, $686,260 was appropriated for the development and construction of a state veterans cemetery, the first of its kind for Georgia's war veterans. While there were already two national cemeteries in Georgia, one of them, in Marietta, had been full since 1978, and the other, in Andersonville, was a considerable distance from many of the state's 700,000 veterans and their families. The new state cemetery covered 58 acres of land and included 12,000 burials sites, a 12-acre water retention lake, a ceremonial area, a maintenance facility, and a committal shelter. The cemetery was projected to be completed by November 1999.

Significant Capital Outlay Projects

Central facility of the Georgia Public Health Laboratory

In FY 1995, the Governor recommended and the General Assembly approved bond funds for a state-of-the-art Public Health Laboratory. For over 30 years, the state's laboratory had been housed near the Capitol in the Health Building on Trinity Avenue. Concerns for safety and appropriate space led to the construction of the new laboratory, which tested specimens from public and private health care providers and agencies statewide, and provided laboratory support for investigations of disease outbreaks and public health programs.

The new 68,000-square-foot central facility on Clairmont Road in Decatur was a measure of the Governor's commitment to improving the public's health in Georgia. A beautiful building, with an exterior of Georgia granite blocks and recycled copper shingles, was completed under budget ($10.2 million) and ahead of schedule. The airy and open laboratory had space for staff and equipment that would carry it into the next century, and included special laboratory areas with safety features that allowed for testing for airborne pathogenic materials like tuberculosis, for fungal specimens and for other disease agents. In addition to a range of microbiology/ immunology and chemistry units, the building included training and teaching capability and space for environmental health testing.

The Public Health Laboratory building was selected as the recipient of R&D Magazine's 1998 "Laboratory of the Year" Award. With this award, the building joined the ranks of facilities such as Bell Laboratories and Genencor International Technology Center, and was the only state public health facility to ever receive the award.

New forensics unit

For FY 1999, the Governor recommended and the General Assembly approved $17.8 million in bonds to construct a 196-bed maximum security forensics building at Central State Hospital in Milledgeville. Georgia's existing 90-bed forensics unit was built in 1946 and was not designed to be a maximum security treatment facility. However, it housed the state's highest risk forensics patients, including persons found not guilty by reason of insanity or incompetent to stand trial, and inmates from the Department of Corrections who required psychiatric hospitalization. The overcrowding at the old facility created risk management concerns in terms of patient escapees and patient and staff security. Additionally, less secure regional hospitals were having to maintain higher risk forensic patients. A consultant retained by the Departments of Human Resources and Corrections estimated that the state should have a capacity of between 150 to 200 beds, and that the facility design should include the ability to expand in 50-bed increments to meet future demand.

IV. Economic Development

In today's economic climate, growing jobs at home requires some of the same things as attracting them from other places—good schools, a positive business climate, targeted infrastructure improvement, coordination and planning in our development efforts... We have to have a comprehensive strategy that fits all of the state's investments and many programs into a big picture like pieces of a jigsaw puzzle.

Governor Zell Miller, May 19, 1993

Governor's Development Council

In the past, we thought of development as something we brought in from outside our borders. In the future, we must think of development as something we produce from within, but that links up with emerging trends in every corner of the global economy.

Governor Zell Miller, November 23, 1992

When Governor Zell Miller took office in 1991, Georgia was in the midst of a recession, and the economic outlook for the 1990s was not favorable. Industries which had traditionally been the mainstay of Georgia's economy were suffering as a result of global market forces. Governor Miller recognized the fundamental shifts taking place in the economy and committed his administration to reorienting the state so that Georgia could become competitive in the new economic environment.

Recognizing the need to cultivate a "new infrastructure" in order to compete in a global, knowledge-based economy, Governor Miller committed his administration to strengthening the state's economic foundations. During the eight years of his administration, Miller strove to employ new approaches to economic development. These new approaches included public-private partnerships; comprehensive strategic planning and targeting the state's development resources; investment in the development of cutting edge technology and its transfer to the private sector; promotion of a skilled workforce; assistance to existing industry; a focus on expanding international trade; and investment in the rural areas of the state. Together, these new approaches were employed to promote a high quality of life throughout the state and to make Georgia a better place to do business.

Prior to the Miller Administration, Georgia's economic development efforts were focused almost exclusively on industrial recruitment, in particular large Fortune 500 corporations, with no particular effort to target firms meeting Georgia's particular needs. While Governor Miller realized the success that this approach had brought to the state, he saw the need for a new approach to economic development to prepare the state to compete in the new millennium. He decided the best mechanism for achieving this shift was a newly constituted Governor's Development Council embodying a true public-private partnership.

The tool Zell Miller chose was not a new one—the Governor's Development Council had been created in 1989 under Governor Harris—but the Miller Administration's approach to the GDC plowed new ground. Under Governor Harris, the GDC had been a forum for agency heads to discuss common issues and problems. However, this discussion did not lead to the development of coordinated strategies. During his first year in office, Governor Miller envisioned a new Council composed of both agency heads and private business leaders. Realizing effective economic development required all of the state's resources, public and private, to be brought to bear on the issues, Governor Miller sponsored legislation reconstituting the GDC to include representatives of a broad range of business and industry. This new GDC, composed of nine private and six public sector members, was charged first with assessing where Georgia was in terms of all aspects of economic development and then creating a statewide economic development strategy to focus and leverage the state's resources for maximal results. J. Mac Holladay, who had substantial experience formulating economic development strategies for several states, was hired as chief operating officer of the Council. He and a small staff with assistance from many agencies crafted an innovative economic development strategy for the council and the Governor.

Additionally, the Governor leveraged the state's investment in the GDC to obtain private funding. The Georgia Corporation for Economic Development, a nonprofit organization composed of representatives from private sector organizations with a vital interest in the economic health of the state, was created to obtain private resources for and to help promote the state's economic development efforts. With this valuable support, the Governor transformed Georgia's approach to economic development.

Strategic planning

Governor Miller and the Development Council saw the need for a comprehensive planning effort which focused available state resources where there was the greatest promise of reward. In 1994, the GDC produced the first state strategic plan for economic development to integrate all of the state's resources, public and private, to meet the challenges of competing in the 21st century.

During the next several years, the council worked with the Governor to put into place policies and mechanisms to implement and strengthen this plan. One key GDC effort was the promotion of a regional focus on economic development. Statewide, 11 regions were created outside Atlanta to bring together regional resources to develop regional strategic plans. This effort ultimately culminated in the Governor's FY 1999 initiative to place regional specialists in 12 regions throughout the state for strategic planning and economic development assistance.

By 1997, the council had accomplished its mission and was dissolved by the Governor. However, as recommended by the GDC, the strategic planning process was institutionalized with the creation of the Strategic Planning and Research Division within the Department of Industry, Trade, and Tourism (DITT) to take over the comprehensive strategic planning efforts begun by the GDC.

Targeting industries with potential

Under Governor Miller's leadership, the Department of Industry, Trade, and Tourism began targeting industries and markets which offered the greatest potential for business recruitment, expansion, or export growth. By the end of his administration, DITT's business recruitment project managers and international trade specialists both worked in industrial sectors that offered the greatest potential for the state.

This targeting approach was pioneered by Georgia Power and NationsBank in partnership with the Georgia Department of Industry, Trade and Tourism through Operation Legacy, which very successfully marketed the state prior to and during the 1996 Olympic Games. Operation Legacy targeted seven primary industry areas: advanced communications, aerospace, automotive, agribusiness, information-related industries, electronics and the sports industry. Over 400 companies were exposed to Georgia and its business opportunities, and 125 companies took part in Legacy Community Tours during the Games with 20 Georgia communities acting as hosts for these tours. Thirty-four new Georgia locations and expansions were completed by companies that took part in Operation Legacy programs. These new locations and expansions created over 5,600 jobs and led to capital investments of over $250 million in the state.

The success of Operation Legacy led Governor Miller to fold Operation Legacy into GDITT as a new division, expanding its membership and using its approach to market Georgia. This division became part of a public-private partnership that carried on a targeted marketing effort focused on bringing the nation's most promising businesses to Georgia.

One clear target of Governor Miller and the GDC was the advanced telecommunications industry. Governor Miller realized that global market opportunities, the evolving capacity of advanced communications, and the deregulation of the telephone industry provided a clear opportunity for Georgia to capitalize on its assets. The state's high quality of life, robust business climate, unique educational opportunities, non-traditional incentives, and the presence of the Georgia Center for Advanced Telecommunications Technology (GCATT), offered fertile ground for the development of this industry. Based on this vision, the Governor's Development Council laid out a strategy to establish the state as the preeminent global center of advanced telecommunications by 2010. This strategy included expanding the economic development potential of GCATT, working with the Public Service Commission to promote telecommunications competition in Georgia, marketing the state's telecommunications advantages, developing the highly skilled workforce required by the industry, and providing venture capital and other assistance to entrepreneurs in the field. The goal was announced by Governor Miller at the dedication of the GCATT building in 1996: "By the end of the first decade of the new century, we intend to be the premier center in the world for advanced telecommunications."

Assisting existing businesses

Another fundamental shift in the state's economic development paradigm came from a broadening of the state's economic activities to include assistance to existing Georgia businesses to encourage and facilitate expansion. Toward this end, a key part of the Governor's Business Expansion Support Act of 1994 (BEST) was the provision, for the first time in the state's history, of tax incentives for existing companies undergoing expansions. These incentives for expanding companies were the same as those offered to companies relocating to the state.

In addition to BEST, several programs were developed or expanded to increase assistance to existing business. Governor Miller and the GDC supported expansion of the international trade program within the Department of Industry, Trade and Tourism to provide increased assistance to Georgia firms interested in exporting. The council recommended and the Governor obtained funding for a new state export finance loan program for Georgia's small and medium sized companies who might not qualify for EXIM bank financing, but were still good credit risks.

Finally, Governor Miller and the GDC recognized that in many areas of the state, businesses and communities could not progress and deal with common problems unless regional economic development approaches and strategies were devised. The GDC encouraged regional partnerships of businesses and communities, but many of them struggled because of the lack of support staff and operating funds. In 1998, Governor Miller successfully maneuvered an initiative through the General Assembly to significantly strengthen this regional approach to economic development. This regional initiative placed community and economic development specialists from the Departments of Community Affairs and Industry, Trade and Tourism in 12 regions throughout the state. These specialists, in concert with other state resources and personnel, helped regions act together for economic development, focusing particularly on assisting existing industry in each region with growth and expansion. The specialists also helped the regions formulate effective economic development strategies and worked with regional policy advisory councils on all aspects of community and economic development.

Developing and transferring new technologies

The Governor recognized the increasing importance of commercializing new technologies in order to find new core industries for the state and to create higher value-added jobs. He worked to foster partnerships between state universities and companies, both to spur innovation and to facilitate the transfer of new knowledge into the private sector. In FY 1993, Governor Miller made state government a partner in a major effort to improve Georgia's research capabilities in emerging technology areas that offered significant potential for economic and industrial growth. Through the Georgia Research Alliance (GRA), a partnership of the state's six research universities, private business and state government, public and private funds were applied toward advanced research facilities, endowments to attract eminent scholars, and research grants in telecommunications, environmental technology, and biotechnology. The chairman of the GRA Board was also a member of the Governor's Development Council.

Additionally, in FY 1994, the Governor proposed the Traditional Industries Program (TIP) to improve the competitiveness of three of the state's most important traditional manufacturing industries: pulp and paper, textile and apparel, and food processing. As part of TIP, the Governor invested in technical assistance, research and development, and technology transfer to these three historically important industries.

Workforce development

A further step in creating a "new infrastructure" for the state's economic development was an emphasis on developing a skilled workforce that was adaptable to the needs of the 21st century. Clearly, a focus on improving education in Georgia was central to the Miller Administration. However, in addition to landmark educational programs which would generate important long-term rewards, Governor Miller also worked to improve the structures that helped companies meet immediate workforce needs. During the Miller Administration, over $212 million was invested in the construction of new technical education facilities at 41 sites. Another $104 million was invested in equipment for technical education facilities.

Moreover, the Governor stressed the importance of a comprehensive strategy for meeting the state's workforce needs. In 1997 he appointed a Workforce Taskforce, composed of both public and private sector representatives, to consider the status of the state's human resources and labor force needs and make recommendations. In 1998, a key recommendation of the taskforce, the creation of a Governor's Workforce Policy and Planning Council, became a reality. This body was responsible for recommending comprehensive workforce development policies to the Governor and for ensuring that all the state's resources, public and private, in workforce development were effectively utilized.

Rural development

At the same time as the Governor increased the state's focus on assisting existing businesses, he also highlighted the need to provide additional incentives and assistance to businesses operating in rural areas. The Business Expansion Support Act of 1994 provided increased tax incentives for firms relocating or expanding in those areas of the state most in need of development.

The Governor also invested in infrastructure to assist these areas in developing. During his administration, $1 billion was invested in developmental highways to facilitate access to Georgia's more remote areas. In addition, $7.5 million of the Regional Economic Business Assistance grants allocated between January 1994 and April 1998, went to 32 projects located in rural Georgia.

Finally, the Governor instituted programs to meet the development needs of rural communities. First, based upon GDC recommendations, the Governor created the Georgia Academy for Economic Development, a training program for local leaders, to address the most critical element in the development process. Additionally, with his Fiscal Year (FY) 1999 regional initiative, the Governor placed regional representatives throughout the state charged with identifying the economic development needs of each region. This information was to be folded into the state's strategic plan for economic development, ensuring that rural Georgia would be fully represented in economic development planning and service delivery.

Results: Success

There can be little doubt that Governor Miller's efforts to steer Georgia from a traditional, industrial economy to a knowledge-based economy in the global marketplace yielded substantial rewards for the state. Georgia's Gross State Product increased by over $80 million between 1990 and 1998, an increase of 52 percent. Between 1990 and 1997, growth in Georgia's GSP was almost 17 percentage points higher than growth in the national Gross Domestic Product.

This growth translated into better opportunities for Georgia's citizens. Over 4,500 more new jobs and almost $2 billion more in capital investment were created by Georgia's new and expanding manufacturing companies in 1997 than in 1990. Cumulatively, *Forbes* magazine credited Georgia with creating 622,000 new jobs between 1990 and 1996 – an average of 2,166 new jobs per week. These new jobs helped to reduce Georgia's unemployment rate to 4.6 percent in 1997, a 33 percent decrease from when Governor Miller entered office.

In 1998, more than 3.6 million Georgians were working, more than at any other time in the state's history. Moreover, Georgia ranked first in the nation in the number of high-tech jobs created between 1990 and 1996. By 1998, 130,000 Georgians were employed in high-tech jobs compared to 86,000 in 1990.

More and better jobs brought increased incomes for Georgians. Under Governor Miller, the state's per capita income increased by 33.8 percent from $17,977 in 1990 to $24,061 in 1997, placing Georgia 12th in the U.S. in per capita income growth during this period. From 1992 to 1997, Georgia ranked ninth in the nation in per capita income growth, with a rate of 27 percent. As a result, both metropolitan and rural Georgians saw greater increases in per capita income than U.S. residents as a whole. From 1990 to 1995, per capita income increased by 28.2 percent in non-metropolitan Georgia ($13,601 to $17,436) and by 24.8 percent in Georgia's metropolitan areas ($19,255 to $24,030). These increases were significantly greater than the national non-metropolitan (22.1 percent) and metropolitan (21.6 percent) gains during the same period.

In addition to this rapid rate of growth, Georgia's per capita income approached the national average. In 1997, Georgia's per capita income reached 94 percent of the national average, placing Georgia third in the Southeast, behind only Virginia and Florida.

Not surprisingly, Georgia's noteworthy economic growth brought new people to the state. Between 1991 and 1997, Georgia's population grew by more than 13 percent, placing the state sixth in the nation in growth. In fact, Georgia was the only state east of the Mississippi River to rank in the nation's top 10 in terms of population growth. Moreover, three Georgia counties—Paulding, Forsyth, and Henry—were among the 10 fastest-growing counties in the nation between 1990 and 1996.

The Governor's Development Council

Governor Zell Miller
Chairman

Ray Weeks
Vice Chairman
Chairman of the Board
Weeks Corporation

Lonice Barrett
Commissioner
Georgia Department of Natural Resources

James H. Blanchard
Chairman
Synovus Financial Corporation

Tim Burgess
Director
Office of Planning and Budget

Paul Burks
Executive Director
Georgia Environmental Facilities Authority

Randolph B. Cardoza
Commissioner
Georgia Department of Industry, Trade, and Tourism

Thomas G. Cousins
Chairman of the Board and President
Cousins Properties

J. Mac Holladay
Chief Operating Officer

Allen Franklin
President and CEO
Georgia Power Company

Jim Higdon
Commissioner
Georgia Department of Community Affairs

Wayne Shackelford
Commissioner
Georgia Department of Transportation

William J. Vereen
President, Treasurer, and Chief Executive Officer
Riverside Manufacturing Company

Carl Ware
President, Africa Group
The Coca-Cola Company

John A. Williams
Chairman
Post Properties

Arthur Gignilliat, Jr. President and Chief Executive Officer Savannah Electric and Power Company	Marguerite Neel Williams General Partner Williams Investments, Ltd.

Note: Originally, Charlie Brown with Technology Park Atlanta was Vice Chairman. Also, Bill Dahlberg was on the Council when he headed Georgia Power.

Growth in Georgia's Gross State Product Outpaces

Growth in US Gross Domestic Product, 1990-1997

	US - GDP	Georgia - GSP
1990	5,743,800,000,000	140,093,000,000
1991	5,916,700,000,000	147,205,000,000
1992	6,244,400,000,000	158,770,000,000
1993	6,558,100,000,000	170,102,000,000
1994	6,947,000,000,000	183,042,000,000
1995	7,265,400,000,000	195,615,000,000
1996	7,636,000,000,000	208,577,000,000
1997	8,079,900,000,000	220,250,000,000
Growth 1990-1997	**40.67%**	**57.22%**

Top 10 States in Population Growth, 1990-1997

Nevada	30.71%
Arizona	21.53%
Idaho	16.35%
Utah	16.33%
Colorado	15.25%
Georgia	**13.03%**
Texas	12.05%
Washington	11.93%
New Mexico	11.68%
Oregon	10.99%
Delaware	10.91%

Georgia's New and Expanded Manufacturing Industry Announcements, 1990-1997

	New Industries			Expanded Industries			New & Expanded Industries		
	Companies	Jobs Created	Capital Investment	Companies	Jobs Created	Capital Investment	Companies	Jobs Created	Capital Investment
1990	164	7,725	574,335,807	397	2,814	983,827,681	561	10,539	1,558,163,488
1991	126	6,852	345,492,636	382	4,312	752,794,870	508	11,164	1,098,287,506
1992	134	7,236	363,270,129	430	5,586	1,710,070,005	564	12,822	2,073,340,134
1993	110	4,461	271,012,368	447	9,340	1,542,813,629	557	13,801	1,813,825,997
1994	132	9,763	746,899,408	532	6,886	1,697,537,508	664	16,649	2,444,436,916
1995	136	9,823	795,295,450	655	9,723	2,335,544,355	791	19,546	3,130,839,805
1996	97	5,607	1,824,111,163	242	6,430	968,579,436	339	12,037	2,792,690,599
1997	114	8,243	1,954,000,000	269	6,817	1,525,000,000	383	15,060	3,479,000,000
Total	1,013	59,710	6,874,416,961	3,354	51,908	11,516,167,484	4,367	111,618	18,390,584,445

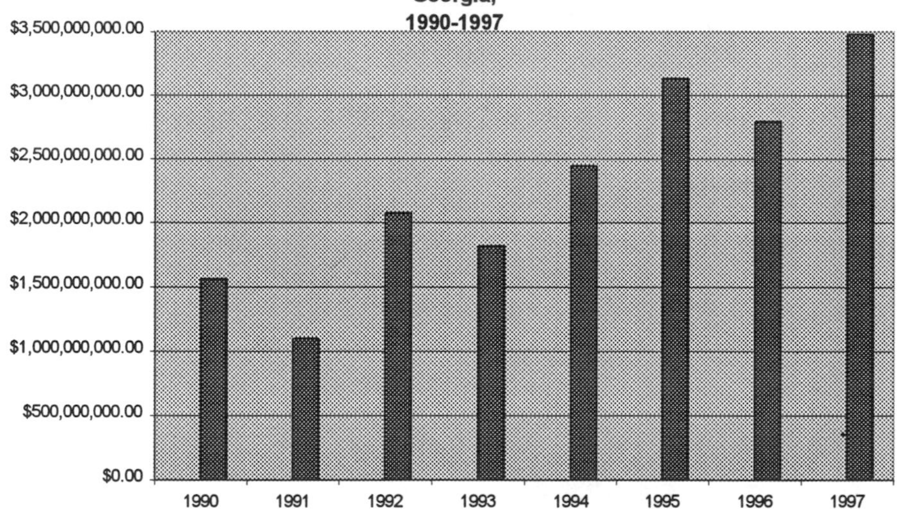

Percent Change in Per Capita Income (1990 - 1995)

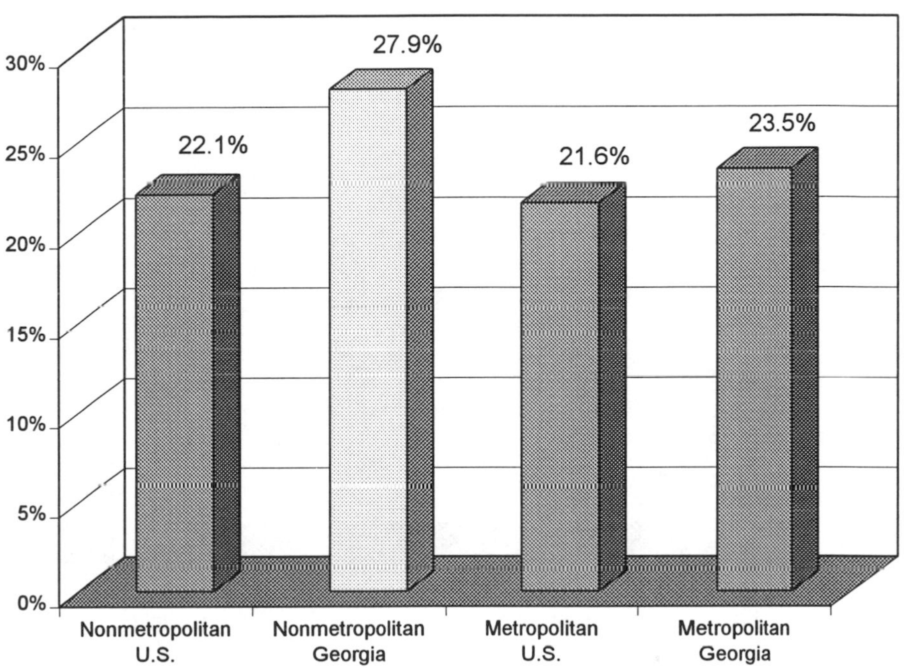

Focus on Existing Industry

The ongoing health of the businesses that are already here is extremely important. After all, eight of ten new jobs are created within exiting businesses....If we're so busy concentrating on out-of-state recruitment that we don't take time for our existing industries, we're going to lose jobs faster than we gain them.

Governor Zell Miller, May 19, 1993

Economic development regions

Governor Miller placed a strong emphasis on regionalism and regional development in his eight years in office. Through the Governor's Development Council he fostered regional economic development utilizing grants, technology and tax credit incentives. He provided planning standards to guide the preparation of regional comprehensive plans by the Regional Development Centers of the state and oversaw their implementation. The end of 1998 saw the completion of regional plans covering the state.

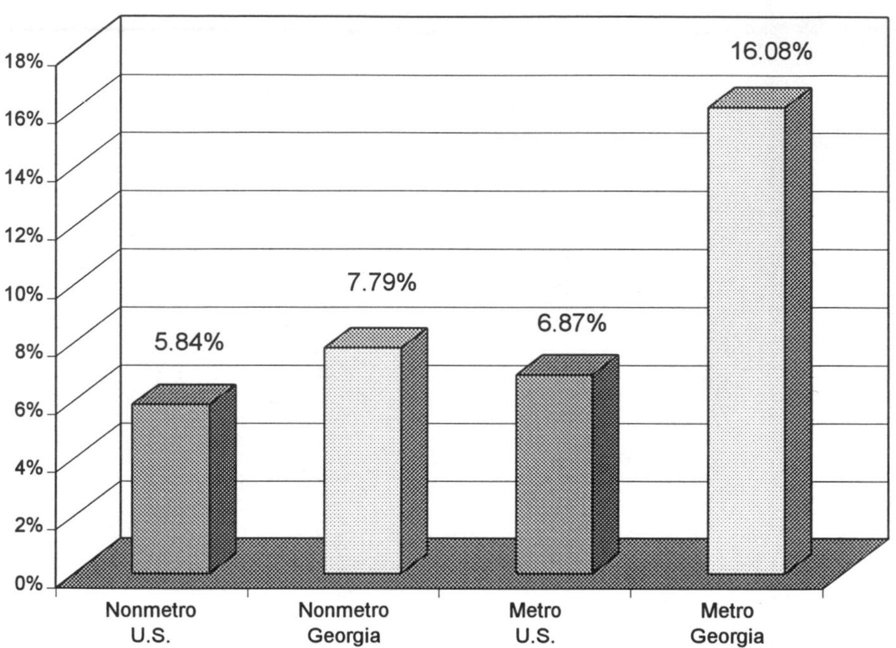

The Governor worked to ensure that the state offered incentives for regionalism and regional development. One such incentive was the Regional Assistance Program (RAP). Implemented in 1997, RAP provided competitive grant funding for local governments, development authorities and regional development centers for regional projects. Eligible projects included industrial parks, water and sewer treatment facilities, transportation and communication facilities, marketing and recruitment programs, tourism and other projects important to regional economic development. In the first year of RAP, six projects involving 18 counties were selected to receive $1.75 million in funding.

Another regional incentive created by Governor Miller was the Regional Economic Business Assistance (REBA) Grants, which in addition to providing direct assistance for the expansion and relocation of individual companies, also funded regional infrastructure improvements. From REBA's creation in 1994 through April of 1998, 54 regional projects received $5.5 million from this program. In addition to the Regional Assistance Program and REBA, the State of Georgia acted as co-applicant with local governments

Georgia State Development Regions
House Bill 1650 (12)

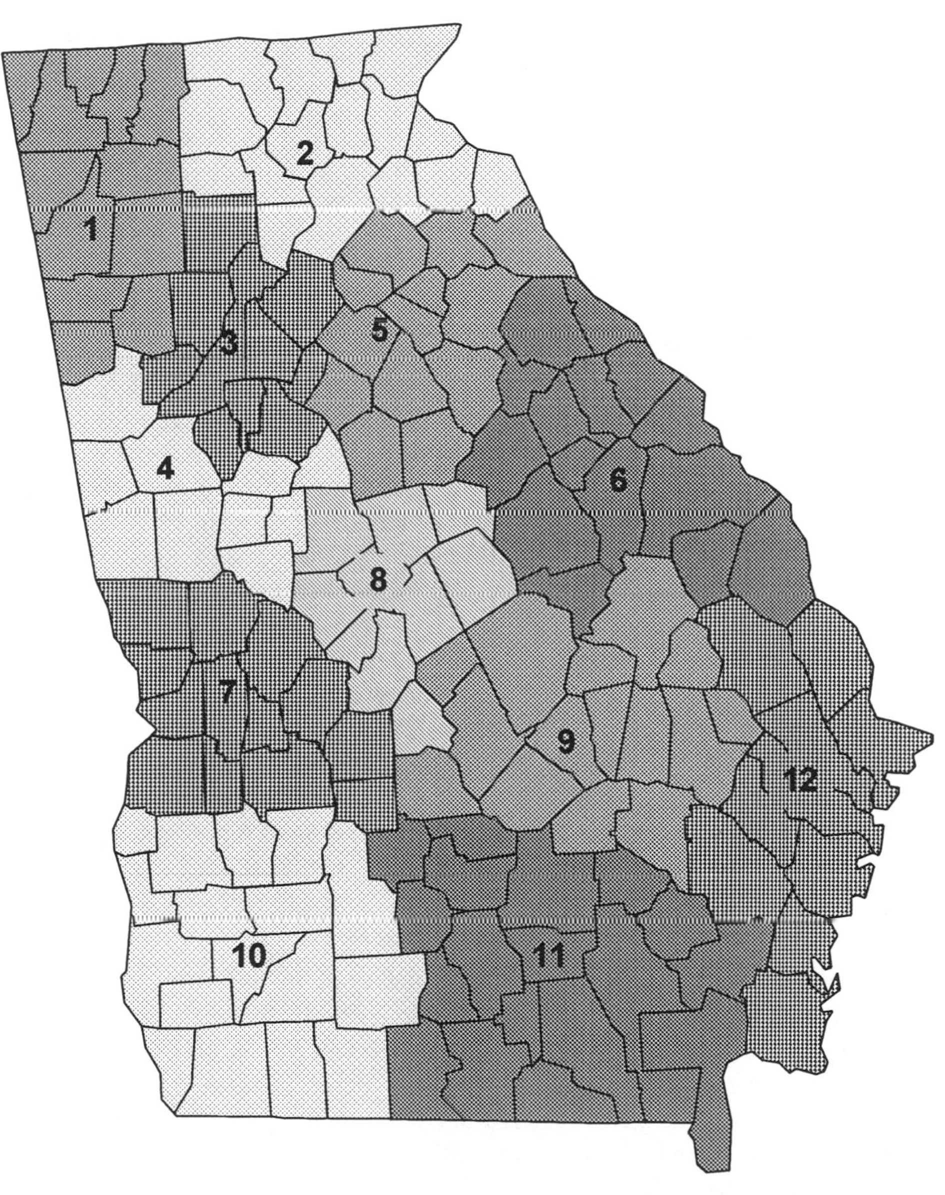

As of July 1, 1998

to obtain four designations and $109 million under the 1994 federal Empowerment Zone/Enterprise Community (EZ/EC) program. Atlanta (EZ) received $100 million; Albany (EC) received $3 million; Crisp and Dooly counties (EC) together received $3 million; and the Central Savannah River Area Regional Development Center (EC) received $3 million on behalf of six counties: Burke, Hancock, Jefferson, McDuffie, Taliaferro, and Warren.

The Governor infused technology into the state's regional planning and development by partnering the Department of Community Affairs and the state's 16 Regional Development Centers (RDCs) in the development of land use, community facilities and other Geographic Information Systems (GIS). He provided the fiscal resources necessary for local governments and/or RDCs to acquire hardware and software, aerial photography, digital orthophoto quadrangle photography, global positioning system (GPS) capability, networking capacity and systems training.

In response to requests from local officials and private sector leadership for uniform community and economic development regional boundaries and calls for state staff to be located outside of Atlanta, Governor Miller created 12 state community and economic development regions. These 12 regions were made law with the passage of House Bill 1650 in 1998. This 12-region configuration was adopted by the state's economic development community to serve as the foundation for future regional economic development planning and service-delivery efforts. The Governor invested over $4 million to staff the 11 non-Atlanta regional state development offices with four positions each. Two positions served as state resource coordinators, bringing state, federal and other players to the table on a variety of projects and opportunities. This staff also helped facilitate multi–jurisdictional efforts and provided technical assistance to local governments when needed. The other two positions included an economic development representative and a workforce development and planning officer.

Expanding Georgia's business assistance programs

Governor Miller recognized that the quality of life in Georgia depended on ensuring that businesses in the state flourished. Upon taking office, he found that the breadth and accessibility of services offered to Georgia businesses were limited. Consequently, providing increased assistance to existing businesses, stimulating entrepreneurs, and supporting the development of new companies were key components of the Governor's comprehensive economic development strategy. Realizing the importance of the assistance that Georgia Tech's Economic Development Institute (EDI) and the University of Georgia's Business Outreach Services(BOS) were providing to companies and entrepreneurs throughout the state, Governor Miller worked to increase both the breadth and accessibility of these programs.

Under Miller's leadership, the scope of services offered by EDI expanded beyond the traditional "industrial extension" role to include services such as performing economic impact assessments, providing assistance to companies seeking ISO certification to export to most international markets, and assisting businesses considering relocating or expanding in Georgia. Additionally, UGA's Business Outreach Services increased the number of its offices from 15 to 20. Finally, the state's involvement with growing new businesses through incubators increased, bringing some noteworthy successes.

During the Miller Administration, EDI received new state and federal funding to expand its regional office network from 13 to 19 locations in 1994. Ten of the 19 EDI regional offices were co-located with the UGA's Business Outreach Services, in an effort to increase cooperation and achieve cost savings. These regional offices provided management consultation primarily to small and medium sized companies to help increase productivity through the implementation of advanced technology. Between 1994 and 1997, Georgia companies reported over 2,000 jobs created or saved as a result of EDI's increased services, and client companies reported over $50 million in increased sales.

Governor Miller also provided funding for EDI to develop a tool to help Georgia's communities and regions evaluate the costs and benefits of proposed development in their areas. This Local Impact Model (LOCI), considered both the increased revenues brought into the community by the new investment and job growth, as well as the additional cost to the community of serving the new development. With this information, local governments could make more objective decisions about the desirability and magnitude of any incentives to be offered. Between 1995 and 1998, EDI used LOCI to analyze the impact of 58 prospective investments in new plants and equipment throughout the state. Of these, 16 resulted in plant announcements totaling over $382 million in new investment and more than 4,000 new jobs.

In 1995, EDI began helping businesses that were considering moving to or expanding within Georgia. EDI engineers and business specialists would spend 20 to 30 days helping companies prepare for and start new manufacturing operations quickly and efficiently. Companies were assisted with planning functions such as the design of plant layouts, identification of subcontractors, and the performance of market assessments and energy studies as well as with some implementation. Between 1995 and 1998, EDI aided more than 50 companies moving to or expanding operations in the state and also helped attract millions of dollars in subcontracting work to Georgia.

As an added service provided to companies beyond traditional "industrial extension" work, EDI assisted Georgia companies with achieving

ISO-9000 certification, which opened international export markets to them. This registration process required companies to adopt a quality management system that touched all facets of their business. EDI conducted training courses about ISO-9000 registration, assisted companies in the registration process, and conducted mock audits to give companies a "dry-run" before facing the extensive audit required for registration. EDI began certification assistance in 1991, and by 1998 it had assisted more than half of the 415-plus ISO-9000 certified companies in the state.

Governor Miller also realized that many small and medium sized companies in the state did not have sufficient knowledge of environmental and energy-saving technologies to meet environmental requirements in the most cost-effective manner. The Georgia Environmental Partnership (GEP), was established to focus the state's technical assistance providers on solving critical environmental issues facing Georgia businesses. GEP was a coalition of EDI, The University of Georgia's School of Biological and Agricultural Engineering, and the Pollution Prevention Assistance Division (P^2AD) of the Georgia Department of Natural Resources.

GEP leveraged the financial and human resources of its members to promote the adoption of pollution prevention, energy efficiency, and environmental compliance among companies of all sizes throughout the state. GEP also served as an outreach and training tool to reach companies in Georgia's most pollution intensive industries. By 1998, GEP representatives had participated in 10 major trade shows and environmental conferences in the state, and conducted six industry-specific workshops. Based on these initial successes, Governor Miller increased funding for the GEP in his FY 1999 budget to expand the partnership's regional environmental network system, which fostered awareness and mentoring, and to work toward the development of a recycling market for industrial wastes.

Governor Miller also worked to bring the services of UGA's Business Outreach Services (BOS) closer to businesses throughout the state. This Small Business Development Center (SBDC) program offered business consultation and training to small businesses and aspiring entrepreneurs. Under Governor Miller, Business Outreach Services expanded from 15 to 20 offices throughout the state. As a result, 87 percent of BOS' consulting and training personnel were located outside of the Athens area. The SBDC program consulted with more than 44,500 small business owners and aspiring entrepreneurs in Georgia during the Miller Administration. In all, more than 122,000 individuals attended the 6,700 business training programs offered around the state. The success of these programs was shown by an economic impact study of the SBDC program toward the end of the administration. This study indicated that businesses receiving SBDC assistance increased employment by 12.22 percent, while employment for all Georgia businesses increased by only 1.45 percent for the same time framework. The average increase in sales per business for SBDC clients was 15.4 percent compared to an average increase for all Georgia businesses of 7.4 percent.

Finally, Governor Miller worked to increase the state's involvement with growing new businesses. Under his leadership, Georgia invested over $24 million in the Georgia Center for Advanced Telecommunications Technology (GCATT), a high-tech communications research facility located adjacent to Georgia Tech and Turner Broadcasting in Atlanta. The development of this center was part of a broader strategy to make Georgia the premier center in the world of advanced telecommunications.

When GCATT opened in 1996, an additional $4 million was invested in the development of the state's third Advanced Technology Development Center (ATDC) business incubator, located within the center, which was devoted exclusively to start-up companies and landing parties in the fields of communications, computing and digital media. Demand for space at the 25,000 square foot ATDC incubator quickly outstripped availability, and within a year it was full with 14 companies located there.

Regional Offices Opened Under Governor Miller

Economic Development Institute	Business Outreach Services
Atlanta	Dalton
Dalton	Carrollton
Cartersville	LaGrange
Norcross	Warner Robbins
Morrow	Valdosta
Griffin	

With its first two incubators, one at Georgia Tech and the other in Warner Robins, ATDC came to be widely considered as one of the nation's premier university-associated economic development centers. In 1996, ATDC was selected from a field of 550 eligible incubators in North America as the unanimous winner of the Randall M. Whaley Award, conferred on the "outstanding business incubator of the year" by the National Business Incubator Association. Between 1994 and 1998, ATDC was incubating some 40 early

Regional Office Expansions
Business Assistance

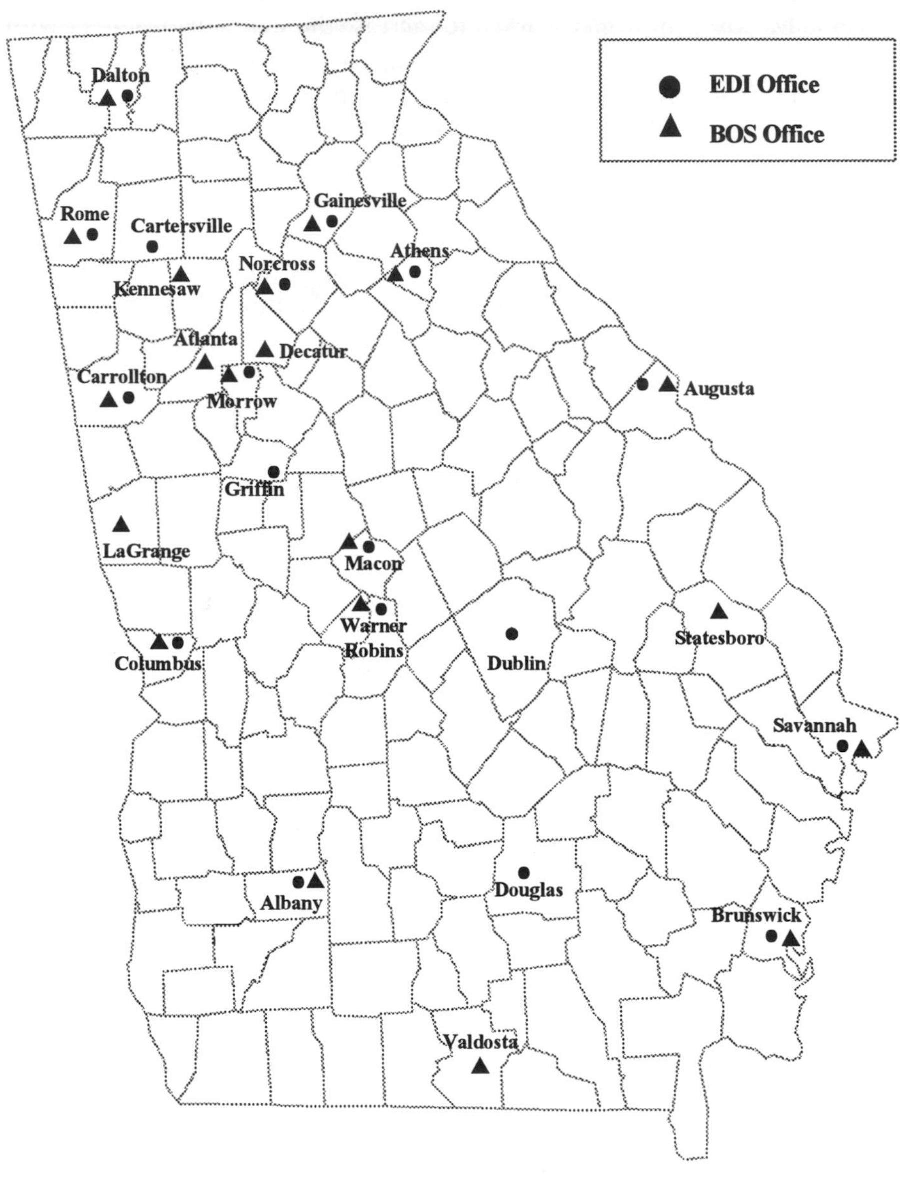

stage technology programs at any one time, and graduated 25 companies, including MindSpring. In 1997, ATDC member and graduate companies generated $340 million and employed nearly 2,800 people. Based on the success of the three ATDC incubators, Governor Miller funded three more in his FY 1999 budget to develop start-up companies in the life sciences, one of which utilized the facility that had been vacated by the closing of the Georgia Mental Health Institute.

Strengthening Georgia's international business position

As the global economy evolved over the last several decades of the 20th century, so did Georgia's level and type of interaction in the global market. In the 1970s, former Governor Carter led the state's first trade mission to Recife, Brazil, with the goal of increasing export opportunities for Georgia companies. However, the state's efforts were quickly diverted away from trade and toward attracting the "new wave" of foreign direct investment coming into the United States

The state's first overseas offices, in Brussels and Tokyo, were established under the Carter Administration in 1973 and 1974. Not long afterward, newly-elected Governor Busbee spearheaded the formation of the Southeast U.S.-Japan Association, followed several years later by the creation of the Southeast U.S.-Korea Association. In 1981, an additional foreign office was established in Canada to recruit direct investment from Canada to Georgia. Governor Harris furthered this effort to attract foreign investment in 1985 with the establishment of a contract with a consulting firm in Korea focused principally on promoting investment in Georgia.

In the early 1980s there was a renewed awareness of export opportunities and a recognition among the states that trade promotion needed to be an important element of any international economic development plan. By 1984, Georgia had a small international trade unit with a nominal budget. It disseminated international trade leads, offered limited export counseling services, and encouraged Georgia companies to participate in international trade shows. During the second half of the Harris Administration, the budget and level of activity of this trade unit gradually increased, reaching $500,000 with a seven-person staff in 1990. In 1987, Georgia's first overseas contract principally for the promotion of Georgia exports was established with a trade representative in Taiwan.

Georgia's international economic development efforts surged ahead under Governor Miller with major efforts in both trade promotion and recruitment of new foreign direct investment to the state. Successes in both of these areas placed Georgia on the map as a global center of commerce.

International trade promotion: At the beginning of his administration, Governor Miller launched his International Trade Initiative, which was officially announced at a Georgia Chamber of Commerce Prelegislative Forum in 1991. The goal of this initiative was to bring international trade to a position of importance and prominence in Georgia's economic development efforts. When Miller assumed office in January 1991, the state was well behind the nation in exports. Recognizing the increasing globalization of commerce, Governor Miller established the International Trade Division within the Department of Industry, Trade, and Tourism to encourage and assist Georgia companies to do business internationally. This move was part

Georgia's International Representation

Location	Administration	Date
Brussels, Belgium	Carter	1973
Tokyo, Japan	Carter	1974
Toronto, Canada	Busbee	1981
Seoul, South Korea	Harris	1985
Hsin Chu City, Taiwan	Harris	1987
Mexico City, Mexico	Miller	1993
Shanghai, China	Miller	1996
Greenpoint, South Africa	Miller	1996
Jerusalem, Israel	Miller	1996
Kuala Lampur, Malaysia	Miller	1996
Sao Paolo, Brazil	Miller	1996

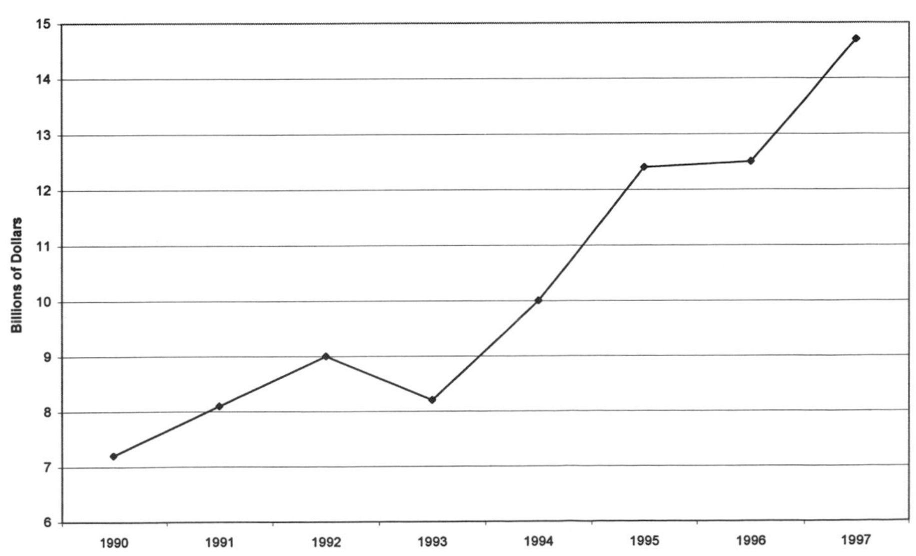

of Governor Miller's efforts to assist existing businesses in Georgia. By the end of his administration, this progeny of the tiny original international trade unit, was responsible for promoting the sale of Georgia products and services abroad and for coordinating all aspects of international trade and export in the state.

The International Trade Division worked to create an export culture in Georgia by encouraging small and medium sized businesses to do business internationally. In September 1995, the Regional Export Assistance Center (EAC) opened, making Georgia the only southeastern state to integrate federal and state export programs. This federal-state partnership brought together trained export specialists from the US Department of Commerce, the State Department of Industry, Trade and Tourism, the EXIM Bank, the Small Business Administration and other organizations to assist Georgia companies in evaluating their export potential, finding appropriate international markets, planning market entry, and obtaining export financing.

During Governor Miller's administration the center responded to over 7,640 information requests and received over 2,660 visitors. Center staff also responded to over 10,000 customer requests through telephone assistance, in person consultation, or through assistance with the center's resource library. To further assist small businesses, Governor Miller created an export revolving loan fund, called the Georgia Export Finance Fund, capitalized by $2 million in state appropriations. Georgia companies were also given access to federal export funding through the EAC. During the first two years of the center's operation, 1995 to 1997, Georgia exports rose by $2.3 billion – an increase of 18.5 percent.

Another key aspect of Governor Miller's focus on international trade was targeting specific markets and industries with superior export potential. First, Governor Miller dramatically expanded Georgia's representation internationally. Under Governor Miller, Georgia entered into contracts with trade representatives in Mexico, Brazil, China, Southeast Asia, the Middle East, and South Africa to promote Georgia products and services. Additionally, the Governor maintained representatives in Tokyo, Brussels, Canada, Taiwan, and Korea. As a result of these contracts, Georgia's exports to Canada, Japan, and Mexico, the state's primary trading partners, remained strong, and the state's exports to emerging markets increased notably. For example, under Governor Miller the state's business with Mexico increased by 95 percent, placing Georgia third in the U.S. for five of Miller's last seven years in terms of exports to Mexico. In the first year of Georgia's Brazil contract, which was initiated in 1996, exports to that country increased by almost 30 percent.

At the same time he was broadening Georgia's markets, Governor Miller targeted specific industries, focusing the state's resources on those with the most promise for exports. In addition to growth potential, the existence of numerous small and medium sized companies within a given industrial sector was particularly important in the selection of targeted industries. The new targeted approach enabled Georgia to expand successfully in several new product areas, while still maintaining a solid performance from the state's traditionally strong export products, such as paper. The state's performance in the high-tech sector was especially impressive. Exports of industrial machinery and computers rose by 90 percent between 1990 and 1996. Electrical equipment showed a 118 percent gain, and medical and optical instruments increased by 206 percent during this period.

This attention paid off for the state. Under Governor Miller's leadership, Georgia's total exports increased by 104 percent from $7.2 billion in 1990 to $14.7 billion in 1997. In 1997, Georgia ranked 15th in the U.S. in terms of dollar value of exports. Most importantly, exports increased as a share of Georgia's economy. In 1990, export goods were 5.15 percent of Gross State Product; in 1997, exports made up 6.7 percent of GSP. In all, it is estimated that 114,000 jobs were created due to increased exports during the Miller Administration.

Georgia's Exports to Targeted Markets

Market	1990 Exports	1997 Exports	Total Growth	Percentage Growth
Brazil	71,646,000	549,246,000	477,600,000	666.6%
Canada	1,253,818,000	2,912,016,000	1,658,198,000	132.3%
China	49,192,000	257,944,000	208,752,000	424.4%
Europe	2,166,629,000	3,707,229,000	1,540,600,000	71.1%
Israel	54,329,000	107,810,000	53,481,000	98.4%
Japan	717,932,000	1,454,047,000	736,115,000	102.5%
Korea	265,466,000	260,990,000	-4,476,000	-1.7%
Mexico	435,118,000	823,686,000	388,568,000	89.3%
South Africa	45,153,000	165,197,000	120,044,000	265.9%
Southeast Asia	225,612,000	680,309,000	454,697,000	201.5%
Taiwan	177,465,000	295,795,000	118,330,000	66.7%
TOTAL TARGETED COUNTRIES	**$5,462,360,000**	**$11,214,269,000**	**$5,751,909,000**	**105.3%**

Recruiting international businesses to Georgia: In addition to encouraging and promoting Georgia exports abroad, the Department of Industry, Trade, and Tourism under Governor Miller was successful in recruiting foreign companies to Georgia. Governor Miller's commitment to travel where needed to close these international deals was an important factor in this success. In 1997 alone, 30 new companies were brought to Georgia from overseas, creating 3,840 jobs and over $1.5 billion dollars in capital investment. These included a manufacturer of convertible and truck tops employing 250 people in Eastman, a company producing polyester fiber employing 1,800 in Augusta, a manufacturer of ice-making machines employing 200 people in Griffin, a company producing wood chip products employing 150 people in Cleveland, and a PVC pipe manufacturer employing 150 people in Adel. In addition, 41 existing foreign-owned companies in Georgia expanded in 1997, creating 1,050 new jobs and investing over $200 million in the state.

Announced International Investment, 1990-1997

Year	Investment
1990	938,653,117
1991	678,951,320
1992	305,455,933
1993	898,394,585
1994	787,180,818
1995	958,715,674
1996	1,888,880,949
1997	1,908,869,210
TOTAL	$8,365,101,606

Total Investment from Counties with Georgia Foreign Offices, 1990-1997

Foreign Office Location	Investment
Canada	$492,296,641
Japan	$1,689,944,688
European Union:	
Austria	3,377,540
Belgium	83,529,168
Denmark	106,061,875
Finland	19,447,805
France	157,701,364
Germany	424,711,692
Ireland	15,006,162
Italy	58,892,658
Luxembourg	135,000
Netherlands	231,579,035
Spain	30,750,000
Sweden	429,867,511
United Kingdom	870,109,934
Total EU	$2,431,169,744

Governor Miller's Business Recruitment Missions & Trade Missions

Trade Mission	Dates	Cities Visited
Austria/Switzerland/Germany	5/26/91-6/1/91	Vienna, Zurich, Stuttgart
Japan	10/2/91-10/9/91	Tokyo
United Kingdom	4/21/92-4/30/92	Manchester, London
Taiwan/Hong Kong/Singapore	8/24/92-9/4/92	Taipei, Hong Kong, Singapore
*Germany/Italy/Belgium	4/14/94/30/93	Munich, Rimini, Bologna, Milan, Brussels
Mexico	9/1/93-9/3/93	Mexico City
Japan	10/3/93-10/15/93	Osaka, Kyoto, Kagoshima, Nagoya
Finland/Sweden	4/24/95-4/29/95	Gotenborg, Stockholm, Helsinki
France	6/12/95-6/17/95	Paris, Lyon
Japan/Korea/Australia	10/2/95-10/15/95	Tokyo, Seoul, Canberra, Melbourne
Germany	6/11/96-6/19/96	Frankfurt, Heidelberg, Berlin, Dusseldorf, Karlsruhe, Cologne
United Kingdom/Denmark	10/5/96-10/12/96	London, Copenhagen
◆ Canada	5/19/97-5/23/97	Montreal, Toronto
◆ South Africa	6/21/97-6/26/97	Johannesburg, Durban, Capetown
◆ Brazil/Argentina	7/14/97-7/18/97	Sao Paulo, Buenos Aires, La Plata
Japan/Korea	10/2/97-10/10/97	Tokyo, Seoul
Germany	7/12/98-7/18/98	Stuttgart, Munich
Netherlands/United Kingdom	9/20/98-9/26/98	Amsterdam, London

***Lt. Gov, Pierre Howard represented Governor in Germany and Italy, Governor joined mission in Belgium.**

GDITT Missions

France	3/21/94-3/26/94	Nice, Paris
◆ Brazil/Argentina	8/19/95-8/25/95	Rio De Janeiro, Sao Paulo, Buenos Aires
Italy	5/25/96-6/1/96	Florence, Rimini, Parma
◆China	5/17/98-5/24/98	Hong Kong, Shanghai, Nanjing, Beijing

◆ Trade missions which included recruited Georgia companies as participant

Tourism

Georgia's tourism and travel industry grew steadily in importance in the late 1970s and throughout the 1980s, especially with the growth of the state's convention business. However, beginning in the early 1990s the pace of growth of Georgia's tourism and travel industry accelerated significantly. In 1991 a study conducted by the Department of Industry, Trade and Tourism (DITT) showed that the industry had a direct $10 billion impact on the Georgia economy. By 1997 that impact had grown to $16 billion. Between

1991 and 1997, tourism jobs grew from approximately 360,000 to 495,000 – a 37 percent increase, and income paid to industry workers grew from $6 billion to $11 billion.

In nurturing and supporting the growth of the tourism and travel industry, Governor Miller provided critical state infrastructure, worked with local communities and regions on product development, began new marketing initiatives and focused more attention on letting Georgians know what travel opportunities are available right here in Georgia. This focus was based on the realization that, for certain regions and communities in the state, the tourism and travel industry was the most important industry and the greatest opportunity for growth and development.

Governor Miller's largest and most important infrastructure investment for the tourism and travel industry was the expansion of the Georgia World Congress Center (GWCC). This investment included $75 million for exhibit space expansion (Phase III), $31 million for the GWCC Plaza and parking deck, and $10.5 million for the planning and design of the $200 million Phase IV expansion of the GWCC. These infrastructure investments kept the GWCC and Atlanta among the top five cities in the country in convention and trade show business. Phase IV would assure that Atlanta maintained that position throughout the next decade.

To ensure that tourists coming to Georgia by road were impressed by Georgia's hospitality and welcomed properly to the state, Governor Miller provided the support and funding to replace three outdated facilities at Ringgold (I-75 North), Lavonia (I-85 North) and Augusta (I-20 East) with larger and new state-of-the-art visitor information centers. These centers cost a total of $30 million, but required only $5 million from the state to match $25 million in federal funding. Ringgold and Lavonia were replaced and opened before the 1996 Olympics. In addition, the Governor provided over $500,000 in capital repairs to 11 visitor centers prior to the Olympics so that Georgia would be ready to welcome the world.

During Governor Miller's administration, over 1.25 billion visitors passed through the 11 state Visitor Information Centers. To ensure that adequate maintenance of these heavily used centers continued, in FY 1999 Governor Miller proposed and the General Assembly approved the transfer of the maintenance of these Centers to the Department of Transportation (DOT).

Growth in the tourism industry depended on the tourist or convention "product" that communities and regions had to sell to travelers, so another emphasis of the state's tourism development program under Governor Miller was improving and expanding that product. The Department of Industry, Trade and Tourism, through its regional tourism representatives and through two contractors, placed increased emphasis on hospitality training for the industry and re-energized and expanded the Main Street program that primarily benefited small cities and towns in rural Georgia.

Governor Miller also worked with a number of local communities on adding to their tourism product base. In FY 1994, the Governor worked with the mountain region and the Department of Natural Resources on the development of the Brasstown Valley resort. The $24.7 million resort included a main lodge and associated villas (135 rooms), a 175 seat restaurant, meeting rooms, a golf course and other recreational amenities. The Stormont-Trice Corporation (a resort development and operation company) became a partner with the state in the resort, constructing it and contracting with the state for its long-term operation and maintenance. The resort provided a major anchor that helped to spur the growth of the tourism industry in North Georgia.

Two projects in Macon also represented a significant expansion of Georgia's tourism product. With Governor Miller's strong leadership, the city of Macon and the Macon Chamber of Commerce partnered with the state to develop and promote the Georgia Music Hall of Fame and the Georgia Sports Hall of Fame. The geographic centrality of Macon and the revitalization efforts underway in downtown Macon made the city an ideal location for the Halls of Fame. Macon's downtown revitalization efforts were targeted at expanding its convention facilities and renovating facilities and public areas to attract more visitors. The two Halls of Fame provided the vital extra "products" needed to significantly increase the attraction of visitors to Macon.

Additionally, Governor Miller provided funding for Savannah, Augusta and Albany to improve their tourist/convention "product." The state's investment in the Georgia International and Maritime Trade Center in Savannah provided the city with the convention and trade show facilities needed to meet a demand that the city had been unable to accommodate for years. A new convention hotel was constructed by private investors adjacent to the center.

The development of Fort Discovery in Augusta was a vital addition necessary to attract visitors to the Riverwalk area in downtown Augusta. The city also benefited from the addition of the Golf Hall of Fame, designed to build on the visibility of the renowned Masters tournament. Finally, Governor Miller supported the development of the Albany River Center, a focal point for visitors to the Albany area. The River Center was part of a major local downtown revitalization effort and Governor Miller provided the full funding for the planning and design of the Center.

In addition to product development, the Miller Administration undertook new marketing initiatives. These included the Georgia Global Now campaign, a new International tourism marketing plan that targeted selected countries; the reestablishment of the regional co-op advertising program; minority marketing; and an in-state television marketing campaign.

The Georgia Global Now advertising campaign, which leveraged the attention drawn to the state by the 1996 Centennial Olympic Games, represented an investment of more than $10 million. This investment spanned a three year period leading up to the Olympics and extending for a year after the Games. The aim of this campaign was to market all of Georgia to the "influential traveler." The campaign defined "influential traveler" as the business decision-maker who influenced the location, export, and/or meeting/conference decisions of a company. The focus of Georgia Global Now was to market Georgia's image, so that the attention focused on Atlanta during the Olympics would be leveraged to make people aware of the business and vacation opportunities available in the rest of the state.

Governor Miller also provided funding, especially after the Georgia Global Now campaign, to attract visitors from foreign countries identified as particularly good markets for Georgia tourism. Germany and Great Britain were the primary targets in Europe, but Austria, Ireland, Switzerland and the Benelux countries were also targeted. This effort was expanded to include South American countries towards the end of the Miller Administration in response to an increasing number of South American tourists coming to the U.S.

Another overlooked market for which Governor Miller provided funding was American minorities, particularly those with special ties to Georgia. A 1998 Tourism Marketing Assessment conducted for the Department of Industry, Trade, and Tourism indicated that African-Americans were more likely than white Americans to have visited Georgia on a vacation. The study showed that the level of awareness of Georgia, rate of visitation, and overall rating of Georgia as a vacation destination was higher among African-Americans than for all others. In fact, no southern state was seen as a better vacation destination for African-Americans than Georgia.

Realizing that there was a need to make Georgians more aware of the travel and vacation opportunities available within the state, Governor Miller supported several marketing initiatives that were focused in-state. The regional cooperative advertising program that was almost eliminated in the budget cuts of the early 1990s was re-established and made available to all nine tourism regions. DITT provided $30,000 in funds for marketing to each region willing to match the state dollars. For most of the tourism regions in Georgia, the primary market was metro Atlanta. The state support through the cooperative advertising program was vital to these regions in formulating and implementing effective marketing and advertising programs that focused on their primary markets.

Even more significant for tourism outside Atlanta was the five-week television campaign which ran in metro-Atlanta in 1998, highlighting the vacation and travel opportunities in the rest of the state. This campaign increased awareness among Atlantans of Georgia as a destination by 22 percent and increased intent to travel in Georgia in the next year by nine percent.

The progress under Governor Miller in raising awareness of Georgia as a travel and vacation destination was clearly demonstrated by a 1998 survey funded by the Governor to assess where Georgia was as a travel/tourism destination and what the state needed to do to improve and expand the prospects for this important industry. In 1990, a nationwide survey showed awareness of Georgia as a vacation destination at 7 percent; by 1998 that awareness had increased to 13 percent. In that same time frame, surveys showed that individuals expressing an intention to take a future trip to Georgia increased from 31 percent in 1990 to 52 percent in 1998.

Public-Private Partnerships

Business and government share many of the same goals... that we can work together to achieve, and when we put our public and private resources on the table together and use them in complementary ways, then it becomes possible to do more with less.

Governor Zell Miller, May 5, 1994

Georgia Research Alliance

Silicon Valley and Route 128 in Boston developed largely because of the innate strength and excellence of Stanford University and MIT respectively. To leverage Georgia's strong pro-business environment and the research capabilities of Georgia's research universities, Governor Miller made state government a partner with Georgia's six research universities and the state's high-tech business leadership in the Georgia Research Alliance (GRA). The first state funding was included in the FY 1993 budget, starting GRA on an aggressive campaign to turn research productivity into economic development results, with the vision and commitment that Georgia would be among the top five states in the nation with a technology-driven economy by 2010.

When Governor Miller took office, Georgia was focusing most of its economic development efforts on recruitment. Miller realized that Georgia's industrial base, which was dominated by textiles, apparel, food processing and forest products, needed to change significantly as the economy became more global and more technology driven. "I believe that Georgia must make the decade of the 90's the decade of technology," he said. " To accomplish this, the public and private sectors must come together, in partnership, to develop a technology policy for our state to steer a course of economic prosperity into the 21st century." He was determined to position Georgia for the next millennium by helping support and build a new industrial base through investment in research in critical technology areas. A study by the Georgia Tech Economic Development Research Program identified a number of critical technologies where Georgia had some competitive advantage. Governor Miller and GRA used this information to identify the areas where research should be focused.

The GRA approach was different from previous efforts to foster development in specific technology areas. The previous approach, known as the Research Consortium, invested primarily in research buildings on specific campuses whose selection was often driven by the research priorities of a specific university rather than the economic development needs of the state. The state had no overall strategy that helped set research priorities, and the investments were one-time with no follow-up support.

Governor Miller and GRA established a strategy that focused on specific research areas in three broad industry areas: advanced communications, biotechnology, and environmental technology. Rather than building technology parks as other states had done, Georgia focused its investments at the front-end of the process. The strategy was based on the critical mass model which held that the emergence of a large enough pool of scientific researchers and entrepreneurs in a supportive business environment would lead to sustained and rapid creation of start-up companies as well as attracting businesses who would benefit from the research. This strategy required four elements to succeed: applied, leading-edge research at university, government, or industry research labs; a supportive environment that provided venture capital, attorneys, and bankers who understood the needs of start-up companies, along with a positive climate for risk-taking; a skilled workforce, from assembly line workers to skilled technicians to experienced engineers and scientist; and enough related industry to ensure both suppliers and customers.

From the very beginning, GRA was set up to create a critical mass of research and development activity in targeted areas that would lead to enough new company formations to spawn whole new industries in the state. It was a multi-year strategy that aimed to support the research areas identified, not with industrial parks as many other states had done, but with sophisticated research buildings, labs, equipment, eminent scholars and seed grants.

One revolutionary aspect of the strategy was to draw on the complementary strengths of six universities, both public and private, including Georgia Tech, University of Georgia, Emory University, Georgia State University, Medical College of Georgia and Clark-Atlanta University. The multi-university strategy led to research centers such as the Georgia Center for Advanced

Telecommunications Technologies (GCATT) where faculty from several universities had research facilities and where some faculty held joint university appointments. Another aspect of the strategy was to form public-private research partnerships that not only used the state investments to leverage private funds but also allowed private companies to be drivers in the establishment of research priorities. In fact, the Board of Directors of the Georgia Research Alliance was dominated not by higher education, but by private-sector leaders in the targeted industries. The public-private partnerships spawned research centers like GCATT that were also technology commercialization centers that incubated products and companies in addition to containing research labs.

During his administration, Governor Miller supported the GRA strategy with a substantial state investment of over $200 million for research labs and equipment, and endowments to support 27 eminent scholars in advanced communications, biotechnology, and environmental technologies. This state investment generated half a billion dollars in investments from federal and private research partners.

Distribution of Funds by Strategic Area
(F.Y. 1993-F.Y. 1998Amended)

Biotechnology	$ 85,633.032
Advanced Communications Technology	$ 62,006,830
Environmental Technologies	$ 45,644,138
Other	$ 4,889,000
	$201,173,000

Distribution of Funds by Investment Category
(F.Y. 1993-F.Y. 1998Amended)

Eminent Scholars	$ 19,500,000
Facilities	$ 76,623,987
Equipment	$101,599,013
Development Funds/Investments	$ 3,450,000
	$201,173,000

Distribution of Funds by Member Institution
(F.Y. 1993-F.Y. 1998Amended)

Clark Atlanta University		$ 10,447,811
Emory University		$ 21,867,387
Georgia Institute of Technology		$ 44,565,839
Georgia State University		$ 23,049,837
Medical College of Georgia		$ 17,068,699
University of Georgia		$ 50,423,427
Other:	GCATT	$ 24,700,000
	Center for Food Safety and Quality Enhancement	$ 7,000,000
	Technology Development Investments	$ 2,000,000
	Misc.	$ 50,000
		$201,173,000

This investment moved Georgia from 19th place in the nation in 1992 to third place in 1996 and a projected first place by the end of the Miller Administration in state spending for science and technology. It also created a rich research base and climate which succeeded in attracting high-tech companies to Georgia and providing the impetus for new company start-ups.

The success of the Research Alliance attracted unprecedented levels of venture capital to the state, further stimulating start-up companies. Georgia led the Southeast in venture capital investment in 1998. According to the Price Waterhouse National Venture Capital Survey, Georgia ranked 12th in the nation in total dollar investment with over $94.1 million in the first quarter of 1998, which was more than five times the amount of the first quarter of 1995. In 1998, Georgia also ranked seventh in the number of deals, with 51 percent of the money invested in technology companies. The success of Governor Miller's investment strategy was evidenced by the fact that Atlanta joined San Francisco, Boston and London as a regular stop for the prestigious venture capital conferences put on by Red Herring. Called Venture Market South, this widely respected venture capital conference attracted some 500 venture capitalists and investment bankers to Atlanta each spring.

To improve the pool of early-stage investment, GRA participated in the creation of Alliance Technology Ventures, a Georgia-based venture capital fund, in 1994. Alliance Technology Ventures, along with other venture capital firms in Georgia and the region, actively invested in early-stage ventures based on discoveries coming out of GRA research programs.

The key to the success of the Georgia Research Alliance was the recruitment of eminent research scholars of world renown to Georgia. Governor Miller viewed these scholars as so important to Georgia's economic development that he was personally involved in their recruitment, highly unusual for a governor. Endowments of matching state and private funds were created to support research chairs, and eminent scholars were recruited internationally to hold them. The lure that attracted many of these scholars to move to Georgia was the millions of dollars of state-of-the-art research equipment provided through GRA.

These research stars figured prominently in most of GRA's success stories as they captured a disproportionate share of funded research, attracted the best graduate students, and created the most appeal for high-tech companies in their fields. According to a *Wall Street Journal* article in spring of 1998, Georgia's strategy of recruiting eminent scholars was not only successful in its own right, but also redefined economic competition among states. Because of the success of this program, GRA continues to focus its research in areas of greatest potential.

Eminent Scholar Chairs Created During Miller Administration

Biotechnology	Advanced Communications Technology	Environmental Technologies
Structural Biology	Technology Transfer	Water Quality
Cell Signaling	Telemedicine	Environmental Policy
Neuropharmacology	Advanced Telecommunications	Atmospheric Chemistry
X-Ray Crystallography	Medical Imaging	Molecular Immunogenics
Microbial Physiology	Technology Enhanced Learning	Environmental Technology
Molecular Genetics	Distance Learning	Sensors & Instrumentation
Vaccine Development	Multichip Packaging	
Molecular Biology	Digital Commerce	
Molecular Immunology	Wireless Systems	
Animal Vaccine Development		
Agricultural Biotechnology		
NMR Spectroscopy		
Tissue Engineering		

As a result of research conducted within GRA, Georgia had a pipeline of homegrown ideas and concepts at different stages of development by the end of the Miller Administration. A 1997 McKinsey and Company strategic review of GRA concluded that Governor Miller's investment was successful. The Georgia Research Alliance was building an academic base to support the research efforts, demonstrated by the number of Ph.D's awarded in the sciences and engineering and the number of scholars recruited. Intellectual capital formation was demonstrated through patents issued, new patent applications filed, invention disclosures, licenses/options executed, and royalties received. GRA was helping its member institutions to sustain the effort through increased R&D expenditures. The chosen research areas performed well, and the growth of high-tech/high-wage jobs accelerated as a result of GRA's efforts.

Some of the ideas and concepts developed with the help of GRA led to new business start-ups; others served as magnets to attract business to Georgia; and yet others helped existing companies become stronger and more competitive. At the encouragement of the Governor, GRA increased its focus on the end of the development phase, which was the commercialization of research discoveries. The state was already supporting two incubators for start-up companies under the auspices of the Advanced Technology Development Center (ATDC). The location of a third ATDC incubator with

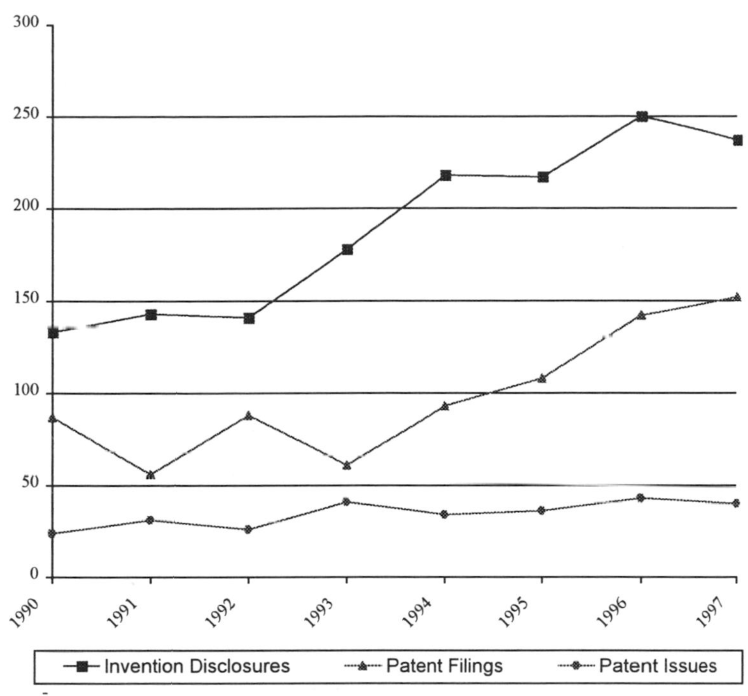
300
250
200
150
100
50
0
1990
1991
1992
1993
1994
1995
1996
1997
Invention Disclosures
Patent Filings
Patent Issues

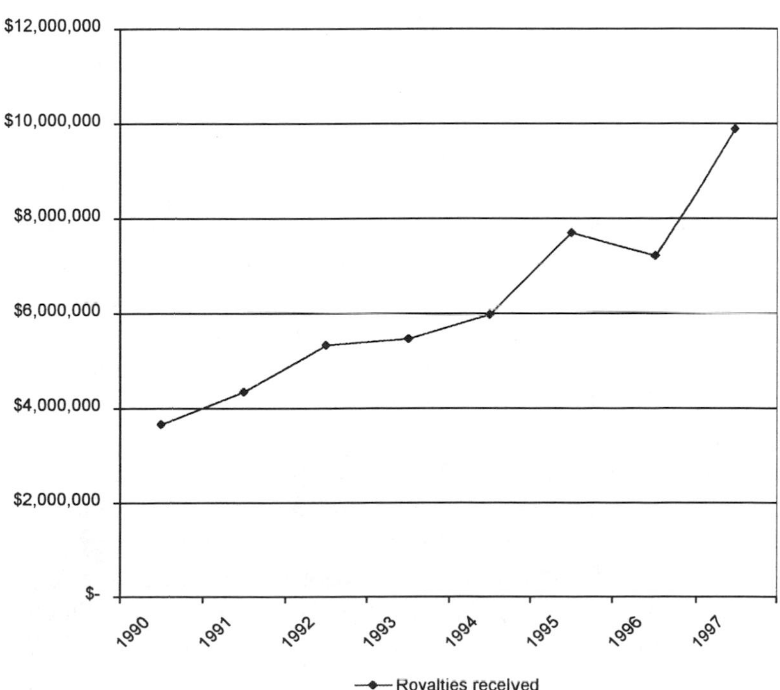
$12,000,000
$10,000,000
$8,000,000
$6,000,000
$4,000,000
$2,000,000
$-
1990
1991
1992
1993
1994
1995
1996
1997
Royalties received

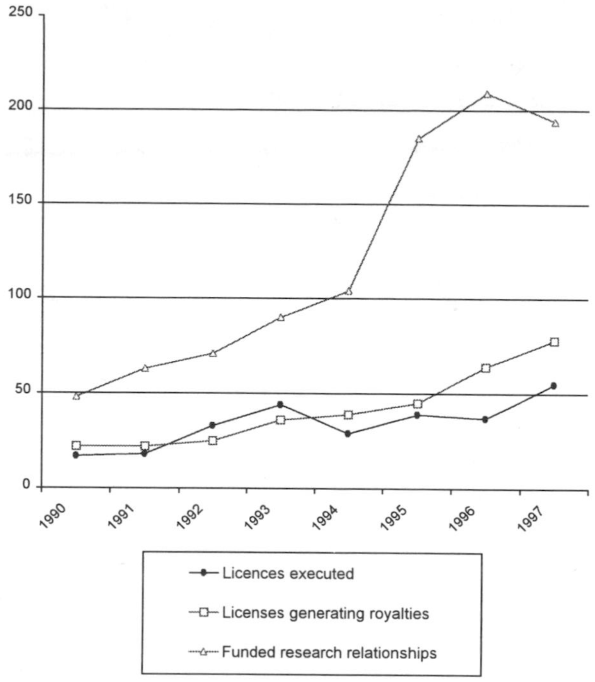

the Georgia Center for Advanced Telecommunications Technology (GCATT) became a model for combined research and commercialization centers. Reporting on the acquisition of a local Atlanta start-up (Astra Com) by a large communications company (Ciena) with plans to expand ten-fold in the city, a February 1998 *Wall Street Journal* article declared the GRA incubation model a success. Governor Miller succeeded in persuading the 1998 General Assembly to fund three more incubators under the auspices of GRA to provide an opportunity for commercialization of discoveries in biotechnology and life sciences. The incubators would allow discoveries coming from Georgia labs to be commercialized in Georgia rather than in other states. Interest was so high in Georgia incubators that at least one of the three proposed incubators was filled with prospective clients before it was even off the drawing board.

The state's investment in the Georgia Research Alliance was a long-term investment in Georgia's economy which would ultimately not only solidify Georgia's reputation as an advanced technology state, but also create high-paying, good-quality jobs for Georgians. Georgia led the nation in high-tech job growth from 1990 to 1996, according to the American Electronics Association. During the same time period, the state ranked 11th in the nation in total number of jobs created, and was one of the few states to add high-tech jobs every year since 1990. While the HOPE scholarship and other investments in higher education certainly played a large role in this growth, Governor Miller's investment in and commitment to the Georgia Research Alliance helped to create an environment conducive to high-tech company growth. It was Governor Miller's leadership throughout the 1990s, that enabled Georgia to exert the deliberate strategy and civic will needed to create a knowledge-based economy.

The Georgia Center for Advanced Telecommunications Technology (GCATT): The Georgia Center for Advanced Telecommunications Technology (GCATT) was created under the Georgia Research Alliance (GRA) umbrella to establish a research-driven growth-engine for the advanced communications industry, preparing Georgia for a leadership role in this emerging industry, and ensuring Georgia's full participation in the information age economy. Over the years, the term "advanced telecommunications" became "advanced communications," in recognition of the convergence of cable TV, computing, consumer electronics and mass media content with the traditional telecommunications technologies.

Like its sister GRA centers (the Georgia Biotechnology Center and the Georgia Environmental Technology Consortium), GCATT was designed to conduct basic and applied research, and to commercialize the technologies developed. However, given the interdisciplinary nature of Georgia Research Alliance (GRA) research programs which are spread across its six member schools, GCATT was the only one of these three centers to have a physical presence through its own building.

The 150,000 square foot state-of-the-art GCATT building adjacent to the campus of the Georgia Institute of Technology (Georgia Tech) opened in 1996. It was built with a $24.7 million investment by Governor Miller in FY 1995, combined with additional private funding. The GCATT facility itself was a testimony to what could be accomplished through the efforts of partners working together toward a common objective. The building was a showcase for advanced communications technology in the state. It housed 60 labs and 400 researchers, 14 incubator companies with approximately 100 employees, state-of-the-art conference facilities, and headquarters for three of the state's largest high-tech associations. Governor Miller's personal interest and involvement guaranteed the project's success, and GCATT was destined to become a symbol of his vision and leadership in taking the state to the next level of competitiveness in advanced communications.

At the dedication of the facility in 1996, Governor Miller charged this $28 million investment (88 percent public dollars), with making Georgia the premier center in the world for advanced communications by the year 2010. With such communications powerhouses as AT&T, BellSouth, Cox

Enterprises, Lucent Technologies, Turner Broadcasting System, and Equifax, GCATT had the corporate partners to make Governor Miller's vision a reality.

Spurred on by the strong support of Governor Miller, GCATT enjoyed many successes during his administration. A prime example was the role GCATT and proximity to Georgia Tech played in the location of a 11,000 square foot Lucent Technologies wireless communications laboratory in an adjacent building. Another *coup* was the relocation of Philips Consumer Electronics North American headquarters to be near the advanced research capabilities embodied in GCATT. Citing similar reasons, ALLTEL, a telephone electronics provider, announced plans to build a 2,000-employee complex in metro Atlanta in 1998. In addition to attracting facilities like these, GCATT's partnership with ATDC to provide an in-house incubator resulted in the successful launch of many new small communication companies.

GCATT's accomplishments were not limited to company start-ups and recruitment, and many preceded the GCATT building. During the Miller Administration, GCATT led the creation of a policy report on the future of Georgia's regulatory environment for telecommunications. The report formed the basis for Georgia's 1995 Telecommunications Competition Act, a law that in turn influenced the federal Telecommunications Act of 1996. In addition, GCATT regularly hosted a public policy series and brought together entrepreneurs and venture capital investors.

Although GCATT was a young venture, it succeeded in establishing leadership in electronic commerce early on. During the Miller Administration, it hosted an international conference on business in the new digital marketplace, and a national symposium on corporate information security. GRA's investments also supported the establishment of the Center for Digital Commerce at Georgia State University in 1997, and led to the development of the Information Security Center at Georgia Tech in 1998. Other GCATT centers included the Communications Systems Center, also at Georgia Tech; the Telemedicine Center at the Medical College of Georgia; the Learning, Performance and Support Laboratory at the University of Georgia; and the Interactive Media Technology Center at Georgia Tech. Each of these GCATT centers could boast of its accomplishments.

The Communications Systems Center designed a high-speed digital backbone network for the State of Georgia, developed a high-speed network that served as a testbed for hardware and application development associated with the next generation Internet, and engineered the Georgia Information Network for Public Health Officials. The latter received the Best NII Project in the Area of Public Health award by the Nation Information Infrastructure Consortium in December 1995.

The Telemedicine Center developed a comprehensive statewide telemedicine program linking hospitals, health departments, community public health centers, and state prisons. By the end of 1998 the network included 58 sites around the state available for use 24 hours a day.

The Learning, Performance & Support Laboratory's "Science Connections" 1997 project brought the benefits of a low-cost, high-performance Internet connection to rural school students, helping to maximize network technology available to students.

The Interactive Media Technology Center at Georgia Tech worked with the Atlanta Ballet on "Dance Technology," a project to integrate technology and the performing arts in innovative and creative ways.

By the end of the Miller Administration, each state dollar invested in GCATT was generating six dollars in additional private and/or federal government funding. It is clear that GCATT, as part of the Georgia Research Alliance, played its role well in building a critical mass for high tech in Georgia. The *Atlanta Journal-Constitution* wrote on July 12, 1998, "In part because of GCATT, Atlanta is becoming a high-tech mecca. Georgia taxpayers will get back much more than they have spent on the project through tax revenues generated by GCATT-related businesses. GCATT will also save money for consumers by spurring development of new kinds of telecommunications equipment. At the GCATT headquarters in Midtown, the alchemy is working: state and private dollars are stirring up pots of high-tech gold for Atlanta."

Traditional Industries Program

Georgia's traditional industries—pulp and paper; food processing; and textile, carpet, and apparel—had historically been the backbone of the state's industrial base. Virtually every county in Georgia was home to at least one of these industries, which combined employed 242,700 Georgians, half of the state's manufacturing workforce. Despite their size, these leading industries faced serious international challenges to their competitive position, especially from companies in low-wage regions of the world.

Governor Miller established the Traditional Industries Program (TIP) in 1994 to bring industry leaders and university-based researchers together to develop and implement practical solutions to problems critical to the competitiveness of these three Georgia industries. The aim was to apply technology to keep industries viable in the state. The program was the existing industry complement to the Georgia Research Alliance, which focused on creating and attracting new companies in industries of the future. Like GRA, TIP was a public-private partnership, in which industry identified critical competitiveness problems, then worked closely with researchers from Georgia's colleges, universities, and research institutes to solve them.

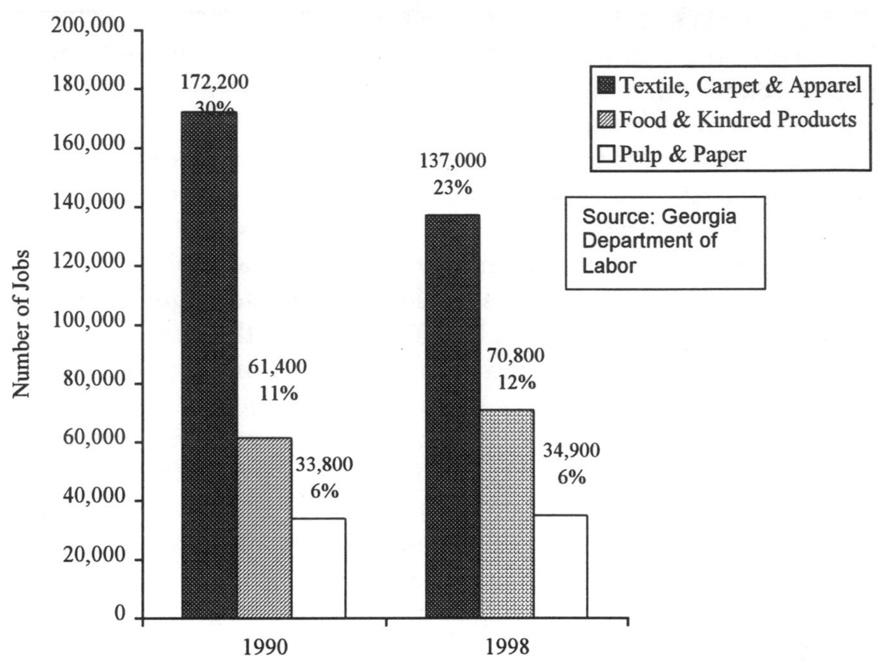

Percentages refer to percent of total manufacturing employment. For purposes of comparison, all figures are from June.

Beginning in 1994, the Miller Administration invested over $44.4 million in research (including two lab facilities), technology development, and direct technical assistance to Georgia's traditional industries, and industry matched the state's investment.

FY 1994 - FY 1999 Appropriations (Bonds & General Funds)

Food Processing	$12,156,333
Pulp & Paper	$11,502,334
Carpet, Textile & Apparel	$10,553,333
Large Infrastructure Projects	
Center for Food Safety & Quality Enhancement	$7,000,000
Herty Lab	$3,200,000
Total	$44,412,000

While each of the three industry groups—known as FoodPAC (food processing), CCACTI (carpet, textile, and apparel), and TIP^3 (pulp & paper)—assumed a separate identity under the Traditional Industries umbrella, they had a common director and shared certain characteristics. Each industry group was chaired by a private sector member, and while university researchers sat on the various committees, voting rights were reserved for private sector members. Thus, industry members were able to keep the research focused on solutions to practical problems that were critical to their competitiveness. Projects were funded for a year at a time, for a maximum of three years. Each of the three groups looked at problems related to environmental quality and the manufacturing process. In addition, TIP^3 focused on fiber supply, and FoodPAC on food safety issues. Participating industries enjoyed a number of benefits, including jobs saved and, in some cases, added; environmental regulatory compliance; new products or new uses for byproducts; new manufacturing technologies; energy and resource savings; and overall cost savings.

The membership in the three TIP groups reflected the organizational structure of the industries they represented. CCACTI, for instance, maintained a close connection to the Carpet and Rug Institute and the Georgia Textile Manufacturers' Association, whose president chaired CCACTI. TIP^3's membership included most of Georgia's major mills, and was chaired by the president of the Georgia Pulp and Paper Association. Both TIP^3 and CCACTI thus had membership that was either virtually all-inclusive or very representative, and whose members had common problems. FoodPAC, however, represented an industry with over 800 locations in the state and few common denominators. Members represented large grocery chains; fast food companies; and meat, fish, fruit, nut, vegetable, and dairy processors. Despite this mixed membership, the FoodPAC steering committee was very conscientious about recommending funding for projects that affected products critical to the state.

Herty Foundation: Created by the General Assembly in 1939, the Herty Foundation's mission was to enhance the competitiveness of the pulp and paper industry in Georgia and across the nation through the Herty Research and Development Center in Savannah. A participant in TIP^3, the Herty Foundation supported the industry by providing quality, flexible responses to development trials, accurate laboratory testing services, and rapid answers to product and process development problems in a pilot plant setting that protects and ensures the confidentiality of the work being done.

Georgia's pulp and paper mills were producing in excess of 7 million tons of paper products per year during the Miller Administration, and led the nation in the production of paperboard. The total economic impact of the industry on Georgia's economy was approximately $8 billion. Since the pulp and paper industry was the most capital-intensive of all industries, the Herty Foundation played an important economic role by assisting companies that could not afford their own pilot equipment. The use of Herty's facilities constituted a substantial saving for companies that would otherwise have to interrupt their for-profit production runs.

Governor Miller recognized the important role that the Herty Foundation played in supporting the pulp and paper industry, and assisted the foundation in preparing itself to meet industry demand in the next century. During the Miller Administration, the state invested almost $10 million for important modernization and development projects at Herty, including the upgrading of existing paper-making equipment; the purchase and installation of new paper-making equipment; the improvement of wastewater treatment facilities to allow the Foundation to expand production activities while meeting environmental quality standards; the renovation of Herty's existing manufacturing facility the construction of a new, state-of-the-art laboratory facility; and the purchase of modern lab equipment.

This modernization effort had a profound impact on the level and quality of service offered to the companies using Herty. Before modernization (1990), Herty's average annual revenue was $1.7 million. After 1993, Herty's average annual revenue increased by 235 percent, to $4 million by 1998. Before modernization, only 6 percent of this revenue came from Georgia companies. After modernization, the revenue derived from Georgia-based industry increased to 13 percent. At the end of the Miller Administration, the Herty Foundation was the largest facility of its kind in the United States, and enjoyed a national reputation for its efforts. Herty customers included such companies as Georgia Pacific, International Paper Company, Interstate Paper Company, Weyerhaeuser Paper Company, Stone Container Corporation, Proctor and Gamble, and Armstrong World Enterprises.

In addition to working with Georgia's pulp and paper industry, Herty established alliances with Georgia educational institutions. Herty evaluated pulpwood for the University of Georgia's School of Forestry, and conducted classroom exercises for the Institute of Paper Science and Technology. Herty's management met regularly with educators at other public colleges and universities to determine how the Herty facility could be used to sponsor further research and development efforts.

Supporting and leveraging the 1996 Olympics

The 1996 Centennial Olympic Games were one of the defining moments of the 20th century for Atlanta and Georgia. The Games solidified Atlanta's position as one of the world's great international cities and gave Atlanta and

Georgia worldwide recognition that no marketing campaign could ever have achieved. Additionally, the Olympics brought important improvements to Atlanta's infrastructure at little cost to taxpayers. The Atlanta Committee for the Olympic Games (ACOG) obtained private funding to build most of the facilities needed for the games, leaving Atlanta a new stadium which was converted to a baseball stadium without any cost to the Georgia or Atlanta taxpayers. ACOG also renovated all of the dorms at Georgia Tech and put over $47 million into building new dorms for both Georgia Tech and Georgia State University. Finally, the Olympics led to the installation of new telecommunications infrastructure by the private sector, giving Atlanta more fiber optic trunk lines than any other major metropolitan area in the country.

Infrastructure improvements: In preparing for and staging the Olympic Games, Governor Miller recommended and the General Assembly approved significant financial resources, including over $235 million in infrastructure and funding for safety and security. The state provided $154 million for new dormitories to house Olympic athletes and officials on the campus of Georgia Tech, which served as the Olympic Village. After the Games, the dorms were used by both Georgia Tech and Georgia State University. ACOG also contributed $47 million to the construction of these dorms. In addition, the Governor recommended early funding for several improvements that had already been identified in the long-term plans for state facilities. The Georgia World Congress Center Plaza and parking deck ($31 million) was built ahead of schedule, providing parking and pedestrian access between the WCC and the Georgia Dome. Similarly, early funding of improvements from the master plan for Stone Mountain Park enabled the park to handle Olympic visitors and present a fresh look to the world.

The Georgia Department of Transportation completed all road improvements in the Atlanta area needed to accommodate the Olympics. In all, more than 100 Olympic transportation projects costing $750 million were completed, with $450 million in projects for the metro Atlanta area. The traffic management plan for the Olympics was a state-of-the-art computer-controlled management system which was run out of the DOT's Traffic Management Center (TMC). Finally, grants were provided to communities and colleges throughout the state that became training sites for Olympic teams. These grants were used to improve athletic facilities and equipment needed by the teams.

Centennial Olympic Park: Arguably the most lasting tribute to and symbol of the Olympic Games' importance to Georgia was Centennial Olympic Park, the first new urban park in the nation in a quarter century. The willingness of the State of Georgia to take the lead in the development and future operation of the Park was crucial to the transformation of this Olympic dream into reality. At the urging of ACOG chair Billy Payne, who emphasized the importance of a central gathering place in downtown Atlanta, Governor Miller directed the GWCC Authority to conduct a feasibility study in 1994, and gave the official go-ahead to begin purchasing property for the 21-acre site. The initial construction funding came from philanthropic donations of $25 million, an Atlanta Chamber of Commerce fund-raising campaign of $10 million, and a guarantee from the Atlanta Committee for the Olympic Games to provide $15 million from the sale of commemorative bricks. Approximately 325,000 commemorative bricks were purchased and installed before the Centennial Olympic Games. Brick sales continued through the Games, for a total sale of 468,874 commemorative bricks, making this program the most successful of its kind ever.

Designed and built in less than two years, the park became the central gathering place Billy Payne had envisioned during the Centennial Olympic Games (July 19 – Aug. 4, 1996). ACOG estimated over 5.3 million persons visited the park between July 13 and August 14. Following the Games, final construction of the permanent state park began. Funding for this second phase included a $3.75 million donation from the Southern Company, $2.25 million from the GWCC Authority and a $6 million matching contribution from the Robert W. Woodruff Foundation. A gala rededication weekend reopened the park at the end of March 1998, attracting throngs of citizens eager to relive and reconfirm the uplifting Spirit of the Centennial Olympic Games. Among the Park's many special features was Centennial Plaza with its famous interactive Fountain of Rings. Music of all types was performed on the Great Lawn and in the Southern Company Amphitheater. A unique series of five quilt plazas—the Quilts of Dreams, Remembrance, Origins, Olympic Spirit, and Nations—told the dramatic story of Atlanta's Centennial Olympic Games. Beautifully landscaped, cascading water gardens wove through these quilt plazas.

The completed park performed the dual mission Governor Miller envisioned for this largest new center city park developed in the United States in the past 25 years. As an important community gathering place and entertainment venue, it became Atlanta's lasting legacy, both physically and emotionally, from the Centennial Olympic Games. It also became a dynamic economic catalyst in the commercial and residential revitalization of a central but under-utilized downtown section of Georgia's capital city.

In addition to providing authorization and support for the development of the Centennial Olympic Park, Governor Miller also committed the resources of the Georgia World Congress Center to the ongoing operation of the park. The Governor recommended and the General Assembly approved a one-time appropriation of $2.5 million in the FY 1996 amended budget to pay off the remaining balance on a construction loan from the Georgia Dome. The Congress Center had been making the payments on this loan using revenues from the hotel/motel tax, of which it received one-quarter of each cent collected. Retirement of the Georgia Dome debt enabled the Congress Center to dedicate its hotel/motel tax revenues, which totaled about $1 million a year, to the permanent operation of the Centennial Olympic Park.

Operation Legacy and Georgia Global Now: Governor Miller effectively utilized the Olympics to leverage economic development for the state through Operation Legacy, a public-private partnership with businesses such as Georgia Power and NationsBank. Operation Legacy targeted key industries and used the occasion of the Olympics to invite their CEOs to visit Georgia. Invited in groups by industry type, the executives toured Olympic venues and also learned why Georgia would be a prime location for a new company facility.

Operation Legacy attracted 34 new facilities or expansions employing about 5,600 people with capital investments totaling more than $250 million. After the Olympics, Operation Legacy was folded into the Georgia Department of Industry, Trade and Tourism (GDITT). The department continued to target many of the industries identified by Operation Legacy.

In parallel with Operation Legacy, GDITT undertook a special marketing program known as Georgia Global Now. Over a three-year period, more than $10 million in state funds was provided for this program. This investment leveraged the attention focused on Atlanta because of the Olympics into a promotion and celebration of the entire state as a place to do business and to visit.

Olympic security: Governor Miller and the General Assembly provided over $26 million to help with the security needed for staging the Games. Two-thirds of the Olympic venues were on state property at sites like the Georgia Dome, the World Congress Center, the Georgia Institute of Technology and Stone Mountain Park. Overtime expenses for about 2,600 state personnel from 19 agencies, including 2,400 sworn law enforcement personnel, were funded to provide security at or around venues on state property and for other activities as determined by the State Olympic Law Enforcement Command (SOLEC).

On January 22, 1996, Governor Miller issued an Executive Order establishing the State Olympic Law Enforcement Command, placing all of the state's public safety resources under one command for the Olympic Games. In this unique move, Governor Miller incorporated Georgia's emergency response capabilities and experience into a wide, coordinated range of services that extended far beyond the traditional public safety umbrella. The

State of Utah adopted this innovative design for its public safety effort during the 2002 Winter Games in Salt Lake City.

Governor Miller's Executive Order also appointed executives to a SOLEC Command Post made up of the director of the Georgia Bureau of Investigation, the commissioner of the Georgia Department of Public Safety, the adjutant general of the Georgia Department of Defense, and the director of the Georgia Emergency Management Agency, who was designated chief of staff. SOLEC's chief of staff immediately arranged the organization into five major components: operational support, competition venues, function venues, specialized management centers and Torch Relay security.

SOLEC operated from early 1996 through the Paralympic Games, which followed the Olympics, assuming a primary role in the public safety arena in coordination with local and federal agencies. During its time of operation, SOLEC executives met regularly with leaders from key agencies to coordinate public safety throughout the Olympic theater. Over the five month period prior to the Olympic Games, SOLEC became a primary public safety partner for planning and coordination. During this period, operational plans were completed, roles and responsibilities were defined and resources were identified.

SOLEC merged all aspects of public safety (law enforcement, emergency services and medical care). As a part of this process, technical assistance visits were made to Olympic communities; specialized training was developed and conducted; and legal issues were resolved. Special needs from other agencies participating in the Olympics were identified, such as support to the Metropolitan Atlanta Rapid Transit Authority, equine disease control, traffic, housing, food services and logistics. By the start of the Games, SOLEC had doubled the number of personnel and added several new agencies to meet the expanded responsibilities of this comprehensive public safety approach.

The Torch Relay was the first major event of the 1996 Summer Olympic Games. Amid the ancient ruins of Greece the official Olympic Torch was lit on March 30, 1996, and began its journey to Atlanta. The Olympic Flame arrived in the United States on April 27, 1996, in Los Angeles, the American host city that preceded Atlanta. Accompanied by 46 State Olympic Law Enforcement Command (SOLEC) officers, the flame traveled across the United States for 84 days over 15,280 miles through over 335 cities. Approximately 10,000 torch bearers carried the Olympic Flame on its journey across America. Governor Miller received the Olympic Torch on the behalf of all Georgians at its arrival on Georgia soil in Savannah two weeks prior to the Games. After traveling throughout Georgia, the flame arrived at the Olympic Stadium in Atlanta for Opening Ceremonies on Friday, July 19, 1996.

SOLEC personnel provided escorts in marked Georgia State Patrol cars for the Torch Relay caravan, and escorted torch bearers on foot in crowded areas where tighter security was needed. Other SOLEC personnel worked with local, state and federal agencies throughout the United States in advance of the torch's arrival.

During the Games, the focal point of the SOLEC command and control system was the newly constructed State Operations Center (SOC). Representatives from public safety and emergency management agencies staffed the SOC and provided support to Olympic communities throughout the state. The center was in close contact with SOLEC's command posts at the competition/function venues and special management centers, ready to respond whenever a situation might exceed existing resources or scope of authority, such as cases involving mass casualties or injuries. Staff and resources were available through the SOC on a 24 hour basis. This structure encouraged decisions to be made at the lowest level, enabling field commanders to operate more effectively. After the Olympics and Paralympics, the State Operations Center became the command center for the Georgia Emergency Management Agency, which responded to all declared disasters in Georgia.

The most tragic occurrence during the Games was the bombing at Centennial Olympic Park. In the early morning hours of July 27, a pipe bomb exploded in the park, injuring over 118 people and resulting in the death of two individuals. The planned public safety response was immediately activated through the SOC. Crisis counseling assistance was provided to care for the victims and their families. The state's public safety response was exemplary. By the following day, the Games continued without any delay.

Immediately following the bombing incident, the park was closed for three days to allow for evidence gathering and clean-up. At the "reopening ceremonies" of the park three days later, Governor Miller spoke to the large crowd assembled about the resolve of the people of Georgia to look terrorism in the face and not be deterred. After reopening, daily attendance averaged between 250,000 and 300,000 persons. The largest crowds were experienced on August 2 and 3 with over 300,000 persons each day, indicating the public's resolve to not be deterred by terrorist acts.

The Centennial Olympic Games were a great success for Georgia and Atlanta. The crowds were massive but were in a festive and cooperative mood. Governor Miller's commitment to keeping citizens and Olympic athletes and visitors safe was realized successfully.

Improving Georgia's workforce

As our economy races toward the future, business and industry are undergoing rapid technological change. This evolution is creating more job opportunities than it's closing off, but the key to this new, emerging breed of jobs that is coming to dominate our employment growth is technical skills.

Governor Zell Miller, February 17, 1994

Expansion of technical and adult education

During the Miller Administration, the state invested almost $212 million in the construction of new technical and adult education facilities at 41 sites, including 17 satellite campuses attached to the state's 32 technical institutes. In addition, existing facilities were renovated, retrofitted and expanded. All technical institutes received new equipment totaling an unprecedented $104 million.

With 32 technical institutes, 17 satellites, one locally-governed technical institute, and associated programs housed at four colleges of the University System of Georgia, every Georgian was within a 45-minute drive of a technical and adult education campus. The expansion under the Miller Administration also provided additional capacity to handle increased student enrollment. From FY 1991 to FY 1997, credit enrollment at technical institutes grew by 80 percent. By FY 1998, nearly 240,000 students were enrolled in postsecondary technical programs. This growth was essential to Georgia's economic performance in the 1990s and critical to the state's continued development beyond the year 2000.

Beyond the Miller Administration, however, enrollment growth would no longer be totally facility-dependent. The Governor instigated the development of the virtual technical institute with a $471,858 appropriation in FY 1999. Under the auspices of the Department of Technical and Adult Education, the virtual technical institute was designed to enable students to take classes via the Internet from their homes, workplaces or public libraries.

Quick Start

Quick Start, a unit of the Department of Technical and Adult Education, was a major recruiting tool for Georgia's economic developers, and under the Miller Administration it also became a vital resource in encouraging and supporting business expansion, the main source of job growth in Georgia. Quick Start was created in 1967 to provide on-site employee training free of charge to companies coming into Georgia. It worked extensively in cooperation with other state agencies, particularly the Department of Industry Trade and Tourism, Georgia's business and industry recruiter. Under the Miller Administration, Quick Start was expanded to include employee training for

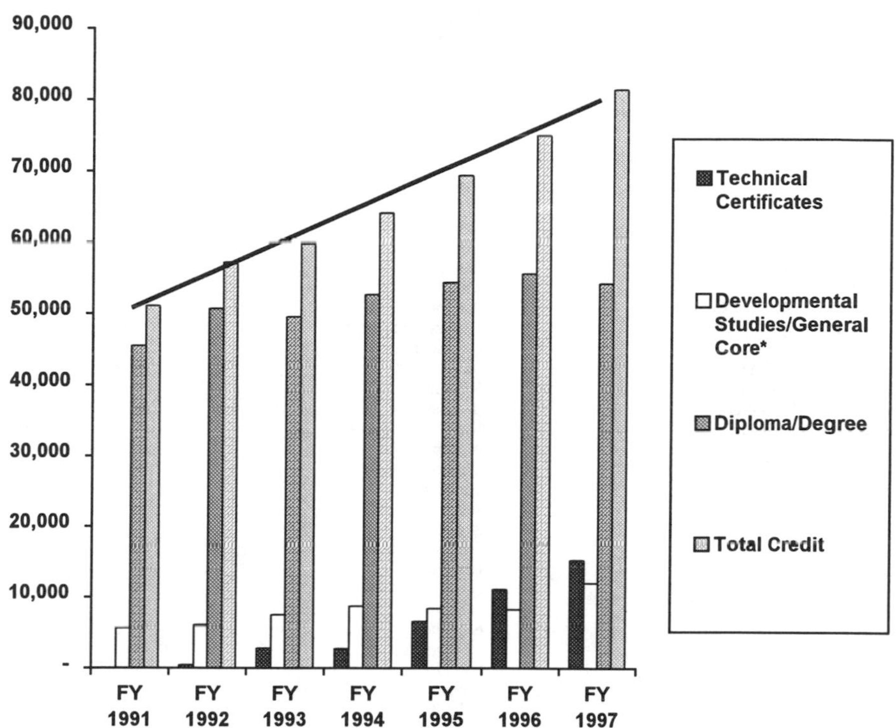

expansions by existing Georgia companies. From its creation in 1967 until the end of the Miller Administration in 1998, Quick Start had trained a total of over 300,000 workers for over 2,800 Georgia companies. Over half of all Quick Start projects and more than half of its trainees were served during the Miller Administration.

The year before Governor Miller took office, Quick Start served 127 companies and 9,455 trainees at a per-trainee cost of $561. At the end of his term, Quick Start's accomplishments underscored the governor's pro-business, pro-education attitude with FY 1998 figures of 251 companies and over 30,000 trainees served, while the per-trainee costs had plummeted to below $320. The spectacular growth in Quick Start operations was possible because of the increased financial and policy support Governor Miller gave the program, along with increased program efficiency. During the Miller Administration, Quick Start's budget almost doubled.

Quick Start's reputation for quality services placed Georgia in the forefront of economic development incentive training programs across the

DEPARTMENT OF TECHNICAL AND ADULT EDUCATION
New Buildings During the Miller Administration

Technical Institute	Project	Appropriation
Albany	Industrial Technology Center	1,052,000
Albany	Classroom	4,131,000
Albany-Early County	Satellite	3,639,225
Altamaha-Appling County	Satellite	3,459,225
Athens	Academic/Classroom	4,300,000
Athens-Elbert County	Satellite	7,183,875
Augusta	Library/Conference Center	4,988,000
Augusta	Automated Mfg Technology Center	720,000
Augusta-Burke County	Satellite	5,240,000
Augusta-McDuffie County	Satellite	6,222,179
Ben Hill-Coffee County	Satellite	3,782,644
Ben Hill-Irwin	Classroom	2,003,000
Carroll-Douglasville	Satellite	8,350,000
Chattahoochee	Classroom	3,743,000
Chattahoochee-Paulding County	Satellite	4,849,942
Columbus	Library/Multipurpose	5,282,000
Coosa Valley	Classroom	2,887,000
Coosa Valley-Gordon County	Satellite	3,014,865
Coosa Valley-Gordon County Phase II	Satellite	136,600
Coosa Valley-Polk County	Satellite	3,944,225
DeKalb-Newton County	Satellite	8,912,000
Flint River	Multipurpose	3,199,000
Griffin	Classroom	1,298,000
Heart of Georgia-Dublin	Health Occupations	1,020,000
Heart of Georgia-Dublin	Business Center	7,283,000
Heart of Georgia-Eastman	Aerospace	2,975,000
Heart of Georgia-Eastman	Expansion	4,321,200
Lanier	Classroom	3,565,000
Lanier-Forsyth County	Satellite	7,163,246
Macon	Aerospace	5,600,000
Macon-Milledgeville	Satellite	5,289,784
Middle Georgia	Relocation	13,700,000
Moultrie-Tift County	Satellite	4,172,995
North Georgia	Industrial Training Center	1,027,000
North Georgia-Union County	Satellite	5,569,849
Ogeechee	Health Occupations	5,725,000
Okefenokee	Classroom	3,060,000
Pickens	Economic Development Center	1,195,000
Sandersville	New Technical Institute	6,325,000
South Georgia	Business & Industrial Development Fac.	5,700,000
South Georgia	Transportation Center	5,653,000
South Georgia-Crisp County	Satellite	5,734,625
Swainsboro	Classroom	2,005,000
Thomas	Allied Health Bldg.	5,400,000
Valdosta	Multipurpose	7,753,000
Walker	Library	4,806,000
West Georgia	Economic Development Center	4,300,000
TOTAL		$211,681,479

nation. The use of knowledge gained through Quick Start to develop programs and services for delivery through Georgia's technical institutes was a model of government efficiency.

The Quick Start that Governor Miller inherited used few computers for training projects. The most technology-intensive project at that time required the use of two Apple II computers (outdated even then) and a dot matrix printer. When a company requested that its training manuals be printed on a laser printer instead, the request was met only after much debate.

The Quick Start that Governor Miller passed on to his successor consistently impressed even the highest profile companies with its efficient use of

State Technical Education

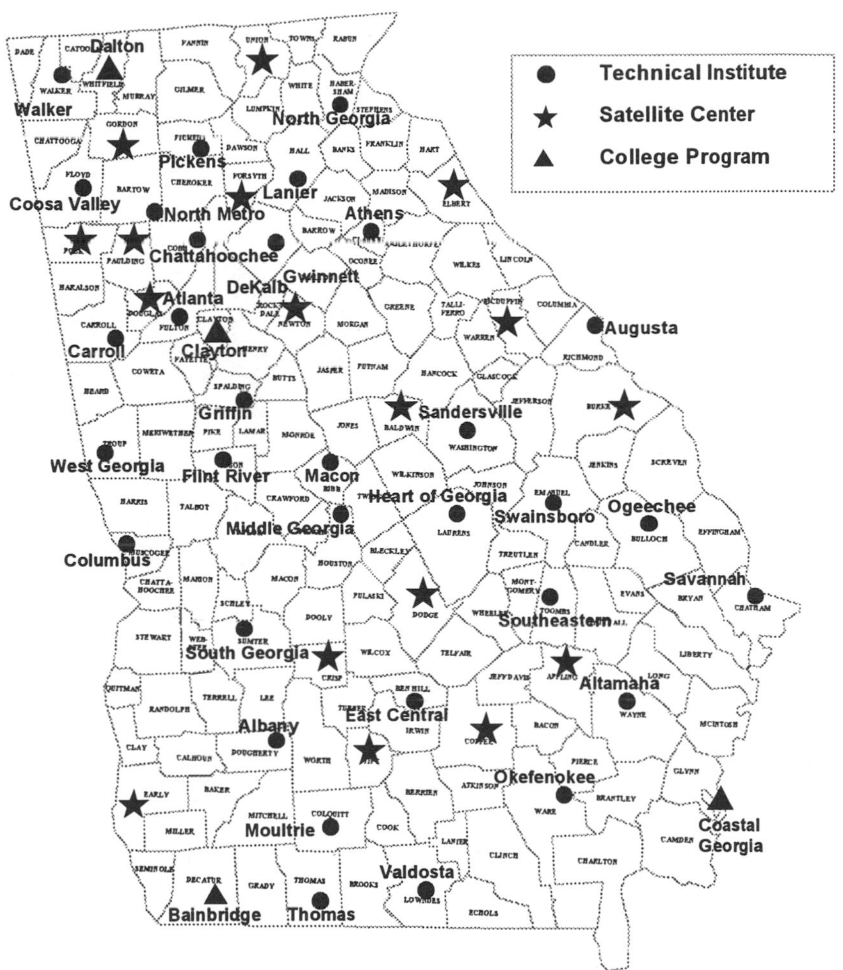

leading-edge technology to deliver the latest in whatever kind of training made bottom-line sense to companies. Intelligent purchasing of the right technology to support training development enabled Quick Start to take the lead among similar programs while, at the same time, producing impressive cost reductions. Quick Start continued to deliver printed manuals when appropriate, but it increasingly used computer-based training, broadcast-quality video, and the very latest in job aids available to make training available to employees when and where they needed it. These tools were developed in-house as part of a system of capability-based service, a system

any business would be proud of, and one that continued its benefits to the state long after any particular Quick Start project was complete.

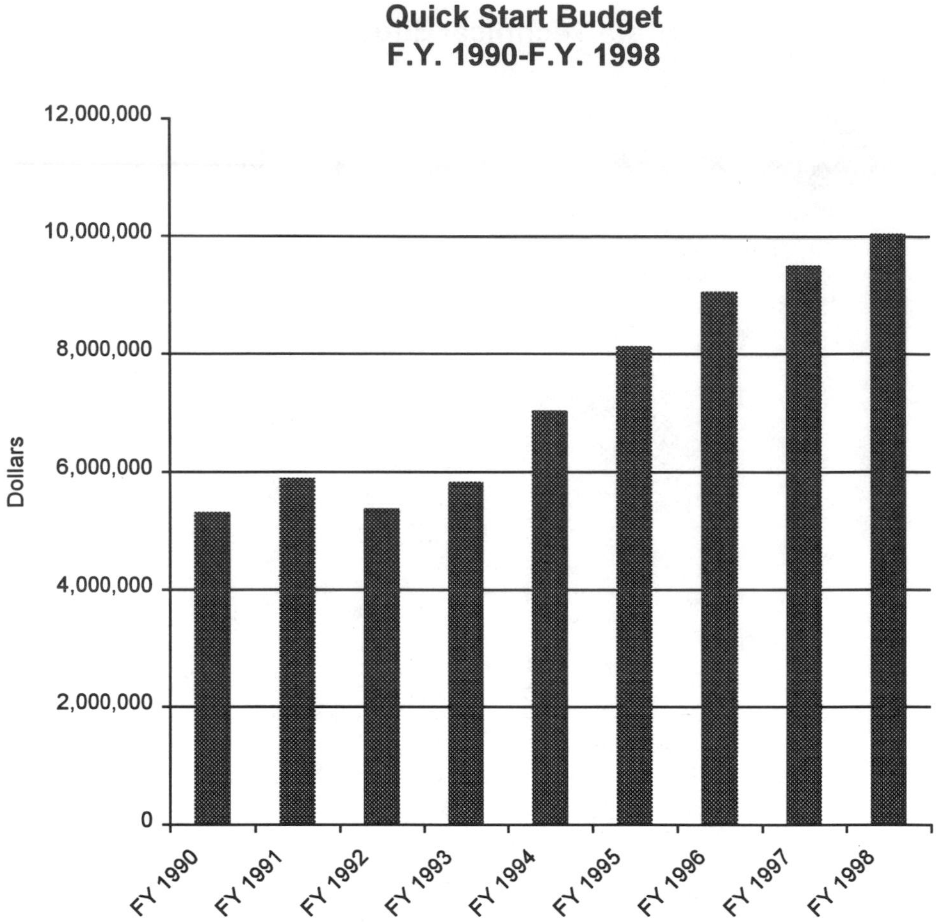

The enhancement of Quick Start's training capabilities to include state-of-the-art computer technology for computer-based multi-media training programs utilizing three-dimensional modeling and animation directly contributed to attracting and/or encouraging expansion of such companies as SKC (the largest capital investment ever made in Georgia), Ciba Vision, General Mills, Anheuser-Busch, and Metal Container.

During Governor Miller's administration, Quick Start's capabilities were expanded to provide productivity enhancement programs in world-class manufacturing, total quality management, just-in-time inventory control, and ISO 9000 training. These training strategies enabled Georgia's companies to improve quality and productivity, thus improving their competitive position.

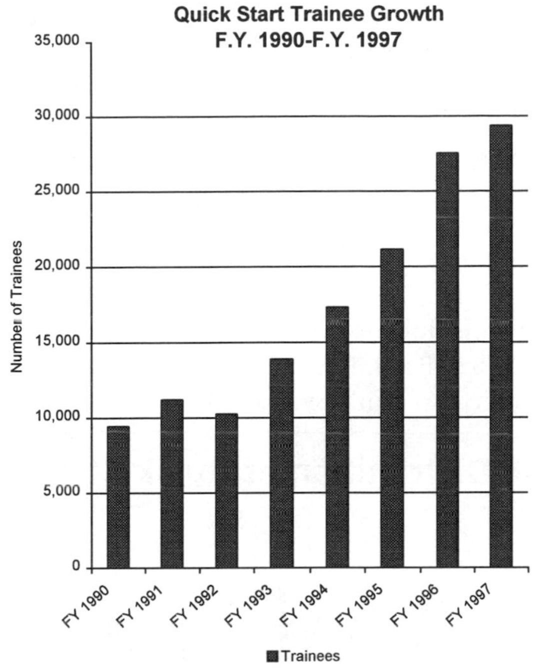
Quick Start Trainee Growth
F.Y. 1990-F.Y. 1997
35,000
30,000
25,000
20,000
15,000
10,000
5,000
0
Number of Trainees
FY 1990
FY 1991
FY 1992
FY 1993
FY 1994
FY 1995
FY 1996
FY 1997
Trainees

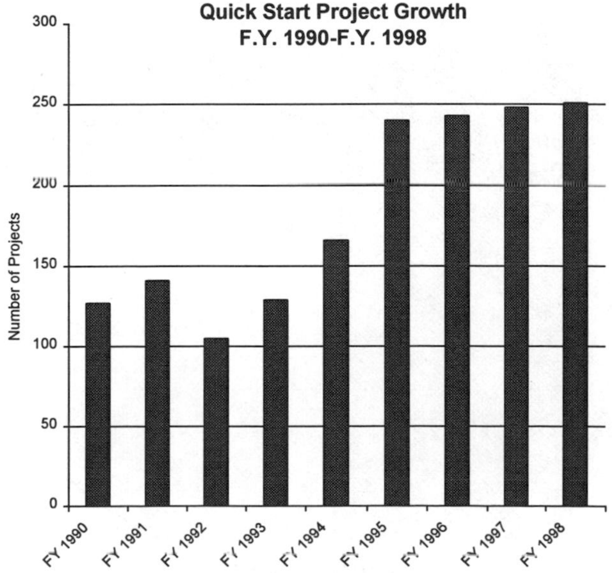
Quick Start Project Growth
F.Y. 1990-F.Y. 1998
300
250
200
150
100
50
0
Number of Projects
FY 1990
FY 1991
FY 1992
FY 1993
FY 1994
FY 1995
FY 1996
FY 1997
FY 1998

The expansion of Quick Start's scope of services to include customer service and office-oriented operations met the needs of companies such as AT&T Universal Card Services Corp., Cooper Lighting First Center, E*Trade, Equifax, Smart Corporation, Pitney Bowes, and GEICO. This initiative led to the creation and statewide implementation of the Certified Customer Service Specialist program, as well as to Georgia's Service Industry Academies in Columbus and Savannah. These academy partnerships between businesses, chambers of commerce, and technical institutes were innovative approaches to building a pool of qualified workers. Partners in the Columbus Service Industry Academy included companies such as AFLAC, AT&T, Blue Cross/Blue Shield, Char-Broil, First Union National Bank, Regions Bank, SunTrust Bank, SouthTrust Bank, Synovus Service Corp., and Total System Services.

Geographic Distribution of Quick Start Projects

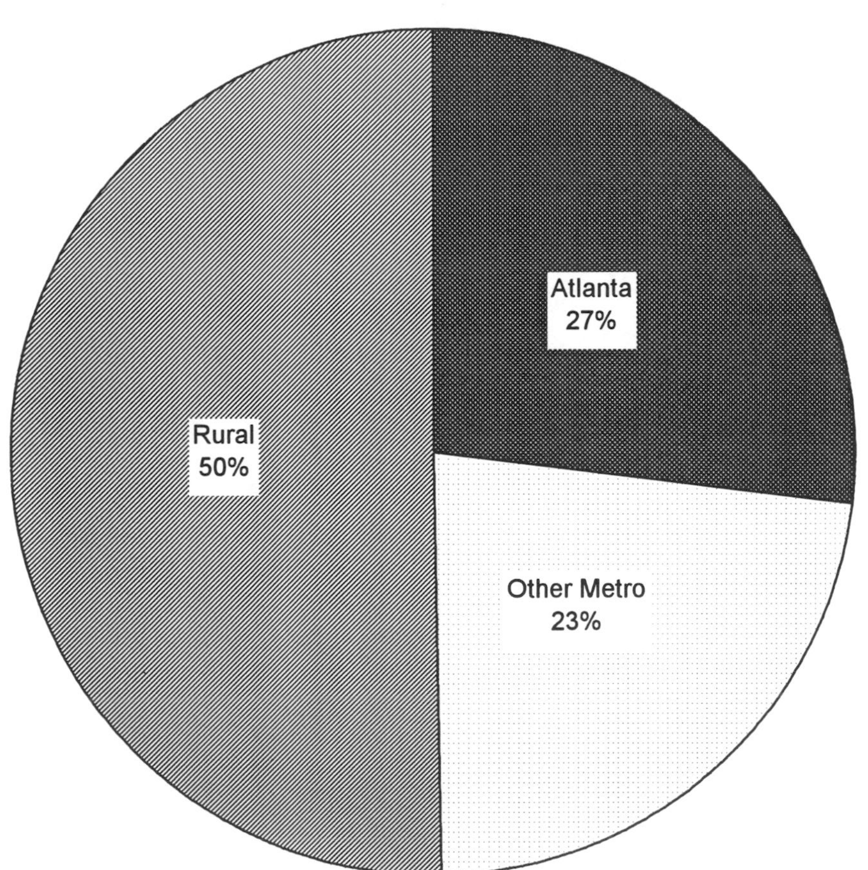

Quick Start could also assist companies in making hiring decisions and defining their organizational structure through the use of job profiling tools. Among other things, these tools enabled companies to match applicants with jobs based on a job's skill requirement and an applicant's actual skills. Using Quick Start's job profiling tools and services, a company could increase both its efficiency and effectiveness.

Through its position as a vital partner to Georgia's new and expanding companies, Quick Start was knowledgeable both about the current state of manufacturing and service technology and workforce needs. Quick Start's knowledge and capabilities were essential to the development and implementation of Georgia's Certified Manufacturing Specialist (CMS) and Certified Customer Service Specialist (CCSS) programs. Governor Miller's support for these programs helped to ensure that Georgia had excellent training available to supply Georgia's businesses with the skilled workers they needed to be successful.

The specialist programs provided the stepping stone into entry-level jobs and further education. For instance, in the plastics industry a person might begin with the CMS program, learn how to become a basic operator, then pick up additional technician training all the way through a three-year mold-making apprenticeship program which would allow entry into a high-skill, high-wage specialization in great demand. Through a combination of approaches, the same individual might earn a diploma and/or a degree, proceeding into four-year programs provided through agreements with the University System.

During the Miller Administration, all of Georgia benefited from Quick Start projects. Half of the projects were in rural areas, allowing communities across the state to upgrade their workforce.

Project Geographic Distribution
FY 1990-FY 1998

MSAs	Number of Companies
Albany	34
Athens	35
Atlanta	444
Augusta	78
Columbus	76
Macon	53
Savannah	46
Rural	840
Total	**1606**

Under the vision and leadership of Governor Zell Miller, Quick Start moved from the middle ranks of the nation's programs into a leadership position. The Governor supported the development of Quick Start into the premier provider of high quality, leading-edge training as well as an essential part of a system that continued to build Georgia's infrastructure for the future by developing and strengthening its capabilities to respond to the needs of Georgia's business and industry and, most importantly, the citizens of the state.

Adult literacy

When Governor Miller took office, the 1990 census showed that nearly 30 percent of Georgia's adult population had never completed high school, and only a few of the state's 159 counties had full-time adult literacy teachers. Learning centers providing adult literacy services operated for only two to six hours per week.

To expand and improve literacy services in the state, the Governor more than doubled funds for adult literacy. By the end of his administration, every

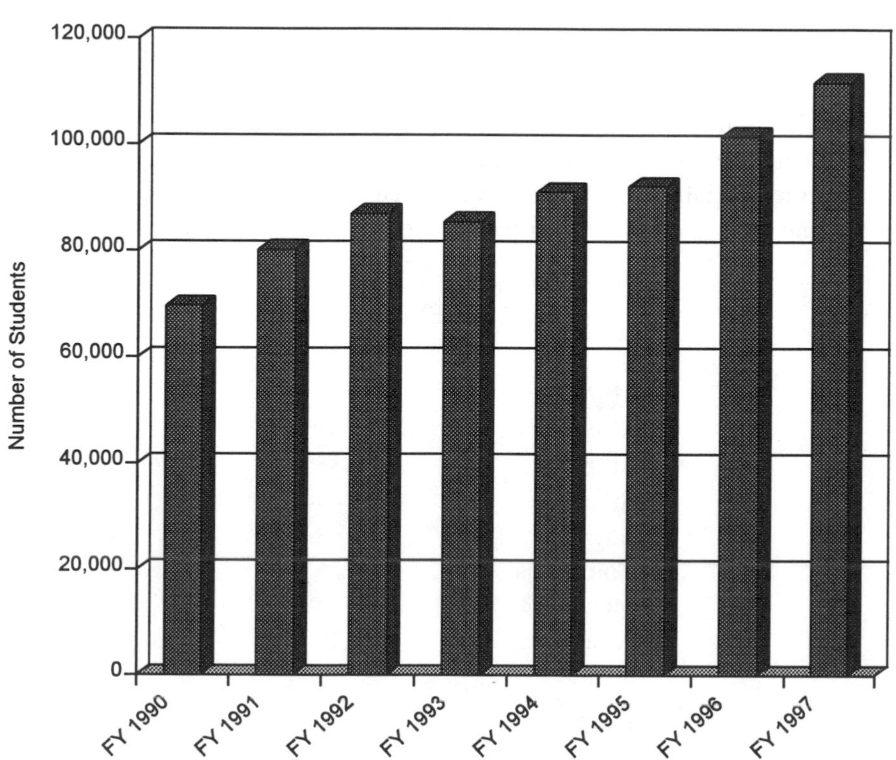

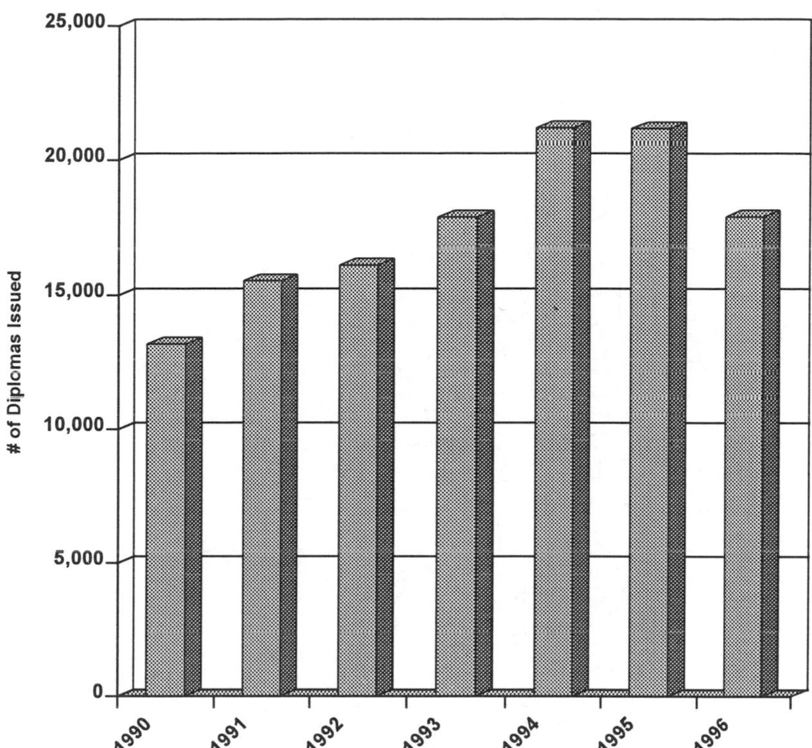

county had at least one full-time adult literacy teacher, and more than 1,100 computers were provided for adult literacy labs. There was no doubt that the full-time adult literacy teachers had an impact. Analysis showed a 91 percent increase in student enrollment between FY 1994 and FY 1997 for those counties that had received a full-time adult literacy teacher, versus a mere eight percent increase for the counties that did not yet have their own teacher. To build on the success of the full-time adult literacy teachers and further improve the delivery of community literacy services, another 110 part-time teachers were funded in FY 1999.

At the Governor's initiative, the state began paying the fee the first time an adult took the General Education Diploma exam, and all adults who passed it received a $500 HOPE scholarship voucher to continue their education. During the Miller years, enrollment in adult literacy programs increased from about 80,000 to more than 100,000 and the number of GEDs issued increased from 13,000 to about 20,000 a year. From January 1990 to October 1998, over 152,000 GEDs were issued in Georgia.

CERTIFIED LITERATE COMMUNITY PROGRAM

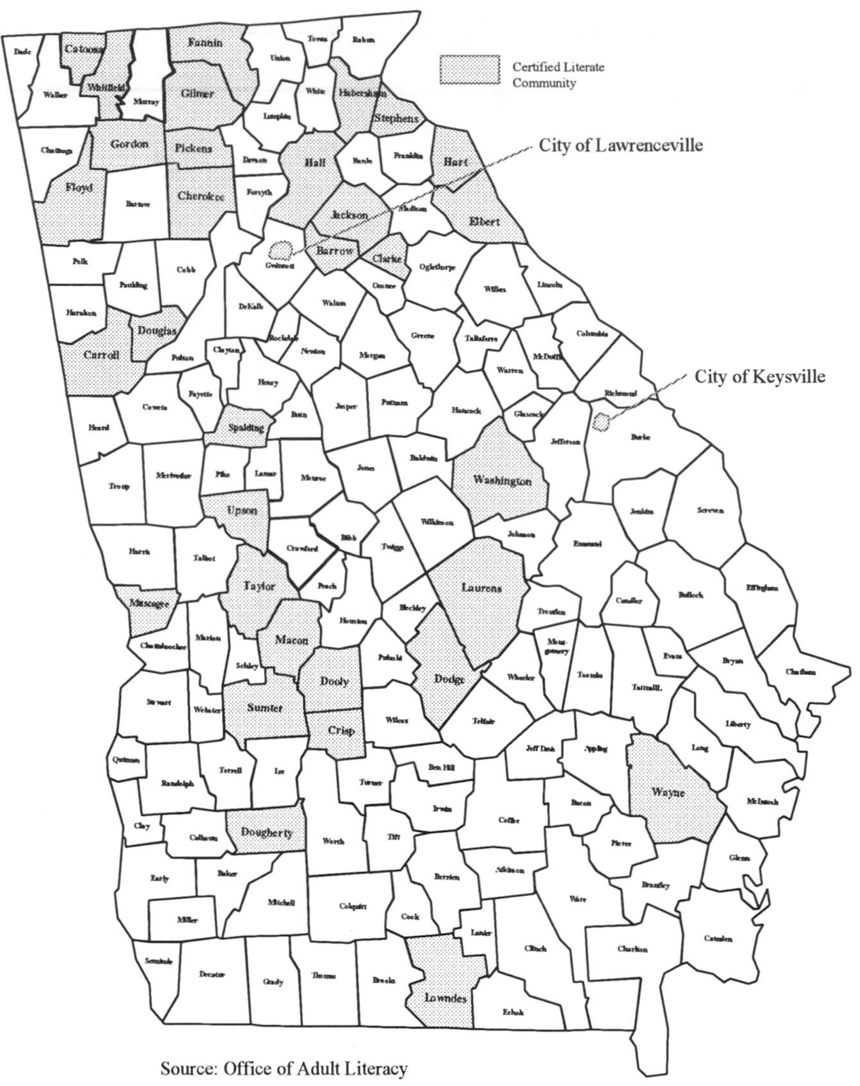

Source: Office of Adult Literacy

To support literacy training in the workplace, the Governor initiated the Georgia Tax Credit for Adult Basic Skills Education. Employers became eligible for a state tax credit if they provided or sponsored basic skills education for their employees. In addition, companies that made significant progress in this area received the Governor's Award for Achievement in Workplace Learning. Between 1991 and 1997, 391 companies received this award.

Governor Miller's commitment to improving Georgia's adult literacy extended to individuals, companies, and communities. By the end of his administration, 34 Georgia communities were participants in the Certified Literate Communities Program (CLCP), started in FY 1991. An additional 25 communities were in various stages of organizing programs. Program participants made literacy a community-wide commitment and mobilized resources to improve literacy levels of children, families, and workers in their communities. During the Miller Administration, First Lady Shirley Miller was Georgia's chief spokesperson for adult literacy, and served as co-chair of the Georgia Council on Adult Education.

Libraries

During the Miller Administration, Georgia's public libraries not only received a needed face-lift, but also moved into the 21st century. The Miller Administration funded over $52 million for library construction and renovation, resulting in better access to more modern library facilities across the state. In addition, the modernization effort included another $2.7 million for Internet connections through PeachNet, over $900,000 for computers and printers, and $1.5 million for access to GALILEO, the Georgia Library

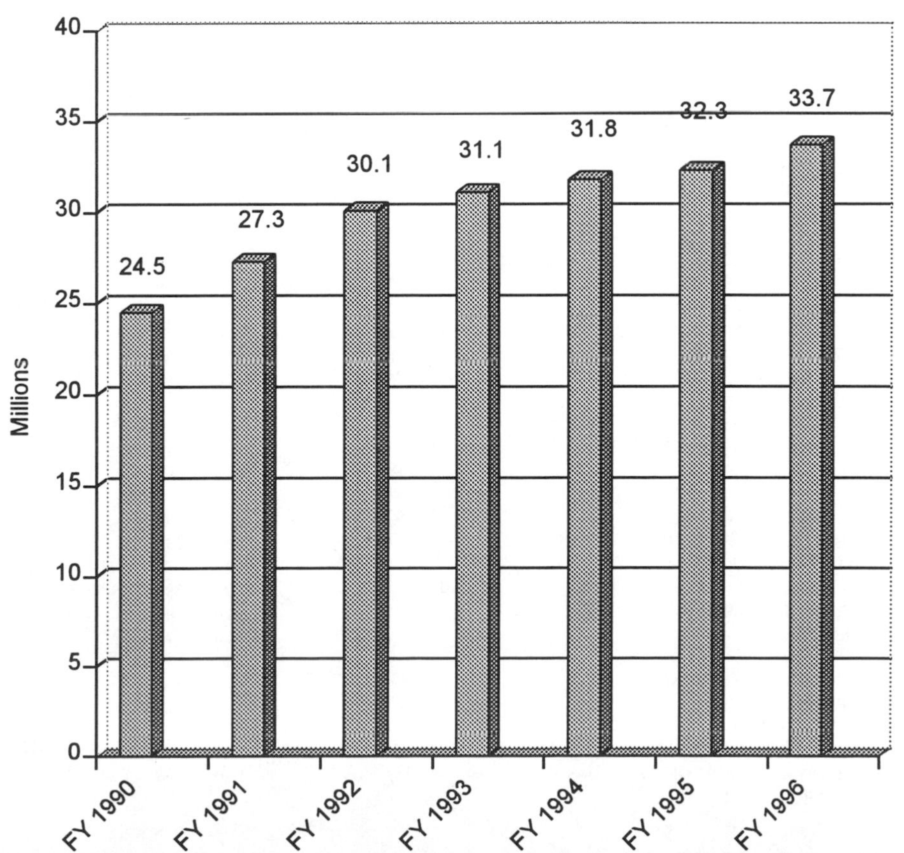

Industry-specific Regional Economic Business Assistance (REBA) Projects						
Number of Projects	Grant Amount	Private Investment	Jobs Created	State Cost per Job	Total Direct Public Benefits first 10 yrs	Average Annual Benefit
49	$16,978,035	$1,976,135,000	18,622	$912	$353,117,902	$720,649

SYSTEM	Libr. # of	Population	Circ./ Cap.	Incentive/ Capita	Total $ Amount	Tot'l # of Books*
THOMAS COUNTY	6	40,972	9.30	1.64	67,194	2,936
GWINNETT-FORSYTH REGIONAL	9	514,718	8.91	1.64	844,138	36,887
MIDDLE GEORGIA REGIONAL	13	257,687	8.59	1.64	422,607	18,467
HART COUNTY	1	21,331	7.51	1.64	34,983	1,529
SARA HIGHTOWER REGIONAL	4	118,512	7.27	1.64	194,360	8,493
DESOTO TRAIL REGIONAL	8	56,955	6.92	1.64	93,406	4,082
OCMULGEE REGIONAL	6	55,627	6.75	1.64	91,228	3,986
BRUNSWICK-GLYNN COUNTY REGIONAL	8	166,862	6.58	1.64	273,654	11,958
MOUNTAIN REGIONAL	4	38,479	6.13	1.64	63,106	2,758
COBB COUNTY	16	543,764	5.98	1.64	891,773	38,968
ATHENS REGIONAL	13	169,577	5.66	1.64	278,106	12,153
BROOKS COUNTY	3	16,063	5.22	1.64	26,343	1,151
SCREVEN-JENKINS REGIONAL	2	21,781	5.14	1.64	35,721	1,561
DOUGHERTY COUNTY	5	97,444	5.12	1.64	159,808	6,983
DEKALB COUNTY	22	593,375	4.91	1.64	973,135	42,524
CHESTATEE REGIONAL	8	138,342	4.90	1.64	226,881	9,914
CONYERS-ROCKDALE	1	66,296	4.88	1.64	108,725	4,751
NORTHEAST GEORGIA REGIONAL	6	81,632	4.87	1.64	133,876	5,850
PEACH PUBLIC	2	22,372	4.64	1.64	36,690	1,603
ELBERT COUNTY	2	19,478	4.31	1.20	23,374	1,021
CHATTOOGA COUNTY	3	22,321	4.26	1.20	26,785	1,170
FLINT RIVER REGIONAL	8	203,095	4.09	1.20	243,714	10,650
SOUTHWEST GEORGIA REGIONAL	3	41,511	4.09	1.20	49,813	2,177
SEQUOYAH REGIONAL	6	146,347	4.02	1.20	175,616	7,674
SOUTH GEORGIA REGIONAL	6	90,941	4.02	1.20	109,129	4,769
UNCLE REMUS REGIONAL	8	104,062	3.87	1.20	124,874	5,457
CLAYTON COUNTY	5	207,409	3.84	1.20	248,891	10,876
HOUSTON COUNTY	3	100,398	3.75	1.20	120,478	5,265
NEWTON COUNTY	1	51,693	3.75	1.20	62,032	2,711
RODDENBERRY MEMORIAL	1	21,111	3.74	1.20	25,333	1,107
ATLANTA-FULTON PUBLIC	35	689,606	3.72	1.20	827,527	36,161
FITZGERALD-BEN HILL COUNTY	1	17,172	3.66	1.20	20,606	900
COASTAL PLAIN REGIONAL	6	82,719	3.64	1.20	99,263	4,338
MOULTRIE-COLQUITT COUNTY	3	37,658	3.43	1.20	45,190	1,975
CHEROKEE REGIONAL	4	74,680	3.34	1.20	89,616	3,916
CHATHAM-EFFINGHAM-LIBERTY REGION	19	325,811	3.31	1.20	390,973	17,085
KINCHAFOONEE REGIONAL	6	28,942	3.29	1.20	34,730	1,518
EAST CENTRAL GEORGIA REGIONAL	14	321,231	3.25	1.20	385,477	16,844
BARTRAM TRAIL REGIONAL	3	34,504	3.25	1.20	41,405	1,809
STATESBORO REGIONAL	6	104,416	3.21	1.20	125,299	5,475
CHATTAHOOCHEE VALLEY REGIONAL	10	221,046	3.02	1.20	265,255	11,591
WEST GEORGIA REGIONAL	9	250,564	2.90	1.20	300,677	13,139
JEFFERSON COUNTY	3	17,601	2.87	1.20	21,121	923
OKEFENOKEE REGIONAL	6	82,761	2.79	1.20	99,313	4,340
TROUP-HARRIS-COWETA REGIONAL	6	143,022	2.78	1.20	171,626	7,500
LAKE BLACKSHEAR REGIONAL	6	66,309	2.60	1.20	79,571	3,477

SYSTEM	Libr. # of	Population	Circ./ Cap.	Incentive/ Capita	Total $ Amount	Tot'l # of Books*
LEE COUNTY	2	20,503	2.45	1.20	24,604	1,075
PIEDMONT REGIONAL	6	79,403	2.45	1.20	95,284	4,164
HENRY COUNTY	4	74,382	2.36	1.20	89,258	3,900
BARTOW COUNTY	3	65,096	2.25	1.20	78,115	3,413
PINE MOUNTAIN REGIONAL	7	63,161	2.13	1.20	75,793	3,312
SATILLA REGIONAL	7	51,145	2.01	1.20	61,374	2,682
OHOOPEE REGIONAL	6	51,580	1.78	1.20	61,896	2,705
OCONEE REGIONAL	5	82,397	1.76	1.20	98,876	4,321
NORTHWEST GEORGIA REGIONAL	5	197,343	1.46	1.20	236,812	10,348
TOTAL ENHACEMENT		7,213,207	4.60		9,985,436	436,338 *
TOTAL ADJUSTED BASE		7,676,784			4,486,999	162,134 *
SUBTOTAL ESTIMATED # OF BOOKS						598,472
FED'L GRANTS					1,485,346	53,671 *
SCHOOL MEDIA CENTER QBE INCREASE						400,000
GRAND TOTAL EST. # OF BOOKS (STATE & FEDERALLY FUNDED)						**1,052,143**

The above recommendation gives all systems $1.20/capita. It further awards systems with above average circulation (above the line) an additional $.44/capita.
*Assumes a 50/50 split between adult and children's books, with adult books priced at $35 and children's books at $17.
**Assumes the normal 75/25 split between adult and children's books, priced as above.
All figures are 1996 figures.

Online. As a result, every county in Georgia, regardless of size, population, economic situation, or location had access to the same electronic resources.

Governor Miller's book initiatives: While electronic resources were critical in an instant world, books and other media resources were no less important. As public libraries and school media centers became more efficient resources for a wider variety of information, they experienced an unexpected side-effect—the demand for books increased. Governor Miller undertook several initiatives to meet the increasing appetite for information and entertainment provided by books. Early in his tenure, he raised the state's material allocation for public libraries by two cents to 56 cents per capita. Library holdings received an additional boost in FY 1998 when the Governor dedicated $10 million for public library book purchases, in an effort to increase reading across Georgia.

School media centers also saw their holdings increase when the 1998 General Assembly funded Governor Miller's FY 1999 recommendation for the largest increase for school media materials in the history of the Quality Basic Education formula. This 20 percent increase of almost $4.3 million would be a continuing feature of the QBE formula for years to come, helping to meet the increased demand and offset the increased cost of books.

By the most conservative estimates, the extra funds provided in FY 1999 enabled school media centers to purchase an additional 400,000 new books for the 1998-1999 school year. Public libraries were able to add an estimated 450,000 books to their collections. Combined with the regular allocation for books to public libraries, Governor Miller made over 1 million new books available in one year to Georgia's citizens and students.

In addition to the investment in books, $200,000 was appropriated to enhance and expand summer reading programs. Governor Miller's efforts to promote reading appeared to succeed. Between FY 1990 and FY 1996 book circulation increased 27 percent, slightly outpacing population increases. The impact on reading from the $10 million book investment and the boost to summer reading programs should be reflected in circulation figures for FY 1999 and FY 2000.

Incentives for job creation

Job creation was a major concern of Governor Miller's when he took office. He focused state efforts on areas which industry identified as crucial to Georgia's future economic growth— education, workforce, research, and infrastructure. Governor Miller also instituted several successful incentive programs to better retain businesses, support business expansion and attract new business into the state. The Regional Economic Business Assistance (REBA) program, the Job Tax Credit and the Investment Tax Credit were three key programs created to combat business incentives offered by other states, assist Georgia businesses looking to expand, and position Georgia as the best state for employers to locate.

REBA was created in 1994 to provide financial assistance for community and economic development projects. Projects fell into two categories: direct, which assisted a specific company, and regional, which provided community improvements. Project activities included infrastructure and other public works or improvements; the development, promotion and retention of trade, commerce, industry and employment opportunities; the provision of transportation systems related to specific economic development projects; and the formulation and implementation of regional or multi-county plans for community or economic development cooperation. From FY 1995 through FY 1999, the Governor committed over $31 million to REBA. By the end of FY 1998, REBA funds had assisted 124 projects with $27.5 million.

The vast majority of REBA funds were used for direct project assistance, to help bring a specific employer to a Georgia community or to encourage the expansion of an employer in the community. Between January 1994 and April 1998, nearly $17 million of REBA funds were used to assist 49 different industry-specific projects. The state's $17 million investment in these 49 projects secured roughly $2 billion in private investment and created 18,622 jobs for Georgians. In addition, the average public benefit of these projects exceeded $720,000 per year. During the same time, another 54 regional projects received $5.5 million in REBA funding.

The Job Tax Credit and Investment Credit programs were created as part of the Business Expansion and Support Act (BEST) and allowed Georgia businesses to claim a tax credit for the creation of full-time jobs or the investment of capital in the manufacturing, warehousing and distribution, processing, tourism, and research and development industries. Furthermore, the program was organized to provide higher tax and investment credits to companies that created jobs or invested capital in the state's least developed counties. Companies creating five or more jobs in any one of the 53 least developed counties (tier 1) could receive a $2,500 tax credit. Expanding companies investing $50,000 in a tier 1 county could receive a five percent credit. Companies creating 15 or more jobs in the 53 middle-ranked counties (tier 2) could receive a $1,500 credit. An investment of $50,000 in a tier 2 county by an expanding company resulted in a three percent credit. Companies creating 25 or more new jobs in the 53 most developed counties (tier 3) could receive a $500 tax credit. Companies expanding in tier 3 counties could receive a 1 percent credit for an investment of $50,000. From 1991 to 1995, the Job Tax Credit program created more than 12,000 new jobs. In 1995, the first year the credit applied to all 159 counties, 7,140 new jobs were created and businesses were allowed over $7.8 million in tax credits.

The Employment Incentive Program (EIP), a CDBG-funded grant program, was designed to support local government projects that facilitated and enhanced job creation and retention. From FY 1991 to FY 1997, 110 projects were funded, involving a public investment of $21,080,765. These public dollars leveraged $692,906,779 in private investment, creating 5,352 new jobs and retaining 1,091 jobs. Low and moderate-income persons acquired 82 percent of the 5,352 new jobs. For every public dollar, the program leveraged nearly $33 in private investment.

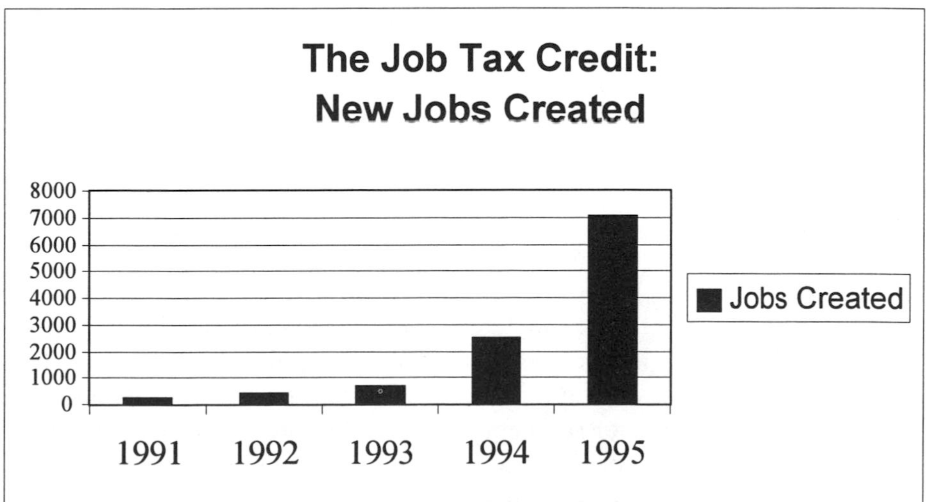

The Job Tax Credit Program 1996

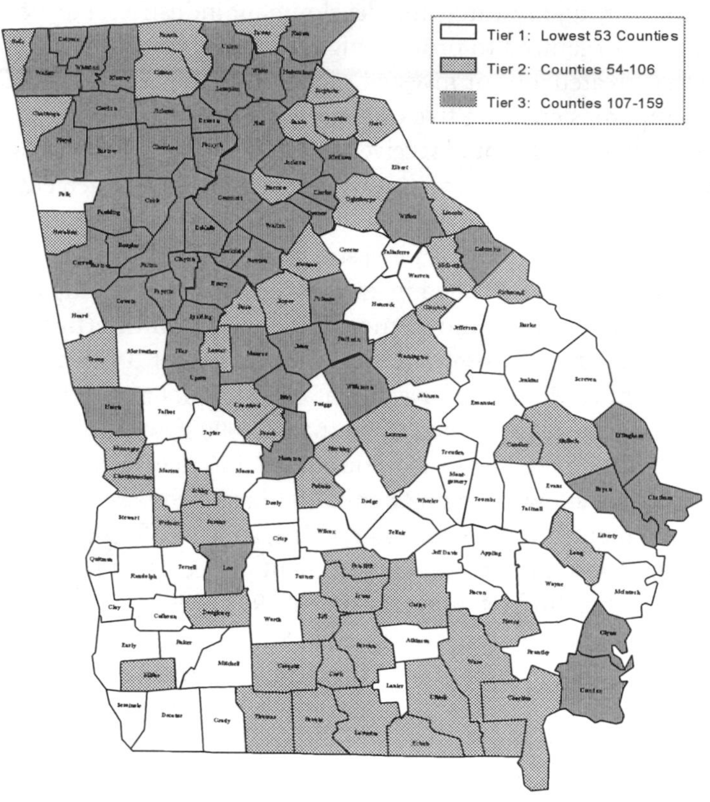

Source: Georgia Department of Community Affairs

Fostering Growth in Rural Georgia

What I am working hard to do is build economic growth into a balanced pattern all across the state, a pattern that brings growth to every part of the state, not just metro Atlanta.

Governor Zell Miller, May 26, 1994

During the 1980s, many people claimed there were "two Georgias"—metro Atlanta and the rest of the state. Governor Miller worked to eradicate the disparities between these "two Georgias" by emphasizing growth in the rural areas of the state during his tenure. He promoted community betterment, created incentives for rural employers, and improved infrastructure in rural Georgia. The result of Governor Miller's efforts was that Georgia's non-metropolitan areas exceeded the national growth rates in population from

1990 to 1996 and per capita income from 1990 to 1995. On May 15, 1996, the *Wall Street Journal* wrote, "Employment in Georgia's five other (non-Atlanta) metro areas and rural communities grew 3.4 percent in 1995—twice as much as initial estimates and faster than the revised rate of every other southeastern state."

The Main Street Program and the Better Hometown Program were public-private community betterment partnerships between the Georgia Department of Community Affairs, Georgia Department of Industry, Trade and Tourism, the Georgia Power Company, the Georgia Municipal Association, The University of Georgia and many other technical assistance providers. These programs promoted community betterment in small and medium size cities with populations between 1,000 and 50,000. Main Street and Better Hometown communities had access to technical assistance and advice designed to stimulate downtown revitalization. The 55 communities that qualified for these programs while Miller was Governor hailed them as the best programs created in many years for smaller communities.

The Governor took a strong interest in luring and creating jobs in Georgia's rural areas. Toward this end, his administration steered over $7.5 million in incentive grants from the Regional Economic Business Assistance (REBA) program to 32 projects in rural Georgia from the creation of REBA in January of 1994 through April of 1998. The Governor also encouraged communities to use the Business Retention and Expansion Process (BREP) as a tool for communities working with local chambers of commerce and development authorities to identify barriers and assess opportunities for growth. The process involved in-depth, personal interviews with plant managers and industry executives to identify the perceptions and potential problems of private sector firms concerning issues like future plans, international trade, labor and manpower, local government services, energy requirements and community linkages. The Business Expansion and Support Act (BEST) also organized the state's incentives for business investment so that industries garnered larger incentives for expanding or locating in the poorer areas of the state. BEST divided the state into three tiers of 53 counties each, based on economic indicators. A business would receive the largest tax incentives for locating or expanding in a county in the lowest tier (lowest economic status), comparatively lower incentives for locating in a second tier county (moderate economic status), and the smallest incentives for locating in the highest tier (high economic status).

The pulp and paper; food processing; and textile, carpet and apparel industries constituted 45 percent of the state's manufacturing employment and an even larger portion of the manufacturing base in rural Georgia. The Governor recognized the importance of these industries to the state's rural areas and saw that they were undergoing major transitions to compete in a global marketplace. To help them improve their technology and solve problems that affected their ability to compete, the Governor developed the Traditional Industries Program in FY 1994. By FY 1999 he had committed over $44.4 million for research and development to infuse these industries with technology to help keep them competitive and enable them to continue providing jobs and economic stability to Georgia.

Under the leadership of Governor Miller, the state greatly improved the infrastructure of rural Georgia so that it could accommodate greater gains in economic development. The Governor's Road Improvement Program (GRIP) was initiated in 1985 and consisted of 14 corridors with over 2,600 miles of roadways that were slated to be upgraded to four lanes. Under Governor Miller, over $1 billion was invested in GRIP and approximately 55 percent of the system was completed. Upon completion, this network of economic development highways would place 98 percent of Georgia's population within 20 miles of a multi-lane highway.

Governor Miller also committed $35,350,000 to upgrade 28 strategically located publicly owned airports that primarily benefit rural areas. These general aviation airports were identified in the Georgia Statewide Aviation Systems Plan as airports with regional impact. Miller's airport initiative provided a statewide network of airports with the necessary facilities to serve corporate aircraft. They provided a competitive advantage in attracting industry and stimulating long-term economic development to communities in Georgia that might not otherwise have opportunities for growth and development. With these upgrades, virtually every community in Georgia was within a 45-minute drive of a regional airport.

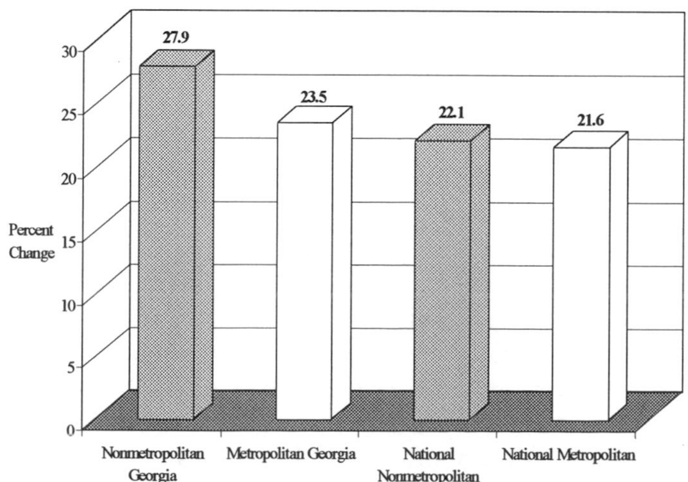

Better Hometowns and Main Street Cities

Using the Georgia Environmental Facilities Authority (GEFA), Governor Miller committed over $174 million to provide low interest loans to small local governments (communities of under 25,000) for water and wastewater infrastructure construction. This $174 million was 58 percent of the state's total loan funds dedicated for water and wastewater infrastructure in Georgia during Governor Miller's tenure. With this money, rural Georgia communities built infrastructure capable of supporting a more diversified industrial base and larger industrial facilities.

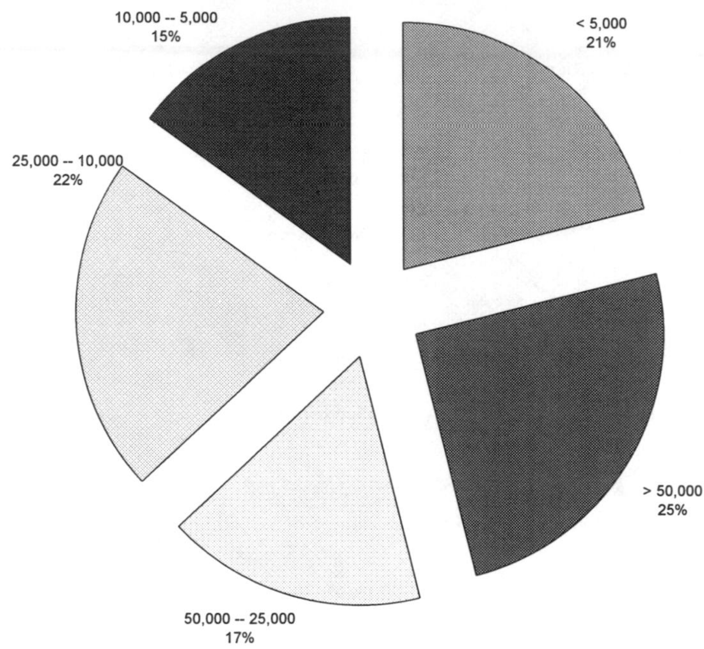
Georgia Environmental Facilities Authority
Loan Dollar Distribution by Recipient Population Groups
Fiscal Years 1992 -- 1997
10,000 -- 5,000
15%
< 5,000
21%
25,000 -- 10,000
22%
> 50,000
25%
50,000 -- 25,000
17%

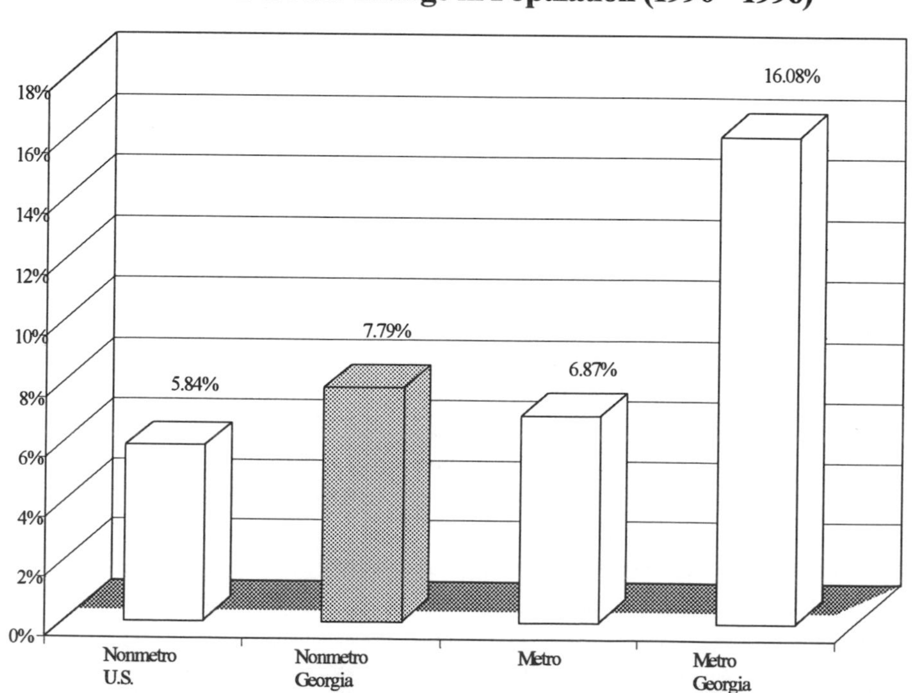
Percent Change in Population (1990 - 1996)
18%
16%
14%
12%
10%
8%
6%
4%
2%
0%
5.84%
7.79%
6.87%
16.08%
Nonmetro U.S.
Nonmetro Georgia
Metro
Metro Georgia

The Governor's commitment helped rural Georgia make great strides in the 1990s. From 1990 to 1995, per capita income in nonmetropolitan Georgia increased 28.2 percent ($13,601 to $17,436). This rate of growth was greater than Georgia's metropolitan areas (24.8 percent) and was significantly greater than the national nonmetropolitan increase of 22.1 percent ($14,472 to $17,675) during this same period. In addition to its rapid rate of growth, Georgia's nonmetropolitan per capita income began to approach the national nonmetropolitan average during the Miller Administration. In 1990, Georgia's nonmetropolitan per capita income was 93.98 percent of the national average. In 1996, this figure grew to 98.65 percent of the national average. This rise in per capita income occurred while the population of rural Georgia also experienced significant increases. Population growth from 1990 to 1996 in nonmetropolitan Georgia (7.79 percent) outpaced both the national nonmetropolitan (5.84 percent) and the national metropolitan (6.87 percent) growth rates.

Investing in Georgia's Urban Centers

We have new tourism infrastructure that has been opening across the state... So we are developing an increasingly large and diverse tourism product in Georgia.

Governor Zell Miller, September 10, 1997

Assistance to non-Atlanta metro areas

Georgia's non-Atlanta metro areas (often called Georgia's second tier cities) had great potential for growth because they had the infrastructure and the workforce to support most industries. They generally already had the capacity for expansion and growth or could put it in place in a short period of time. The state tried to direct industries to these communities since they usually were the most prepared for growth. Each of these cities had vital economic development organizations and chambers, and they were viewed by statewide economic developers as Georgia's untapped resource for growth.

Governor Miller systematically worked with the leaders of Georgia's non-Atlanta metro areas to provide state financial support for projects that these cities considered important, directly or indirectly, for their economic development. All these projects involved state participation with local public and private partnerships or coalitions in which the local effort was much more substantial than the state's—usually part of a major multi-year plan for downtown revitalization and expansion. These projects included the Georgia International and Maritime Trade Center in Savannah, the Georgia Music and Sports Halls of Fame in Macon, the Discovery Center in Augusta, the Performing Arts Center in Columbus, and the River Center in Albany.

In each of these cities, local public-private coalitions or partnerships produced overall development plans that identified priorities for development and specified how each would be funded (private, local, federal, state). In each case the state was asked to provide a key element of the plan which would contribute significantly to economic development of quality of life improvements.

Savannah: Savannah's International and Maritime Trade Center was the first project funded. It was to be a major new convention and trade show center that would enable Savannah to handle the already demonstrated demand for such space in the city. It was a $75 million project, and the Governor Miller recommended and the General Assembly provided $18.25 million (about 25 percent) for the project. A private development company built a convention hotel next to the trade center. This project was expected to transform Savannah's convention business, increasing it to as much as double its prior size.

Macon: Macon developed a master plan for downtown improvement and realized that it needed several different type of attractions as a draw primarily for tourists and conventioneers, then went after both the Music and Sports Halls of Fame being proposed by the state. Macon provided the land for these attractions and made $1.7 million in street and pedestrian improvements to accommodate them. The city also spent $18 million to renovate and expand its convention facilities, $4 million to renovate the classic Douglass Theater, and $3.3 million to construct the Peyton Anderson Community Service Center near the two Halls of Fame. The state invested $14.9 million in the construction of the two facilities. The value of the land donated by Macon and the improvements made by the city to facilities that complemented the Halls of Fame amounted to an estimated $27 million. Private sector investments by the end of the Miller Administration amounted to $15.8 million. Of the cities mentioned here, only the two Halls of Fame in Macon were operated by the state. These two attractions were expected to become self-supporting.

Columbus: Columbus developed a downtown improvement plan that approached a $200 million total investment. The element of the plan with which Columbus wanted state help was the Columbus Performing Arts Center. The center was a quality of life improvement that Columbus felt was important both to attract more advanced technology industries and to help revitalize the downtown area. The Center was also to be utilized by Columbus State University's performing arts programs. Governor Miller obtained $15.25 million in state assistance for this $57 million facility.

Augusta: The Discovery Center in Augusta was an integral part of the development of the Riverwalk area of Augusta. This area was the core of

Augusta's downtown redevelopment plan, and the state's investment of $10 million to develop the Discovery Center was important to generating activity and business in Augusta's downtown. The center, known as Fort Discovery, was an interactive science and math center that featured 250 exhibits that were both educational and fun for kids.

In addition, in FY 1997, Governor Miller supported the appropriation of $6 million in bonds toward the construction of the Georgia Golf Hall of Fame located in Augusta. This financing represented the state's portion of an ambitious project designed to honor golf's greatest players and impart the history and appreciation to the public of a game that enjoyed worldwide popularity. The grace and tradition of the world-renowned Master's tournament was a fitting backdrop for this facility and the sport it represented. Financing for the Hall of Fame was a collaborative effort between the state, the city of Augusta, and the private sector with each participant contributing approximately one-third of the Hall of Fame's construction cost.

Albany: Albany developed a long range downtown revitalization plan whose first phase would cost $62.5 million and utilize funding from several sources. From the state, Albany sought $15 million to fund the Flint River Center, one of the core elements of this plan. Governor Miller recommended $1,447,727 in the FY 1998 amended budget to plan and design this facility on a site provided by the city. The Flint River Center would be a focal point that interpreted the river and its impact on the region and directed visitors to all areas of interest in the Albany area.

Georgia Music Hall Of Fame

The State of Georgia produced a musical dynasty whose contributions helped shape and define American music. The Peach State can claim such influential luminaries as the "Father of Gospel Music" Dr. Thomas Andrew Dorsey, the "Mother of the Blues" Gertrude "Ma" Rainey, the "Godfather of Soul" James Brown, the "Architect of Rock 'n' Roll" Little Richard Penniman, the "Father of Commercial Country Music" Fiddlin' John Carson, and the "First Lady of Contemporary Christian Music" Amy Grant. These are but a few of Georgia's internationally famous musical sons and daughters.

In 1977, Zell Miller took the first step in creating an institution to honor and preserve the state's rich musical heritage when as Lieutenant Governor he appointed the Senate Music Industry Committee, charging its members to attract investment in Georgia music and to encourage new talent. Two years later, under the auspices of this Senate committee, the newly-formed Friends of Georgia Music organized Georgia Music Week and held the first annual Georgia Music Awards ceremony. The first to receive GEORGY Awards were the legendary Ray Charles (Albany) and music publisher Bill Lowery

(Atlanta). By 1998, a total of 75 Georgians including Governor Miller had been honored with induction.

Over the intervening years, the awards grew in prestige and popularity, and live broadcasts of the awards ceremony reached over 350,000 viewers annually. In 1989, then-Lieutenant Governor Miller chose Macon as the future site of the Georgia Music Hall of Fame, the state's official museum. During the 1991 legislative session, the General Assembly created the Georgia Music Hall of Fame Authority, and Governor Miller appointed its members to guide the development of the museum and oversee its construction and operations.

Economic development and market feasibility studies endorsed the music hall of fame concept. Based on its potential for cultural tourism, Governor Miller endorsed and the General Assembly approved $6.5 million in general obligation bonds to finance construction of the Music Hall of Fame. Construction of the 43,000 square-foot building started in 1994, and staff began gathering artifacts that documented Georgia's significant musical history. With Governor Miller's assistance, the state provided an additional $3.9 million in annual operating support for the Music hall of Fame, including $1,155,051 authorized in the 1998 legislative session.

On September 22, 1996, Governor Miller cut the ribbon and opened the Georgia Music Hall of Fame to the world. During the first year's operation, visitors from all 50 states and 36 foreign countries toured the Music Hall of Fame, expressing delight with the innovative exhibits and beautiful facilities. With over 90,000 visitors during the second year of operations, the museum experienced a 51 percent increase in ticket sales and over 100 percent increase in fees generated by after-hours events.

The Georgia Music Hall of Fame became the keystone of downtown Macon and the place for business and community gatherings. The facility was an extraordinary, one-of-a-kind museum that was equal measures of education and entertainment. The 12,000 square-foot exhibition hall was a stage set called "Tune Town" where a perpetual music festival was underway. In this fictional village the sounds and the stars of the Peach State came alive. Exhibits documented the lives, careers, and accomplishments of over 450 artists, including the 75 inductees.

The museum covered the state's musical heritage from precolonial Native American sounds to the hottest urban cuts, including country, gospel, rhythm and blues, jazz, and swing, pop, classical, rock 'n' roll, and folk. Music scholars, ardent fans, and casual listeners could learn through all their senses, surrounded by over 3,000 display items, and over 80 hours of audio and video presented in two theaters, five music-themed clubs, and 20 individual listening stations.

After a trip through Tune Town, visitors wishing for an in-depth look at Georgia music history could join scholars and students in the Zell Miller Center for Georgia Music Studies. Research assistants provided visitors access to the Center's informational resources, historic documents, and musical artifacts. The center's library contained over 600 reference books, 1,000 periodicals, 8,000 sound recordings, 450 videotapes and electronic media, and volumes of printed music, photographs, and manuscripts.

The center's staff helped students and researchers trace the state's diverse musical roots through the examination of musical artifacts and memorabilia. The collections included 159 musical instruments, 186 performance outfits, 1,938 promotional pieces, and 25 vintage sound recording and playback devices. Some highlights of the archives included the handwritten score to "Gone With The Wind" by composer Max Steiner; two very rare Steinway pianos, one dating to 1854; the original recording console from STAX Records; nineteenth century banjos; a calliope; and fine examples of Georgia instrument-makers' artistry.

For serious scholars and authors, historical documents included business papers, itineraries, hours of oral history interviews, and personal letters providing original sources for publication and media productions. The center provided Internet access to other music-related websites around the world. The staff used these resources in sharing Georgia's music history with a worldwide audience. The "Otis Redding 25th Anniversary Special" radio documentary reached over 10 million listeners throughout the United States, Canada, and Europe. "Georgia Music Minutes" were aired throughout the state daily on 125 radio stations. The Georgia Music Hall of Fame was featured on numerous television shows domestically and abroad, and the museum website—www.gamusichall.com—provided global communication and information to music lovers everywhere.

Education was of paramount importance at the Music Hall of Fame. Over 30,000 school children toured the facility during the Miller Administration. Museum educators reached thousands more through the Georgia Statewide Academic and Medical System (GSAMS) interactive television network. Thanks to Governor Miller's keen interest in the development of remote site learning, students who might not be able to visit the museum could share in educational programming. Museum staff linked up with other states in addition to the more than 400 GSAMS sites in Georgia.

A 2,400 square-foot children's interactive exhibit, "The Music Factory," was slated to open in spring of 1999, spotlighting arts education for ages 4-10 but providing fun for music lovers of all ages. Here visitors could explore Georgia geography through music, learn how instruments were made, explore music fundamentals, take music lessons and compose music via interactive computers, and get hands-on experience in a variety of music-related professions.

From the museum's inception, economic development consultants encouraged the state and the City of Macon to form a partnership that would transform the Georgia Music Hall of Fame into a downtown revitalization and historic preservation success story. With the Music Hall of Fame's opening, the economic potential of the Macon downtown entertainment corridor was realized with 38 new or expanded businesses in downtown, a coliseum renovation, and infrastructure improvements valued at over $45 million.

Members - Georgia Music Hall of Fame

Year	Category	Inductee
1979	Non Performer	Bill Lowery
	Performer	Ray Charles
1980	Non Performer	Zenas "Daddy" Sears
	Performer	Ray Stevens
		*Johnny Mercer
1981	Non Performer	Dr. Thomas A. Dorsey
	Performer	Joe South
		*Otis Redding
1982	Non Performer	Boudleaux Bryant
	Performer	Brenda Lee
		*Duane Allman
1983	Non Performer	Albert Coleman
	Performer	James Brown
		*Harry James
	Pioneer	Piano Red Perryman
1984	Non Performer	Buddy Buie
	Performer	Little Richard Penniman
		*James Melton
	Pioneer	Fiddlin' John Carson
1985	Non Performer	Zell Miller
	Performer	Bill Anderson
		*Graham Jackson
	Pioneer	Eva Mae LeFevre
1986	Non Performer	Phil Walden
	Performer	Tommy Roe
		*George Riley Puckett
	Pioneer	Hovie Lister
1987	Non Performer	Alex Cooley
	Performer	Jerry Reed
		*Felton Jarvis
	Pioneer	Bob Richardson
1988	Non Performer	Robert L. Shaw
	Performer	Billy Joe Royal
		*Gid Tanner
	Pioneer	Joe Williams
1989	Non Performer	Harold Shedd
	Performer	Gladys Knight
		*Fletcher Henderson
	Pioneer	Lee Roy Abernathy
1990	Non Performer	Chips Moman
	Performer	Ronnie Milsap
		*Blind Willie" McTell
	Pioneer	Wendy Bagwell
1991	Non Performer	Ray Whitley
	Performer	Lena Horne
		*Roland Haynes
	Pioneer	Joseph "Cotton" Carrier
1992	Non Performer	Emory Gordy, Jr.
	Performer	Connie Haines
		*Gertrude "Ma" Rainey
	Pioneer Group	The Tams
		The Lewis Family
1993	Non Performer	J. R. Cobb
	Performer	Curtis Mayfield
		*Sam Wallace
	Group	Dennis Yost & Classics IV
1994	Non Performer	Gwen Kesler
	Performer	Issac Hayes
		*Chuck Willis
1995	Non Performer	Joel Katz
	Performer	Chet Atkins
		*Ray Eberle
	Pioneer	Elmo Ellis
1996	Non Performer	Rodney Mills
	Performer	Mac Davis
	Pioneer Group	Joe Galkin
		Atlanta Rhythm Section
1997	Performer	William Bell
		*Boots" Woodall
	Pioneer Group	Dave Prater
		Atlanta Symphony Orchestra
1998	Non Performer	J. Lee Friedman
	Performer	Peabo Bryson
	Pioneer Group	Emma Thompson Kelly
		Allman Brothers Band

***Deceased**

During the initial year of operation, the Music Hall of Fame's visitors came because the experience was highly recommended by friends and family. But, as newspapers, television, and magazines raved about the new museum experience, this trend changed. By the end of the Miller Administration, the majority of out-of-town visitors, particularly non-Georgians, came specifically to visit the Music Hall of Fame. International visitors made up 10 percent of the museum audience. Customer satisfaction as captured on museum visitors' surveys was extremely high and non-traditional audience participation in museum programs was excellent. The average length of time the Music Hall of Fame visitors spent in Macon was 3.2 nights, compared to a state average of 2.7 nights.

Tourism increased as a result of this public-private partnership and in 1997 tourists in Bibb County spent $310 million that generated $13.4 million in local tax revenue and sustained 8,593 jobs, providing $167.74 million in resident income. The state's share of this increased heritage tourism amounted to $23.75 million in tax revenues. The economic impact of the Music Hall of Fame was $38 million for the local economy and a rate of return for the state of $2.12 in tax revenue for each dollar of annual operating support provided by the General Assembly.

Visitors to the Georgia Music Hall of Fame confirmed Governor Miller's dream of a place of celebration for Georgia Music and the preservation of the histories of the talented musical artists who called Georgia home. Their heart-felt praise was reflected in comments such as: Marvelous museum—Pittsburgh; Tres joli— France; Spiritual, soulful, fulfilling—Byron; We danced and loved it—Warner Robins; Wonderful place—England; Hats off to Georgia— Louisiana; Wunderbar—Germany; Amazing resource—Chicago; Fantastic—Tasmania; This Yankee was impressed!—Boston.

Sports Hall Of Fame

Georgia had a great sports heritage that needed to be preserved and presented to each new generation. Georgia's sports heritage included not only sports legends who were born in Georgia like Ty Cobb, Ralph "Country" Brown, Johnny Mize, and Jackie Robinson, but also those who spent their career in Georgia like Hank Aaron, Tommy Nobis and Dale Murphy. To preserve and present this heritage, the General Assembly, under the leadership of Governor Miller, supported the construction of a sports museum.

The Sports Hall of Fame had its roots in the State of Georgia Athletic Hall of Fame, which was organized in 1963, then merged with the Georgia Prep Hall of Fame, which covered high school, college, professional and amateur sports. The first class of inductees into the expanded Hall of Fame came about in 1964 and included such sports heroes as Ty Cobb, Bobby Jones, Luke

Appling, Bill Alexander, Bobby Hooks, Bob McWhorter, Albert Slaton and Bobby Walthour.

The Sports Hall of Fame was officially created with the passage of legislation in 1978. The initial board for the Sports Hall of Fame was appointed to supervise the direction of the Hall of Fame and to select inductees. During the early 1980s a lot of attention was directed toward the construction of a permanent home for the Sports Hall of Fame. Originally a site was sought in the Atlanta area with the World Congress Center as one possibility. Finally in the early 1990s, the General Assembly selected downtown Macon as the site for the museum, where the Sports Hall of Fame could join forces with the

Members - Georgia Sports Hall of Fame

Year Inducted	Year Inducted	Year Inducted
1975 Henry L. "Hank Aaron	1985 John Donaldson	1984* Oscar Bane Keeler
1980 Tommy Aaron	1978 Vince Dooley	1960* Dwight Keith, Sr.
1994 Lucinda Williams Adams	1957* R.L. "Shorty" Doyal	1996 Kim King
1964* William A. Alexander	1995 Allen M. Doyle	1974 Dorothy Kirby
1974* Paul Anderson	1993 Paula A. Duke	1995 Charles "Ray" Knight
1966* Frank B. Anderson, Sr	1992 David Dupree	1960* Henry L. Langston
1996 William Andrews	1977* Sterling A. Dupree	1982 Milton "Red" Leathers
1964* Lucius "Luke Appling	1980 Edith McGuire Duvall	1972 Carlton Lewis
1990 Howard "Doc" Ayers	1987 Partick E. Dye	1996 L. J. "Stan" Lomax
1992 Harry Babcock	1972* Joel H. Eaves	1986* Billy Lothridge
1992* James C. Bagby, Jr	1977* Sam J. "Sambo" Elliott	1988* Jim Luck
1982*James C. Bagby,Sr	1985 Leonidas Epps	1958* Quinton Lumpkin
1981 Thomas William Barnes	1975* William E. "Bill" Fincher	1990 Steve Lundquist
1977* David "Red" Barron	1978 J. Timothy "Tim" Flock	1987 Thomas L. Lyons
1973* Weems O. Baskin	1995* Vera "Punkin" Flock	1981* Herbert Maffett
1980 Maxie Baughan	1976* Theo "Tiger" Flowers	1976 Dan Magill
1960 Wright Bazemore	1969* Allen Ralph "Buck" Flowers	1995* Earnest Lynwood "Baggy" Mallard
1958* Joseph W. Bean	1983* Mary Louise Fowler	1971* Earl Mann
1959 Ray Beck	1988 Douglas L. "Buddy" Fowlkes	1974 Martin W. "Marty" Marion
1984* Joseph J. Bennett	1978* Alexa Stirling Fraser	1959 George Mathews, Jr.
1989 Daniel A Birchmore	1986 Walter Frazier, Jr.	1995 William H. Mathis
1990 Furman Bisher	1993 James R. Gabrielsen	1992 Alex McCaskill
1990 Mel Blount	1961 George Gardner	1957* Harold E. McNabb
1979 Arnold Blum	1993* Frances P. King Garlington	1980* H. Boyd McWhorter
1994 John Pennington Bond	1989 Jospeh Geri	1964* Robert McWhorter
1991 Emerson Boozer	1986 Joe H. Gerson	1971* Harry Mehre
1987 Harley Bowers	1962* Sam Glassman, Sr.	1980* Ralph Metcalfe
1980 Edmund R. "Zeke" Bratkowski	1985* William L "Dynamite" Goodloe, Jr.	1992 Hal M. Miller
1994 George H. Brodnax	1965* Bryan M. "Bitsy" Grant	1975 Fred Missildine
1990 Pete Brown	1987*Joseph A. "Cy" Grant	1993 A. Thomas "Tommy" Mixon
1994 Ralph "Country" Brown	1961* Thomas E. Greene	1915* John H. Mize
1971 Frank Broyles	1984 George C. Griffin	1987* Johnny Moon
1986* Morris M. Bryan, Jr	1979 Charles Grisham	1976 Virlyn Moore, Jr.
1986 Bobby Lee Bryant	1985* Watts Gunn	1967* Charles Morgan
1956* Selby H. Buck	1995 Rufus Guthrie	1986 Anthony "Zippy" Morocco
1959* Sam Burke	1972* Joe Guyon	1975 Larry Morris
1959* H.D. Butler	1982* Edward B. Hamm	1981 George A. Morris, Jr.
1966* Wallace "Wally" Butts	1988 Leon Hardeman	1977 Elmer B. Morrow
1981 Marion Campbell	1974* James "Doc" Harper	1989* Wallace Moses
1984 Jimmy Carnes	1991 Charles W. Harrison	1972* Tom Nash, Jr.
1962* D.B. Carroll	1993 Tommy Hart	1994 Larry G. Nelson
1957 John R. Carson	1981 William C. Hartman, Jr.	1985 Phil Niekro
1991* Hugh Casey	1981 Leonard Moore Hauss	1993 Willard L. Nixon
1956* Clint Castleberry	1991 William R. Healy	1983 Tommy Nobis
1962 Gus Vassa Cate	1983 James T. "Jim" Hearn	1962* Jim Nolan
1969* Jim Cavan	1992* William Waller "Tiny" Hearn	1962* George H. O'Kelley
1968* Edgar Chandler, Jr.	1967 John Heisman	1978 James E. "Jimmy" Orr

Members - Georgia Sports Hall of Fame

Year Inducted	Year Inducted	Year Inducted
1969* Spurgeon Chandler	1962 William Henderson	1991 Jessie Outlar
1958* W.O. Cheney	1989 Jimmy L. Hightower	1956* Vernon "Catfish" Smith
1976 James P. "Buck" Cheves	1985* J.C. "Jake" Hines	1972 Alline Banks Sprouse
1993 Ellis Clary	1988 Graham Hixon, Jr.	1979* George "Tweedy" Stallings
1964* Tyrus Raymond Cobb	1995* Morton Strahan Hodgson	1976 Charles Yates
1982 Lew Cordell	1973* Howell T. Hollis	1977* Rudolph P. "Rudy" York
1991 Pete Cox	1987 Isabelle D. Holston	1997 Dale Murphy
1973 Wayman O. Creel	1964* Robert G. Hooks	1979* Frank "Hop" Owens
1992 Bill Curry	1985 Fred W. Hooper	1961 Thomas H. Paris, Sr.
1979 Alice Coachman Davis	1961 Oliver Hunnicutt	1974 Jim Parker
1990 "Lamar Race Horse" Davis	1980 John "Whack" Hyder	1979 William A. "Billy" Pashcal
1983 Robert T. "Bobby" Davis	1956* Joe H. Jenkins	1983 Reid Patterson
1994* Van Andrew Davis	1996 Andy Johnson	1991 George E. Patton
1992* Claud Derrick	1990* William "Bo" Johnston	1984 Melvin Pender, Jr.
1992 Gardner Dickinson	1964* Robert T. Jones, Jr.	1986 Martha Hudson Pennyman
1965* Robert L. 'Boddy" Dodd	1984 Roger Kaiser	1958* George M. Phillips
1991 Daniel Reeves	1984 William Thomas Stanfill	1980 Garland Pinholster
1989 Randall P. Rhino	1957* Eric P. Staples	1960* Julian H. "Joe" Pittard
1989 Ken Rice	1964* Albert H. Staton	1995 Dan Pitts
1996* Paul Rapier Richards	1971* Herman J. Stegman	1982 George Poschner
1978* Nolen Richardson	1994* Patrick D. "Pat" Stephenson	1977* Henry R. "Peter" Pund
1994* Elmer R. Riddle	1996* Donald "Duck" Priestly Stephenson	1979 Johnny Rauch
1989* L.W. "Chip" Robert	1961* Kimsey R. Stewart	1979* B.L. "Crook" Smith
1957* Charles N. Roberts	1965* William L. "Young" Stribling	1969* Joseph T. "Phoney" Smith
1958 Jack Roberts	1974* Everett Strupper	1995 Rankin Smith
1987 Hugh Royer, Jr.	1966 Louise Suggs	1995 Royce Smith
1967* Nap Rucker	1977 Francis A. Tarkenton	1980* Sherrod Smith
1987 Erskine Russell	1957* Johnny G. "Stumpy" Thomason	1994 E. Cleve Wester, Jr.
1975 Doug Sanders	1956* Claude T. "Gabe" Tolbert	1993* Ivey Wingo
1978* Harold Sargent	1967* Forrest "Spec" Towns	1988 Rayfield Wright
1958* Sidney Scarborough	1975 Cecil H. Travis	1976 Whitlow Wyatt
1983 James B. "J.B." Scearce	1988* Amater Z. Traylor	1978* Doug Wycoff
1992 Stephen J. Schmidt, Sr.	1965 Charley Trippi	1998 Jim Breland
1961* Alfred W. Scott	1996 R.E. "Ted" Turner	1998 Bill Elliot
1986 Jacob "Jake" E. Scott, III	1976 Wyomia Tyus	1998 Lyn Lott
1985 William L. Shaw	1956* John Varnedoe	1998 Clifford Holmes McGaughey
1966* Ivy M. "Chick" Shiver	1990* Henry Wagnon	1998 Edwin Moses
1996 Cecil J. "Pete" Silas	1993 Bobby Walden	1998 Calvin G. Ramsey
1993* Henry L. "Suitcase" Simpson, Sr.	1988 LeRoy T. Walker	1998* Jack Roosevelt Robinson
1983 Mildred McDaniel Singleton	1976 Perrin Walker	1998 Rich Yunkus
1967* Frank Sinkwich	1979 Sidney "Beau Jack" Walker	1998* Alf Anderson
1960* James Skipworth, Jr.	1964* Bobby Walthour, Sr.	1998* Walter G. Carpenter
1960* Thomas J. Slate	1996* W.H. "Tubby" Walton, Sr.	1998* Wililam A. Winn, Jr.
1959* Mark Smith	1959* A. Drane Watson	*** Deceased**

Music Hall of Fame to help create a tourist destination that would draw visitors from I-75 and I-16.

The Sports Hall of Fame opened in December 1998. The 43,000 square-foot museum was on a site adjacent to the Georgia Music Hall of Fame and Douglass Theater. Under the leadership of Governor Miller, the General Assembly authorized $8.4 million in planning, design and construction funding. The museum's exhibits are educational as well as entertaining, with a balance between static and interactive displays to foster a higher level of learning and entertainment. Display themes captured a variety of perspectives at different levels of sports—grade and middle school sports, high school, amateur, college and professional. In addition to exhibit areas, the museum included instructional facilities, an auditorium, a gift shop, food service areas, exhibit support space, library and archives area, and administrative offices.

In addition to funding authorized for planning, design and construction, $2,266,386 was authorized in annual operating subsidies for the Sports Hall of Fame. In the FY 1998 amended budget, $740,000 in state general funds was authorized to aggressively promote the Sports Hall of Fame in advance of its December 1998 opening and for equipment, gift shop build-out, and critical positions. The legislature also authorized $770,187 in FY 1999 for operating support, but it was projected that revenues generated from visitors would eventually make the Sports Hall of Fame operationally self-supporting.

Georgia World Congress Center Authority

During the Miller Administration, the Georgia World Congress Center achieved a number of significant accomplishments. Between 1991 and 1998, the Congress Center Authority expanded the facility to 950,000 square feet, completed development of the Georgia Dome, constructed the adjacent International Plaza, and developed Centennial Olympic Park. As a result of this growth, the Authority became the only public authority in the nation that owned and operated a major stadium, an international convention center, and a major urban park, even as it remained operationally self-supporting. In fact, it was the quality and breadth of these facilities that enabled the GWCC to host more than one quarter of the events of the 1996 Summer Olympics. The growth that occurred during Governor Miller's two terms significantly enhanced the complex's attractiveness as a venue for national and international trade shows, major sporting events, and the community at large.

Georgia World Congress Center: Owned by the State of Georgia and operated by the Georgia World Congress Center Authority, the Georgia World Congress Center opened in 1976 with a total of 750,000 square feet, of which 350,000 square feet was exhibit space. Another 1.1 million square feet were added in a 1985 expansion. In 1988 the Congress Center hosted the Democratic National Convention. That same year, the General Assembly approved $5 million general obligation bonds for land acquisition and design development of 300,000 square feet of additional exhibition space, $13 million in general obligation bonds for a parking and truck marshaling facility, and $14 million general obligation bonds to acquire land for a domed stadium.

Even during the state budget cutbacks of 1991 and 1992, Governor Miller recommended $75 million for the Phase III expansion of the World Congress Center. This expansion, which added 310,000 square feet of space in two new exhibit halls, brought the GWCC to second place in the nation in terms of prime exhibit space. To maintain this status, the 1998 General Assembly approved Governor Miller's recommendation of $10.5 million for the planning and design of a Phase IV expansion of the GWCC. This expansion would add 500,000 square feet of exhibit space, 200,000 square feet of meeting rooms, an additional ballroom, registration areas, and a new entrance, thereby allowing Atlanta both to attract and retain larger trade shows and to accommodate more meetings and shows simultaneously. This Phase IV expansion was projected to create 19,000 new jobs each year in Georgia and generate $53 million in new tax revenues.

Governor Miller also supported facility enhancements which improved appearance, visitor convenience, and operating efficiencies for the World Congress Center and Georgia Dome. The International Boulevard viaduct extension, finished in 1994, alleviated traffic congestion by providing a secondary entrance and exit to the facilities and establishing a more immediate link to state and federal highway systems. The 5.5 acre International Plaza, completed in 1996, provided 2,000 additional parking spaces and at the same time added a park-like outdoor environment linking the GWCC, Dome and Omni Coliseum.

Georgia Dome: After the world's largest cable-supported domed stadium opened in 1992, people from around the globe streamed through its doors to attend an incredible variety of sports, entertainment, business, and social events. These events included Atlanta Falcons football, Centennial Olympic Games competitive events, the Chic-fil-A Peach Bowl, SEC football and basketball games, NCAA basketball tournaments, the U.S.A. Indoor Track and Field Championships, and Atlanta Hawks basketball, plus a myriad of motor sports, concerts, trade and consumer shows, and smaller events. In addition, Gov. Miller's personal involvement secured the selection of the Dome as the site of the 1994 Super Bowl XXVIII.

The economic impact of the Georgia Dome was substantial. In FY 1997 alone, the 71,200-seat Dome attracted almost 2.4 million guests. These visitors spent more than $190 million in "new dollars," which produced over $414 million in total impact on the state's economy. Additionally, the Georgia Dome caused the generation of $20 million in new tax revenue and 7,130 full- and part-time jobs.

Centennial Olympic Park: Centennial Olympic Park, the largest new center-city park to be developed in the U.S. in the last 20 years, became a reality under Governor Miller. The willingness of the State of Georgia to take the lead in the development and future operation of the park was crucial to the transformation of this dream into reality. At Miller's direction in 1994, the GWCC Authority conducted a feasibility study and received the official go-ahead to begin purchasing property for the 21-acre site. The initial construction funding came from philanthropic donations of $25 million, an Atlanta Chamber of Commerce fundraising campaign of $10 million, and a guaranteed $15 million from the Atlanta Committee for the Olympic Games' from its commemorative brick sales. Approximately 325,000 commemorative bricks were purchased and installed before the Centennial Olympic Games. Sales continued throughout the duration of the Games, which brought the grand total of commemorative bricks to 468,874 and made this program the most successful of its kind ever.

The park was Atlanta's central gathering place during the Olympics (July 19 to Aug. 4, 1996). During the Games, the park hosted the Festival of the American South, a multi-cultural, multi-media expression of southern life. Even an anonymous terrorist's bomb that caused two deaths and injured 118 in the early morning hours of July 27, 1996, could not extinguish the spirit of unity that the Games engendered for the millions of visitors who came to Centennial Olympic Park from around the world.

Following the Games, the park was reconfigured into a permanent feature of downtown Atlanta using funding provided by the Southern Company donation, the Robert W. Woodruff Foundation and the GWCC Authority. The park was reopened during a gala weekend in March 1998. Governor Miller provided an ongoing mechanism to fund the permanent operation of the park by convincing the 1996 General Assembly to pay off an outstanding loan remaining from the construction of the Georgia Dome. The GWCC Authority had been making loan payments with revenue from the hotel/motel tax, of which it received a quarter of each cent. Paying off the loan enabled this fund source to be dedicated to the ongoing operation of the park.

Among the Park's many special features were Centennial Plaza with its popular Fountain of Rings, the Great Lawn and the Southern Company Amphitheater, which lent themselves to performances, and the five quilt plazas, which told the dramatic story of the Atlanta Olympics. Beautifully landscaped, cascading water gardens wove through these quilt plazas.

The reopened park served as an important community gathering place and entertainment venue and as Atlanta's lasting legacy, both physically and emotionally, from the Centennial Olympic Games. It became a economic catalyst in the commercial and residential revitalization of a central but under-utilized section of Georgia's capital city.

The impact of Georgia's substantial investment in GWCC Authority facilities was clear. During Governor Miller's administration, over 22 million visits were paid the Authority's facilities. As a result, the GWCC stimulated more than $9.5 billion dollars in economic impact and brought over $362

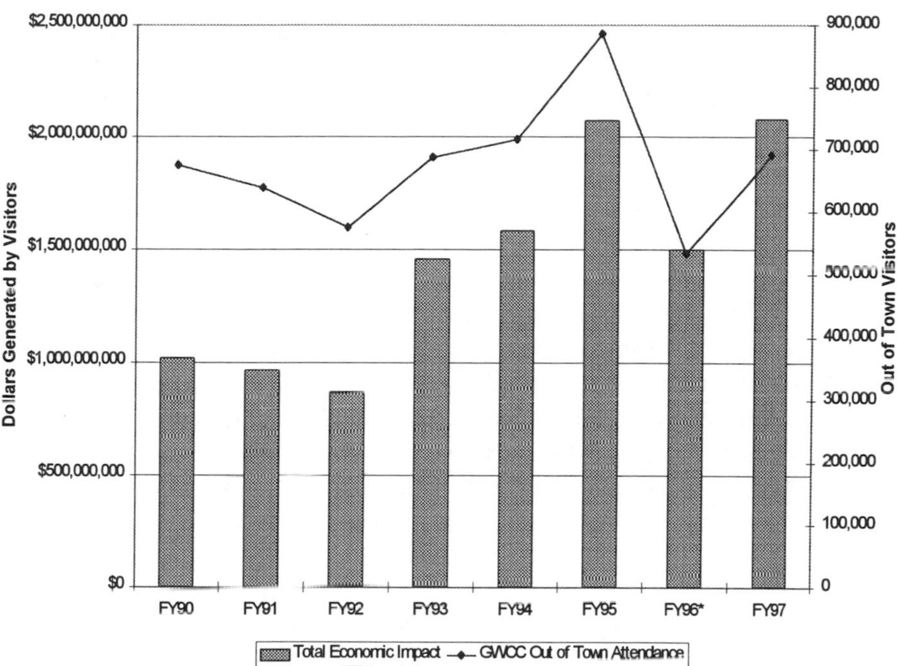

million in tax revenues to the state. Even after debt service on construction bonds was taken into consideration, the GWCC still provided over $220 million in revenue for the state.

Improving Georgia's Infrastructure

The single most important factor in luring international business to Georgia is transportation. This global community in which we now life increasingly demands quick, efficient movement of people and goods.

Governor Zell Miller, April 14, 1992

Few would deny that economic growth and development require an adequate transportation system, and state transportation policies and programs played vital role in shaping Georgia's growth. Georgia was the fourth fastest growing state in the nation from 1990 through 1997. In those seven years the state's population grew by 1,008,000 people. It was important to know where that growth was occurring so that transportation infrastructure improvements could be planned according to changes in the business community and labor market.

Highway investments

Georgia's tremendous growth resulted in increased automobile traffic and vehicle miles of travel. From 1990 to 1997, the number of vehicle miles traveled on the state's roads increased from 200 million a day to 243 million. By the end of the Miller Administration, Georgia's public road system was serving 93.1 billion vehicle miles of travel and over 217 tons of freight annually, which emphasized the importance of an effective and efficient highway system. The focus of state investments in public road infrastructure under the Miller Administration was consistent with the state's overall agenda to enhance opportunities for economic growth and quality of life. During Governor Miller's tenure, the state continued to expand its network of four-lane economic development highways, providing four-lane access to many more Georgia communities. In addition to improving traffic flow, these transportation infrastructure improvements helped businesses decrease their shipping costs and expanded their access to markets. Workers also benefited from increased employment opportunities as travel times and costs were reduced. Adequate transportation infrastructure was essential to numerous economic sectors in Georgia, including service, tourism, agriculture, and manufacturing.

Under the leadership of Governor Miller, the General Assembly invested over $1 billion for the Governor's Road Improvement Program (GRIP) and $87 million for additional four-laning and multi-laning over an eight-year period, including $145 million and $20.7 million authorized in 1998 legislative session for the GRIP and the four-laning program respectively. The $1 billion invested for GRIP equated to a two-fold increase over the amount invested by the previous administration.

Although expanding the network of four-lane developmental highways and passing lanes was needed, it was not inexpensive. Preconstruction and construction activity for a typical highway project was highly capital-intensive, time-intensive and very costly. It required data analysis, public hearings, design, environmental analysis and assessment, property title researches, property appraisals and acquisitions, right-of-way plans and, finally, the actual construction. The typical highway construction project took almost five years from its conception to the beginning of construction and cost an average of $1.8 million for every mile of roadway. Based on construction costs at the close of the Miller Administration, the $1 billion invested for GRIP was equivalent to approximately 560 miles of road construction.

Over the course of the Miller Administration, the number of miles opened or under construction increased to 1,440 miles, with approximately 58 percent of all corridors scheduled for completion by the end of FY 1999. The four-laning and multi-laning program was designed to address the need

The Governor's Road Improvement Program (GRIP)

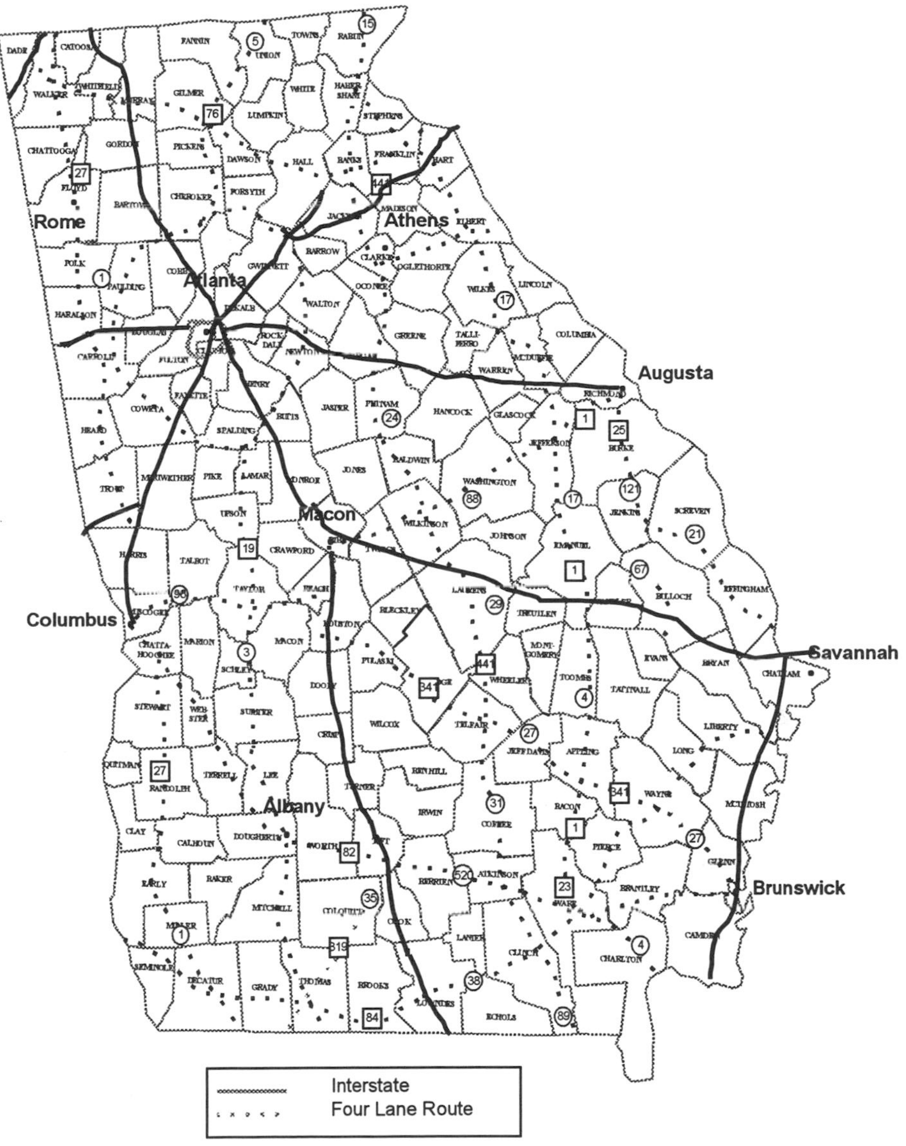

for passing lanes on the state road system throughout Georgia. Upon completion, the economic development highways, coupled with passing lanes on the state road system, would provide major interstate connections for regional access, capture tourist and traveling markets, and place 98 percent of Georgia's population within 20 miles of a multi-lane highway. Moreover, GRIP and the multi-laning program would give Georgia communities the ability to compete in the global economy by connecting all of our small and medium size cities to the interstate system with safe, efficient four lane roads.

The economic effects associated with completed GRIP corridors have been positive, particularly with respect to rural counties in or near a completed GRIP corridor, according to studies conducted by The University of Georgia and the Georgia Department of Transportation in 1996. The DOT study indicated that 50 counties credited GRIP with bringing in 166 new businesses and creating a total of 9,753 new jobs. Additionally, the study noted that 71 businesses expanded as a result of GRIP adding 4,439 new jobs. Another 65 percent of the responding counties attributed the lack of GRIP access for the loss of 19 potential business opportunities that would have created 5,030 additional jobs. The UGA study went on to suggest that the economic impact of the developmental highway system may reveal even larger gains as the completed system begins to influence regional growth. The importance of the developmental highway system improvements as lifelines for Georgia's future commerce was certainly recognized and reflected in the acceleration of funding for GRIP under Governor Miller.

GRIP Funding

Miller Administration

	Amount by Legislative Session
FY 1991-1992	$125,555,000
FY 1992-1993	100,000,000
FY 1993-1994	125,000,000
FY 1994-1995	125,000,000
FY 1995-1996	135,000,000
FY 1996-1997	100,000,000
FY 1997-1998	150,000,000
FY 1998-1999	145,000,000

Total State Investment, Miller Administration $1,005,555,000

Harris Administration

	Amount by Legislative Session
FY 1985-1986	$40,000,000
FY 1986-1987	81,000,000
FY 1987-1988	74,000,000
FY 1988-1989	91,000,000
FY 1989-1990	2,000,000
FY 1990-1991	135,000,000

Total State Investment, Harris Administration $ 423,500,000

At the same time as it was building GRIP and four-laning other roads, the DOT also effectively maintained Georgia's existing roads, as reflected in the excellent rating that the highway and public road system received. Georgia's highways were ranked first in the nation in pavement quality and maintenance categories by federal highway sources and national public policy groups. In September 1997, Georgia's urban highways were voted the best in the nation according to a report issued by the Environmental Working Group, a nonprofit environmental research organization based in

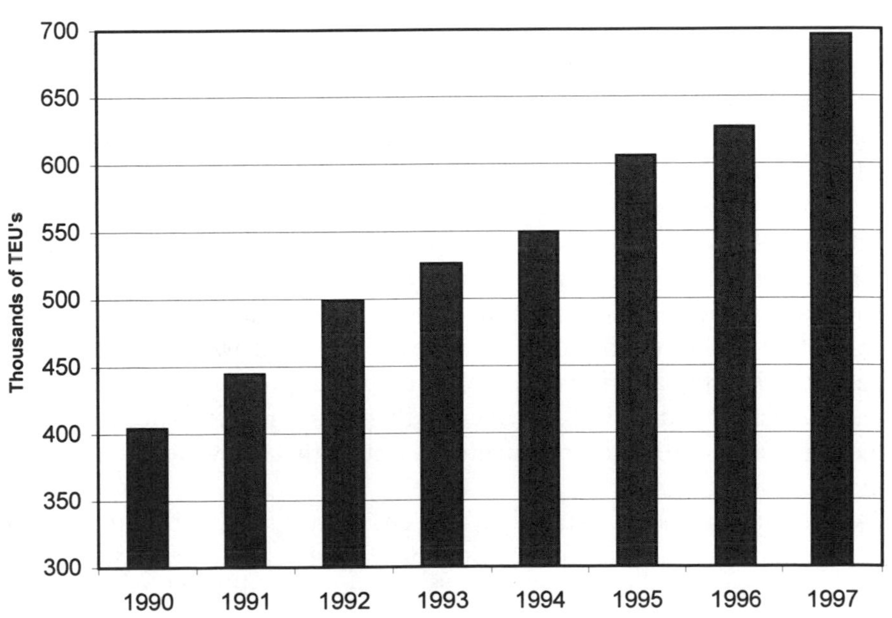

Washington, D.C., and the Surface Transportation Policy Project, a nonprofit coalition of approximately 175 groups. According to this group's report, none of Georgia's urban highways and interstates was classified in poor or mediocre condition. The Highway Information Quarterly classified fewer than 10 percent of these highways and interstates in fair condition with the rest of the state's urban mileage in good condition or better.

In consecutive years 1996 and 1997, The Road Information Program (TRIP) found Georgia's highways to be the best in the nation. Georgia 400, Atlanta's first and only toll road, received the Federal Highway Administration (FHWA) 1994 Biennial Excellence in Highway Design award in the Urban Highway Category which is FHWA's highest award. Georgia 400 connected I-285 in Atlanta's northern suburbs with I-85 near downtown. This $287 million project was recognized for its unique features such as an advanced computerized toll plaza, MARTA rail transit line in the medium, and extensive landscaping.

Georgia roads also received excellent ratings in asphalt and concrete pavement quality. In January 1997, the American Concrete Pavement Association's (ACPA) national award for "excellence in concrete pavement" was presented to the Georgia DOT for the quality of more than 1,200 concrete patches that improved rideability of 240,000 square feet of pavement. The Department also received the American Concrete Pavement Association's 1996 Presidential Award for its long-standing commitment to concrete pavement restoration in the state. Through restoration processes, the Department extended pavement life for 30 to 40 years, and was the first transportation agency to identify formal and methodological approaches to concrete pavement maintenance.

In February 1997, the Sheldon G. Hayes Award, the Hot Mix Asphalt Pavement industry's highest award, was presented to the Georgia DOT for a 61.8 mile project in Lowndes County. This award was given annually for the best-rated pavement used on projects utilizing 50,000 tons or more of hot mix asphalt. The Quality in Construction Award from the National Asphalt Pavement Association was given for a project in DeKalb and Fulton Counties consisting of the construction of express lanes. This award recognized the nation's highest quality hot-mix asphalt pavement project as determined by a panel of independent judges. Overall, these rankings enhanced Georgia's national reputation and prominence as a state that knew how to build and maintain good highways.

Georgia was also recognized for the sensitivity it showed the environment in highway construction. In 1993 Georgia was rated first among the 50 states for standards and specifications on erosion control. DOT policies also required special provisions to protect wildlife in bridge construction, such as curtailing construction during spawning seasons, monitoring water quality, restricting blasting in the water when particular species were known to be present, and requiring training manatee spotters on projects within the manatees's range. DOT also adopted a Statewide Bicycle and Pedestrian Plan in August 1997 and funded over $50 million in multi-use trail and bicycle/pedestrian facilities during the Miller Administration.

In addition to road expansions and quality improvements, Governor Miller supported enhancements to Georgia's traffic management system in metro Atlanta to improve both the flow of traffic and the air quality on our existing roads. In 1996, the Department of Transportation began the HERO (Highway Emergency Response Operators) program, in which distinctive green-yellow trucks patrolled Atlanta's expressways to assist with disabled vehicles and crashes. HEROs worked with other emergency response agencies to help reduce response times, clear travel lanes quickly, and keep traffic flowing smoothly. During its first two years (1996-1998), this incident management program assisted over 41,000 motorists and worked approximately 7,000 accidents.

Another enhancement was the Traffic Management Center (TMC), completed in 1996 to improve the flow of traffic on Atlanta's interstates. Cameras on I-75 and I-85 inside the perimeter and along the northern arc of I-285 sent digital signals to the TMC via 63 miles of fiber-optic cable. This system made traffic information available instantly to local transportation control centers in Clayton, Cobb, DeKalb, Fulton and Gwinnett Counties, and the City of Atlanta. Operators at the TMC and associated control centers continuously monitored traffic flow and communicated problems to motorists via electronic message boards mounted above the roadway on each interstate segment.

The traffic flow of metro Atlanta's interstates was also improved by opening high Occupancy Vehicle (HOV) lanes inside I-285 on I-75, I-85 and I-20 East. Use of these lanes was restricted 24 hours a day, seven days a week to vehicles occupied by at least two persons. The Department of Transportation also promoted carpooling during the Miller Administration with the construction of additional park and ride lots.

Airport enhancements

The state airport system was defined in terms of its capacity and capability to serve the needs of the general aviation industry. Georgia's 101 public-use general aviation airports provided local residents and businesses with easily accessible, quality aviation facilities for both corporate and recreational flying. These general aviation airports also comprised an important industry in the state that generated numerous economic impacts. Businesses depended on aviation access to transport goods and services, and they evaluated a community's local airport capabilities when considering new locations and expansion. Although the economic benefit to any community and its ability to attract new industry based on the presence of an airport was difficult to isolate, the Department of Transportation estimated that the combined impact of the 101 general aviation airports totaled about $333 million in annual economic activity, $104 million in wages and salaries, and 5,168 jobs.

Under the leadership of Governor Miller, the General Assembly authorized and committed a substantial investment of state funds for expansion and enhancement of regional airports. In the FY 1998 amended budget, $35,350,000 in state general funds was committed to upgrade 28 strategically located publicly owned airports. These general aviation airports had been identified in the Georgia Statewide Aviation Systems Plan as having regional impact. In addition, they were spread geographically across the state so that every part of Georgia was within 45 minutes driving time of one of them. Miller's $35 million investment gave Georgia a comprehensive network of airports that could provide the necessary facilities to serve corporate aircraft, guaranteeing that no part of the state was excluded from economic development for want of a top-level airport. The investment of state funds for airport enhancements provided a competitive advantage in attracting industry and stimulating long-term economic development for communities in Georgia that might not otherwise have had that window of opportunity for growth and development.

Due to the efforts of Governor Miller, Georgia became a national leader in developing its aviation infrastructure. The $35 million appropriation placed Georgia second among southeastern states behind only Florida in state funding assistance for airports. In June 1998, the Aircraft Owners and Pilot Association (AOPA) presented Governor Miller its Presidential Citation for his "exemplary leadership and extraordinary commitment to economic development in Georgia" in spearheading the campaign for funding to improve Georgia's general aviation airports.

Approximately $26 million of the total $35.35 million allocation was used for capital improvements that upgraded 20 general aviation airports to a Level III, top-rated airport that could accommodate corporate jets. These upgrades allowed for runway extensions to 5,500 feet, construction of the required taxiways to serve the extended runways, necessary runway and taxiway lighting systems, and the installation of state-of-the-art electronic weather, navigational and approach aid systems to establish the airport for all weather operations. The remaining $9.35 million was used to accelerate the process of making navigational, maintenance and operational improvements at existing Level III regional airports. Without the $35 million special appropriation, it would have taken 15 years to complete all of the needed improvements at the airports.

Funding was awarded to the airports by an executed grant between the Department of Transportation and the airport owners, and became available as the airport owner accomplished the work. State funds were limited to 75 percent of the cost of the project. Planning, environmental assessment, design and construction were eligible grant elements for state funding assistance. All land acquisition costs were to be financed with local and/or federal funding assistance.

In addition to the $35 million to create a statewide network of Level III regional airports, the Miller Administration also invested over $17 million for airport aid and development projects over its eight years, including $2.24 million in the FY 1999 budget to address critical navigational and maintenance needs at the remaining public airports not slated for upgrades or expansion. This commitment of state grants for publicly owned airports increased the capability of the Georgia's public airports to meet existing and future aviation mobility needs and enhanced Georgia's airport system as an extremely valuable transportation resource for the state's residents, businesses and visitors. "Thanks to Governor Miller's efforts... the state will make significant airport improvements that will bring major economic benefit to Georgia communities," commented AOPA President Phil Boyer during ceremonies in the State Capitol to honor the Governor.

Passenger rail

During the last half of the 20th century, people flocked to Georgia, establishing it as the economic mecca of the southeastern United States. Transportation was key to this success and growth. The state had long been able to boast that its efficient, integrated, and well-maintained transportation system was one of the best in the nation. However, the strength of the growth and success caused some negative spillover. Georgia's growing population meant increasing automobile traffic and congestion. Transportation congestion, in turn, created air quality problems. Air quality and transportation congestion became two quality of life issues that impacted all Georgia residents and could have a significant negative impact on economic development for our major cities and communities.

Commuter rail and inter-city passenger rail offered long-term transportation options for addressing metro Atlanta's air quality problems and traffic congestion while at the same time extending the economic impact and benefit of metro Atlanta to other cities in Georgia. To supply this missing link in our transportation system, Governor Miller and the General Assembly committed $4 million to initiate inter-city passenger rail in the 1997 legislative session and $8,380,000 for commuter rail in the 1998 session. These appropriations constituted Georgia's first major step forward in implementing an inter-city rail system and making commuter rail a reality for the thousands of Georgians who commute to Atlanta on a daily basis.

Several studies undertaken by the Department of Transportation identified both commuter and inter-city rail corridors that link metropolitan Atlanta, other Georgia cities and additional southeastern destinations. The studies were of particular interest to the Georgia Rail Passenger Authority, an independent body created for the purpose of constructing, financing, operating and developing rail passenger service in Georgia. Although the law creating the authority had existed in the Georgia Code since 1985, authority members were not appointed until the Miller Administration. Initially the Authority was appointed to explore realistic possibilities for passenger rail service in Georgia.

The purpose of inter-city rail was to meet the demand for longer-distance travel between cities, typically over 60 miles. It generally competed with driving and air trips. Georgia's inter-city rail system would begin with an Atlanta-to-Macon line that included some type of connection to Hartsfield Airport. Aside from Athens, Macon was the closest metro area to Atlanta and offered the best opportunity for a first inter-city rail link. The Atlanta-to-Macon line was one of a core network of destinations identified in the "Georgia Intercity Rail Passenger Plan" for inter-city rail links. Other links included Athens, Augusta, Savannah, Jacksonville, Albany and Columbus. An extended network with additional destinations included Chattanooga, Greenville, Columbia, Charleston, Tallahassee, Montgomery and Birmingham. The $4 million authorized by the state legislature, coupled with anticipated federal funds, would enable the state to complete an environmental assessment and impact analysis of the high-speed rail link between Macon and the City of Atlanta. The assessment would take about 12 months to complete, and the full environmental impact analysis would require an additional 12 to 18 months due to amount of rail line alteration needed.

Commuter rail service moved workers living in suburban areas to and from a central business district with few stops over long distances, usually up to 40-50 miles. Commuter rail was found to be feasible in six existing rail corridors. The "Commuter Rail Plan" study recommended a two-phase staging plan to implement service on three corridors (Athens, Senoia and Bremen) by the year 2000 and the remaining three corridors (Madison, Canton and Gainesville) by year 2010. Georgia's commuter rail service would begin with the Atlanta-to-Athens line through Gwinnett County, since this line was projected by consultants to be the most heavily used in the system. It also was one of the easier, less costly lines to complete. To initiate the Atlanta-to-

Athens line, the state advanced-funded the full cost of the environmental analysis ($875,000) and funded the state's 50 percent share ($3,250,000) of the design and engineering plus related legal expenses ($175,000) associated with the corridor. This funding helped the state obtain federal authorization and funding for the commuter rail system. An additional $4 million in planning funds was also provided for the secondary phase extension corridor which includes Canton and Cartersville.

The studies undertaken by the Department of Transportation concluded that passenger rail was feasible and would generate long-term benefits to Georgia. Upon completion of the commuter rail project, commuters who switched from driving to rail service were projected to save $2,200 a year in automobile depreciation alone, and commuter rail was estimated to directly produce about 4,200 jobs by the year 2010 and create 5,940 jobs through indirect impacts.

Upon its completion, the inter-city rail project could bring $115 million in wages, indirect income and employee benefits to Georgia; create 1,000 new permanent jobs, half of which would be located outside the metro Atlanta area; and produce about $2.2 billion in economic benefits to the state, with 75 percent of these benefits occurring outside Atlanta.

Georgia Ports Authority

When Governor Miller assumed office, the Georgia Ports Authority was struggling to recover from the loss of its largest shipping line in the late 1980's. Because a key part of Governor Miller's comprehensive economic development strategy was an emphasis on maintaining Georgia's position as a South Atlantic center for international commerce, he was committed to helping Georgia's ports overcome this setback. While in office, Governor Miller directed over $220 million for capital investments to Georgia's ports—more than any previous administration. This investment began as a major part of the Governor's Georgia Rebound program in FY 1993 and continued throughout his administration. Driven by goals identified in Focus 2000, the Georgia Ports Authority's strategic plan to lead Georgia's ports into the 21st century, major projects were completed during the Miller administration which significantly increased the capacity of Georgia's ports.

Under Governor Miller's leadership, the Port of Savannah experienced a period of sustained growth. As the shipping industry turned increasingly to the use of containers, Savannah's harbor was widened and deepened to 42 feet to allow the newest and largest container ships access. A significant investment also increased the capacity of Savannah's facilities for handling container shipments. In all, six new container cranes were purchased and two new container berths were constructed. As a result, the volume of container

Growth in Economic Impact of Georgia Ports

	1988	1998	% Change
Sales	7,243,000,000	23,000,000,000	217.55%
State & Local Taxes	189,000,000	585,000,000	209.52%
Employment	63,700	80,100	25.75%
Source: Georgia Ports Authority ***NOTE: These figures are from studies done in 1988 and 1998. Numbers from 1990 are not available.***			

traffic shipped through the Port of Savannah increased by 72 percent from 404,100 TEUs in 1990 to 695,700 TEUs in 1997. In 1998, Savannah ranked 11th in the U.S. in container throughput. Breakbulk operations were also facilitated by improvements made at Savannah's Ocean Terminal. Thanks to these improvements in both breakbulk and container facilities, Savannah ranked second in the South Atlantic in total tonnage shipped in 1998.

Governor Miller also set the stage for the expansion of the port at Brunswick. State motor fuel tax revenues and federal funds were used to fund the replacement of the Sidney Lanier Bridge. This new bridge, in combination with the harbor deepening that was pending federal approval at the end of the Miller Administration, would allow the port to serve newer and larger vessels. Additionally, an extensive upgrade of the Colonel's Island Bulk Grain Facility was undertaken, as well as other expansions of warehousing and storage capacity. This investment brought clear rewards. Since 1992, traffic through Brunswick increased by over 35.5 percent, reaching 2.3 million tons in FY 1997. By the end of the Miller years, Brunswick was not only better equipped to serve the bulk and breakbulk shippers in South Georgia, but also was recognized as having one of the best automobile terminals in the nation.

In all, Governor Miller's commitment to Georgia's ports produced a 32 percent increase in overall tonnage handled by the Georgia Ports Authority between 1990 and 1997. As a result, the total traffic shipped through Georgia's ports reached 10.8 million tons in 1997. During this same period, combined general cargo tonnage between the Port of Savannah and the Port of Brunswick increased over 50 percent from 2,161,000 tons to 3,283,900 tons. The annual economic impact of this activity was clear. A 1998 economic impact study indicated that Georgia's ports and port-related activities were generating $23 billion in revenue, $1.8 billion in personal income, and $585 million in state and local taxes annually. In 1998, Georgia's maritime activities impacted the employment of over 80,000 people, involving one in 45 jobs across the state.

List of Investments

1992	Replaced Savannah's Berth 50 for liquid bulk imports
1993	Deepened Savannah River Channel from 38' to 42'
	Renourished Tybee Island
	Expanded Mayor's Point Terminal in Brunswick by 70,000 sq.ft.
1994	Expanded Savannah's Container Berth 6, including 30 acres of paving and upgrading and the modification of two container cranes
	Purchased four new container cranes for Savannah
1995	Purchased material handling equipment using federal funds
	Paved container area for Home Depot
1996	Began construction of Savannah's Container Berth 7
	Expanded and upgraded existing grain facility on Colonel's Island in Brunswick
1997	Completed Container Berth 7 in Savannah
	Conducted feasibility study for Brunswick Harbor deepening
	Expanded Colonel's Island automobile processing facility and purchased an additional facility for automobile processing
1998	Purchased two new container cranes for Savannah
	Expanded Savannah's Ocean Terminal, including extending Container Berth 12 and constructing a new transient shed
	Conducted feasibility study for Savannah and Brunswick Harbor deepenings
	Purchased ship unloader for Colonel's Island in Brunswick

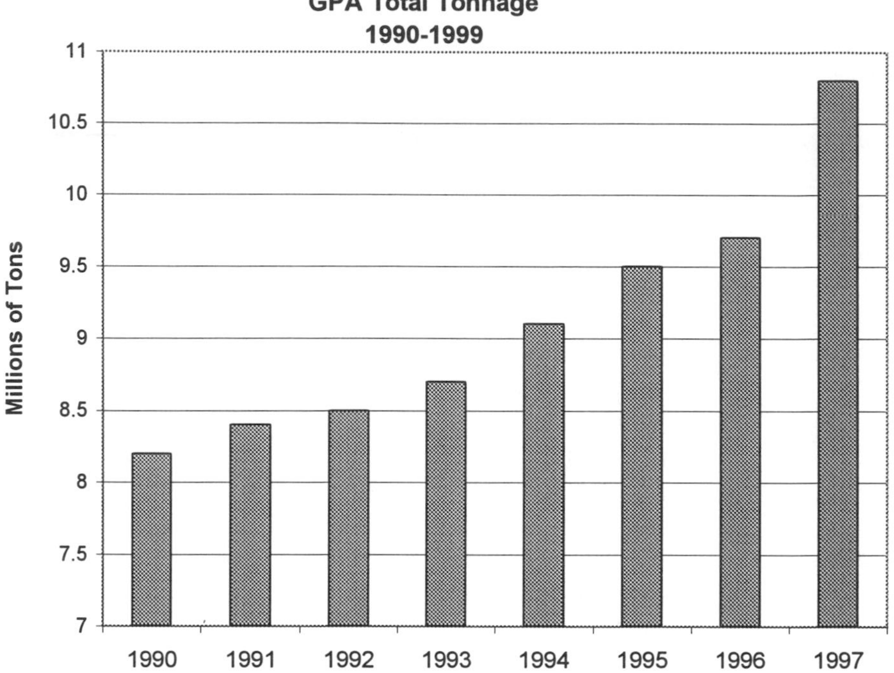
GPA Total Tonnage
1990-1999
Millions of Tons
11
10.5
10
9.5
9
8.5
8
7.5
7
1990
1991
1992
1993
1994
1995
1996
1997

Georgia Ports Improvements - Miller Administration

Funds	Authority Funds	Total Funds	Project	Fiscal Year
	2,500,000	2,500,000	Berth 50 replacement for liquid bulk imports in Savannah	1992
32,480,000	5,437,000	37,917,000	Savannah River channel deepening from 38' to 42', including renourishment of Tybee Island beach ($4,822,998)	1993
	5,500,000	5,500,000	70,000 square ft. expansion of Mayor's Point Terminal in Brunswick (Revenue Bonds)	1993
23,595,000		23,595,000	Expansion of Container Berth 6, 30 acres of paving and upgrading, container cranes	1994
24,665,000		24,665,000	Purchase of four new container cranes for Savannah	1994
	7,500,000	7,500,000	Purchase of material handling equipment using federal funds reimbursement to the State for the Savannah Harbor Deepening	1995
	12,000,000	12,000,000	Container paving including area for Home Depot	1995-96
34,000,000		34,000,000	Start of construction of Container Berth 7 in Savannah (Completion 1998)	1996
8,600,000		8,600,000	Expansion and upgrade of existing grain facility on Colonel's Island in Brunswick	1996
20,000		20,000	Completion of Container Berth 7 in Savannah	1997
550,000	550,000	1,100,000	Feasibility study for Brunswick Harbor Deepening	1997
	15,000,000	15,000,000	Expansion of Colonel's Island automobile processing facility ($7.5 million)and purchase of an additional facility for automobile processing ($7.5 million).	1997
13,000,000		13,000,000	Purchase of two new container cranes for Savannah	1998
14,490,000		14,490,000	Expansion of Savannah's Ocean Terminal including the extension of Container Berth 12 ($8.7 million) and the construction of a new transient shed ($5.79 million).	1998
5,500,000		5,500,000	Feasibility study for Savannah and Brunswick Harbor deepenings	1999
1,000,000		1,000,000	Purchase of ship unloader for Colonel's Island in Brunswick.	1999
54,760,000		54,760,000	Indirect improvements due to dike construction and harbor maintenance	1992-1999
212,660,000	**48,487,000**	**261,147,000**	**Grand Total - Miller Administration funding for Georgia Ports Authority**	**1992-1999**

V. Natural Resources

The vast ecosystems of the earth move across the centuries with a tremendous power that is far beyond our control. But at the same time, what we do during our brief tenure on earth can and does alter them in remarkable ways. For the moment in which we are here, we are the stewards of those systems. We hold the earth in our hands. The stewardship of the earth is a much heavier and more far-reaching responsibility than simply exploiting natural resources for our needs and desires of the moment.

Governor Zell Miller, February 29, 1992

Preserving Georgia's Natural Environment

I grew up living, playing, walking among places with names that described their natural features—names like Frogtown Gap, Trackrock Gap, Wolf Creek and Choestoe, which means "land of the dancing rabbits." It pains me to think that unless everyone who lives in and visits these mountains understands and cares for their fragile environment, those names will eventually be all that remains to remind us of the beautiful natural creatures and features that once characterized these places.

Governor Zell Miller, April 16, 1994

Preservation 2000

Governor Miller established the Preservation 2000 Program in 1991 to preserve Georgia's natural beauty for future generations. His goal was to acquire and protect 100,000 acres of natural and environmentally sensitive land. Unaltered, old-growth forests and wetlands, including river bottom hardwood forests, bays and other naturally occurring water features, were priority acquisitions under the program.

Preservation 2000 was very successful and reached Governor Miller's goal of acquiring 100,000 acres in May of 1996. By January of 1998, the state had acquired or taken options on 105,602 acres at 56 locations throughout Georgia, including old-growth forests, wetlands, and other naturally occurring water features. Total funding for Preservation 2000 included $65 million in general obligation bonds from the state plus $57 million in private and corporate donations of land and funds, making Preservation 2000 a $122 million endeavor.

Smithgall Woods-Dukes Creek Conservation Area: One of the most outstanding Preservation 2000 properties was the Smithgall Woods-Dukes Creek Conservation Area. Located near the City of Helen, it was acquired in 1994. Although the property was valued at $21.6 million, Charles Smithgall,

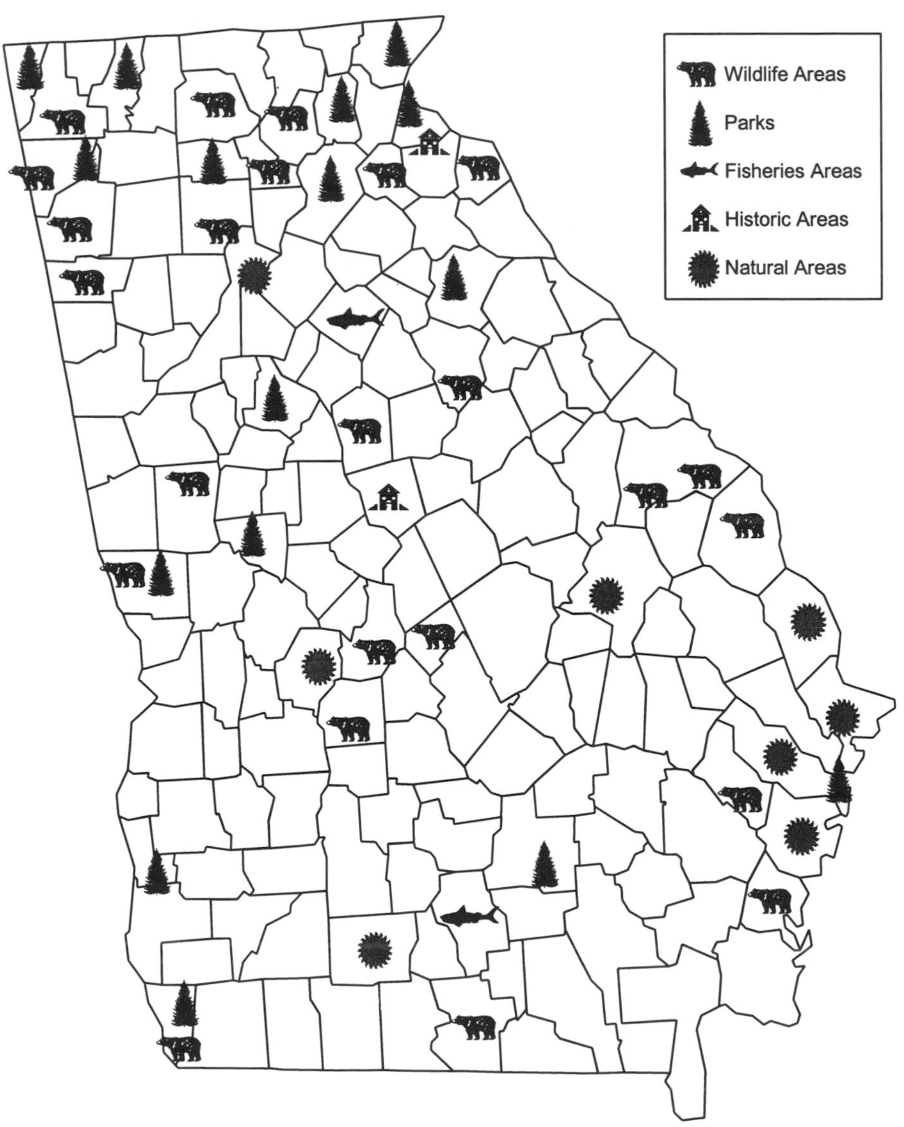

the noted businessman and conservationist who owned it, donated half of the property's value. Included in the gift-purchase were buildings, roads, maintenance facilities and equipment already on the grounds. Governor Zell Miller dedicated the property as a Heritage Preserve, ensuring that the spectacular 5,562-acre estate would remain protected for future generations.

Most of the land was mature, second-growth hardwood and mixed pine-hardwood forest. A few small openings served as wildlife food plots. The property also featured 12 miles of mountain streams, including North Georgia's premier trout stream, Dukes Creek, which offered anglers a secluded fishing experience. Daytime visitors could also enjoy the new visitors' center, hike the Cathy Ellis Memorial Trail, bike, observe and photograph wildlife, hunt and participate in guided tours and educational programs. Overnight guests stayed at the Conservation Center, a magnificent mountain home situated along a bubbling stream. This elegant center primarily served group retreats.

Charlie Elliott Wildlife Center: In 1993, Governor Miller's Preservation 2000 Program acquired a 6,000-acre tract of land in Jasper and Newton counties which became the Charlie Elliott Wildlife Center. Managed by the Georgia Department of Natural Resources' Wildlife Resources Division (WRD), it was named for Charlie Elliott, a native Georgian and one of the nation's best-known conservationists and outdoorsmen. Governor Miller approved funding for architectural design of the visitors' center, which opened to the public in 1997. By the time he left office, the wildlife center included three multiple-use areas — an educational complex, the Clybel Wildlife Management Area, and the Marben Public Fishing Area. Together, these programs offered wildlife education and recreational opportunities that were unmatched anywhere else in the state.

The wildlife center's general mission was to provide a comprehensive wildlife education program, hunting, fishing and other wildlife-related recreational opportunities while managing a diversity of wildlife species and habitats. Its educational mission was to instruct Georgia's citizens about wildlife, natural resources, and the outdoors so they might become wise stewards of the environment. The first two educational programs, the outreach program and the Brooke Ager Discovery Room, immediately attracted the interest of teachers throughout middle Georgia. These programs reached more than 40,000 students a year. The wildlife center's staff held teacher workshops throughout the state to teach wildlife biology, aquatic biology, orienteering, and Project WILD materials, and show teachers how to develop and use schoolyard wildlife habitats. More than 2,000 teachers attended these workshops every year.

The visitors' center was the first building constructed within the education complex. A nature center and adult conference facility were slated for construction later. WRD also planned to add youth dormitories and a dining hall. Featuring an auditorium, a beautiful exhibit about the life and work of Charlie Elliott, and a replica of his library, the visitors' center served as the focal point and as a starting point for people visiting the wildlife center.

Without a doubt, the wildlife center was an ambitious and extensive undertaking. However, thanks to Governor Miller and generous corporate support, it became a tremendous resource for Georgia's citizens and visitors. Through its dynamic programs, educated staff, and state-of-the-art facilities, the Charlie Elliott Wildlife Center promised to provide tomorrow's leaders and voters with information they would need to make responsible decisions about wildlife and the environment.

Tallulah Gorge State Park: Among the most impressive achievements of Preservation 2000 was the creation of Tallulah Gorge State Park through a public-private partnership between the Department of Natural Resources and the Georgia Power Company, which owned the property. The state received a long-term, no-cost lease, and Georgia Power continued to pay property taxes to Rabun and Habersham Counties, which the property straddled.

Within the park's 3,000 acres was one of the most significant geological features in the eastern United States, a spectacular chasm two miles long and 1,000 feet deep. Breathtaking views and the gorge's rich history as a popular Victorian resort quickly made this new park a favorite stopping point along the main route between Atlanta and the Great Smoky Mountains. In 1996, the park opened a new interpretive center dedicated to the memory of Georgia conservationist Jane Hurt Yarn. Partially funded by the Georgia Power Company, the $3 million center featured an award-winning film and simulated rock outcroppings that made visitors feel as if they were traveling through the gorge. Exhibits included natural history, the Victorian resort area, Karl Wallenda's famous tightrope walk across the gorge, hydroelectric power generation and the Tallulah Falls Railroad.

In May of 1995, the Georgia Power Company and the Department of Natural Resources made a similar agreement for another Preservation 2000 property, paving the way for the creation of the 3,100-acre Sprewell Bluff State Park and Wildlife Management Area on the Flint River in central Georgia.

RiverCare 2000

Recognizing that Georgia had to have healthy rivers if the state's residents and visitors were to continue enjoying a high quality of life, Governor Miller

RiverCare 2000 Program
Properties Closed or Under Option
September 30, 1998

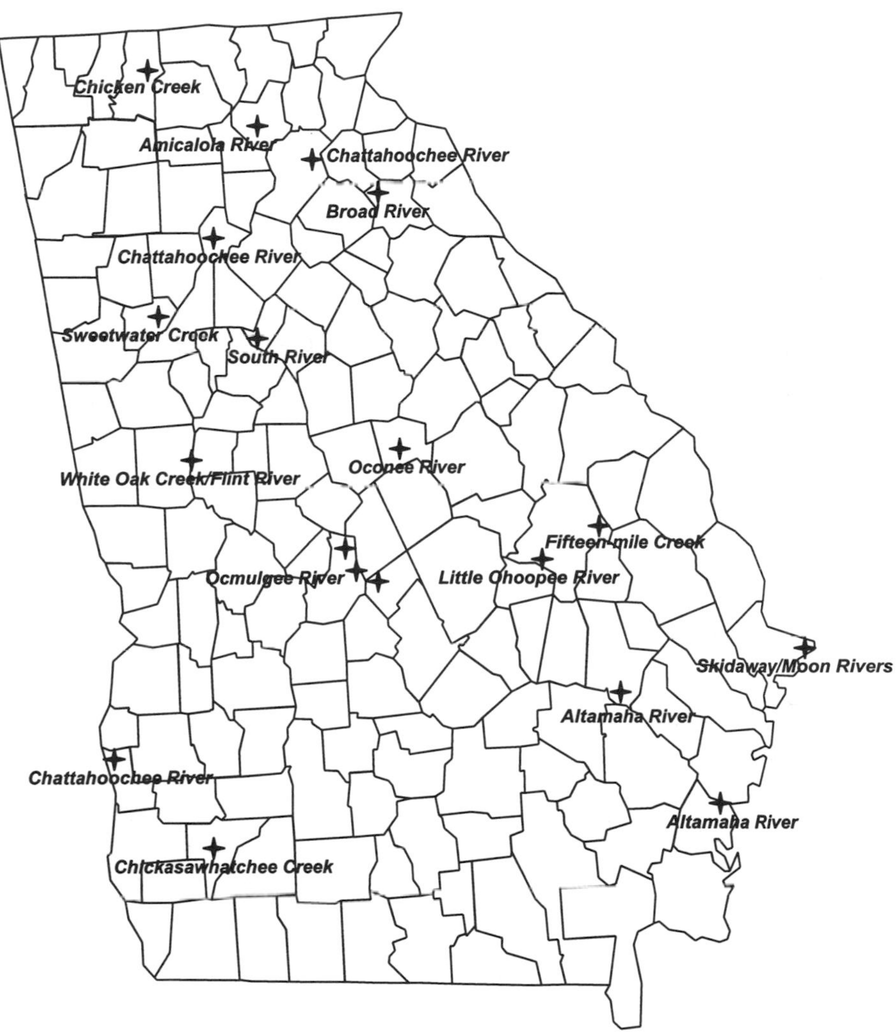

announced in 1995 his intention to establish the RiverCare 2000 program. The guiding principle of RiverCare 2000 was to share with the state's citizens the Governor's appreciation and deep regard for the importance of Georgia's 70,000 miles of rivers and streams.

Programs implemented by governments, industries, farmers, foresters and others had greatly improved the quality of the state's rivers over the prior 20 years. Unfortunately, Georgia's rivers still faced significant challenges: control of polluting storm-water runoff; erosion and subsequent sedimentation from land disturbing activity; restriction of public access to rivers for recreational use; and unwise development of flood-prone areas. Development and other land-disturbing activities were destroying historic and prehistoric resources and reducing the populations of many native wildlife species.

RiverCare 2000 Projects Completed / County	
Amicalola River / Dawson Forest WMA	Dawson
Broad River Heritage Trail	Madison
Chattahoochee River	Chattahoochee, Clay, Quitman
Chickasawhatchee Creek	Baker
Echeconnee Creek	Houston
Fifteen-mile Creek / Wolf Branch / George L. Smith Park	Emanuel
Flint River – White Oak Creek	Meriwether
Ocmulgee River	Bleckley, Twiggs
Ocmulgee River / Oaky Woods WMA	Houston
Oconee River / Berry Farm	Baldwin
Ohoopee Dunes	Emanuel
Skidaway River	Chatham
Sweetwater Creek	Douglas

RiverCare 2000 Projects Under Review / County	
Chattachoochee River / Lake Lanier	Hall
Altamaha River / Vivian's Island	McIntosh
Alcovy River	Newton
Altamaha River / Darien River	McIntosh
Amicalola River / Dawson Forest WMA	Dawson
Broad River / Watson Mill Bridge	Madison
Ocmulgee River / Oaky Woods	Houston
Altamaha River	Long, Tattnall
Chattahoochee River	White
Ocmulgee River Greenway	Bibb, Twiggs
Alcovy River Greenway	Newton
Broad River Heritage Trail	Elbert, Madison, Oglethorpe, Wilkes
Coosa, Etowah, Oostanaula Rivers Greenway	Floyd
Ebenezer Creek Greenway	Effingham
Etowah River Greenway	Cherokee
Flint River Greenway	Dougherty
Ocmulgee Heritage Greenway	Bibb, Jones
Oconee River Greenway	Clarke

RiverCare 2000 Program

Proposed Riverway Demonstration Projects
September 30, 1998

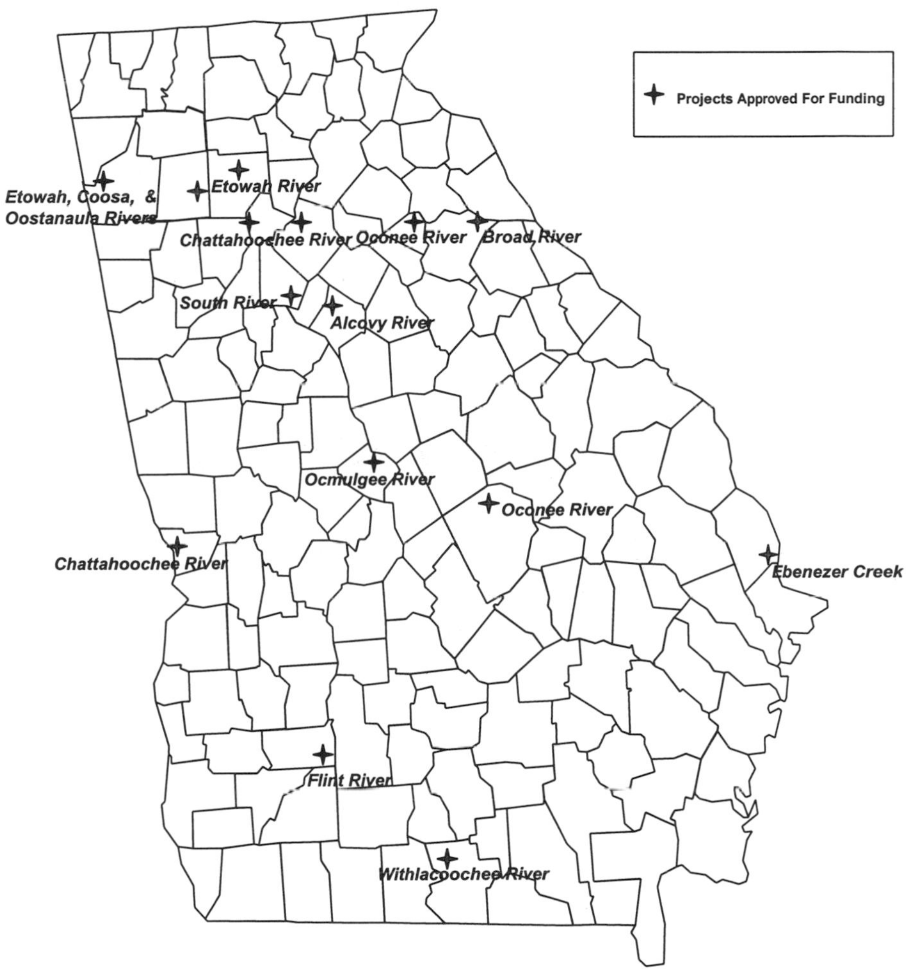

RiverCare 2000 was established in 1995, modeled after Preservation 2000, as a conservation program to meet those challenges by increasing state-preserved land in Georgia's river corridors and by improving the knowledge and management of riverbank property among all of the state's owners. RiverCare

GEORGIA DEPARTMENT OF NATURAL RESOURCES

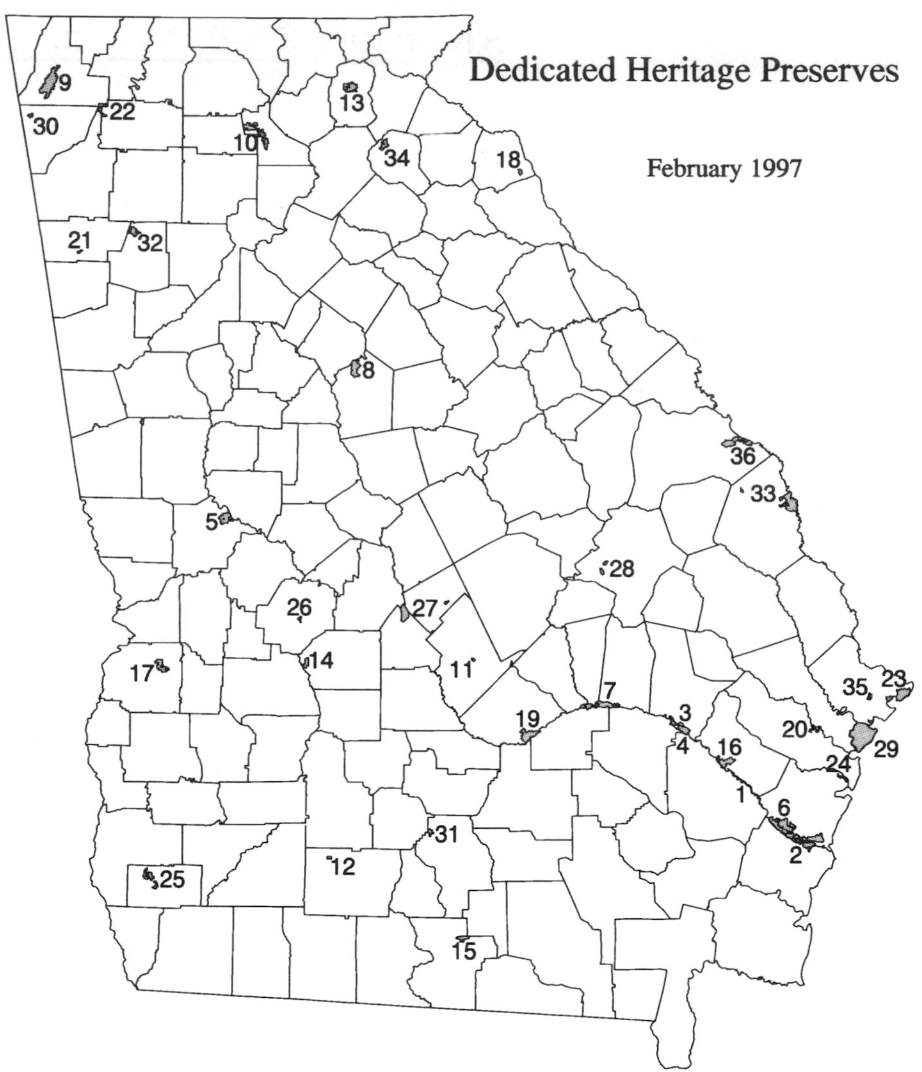

was managed by the Department of Natural Resources with guidance from more than 100 citizens serving on four advisory bodies.

RiverCare consisted of three related tasks: assessing important river and stream resources throughout the state, identifying effective management tools for river corridors, and acquiring riverfront property for preservation. The river assessment report was approved by its coordinating committee and made widely available on the World Wide Web. The river management recommendations received the coordinating committee's approval in 1998 and were published on the web late in the year.

RiverCare also worked with 15 communities to establish riverway demonstration projects, in which the state acquired riverside property for recreation and education, and local governments managed it under operating agreements. River demonstration projects included the Roswell-Chattahoochee Greenway in northern Fulton County, the Etowah-Coosa -Oostanaula Rivers Project in Floyd County, the Ocmulgee Heritage Greenway in Macon and the Oconee Rivers Greenway in Clarke County. At each of these sites, the state acquired up to $1.5 million in land which local governments or federal agencies leased from the state for improvement and management.

As of July of 1998, the RiverCare land acquisition program, funded with $45.8 million in state, federal and private funds, had placed under option about 13,400 acres at 17 sites, protecting 38 miles of rivers and streams, and had purchased 9,964 acres. RiverCare 2000 acquisition funds included $40 million in state bonds, $3.4 million in remaining Preservation 2000 bonds, $1.4 million in federal matching funds from the U.S. Environmental Protection Agency and $1 million in private donations. Governor Miller designated $15 million of the $20 million in RiverCare 2000 funds in Fiscal Year (FY) 1999 for land purchases in the Chattahoochee River corridor, one of the most abused rivers in the nation.

Heritage Preserve dedication of wildlife lands

The Georgia Heritage Trust Act of 1975 helped the state preserve its natural and historic heritage. Any state-owned land which the Department of Natural Resources managed and the Board of Natural Resources identified as having significant historical, natural or cultural value could be dedicated by the Governor as a heritage preserve. Once dedicated, a preserve could be put only to the uses for which it was designated. These uses could be changed only after formal review and approval by the Board of Natural Resources, the General Assembly, and the Governor.

Prior to Governor Miller's administration, only four properties totaling 27,305 acres, had been dedicated as heritage preserves. However, Governor Miller used the ability to dedicate as heritage preserves the more unique wildlife management areas, public fishing areas and natural areas which the state acquired in whole or in part under his Preservation 2000 program. In all, he dedicated 108 sites totaling 254,839 acres as Heritage Preserves to conserve and protect their significant natural, recreational and cultural resources for the benefit of present and future generations.

DEDICATED HERITAGE PRESERVES IN GEORGIA, February 1997

PROPERTY (COUNTY)	ACREAGE	YEAR DEDICATE
1. Altamaha--Rayonier NA (Long, McIntosh, Wayne)	1,331	1984
2. Altamaha WMA (McIntosh)	18,109	1996
3. Big Hammock NA (Tattnall)	801	1996
4. Big Hammock WMA (Tattnall)	5,566	1996
5. Big Lazer Creek WMA and PFA (Talbot)	5,831	1996
6. Buffalo Swamp portion of Altamaha WMA (McIntosh)	6,258	1996
7. Bullard Creek WMA (Appling, Jeff Davis)	8,442	1996
8. Charlie Elliott Wildlife Center (Jasper, Newton)	6,059	1996
9. Crockford-Pigeon Mountain WMA (Walker)	15,527	1996
10. Dawson Forest WMA (Dawson)	8,770	1996
11. Dodge County PFA (Dodge)	444	1996
12. Doerun Pitcherplant Bog NA (Colquitt)	650	1996
13. Dukes Creek Conservation Area (White)	5,604	1994
14. Flint River WMA (Dooly)	2,358	1996
15. Grand Bay WMA (Lowndes)	2,293	1996
16. Griffin Ridge WMA (Long)	5,616	1996
17. Hannahatchee WMA (Stewart)	4,913	1996
18. Hart County WMA (Hart)	968	1996
19. Horse Creek WMA (Telfair)	7,370	1996
20. Jerico River NA (Liberty)	776	1996
21. J.L. Lester WMA (Polk)	477	1996
22. Johns Mountain WMA (Floyd, Walker)	2,641	1996
23. Little Tybee and Cabbage Islands NA (Chatham)	7,721	1992
24. Little Wahoo Island NA (McIntosh)	1,013	1996
25. Mayhaw WMA (Miller)	4,681	1996
26. Montezuma Bluffs NA (Macon)	499	1996
27. Ocmulgee WMA (Bleckley, Pulaski)	6,310	1996
28. Ohoopee Dunes NA (Emanuel)	1,809	1996
29. Ossabaw Island WMA (Chatham)	25,152	1978
30. Otting Tract WMA (Chattooga)	699	1996
31. Paradise PFA (Berrien, Tift)	1,240	1996
32. Sheffield WMA (Paulding)	3,303	1996
33. Tuckahoe WMA (Screven)	11,451	1996
34. Wilson Shoals WMA (Banks)	2,727	1996
35. Wormsloe HS (Chatham)	822	1981
36. Yuchi WMA (Burke)	7,660	1996
TOTALS:	185,892	

Property Types

HS: Historic Site
NA: Natural Area
PFA: Public Fishing Area
WMA: Wildlife Management Area

Properties dedicated under Heritage Trust Act of 1975, O.C.G.A. Sec. 12-3-70, et seq

h:\pres2000\preserve\sites&ac.wb6

Nongame-Endangered Wildlife Program

During the 1980s. the General Assembly created the Nongame-Endangered Wildlife Program to conserve and manage Georgia's nongame wildlife, with special attention to endangered species. It was part of the Department of Natural Resources' Wildlife Resources Division. Despite the fact that it was operated from within state government, the program received only minimal state funding for administrative support, and relied on private donations to fund its wildlife surveys and conservation projects.

Weekend for Wildlife: In 1989, a small group of wildlife enthusiasts and the Georgia Department of Natural Resources hosted the first of what would become one of the most popular and innovative events held in the Southeast to benefit nongame wildlife. The location was the five-Star Cloister Resort at Sea Island, Georgia; the beneficiary was DNR's financially struggling Nongame-Endangered Wildlife Program; and the event was Weekend for Wildlife. The event generated funding for the nongame program through registration fees and an auction, and took participants on unique safaris to some of the state's most unusual coastal destinations, many of which were off limits to the general public. Safari destinations included the Altamaha River Wildlife Management Area, Sapelo Island and its companion Blackbeard Island, Hofwyl-Broadfield Plantation, King's Bay Naval Submarine Base, Little St. Simons Island, Ossabaw Island, privately-owned St. Catherines Island, and White Oak Plantation. Other tours include canoeing, skeet shooting and joining Coastal Resources Division staff for a day aboard the *R. V. Anna.*

In 1998, the DNR along with 450-plus guests celebrated the 10th Anniversary Weekend for Wildlife at Sea Island. Attendees included Governor and Mrs. Zell Miller, several members of the Georgia General Assembly, nationally-known wildlife advocates such as *Wild Kingdom's* Jim Fowler, leaders of some of Georgia's top industries, and first-time and veteran "weekenders." The event was advertised only by word-of-mouth and *pro bono* inclusion in National Geographic *Traveler* magazine and Sea Island's *Shorelines.* However, it drew participants from throughout Georgia as well as from Florida, Louisiana, Michigan, Minnesota, Mississippi, Missouri, North Carolina, Ohio, Pennsylvania, South Carolina, Virginia, and Washington.

Guests of honor at Weekend for Wildlife have included world-renowned bird artist Roger Tory Peterson, Jim Fowler, and best-selling *Birds of North America* author Chandler Robbins. However, perhaps the greatest attraction the Weekend for Wildlife offered was the regular attendance of Governor and Mrs. Zell Miller and their family. Consistent supporters of the weekend, the Millers became part of the on-the-ground team that made the Weekend a premier event. The Governor's keynote address became a tradition at the

Saturday evening banquet, and as honorary chairwoman of the event from 1996 to 1998, Mrs. Miller gave her endorsement both literally and figuratively to obtaining and recognizing corporate and private sponsorships.

During its 10-year history, the Weekend for Wildlife raised more than $1 million for the nongame program's dedicated funding source, the Wildlife Conservation Fund. Recruiting sponsors to cover the cost of the weekend enabled these monies to go directly into the fund to support conservation and education projects related to nongame wildlife—such as songbird conservation, right whale recovery, reptile and amphibian surveying. But perhaps more important than actual dollars, the Weekend for Wildlife generated new supporters of wildlife conservation and broke down many barriers between government and industry. Like no other event, it provided a communication forum for industry, wildlife experts, wildlife enthusiasts and state agency representatives.

Among the event's corporate sponsors were Browning-Ferris Industries, the Coca-Cola Company, the Georgia Pacific Corporation, Georgia Power Company, Georgia Transmission Corporation, Oglethorpe Power Company, Philip Morris Management Corporation, Sea Island Company, Synovus Financial Corporation, Wachovia Bank, and Waste Management Corporation. Private sponsors include Marguerite Williams and Diane Parker of Thomasville. Additional support for the event and its beneficiary came from donations of items for verbal and silent auctions. The 10th anniversary weekend featured 170 items from 108 donors. About 30 Georgia businesses also contributed cash, door prizes and other items to show their support of the department and its efforts to conserve nongame wildlife.

Wildlife vehicle tags: Another source of funding for the Nongame-Endangered Wildlife Funds was a state income tax checkoff. During its first decade, the checkoff provided approximately $2.7 million, but funds had begun to decline by the mid-1990s. To create a more stable funding mechanism for nongame wildlife conservation, Governor Miller and DNR created the "Give Wildlife A Chance" vehicle tag project in 1995. The legislation passed with the Governor's help in 1996 and the state introduced the tag to vehicle owners in 1997.

DNR test-marketed six tag designs—screech owl, bluebird, hummingbird, wood duck, gray fox and bobwhite quail—by creating an exhibit and traveling the state asking citizens to vote on their favorite design. Georgians all over the state overwhelmingly chose the bobwhite quail in a longleaf pine-wiregrass habitat as the favored design. The design was appropriate, as the quail was the state game bird and Georgia had long been known as the quail capital of the world.

DNR undertook an intensive marketing campaign to notify the public that the tag was available and that the state's nongame wildlife would benefit from the funds raised. Governor and Mrs. Miller received tags numbered "1" and "2" in appreciation of their continuing support for the Nongame-Endangered Wildlife Program. Original sales projections for 1997 were 100,000 tags, but Georgians' enthusiasm exceeded all expectations. They bought more than 600,000 wildlife tags that year.

In its first year, net conservation revenues were $14 per tag. However, under legislation passed in 1998, DNR began paying a production cost of $1.59 per plate, yielding a net conservation revenue of $12.41 per tag. The unprecedented success of the wildlife tag was partly due to a great team effort between DNR, the Department of Revenue and the 159 county tax commissioners, with consistent support from the Governor's Office. By July 1998, purchase of these commemorative license plates had raised more than $8 million for nongame wildlife conservation. These funds supported much-needed conservation projects such as cave inventories, robust-redhorse fish surveys, rare plant surveys, environmental education outreach and habitat acquisition.

Managing Georgia's Natural Resources

It is very important for us to understand how our natural resources and systems work, and to manage our natural environment, not only because it is beautiful, but also because it is essential to life itself.

Governor Zell Miller, May 26, 1995

Protecting Georgia's coast

In 1992, the General Assembly strengthened the Coastal Marshlands Protection Act of 1970 and the Shore Protection Act of 1979 to incorporate the designation of "vital areas" of marshland and beaches. The amendments also included most of the existing rules and regulations, made changes required by litigation and provided for leasing of state-owned water bottoms for commercial purposes. This solved the "gratuities" question under the State Constitution and allowed the Coastal Marshlands Protection Committee to continue to issue permits for new marinas to serve the boating public. Both laws were administered by the Coastal Resources Division of the State Department of Natural Resources. In 1997, in response to the steady population growth in coastal Georgia, the Coastal Resources Division opened a satellite office in Savannah to provide a greater level of customer services. It also increased coordination with federal, state and local government agencies in areas where these agencies had mutual interests.

Another important customer-service initiative was the coordination of private recreational dock permits between the U.S. Army Corps of Engineers and the Department of Natural Resources. In 1996, the Coastal Resources Division received permission to from the Corps to issue licenses for these facilities. A process that once took at least three months was reduced to as little as 15 minutes.

Protection of tidewaters: In 1992, 215 unauthorized river houses lined the banks of the Altamaha and other coastal rivers. They could not be regulated under existing property laws because they were on the water, but they were not covered by watercraft laws because they had no engines. The river houses were not only "squatters" on public waterways, but many also polluted the waterways by dumping raw garbage and sewage into the river.

In 1992, Governor Miller persuaded the General Assembly to enact the Protection of Tidewaters/Right of Passage Act, authorizing the Department of Natural Resources to require all river houses to be permitted immediately, then requiring all owners to remove their river houses by July of 1997. In all, 110 boat owners upgraded their river houses to provide adequately for waste and received permits to remain on the river until 1997. Unfortunately, 47 owners did not comply with the law and fought the department in state court. Once their appeals were completed, DNR could clear the Altamaha and other Georgia rivers of the remaining few unsightly structures, which had increased pollution and reduced the enjoyment of the rivers for many Georgians.

Coastal Zone Management: On Earth Day, April 22, 1997, Governor Miller signed the Georgia Coastal Management Act into law, giving the state the authority to enter the national Coastal Zone Management (CZM) program. Under the Governor's direction, the Coastal Resources Division of the Georgia Department of Natural Resources began working with the public, elected officials, and other agencies and organizations to develop the Georgia Coastal Management Program (GCMP). The GCMP sought to balance economic development in Georgia's coastal area with preservation of natural, environmental, historic, archaeological, and recreational resources. Using existing state laws, the GCMP established a network of agencies with management authority in the eleven-county coastal area.

Governor Miller pushed for Georgia's participation in the national CZM program for the benefit of all Georgians, especially those in coastal counties. By 1998, Georgia's coastal region had grown in population to over 520,000, a 14 percent increase from 1990. During this period, the region's average monthly employment also rose 14 percent, and per capita income increased by more than 23 percent. The Georgia Coastal Management Program provided assistance in dealing with the conflicting demands of a growing population in an environmentally sensitive area.

In January 1998, approval of the GCMP by the U.S. Secretary of Commerce completed the network of ocean-facing states that participate in the national Coastal Zone Management program. The federal Coastal Zone Management Act provided funding for program and administration to states with approved coastal management programs. In Georgia, the DNR Coastal Resource Division contributed about 60 percent of its federal administrative allocation to fund Coastal Incentive Grants (CIG), which provided funds to local communities and organizations for coastal management projects. These grants allowed coastal issues to be addressed at the grassroots level, according to annual funding themes and criteria established by a citizens' Coastal Advisory Committee.

Georgia provided nearly $2 million in CIG funds in FY 1998 for 42 grants to six universities, five counties, five cities, and various planning authorities such as the Soil Conservation Commission, Coastal Regional Development Center, and Georgia Emergency Management Agency. Projects included developing storm surge models to predict hurricane impacts; educational signs on nature trails; scientific investigation of ground water and surface water use; and teaching children drown-proofing. Since CIG funds could be used as required match for other federal funds, Georgia used a portion of its 1998 money to leverage an additional $800,000 in federal funds to address critical coastal issues. As a result of these efforts, Georgia received at least $1 million a year in federal funds through participation in the CZM program.

Other benefits of Georgia's participation in the national Coastal Zone Management program included an increased level of technical assistance and the authority to review federal activities to make sure they were consistent with state coastal resource laws. These benefits increased Georgia's ability to balance conservation with wise development along the coast. The state immediately developed procedures with the U.S. Army Corps of Engineers and the Federal Emergency Management Agency to ensure that projects were not undertaken along Georgia's coast which were in violation of state law. These procedures did not involve new permits and added no additional time to the processing of permit requests, thus keeping Georgia's promise to develop a GCMP that added no new regulatory layers. Increased technical assistance was provided in many ways, including establishing a site office in Chatham County that placed staff closer to clients, creating more efficient and effective delivery of government services along Georgia's coast.

Marine fish conservation: Population growth on Georgia's coast resulted in the need to conserve Georgia's most important marine sportfish, and laws were passed during Governor Miller's two terms to accomplish that. In 1992, the Governor signed a bill which authorized the Board of Natural Resources to establish size and creel limits for 17 marine fish species important to sport anglers in Georgia's coastal waters. Then in 1998, Governor Miller signed amendments to the 1992 law to protect another eight species or species groups of fish. These conservation initiatives were designed to keep Georgia's sportfish population healthy and available for future generations to catch and enjoy, and in the process to sustain economically important charter-fishing operations.

Offshore artificial reef program: Because Georgia had few natural offshore reefs, an artificial reef program was begun to place manmade materials on the ocean bottom that would increase fisheries habitat and provide safely accessible recreational opportunities for both anglers and divers. Although this program was begun in the early 1970s, the first state dollars ever appropriated for artificial reef construction came from the Miller Administration. Totaling $500,000 during the Miller years, these funds doubled the number of offshore artificial reefs, and added a series of coastwide reefs specifically sited closer to shore for anglers with smaller, less equipped boats. By 1998, literally thousands of tons of concrete, over 2,100 designed fisheries enhancement units with anticipated life spans of over 200 years, 55 M-60 battle tanks and several scrap vessels up to 195 feet in length had been added to the state's offshore artificial reefs. In addition to providing long-term improvements in offshore fisheries habitat and recreational experiences, the offshore artificial reefs also helped generate millions of dollars annually for Georgia's coastal economy.

Sapelo Island restoration: With Governor Zell Miller's full support, the Sapelo Island Restoration Foundation was established in 1992 as a non-profit organization. The Governor appointed the foundation's members, and former Governor George Busbee served as chair. The foundation raised funds to restore the historic R. J. Reynolds mansion and the lighthouse on Sapelo Island. By 1998 the foundation had raised more than $600,000 in private donations, received $500,000 from the Georgia legislature, and obtained a federal grant of $176,000. Work at the lighthouse complex was completed at a cost of $458,000 included full restoration of the 1820 lighthouse, range beacon, oil houses and water cistern. Governors Miller and Busbee participating in the relighting of the lighthouse on September 6, 1998, returning it to service as Georgia's third working lighthouse.

The Reynolds mansion restoration was also underway by the end of Miller's time in office, including the installation of new slate and tile roofs, downspouting and flashing; total rewiring of the building and other electrical repairs; and replacement of outdated air conditioning compressors and air handling units. Future projects included the restoration of the historic gardens around the mansion, to be funded by the Turner Foundation, and restoration of the priceless Menaboni murals in the mansion, to be funded by the Coca-Cola Company. The grounds and landscaping and mural restoration, plus plumbing upgrades, exterior painting and furnishings were expected to cost a total of $2.3 million.

Water resources management

Several major water management issues emerged for the State of Georgia during the Miller Administration. In order to avert a water war over resources in the western part of the state, Georgia began working with Florida and Alabama to manage shared water resources. This effort was begun by Governor Miller with an appropriation of $250,000 in FY 1994. These funds, along with $250,000 each from Alabama and Florida, were used to match $3,000,000 from the U.S. Corps of Engineers for a comprehensive study of water demand and availability in the Apalachicola-Chattahoochee-Flint and Alabama-Coosa-Tallapoosa river systems. Georgia, Florida and Alabama subsequently entered into compacts that called for the development of water allocation formulas for each state.

In southeast Georgia, most of the water used by citizens, agriculture, industry and local government in 24 counties came from the Floridian Aquifer. The increasing level of water usage in this area was contributing to existing saltwater intrusion in the Brunswick area and the potential of saltwater intrusion in Savannah. The economic well being of coastal Georgia depended on maintaining the capability to use this aquifer to support future development in this region of the state. Understanding groundwater was a difficult and expensive undertaking that required solid scientific data and water management strategies. State support for the development and implementation of a comprehensive management plan was necessary to allow for the sustainable use of this valuable resource for the future and to provide adequate protection for coastal groundwater resources. The Governor initiated an eight-year project in FY 1999 with $1,000,000 in state funds to be matched with $500,000 from the pulp and paper companies who depended on the aquifer. These funds were used to collect scientific data needed to fully understand the aquifer and to develop an appropriate management plan to protect coastal groundwater. The eight-year project was projected to cost $14 million.

Although agriculture was the largest user of groundwater in Georgia, there were no reporting requirements under the agricultural water use permitting process. To develop both a strategy to protect coastal Georgia from saltwater intrusion and a water allocation formula for Georgia, Florida and Alabama, EPD had to have reliable agricultural water use information. Rather than impose a cumbersome reporting requirement on all farmers with water withdrawal permits, meters were installed on a small, but statistically valid sample of farms to provide EPD with a reliable estimate of agriculture water use that could be used for water resource management. The Governor initiated this five-year study with $250,000.

ACT/ACF river basin interstate compacts: During their 1997 sessions, the legislatures of Georgia, Alabama, and Florida adopted the first and only interstate compacts to allocate water in the southeastern United States. All three legislative bodies passed compact legislation for the Apalachicola-Chattahoochee-Flint (ACF) river system, and the Georgia and Alabama legislatures passed compact legislation for the Alabama-Coosa-Tallapoosa (ACT) river system. The language of the compacts differed only in the names of the river basins and the states involved. Congress ratified both compacts, and President Clinton signed them into law in November 1997. The compacts required that, in 1998, the states would develop water allocation formulas.

The compacts represented the best way currently known to settle the disputes over the use and management of interstate waters of the ACF and ACT systems that started in the late 1980s. These river basins made up 38 percent of Georgia's total land area, provided drinking water to more than 60 percent of Georgia's population, and supplied water for more than 35 percent of Georgia's irrigated agriculture. Significant portions of Georgia's industrial production and recreation-based economy depended on the water in these basins. The fish and wildlife resources that depended on these waters were also vital to Georgia.

Reducing pollution in the Chattahoochee River: Three sources of pollution affected the Chattahoochee River and West Point Lake downstream of Atlanta: phosphorous from wastewater treatment plants, overflow from Atlanta's sewers, and storm run-off from the entire metro Atlanta area into the Chattahoochee basin. Water quality in the Chattahoochee River south of Atlanta improved after 1992 because pollution from two of these sources declined. The phosphorus discharged into the Chattahoochee River dropped about 86 percent during the Miller Administration because of a statewide ban on phosphorous detergents and improvements to wastewater treatment facilities. Reducing phosphorous improved the quality of West Point Lake by limiting the growth of nuisance algae that fed on the phosphorous. Between 1992 and 1998, the City of Atlanta completed construction of two combined sewer-overflow treatment facilities, significantly reducing the amount of untreated sewage overflowing into tributaries of the Chattahoochee River.

The reduction of stormwater runoff in metro Atlanta, as in the rest of the nation, would take decades to carry out, but a major step occurred in 1993, when Georgia's Environmental Protection Division issued stormwater runoff permits to metro Atlanta governments, requiring for the first time that local governments address this issue and improve the quality of stormwater runoff.

Safe watershed dams

Georgia's watershed dams were exempted from compliance with the Safe Dams Act of 1978. At the beginning of his term, Governor Miller opted voluntarily to bring Georgia's watershed dams into compliance with the law. A 1991 Environmental Protection Division (EPD) assessment of Georgia's Category 1 Federal Watershed Dams (dams whose failure may cause loss of life) identified 139 of the structures as requiring maintenance upgrades. From 1991 to 1999, the Governor spent $785,000 to complete maintenance upgrades on these dams and bring them into compliance with the law. At the end of Governor Miller's tenure in office, 13 upgrades were completed with an additional 32 under contract. In addition, plans for upgrades on 44 of the structures were under review by the EPD.

Category 1 Federal Watershed Dams

(Failure may cause loss of life)
Maintenance Upgrades

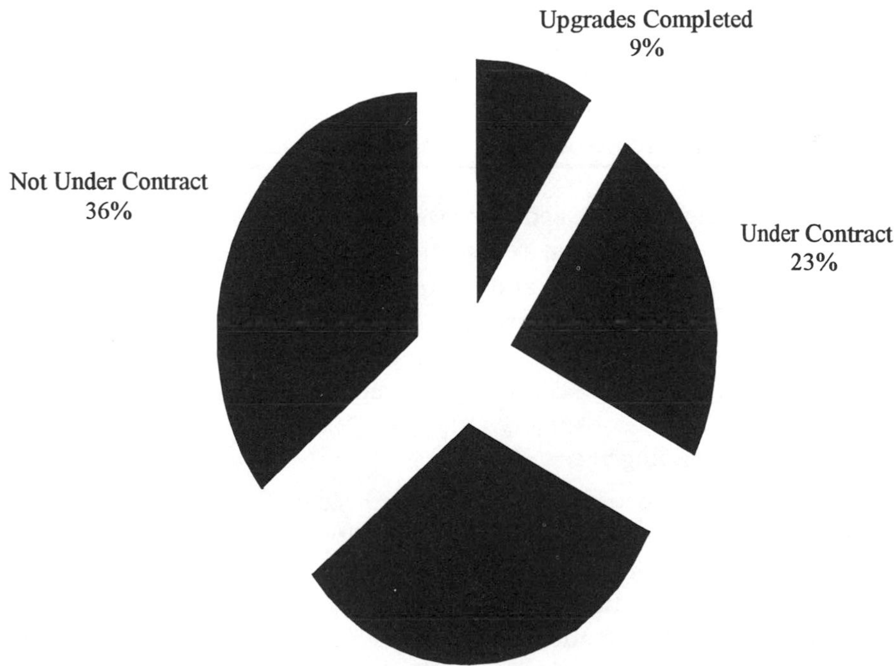

The 1991 EPD assessment also identified 10 Georgia dams as needing structural upgrades with an estimated cost in excess of $7.1 million. Governor Miller supported two bond issues totaling $3.84 million dedicated to these structural upgrades. With these funds, construction began on the Etowah #12 dam and the Racoon #7 dam with the other eight dams in various pre-construction phases.

Category 1 Federal Watershed Dams
(Failure may cause loss of life)
Structural Upgrades

Priorit	Structure	Location	Estimated
1	Etowah	Dawson	$1,100,30
2	Racoon	Barto	$999,70
3	North Broad	Frankli	$700,00
4	Sandy Creek	Jackson	$795,00
5	Soque	Habersha	$661,00
6	Potato #6	Upson	$559,00
7	Hightower	Towns	$622,00
8	Pine-Log	Gordon	$688,00
9	Mill-Canton	Cheroke	$357,00
10	Palmetto	Harris	$650,00

The upgrading of watershed dams was a slow process. In addition to the multitude of pre-construction assessments and planning requirements, the state had to gain the support and commitment of any local government impacted by the watershed. Before any construction on a dam could begin, the state had to have signed contracts with these local governments to maintain dams after the state had completed upgrades.

Flathead catfish management

The illegal introduction of nonnative flathead catfish into the Altamaha River system severely impacted several groups of native fishes. This predator, which could weigh more than 100 pounds, reduced by 80 percent the population of redbreast sunfish, a popular sport fish. Populations of various species of bullhead catfish and suckers also declined dramatically as the flathead catfish population has increased. Downstream of Jesup, the flathead catfish population grew until it was far denser than any known population within the fish's native range. Responding to an outcry from the fishing public, Governor Miller recommended one position and operating funds, later approved by the General Assembly, to bring this illegally introduced species under control.

The new biologist surveyed anglers in the counties along the river. Although 54 percent of respondents had fished for flatheads, more than half of them wanted the flathead population reduced to allow the recovery of redbreast sunfish. By electrofishing during the program's first full year, the biologist removed 3,781 flathead catfish which weighed a total of 17,662 pounds from a 36-mile target area of the Altamaha River system. The fish were processed for human consumption by the Rogers Correctional Institute and donated to various charities, including the Second Harvest Food Bank in Savannah.

This initial effort reduced the population in the 36-mile target area by 73 percent, and the redbreast population showed signs of recovery. Each year, the biologist expanded the removal zone as well as maintaining the area from which the catfish had already been removed. He also periodically surveyed anglers to be sure the program continued to meet their expectations.

Law enforcement/boating safety

Georgia, the largest state east of the Mississippi, was blessed with great scenic beauty and many outstanding natural resources. The state had more than 70,000 miles of rivers and streams, 660 square miles of public lakes and reservoirs, 850 square miles of estuaries and 100 miles of coastline. During the Miller Administration, state government managed more than 70 wildlife management areas, covering about one-million acres of forest, that were used chiefly for hunting, fishing, recreational boating and other outdoor-oriented activities.

The Georgia Department of Natural Resources (DNR) Law Enforcement Section administered the state's hunter education and boating safety programs. Its conservation rangers enforced laws and regulations concerning game and nongame animals, threatened and endangered species, and nonnative animals. They rescued lost or injured persons; they investigated hunting and boating accidents and violations of wildlife laws; and they investigated and enforced environmental laws which prohibited littering roads and waterways, burning scrap tires, and illegal commercial dumping.

Recreational boating was a rapidly growing activity in Georgia during the 90s. More than 330,000 boats, including 25,000 personal watercraft, were registered in the state in 1998. Boating accidents injured seriously or killed a number of Georgians each year, and intoxicated operators were frequently involved. During 1997, 28 people died in boating accidents and 61 people drowned in Georgia waterways. The number of persons arrested for boating under the influence of drugs or alcohol was also increasing. The number of personal watercraft, commonly referred to by brand names like Jet Skis WaveRunners and Sea Doos, more than doubled from 1994 to 1997. The increase was equally dramatic in boating accidents that involved personal watercraft. In 1990, only eight percent of all boating accidents involved personal watercraft. By 1996 that figure had increased to 46 percent, and the 1997 total of 62 personal watercraft accidents was the highest to date. Conflicts between traditional boaters and users of personal watercraft became commonplace, and many lakeside residents and boat owners began calling for restrictions on the use of personal watercraft. In a survey of registered boat owners in Georgia, 82 percent agreed or strongly agreed that the Department of Natural Resources should strictly regulate personal watercraft.

Governor Miller recognized that, as the population grew and as demands on Georgia's natural resources increased, the state had to become more vigorous in dealing with activities that harmed natural resources or seriously interfered with people's enjoyment of them. During the 1995 legislative

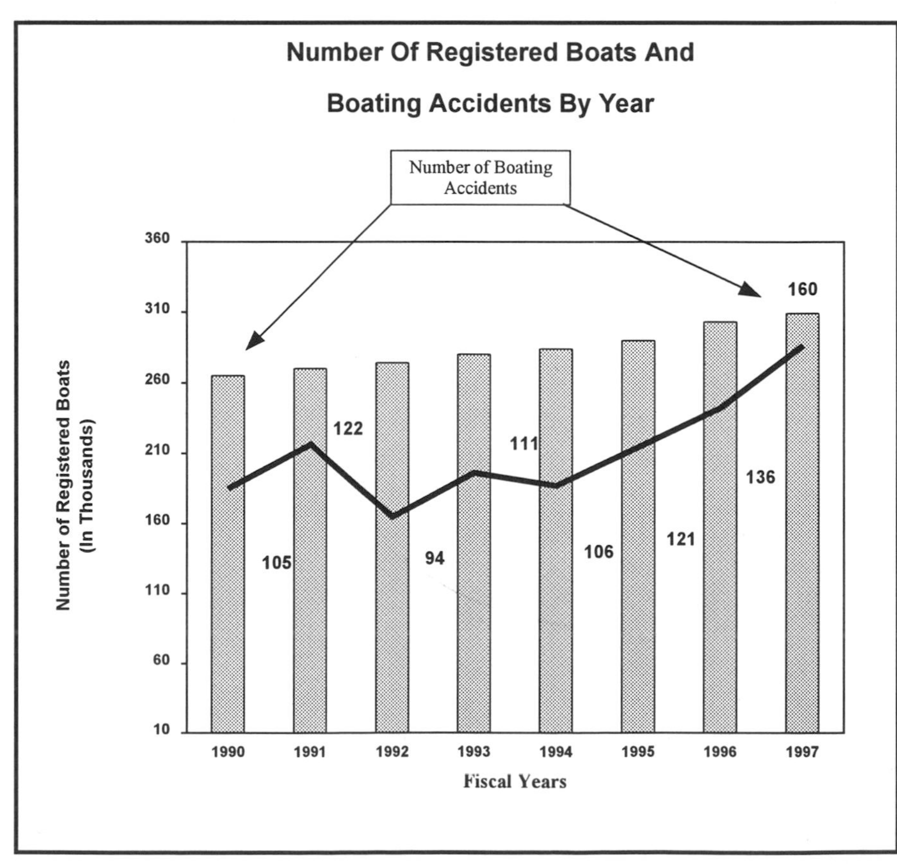

session, he spearheaded the enactment of several new laws to regulate personal watercraft. One prohibited the operation of a personal watercraft at speeds of more than five miles per hour within 100 feet of any docks, bridges, moored boats, persons in the water or shoreline. In 1996, DNR's boating safety officers began an extensive public awareness campaign to educate boaters on the new law and let them know that beginning in 1997 it would be strictly enforced.

Governor Miller also supported improvements to Georgia's antiquated and obsolete system of registration for its 330,000 boats. He approved funding to upgrade the system's hardware and software. The conversion, completed in early 1998, greatly improved the Department of Natural Resource's ability to register boats and increased customer convenience.

In 1998, the Governor supported additional boating safety laws to strengthen the penalties for boating under the influence of alcohol or drugs. The new laws also established a minimum age requirement for the operation of a boat, and extended the 100-foot law to all boats. The Governor also persuaded the General Assembly to fund 20 new law enforcement rangers in the Department of Natural Resources in FY 1998. Ten of them were assigned to patrol inland rivers and reservoirs that had high levels of recreational boating use, and another eight patrolled coastal waters for violations of boat safety and commercial fishing laws. The remaining two ranger positions were wildlife investigators. To protect Georgia's natural and historic resources, the state sometimes had to conduct long-term surveillance operations and covert investigations. These operations could last for weeks or months, and were used on cases involving commercial exploitation of game species; the sale or destruction of endangered or protected species, the unauthorized digging of archeological sites and sale of artifacts; or illegal shrimping. The additional two rangers improved the state's ability to reduce these hard-to-detect crimes that often had a major resource impact.

The new law enforcement positions also greatly improved the quality of DNR's conservation and safety education programs throughout the state. DNR conducted hunter education programs for more than 20,000 people each year, provided instructors for voluntary boating safety courses, and conducted conservation and safety education programs in public schools.

Most people voluntarily obeyed conservation and boating laws because they understood how compliance benefited them as individuals and society at large Many violations occurred because the offender did not adequately understand these laws.. Perhaps the most important element of DNR law enforcement was educating the users of Georgia's natural and historic resources about the laws that apply to their activities. A preventive approach helped reduce the number of enforcement actions, and therefore the cost of law enforcement.

With this philosophy in mind, Governor Miller urged DNR's conservation officers to become more customer-service oriented. DNR discovered that law enforcement is usually more effective when it is friendly as well as firm. Conservation rangers began spending more time in educational roles. A ranger from the Law Enforcement Section visited every elementary school in the state each year, to talk about Georgia's natural resources. When on patrol, rangers were more likely to issue a warning than a ticket, if the offense was minor and based on genuine ignorance rather than an intentional violation of the law. Hunter safety and boating education courses, once taught only in group settings by volunteers, became available in take-home and Internet formats, so that busy outdoors-persons could conveniently learn how to use natural resources safely and wisely. Governor Miller set in motion a healthy and creative rethinking of conservation law enforcement that would continue to improve conservation management in the years to come.

Sporting licenses

In return for a modest $1.50 increase in Georgia's hunting and fishing license fees as part of his Georgia Rebound initiative in 1992, Governor Miller created new opportunities for Georgia's sportsmen and women and updated the state's antiquated system for providing licenses. The proceeds of the license fee increase went in their entirety to provide additional land for hunting and fishing through Preservation 2000.

Under the Governor's leadership, the 1995 General Assembly passed legislation authorizing the Department of Natural Resources to sell a new, comprehensive sportsman's license. This single license, which cost $60 a year, covered all resident noncommercial sport hunting and fishing privileges in the state, with the exception of the federal duck stamp. DNR expected to sell 10,000 sportsman's licenses during 1996, which was the first year they were available. However, 17,704 licenses were sold at a net revenue to the state of over a million dollars. The following year, the sale of 19,972 of these comprehensive licenses provided nearly $1.2 million in net revenue. Sale of the sportsman's license also increased the number of state waterfowl stamps sold, which provided more money for waterfowl management. In addition, the sales increased the state's eligibility for federal aid in wildlife and sportfish restoration funds. These funds were a major source for DNR's wildlife and sportfish management programs, which improved the hunting and fishing opportunities the state provided its sportsmen and women.

In his FY 1998 budget, the Governor provided over $2 million to allow the Department of Natural Resources to implement a new point-of-sale licensing system. This electronic system ensured that Georgia's hunters and anglers could purchase all types of licenses at all locations. The system also allowed DNR to create for the first time a database of licensed sportsmen and women, to be used for research and surveys so that the department's efforts would better meet their needs.

This point-of-sale system was only one way to purchase a license. Under the Miller Administration, Georgia became the first state in the nation of offer hunting and fishing licenses through the telephone and the Internet as well as through license vendors, making it easy for Georgia's million-plus anglers and hunters to buy their licenses.

Forest resource management

Under the Governor's guidance, the Forestry Commission underwent important organizational and policy changes during the 1990's. These changes reduced costs while improving the efficiency and types of services the commission offered to Georgians. As a result of a creative and thorough analysis of the effectiveness of fire-fighting methods, the commission phased out less effective techniques and aggressively adopted more effective techniques and management styles. None of these changes adversely impacted the quality of the Forestry Commission's services or fire-fighting capability, which remained the best in the Southeast with a ten-year average fire size of 3.96 acres.

The impact of the Forestry Commission's changes was broad. Analysis showed that with the onset of technology, air detection patrols and cellular phone use by citizens, fire towers were no longer important in the detection of fires. Therefore, Georgia significantly reduced the number of fire tower operators in the state. The addition of technology was recognized as important to improving fire prevention and detection. The purchase of GPS locating systems improved the commission's ability to map the exact location of fires and improve response times.

The commission added weather information and tracking equipment to determine high-risk days for fires and wind direction for prescribed burns and burn permits. Establishing the burn permit program, which required citizens to obtain a burn permit from the Forestry Commission before conducting any outside burns, reduced the number of fires and the time spent responding to citizen calls.

Another organizational change was establishing contracts for service with Atlanta metro-area county commissions. The primary mission of the Forestry Commission was to prevent and suppress forest fires. Since these urban counties contained very little forest, they did not need the commission's services. Contracting with the county commissions for the limited services these areas required greatly reduced costs without sacrificing service.

The method for responding to forest fires also changed. Prior to 1998, the commission relied on county units to fight fires within their respective counties. Under Governor Miller's guidance, the Commission moved to fighting fires with the closest resource available. This change reduced response times significantly and at the same time reduced the need for personnel, since county offices were able to consolidate. In fact, all of these changes resulted in a 10 percent reduction in force between FY 1996 and FY 1999, thus reducing the cost of fire-fighting while improving services.

The Forestry Commission also became more proactive in aiding forest-related industries in the state, helping to create 10,036 new jobs and increase the forest-based economic impact by 61.2 percent in Georgia from 1991 to 1998. Georgia forest exports continued to increase during the Miller Administration. From 1991 to 1998, forest exports to other countries increased 40 percent, and products sent to other states grew by 62 percent.

Finally, the move to assume the responsibility for the compilation of the Forest Inventory Analysis from the federal government on a five-year cycle instead of the previous ten-year cycle proved to be a success with landowners and forest product industries. The compilation of vital information about forest resources, health and productivity levels significantly impacted forest planning to the benefit of the state's forestry industry. From 1990 to 1998, forestry grew from a $12.1 billion state industry to a $19.5 billion state industry.

Average Fire Size for Southeastern States (1986-1996)

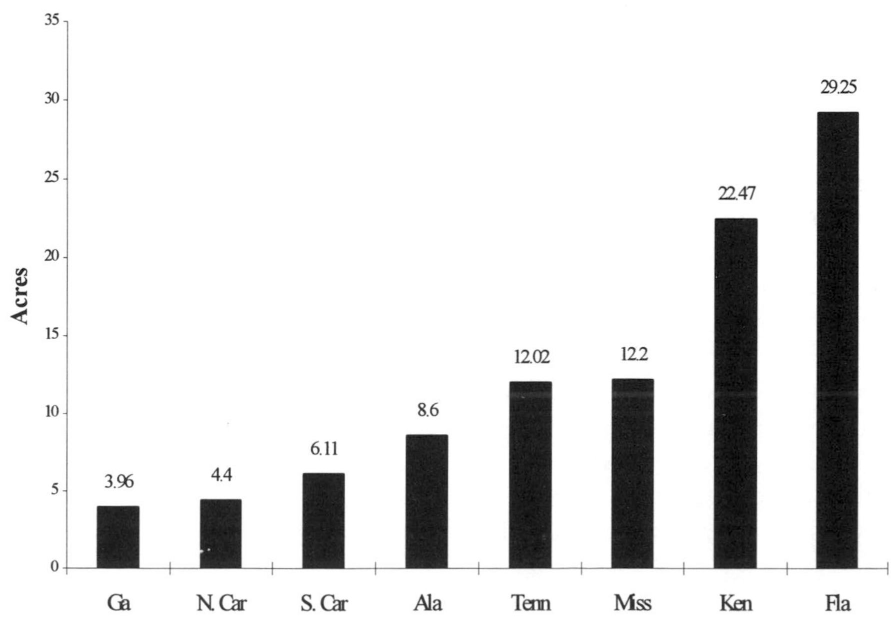

In addition to improvements for the Forestry Commission, the Miller Administration launched the Forestry for Wildlife Partnership. The partnership recognized that while 64 percent of the state was covered by forests, most of that timberland and the wildlife habitat it contained was in private, corporate ownership. The Forestry for Wildlife Partnership was created to encourage and help corporate landowners to incorporate wildlife conservation efforts into their forest management plans. The DNR Wildlife Resources Division worked with 14 corporate forest landholders to develop the partnership, which was voluntary, flexible, noncompetitive and driven by its private partners. The Forestry for Wildlife Partnership was one of several state programs designed to foster the conservation of the environment and of wildlife and wildlife habitat as a land management objective. Together, these partnerships had the potential to conserve habitat on more than 10 million acres of Georgia land.

Reducing and Preventing Pollution

It is clear that the only really safe way to handle toxic pollutants is not to produce them in the first place. It can be done. The production of toxic pollutants can be reduced, and they can be disposed of in a responsible manner. It must be done. And I intend for it to begin during my administration as Governor.

Governor Zell Miller, July 23, 1991

Pollution Prevention Assistance Division (P^2AD)

In the 1980s, the prevailing philosophy dictated that hazardous waste be managed by treatment and disposal programs using pollution control technology. The Georgia Hazardous Waste Management Authority, therefore, proposed to build a hazardous waste management facility, including an incinerator, to manage the state's hazardous waste. There was significant opposition to this plan. When Governor Miller took office in January of 1991, he immediately restructured the Authority to reduce its political appointments and increase the scientists and engineers among its membership, and expanded its mission to include the development of programs to reduce hazardous waste at the source through voluntary measures. With these changes in place, the newly constituted Authority determined that a state-sponsored hazardous waste management facility was neither economically viable nor needed in Georgia at that time. As a result, the Authority became dormant.

The Georgia Pollution Prevention Assistance Division (P^2AD) was subsequently created as a non-regulatory division of the Georgia Department of Natural Resources in October 1993. It was designed by Governor Miller as a "One Stop Shop" to help Georgia businesses and citizens find ways to reduce their generation of solid and hazardous waste, emissions, and releases of pollutants into the air, water, and land. To accomplish this goal, P^2AD developed a variety of innovative technical and financial assistance programs. The division's activities were designed not only to provide technical assistance to companies, but also to guide them in developing pollution prevention programs tailored to their specific needs.

Technical assistance: Technical assistance from P^2AD could take many forms, including access to the Division's Information Center and library, workshops and training sessions, on-site pollution prevention assessments, and publications (case studies, tip sheets, quarterly newsletter). During the Miller Administration, P^2AD also operated the state's Household Hazardous Waste and Radon Awareness programs. From its creation through the end of the Miller Administration, the Technical Assistance Program handled an ever-increasing number of requests. Additionally in this four-year period, staff made 283 presentations at various conferences and events.

Fiscal Year	Completed Technical Requests
1994	237
1995	330
1996	375
1997	717
Total	**1,659**

The division surveyed past clients of P^2AD to determine their rate of implementation of pollution prevention solutions as well as the resulting cost savings and waste reduction achieved. Clients reported substantial reductions in hazardous waste, solid waste, wastewater and air emissions, with cost savings of \$600 to \$236,000 per company. Some of those who developed comprehensive pollution prevention programs reported annual savings in the millions of dollars.

Department of Energy grants: In 1993 and again in 1994, projects sponsored by P^2AD were selected for funding under the National Industrial Competitiveness through Energy, Environment, and Economics ($NICE^3$) program. One of the grants focused on an improved process for batch-dying nylon carpet, while the other concentrated on improved lime mud regeneration techniques applicable to the pulp and paper industry. Savings from the carpet project in a dyehouse which processed 50 million pounds of carpet per year, were estimated to be \$1,451,000. Savings estimated for operating costs of a typical improved mud regeneration unit were \$648,200 per year over a conventional rotary kiln system.

Georgia Environmental Partnership (GEP): P²AD invited the Georgia Tech Economic Development Institute and The University of Georgia's Department of Biological and Agricultural Engineering to join it in a three-way partnership called the Georgia Environmental Partnership. All three organizations provided technical assistance to industry and business, and GEP enabled them to coordinate the assistance they provided on environmental problems. Partnership activities included joint on-site pollution prevention assessments, workshops, the establishment of regional environmental networks, and greater interaction with the Governor's Traditional Industries Program, an industry-directed research program that served the pulp and paper, carpet and textile, and food processing industries.

Recognition programs: One way P²AD encouraged companies to pursue pollution prevention in their activities was through positive recognition. The division initiated two programs of recognition: Pollution Prevention Partners (P³) and the Governor's Award for Pollution Prevention. Companies which committed to continuous pollution prevention and environmental improvement could be certified as P³ Partners at three levels: entry, achievement and model. The Governor's Awards were given yearly in several categories to recognize specific pollution prevention projects.

Department of Defense partnership: In April 1998, P²AD entered into a formal partnership with the Department of Defense installations in Georgia. The objective of the partnership was to create a working relationship with the military services, the Georgia National Guard, and P²AD, that recognized and promoted pollution prevention as the standard way of doing business. Pollution prevention issues were identified by the group and selected inter-service work teams from the partners began seeking solutions to these issues.

Agricultural Pollution Prevention (AgP²): In partnership with The University of Georgia and the Cooperative Extension Service, P²AD developed a comprehensive pollution prevention program for Georgia's agricultural and horticultural communities. Staff from the AgP² Program addressed animal waste management, bioconversion and by-production utilization; pesticide stewardship; and horticultural pollution prevention. The program also developed a voluntary assessment system for farmers called Farm*A*Syst, and participated in numerous workshops and assessments around the state.

Recycling market development: P²AD had responsibility for reducing solid waste generated by businesses, industry and institutions. The division identified five industries that generated solid wastes in large quantities in Georgia: carpet/textile, wood processing, construction and demolition, food processing and municipal biosolids. P²AD and its university partners began in-depth waste characterization studies of these five solid waste streams to identify ways to reduce their generation and to foster the development of recycling markets for their by-products.

Neighborhood Environmental Partnership (NEP): In 1996, the City of Atlanta received an EPA environmental Justice Through Pollution Prevention grant. As a result, NEP was established as a cooperative effort between P^2AD, the City of Atlanta and Clark-Atlanta University's Southern Center for Studies in Public Policy. It was designed to serve as a vehicle for non-adversarial communication between industries and neighborhoods on issues of mutual concern, to provide technical assistance to industries in their efforts to reduce the generation of pollution, and to facilitate community access to timely environmental information. During the initial phase, two Atlanta neighborhoods with significant low-income, minority populations located near manufacturing facilities were selected as pilot projects. Based on the lessons learned during this phase, NEP would expand into a citywide effort.

Cleaning up hazardous waste

At the same time he was working to minimize pollution and waste, the Governor also raised the concern of the threat to human health and the environment posed by the potential release of harmful substances from abandoned hazardous waste sites. In the 1992 legislative session, he called for an expanded state law to clean up abandoned sites that neither the federal Superfund nor then-existing state law could address. In response, the General Assembly passed the Georgia Hazardous Site Response Act, which the Georgia Environmental Protection Division (EPD) administered. It was highly controversial legislation, and passed only through the personal leadership of the Governor and the hard work of his floor leaders in the House and Senate.

The act alerted the public to the existence of contaminated sites through several means: reporting requirements, annual publication of a list of contaminated sites (known as the Hazardous Site Inventory), and deed notices for properties with significant contamination. The Act also established the Hazardous Waste Trust Fund, which EPD used to investigate and clean up sites when the persons responsible for contamination were unable or unwilling to do so. The fund received income from fees on solid and hazardous waste, fees on releases of hazardous substances, and fines collected under Georgia's various environmental laws. These fees also encouraged waste generators to consider ways to reduce the waste they generated and to manage their wastes in a more environmentally acceptable manner.

In 1998, the Hazardous Site Inventory contained 400 sites. Whenever possible, those who had been responsible for the contamination were held responsible for cleaning up these sites. For sites where those responsible were

Hazardous Waste Trust Fund Sites

Site Name	County	Cost
4th Street Landfill (Brunswick Airport)	Glynn	$150,000
A&D Barrell & Drum Company	Fulton	150,000
Arivec Chemicals	Douglas	500,000
Barlow Creosoting	Clinch	3,898,100
Barnett Shoals Road	Clarke	200,000
Baxley Creosoting	Appling	1,276,800
Ben Gober Landfill	Gwinnett	3,000,000
Ben Hill County Disposal Site	Ben Hill	2,000,000
Berrien Products	Berrien	882,000
Bumper Distribution	Fulton	205,000
Butler Island Drum Dump	McIntosh	125,000
CR&A Battery Company	Douglas	500,000
Carolina Commercial Heat Treating	Rockdale	120,000
Cascade Lot	Fulton	200,000
Ceco Concrete Construction	Lowndes	230,000
Cedartown Battery Site	Polk	250,000
Chemresol	Glynn	500,000
Chemtall	Liberty	1,400,000
City of Damascus Groundwater	Early	200,000
City of Ideal Pesticide Site	Macon	780,000
Conyers Battery Exchange Dump	Rockdale	1,214,000
Crymes Landfill	Gwinnett	3,000,000
David Jones Tax Parcel #280-12	Walker	100,000
DeKalb Pest Control	DeKalb	80,000
Eleventh Street Landfill	Bibb	2,000,000
Elite Coating/Hargis Enterprises	Wilkinson	320,000
Escambia Treating Co.-Brunswick	Glynn	18,320,900
Escambia Treating Company - Camilla	Mitchell	830,000
Farmers Favorite Fertilizer	Colquitt	1,200,000
Former Atlanta Fish Warehouse	Fulton	250,000
Former Atlantic Engineered Products	Glynn	320,000
Former Circle K Lead Dump	Chatham	892,000
Futch Wire Burn Site	Effingham	601,000
Georgia Metals Lead Dump	Cobb	147,800
Goldberg Brothers	Richmond	50,000
Gordon Service Company Landfill	Wilkinson	162,000
Gordon Services Company	Wilkinson	3,500,000

financially unable or unwilling to do remediation, EPD could use money from the trust fund to investigate and hire contractors to clean up the sites. EPD could then seek to recover the state's costs from the responsible parties. From 1992 through 1998, EPD committed $37 million from the trust fund to

Site Name	County	Cost
Gravel Pit Road Site	Richmond	110,000
Griffith Waste Oil	Jackson	347,800
HanHar Metals	Long	1,220,000
Hargis Enterprises	Wilkinson	373,100
Herndon Homes Housing Project	Fulton	9,146,800
Holley Electric Company	Wayne	108,000
Hyde Park Neighborhood	Richmond	80,000
Kendrick Sanitation Service Site	Upson	1,200,000
Lastinger Dump	Glynn	15,000
Liberty Waste Oil Drum Dump	Colquitt	259,600
Lyndal Chemical (aka: Chemical Processing of Georgia)	Whitfield	120,000
M&J Solvents	Fulton	500,000
Martin Fireproofing Company	Elbert	500,000
McClusky Farm	Gwinnett	2,200,000
Metropolitan Sandblasting	Paulding	80,000
Morgan Post Treating Co.	Clinch	611,500
Moultrie Wood Treating Co.	Colquitt	350,100
Murrow Brothers Delinting Waste	Oconee	200,000
Muse Scrap Drum Dump	Carroll	320,000
Nashville Old City Landfill	Berrien	1,700,000
Nobles Sludge Pits	Carroll	620,000
North Georgia Agricultural Services Inc.	Madison	750,000
Oil Processing Corp.	Jefferson	100,000
Old City Landfill	Jeff Davis	2,000,000
Old Hazelhurst Solid Waste Disposal Site	Jeff Davis	2,000,000
Old Sterling Landfill	Glynn	1,700,000
Old Willacoochee Wood Preservers	Atkinson	250,000
Palmetto Tire Fire	Coweta	150,500
Paramore Railcar	Tift	6,600
Paul Avenue Disposal Site	Fulton	12,600
Peach Metals	Peach	80,000
Pelham Phosphate	Mitchell	200,000
Powersville Landfill	Peach	793,500
Rummel Fibre Company	Floyd	360,000
Sardis Road Creosote Site	Cobb	446,400
Sharon Pit (Landfill)	Chatham	1,700,000
Shaver's Farm	Walker	3,000,000
Smith Wrecking Service	Screven	750,000
Southern Industrial Park - Parcel #5	Gwinnett	750,000

80 investigations and cleanups, 29 of which were completed by 1998. Responsible parties were responsible for cleaning up another 132 sites.

The provisions of Georgia's Hazardous Sites Response Act encouraged voluntary clean up of contaminated sites by responsible parties. The state's Annual Hazardous Site Inventory identified as many as 400 sites. Of those,

Site Name	County	Cost
Stan Sax	Brooks	45,000
Sun Labs	Fulton	1,088,500
Sycamore Pesticide Site	Turner	500,000
T Street Dump	Glynn	1,700,000
Terhune Company	Polk	250,000
Terry Creek Dredge Spoil Area	Glynn	175,000
Tift Site	Fulton	727,000
Truman Parkway, Phase II	Chatham	1,000,000
Twin City Mfg. Co.	Emanuel	150,000
U. S. Plating Burn Site	Fulton	150,000
Vandy Musgrove Property	Dougherty	500,000
Virginia Avenue Drum Dump	Walker	167,100
W.F. Harris Wood Treating Co.	Upson	1,080,000
Wallace Lake Road Dump	Douglas	200,000
Waynesboro Old City Dump	Burke	2,000,000
Westrek	Troup	575,000
Whitehall Street Wire Burning Site	Fulton	150,000
Whitlock Junkyard PCB Spill	Stephens	750,000
Williams Property Pesticide Dump	Mitchell	80,500
Winder-Barrow Speedway	Barrow	220,000
TOTAL CLEAN-UP COSTS FOR ALL SITES	231 Sites	$96,174,200

132 were to be cleaned up by responsible parties. The remaining 268 sites, which consisted of 122 privately-owned abandoned sites and 146 state and local government sites were to be cleaned up with the Hazardous Waste Trust Fund (HWTF). In addition to funding such clean up activities, 10 percent of the HWTF receipts was used to reduce hazardous waste at the source through a variety of pollution prevention methods. Governor Miller provided $60.8 million for the Hazardous Waste Trust Fund during his administration.

Scrap tire management

At the same time he was addressing abandoned hazardous waste sites, the Governor also targeted the growing number of scrap tires dumps, which posed a particular threat to the environment because of their potential to burn, releasing toxic fumes into the air and oil into the groundwater. In 1992, simultaneously with the Hazardous Site Response Act, the Governor also persuaded the General Assembly to amend state laws on solid waste management to include the proper disposal of the six to seven million scrap tires generated in Georgia each year.

At that time there were approximately eight million illegally dumped tires in piles ranging from 200 to three million tires each. The 1992 legislation created the Solid Waste Trust Fund to fund the clean-up of existing dumps, either by contracting with private companies or by awarding grants to local governments to clean up dumps within their jurisdictions. Grants were also offered to local governments for the development and implementation of waste management and educational programs. The trust fund was funded with revenues generated by a $1 per tire fee charged to consumers and collected by retailers. This source provided $24 million, which when added to revenue from solid waste fines, yielded $32 million for the Solid Waste Trust Fund to clean-up scrap tire dumps throughout the state during the Miller Administration. EPD identified some 300 significant tire dumps throughout the state, containing more than five million tires. By the end of the Miller Administration, the trust fund had cleaned up 85 of those sites which contained four million of the five million tires. The fee and the trust fund were set to expire in the year 2002, with the expectation that by that time the trust fund would have completed the task of cleaning up the tire dumps and Georgia's tire recyclers would have become self-sustaining.

The new scrap tire law put the Georgia Environmental Protection Division (EPD) in charge of preventing the creation of new scrap tire piles by regulating tire carriers, generators and processors. EPD issued 218 scrap tire carrier permits, and six scrap tire processors began producing rubber chips and crumb rubber from discarded tires. In January 1995, whole, shredded and chipped tires were banned from the state's landfills, and by the end of the Miller Administration, EPD-approved facilities were recycling more than 10.5 million scrap tires a year. Most tires became chips which served as supplemental fuel for the paper industry, as a substitute for gravel in septic tank drain lines and for various civil engineering projects.

Trust Funds Appropriations by Year

Fiscal Year	Hazardous Waste Trust Fund	Solid Waste Trust Fund
1994	$4,300,000	$3,000,000
1995	$8,918,534	$5,363,868
1996	$11,512,235	$5,276,344
1997	$20,800,013	$5,396,990
1998	$7,380,472	$6,792,756
1999	$ 7.895,077	$6,132,574
Totals	**$60,806,331**	**$31,962,532**

Solid waste management

Governor Miller led the state in reducing Georgia's waste stream and in making significant improvements to solid waste management. In 1990, few local recycling programs existed statewide; by 1996 however, recycling programs and services existed in over 500 communities covering roughly 96 percent of the state's population. Similarly, solid waste public education efforts were carried out in only a handful of cities and counties in 1990, but by 1996 about 260 cities and counties had education programs in place covering nearly 83 percent of the state's population. Of the approximately 180 local public solid waste landfills operating in 1990, only eight were lined. In 1996, 101 landfills remained, of which 35 were lined facilities. By 1998, Georgia had at least 14 years of remaining landfill capacity, because the newly permitted landfills were designed with much larger capacity.

In 1990 there were no certified landfill operators in Georgia. In 1996, there were over 625 certified landfill operators. Essentially all operators had been trained and certified, and over 99.9 percent of the state's population was covered by a solid waste management plan.

The imposition of a $1 retail sale fee per tire on all new replacement tires began on July 1, 1992, with the proceeds going into the state's Solid Waste Trust Fund. By 1998, nearly four million scrap tires had been recycled with these funds.

In 1990 the governmental cost of solid waste management came mostly from the property tax. Under the governor's leadership, 63 percent of local governments providing residential collection in 1996 charged a user fee for the service.

A new division of DNR, the Pollution Prevention Assistance Division (P^2AD) was established in 1993 to offer technical assistance to businesses to reduce, reuse, and recycle materials and to lower demand for raw materials, water, and energy. Although Georgia's 1990 recycling rate was unknown, by 1995 at least one-third of the potential solid waste generated in the state was recycled, placing Georgia among the top ten states in the nation.

Before 1993, a violation of the Georgia litter control law was a misdemeanor punishable with a maximum fine of $300. The law made no distinction whether the quantity was large or small, whether the waste was hazardous or biomedical, or whether the violation was committed for profit. To remedy these deficiencies, the General Assembly, at the urging of Governor Miller, passed the Georgia Waste Control Law in 1993. This legislation was written under Georgia's criminal code and could be enforced by any of the 30,000 peace officers in Georgia. The legislation also expanded the definition of dumping to include discharging sludge and emitting air contaminants.

While the act of littering and the penalties associated with litter control remained the same, stiffer penalties were established for more serious violations. Penalties became more progressively more severe depending on the amount of waste dumped, discharged or burned, and depending on whether the waste was hazardous or biomedical. Whether the violation was committed for profit was also a factor. By addressing environmental crimes in Georgia's criminal code, Governor Miller sent a strong message to people who polluted or profit or failed to show proper respect for the state's environment. The 1993 Waste Control law became an effective enforcement tool that allowed every peace officer and prosecutor in Georgia to join the fight against environmental crime.

A national panel of judges representing government, industry and citizen groups selected Georgia Clean and Beautiful as a winner in the 1997 Keep America Beautiful (KAB) State System Awards program. Georgia Clean and Beautiful received a second place award for its role in promoting the growth of the Keep America Beautiful (KAB) system, in providing leadership and networking opportunities for local KAB affiliates in Georgia, and in facilitating public-private partnerships to prevent litter and improve waste handling practices across the state.

In 1995, under Governor Miller's direction, several state agencies began working together for the first time to combat litter. Five state agencies consolidated their independent approaches to Georgia's litter problem into a coordinated effort called the Georgia Peachy Clean Team. They sponsored a statewide media campaign and established an annual statewide cleanup effort. In the first two weeklong cleanups, more than 11,000 volunteers cleaned 1,750 miles of roadway, 70 acres of vacant lots and 134 illegal dumps. Peachy Clean Team members included the Departments of Community Affairs, Natural Resources, Public Safety and Transportation, the Georgia Environmental Facilities Authority and the state's local Keep America Beautiful affiliates.

Underground petroleum storage tanks

In 1994, Governor Miller recognized the need to consolidate the state's response to the Environmental Management Rules and Regulations for underground tanks storing fuels for vehicles and emergency power generators. An inventory of tanks owned by the State of Georgia tallied some 2300 tanks at almost 1000 sites, spread among 18 different units of state government. Each agency/department was responding differently from the others, and all were requesting large sums of monies for those efforts.

The Governor consolidated the state's remediation efforts within a single agency and reduced to a minimum the number of tanks owned by the state.

By consolidating, he achieved a coordinated response based upon the operating costs and environmental risk of each site, regardless of agency ownership. By reducing the number of state-owned sites, he simultaneously reduced future environmental risk and avoided the outlay of funds to replace unneeded tanks. Combined, these two actions enabled the state to reduce from about $100 million to less than $40 million the funding needed to remediate the tanks it kept and remove the ones it stopped using.

However, consolidation and reduction of underground fuel tanks required a new procedure for acquiring fuel for the state's vehicles. As part of the Governor's privatization effort, a new vehicle fuel-purchasing card was created and was managed by the private sector. Similar to a MasterCard or Visa, this card enabled fuel purchases at over 6000 sites statewide — shifting some 70 percent of the state's fuel purchases to local neighborhoods.

The Governor recommended a four-year tank remediation plan to the General Assembly. The funding for this plan included three payments of $5 million in bond monies in FY 1996, FY 1998 and FY 1999. Additional funding for the remediation of Department of Transportation fuel tank sites came from motor vehicle fuel tax revenues. Georgia began this task in July 1995 and became one of the first states to achieve the program's goals within the timeline established by the Environmental Management Rules and Regulations.

Investing in local environmental facilities

Governor Miller demonstrated his dedication to helping local governments in Georgia meet the needs of growth and development. Using the Georgia Environmental Facilities Authority (GEFA), his administration dedicated over $300 million to provide low interest loans to local governments for water and wastewater infrastructure construction. This was a large expansion of the program from the $168 million dedicated to it from FY 1985 to FY 1991. Most of these loans went to smaller municipalities, enabling rural Georgia to meet the infrastructure needs of development and deal with pollution problems. From FY 1992 through FY 1997, communities of under 25,000 residents received 58 percent of the loan funds and communities with populations under 5,000 received 21 percent. Governor Miller's commitment to this program would enable this state-funded water and sewer revolving loan program to become self-sustaining at a $20 million level through loan repayments by FY 2001.

In 1994, desiring greater efficiency in government, Governor Miller requested and the General Assembly approved the consolidation of the federal Clean Water State Revolving Fund (SRF) with the Georgia Environmental Facilities Authority state-funded loan programs. In 1997, the

U.S. Environmental Protection Agency approved GEFA for the very first Drinking Water SRF Program in the nation, allowing GEFA to offer a comprehensive financing program to local governments for any type of water and sewer project envisioned by the community. By the time Governor Miller left office, GEFA was able to commit some $80 million per fiscal year in state and federal funds to local water and sewer projects.

Georgia Environmental Facilities Authority
Water and Sewer Loan Activity 1992 - 1998

F.Y.	Emergency Loans	State Bonds	Program Repayments	TOTAL
1985-1991	$0	$132,458,755	$35,899,657	**$168,358,412**
1992	$811,068	$41,408,986	$2,382,530	$44,602,584
1993	$220,000	$19,404,339	$2,098,000	$21,722,339
1994	$780,259	$19,878,660	$22,483,975	$43,142,894
1995	$689,000	$18,987,925	$14,639,036	$34,315,961
1996	$744,946	$19,176,100	$28,318,373	$48,239,419
1997	$667,500	$19,962,629	$13,350,637	$33,980,766
1998*	$676,875	$20,000,000	$15,500,000	$36,176,875
1999*	$643,031	$20,000,000	$17,500,000	$38,143,031
TOTAL	**$5,232,679**	**$178,818,639**	**$116,272,551**	**$300,323,869**

**Projections based on commitments to date*

Georgia Environmental Facilities Authority
Loan Dollar Distribution by Recipient Population Groups
Fiscal Years 1992 -- 1997

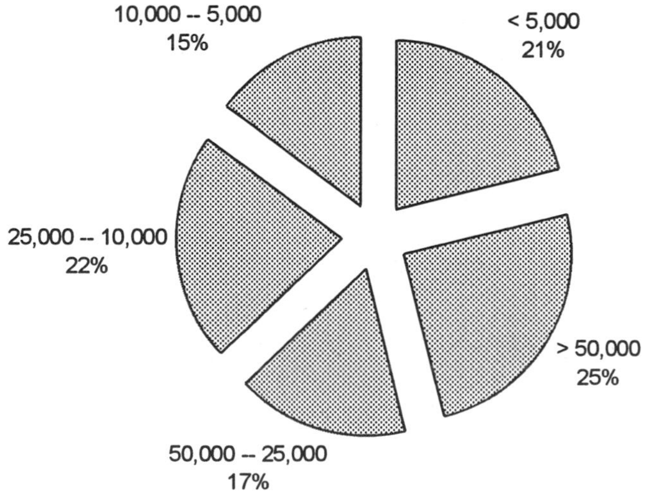

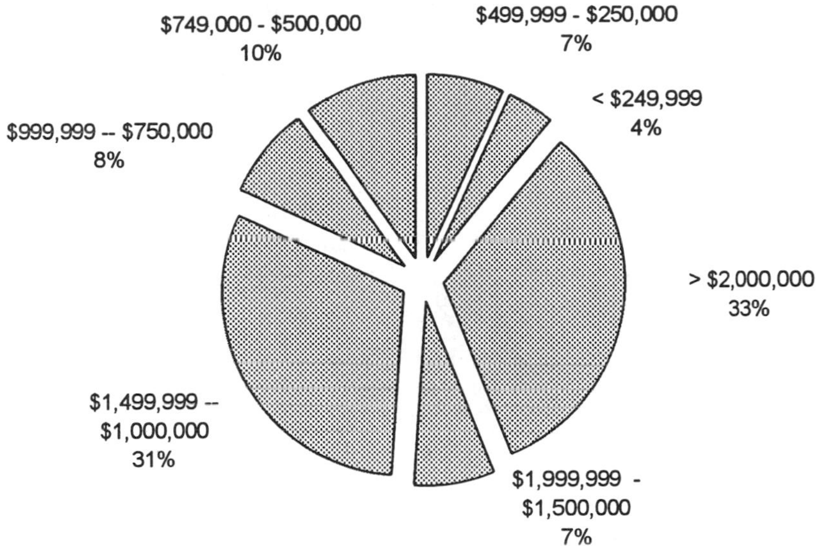

Air quality improvements for metropolitan Atlanta

In 1970 Congress adopted national ambient air quality standards for six pollutants that had the potential to cause adverse health effects: carbon monoxide, lead, nitrogen dioxide, particulate matter, sulfur dioxide, and ozone. During the Miller Administration, Georgia met the national standards for all these pollutants except ozone in the 13-county metropolitan Atlanta area. Following the establishment of national air quality standards, 21 areas in the southeastern United States failed to meet the ozone standard. By 1998 only four ozone non-attainment areas remained: Atlanta, Birmingham, Louisville and north central Kentucky.

The failure of the 13-county metropolitan Atlanta area to meet mandatory federal air quality standards threatened the health of Georgians. A continued failure to meet federal air quality standards could jeopardize federal highway funding for the Atlanta area and seriously impact the area's future economic growth and development as well as affecting the health of its citizens. Since metro Atlanta's economy drove Georgia's economy, both the health and the economic aspects of ozone were a problem for the state.

Metropolitan Atlanta's ozone problem started well before Governor Miller took office. In 1979, the U.S. Environmental Protection Agency adopted national air quality standards for ozone. The Environmental Protection Division (EPD) of the Georgia Department of Natural Resources began monitoring for ozone in 1980, and immediately found that the Atlanta

Local Environmental Facilities Projects
F.Y. 1992 - F.Y. 1998

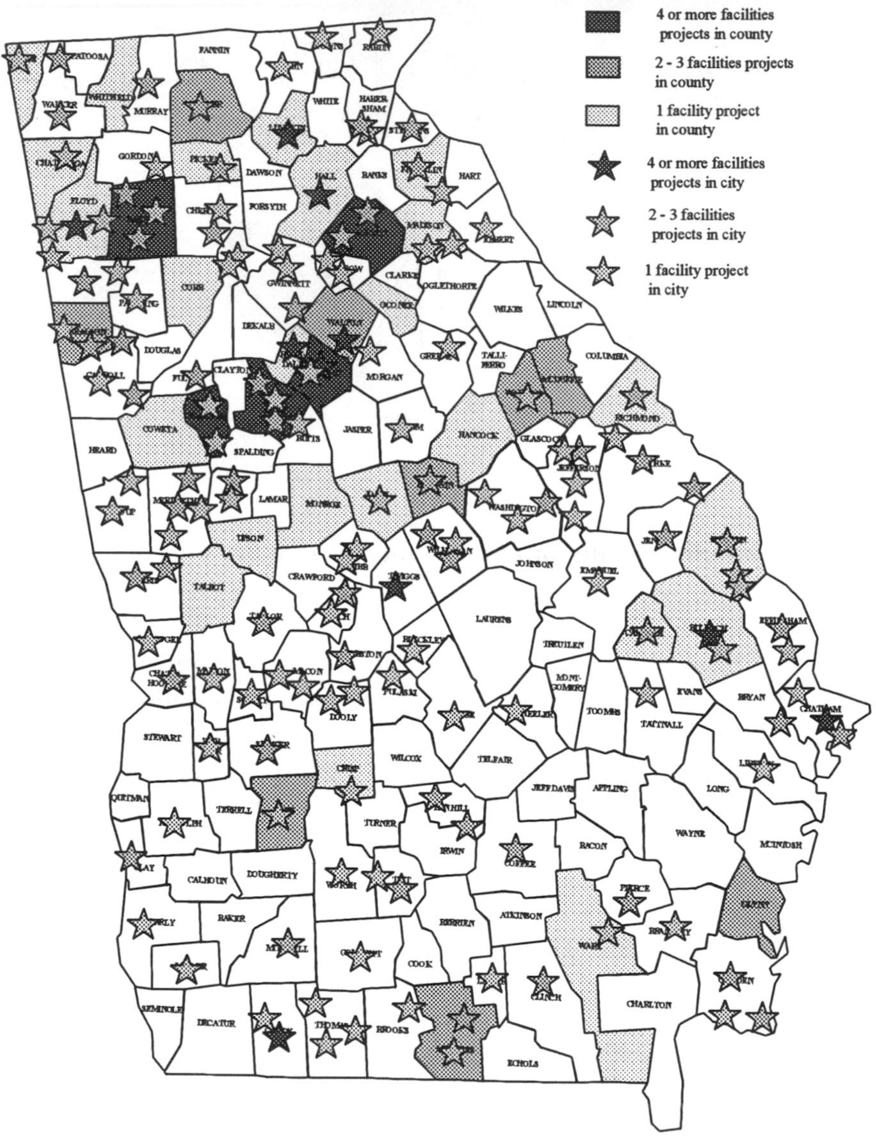

area did not meet the standards. No one knows how long before 1980 the problem had existed. The ozone problem in metropolitan Atlanta was not solved during the Miller Administration, because a feasible solution was not identified until April 1998, and that solution would take five to seven years to implement.

The Environmental Protection Division (EPD) of the Georgia Department of Natural Resources, was responsible for developing and carrying out a state implementation plan to bring the Atlanta area into compliance with state and federal ozone standards. EPD began programs to control ozone in 1980, and those earlier plans applied the conventional national wisdom of controlling emissions of one of the two families of chemicals, called volatile organic compounds (VOCs), from which ozone was formed. VOCs were reduced significantly through the 1980s by businesses, industries, and through a motor vehicle emission inspection program in Cobb, DeKalb, Fulton, and Gwinnett Counties, but those measures weren't enough. The phenomenal growth of the Atlanta area, which increased by 1.3 million people from 1980 through 1997, offset much of the progress from these emission reductions.

By the early 1990's, Georgia EPD had learned from the evolving science of ozone prediction that control of the other family of ozone-forming chemicals, nitrogen oxides (NOX), would also be necessary to solve the problem in the Atlanta area. Unfortunately, the only ozone control solutions identified by computer models at that time were infeasible, since they would have required a 90 percent reduction in NOX emissions. Achieving that would have required metro Atlanta to park 90 percent of its cars, trucks, and buses, among other things. It made no sense to enact draconian measures which might ruin the economy of metropolitan Atlanta and Georgia. Many other large urban areas across the nation also had ozone problems, and they were not pursuing draconian measures. Georgia EPD recommended waiting while both the science of predicting ozone and the technology for controlling emissions improved. Governor Miller accepted that, but while waiting, the Miller Administration made continual reductions in ozone forming emissions to stay in compliance with requirements of the Federal Clean Air Act. Despite Atlanta's growing population, NOX and VOC emissions were reduced three percent per year from 1991 through 1997 through state control programs.

Late in 1997, after three years of intense work with the U.S. EPA and 37 other states that also had ozone problems, Georgia EPD had the best technical ozone prediction tools available, and tried once again to find a feasible solution. Using the advanced science developed by this state-federal group, Georgia EPD identified a feasible solution to the problem. The new plan, reported in April 1998 had three crucial elements: state regulations to change gasoline sold around Atlanta to a lower NOX formulation; further reductions in NOX emissions from power plants and industries in Atlanta and much of North Georgia; and a Voluntary Ozone Action Program to encourage people to drive less and reduce the vehicle emissions that create half of the ozone-forming NOX.

The cleaner vehicle fuels and the emission reductions at industries and power plants, which Georgia EPD began to implement through its traditional regulatory authorities, would take several years to put into effect. However, Governor Miller recognized that the third crucial element of the ozone control program could and should begin immediately, and he enthusiastically supported and promoted the Voluntary Ozone Action Program (VOAP). The VOAP idea came from Atlanta's experience during the 1996 Olympics when people voluntarily carpooled, took public transit, worked alternate schedules, and telecommuted to ease anticipated traffic congestion. Not only did traffic move well, but in addition there were no days of high ozone concentrations during the Olympics, indicating voluntary actions by lots of people would help to solve the ozone problem.

The Voluntary Ozone Action Program promoted simple and effective voluntary actions which employers and employees could take to help improve air quality in the metro Atlanta area during the ozone season, May to September. The goal of the VOAP was to reduce vehicle emissions at the right times to shave ozone peaks. VOAP focused mainly on collective and individual actions to change or reduce vehicle volumes and traffic patterns on days when ozone concentrations were predicted to be high.

Understanding that state government had to lead by example to make VOAP successful, Governor Zell Miller issued an Executive Order on December 4, 1997, directing all state agencies and units of the University System located in the 13-county metro Atlanta area to become VOAP partners. He also sent letters to the regional administrators of all federal agency offices, to local governments, and to the top 100 employers in the 13-county region, challenging them to become VOAP Partners and work together with the state to maximize the success of VOAP. Essentially all state agencies completed a VOAP plan by March 31, 1998, and began implementing their plans in spring of 1998. Full implementation by state agencies was slated for 1999 and every year thereafter, with the objective of reducing single occupancy vehicle commuting by 20 percent for state employees in metropolitan Atlanta.

Solving Atlanta's ozone problem required its 2.5 million vehicle owners to understand that their vehicles created a large part of the ozone-forming pollutants, and that the problem could not be solved without their help to reduce the area's total vehicle miles of travel. So Governor Miller proposed and obtained $1,000,000 in the state budget to fund a large public education campaign to make VOAP a success sooner.

By October 1998, the impact of the first summer of VOAP was clear. A survey of metro Atlanta residents indicated that 93 percent believed cars and traffic contributed to air pollution. Department of Transportation traffic counts indicated that traffic volumes had been reduced by as much as five percent on days when ozone levels had been projected to exceed federal standards. VOAP had clearly begun the process of educating Atlanta's drivers and encouraging them to reduce driving time on days when high ozone concentrations were predicted.

Governor Miller initiated several other programs to reduce air pollution in the Atlanta area. His strategy focused on encouraging and supporting alternatives to present practices rather than severe regulatory systems. In addition to his strong support of VOAP, he initiated the planning and design of commuter rail and inter-city rail service. He increased the number of alternative fuel vehicles in operation in Atlanta by incorporating them into the state motor vehicle fleet, providing $1.3 million in matching DOT funds for MARTA to begin replacing diesel buses with buses fueled by compressed natural gas and providing tax credits to private citizens and businesses who leased, purchased or converted a vehicle to low-emission fuel. He ensured the success of the tougher new vehicle emission tests by helping establish enough independent inspection stations to make testing convenient to 2.5 million car owners.

The 1998 vehicle emission inspection program for the Atlanta area required all vehicles to meet tougher tailpipe standards. Building on the existing program, all testing was done by private businesses (service stations, independent test stations, auto maintenance shops) that chose to participate. The new equipment to test older vehicles cost $25,000 to $30,000 per site. To insure that an adequate number of test sites had the required equipment, the Governor increased amount of the fee that sites with the new equipment could retain in a one-year incentive program, funded at $6 million.

Since cars registered in counties where the emissions test was mandatory, had about 20 percent lower emissions than cars from other counties, the vehicle testing program was a major component of Governor Miller's overall strategy to improve the air quality in the metropolitan Atlanta area. The list of counties where cars had to be tested was also expanded from four to thirteen in the Atlanta area in 1996.

Preserving Georgia's History

The sense of place is a powerful thing. The sensory experience of actually being where history happened brings our heritage out of the realm of the imaginary and into the realm of reality. If we can stand in the very place where history happened, if we can walk the same paths our heros once walked and look out of the same windows through which they once looked—history comes alive. Historic preservation enriches our understanding of what it must have been like for our forebears, and weaves our rich heritage into our daily lives in a tangible way.

Governor Zell Miller, February 18, 1992

The passage of the Georgia Planning Act in 1989 required local governments statewide to consider historical and environmental resources in their planning efforts. The participation of the state preservation office in this process verified the necessity for state participation and review. This legislation, which encouraged the important role of the state preservation office, put into place the building blocks of the preservation movement in Georgia over the last decade.

A higher profile for historic preservation

After the Georgia Planning Act became law, Governor Miller and the General Assembly took many additional actions which greatly enhanced the role of historic preservation in public policy, increased its visibility and strengthened public support. Enacted in 1991, the Georgia Environmental Policy Act required that historic resources be taken into account for state-funded projects. In 1992, the Council on American Indian Concerns was established. In 1993, the Georgia Civil War Commission, the Georgia State Capitol Commission and the Centennial Farms Program were begun, and funding was provided to conduct a survey of state-owned buildings.

The Georgia Heritage 2000 Program was begun in 1994, and for the remainder of the Miller Administration it administered more than $1,000,000 in grants to historic properties. The same year, the historic preservation function in the Department of Natural Resources was elevated to division status to provide more emphasis and visibility on preserving the state's historical structures. In 1997, the Joint Study Committee on Historic Preservation was created and the following year it was reauthorized. In 1998, the Archaeology Education and Protection Program was established within the Historic Preservation Division (HPD), and the General Assembly enacted Senate Bill 446 for State Agency Historic Property Stewardship, Historic Preservation Grants, Historical and Cultural Museum Assistance. In addition, the regional planner program and the state-funded survey program were continued to support and encourage preservation at the regional and local levels.

The primary goal of the historic preservation program in Georgia was to achieve widespread public awareness and involvement in preservation by using the past to benefit the future. This was done at several levels, ranging from general information for the interested public, to professional conferences and publications, to heritage education programs for teachers. During Governor Miller's administration, Georgia became known as a state that produced quality technical publications and conferences and computer-friendly processes for exchanging information. This was an ongoing process, and would continue to be a priority.

The Department of Natural Resources' Historic Preservation Division (HPD) also gave priority to special initiatives that promoted the preservation of properties associated with previously under-represented groups. HPD formed the Georgia African American Heritage Committee and Network to highlight the special role of Georgia's African Americans in the state's history and to encourage the preservation of historic properties associated with black history. Together, the network and HPD sponsored several public awareness projects, including a poster series, a driving tour, a preservation resource guide, and many workshops, including "If Georgia Walls Could Talk." In 1994, the Georgia African American Historic Preservation Network and HPD received a National Honor Award from the National Trust for Historic Preservation which recognized Georgia's achievements and leadership in promoting and strengthening African American preservation.

In 1997, HPD cosponsored "HerStory," the first state-sponsored conference in the nation to focus on preserving and interpreting women's history through the built environment. The Women's History Initiative at HPD received special funding through the General Assembly in 1998 to continue the study of women's history by creating a project to identify and nominate to the National Register of Historic Places significant properties associated with Georgia women.

Initiated in 1993, the Centennial Farms program was cosponsored by HPD, the Department of Agriculture, and other private and nonprofit organizations. By focusing in on the agricultural history of Georgia that went back many generations, it reinforced the importance of this dominant industry to a state that was rapidly urbanizing. It was of great significance to all Georgians to highlight a way of life that could be lost due to rapid urbanization.

Technical assistance and tax incentives

The Historic Protection Divison offered technical information to the public in a variety of ways. HPD extended design assistance and technical advice to Georgia communities through the Office of Preservation Services in Athens, and the Main Street Downtown Design Team program. This free architectural and technical advice provided Georgia communities of varying sizes the expertise of architects, planners, and historians in focusing on ways to improve the look and the viability of their communities. HPD also worked closely with the college-level historic preservation programs in the state, and with K-12 programs through the Heritage Education Program sponsored by the Georgia Trust for Historic Preservation.

In technology applications, DNR was one of the first state agencies put an agency web site on the Internet. HPD also moved quickly to make all its publications available on-line, and became a national leader in incorporating GIS

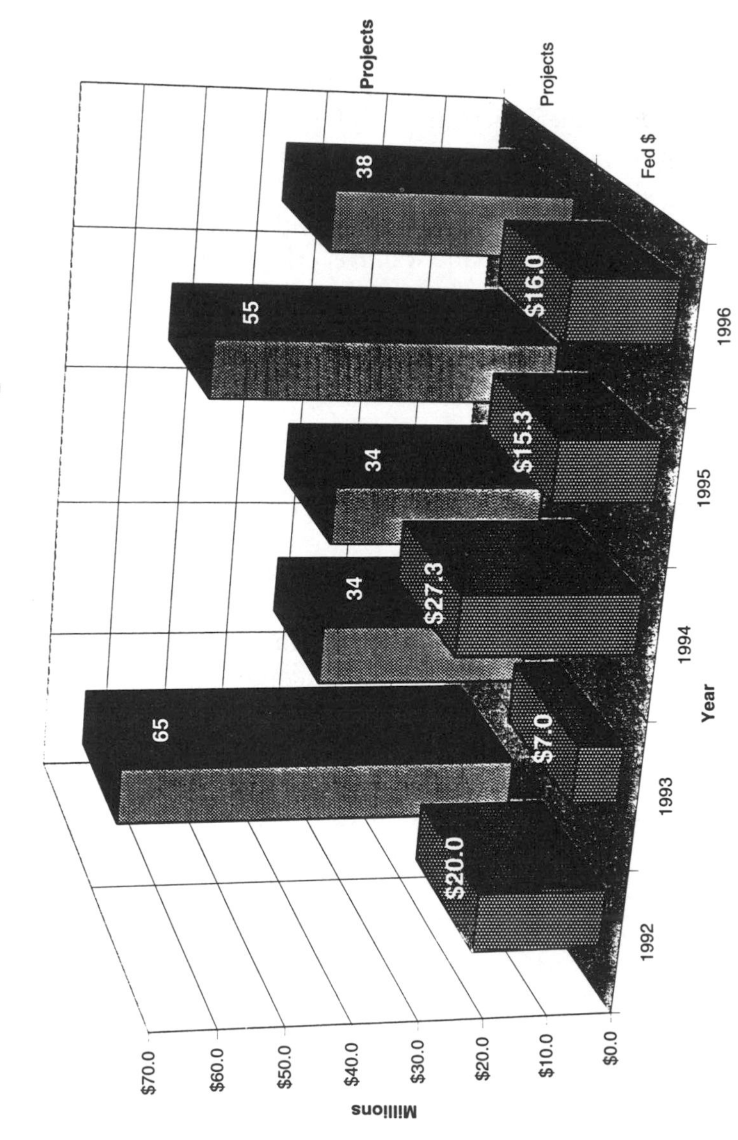

Renovation Projects Through Main Street Program

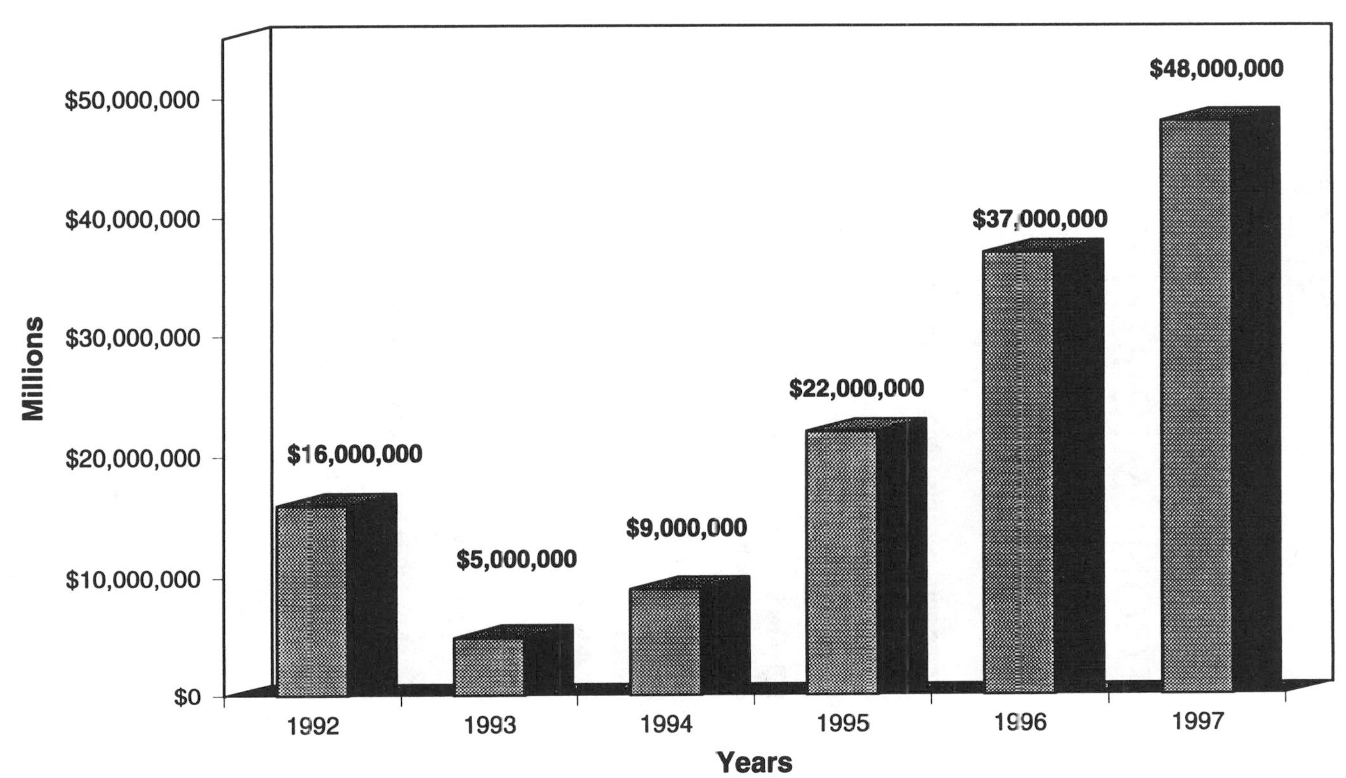

ECONOMIC BENEFITS OF COMMUNITY REVITALIZATION INITIATIVES

Historic preservation benefits Georgia's economy through the creation of jobs for its citizens and sales for businesses. From 1992 through 1996, the economic impact of construction activity for the rehabilitation of historic buildings has generated the following:

- **7,550 jobs** in the construction industry and in other sectors of the Georgia economy
- **$201 million** in earnings, including wages for workers and profits for local businesses
- **$559 million** in total economic activity
- **$1 million** spent on rehabilitation in Georgia means:

    31 jobs in construction and other sectors

    $819,000 in household and business earnings

    $2.3 million in total economic activity

technology in program management, making information available to all Georgians rapidly and in an organized format.

Under the Miller Administration, the building blocks of a strong preservation program for the new millennium were put into place in Georgia. The reauthorized Joint Study Committee on Historic Preservation would

ENCOURAGING HISTORIC PROPERTY REHABILITATION THROUGH TAX INCENTIVES

Between 1992 through 1996, federal and state tax credits for the rehabilitation of historic structures have generated:

- **$101 million** in private investment in historic properties
- More than **$85 million of private investment** in 228 properties throughout the state through the federal program
- **$16 million** of private investment through the state incentive program
- This record puts Georgia in the **top five states** in terms of the number of projects receiving final certification, and in 1995 and 1996, it ranked **number one**

What this means is that together, the federal and state programs have:

- Served as a catalyst for the rehabilitation of properties for affordable housing
- Created unique space for professional and commercial activities
- Created 7,550 jobs
- Generated $271 million in earnings
- Increased property values
- Improved community infrastructure

continue to focus on achieving those goals that will strengthen our knowledge and appreciation of Georgia's greatest assets: its people and its communities.

During most of Governor Miller's second term, Georgia ranked first or second in the nation for the number of completed federal tax-incentive projects.

Encouraged and supported by technical assistance from the Department of Natural Resources' Historic Preservation Division (HPD), hundreds of property owners took advantage of the tax-incentive program and renovated historic properties across the state. By 1998, landowners had invested $600 million to rehabilitate historic commercial properties through the federal tax-credit program that HPD administered, and a smaller amount through the state property-tax freeze program. In 1997 alone, Georgia's property-tax assessment incentives for both commercial and residential historic properties generated $83 million in private investment. In Atlanta the successful use of the tax-incentive program in the preservation and reuse of many of Atlanta's historic buildings may be the most lasting legacy of the Olympic Games. Throughout the state, this work revitalized neighborhoods where properties were previously underutilized, and it employed people in the construction and tourism industries. HPD projected that as the state moved into the next century, funds spent on restoration of existing properties would outpace the cost of new construction nationally.

The economic legacy of preservation projects existed in many other areas as well, in programs administered by HPD and by other state agencies. Georgia's Main Street Program, available to more than 40 communities by 1998, generated more than $150 million in private funds for renovation between 1992 and 1998. The federally funded Intermodal Surface Transportation Efficiency Act brought $70 million to Georgia during the Miller Administration for renovation of more than 100 historic properties, including the Sapelo and Tybee Island historic lighthouses. The affordable housing program sponsored by the Department of Housing and Urban Development not only brought additional funding to Georgia, but also spotlighted projects in Atlanta and Macon as national models for redevelopment of historic properties. The Civil War Commission also helped the state acquire historic properties, generating tourist dollars and preserving important historic resources.

By autumn of 1998, HPD completed a comprehensive multi-year economic benefits study that would graphically detail the costs and benefits of preservation as an economic tool in Georgia's communities and neighborhoods.

A national leader in historic preservation

Long before the idea of privatization became popular, preservation programs had actively encouraged private enterprise as the economic engine of preservation reform. After the National Historic Preservation Act was passed in 1966, preservation began to generate more partnerships between different levels of governmental entities, nonprofit organizations, and the business sector. During Governor Miller's administration, Georgia was a national leader in successfully using federal and state legislative tools to advance economic and educational awareness of preservation's benefits.

The Historic Preservation Division and the private Georgia Trust for Historic Preservation, with its network of almost 10,000 members, formed a partnership that put into place effective preservation programs that affect all levels of public and private decision-making. Georgia's successful partnership was highlighted as one of three case studies in the 1998 National Trust publication "Partnerships for Preservation: Preservation Offices and Statewide Nonprofits."

During the Miller Administration, the Georgia HPD consistently ranked within the ten most successful historic preservation programs nationally. Georgia benefitted from the dynamic leadership of nationally known advocates, and maintained a reputation as a "can-do" state. The U.S. Department of Interior recognized the quality of HPD and made Georgia one of few states to receive broad control of the National Register review program and the environmental review program. In turn, HPD arranged for regional and local governments to take on more of the standard review responsibilities regarding environmental impacts and local property designations.

Georgia's historic preservation program was nationally recognized for the speed of its response, the expedited delivery of funding, its broad range of direct and technical assistance, and the comprehensive information it put together following the flooding caused by Tropical Storm Alberto in 1994. In a national first, the federal government provided a $2.5 million grant specifically for rehabilitating historic properties damaged by the flooding. This grant assisted owners of more than 100 historic properties in 20 communities damaged by the storm, including commercial facilities, museums, community centers, public buildings, private residences, and archaeological sites. Technical assistance for community planning, economic revitalization and heritage tourism complemented the building rehabilitation projects. A stateside disaster plan process was put in place to deal with disasters of any sort as they might occur. Two publications and a video were produced which were used by other states as flood and other natural disasters occurred.

In 1994 assistance from the Governor's discretionary fund enabled HPD to complete a survey of state-owned properties and publish information on the 1,175 historic properties identified in *Held in Trust: Historic Buildings Owned by the State of Georgia.* The attention which this publication brought to the state's responsibilities led to the passage of Senate Bill 446 in 1998, which addressed the stewardship of publicly owned historic properties. Under the Miller Administration, the state took its responsibilities for stewardship seriously, allocating funding for restoration of Rhodes Hall, which was leased from the state by the Georgia Trust for Historic Preservation; for the Old State Capitol in Milledgeville; and for the State Capitol in Atlanta.

The state further emphasized its concern for historic properties with the formation of a public-private partnership to acquire the Nichols-Hardman Farm and with the acquisition of the Griswoldville Civil War site in 1997. These projects required an ability to work successfully with nonprofit and local groups as well as with a variety of state agencies. DNR and HPD were active participants in this process, which made preservation available to a broader public then ever before.

Rhodes Hall

Rhodes Hall was one of the few remaining "castles" on Atlanta's Peachtree Street. Built in 1902-04 by furniture magnate A.G. Rhodes and used as his family home for more than 20 years, the building was given to the state in 1929 by the Rhodes family with the stipulation that the state use it for "historical purposes." From 1930 until 1965, Rhodes Hall housed the state archives. After the state built a new archives building south of the Capitol, Rhodes Hall was leased to the Georgia Trust for Historic Preservation. The Georgia Trust also began a fund-raising drive to restore the interior of the building.

By the time Governor Miller took office, Rhodes Hall had developed some structural problems. With Governor Miller's support, the state agreed to perform some long-deferred maintenance, then entered a 50-year lease with the Georgia Trust. Governor Miller included more than $1 million in his budget over the course of several years to stabilize the building structurally, make repairs to a severely leaking roof and correct cracks and other flaws in the stonework. As a result of this joint commitment to restore the hall's former beauty, this historic building emerged as a fine house-museum and a venue for weddings and other social events.

Jefferson Davis Memorial State Historic Site

This important historic site marked the location of the surrender of Confederate President Jefferson Davis on May 10, 1865. This historic site was first established by the state about 1915 but was turned over to Irwin County in 1977. For 20 years the county operated it as an historic site, but in 1997 it was returned to the state. The General Assembly provided funding to operate the site, and a rededication was held on May 3, 1997.

State Parks

ParkPass

Georgia had some of the best state parks in the South, and with 15 million visitors each year, it was understandable that some facilities were being "loved to death." While revenues from activities such as camping and golf supported a large part of operating costs, they simply could not fund all the needed repairs.

The idea of charging state park visitors a parking fee first arose in the early years of the Miller Administration, at a time when many other states and some parks in the National Park Service, were already testing the waters with such fees. The early 1990s were also a time of fiscal austerity, when state agencies were asked to cut budgets just as repair and maintenance needs in state parks and historic sites were growing. Faced with these competing demands, the Parks, Recreation and Historic Sites Division of the Department of Natural Resources proposed the ParkPass for Georgia state parks.

In April 1991, Governor Miller signed into law the ParkPass authorizing legislation. Collection of the $2 per vehicle parking fee began in June of 1991. ParkPass fees were collected at all 48 state parks, but the daily pass was not required at the historic sites. By the end of the Miller Administration, the ParkPass had generated more than $10 million, which had renovated campgrounds, built group shelters and trails, improved roads, and replaced boat docks. All funds collected were used for repair projects. Each year, as more kiosks were installed at park entrances, ParkPass collection improved, reaching $1.9 million in FY 1998.

Although the ParkPass was initially quite a change for Georgia park users, it gained acceptance because of the improvements it made. The Parks Division placed signs and other markers informing visitors each year of the projects undertaken with ParkPass funds, and a "While You Were Gone" bulletin board at each site showed visitors what renovations took place in the off-season.

ParkPass Funds Collected

FY 1991 (June only)$3,768	FY 1995 $1,470,256
FY 1992 $1,344,506	FY 1996 $1,505,630
FY 1993 $1,386,490	FY 1997 $1,778,543
FY 1994 $1,507,089	FY 1998 $1,904,757

Privatization initiatives

With Governor Miller's strong support, the first large-scale privatization initiative in the Georgia state park system took place in 1994-95, with the construction of the Brasstown Valley Resort in Young Harris, Georgia. Built on state-owned land with state bonds providing a low-cost loan for part of its construction, the resort was operated by Stormont Trice Corporation. It was the first facility of its kind in Georgia and proved a lucrative investment for Georgia taxpayers. Under a five-year operating contract, the Department of Natural Resources paid Stormont Trice a fixed amount plus most of the profits to operate the resort. After deducting expenses and its operating fee, Stormont Trice sends the remaining revenues to the North Georgia Mountains Authority to repay the bond debt for development of the project. Three years into the first five-year contract, the proceeds of the resort not only exceeded the pro-forma expectations, but they more than settled the annual bond repayment.

The success of the Brasstown Valley project created demand for a similar project at Georgia Veterans State Park in Cordele. The park's Retreat at Lake Blackshear was a conference center built with state funds, but privately operated by Private Club Associates, a corporation from Macon, Georgia. The retreat opened in November of 1997 in a private partnership that was also expected to prove successful.

Golf course operation was the first existing state park activity to be privatized that resulted in the loss of several state employees. Historically, each golf course was managed as part of the state park where it was located. To prepare for privatization, all seven state-park golf courses were brought together under one manager, so that economies of scale and more efficient operation were likely to generate cost savings. After this reorganization, a consultant who studied the potential for privatizing the courses recommended that only the maintenance function be outsourced. ISS Corporation of Tampa, Florida, won the maintenance contract and began providing service in 1996. Three of the five eighteen-hole courses were placed under this maintenance contract.

DNR also privatized three park lodges in North Georgia. AmFac Parks & Resorts leased all stay-use facilities at Unicoi, Amicalola Falls and Red Top Mountain State Parks. Unlike the management contracts at Brasstown Valley and the Lake Blackshear conference center, AmFac leased the facilities, paid a fee for their use, and kept all revenues. The lease fee equaled the amount of net income that those three facilities formerly produced. AmFac would also make extensive capital improvements that the park system could not have afforded. At the beginning of the 20-year lease, AmFac had to invest $2 million in these three properties to bring the facilities up to good standards, and then was required to invest five percent of revenues each year to maintain the facilities. Six state employees remained at each of the three parks to manage the natural resources and day-use facilities. AmFac hired many of the other former state employees, and the rest left for other jobs.

Central reservation system

For many years, guests of Georgia's state parks expressed dissatisfaction at having to call several parks before they could make a reservation. Eventually, computer software designed for state park reservations became available, and after studying the experiences of states that used this software, the DNR Parks, Recreation and Historic Sites Division developed a central reservation system for Georgia's parks. The division bought the necessary hardware and software and set up the central reservations office at Panola Mountain State Park east of Atlanta. Staffed by four full-time employees and 10 to 17 hourly employees depending on the season, the State Park Central Reservations Center opened in August 1995.

The central reservations system proved helpful to guests and park staff alike. The system allowed potential state park visitors to make different reservations at several parks with one phone call, or to choose another park and make reservations there if their first choice was unavailable. Freed from the responsibility of handling reservations, park staff had more time to attend to the needs of their guests. When Hurricane Opal forced the closing of Fort Mountain State Park, the reservations center notified those with reservations of the closing and helped them find suitable accommodations at other state parks. The park staff, freed from the task of notifying scheduled guests, could concentrate on restoring the park to full operation.

The State Park Central Reservations Center paid for itself within two years of its opening. It was probably the most significant change the Parks Division had made in its history, redefining the way the Parks Division did business with its guests. As the Miller Administration drew to a close, the division was exploring the possibility of using the Internet to provide even more streamlined services.

Corporate and nonprofit partnerships

One of the state's most important challenges was to maximize corporate and nonprofit support of state parks and historic sites while protecting the integrity of the resources. One successful partnership was between the Department of Natural Resources and the Georgia Power Company through the development of Tallulah Gorge State Park. The company granted the state a long-term lease of 3,000 acres for this new park, helped to fund the construction of an interpretive center, and provided two positions to staff it. Georgia Power received an award from the Edison Institute for its contributions to Tallulah Gorge State Park.

DNR also formed partnerships with nonprofit organizations like the Georgia Heritage Association and the Georgia Appalachian Trail Club. The Heritage Association supported programs that benefited the users of

Georgia's state parks and historic sites. It began by taking over the gift shop at Amicalola Falls State Park, which was suffering financial problems and needed attention. The association provided the retail expertise to operate the gift shop and used the net income to improve the shop's inventory and appearance.

The success of the Amicalola Falls gift shop encouraged the Georgia Heritage Association to assume operation of the gift shops at Tallulah Falls State Park and at the Little White House historic site in Warm Springs. In 1998, the association, in a three-way partnership that involved Georgia Power Company and the Tallulah Falls State Park, opened the Georgia Heritage Center for the Arts at the park. This center, which focused on the work of Georgia folk artists, was on the ground floor of the Georgia Power office building.

The Georgia Appalachian Trail Club, a long-time supporter of Georgia's state parks, became a partner in operating a walk-in lodge at Amicalola State Park, where the trail begins. The state built the lodge, and the club organized a group of volunteers, who incorporated themselves as a nonprofit organization named Appalachian Education and Recreation Services (AERS), to cook the meals and clean the rooms. The Hike Inn, which opened in October 1998, was accessible by a five-mile hiking trail from the Amicalola Falls Lodge parking lot and provided more primitive accommodations for hikers. All revenue earned from the lodge was retained by AERS. After AERS deducted its expenses, the remainder was used it for repairs and improvements at Amicalola Falls State Park, as decided jointly by AERS and the Department of Natural Resources.

Golf courses

Governor Miller provided funding for two new 18-hole golf courses at state parks during the course of his administration. The course at Laura S. Walker State Park was funded in FY 1995 at a cost of $2.5 million. The clubhouse, funded in FY 1996, at $1.6 million, was dedicated in honor of State Representative Harry Dixon in May of 1997. The course at George T. Bagby State Park was added in FY 1996 at a cost of $2.4 million. The clubhouse was added in FY 1997 at a cost of $1.4 million and was dedicated in honor of former Clay County economic development council member Walt Bakes in June 1998.

Repairs and maintenance

The Georgia state park system consisted of 65 parks and historic sites, including nearly 2,000 buildings with a value approaching $100 million. Maintenance of these facilities was a challenge. DNR annually received about

$4 million from the General Assembly and as much as $1.8 million from ParkPass revenues for this purpose. Park maintenance staff and in-house construction crews performed the smaller projects, while private contractors handled the larger ones. Despite a focused effort to repair and maintain park facilities, the list of tasks not funded continued to grow. Issuing bonds for major maintenance was sometimes necessary. In FY 1995 Governor Miller helped DNR obtain $4.5 million in bond funds. Maintenance projects completed with these funds included campground renovation at Fort Mountain and Black Rock Mountain State Parks; cottage renovation at Crooked River, Elijah Clark, F.D. Roosevelt, Vogel and Seminole State Parks; new boat docks for Tugaloo and F.D. Roosevelt State Parks and for Ossabaw and Sapelo Islands; renovation of the historic pools and springs at Warm Springs and the Little White House historic site; renovation of the pool and bathhouse at A.H. Stephens State Park; completion of the pioneer village at General Coffee State Park; renovation of historic Camp Rutledge (an original Civilian Conservation Corps group camp) at Hard Labor Creek State Park; replacement of a lake spillway at James H. Floyd State Park; renovation of the dam at Unicoi State Park; major dredging of the lake at Reed Bingham State Park; renovation of an historic structure at Indian Springs State Park; construction of a new parking lot for the museum at Kolomoki Mounds State Park; construction of new horse trails at five state parks; and repairs to other infrastructure, including the removal of some underground fuel storage tanks.

Brasstown Valley Resort

The Brasstown Valley project was initiated in 1987 when the State of Georgia purchased 503 acres of land along Brasstown Creek in Towns County for $2.2 million. From its inception, the project was designed as an economic stimulus for that region of Georgia where jobs were so badly needed. The preliminary plan included a lodge, conference center, cottages, 18-hole golf course, trails and tennis courts. However, the Department of Natural Resources was unable to find anyone who was willing to build the lodge with private funds. In 1992, Governor Miller persuaded the General Assembly to make $4.5 million in bond funding available to jump-start the project. These funds plus interest charges were to be repaid to the state with revenues generated by the project. The availability of state-owned land and partial construction funding at a low interest rate attracted the Stormont Trice Corporation, and ground breaking occurred in May 1993. Construction was completed in March 1995 at a total cost of $24.7 million. The estimated financial impact in the Towns County region during the first five years of construction and stabilization exceeded $50 million.

From the beginning, DNR took great care to protect the existing environmental conditions. Agency staff worked with the local community to find farmers to cut the 200 acres of hay on the property. One farmer agreed to plant corn fields using a no-till system that did not disturb the soil. DNR carried out other conservation projects on the site, preparing wildlife food plots, rehabilitating stream banks, and planting wildflower patches. The team that subsequently designed the Brasstown Valley facilities analyzed slopes, vegetation, hydrology, archaeology and ridge top protection zones. The final master plan for the resort caused no net impact on jurisdictional wetlands, and it protected trout streams, flood plains, significant archaeological sites, botanically significant zones and various wildllife habitats.

Prior to the construction of the resort, a number of archaeological sites were discovered on the property. Beginning in November 1987, the Georgia Department of Natural Resources (DNR) sponsored investigations of these sites. The primary focus of the investigations involved a cluster of five sites situated along the west bank of Brasstown Creek in an area of relatively extensive floodplain development, although a prehistoric soapstone quarry on the eastern perimeter of the property near the present resort complex was also mapped and tested. Four of the five sites in the Brasstown Creek cluster were considered to be important, and a management plan was designed to insure that these resources were either preserved or excavated prior to the construction of the resort. The plan worked out between developers and New South Associates, archaeological consultants to DNR, called for the preservation of the largest site and the excavation of the other three to clear a workable tract of land for completion of the golf course.

Three separate evaluation investigations were conducted at the Brasstown Valley sites. The first of these in November of 1987 resulted in the initial identification and recording of the sites. In July 1988, a second investigation evaluated the importance of the sites. Small test excavations revealed that the sites contained abundant evidence of earlier aboriginal settlement in the form of cultural features (*e.g.*, post holes, pits, hearths, etc.) Consequently, they were tentatively evaluated as important archaeological resources. A final evaluative investigation was conducted in the winter of 1992-1993.

In the summer of 1993, three of the four important sites were excavated by New South Associates. The excavation strategy involved statistical sampling of the three sites with small test pits and the machine-aided stripping of thin layers of top soil from extensive areas of these sites to search for cultural features to reconstruct the settlement plans and subsistence patterns of the various aboriginal groups represented. Excavations revealed a lengthy occupation history spanning the period from about 9000 to 300 years ago. The primary occupations, however, were represented by cultural phases of the

Woodland, Mississippian and Historic Cherokee periods. Nearly six acres of topsoil was machine stripped to expose over 12,000 cultural features, making this the largest scale archaeological project conducted in Georgia since the Works Project Administration days.

Early in the process DNR, in consultation with the Georgia Council on American Indian Concerns, developed a management plan for the project including a plan for addressing the discovery of American Indian burials on the project. An on-site manager from DNR coordinated all aspects of the resource management plan including coordinating the fieldwork, communicating with the public and most importantly securing the site. The plan emphasized consultation with Native American groups in Georgia, North Carolina and Oklahoma. Council members from Cherokee, N. C., visited the site. DNR staff attended council meetings in North Carolina. A tribal council member was added to the team completing the fieldwork.

Important archaeological areas were subsequently avoided in the design and construction of the resort and its golf course. The areas were returned to their natural condition and were not identified in the landscape. The most significant site was never studied beyond the initial investigation and report. Burials were all left in place and not disturbed. Dirt was hand placed over the area. DNR secured the site throughout the process, monitoring the site 24 hours a day during the most sensitive four months. The required permits were obtained, but at DNR's request the specific survey records specifying the sensitive areas were sealed in the Towns County records by order of the Superior Court. The success of this approach to the archaeological sites was confirmed when the Cherokee Natives in Oklahoma recognized the State of Georgia for the excellent job managing the project and invited the DNR Commissioner to attend a National Forum in Oklahoma and to present a report on the project.

Brasstown Valley continued to practice sound management practices in all areas of resource management. The resort developed over three miles of hiking trails. The trout streams were improved with 17 stream structures. Over 20 interpretive signs helped the visitors better understand the history and culture of the mountains. Two large exhibits were installed in the lower lobby gallery of the resort, detailing in picture, words, and image the history of the Native Americans and the sensitive development of the project with the fragile ecosystem of the mountain forest.

Brasstown Valley proved very successful. The development was recognized with environmental design and engineering awards. The public-private partnership aspect was the spearhead for a statewide effort in privatization. The financial projections exceeded every expectation. The quality of accommodations, food and service were a perfect blend of mountain hospitality and professional resort management. The golf course was rated in the top 10 in the state within the first six months of its opening. The economic impact could be seen throughout the region, as the resort created more than 100 new jobs and stimulated another 75 new businesses to open nearby. The resort became a shining example of economic development, environmental sensitivity and public-private partnership.

VI. Law Enforcement

The reason I have worked so hard to get tough on violent crime is because I believe in safety, discipline and respect for others, and I believe that our laws and our prison sentences must make it clear that we expect our citizens to live by those values.

Governor Zell Miller, January 5, 1994

New Initiatives

Violent thugs have affected the lives of too many of us. First, of course, are the actual victims of those who choose to rob, rape and kill. My heart goes out to each and every one of those victims and their families. But we are all touched by the violence. It is that uneasiness the late night store clerk feels in Carrollton. It is the anxiety the secretary in Savannah feels when she walks alone to the parking garage. It is the fear that shoots through the mom in Atlanta as she momentarily loses eye contact with her child in a busy mall, or that nervousness we've all shared when unknown footsteps walk behind us on any given street.

Governor Zell Miller, January 5, 1994

One of the hallmarks of Governor Miller's administration was a "get tough" stance on crime. Before he was elected the citizens of Georgia felt that justice was not being served in this state and violent criminals were not serving the time the judges gave them. To answer these concerns, the Governor proposed legislation, passed by the 1994 General Assembly, that included the toughest crime and sentencing laws in the country. The Governor's legislation made it clear that here in Georgia, life was precious, and if someone damaged or destroyed it, the consequences would be heavy.

"Two strikes and you're out"

"I like baseball, but violent crime is not a game. My mother always taught me that folks deserve a second chance, and I've always believed that. But a third chance at violence, a third chance to kill, rape or commit armed robbery is a completely different matter," explained Governor Miller when he announced his "two strikes" proposal. The Governor's "two strikes and you're out" legislation applied to second violent offenses committed on or after

January 1, 1995. It allowed no parole for persons convicted for the first time of murder, armed robbery, kidnaping, aggravated child molestation, rape, aggravated sodomy and aggravated sexual battery. Offenders convicted of one of these violent offenses for the first time had to be sentenced to a mandatory prison term of at least 10 years. The law also doubled from seven to 14 years the minimum time that an offender must serve in prison for murder and other life sentences before even becoming eligible for parole. These offenders also had to serve the entire prison sentence ordered by the court. "If you commit one of these violent crimes, and the judge sentences you to specific number of years, you are going to serve every bit of that time, "Governor Miller explained. "No parole. No loopholes. No exceptions."

A person who had been previously convicted of one of these offenses and then was convicted a second time for one of these offenses, was required to be sentenced to life without parole: "two strikes and you're out." The Governor stated "If you've been convicted of any of these violent crimes, and you commit a second violent crime, you are gone for life – you will never get out of a Georgia prison again."

Governor Miller increased the penalties for statutory rape by tenfold in Georgia. Georgia's new rape law, passed in 1996, required that a rapist was to be sentenced to 10-20 years if the rapist was older than 21 and the victim was younger than age 16.

The Governor also increased the penalties against persons who used children in drug operations. Individuals who hired or used anyone under the age of 17 to manufacture or sell drugs were guilty of a felony, punishable by imprisonment for up to 20 years or a fine or both.

Victims' rights

Victims' Bill of Rights: "For too long, criminals have had all the rights, and the justice system has bent over backwards to protect them," Governor Miller said. "No more. Georgia will give victims a role they deserve; we will give victims a voice." In 1995, the Governor won approval of a "Bill of Rights" for victims of violent crimes. Among them were the right to be informed of arrest, bail, bond, court proceedings, the appeals process, parole or release considerations; the right to inform the prosecution of opinions about bail or bond release and give input into plea or sentence negotiations; and the right to be informed of availability of victim compensation and victim service programs.

Victim compensation: The victims' rights legislation also increased the maximum compensation awards for victims to $10,000 and provided an award of up to $10,000 for economic loss due to injury or death. Georgia's Victim Compensation Program had begun just before Miller took office, and in its early years provided compensation of up to $1,000 per victim. In 1994, that maximum award had been increased to $5,000 per victim. These compensation monies were funds of last resort made available to victims of violent crimes to help with medical or counseling expenses that were not covered by insurance, or to families of victims of murder to cover funeral expenses for which no other funds were available. They could also serve as stop-gap income replacement in cases where sick and vacation leave had been exhausted and welfare, insurance workers' compensation, insurance or other funding was not available.

As the peace officer training provided by the state began to include information about the Victim's Bill of Rights and the compensation program, and as the maximum amount of the award increased, the demand for victim compensation funding increased. During the course of the Miller Administration, payments to victims increased from only a few hundred thousand dollars per year to $1.8 million in Fiscal Year (FY) 1998. At the same time, however, the traditional sources of funding, charges levied on DUI offenders and parolees, began to decline. The decline resulted from tougher DUI laws, which reduced the incidence of drunk driving, and from criminals' serving longer sentences, which resulted in less time on parole. In 1998, a third source of funds, used by many other states, was authorized by the General Assembly. Beginning July 1, 1998, a fee of $3 per month was charged to those on probation with the proceeds going to victim compensation.

VINE: In April 1997, the Governor announced that the Department of Corrections had developed a computerized notification program for victims. The service provided registered victims with valuable information on the status of their offender. In addition, state officials signed a contract to activate an electronic victim notification program. Known as VINE, the Victim Information and Notification Everyday program allowed crime victims to phone 24 hours a day for updates on the status of any prisoner convicted of harming them. It automatically notified victims via telephone within 10 minutes if their attacker escaped or was released.

With Corrections' VINE program, the registered crime victim or the survivors will be notified if there is a change in the prisoner's status:

- Prior to the inmate's release into the community;
- Prior to the inmate's transfer to a transitional center;
- Upon the death of an inmate;
- Upon an inmate's escape, and
- Upon an inmate's recapture and return to custody.

Drug Dealer Liability Act, Senate Bill 80: The Governor pushed tough legislation through the 1997 General Assembly allowing victims to sue drug dealers in Georgia. The Drug Dealer Liability Act allowed a parent, spouse, or child of a drug user; a child whose mother was an abuser while pregnant; an employer of an abuser; or medical facilities that provide treatment for the abuser, to sue to recover damages against a drug dealer. The drug abuser himself was not permitted to file such a suit.

Boot camps for nonviolent offenders

During his 1990 campaign, Governor Miller discussed the positive results of his Marine boot camp experience. He proposed that a similar experience of military discipline and physical training might have a positive effect on young offenders, especially those who had substance abuse histories. Late in 1990, long-term evaluative studies were being concluded that showed an alternative incarceration program such as a boot camp program was more successful than traditional prison beds with certain offender groups.

In the 1991 legislative session, Governor Miller was successful in passing Senate Bill 177, implementing the Correctional Boot Camp program. During his administration he funded and opened 4,928 boot camp beds statewide. Of the total boot camp beds opened, 2,106 involved new construction and 2,822 were converted from other uses.

Georgia used this system of Marine-style boot camps to punish young, first time offenders. All boot camps stressed manual labor, tough discipline, respect for authority and basic work skills. Great emphasis was placed on comprehensive programming in the evening in the areas of substance abuse, academic education, and life skills. There was also a requirement for unpaid community service, and after release from the confinement of boot camp, each inmate was involved in intensive probation or specialized parole supervision. Tough discipline gave young offenders what might be a final chance to turn their lives around.

Boot camps were proven to be cost effective. Lower-risk offenders were sentenced to a less costly residential component of the boot camp program rather than a high cost prison bed. Costly prison bed-space was reserved for offenders who were a threat to the community. Boot camps gave Georgia the opportunity to better manage prison capacity by directing non-violent young offenders to these facilities and freeing space at traditional prisons for career criminals.

Public and Highway Safety

One of the greatest tragedies of modern society is the carnage on our highways caused by drunk drivers. It is raw violence, often inflicting injury and death on innocent victims.... I want to get chronically drunk drivers off our highways, and I want all other drivers to curtail their drinking or plan ahead for their travel needs when they drink.

Governor Zell Miller, September 23, 1991

Teenage and Adult Driver Responsibility Act

Georgia experienced rapid population growth during the 1990s, which put more and more teenagers behind the wheel of motor vehicles. From 1992 through 1996, the number of licensed drivers ages 16-20 increased by 17.6 percent. Data from the Insurance Institute for Highway Safety indicated that 16 year-olds were eight times more likely to have a vehicle crash than adult drivers. Georgia's highway crash data mirrored that national data. The cause of those crashes was largely inexperience and errors in judgement. Experts in driver safety said it took about two years to learn to drive defensively, and become fully aware of how quickly control of a motor vehicle could be lost. For many drivers, that two-year learning curve coincided with their teen years, when they were more likely to take risks and show off.

Governor Miller initiated major legislation to keep teenage drivers safe. In 1997, he pushed House Bill 681, the Teenage and Adult Driver Responsibility Act, through the General Assembly. The new law provided a graduated driver's license with restrictions for drivers under the age of 18 years. Teens could still get a learner's permit at age 15, but they were required to prove they were enrolled in school, and they had to hold the permit for a full year before becoming eligible for a provisional licence. They also had to be enrolled in school and have a clean record, free from vehicle crashes, moving violations and alcohol or drug charges to obtain a provisional license at age 16. Drivers with provisional licenses were prohibited from driving between 1:00 a.m. and 6:00 a.m., and limits were placed on the number of teenage passengers they could carry. At age 18, teens became eligible for a regular driver's license, but again they had to have a clean record, free from vehicle crashes, moving violations and alcohol or drug charges for the prior year.

Speed often contributed to accidents in which the driver was under 21 years old, and the number of speed related crashes with injuries declined as drivers became older. Therefore, the new law mandated that drivers under age 21 who were speeding at 24 miles per hour or more over the speed limit would have their licenses suspended. Additional restrictions included a zero tolerance policy for drivers up to age 21 who consumed alcohol then operated a motor vehicle, and a mandatory 24 hours in jail for a first time conviction for driving under the influence (DUI) of alcohol or drugs. The bill also provided for license suspension if a driver under the age of 18 dropped out of school without parental permission.

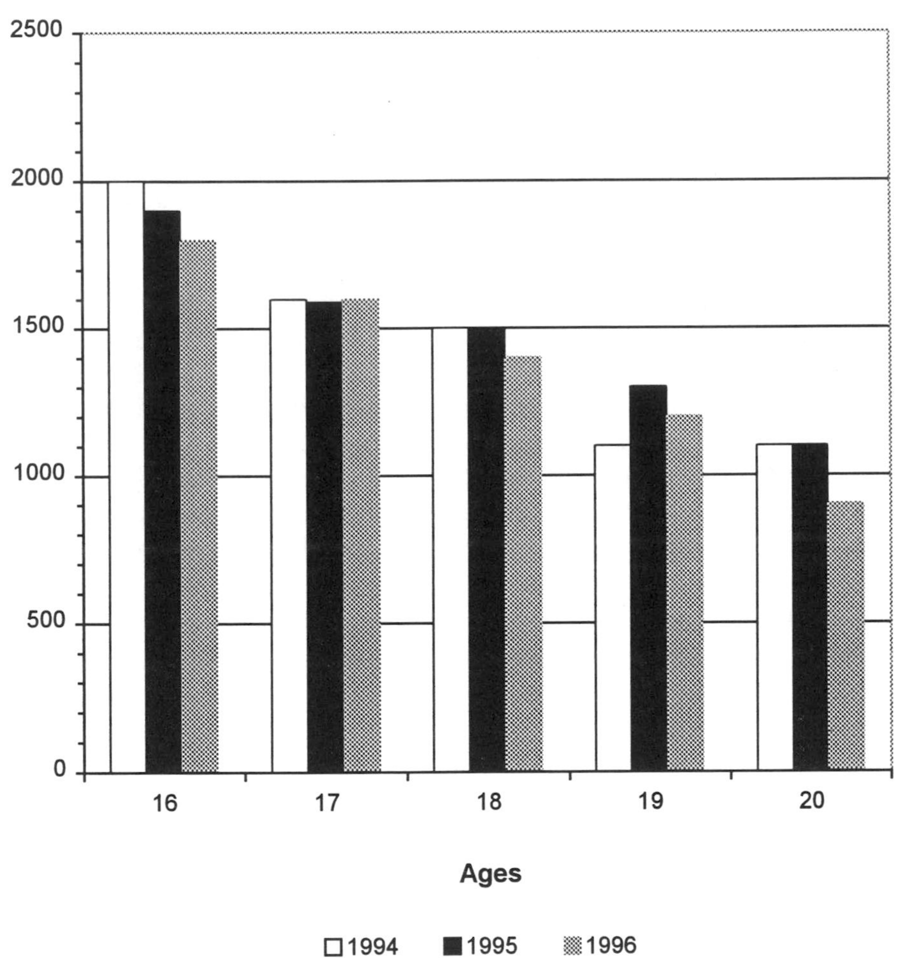

Driving under the influence (DUI)

Throughout his administration, Governor Miller kept a framed picture in his office of a 21-year-old Georgia woman who was senselessly killed by a drunk driver. The photograph was a constant reminder to all who entered his office of the human cost and consequences of drunk driving. Everyday

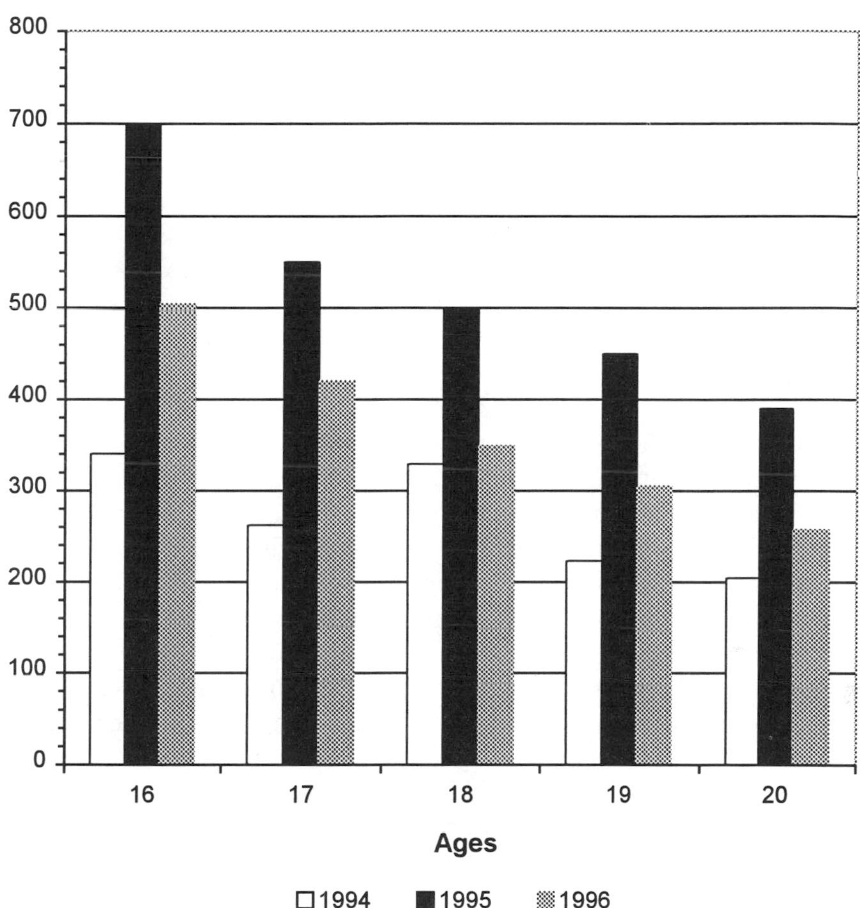

somebody's loved ones were being hurt or killed by drunk drivers, and the citizens of Georgia were looking to government to make their streets and highways safer places to travel.

Governor Miller targeted alcohol-impaired drivers during his administration, pressuring the General Assembly every year of his eight years in office to enact tougher DUI laws and close legal loopholes. Every year the General Assembly responded, but usually with significantly milder changes than the Governor had asked for. Finally, on July 1, 1997, a major DUI law went into effect, containing many of the measures the Governor had been pushing. The new law treated the nolo contendere plea for DUI as a conviction on an offender's driving record, and required the vehicle license plats of habitual violators (convicted of violating three serious driving offenses within five years) to be seized upon a DUI conviction. Drivers began serving mandatory jail time if they were found to have a blood alcohol concentration (BAC) equal to or higher than 0.08 while operating a motor vehicle.

Pressured by Miller, the General Assembly enacted zero tolerance for alcohol use by drivers under the age of 21. A driver who was less than 21 years of age, the legal drinking age, needed blood alcohol content of only 0.02 to be was guilty of DUI. On their first conviction, drivers under age 21 received a required six-month suspension of the driver's license, and a second conviction brought a twelve-month suspension. Governor Miller also made provisions to teach minors of the dangers of driving a motor vehicle while impaired by drugs or alcohol. Drivers in Georgia under the age of 18 were required complete an alcohol and drug course in order to receive a regular driver's license.

Habitual violators of Georgia's DUI laws faced new penalties and restrictions during the Miller Administration. Governor Miller increased fines and impounded the license plates of habitual offenders. He set mandatory jail terms for second and third-time offenders as well as mandatory community service for first, second and third-time offenders. A third DUI conviction was met with a mandated publication of the offender's name, address and photograph in the local newspaper. Governor Miller took away driving privileges from those drivers who were convicted four times of a DUI, and mandated that three-time DUI offenders whose licenses have already been revoked were subject to forfeiture of their vehicle to the state upon their fourth conviction.

To ensure that DUI offenders not only faced stiff penalties, but that they also got help with their alcohol problems, the Governor helped pass legislation stipulating that if two or more convictions on a DUI offense occurred within a five-year period, the defendant had to undergo a clinical evaluation. Offenders who were found need to help with an alcohol problem, had to go through a substance abuse program at their own expense before their suspended license would be reinstated.

Governor Miller also gave the justice system new weapons in the crusade against drunk driving. During the course of his administration, he lowered the legal intoxication limit from 0.12 BAC to 0.10 BAC. He gave judges the right to require second-time DUI offenders to install an automobile Breathalyzer as a condition of probation. He gave every Georgian a simple way to combat drunk driving by helping to set up the "Star GSP" program on all cellular telephones. This special emergency number connected directly to the Georgia State Patrol, enabling motorists to alert the state troopers to suspected drunk drivers.

Occupant protection laws

Each year in Georgia 60 percent of the people killed in traffic crashes had not been using safety equipment. Governor Miller pushed for stronger laws requiring child restraints and seat belt use for minors, and signed a primary seat belt law that became effective on July 1, 1996. The law required seat belt use by front seat occupants, age 18 and older in passenger vehicles. Everyone under age 18 was required to be restrained in all type vehicles at all times. The fine for violating the seat belt law for minors (children ages five to 17) was $25. Governor Miller also strengthened the laws on child restraints for children under age five, increasing the fine to $50 for the first offense and $100 for second and subsequent offenses.

To enforce the new laws Governor Miller directed the Georgia Department of Public Safety to lead the effort to enforce the seat belt and child restraint law with Operation Strap 'N Snap. This "no warnings, no excuses" approach to occupant protection violations made Georgia a national model for occupant protection enforcement.

Governor Miller's efforts to increase seat belt usage in Georgia paid off. Georgia's seat belt usage rate climbed from 40 percent in 1990 to an all-time state high of 68 percent in January 1998, representing an increase in usage of over 70 percent. According to survey data gathered in 1998, 63.1 percent of children observed in motor vehicles were in child safety seats, compared with only 49.3 percent in an identical survey conducted in 1990. This represented a 29 percent increase in the number of children that were restrained by child safety seats.

Driver's license process

Under the direction of Governor Miller, the Department of Public Safety took great strides in providing quality services to all Georgians who needed to renew, modify or apply for a new driver's license. When Governor Miller took office in 1991 there were significant problems in obtaining services due to long lines and unnecessary delays in the delivery of driver's license services.

Governor Miller enhanced the driver's license process in three ways to relieve overcrowding and improve service. First, he opened 29 new renewal-only sites, most of them at Kroger grocery store locations. The renewal only sites catered to the driver who did not need to take a driving test and only needed a renewed or updated license. In FY 1999, he recommended funding to open three additional renewal-only sites. By expanding service locations, the problem of long lines at the busiest locations was alleviated.

Third, in 1997 the Governor established travel teams of Department of Public Safety employees to issue driver's licenses in the field. These teams traveled among the 107 counties without permanent facilities to issue driver's licenses, making the process of obtaining, renewing, or updating a driver's license more convenient for all Georgians.

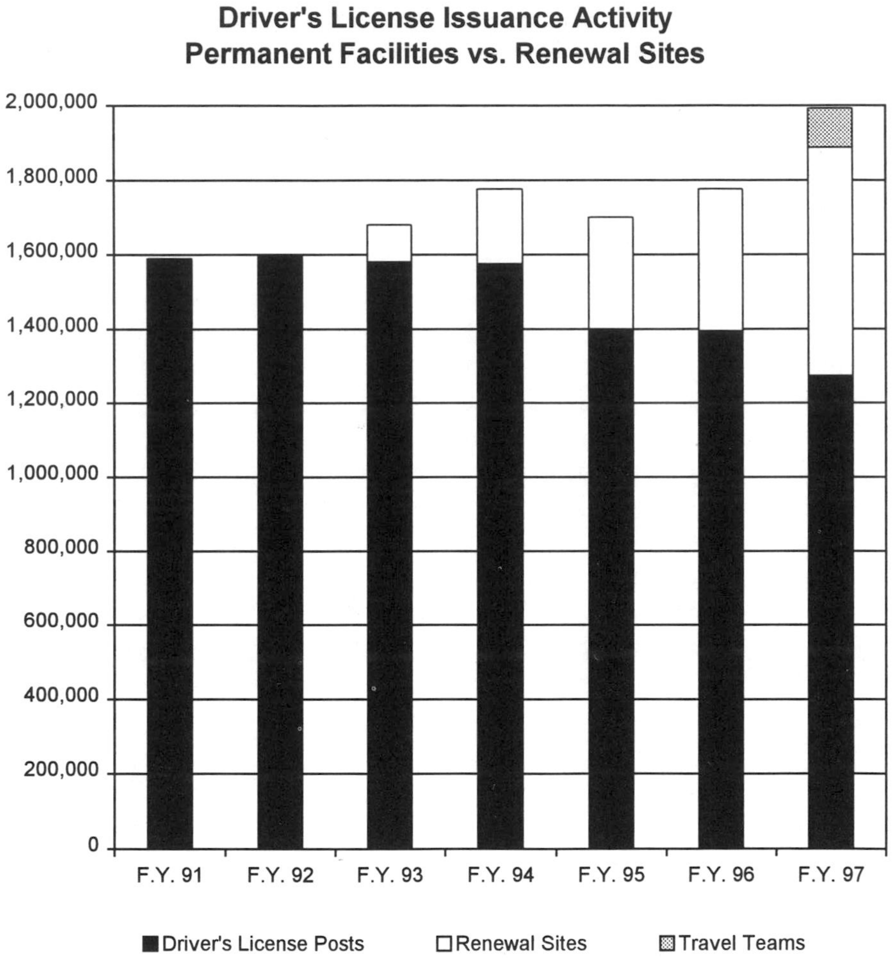

When Governor Miller was sworn into office, it took the Department of Public Safety 45 days to issue a driver's license. By the end of his administration, licenses were issued immediately on site, rather than being mailed to the driver at a later date. The change was made possible by the Digital Imaging License Process, for which the Governor provided funding in 1996. This state-of-the-art computer-based system could immediately store the driver's image, signature, fingerprints and other driver license information. Georgia driver's licenses also had a special security feature built into the laminate to safeguard against duplication, photocopying or alteration.

Peace officer training enhancements

Peace officers were required to attend a basic training course where they learned to perform their duties efficiently and safely. Working in conjunction with the Georgia Peace Officer Standards and Training Council, the Public Safety Training Center offered a basic course for law enforcement personnel. Course work included instruction in areas such as ethics, rules of evidence, media relations, and cultural diversity.

Prior to the Miller Administration, the course lasted just seven weeks. Several times over his tenure, the Governor increased the length and scope of the basic course. Governor Miller's FY 1999 budget recommendation increased the training course to 400 hours of instruction (10 weeks). This increase in the number of hours taught enabled the Public Safety Training Center and Peace Officer Standards and Training Council to add classes in two high liability areas—emergency vehicle driver training and judgmental use of deadly force.

Georgia Bureau of Investigation

It takes many tools to fight crime. At one end, you have to have good law enforcement officers out on the streets.... At the other end, you have to have strong sentencing laws to put violent criminals behind bars.... But in between, you have to have the evidence it takes to convict the criminals in court.

Governor Zell Miller, September 28, 1994

Automated Fingerprint Identification System (AFIS)

The Georgia Crime Information Center (GCIC) made tremendous improvements in service delivery to the law enforcement community during the Miller Administration because of Miller's support for enhancements to existing systems and for the development of new programs. Of major significance were the advancements made in the Automated Fingerprint Identification System (AFIS).

The GBI's AFIS became operational in FY 1990. As a result, a backlog of 700,000 fingerprint cards was eliminated and the manual system of analyzing fingerprint cards was history. In FY 1992, Governor Miller recommended $3.7 million in bond funds to upgrade AFIS to keep up with new technology and to expand the database. Prior to the upgrade, the capacity had allowed for the retention of 1,350,000 individuals' prints. By the close of FY 1997, GCIC maintained fingerprint and criminal history records on 1,869,631 individuals.

Miller also expanded the AFIS system to accommodate electronic transmission of fingerprints from local law enforcement booking stations, allowing local law enforcement agencies to initiate searches without having to go through central office staff. Live scanning devices were placed in high volume booking stations throughout Georgia to transmit the digitized fingerprints of arrested persons directly into the AFIS. After a transmission was received at GBI headquarters, the database of known offenders was searched for a match. The digitized images were also compared to a database containing latent fingerprints found at crime scenes to determine if the fingerprints from the arrested person matched a fingerprint from an unsolved crime. During this process a nationwide search was also launched to determine if the arrestee was wanted anywhere in the United States. Finally, the fingerprint database and the criminal history database were updated with new information and a response was returned to the booking station with the offender's name and a State Identification (SID) number. The SID number could then be used to request a rap sheet that would not only show the offender's previous history if any, but would include the arrest which had just occurred. The entire process took only 45 minutes, compared to the weeks that were needed before the live scan to AFIS interface was implemented.

Georgia's AFIS was the first system in the United States to accept and respond to live scan transmissions from remote sites. Thanks to Governor Miller, six full service remote AFIS workstations became operational before he left office. The Dougherty County Sheriff's Office AFIS remote site was the first to go online in FY 1995, and it was so successful that $550,000 was provided in FY 1998 for five additional remote sites in Bibb, Clarke, Muscogee, Whitfield and Richmond Counties. These remote sites placed the power of the AFIS in the hands of local law enforcement agencies and allowed local fingerprint experts to search the GBI's central database for possible matches with latent fingerprints found at crime scenes, as well as providing the ability to rapidly identify arrested persons.

Activity on the AFIS averaged 468,902 searches, and 308,644 matches a year between FY 1990 and FY 1994. During this period, a backlog of fingerprint cards was processed and eliminated. After remote sites were installed in local law enforcement agencies, the number of searches by local law enforcement agencies increased by 51 percent, from 347,723 in FY 1995 to 524,028 in FY 1996. The small drop in searches and matches between FY 1997 and FY 1998 was the result of processing a backlog of fingerprint cards. The advancements in the GBI's AFIS directly benefited local law enforcement agencies and the citizens they served.

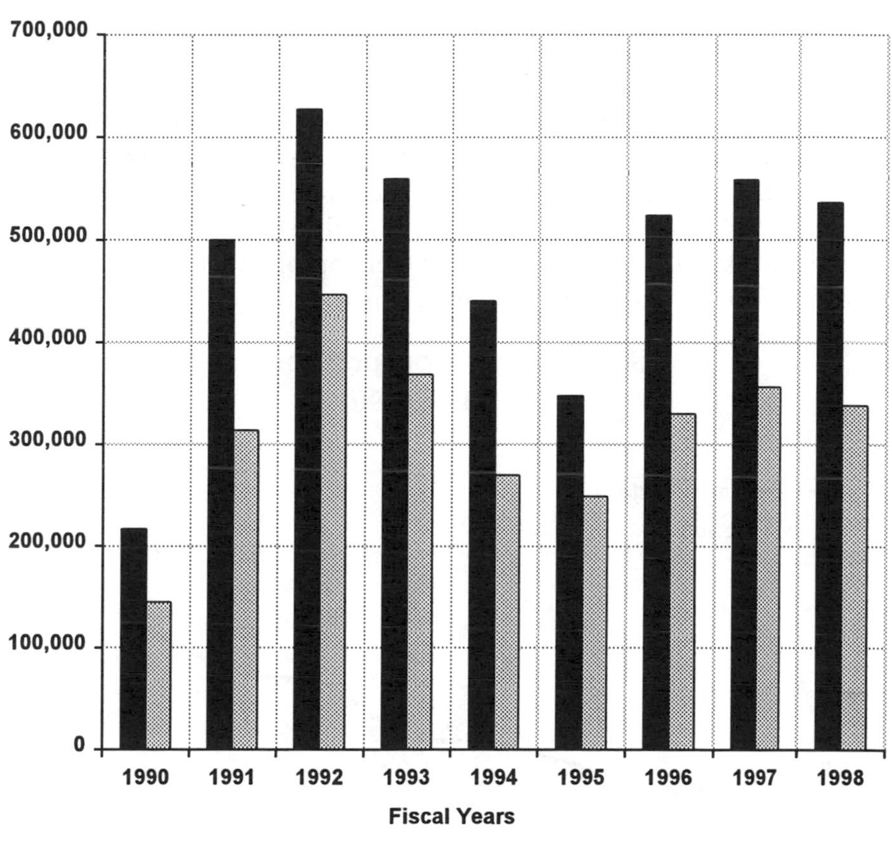

	FY 1990	FY 1991	FY 1992	FY 1993	FY 1994	FY 1995	FY 1996	FY 1997	FY 1998
Searches	216,967	499,923	627,064	559,504	441,053	347,723	524,028	558,246	535,928
Matches	144,325	313,770	447,142	368,675	269,307	248,573	330,032	356,471	337,850

Crime lab (forensic sciences)

Governor Miller recognized the need to meet the ever-increasing demand by local law enforcement and the courts for scientific analysis. Significant resources provided the Forensic Sciences field with new and improved laboratories, 40 additional positions including 15 new scientists, and operating expenses. An increase of $5.9 million or 88 percent, from $6.7 million in FY 1990 to $12.6 million in FY 1999, allowed for new personnel and provided for the purchase of the latest equipment to keep up to date with technological advancements in the scientific field. Construction and equipment for the seventh regional crime laboratory in Summerville, replacement laboratories for Columbus and Moultrie, and new morgue facilities in Macon and Atlanta were the largest building improvements ever appropriated for the Forensic Sciences field at a cost of $10.2 million in bonds.

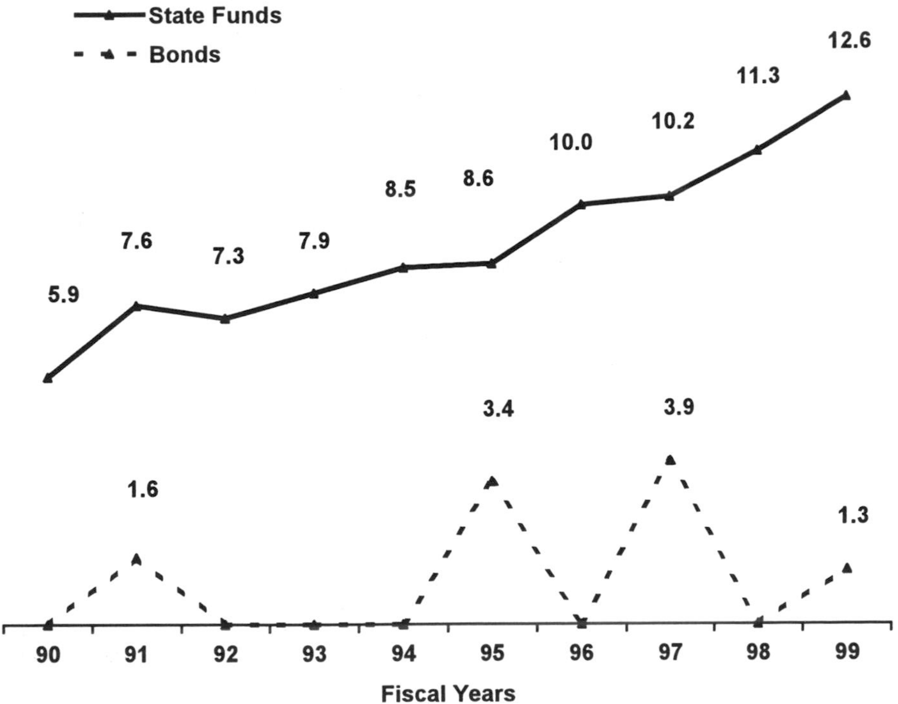

These improvements provided for the expansion of regional medical examiner services at the Moultrie and Summerville Laboratories. The additional resources made significant improvements in the Forensic Sciences' ability to complete more services for its customers and improve the turn-around time of its services. The number of services completed by the laboratories increased 38 percent, from 86,710 in FY 1990 to 119,953 in FY 1997. The number of services completed within 30 days improved, from 53 percent in FY 1995 to 59 percent in FY 1997. This improvement was achieved despite an increase of 24,918 services completed during the same time period. The turn-around time on cases was expected to improve further after increased state funding for FY 1997, FY 1998 and FY 1999 kicked into the overall operations of the laboratories. Adding more scientists, providing incentives for experienced scientists to stay with the GBI, and increasing funding for the laboratories should encourage scientists to handle more cases and handle them faster.

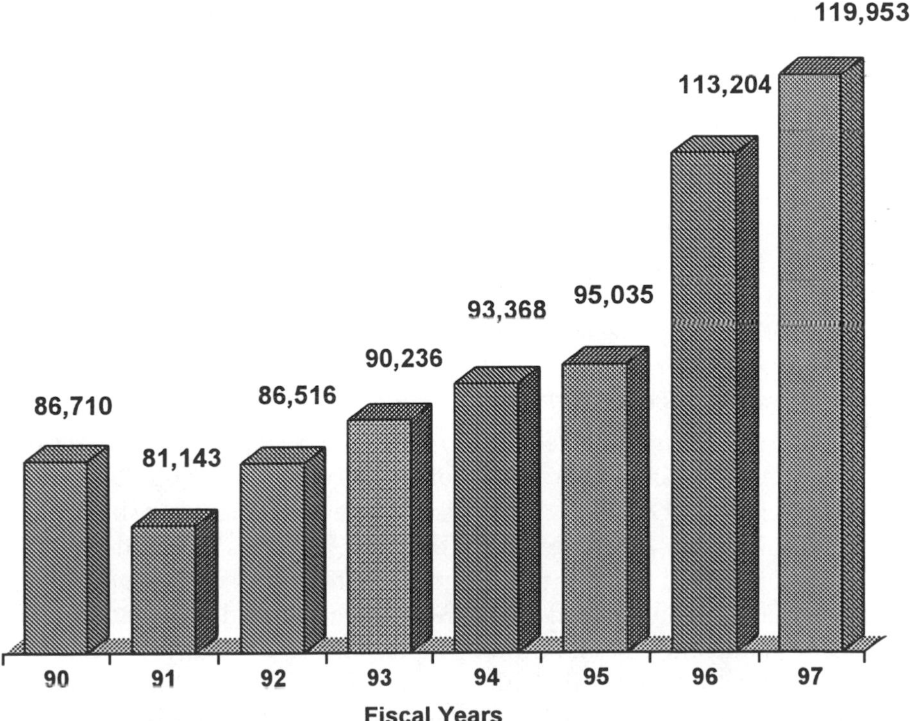

In addition to the new positions, supplemental salary increases were provided for all scientific personnel on top of their annual pay for performance increases. This boost was expected to prove critical in retaining key scientific personnel. In 1998, GBI starting salaries for scientific personnel were ranked second out of eight southeastern states.

Initial funding in FY 1995 allowed a computer database of the **DNA** prints of known criminals to be created, so that a sample taken at the scene of a crime could be compared against the databank for a possible match. Further enhancements in the analysis of DNA afforded GBI the ability to search the database with information from cases where no suspect was known, and to search for Georgia suspects in on a national database. These improvements enabled previously unknown offenders to be identified by their genetic profile with a high degree of certainty and aided in the adjudication of previously unsolved offenses. During the 1990s, DNA technology came to be utilized in crimes of all types, and what once took months to produce could be provided in weeks. Criminal justice was relying on this valuable tool to both convict the guilty and exonerate the innocent.

Child abuse program

To address the sexual and physical abuse of children in the state, Governor Miller created the Child Abuse Program in FY 1996 with 15 special agent positions at a cost of $854,000. One of these agents was assigned to each of the GBI's 15 regional investigative offices throughout the state. These agents were specially trained in this type of investigation and improved the bureau's ability to investigate and prosecute child abuse cases. Violent crime against children increased 11 percent between FY 1990 and FY 1995, from 190 to 211 cases. In FY 1996, with the new agents coming on board, the numbers of cases increased 61 percent to 340 cases, then dropped slightly in FY 1997 to 336 cases. These cases accounted for 19 percent of the total number of cases worked by special agents of the Investigative Division.

Multi-jurisdictional drug task forces

As a result of numerous requests to provide special agents as supervisors for the multi-jurisdictional drug task forces, Governor Miller funded 10 special agents in FY 1995. These supervisors were available to work street to mid-level and in some instances major drug investigations for multi-jurisdictional task forces in 50 counties in the state. They provided experienced, capable leadership and helped to ensure an organized and cooperative effort between not only the GBI and the task forces, but also with other law enforcement agencies. In FY 1997, the task forces accounted for 6,123 investigations and 4,862 arrests, as well as the seizure of nearly $24.2 million worth of illegal drugs, more than $1.6 million in other contraband, 375 firearms from suspects, and $1.2 million in forfeitures.

State Prisons

Today you can enter a Georgia prison, and you will find the inmates clean-shaven and orderly, their cells and dormitories Spartan, and the facilities neat. You will not find a cleaner place in the state.... Our prison inmates rise early in the morning and walk four and a-half miles. Then they work eight hour days. In the evening, they may work on their GED.... Despite more inmates than ever before, escapes are down, use of force to restrain violent prisoners is down. Complaints by inmates about prison staff are down.

Governor Zell Miller, January 14, 1997

Expanding capacity

Passing tougher laws that required prison sentences made no sense if the prison capacity wasn't expanded. To manage the increasing number of criminal offenders being sentenced to state prisons or placed on supervised probation, the Governor opened 20,621 new correctional beds during his eight years in office. The increased capacity included 16,779 prison beds plus 3,842 detention, diversion, transitional and boot camp beds to serve a multitude of different offender types.

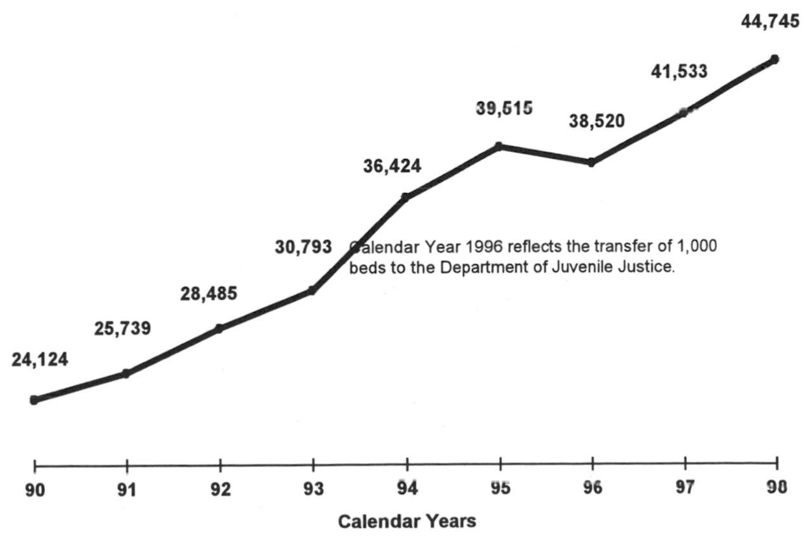

Beds Opened During the Miller Administration

Facility	County	Municipalities	Capacity 1/1/91	Capacity 12/31/98	Net Gain/Loss Remarks
ASMP SP	Richmond	Grovetown	635	1,039	404
Arrendale SP	Banks	Alto	1,443	1,200	-243
Autry SP	Mitchell	Pelham	0	1,514	1,514
Baldwin SP	Baldwin	Hardwick	860	947	87
Bostick SP	Baldwin	Hardwick	504	504	0
Burruss SP	Monroe	Forsyth	400	448	48
Calhoun SP	Calhoun	Morgan	0	1,144	1,144
Central SP	Bibb	Macon	734	775	41
Coast SP	Chatham	Garden City	958	1,230	272
Dodge SP	Dodge	Chester	704	936	232
Dooly SP	Dooly	Unadilla	0	1,114	1,114
GDCP SP	Butts	Jackson	1,581	1,795	214
GSP SP	Tattnall	Reidsville	1,106	1,163	57
Hancock SP	Hancock	Sparta	0	1,322	1,322
Hays SP	Chattooga	Trion	400	1,153	753
Lee SP	Lee	Leesburg	640	720	80
Lowndes SP	Lowndes	Valdosta	300	316	16
Macon SP	Macon	Oglethorpe	0	1,344	1,344
Men's SP	Baldwin	Hardwick	585	650	65
Metro SP	Fulton	Atlanta	690	705	15
Milan SP	Telfair	Milan	150	244	94
Montgomery SP	Montgomery	Mt. Vernon	425	384	-41
Phillips SP	Forsyth	Buford	400	850	450
Pulaski SP	Pulaski	Hawkinsville	0	891	891
Rivers SP	Putnam	Eatonton	100	138	38
Rogers SP	Baldwin	Hardwick	880	1,032	152
Rutledge SP	Tattnall	Reidsville	984	1,014	30
Scott SP	Muscogee	Columbus	580	582	2
St. Mountain SP	Baldwin	Hardwick	874	1,100	226
Smith SP	DeKalb	Stone Mountain	228	0	-228 Closed
Telfair SP	Smith	Smith	0	1,192	1,192
Valdosta SP	Telfair	Helena	0	1,080	1,080
Walker SP	Lowndes	Valdosta	750	870	120
Ware SP	Catoosa	Rock Springs	324	360	36
Washington SP	Ware	Waycross	1,050	1,274	224
Wayne SP	Washington	Davisboro	0	1,048	1,048
West Central SP	Wayne	Odum	192	200	8
Wilcox SP	Pike	Zebulon	0	184	184
	Wilcox	Abbeville	0	1,294	1,294
Sub-Total - State Prisons			**18,477**	**33,756**	**15,279**

In addition to providing start up and operating costs for over 20,000 new beds in the prison system, Governor Miller also provided new construction funds totaling $101 million for an additional 5,584 correctional beds and support facilities, enhanced security systems in prisons statewide with funds totaling $14,945,000, and maintained the prisons' infrastructure through repair and maintenance funding totaling $25,165,000.

In 1996, Governor Miller won approval for legislation that allowed the state to contract with private companies to build and operate prisons. During

Facility	County	Municipalities	Capacity 1/1/91	Capacity 12/31/98	Net Gain/Loss Remarks
Charlton	Charlton	Folkston	0	500	500 Private
Coffee	Coffee	Nichols	0	500	500 Private
Wheeler	Wheeler	Alamo	0	500	500 Private
ST - Private Prisons			**0**	**1,500**	**1,500**
Albany TC	Dougherty	Albany	150	150	0
Atlanta TC	Fulton	Atlanta	156	240	84
Homerville TC	Clinch	Homerville	0	200	200
Macon TC	Bibb	Macon	120	128	8
Metro TC	Fulton	Atlanta	146	124	-22
Savannah TC	Chatham	Savannah	75	76	1
ST - Transitional Centers			**617**	**918**	**271**
Albany DC	Dougherty	Albany	65	68	3
Alcovy DC	Walton	Monroe	50	50	0
Athens DC	Clark	Athens	52	52	0
Atlanta DC	Fulton	Atlanta	40	0	-40 Closed
Augusta DC	Richmond	Augusta	50	50	0
Clayton DC	Clayton	Forest Park	50	50	0
Cobb DC	Cobb	Marietta	50	50	0
Columbus DC	Muscogee	Columbus	52	52	0
Fulton DC	Fulton	Atlanta	33	0	-33 Closed
Gainesville DC	Hall	Gainesville	50	100	50
Gateway DC	Fulton	Atlanta	24	106	82
Griffin DC	Spalding	Griffin	52	52	0
Helms DC	Fulton	Atlanta	75	75	0
Macon DC	Bibb	Macon	40	52	12
Rome DC	Floyd	Rome	50	50	0
Savannah DC	Chatham	Savannah	50	52	2
Thomasville DC	Thomas	Thomasville	40	52	12
Waycross DC	Ware	Waycross	52	56	4
ST - Diversion Centers			**875**	**967**	**92**
Central PDC	Dodge	Cadwell	150	198	48
Colwell PDC	Towns	Blairsville	150	207	57
Davisboro PDC	Washington	Davisboro		216	216
Emanuel PDC	Emanuel	Twin City		220	220
IW Davis PDC	Jackson	Jefferson	150	200	50
Larmore PDC	Fulton	College Park		198	198
Northwest PDC	Polk	Cedartown		204	204
Phillips PDC	Forsyth	Buford		232	232
Patten PDC	Lanier	Lakeland		216	216
Roc/DeKalb PDC	Rockdale	Conyers		206	206
Rogers PDC	Tattnall	Reidsville		232	232
Southeast PDC	Evans	Claxton	150	198	48

Fiscal Year 1997 contracts were signed with private companies to construct three private prisons in Georgia located in Wheeler, Coffee and Charlton Counties, which were scheduled to open in late 1998. The state then contracted for 750 beds at each of the facilities. The state did not have to use its bonding capacity to finance the estimated $60 million construction cost for the three facilities. The cost per inmate day established in each the contracts was less than the Department of Corrections would have spent, generating estimated savings of approximately $4.9 million in the first year of full

Facility	County	Municipalities	Capacity 1/1/91	Capacity 12/31/98	Net Gain/Loss Remarks
Whitworth PDC	Hart	Hartwell	75	207	132
Womens PDC	Evans	Claxton		198	198
ST - Detention Centers			**825**	**3,328**	**2,503**
Treutlen PBC	Treutlen	Soperton		300	300
West Ga. PBC	Haralson	Bremen		192	192
ST - Probation Boot Camps			**0**	**492**	**492**
Bulloch CCI	Bulloch	Statesboro	132	132	0
Carroll CCI	Carroll	Carrollton	124	200	76
Clarke CCI	Clarke	Athens	95	87	-8
Clayton CCI	Clayton	Lovejoy	0	222	222
Colquitt CCI	Colquitt	Moultrie	160	190	30
Coweta CCI	Coweta	Newnan	90	160	70
Decatur CCI	Decatur	Bainbridge	100	105	5
Effingham CCI	Effingham	Springfield	50	56	6
Floyd CCI	Floyd	Rome	220	220	0
Fulton CCI	Fulton	Atlanta	300	0	-300 Closed
Gwinnett CCI	Gwinnett	Lawrenceville	60	126	66
Hall CCI	Hall	Gainesville	240	240	0
Harris CCI	Harris	Hamilton	50	50	0
Houston CCI	Houston	Perry	90	0	-90
Jackson CCI	Jackson	Jefferson	164	174	10
Jefferson CCI	Jefferson	Louisville	125	140	15
Meriwether CCI	Meriwether	Greenville	60	0	-60
Mitchell CCI	Mitchell	Camilla	75	65	-10
Muscogee CCI	Muscogee	Columbus	220	528	308
Richmond CCI	Richmond	Augusta	185	175	-10
Screven CCI	Screven	Sylvania	50	125	75
Spalding CCI	Spalding	Griffin	150	150	0
Stewart CCI	Stewart	Lumpkin	30	40	10
Sumter CCI	Sumter	Americus	280	298	18
Terrell CCI	Terrell	Dawson	45	56	11
Thomas CCI	Thomas	Thomasville	75	125	50
Troup CCI	Troup	LaGrange	80	120	40
Upson CCI	Upson	Thomaston	50	0	-50 Closed
ST - County Correctional Institutions			**3,300**	**3,784**	**484**
TOTAL			**24,124**	**44,745**	**20,621**

operation and almost $74 million over the full 20 year term of the contracts. In addition, a privately-run facility benefitted the local tax base by paying county taxes, which were not required for a state-run facility.

The state took no risk with these facilities in that its contracts were for only one year at a time, and the department maintained absolute control, including the right to take over the prisons if conditions necessitated such action. The Department of Corrections also planned to monitor the operation of the privately run facilities carefully. Finally, the privately run prisons would provide the Department with some basis on which to judge their own institutions' performance and adopt identified best practices internally.

DEPARTMENT OF CORRECTIONS
CAPITAL OUTLAY
FY 1991 – FY 1999

	Construction	Safety/Security	Repair/Maintenance	Totals
FY 1991	9,500,000		1,500,000	11,000,000
FY 1992	7,500,000		2,000,000	9,500,000
FY 1993	3,600,000	4,000,000		7,600,000
FY 1994	14,670,000	2,775,000		17,445,000
FY 1995	33,140,000		4,760,000	37,900,000
FY 1996	29,400,000		5,200,000	34,600,000
FY 1997		1,935,000	2,980,000	4,915,000
FY 1998			1,725,000	1,725,000
FY 1999	3,250,000	6,235,000	7,000,000	16,485,000
	$101,060,000	**$14,945,000**	**$25,165,000**	**$141,170,000**

Making prisons tough but fair

The Georgia Department of Corrections was responsible for 39 state prisons, 25 county prisons, five transitional centers, five inmate boot camps, three parole revocation centers and one pre-transitional center. With 1997 expenditures of about $700 million, the department was charged with managing a growing prison population that had more than doubled from 18,079 in 1987 to almost 38,000 in 1998. In addition, the department's probation division had to supervise approximately 138,000 offenders.

Confronted with a growing inmate population, entangling litigation, spiraling costs for prisoner education and health care, and a problem with inmate discipline and staff morale, the system was in dire need of direction. Governor Miller set the prison system on a steady course of improvement. His administration left taxpayers with a more cost-effective prison system that had improved not only inmate discipline, but also education and rehabilitation.

Under Governor Miller's direction, the Department of Corrections implemented a no-nonsense policy on prisoners to ensure Georgia's prisons were among the toughest but fairest in the country. Despite an increase in inmate population, Georgia's prisons were safer, more secure and more disciplined than ever before. The Department of Corrections' status report for Fiscal Year 1997 showed fewer escapes and suicides, a reduction in inmate grievances and lawsuits, and a drop in serious disciplinary reports.

In December 1995 Miller appointed Wayne Garner commissioner of Corrections. He established clear goals to raise morale for the system's 14,500 employees, create order and discipline among the inmates, improve prisoner health care and education and, at the same time, trim the fat in the budget. The corrections budget was reduced by $55 million, and work and education became key ingredients in improving discipline. Inmates were controlled through hard work, Spartan living conditions and loss of their liberty. Those who wished to do their penance to society and change themselves for the better were allowed that opportunity through education, job-training and substance abuse programs.

By the end of the Miller Administration, Georgia had a tight and Spartan prison system in which prisoners wore uniforms, were clean-shaven, and lived in cells or dorms with no amenities. All inmates had to follow a highly structured routine, work hard, and abide by the rules and regulations of the prison system. All able-bodied inmates in Georgia had to work. To help repay their debt to society, inmates worked up to eight hours per day in the prisons, in communities, on prison farms and in on the job training programs.

A 1997 independent KPMG Peat Marwick audit of state prisons reported "a unanimous consensus that today's prisons in this state are more secure and safer, for both inmate and officer, than ever." Statistics comparing two six-month periods (July 1994-December 1995 and January 1996-June 1997) indicated 600 fewer assaults by inmates against other inmates; 37 fewer assaults by inmates against employees; a decrease from 38 escapes in the first period to 16 escapes in the second; and a decrease in suicides from 11 to four.

In addition, a "benchmarking" audit comparing the GDC to other prison systems revealed that Georgia's prison system was better than the national average in almost all categories. Morale was higher among staff members. "The employees firmly believe that the prisons are safer now because... the officers (not the prisoners) are in control," the audit stated. "The staff, and particularly the officers, based on interviews, believe that they have the full support of the commissioner and that he has given them the clear authority to do their jobs."

"Surprisingly perhaps, the inmates are as appreciative of this new secure environment as the staff," the audit stated. "This emphasis on security and discipline has resulted in a decrease in assaults against officers as well as a decrease in assaults against other inmates. The correctional staff, including administrative and support personnel, now feel safer to walk in areas of the prison where it previously felt apprehensive."

Interviews by auditors revealed that prisoners were required to address the staff in a polite and respectful manner, reminding them daily that they had to follow the set orders and policies of the warden and the Department of Corrections. Inmates were less likely to escape, and if they did, were likely to be quickly returned to serve even more time. In fact, GDC reported a 100 percent recapture rate during this period.

Prisoners, the report stated, "were being held to a stricter disciplinary standard, emphasizing personal accountability which includes hygiene and grooming in addition to a policy which demands that each prisoner participate in some work activity." Work had become essential to improved discipline at the state's prisons, where every able-bodied inmate was assigned a job every day.

The required eight-hour work day for inmates resulted in another important benefit: increased security and cost savings for taxpayers. Inmates helped the prisons operate by working at kitchen, maintenance, and other duties. The result was cleaner prisons with staff members reporting anecdotal evidence of workers fussing at each other if one scuffed another's newly cleaned area. Cleaner prisons promoted higher security with a decreased chance that contraband could be hidden.

With more than 13,000 acres of row crops, pasture, timberland and acreage for other uses on nine prison farms, inmates produced in excess of 40 percent of the prison food requirement. Inmates in the system's model Farm and Food Services program grew lima beans, field peas, beets, carrots, collards, turnips, sweet peas, tomatoes, squash, potatoes, cabbage, spinach, corn, strawberries, blueberries and watermelons. Fruits and vegetables were shipped to Rogers State Prison in Reidsville, where some 132,000 cases of food were canned in FY 1997. Inmates did other jobs in the prison system's dairies, poultry houses, and beef and pork operations to provide food for the prisons. In F. Y. 1997, the Department of Corrections recorded record levels of production, generating 5.2 million pounds of vegetables, 1.6 million dozen eggs and 920,000 gallons of milk. In addition to raising hogs, they raised more than 5,500 heads of cattle on five farms. In FY 1997, prisoners slaughtered and packaged more than 2,500 cows and 7,800 hogs.

Georgia's prison farm program provided more than 30 million nutritionally-balanced meals a year with average food costs that were among the lowest in the country, turning it into a model for other state prison systems. Tennessee and Alabama officials studied and incorporated GDC procedures into their own prison systems. Florida officials visited GDC farm facilities and were considering reopening a prison farm operation in their state.

In addition to farming, prisoners worked in the Georgia Correctional Industries (GCI) program to produce goods, including office furniture, garments, and cleaning chemicals for sale to other government agencies, schools or other tax-supported entities. All work provided job skills that would prove helpful when prisoners reentered society, and with specialized GCI training supported by local tech schools, such as Atlanta's DeKalb Tech, Rock Spring's Walker Tech and Dublin's Heart of Georgia Technical School, prisoners gained marketable skills in metal fabrication, woodworking, chemical manufacturing, upholstery, screen printing, garment production and optical production.

Taxpayers reaped the benefits of a stepped-up GCI program. The GCI net profit has increased dramatically from $43,010 for FY 1995 to $2,815,579 in FY 1997. New products bolstered revenues. A statewide contract to produce and sell file cabinets announced in July 1997, for example, was projected to generate more than $500,000 in revenues for GCI and to save taxpayers another $100,000 by cutting the previous contract by $25 per cabinet.

During the Miller Administration, inmates were given little free time, and were subjected to daytime disciplines similar to working Georgia families. They got up early, walked 4.5 miles every day for their health, worked hard for eight hours, and studied for their GED in the evening. If they behaved, they got some time for recreation. The mandatory walk replaced the use of weight-training equipment, which the prison system donated to local high schools.

Increased educational opportunity and efficiency: The average Georgia inmate spelled at a sixth-grade level, and read and computed math at a seventh-grade level. Poor academic skills figured significantly in the attraction to crime. An emphasis on educational attainment and job training, and therapeutic courses dealing with drug abuse and violent behavior, were cornerstones in inmate rehabilitation. However, the discipline of daily work excluded many inmates from educational programs, which had been offered during the day. Only those who worked nights or were too disabled to work could participate. The Department of Corrections made a high school equivalency diploma more accessible to more inmates by shifting educational programs from daytime to evening and utilizing distance learning technology. The schedule required prisoners to perform a day's work, after which they went to school in the evening (or the day hours for night-shift working inmates) to improve academic skills.

Shifting the primary education program to the evening and utilizing interactive video technology to reach the prisoners not only opened new doors of opportunity for inmates, but also made the prison education program more cost effective. Despite a growing inmate population, the department saved $5 million through the reorganization of its education programs to focus on evening classes and the implementation of distance learning technology. The audit found that night school reduced the number of inmates who had used the daytime education program as a way to avoid having to work, but were not really intent on learning. "Many (prison staff) now believe that prisoners who now attend classes at night are there because they really wish to learn and therefore are more attentive and less disruptive," the audit reported.

Even so, the number of inmates participating in educational programs increased dramatically. In the first year of offering evening classes combined with distance learning, the number of inmates taking classes preparing them for the General Education Diploma (GED) exam increased by 37 percent, and the number of GED tests administered increased by 68 percent.

Improved health care at a savings: As more inmates began serving longer sentences, more of them became sick, especially drug users whose lifestyles and poor nutrition left them more prone to disease. Georgia's prison population was also growing older. As a result, medical costs threatened to eat up more and more of the corrections budget. So the department made changes in its health care program that improved the delivery of basic health care and increased care for mentally ill prisoners while simultaneously holding prison health care costs below those of FY 1995.

The department switched its health care contract from a private vendor, Delaware-based Prison Health Services, to the Medical College of Georgia. At $61 million, the new contract was not any more expensive than the old, but it provided prisoners with state-of-the-art care using advanced medical technology, such as telemedicine, and it kept the dollars spent for prison health care from leaving the state.

To actually diminish spiraling costs, the Governor pushed legislation to allow the Department of Corrections to charge inmates a $5 co-payment for self-initiated visits to the prison medical or dental units. Inmates who truly needed care were never denied access, and inmates who were referred for medical or dental care by prison staff were not charged the co-payment. Under the new system, inmate medical visits dropped 40 percent, and staff members saw a decline in feigned illness. In another cost-cutting measure that saved $1.1 million, dentists were assigned to several facilities instead of just one. Dental staff was reduced by 30 percent with no reduction in inmate care. Another $800,000 was pruned from the bureaucracy for the health services program by eliminating 14 clinical and administrative positions.

As a result of these cost-cutting measures, prison health expenditures in FY 1997 were 4.3 percent less than in FY 1995 despite no reduction in services and a 7 percent increase in the inmate population. In fact, the cost savings freed up funds to improve delivery of mental health services to the state's more than 3,200 mentally ill and mentally retarded prisoners, resulting in a 50 percent decrease in inmate suicides. Representing about nine percent of the inmate population, the mentally ill and retarded inmates required special care and education in addition to enhanced security to meet the threat of psychotic episodes. Class action litigation had challenged staffing levels, staff credentials, levels of clinical supervision of staff, and access to the program for mentally ill and mentally retarded inmates.

The department spent about $5.5 million to resolve these concerns and improve inmate services. Increasing the number of prison psychologists, psychiatrists, and counselors allowed inmates to be cared for and managed more effectively. New antidepressant and antipsychotic medications provided improved treatment, stabilizing inmates and allowing them to participate in work assignments and prison programs. The implementation of 24-hour Crisis Stabilization Units in six state prisons allowed for round-the-clock psychiatric care and reduced the need and the cost of transferring inmates to Central State Hospital in Milledgeville.

In June of 1998, the mental health treatment procedures of the state prison system were evaluated by a team of federal court-appointed psychiatrists. "We congratulate the Department of Corrections, especially the mental health staff, in their successful efforts in developing and implementing a good mental health system.... In particular, we are impressed with the treatment services offered to inmates with serious mental illnesses and the program for inmates (who have) a history of abuse," their report stated.

Decreased litigation: Even though the prison population grew, grievance appeals filed by inmates against the system dropped over 35 percent since 1995 to levels significantly below the national average. Georgia's grievance rate per 1,000 inmates was 526.2 in 1995 and 455.9 in 1996. In comparison, the national average of rate of grievances filed per 1,000 inmates was almost double Georgia's at 868.9 in 1995 and 906.6 in 1996. While 684 suits were filed against the GDC in just six months from July 1994 to December 1995, only 508 suits were filed in the first six months of 1996.

Long-running, costly litigation also came to a close. In July 1997, Senior U.S. District Court Judge Anthony Alaimo lifted a consent order and acknowledged that the State Department of Corrections had met the court's expectations in improving prison conditions at Georgia State Prison in Reidsville and neighboring Rogers State Prison. His decision brought to a close 25-year-old litigation that had impacted the entire prison system and was believed to have cost the state more than $400 million in renovation, construction and attorneys' fees. The department also settled five other class-action suits by July 1997, continuing its aggressive pursuit of closure to outstanding court cases in an effort to save taxpayers the steep cost of litigation.

Saving taxpayers' money: Despite an inmate population which grew by 18.3 percent from FY 1996 to FY 1999, the Department of Corrections held its budget increase to 6.7 percent during the same time. In addition to savings from the reorganization of the education and health service programs, the department instituted efficiency measures in the farm and food services and increased its revenues from the program in which prisoners manufacture goods for sale to other governmental entities.

Another $600,000 was saved when the department privatized its contract for inmate legal services, which were constitutionally mandated for the state's inmates and often involved domestic relations, pending charges and appeals. In August of 1996, the department changed from The University of Georgia Public Legal Counsel Project (PLCP) to the privately-run Center for Prisoners' Legal Assistance (CPLA). The private group delivered more service to the growing population at a cheaper cost to taxpayers, according to a March 1996 report. In the first year of its contract, CPLA received more than 17,000 prisoner requests for legal services, almost 40 percent more than that received by the UGA affiliated group for the four-quarter period prior to the contractual changeover. Yet CPLA still maintained a 99.9 percent compliance rate with the contractual requirement to respond to inmate requests within 14 days.

Additional income was also generated through effective operation of the probation system, which resulted in more than $64 million being collected and returned to crime victims and county and state treasuries during FY 1997. The amount returned exceeded the probation department's $60 million operating budget appropriated by the legislature. Of the total returned, $54 million was in court-ordered fees, fines and restitution collected from probationers, of which approximately $10.5 million went to crime victims as restitution for damages. Using minimum wage as a basis, the equivalent of another $10 million was collected in the form of community service work by probationers on roadsides and in parks and other public properties.

Deporting illegal aliens from Georgia prisons

To increase the capacity of the state's prisons and save taxpayers' money, Governor Miller signed an agreement with the United States Immigration and Naturalization Service (INS) to deport more than 300 convicted alien criminals who were being housed in Georgia prisons. The agreement, signed in June 1995, saved Georgia taxpayers more than $18 million over a three-year period and freed up prison space. Georgia was only the second state to sign an agreement with INS to deport illegal aliens housed in state prisons.

The many improvements to the prison system exemplified the openness to new ideas of the Department of Corrections, under the direction of Governor Miller. The willingness of the department to take innovative approaches toward improvement made Georgia's prisons safer, more secure and more cost-effective. Georgia's prisons became spotless, orderly, secure, regimented facilities where inmates were kept busy with work, educational classes, exercise and rehabilitation programs. The result was fewer escapes and suicides, a reduction in inmate grievances and lawsuits, and a drop in serious disciplinary reports.

Parole

I support the death penalty and have always supported it throughout my career. But the death penalty can only be imposed by unanimous agreement among the men and women who sit in the jury box. In cases where the crime is heinous enough to call for its consideration but the jury cannot quite reach a unanimous decision to impose it, the only other alternative has been a sentence that makes the offender eligible for parole in seven years. In my mind, there is a wide gap between those two options: death or eligibility for parole in seven years. So I proposed a third alternative between the two— a sentence of life without parole.

Governor Zell Miller, April 27, 1993

Prior to the Miller Administration, Georgia had an early release program that was implemented to alleviate prison overcrowding and to prevent a federal takeover of the Georgia prison system. Governor Miller ended the early release of violent criminals in December 1992, sending a message to felons, judges and juries that Georgia was cracking down on violent crime.

During the eight years of Governor Miller's administration, violent and repeat criminals were removed from Georgia's communities. Many began to spend 100 percent of their sentences in prisons, thanks to Governor Miller's "two strikes" legislation, which abolished parole for the most violent criminals who had committed murder, armed robbery, kidnaping, aggravated child molestation, rape, aggravated sodomy or aggravated sexual battery. In addition, he pursued an aggressive prison building program that provided the space to keep violent criminals locked away from law-abiding citizens. The Board of Pardons and Paroles supported Miller's efforts by tightening parole releases and raising the time-served requirement to 90 percent of sentence for some 20 crimes in order to keep violent criminals in prison longer.

Due to the tightening of parole releases, the number of offenders paroled dropped from 16,567 in 1991 to 11,381 in 1998, a decline of 32 percent. Inmates released in 1991 were serving, on average, only 24 percent of their sentences. In 1998 that number had almost doubled to 46 percent of the sentence.

In October 1995, Governor Miller asked the Board of Pardons and Paroles to make child support payment a condition of parole. Parolees who failed to pay child support could be returned to prison as a violation of their parole.

The time served by violent and sex offenders showed even more dramatic increases. During 1991 a total of 2,674 violent offenders were paroled after serving an average of 39 percent of their sentences. In 1998, 798 violent and sex offenders paroled after serving an average of 58 percent of their sentences. This change represented an increase of 49 percent in the amount of sentence

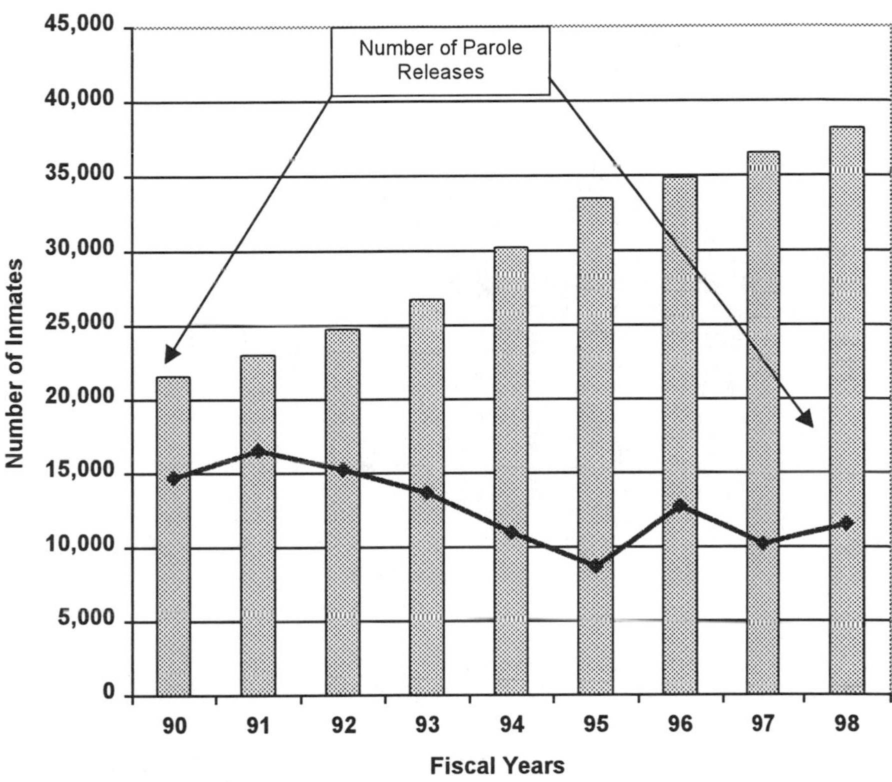

Fiscal Year	Board Releases	Other Releases	Total
90	14,719	3,224	17,943
91	16,567	2,412	18,979
92	15,240	1,863	17,103
93	13,655	2,084	15,739
94	10,942	2,473	13,415
95	8,653	3,706	12,359
96	12,740	4,011	16,751
97	10,188	4,301	14,489
98	11,381	4,470	15,851

served. Those violent offenders who were released were carefully selected as the most deserving of strict community supervision under parole.

In Georgia as in the nation, many death row cases were dragging on for 10 years or more, with one appeal after another. The lengthy delay between imposition of the sentence of death and its execution was the result of legal tactics used by the inmate and was extremely costly to the taxpayers.

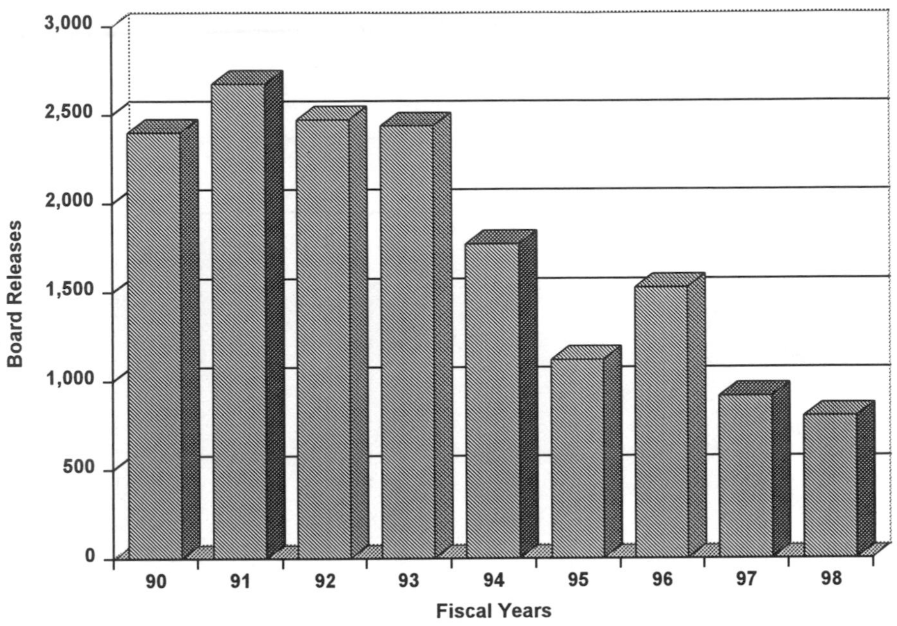

Percentage of time served for violent offenders by release type Fiscal Year 1990 - Fiscal Year 1998

Fiscal Year	Number	Board Releases	Total Releases
90	2399	39%	52%
91	2674	39%	48%
92	2471	41%	52%
93	2434	45%	52%
94	1769	45%	56%
95	1118	47%	64%
96	1523	50%	66%
97	912	53%	72%
98	798	58%	77%

Although he could do nothing to speed up the federal appeals process, Miller pushed a law to passage that limited a person convicted and sentenced to death to only one state court appeal to be made within six months of the conviction so that cases involving the death penalty were not bogged down in state courts for many years.

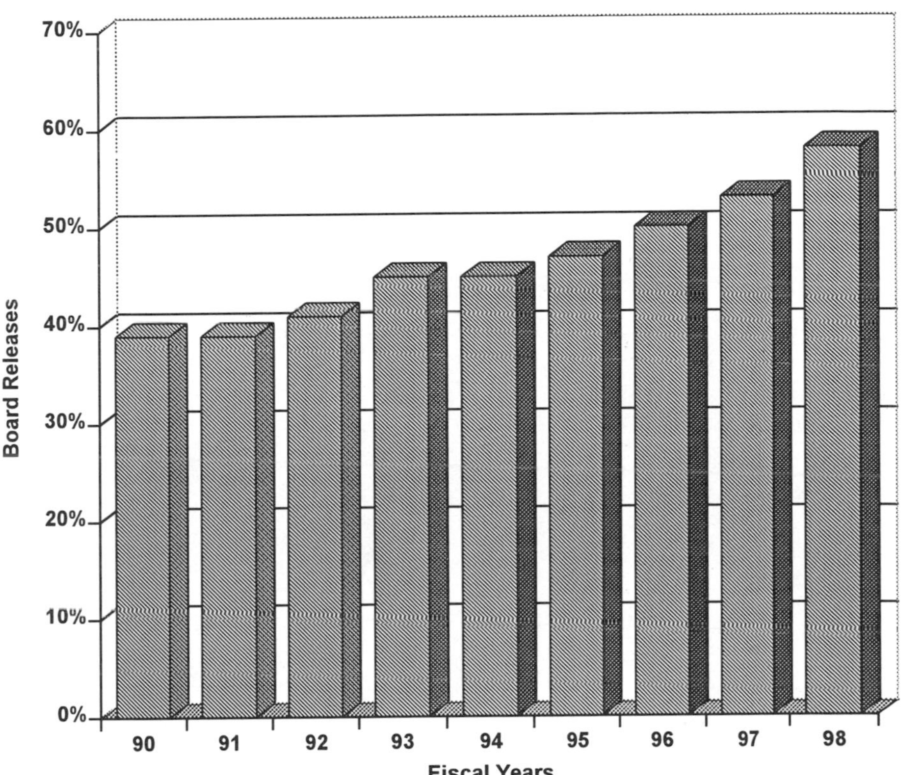

To enhance the public's safety and improve the parole officer's ability to monitor parolees, Governor Miller recommended in FY 1991 a pilot program to use electronic monitoring on parolees. The system allowed parole officers to monitor parolees 24 hours a day and respond quickly to any parole violation. By the end of the Miller Administration, 1,500 units were in operation, providing continuous monitoring of three groups of parolees: those who presented a high risk to the community; those who had a high level of needs; and/or those who continuously and willfully violated the conditions of parole.

VII. Other Accomplishments

Administrative Services

All across Georgia, private businesses are reorganizing their operations. All across Georgia, private businesses are redesigning their products and retooling their services to be more efficient and responsive to what their customers want. We must be doing the same thing in state government.

Governor Zell Miller, October 20, 1995

Commitment to technology

The need for state government to operate efficiently and effectively was a prime concern of Governor Miller's, and the changes that resulted were profoundly felt in the mainframe computer systems operated by the Department of Administrative Services. Most state agencies relied on these mainframe systems for a variety of activities, and Governor Miller endeavored to assure that these systems continued to be a solution and not an obstacle in achieving the goal of an efficient and effective state government. During his administration he obtained appropriations of $8,399,041 in cash and bonds for various replacements and upgrades to the portion of the state's

State Agency Mainframe Computer System Usage

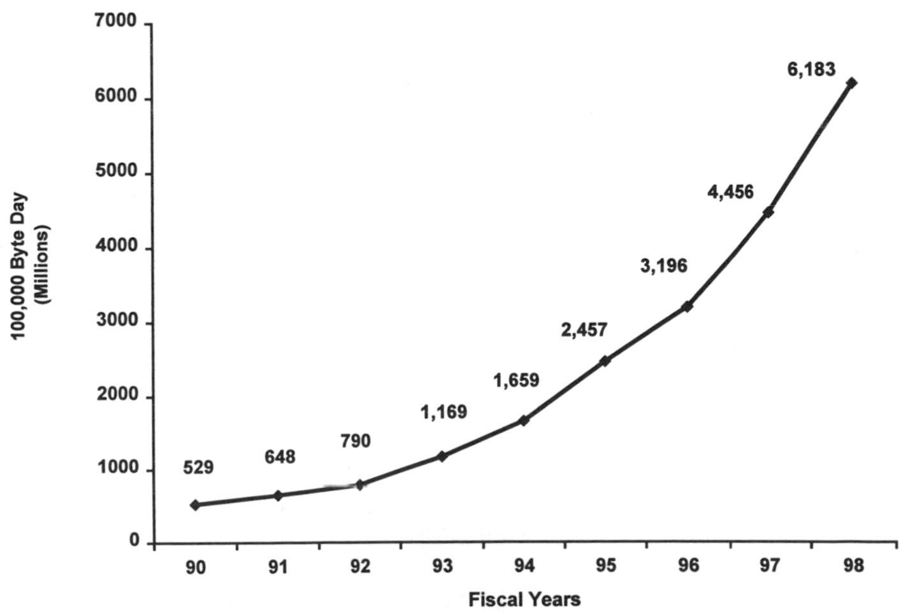

mainframe computer systems devoted to law enforcement activities. The Governor also convinced the General Assembly to appropriate $9,330,000 in bonds to replace and update computer processors in the non-law enforcement portion of the mainframe system used by most state agencies, and to establish a Motor Voter Registration System.

Funding For Statewide Mainframe Computer Improvements	
Law Enforcement Mainframe Computer System:	
FY 1994	$575,000 in 5-year bonds to replace and expand UNISYS mainframe disk storage equipment for the GBI and Department of Corrections portion of the UNISYS mainframe.
FY 1995	$5,000,000 in 5-year bonds to replace the UNISYS mainframe computer used by the GBI, Department of Corrections, and the Board of Pardons and Paroles.
FY 1998	$2,824,041 in cash to upgrade the UNISYS mainframe computer mentioned above.
State Operations (Non-Law Enforcement) Mainframe Computer System:	
FY 1994	$4,700,000 in 5-year bonds to replace a computer processor.
FY 1995	$4,630,000 in 5-year bonds to purchase computer hardware and software for the Motor Voter Registration System.

Purchasing reform

Continuing his far-reaching mission of refining and updating the way state government operated, Governor Miller assisted the Department of Administrative Services in the passage of the Purchasing Reform Act of 1996, which represented the first notable overhaul and revision to laws governing state government purchasing practices since the early 1980s. Carrying out automation measures that had been recommended by the Governor's Commission on Effectiveness and Economy in Government (Williams Commission), this act decentralized state government where practical to allow agencies to react quickly and efficiently in a work environment where change was constant and rapid, and delays meant missed opportunities to serve the citizens in the best, least expensive manner possible.

The Purchasing Reform Act decentralized major portions of the purchasing process, eliminating cumbersome steps and paperwork, and giving state agencies greater authority and responsibility in making purchases. Updating and simplifying the bidding and purchasing requirements and procedures freed the state to automate significant areas of the purchasing process such as small item agency purchases and fuel purchases for state vehicles. The act also created the Georgia Procurement Registry to advertise all state agency and State Purchasing Office bid opportunities on the Internet, publicizing opportunities more widely to the bidding public and encouraging broader participation. The establishment of the Registry resulted in a threefold rise in the number of average bids received per solicitation.

Thus the Purchasing Reform Act became an essential, pivotal instrument in Governor Miller's achieving his primary objectives of expanding access to the bidding process to a much broader audience and giving state agencies the flexibility to aggressively make state government operate with businesslike acumen and prudence.

The Purchasing Reform Act also dovetailed with Governor Miller's efforts to expand the participation of minority businesses in state purchasing. In 1992, Governor Miller issued an Executive Order directing state agencies to work harder to increase the participation of minority businesses in the state purchasing process. The Executive Order called for state agencies to make special efforts to publicize bid opportunities to minority businesses and to designate a staff person to provide assistance to minority businesses wanting to enter the bidding process. The order also set up a system of reporting in which state agencies began sending quarterly progress reports on minority bidding to the Department of Administrative Services. By 1996 more than a third of the minority firms that were solicited bid on state purchases, and a record high level of over $102 million in state contracts was awarded to minority firms.

Privatizing motor vehicle and rapid copy services

As part of Governor Miller's effort to privatize state services whenever practical and economical, the Department of Administrative Services privatized two important functions. First, the department outsourced its Capitol Hill motor vehicle maintenance facility and contracted with a single vendor to provide a network of dealers and repair shops for use by some 1,200 state-owned vehicles. This procurement provided an opportunity to assess the feasibility of privatizing maintenance for all state-owned vehicles statewide. The department's second project involved privatizing rapid copy services at a savings to the state. In 1997 this contract was rebid with a further savings of $250,000 annually to the state.

Agriculture

Georgia agriculture is as old as the state and is the bedrock on which we built our economy starting in colonial days. But it is also as new as the 21st century, with new crops growing in Georgia's fields, new packing and processing plants operating in Georgia's farm communities and new marketing opportunities opening up around the world.

Governor Zell Miller, May 26, 1994

Governor Miller expressed keen interest and support toward agriculture throughout his tenure, sponsoring and supporting a variety of initiatives to ensure Georgia's prosperity in this area. During his administration, $12,720,000 in cash and bonds was directed toward repairs and renovations to the Atlanta Farmers' Market and to other farmers' markets statewide, enhancing their ability to serve the state's farmers and consumers.

The Governor also worked with the Department of Agriculture to protect the consumer through better regulation of residential pesticide treatment businesses. He recommended and secured $258,773 in Fiscal Year (FY) 1996 to fund seven additional positions for the department's Structural Pest Control Inspection Program. This action enabled the department to increase its inspections, both in response to requests and at random to verify that pest control companies had properly treated these structures.

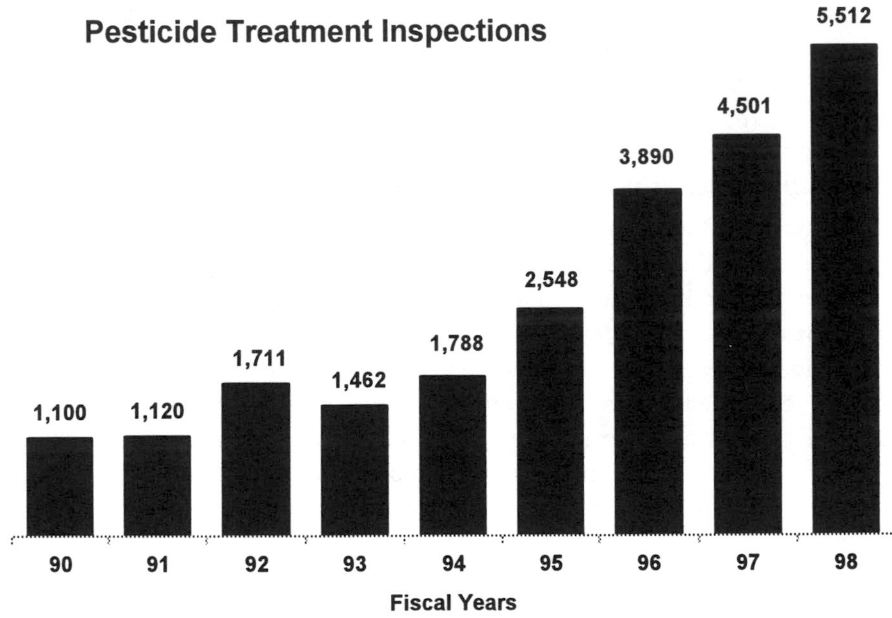

Governor Miller also spearheaded improvements for the University System of Georgia's diagnostic veterinary laboratories in Athens and Tifton. In FY 1994 and FY 1999, over $10 million was appropriated for replacement, expansion and improvements at both labs, $6,300,000 for Athens and $3,877,000 for Tifton. The improved and expanded labs were crucial in assisting the Department of Agriculture to safeguard the health of livestock and other non-poultry animals. In addition, the Governor recommended $500,000 in bonds in FY 1995 to construct a bull testing facility in Tifton to conduct research on cattle breeding and raising.

The tremendous growth of the Georgia poultry industry and the need to protect the health of the live poultry being supplied to poultry processors and ultimately to consumers nationwide, prompted Governor Miller to recommend appropriations during his administration totaling $1,314,500 to expand the network of Poultry Veterinary Diagnostic Labs from four to 10, and replace one existing lab building. The Governor made certain that existing and new Poultry Veterinary Diagnostic Labs were sufficiently equipped to conduct their important tasks by directing $89,234 from the Governor's Discretionary Fund in FY 1994 and later convincing the legislature to appropriate an additional $45,000 in FY 1996 for critically needed laboratory equipment.

Diagnostic Laboratory Construction

***Replacement Laboratories**

Veterinary Diagnostic Laboratories

1. Athens Veterinary Diagnostic Laboratory
2. Tifton Veterinary Diagnostic Laboratory
3. Poultry Veterinary Diagnostic Laboratory (Dalton Branch)

*** New Laboratories**

Poultry Veterinary Diagnostic Laboratories

Bowdon	Douglas
Camilla	Forsyth
Carnesville	Montezuma

The purpose of the Georgia Agrirama at Tifton was to educate persons of all ages about Georgia's rural farm history. The Governor saw that the Agrirama received appropriations during his tenure totaling $162,000 for necessary repairs to museum buildings and for equipment purchases. These efforts aided the museum in continuing to offer an enhanced educational experience and appreciation of an important segment of Georgia's history to everyone.

The Arts and Humanities

Art is not just for artists; it is for everyone. Its intrinsic beauty and balance are capable of bringing joy into the lives of all who view or hear it. But more than that, art is a rich part of our heritage and our identity. It provides us with an interpretive history of our past, a thought-provoking reflection of our present, and sometimes even a glimpse of our future.

Governor Zell Miller, January 29, 1991

Prior to the Miller Administration, state support for the arts consisted mostly of grants to artists and arts agencies. Under Governor Miller's direction, the Georgia Council for the Arts continued those grants, but also began a number of new, creative initiatives to cultivate the development of community arts programs throughout Georgia, promote arts education, and give Georgia artists more exposure. Although the arts bit the bullet along with all other aspects of state government in the lean financial days early in the administration, nevertheless, by the time Miller left office, support for the arts in the state budget had increased by 44 percent, from $2.8 million in FY 1991 to $4 million in FY 1999. The Governor had also instituted several new programs that did not require state funding, like the State Capitol Gallery Series and the Cultural Evenings at the Governor's Mansion.

Organizational Grants Program

The Georgia Council for the Arts Organizational Grants Program awarded almost $21 million in grants during the Miller Administration. State funds supported major institutions such as the Atlanta Symphony Orchestra and the Columbus Museum of Art, as well as smaller organizations all across the state, like the Creative Arts Guild in Dalton, the Perry Players in Perry, and the Augusta Mini-Theatre in Augusta. These funds made it possible for hundred of thousands of Georgians to experience the arts in their communities.

While most of the organizational grants went to arts organizations for general operating support, funds were also available for specific arts projects, technical assistance, leadership development, organization problem solving and fee support to enable communities to bring in artists and arts groups from other parts of the state for performances or exhibitions. This program was designed to be responsive to a broad range of community needs and interests.

Georgia Challenge Program

Governor Miller initiated the Georgia Challenge, a curriculum-based arts education program in 1995 (FY 1996). This program was a partnership between the Georgia Council for the Arts, the State Department of Education and the Coca-Cola Foundation. Each year for the remainder of the Miller Administration, the Governor recommended and the Georgia General Assembly appropriated $700,000 for the Georgia Council for the Arts to provide matching grants to school systems to develop, implement or expand sequential, curriculum-based arts education in kindergarten through fifth grade. The Coca-Cola Foundation provided a $150,000 three-year grant for the administration of the program from 1995 to 1998. Beginning in July of 1998, the Georgia Council for the Arts provided funding for the administration of the program.

The Georgia Challenge Program strove to infuse basic education in the arts into the curriculum on the same level as other core subjects. A special emphasis of this program was to promote a partnership between school administrators, classroom teachers, art specialists, community members and local resources. Grants ranged from $10,000 to $50,000 in any or all of four artistic disciplines: dance, theater, music and visual arts. Funds were awarded based on a one-to-one matching formula, with at least 10 percent of the school system's match in cash. The remaining match could be in in-kind services.

In its first four years, which coincided with Miller's second term, the Challenge Program allocated over $2.7 million to 52 school systems across the state. In Fiscal Year 1996, 19 school systems received grants totaling $683,000; in FY 1997, 31 school systems received grants totaling $623,000; in FY 1998, 21 school systems received grants totaling $662,000; and in FY 1999, 29 school systems received grants totaling $640,000. Over 500,000 students and 27,000 teachers benefited from this program.

Glynn County School System, located along the Southeast Georgia Coast, was an example of the impact this program had. In FY 1997, the school system received a Challenge grant of $37,000. Following a very successful year of Challenge arts programming for students and teachers, the school board voted to hire five new arts teachers for the county's nine elementary schools, filling a void that had existed for over 20 years. This decision represented an investment in arts education of $180,000 a year. The school system stated, "This is our acknowledgment that the arts are inherent with a comprehensive quality education."

Dr. John Culbreath, superintendent of Dougherty County Schools, summed up the Challenge Program best when he said, "Hands-on experiences, active learning and creativity are the hallmarks of the success of the program; the Challenge grant has afforded our students numerous opportunities to maximize students' learning in all areas."

Grassroots Arts Program

The Grassroots Arts Program, initiated by Governor Miller in 1993, provided funding for each of Georgia's 159 counties for arts programs and services. Funds were made available to 36 regional arts agencies, called Grassroots Agencies, which in turn accepted applications from community arts organizations for matching grants. The funds were allocated according to the following formula: One half of the annual appropriation was divided equally among the 159 counties of the state, and the other half was a per-capita allocation based on each county's population. From an original appropriation of $200,000, this program grew to an FY 1999 budget of $425,000.

The goals of the Grassroots Arts Program were to provide an opportunity for every county in the state to receive state arts dollars through a decentralized decision-making process, to encourage multi-county cooperation through the regional Grasssroots Agencies, and to support local arts development in every part of the state. Each Grassroots Agency developed its own guidelines for regranting the state funds within broad parameters that were established at the state level to guarantee some consistency across the state. A committee composed of at least one representative from each of the counties in the region reviewed all applications and made funding decisions.

After the program's inception, hundreds of arts programs were funded across the state in rural communities and inner-city neighborhoods, reaching audiences that previously had had very little exposure to the arts. New partnerships were formed to provide the necessary resources to make the arts happen; new funding sources were tapped for matching funds; and artists and arts groups were discovered in communities where no one had known they existed. The Grassroots Arts Program was an unqualified success. It was an example of how government services could be successfully decentralized with decisions on the expenditure of state tax dollars placed in the hands of citizens at the local level.

State Capitol Gallery Series

The State Capitol Gallery Series was begun in the summer of 1991, and utilized the large reception area of the Governor's Office to showcase the work of artists from various regions of the state. During the Miller Administration, more than 30 arts organizations throughout Georgia were involved in organizing over 34 exhibitions with more than 680 artists and over 1,100 works of art.

The series was managed by the Georgia Council for the Arts, and the majority of arts organizations represented were funded by the agency in the organizational grants category. Some of the arts organizations included the

Okefenokee Heritage Center in Waycross, the Museum of Arts and Sciences in Macon, the Quinlan Arts Center in Gainesville and the Thomasville Cultural Center.

State Capitol Gallery Exhibitions

<u>1991</u>

June 26 - Sept. 14	Georgia Folk Artists, Quinlan Arts Center
Sept. 16-Dec. 27	Emil Holzhauer Exhibition, Macon Museum of Arts and Sciences

<u>1992</u>

Dec. 29 - March 28	Artists of South Georgia, Okefenokee Heritage Center
March 30 - May 16	Landscape Paintings, Lynwood Hall
May 20 - June 29	Georgia Artists at the Capitol, Gertrude Herbert Institute of Art
July 6 - Sept. 19	Georgia Artists from the Paul Jones Collection
Sept. 21 - Jan. 8	Georgia Quilt Exhibition, Georgia Quilt Project

<u>1993</u>

Jan. 11 - March 12	South Georgia Artists, Arts Experiment Station
March 15 - June 11	Athens Artists, Lyndon House
June 14 - Sept. 10	Faculty Exhibition, Valdosta State University
Sept. 13 - Jan. 7	North Georgia Mountains Artists, Gilmer Arts Council

<u>1994</u>

Jan 10 - March 11	Area Artists, Colquitt County Arts Council
March 14 - June 10	Selections, State Art Collection
June 13 - Sept. 9	Selections, Albany Area Arts Council/Albany Area Artists Guild
Sept. 12 - Sept. 30	Historical Quilts, Fort Oglethorpe Senior Citizens
Oct. 3 - Jan. 20	Golden Isles Artists, Golden Isles Arts and Humanities Association

<u>1995</u>

Jan 23 - April 14	LaGrange Area Artists, Chattahoochee Valley Art Museum and Georgia Citizens for the Arts
April 17 - June 23	Selections, State Art Collection, Georgia Citizens for the Arts

	(Capitol renovations precluded summer exhibits)
Oct. 2 - Jan. 5	Eight Atlanta Artists, Arts Station of Stone Mountain

1996

Jan. 8 - March 8	Jailhouse Alley Arts Council, Fort Valley
March 11 - June 7	Native American Artists, Gwinnett Council for the Arts
June 3 - Sept. 6	Classically Southern: Drawings, Paintings and Photographs by Georgia Artists, curated by Richard Waterhouse
Sept. 9 - Jan. 10	Works from Members of the Southeastern Pastel Society

1997

Jan. 13 - Feb. 7	Selections, Elberton Arts Council
Feb. 10 - April 4	Georgia Art Educators Association Exhibition
April 7 - June 6	Special Audiences/Very Special Arts
June 9 - Sept. 5	Atlanta Artists Club
Sept. 8 - Oct. 14	Women on Paper. Augusta Arts Council

1998

Jan. 12 - March 6	Georgia Art Educators Association
March 9 - May 8	Dunwoody Fine Arts Association
May 11 - June 12	Portrait Society of Atlanta
June 15 - Sept. 4	Southern Crescent Alliance of Visual Artists Association
Sept. 7 - Jan. 8	Thomasville Cultural Center

Cultural evenings at the Governor's Mansion

To raise additional funding for arts projects and programs beyond the state appropriations for the Georgia Council for the Arts, Governor and Mrs. Miller hosted a number of cultural evenings at the Mansion, featuring a full-course dinner and an evening of entertainment honoring one or more of Georgia's outstanding artists.

Cultural Evenings at the Mansion:

Date	Honored
April 16, 1992	Playwright Alfred Uhry
May 28, 1992	Violinist Robert McDuffie
June 25, 1992	Novelist Ferrol Sams

July 23, 1992	Artist Benny Andrews
August 18, 1992	Artist Mattie Lou O'Kelley
September 21, 1992	Poet and novelist Byron Herbert Reece
June 8, 1993	Artist Lamar Dodd
September 14, 1993	Potter Lanier Meadors
August 30, 1994	Mountain music group Skillet Lickers and the Golden Gospel Singers
August 29, 1995	Historical drama groups Reach of Song and Swamp Gravy
February 11, 1998	Woodworker Edward Moulthrop, Author Eugenia Price and Tenor Michael Maguire

Folklife Program

In 1991, Governor Zell Miller provided the Georgia Folklife Program with a permanent home within the Georgia Council for the Arts. The goal of this program was to ensure that Georgia's folk cultural heritage was actively documented, presented, preserved and passed on. The Folklife Grants Program was begun in partnership with the Georgia Humanities Council in 1992, and during the remainder of the Miller Administration, requests for grants totaled $412,232. Of these requests, $154,095 was allocated for 38 projects resulting in a total expenditure of $374,465 to support folk and traditional arts in Georgia.

In 1996, the Traditional Arts Apprenticeship Program was initiated to encourage master traditional artists, craftspeople, musicians and dancers to pass on their skills to qualified apprentices. Of the $98,295 in requests received from 33 traditional artists, 18 apprenticeships were funded at a cost of $53,455.

The Folklife Program also conducted folklife field research and maintained an archive of data that included audio recordings, negatives, slides and prints that comprised a unique record of Georgia's folk cultural heritage. In addition, the Folklife Program produced a traveling exhibit called *Missing Pieces or Missing the Point? The Georgia Forum on Folk Art*, and a book on disability entitled *Portrait of Spirit: One Story at a Time.* The sound recording, *Georgia Folk: A Sampler of Traditional Sounds*, was also reissued on compact disc.

Georgia Humanities Council

The Georgia Humanities Council was an independent organization which provided grants to some 81 counties in support of public educational programs that brought citizens together in learning and conversation to promote a better understanding of Georgia's cultural heritage. Governor Miller increased state funding for the council from $50,000 in FY 1990 tp $175,000 in FY 1999. One of the council's most successful programs was "Rights, Responsibilities and Respect," which focused on character education. Initiated in March of 1996, it provided instruction in values, virtues and character in Georgia's schools and conducted workshops for teachers from across the state. The council also supported libraries, schools, colleges and universities, historical societies, museums and other nonprofit humanities-oriented organizations in every region of Georgia.

Governor's Awards in the Humanities

1991

Malcolm Bell, Jr.	Historian, author of *Major Butler's Legacy*
Dan T. Carter	Andrew W. Mellon Professor of History at Emory University
Raymond L. Chambers	Professor of political science and chair, Division of Social Science, Bainbridge College
Gwendolyn Cheatham	Instructional Coordinator, Booker T. Washington School in Atlanta
Anna Harvin Grant	Professor and chair, Department of Sociology and Director of Family Institute, Morehouse College
Carmen Chaves Tesser	Professor of romance languages, The University of Georgia
National Infantry Museum	Fort Benning

1992

Kenneth Coleman	Professor of history, The University of Georgia
Billie Davis Gaines	Cultural leader, Atlanta
W. W. Law	Local historian and cultural leader, Savannah
John Stone	Poet, educator and dean, Emory University School of Medicine
High Museum of Art	Education Programs Department, Atlanta
Fort Frederic Association	St. Simons Island

1993

Marcellus Barksdale	Professor of history, Morehouse College
Hugh Brown	Professor of English, Armstrong State College

Elizabeth Lyon	State historic preservation officer, Department of Natural Resources
Adelaide Ponder	Community cultural leader and preservationist, Madison
Historic Chattahoochee Commission	Columbus

<u>1994</u>

N. Gordon Carper	Dana Professor of History, Berry College
Alton Hornsby, Jr.	Professor and chair, Department of History, Morehouse College
Chris Moser	Documentary producer and director, Lithonia
R. Frank Saunders, Jr.	Professor of history, Georgia Southern University
The Atlanta History Center	Atlanta

<u>1995</u>

Numan Bartley	Merton Coulter Professor of History, The University of Georgia
Jacque Coxe	Director, North Fulton County Teaching Museum, Roswell
Frank Schnell	Archaeologist, Columbus Museum, Columbus
Heritage Education Program	Georgia Trust for Historic Preservation
Annual Writer's Workshop Conference	Clark-Atlanta University Department of English

<u>1996</u>

Delores Aldridge	Grace Towns Hamilton Professor of Sociology and African-American Studies, Emory University
Joyce Blackburn	Author and biographer, St. Simons Island
Adrienne Bond	Associate professor of English, Mercer University
Annette Brock	Professor of social sciences, Savannah State College
Thomas Dyer	Professor of higher education and history, The University of Georgia
Lewis Larsen	State archaeologist, Carrollton

<u>1997</u>

Alfonso Biggs	Collector and preserver of historic African American artifacts, Columbus

Jean Bolen Bridges	Chair, Division of Humanities, East Georgia College
James Gustafson	Woodruff Professor of Comparative Studies and Religion, Emory University
Joseph Jacobs	Attorney and cultural leader, Atlanta
William "Billy" Winn	Editorial page editor, *Columbus Ledger-Inquirer*, historical writer
Museum of Aviation	Warner Robins
Troup County Historical Society	LaGrange

<u>1998</u>

Sophia Bamford	Retired physician and cultural leader, Tignall
Gary Fink	Professor of labor history, Georgia State University
Kay Hightower	Cultural leader and preservationist, Thomaston
Joan B. Huffman	Professor and chair, Social Science Division, Macon State College
Mills B. Lane	Writer, editor and publisher, *Beehive Press*, Savannah
Judy Nail	Director of arts and humanities education, Muscogee County School System
Leon Lawson Neel	Retired businessman, local historian and columnist, Thomasville
Eugene P. Walker	Former teacher and educator, commissioner of the Department of Juvenile Justice

Georgia Building Authority

Property acquisition

Under the direction of Governor Miller, the Georgia Building Authority acquired several facilities, both existing and new, including three in the Five Points area of downtown Atlanta. In chronological order, the more notable of these were:

1991: Tradeport building ($7.4 million) in Clayton County with over 110,000 square feet;

1992: Clark Harrison building ($9.2 million) in Decatur with approximately 100,000 square feet;

1992: former First Atlanta Bank tower ($13.3 million) at Five Points with over 1 million gross square feet;

1993: Peachtree Pedestrian Plaza ($2.9 million) at Five Points;

1994: Olympia building ($3.7 million) at Five Points;

1995: City of Atlanta's and Fulton County's interests in Georgia Plaza Park were acquired ($9.4 million);

1996: Pete Hackney parking deck, which also contained the Capitol Day Care Center, was constructed ($12.7 million) to alleviate a severe shortage of parking spaces in the Capitol Hill area.

Major facility renovations and improvements

Major renovations, restorations, and improvements were made at several facilities, including the State Capitol. The Governor, sensitive to this building's prominent place in the state's history, saw that appropriations amounting to $36.2 million in bonds were devoted to restoring and renovating, in an historically accurate fashion, the public areas, House and Senate Chambers, and the Appropriations Committee meeting room which originally was the Supreme Court's hearing room. In 1998 Governor Miller presided at a ribbon-cutting dedication ceremony for the reopening of the Capitol rotunda, which had been closed for safety concerns due to the danger of falling plaster.

Other major projects included the 2 Peachtree Building (formerly the First Atlanta Bank tower), which was renovated with $81 million in bonds appropriated during Governor Miller's term. When renovations were completed, the per square foot capital cost for this space was approximately half of the cost of new construction, saving the state an estimated $100 million compared to building new similarly sized space. The 244 Washington Street Building was also renovated at a cost of $8.55 million. The top three floors and building mechanical systems of the Trinity-Washington Building underwent renovation at a cost of $13 million.

The Georgia Plaza Park, adjacent to the State Capitol, was converted into the Capitol Education Center ($7.5 million) for use by the Secretary of State. When completed in 1999, this facility would provide meeting rooms, and state-of-the-art facilities for Georgia Public Television and other broadcast media that covered the General Assembly.

Programmatic initiatives

Recycling was a priority of the Georgia Building Authority beginning in 1990, when GBA assumed the responsibility for coordinating recycling programs for state government entities. By the time Governor Miller left office, this program served 150 separate locations in Atlanta, Athens, Milledgeville, Augusta, Macon, Carrollton, and Dahlonega. During the Miller Administration, the program recycled over 21,000 tons of office paper, generated over $2 million in revenues and saved the state over $500,000 in landfill fees.

Energy conservation and utility usage reduction was another area where the authority achieved significant results. In 1992, the central energy plant was expanded to provide hot and chilled water to building systems in the Capitol Hill area. Savings in 1992 alone were over $1 million. In 1994, the authority initiated a lighting retrofit project to replace old inefficient lighting systems in its buildings, reducing energy consumption for lighting by 48 percent. With a cost of only $750,000 and a payback period of only 16 months, this program saved a net of over $1.5 million in less than five years.

The Building Authority also converted its vehicles and other equipment, as appropriate, to operate on Compressed Natural Gas (CNG) which produced a much cleaner exhaust than gasoline. The Authority was the first state agency to operate a CNG fueling station, which it made available to all state agencies to refuel their CNG-powered vehicles.

Historic preservation received significant attention during the Miller Administration, with funds appropriated to correct major deficiencies at several historic Confederate cemeteries. The Building Authority administered grounds maintenance contracts for the historic Confederate cemeteries at Marietta, Resaca, Milner, Kingston, Jonesboro, and Cassville. Comments in the visitor registers at these facilities confirmed that the citizens of Georgia appreciated and supported this service.

State facilities became more accessible to disabled persons through the authority's oversight of the state's compliance with the Americans with Disabilities Act (ADA). In addition to making its own facilities compliant with these requirements, the authority coordinated statewide efforts for all agencies and served as the funding conduit to improve access. From FY 1994 through FY 1998, funding for ADA initiatives totaled over $17.5 million.

Operations

As part of Governor Miller's budget redirection process, facilities programming and planning, and roof maintenance services for all state agencies were centralized in a new, 36-position office within the Building Authority. The facilities planning and programming section also performed reviews of construction plans and specifications to ensure that all new state buildings complied with appropriate building and life safety codes and ADA regulations.

Even with the creation of the new facilities planning and programming section and the addition of over 1.2 million gross square feet to the authority's responsibility, staffing levels for the Building Authority were reduced 21 percent from 705 to 557 positions during the Miller Administration. The reduction was accomplished by completely reorganizing the maintenance and repair function of the authority from stand-alone shops to a maintenance team concept. Not only did this change reduce staffing levels, but tenant surveys conducted before and after this change indicated that productivity, efficiency and effectiveness improved substantially. The maintenance team approach allowed GBA to eliminate 98 positions and outsource several services such as elevator maintenance and major custodial services. The authority also used state corrections system inmate labor in several programs to supplement state employee and contracted activities. In many cases, these inmates were in the process of learning a trade that would allow them to become self sustaining citizens when released.

Between 1990 and 1998, cost reductions for facilities owned by the authority totaled over $17.5 million in real dollar terms. When adjusted for the rise in the Consumer Price Index, this represented savings of over $34 million.

Security was improved in the Capitol area even while the number of personnel decreased. The authority implemented a card access system to the buildings, reducing the number of public entry doors; increased the use of closed-circuit television; installed panic buttons in parking lots; and developed a beat approach for roving security. Like many other urban police forces, a number of the uniformed Building Authority police began to travel on bicycles and motorcycles to expand their patrol area, improve emergency response time, and increase their visibility to the general public.

Department of Defense

We live in a time when a healthy economy, jobs and prosperity increasingly depend on a well-adjusted, productive, literate workforce. Unfortunately, at the same time, the odds seem to be stacking up against us as we struggle toward that end. We must do a better job of nurturing our troubled children and preparing them to make their own way in the 21st century.

Governor Zell Miller, September 6, 1991

Youth Challenge Academy

Governor Miller, who attributed a great deal of his success and discipline to his military service, was an enthusiastic supporter of the Youth Challenge Academy. Operated by the Georgia National Guard, a division of the Georgia Department of Defense, the program provided at-risk youth between 16 to 19 years of age a unique opportunity to earn a high school General Education Diploma and learn valuable life skills.

The academy was based at the National Guard Training Center at Fort Stewart. Two 22-week residential session were conducted each year to give students training and instruction in the four core elements of the program:

academic education, life skills, work skills and military discipline. The academic training unit of the program prepared students for the GED exam. The curriculum encompassed all five areas of the exam: literature, mathematics, science, social studies and written composition. Classroom instruction was augmented by self-paced individual studies. Of the program's ten graduating classes, 1,452 of 1,563 students received their high school equivalency diploma—a 93 percent graduation rate.

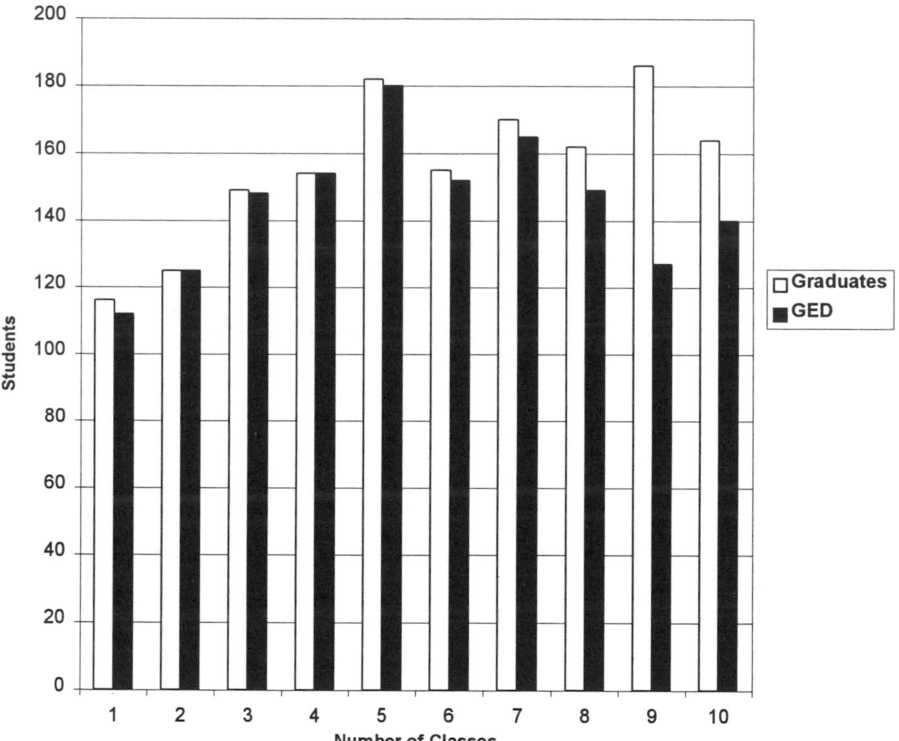

The second component of the academy was life skills. This unit prepared students for the future by familiarizing them with financial and social situations that they were likely to encounter in everyday living. Instruction stressed topics such as establishing and maintaining financial credit, balancing a checkbook, developing a household budget, purchasing insurance and social interaction. These necessary skills prepared the youth to lead productive lives and avoid destructive behaviors. From the program's inception in August 1993 through July 1998, students performed a cumulative 34,624 hours of community service.

Work skills, defined as skills needed to gain and maintain employment, made up the third unit. The skills taught, referred to as paper, people, packaging and practice, were those necessary for success in the work world—learning how to write a resume, fill out job applications, effectively respond to interview questions and dress appropriately for interviews. After studying the precursors to success in the classroom, local businesses gave students an opportunity to apply their new skills through hands-on work experience.

The fourth unit was military structure. During the course of the residential program, students were immersed in a military environment, and courses on military customs, courtesies and drill ceremonies were taught. Students lived in military type dormitories, ate in a military dining facility and participated in vigorous physical activities.

Upon graduation from the residential phase, students moved into a 12-month post-residential phase. Each graduate was assigned a mentor in his/her home community who would assist the graduate in identifying and exploring opportunities while they were transitioning from the program to a new productive phase in life. Of the first eight classes, 1,213 students, or 55 percent found jobs, 16 percent joined the military, 10 percent enrolled in college, 13 percent sought vocational education and 6 percent were still pending placement by mid-1998.

Total Graduates 1213
As of July 97

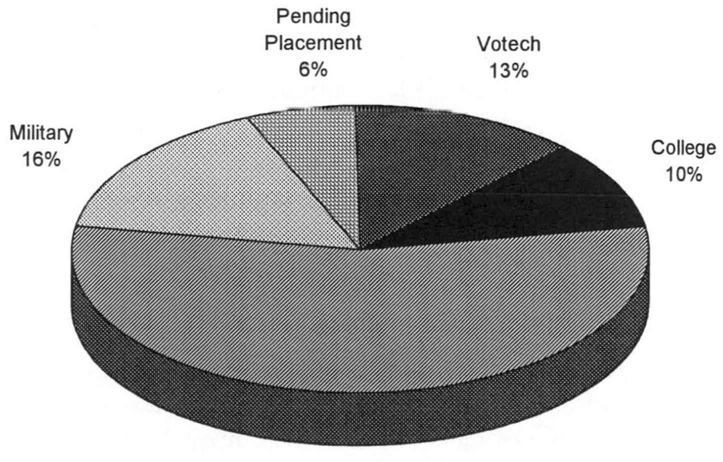

For the first five years of its operation, the Youth Challenge Academy was 100 percent federally funded at an average cost of $4 million per year and an average annual cost per student of $9,167. Then Governor Miller began providing state matching funds, making $1.4 million in state funds available to cover various operating expenses by the end of his administration.

Georgia Emergency Management Agency

Georgia's seven million citizens depend upon GEMA to direct and protect them during disasters, and to help them deal with the dramatic and traumatic damage and destruction left in the wake of disasters.

Governor Zell Miller, May 11, 1994

The Georgia Emergency Management Agency (GEMA) was the lead agency in the State of Georgia for coordination of emergency and disaster response activities. Its number one responsibility was to protect the citizens of Georgia during threats of floods, tornadoes, hurricanes and numerous other emergencies.

Under the leadership of Governor Miller, the Georgia Emergency Management Agency (GEMA) brought together local and state agencies for the first time to build a support network of emergency preparedness that extended from local communities to national levels. With the appointment by Governor Miller of GEMA's director to head the State Olympic Law Enforcement Command, GEMA led the one-team approach to providing security for the 1996 Summer Olympics. The State Operations Center, a 24-hour operational facility manned by GEMA personnel to respond to emergencies, provided a place where all state agencies gathered and worked together to facilitate informed decisions.

During the Miller Administration, with overwhelming support from the Governor, GEMA responded to 12 presidential-declared disasters, including four tornadoes, five floods, one hurricane and one snowstorm. From FY 1990 to FY 1994, an estimated $11 million in state dollars was appropriated for flood and tornado victims. Over $200 million in federal assistance was awarded to aid the state and its citizens in these disasters.

Then came what the Governor called "the single most severe disaster in the history of the state.. In July of 1994, Tropical Storm Alberto flooded South Georgia, taking 34 lives and leaving 50,000 homeless. Dams burst; rivers overflowed; farms, roads, railways and businesses were wiped out. GEMA led the mammoth coordination of relief efforts, which involved 20 state agencies in responding to the urgent needs of victims. Staff from GEMA and Federal Emergency Management Agency personnel set up disaster assistance centers where flood victims could enroll in assistance programs offered through various agencies. Governor Miller secured $97.7 million in state funds, the highest state appropriation ever for a single disaster, to match over $300 million in federal assistance for the recovery efforts for victims who lost their homes, businesses and personal belongings.

In March of 1998, the state was again hit by extensive flooding and tornadoes, which affected 119 counties. GEMA came to the aid of many Georgians affected by this disaster, and Governor Miller approved over $10 million in state assistance.

GEMA responded to the needs of Georgia and its citizens through various ongoing programs and services. Public information was developed, produced and disseminated to local governments and communities in the form of brochures, videos and other materials. GEMA provided professional development, emergency preparedness, and field resourses to public safety personnel and emergency volunteers throughout the state.

NATURAL DISASTERS IN GEORGIA SINCE 1990

DATE	TYPE	COUNTIES	AMOUNT
March 98	Flood/Tornadoes	112	$115,000,000
November 95	Tornado	3	$ 349,533
October 95	Hurricane	50	$ 19,068,744
October 94	Flood	38	$ 11,969,258
July 94	Flood	55	$285,760,873
April 94	Tornado	28	$ 5,254,175
March 93	Snow Storm	105	$ 34,451,483
March 93	Tornado	37	$ 1,456,864
December 92	Tornado	57	$ 2,480,757
March 91	Flood	39	$ 3,644,262
October 90	Flood	24	$ 8,266,909
February 90	Flood	85	$ 15,458,696
		TOTAL	$503,161,554

Office of the Commissioner of Insurance

Insurance and fire safety touched all Georgians. Governor Miller understood the importance of providing the state's insurance and fire safety regulatory arm with the resources it needed to protect the public from improper and unsafe insurance and fire safety practices and designs as well as supply the public information and assistance regarding insurance and fire safety matters. Governor Miller secured $2,233,652 in FY 1993 for staffing and operational improvements the commissioner needed to attain accreditation from the National Association of Insurance Commissioners.

The Governor recommended and achieved funding of $300,000 in FY 1992 for six additional positions to expand fraud investigation. In FY 1996 and FY 1998, Governor Miller advocated proposals totaling $106,943 for adequate staff and equipment to strengthen the department's capability to respond, resolve and, when warranted, investigate a larger number of insurance consumer complaints and inquiries.

Another $153,665 recommended by the governor for FY 1996 and FY 1999 funded additional fire safety engineers to handle the increasing number of fire safety reviews and inspections resulting from the state's steady economic growth.

Consumer Services Closed Cases

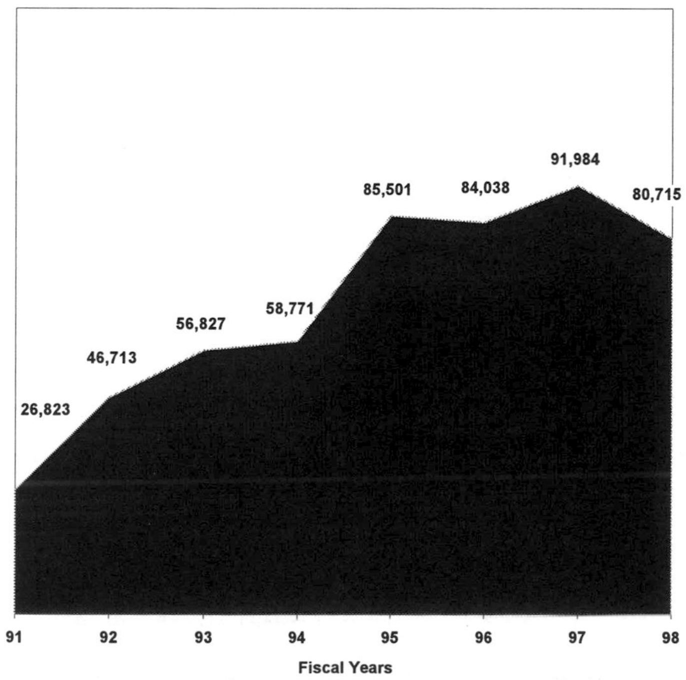

Judicial Appointments

My goal as Governor was to open up the process, giving qualified women and minorities the assurance that they will get fair and equal consideration. I was convinced that we could retain a high level of quality in our judicial system while at the same time making it more representative.

Governor Zell Miller, September 12, 1991

In his inaugural address in January 1991, Governor Zell Miller pledged to help create "a Georgia in which all of us have opportunity to seek our destiny, seize that shining moment and climb as far as strength and wit and perseverance will carry us; never to be blocked by barriers of race or barricades of region, or gender or class." During the course of the next eight years, Miller proceeded to move Georgia's courts in that direction by making a greater impact on the judiciary of the State of Georgia than all his predecessors combined. Through his appointment of African-Americans and women to the appellate and trial courts of the state, he created more opportunities for minorities and women to serve on the bench than at any time in the state's history.

When Zell Miller began his first term as Governor in January, 1991, only six of the 136 judges sitting on the superior courts of Georgia were women and six were African-Americans. The Governor's chief goals were to appoint the best and brightest members of the legal community to fill vacancies on the state's Judiciary, but also to ensure that the attorneys selected reflect the diversity of the citizenry of this state as a whole. In keeping with that pledge, Governor Miller appointed nearly three times more women and African-Americans than all of his predecessors combined during his eight years in office.

Diversifying the selection

A month after taking office, Governor Miller reconstituted the Judicial Nominating Commission, which was charged with screening the pool of applicants for judicial vacancies and providing a "short list" of recommended applicants from which the Governor selected an appointee. By Executive Order dated February 11, 1991, the Governor changed the composition of the Judicial Nominating Commission to require that at all times it included at least one member who was either Black, Hispanic, Asian-Pacific-American, Native American, or Asian-Indian American, and at least one woman. In addition, he opened the judicial selection process by reducing the number of members on the commission affiliated with the State Bar and by granting the Lieutenant Governor and Speaker appointments to the commission.

In swearing in the new members of the commission in 1991, the Governor noted that by mandating the inclusion of women and minorities he wanted to "ensure their participation in the nominating process and to encourage qualified women and minorities to apply, knowing that they will receive due consideration." Governor Miller's efforts were successful, and citizens of Georgia who appeared in courts throughout the state were able to see the diversity of the state's population reflected in the judges who heard their cases.

Appellate courts

Governor Miller's five appointments to the Georgia Supreme Court truly diversified that bench. Of those five justices, two were female and one was African-American. In fact, he appointed the first woman and the first African-American woman to the Supreme Court. By the time he left office, the seven-member Supreme Court had two African-American justices and two female justices, something which was unprecedented in the history of the state's highest appellate court.

Additionally, Governor Miller appointed an African-American to serve on the Georgia Court of Appeals.

Superior courts

Governor Miller has made more appointments to the superior courts of Georgia than to any other courts in this state, and nowhere was the diversity that resulted from his appointments more evident. The superior courts were the most general trial courts where felony cases including death penalty cases were tried, and where all matters relating to divorce, issues respecting the ownership of land, other civil matters, and all actions seeking injunctions were handled.

When Governor Miller began his first term in January, 1991, only four percent of the total superior court judgeships were held by women, and four percent were held by African-Americans. Overlap between these two groups meant that only six percent of the judgeships were not held by white males. During Governor Miller's administration, he appointed 21 women and 15 African-Americans to the superior courts. Overall, 43 percent of Governor Miller's superior court appointments were minority or female.

The change in the Atlanta Judicial Circuit over the course of Governor Miller's administration was a prime example of his pledge to diversify the courts. The Atlanta Judicial Circuit was composed of urban Fulton County and the City of Atlanta. When Governor Miller's term began, there were 11 judges on the Superior Court of Fulton County; two were women and four were African-American. During the course of his administration, this court grew to 17 judges, of which ten were women and six were African-American.

Governor Miller also made the first female or African-American appointments to superior court in many judicial circuits, including: Augusta Circuit (Richmond County); Chattahoochee Circuit (Muscogee County); Eastern Circuit (Chatham County); Gwinnett Circuit (Gwinnett County); Lookout Mountain Circuit (Dade, Walker, and Chattooga Counties), Macon Circuit (Bibb County); Northeastern Circuit (Hall and Dawson Counties); Stone Mountain Circuit (DeKalb County); and Western Circuit (Clarke County).

For the state as a whole, 17 percent of sitting superior court judges were women or minority by the time Miller left office, compared to six percent when he was inaugurated in January, 1991.

State courts

In Georgia, state courts had jurisdiction over trial of criminal misdemeanors and civil actions in which the superior courts did not have exclusive jurisdiction, and over the hearing of applications for the issuance of arrest and search warrants. Of the 86 state court judges on the bench when Governor Miller took office, five were African-Americans and seven were women. During his first six years in office, Governor Miller appointed eight African-Americans and 19 women to the state courts, as many as all of his predecessors combined. Forty-eight percent of Governor Miller's total appointments to the state courts were women or minorities.

As with the superior courts, there were counties in which Governor Miller appointed the first-ever women or minorities as state court judges, including Clayton, Gwinnett, Hall, Lowndes, and Muscogee.

The Miller Record: Total Minority and Female Appointments

Court	**Minority and Female Appointments Total**	**Percentage of Appointments**
Supreme Court	2	40%
Court of Appeals	1	25%
Superior Courts	31	43%
State Court	22	48%
TOTAL	**56**	**44%**

In recognition of his outstanding efforts to diversify and solidify the judiciary of the State of Georgia, Governor Miller was recognized by both the Gate City Bar Association and the State Bar of Georgia for his contributions to the enhancement and diversity of the Georgia judiciary.

Judicial Appointments by Governor Miller:

Supreme Court

Leah Sears	March 6, 1992
Carol W. Hunstein	November 23, 1992
George H. Carley	March 16, 1993
Hugh P. Thompson	March 1, 1994
P. Harris Hines	July 26, 1995

Court of Appeals

Edward H. Johnson	February 28, 1992
J. D. Smith	May 10, 1993
John H. Ruffin, Jr.	August 24, 1994
Frank M. Eldridge	July 16, 1996

Superior Court

Lawton Evans Stephens	Western Judicial Circuit	April 30, 1991
W. Louis Sands	Macon Judicial Circuit	April 30, 1991
Michael E. Hancock	Stone Mountain Judicial Circuit	April 30, 1991
Joe C. Bishop	Pataula Judicial Circuit	May 16, 1991
Linda Warren Hunter	Stone Mountain Judicial Circuit	June 6, 1991
Charles Michael Roach	Blue Ridge Judicial Circuit	July 17, 1991
Fred A. Bishop, Jr.	Gwinnett Judicial Circuit	July 17, 1991
Robert Freeman Mumford	Rockdale Judicial Circuit	September 12, 1991
J. Carlisle Overstreet	Augusta Judicial Circuit	November 1, 1991
Elizabeth E. Long	Atlanta Judicial Circuit	April 20, 1992
William B. Hill, Jr.	Atlanta Judicial Circuit	April 20, 1992
Kristina Cook Connelly	Lookout Mountain Judicial Circuit	April 20, 1992
Hugh Stone	Enotah Judicial Circuit	August 10, 1992
David Barrett	Enotah Judicial Circuit	August 10, 1992
William A. Foster, III	Tallapoosa Judicial Circuit	October 26, 1992
James A. Oxendine	Gwinnett Judicial Circuit	December 21, 1992
Gail C. Flake	Stone Mountain Judicial Circuit	April 13, 1993
C. Andrew Fuller	Northeastern Judicial Circuit	July 29, 1993
Michael Karpf	Eastern Judicial Circuit	August 5, 1993
Gibbs Flanders	Dublin Judicial Circuit	September 27, 1993
E. M. Wilkes	Brunswick Judicial Circuit	September 28, 1993
John D. Allen	Chattahoochee Judicial Circuit	October 27, 1993
Hulane E. George	Ocmulgee Judicial Circuit	May 25, 1994

Harry Jay Altman, II	Southern Judicial Circuit	August 8, 1994
Martha Christian	Macon Judicial Circuit	August 24, 1994
Alice D. Bonner	Atlanta Judicial Circuit	September 16, 1994
Carl C. Brown, Jr.	Augusta Judicial Circuit	December 5, 1994
William Ralph Hill, Jr.	Lookout Mountain Judicial Circuit	February 1, 1995
Penny Haas Freesemann	Eastern Judicial Circuit	May 18, 1995
Gail T. Joyner	Atlanta Judicial Circuit	May 31, 1995
Alford J. Dempsey, Jr.	Atlanta Judicial Circuit	May 31, 1995
Stephanie B. Manis	Atlanta Judicial Circuit	May 31, 1995
Bensonetta Tipton Lane	Atlanta Judicial Circuit	May 31, 1995
Arch Walker McGarity	Flint Judicial Circuit	June 29, 1995
Herbert E. Phipps	Dougherty Judicial Circuit	June 30, 1995
James L. Cline	Ocmulgee Judicial Circuit	July 25, 1995
Johnnie L. Caldwell, Jr.	Griffin Judicial Circuit	July 27, 1995
Tracy Moulton, Jr.	Pataula Judicial Circuit	July 28, 1995
Robert L. Russell, III	Atlantic Judicial Circuit	August 9, 1995
Richard M. Cowart	Southern Judicial Circuit	September 13, 1995
Robert L. Allgood	Augusta Judicial Circuit	September 21, 1995
Bettieanne Hart	Augusta Judicial Circuit	September 21, 1995
Quillian Baldwin	Coweta Judicial Circuit	September 26, 1995
Aubrey Duffey	Coweta Judicial Circuit	September 26, 1995
Douglas C. Pullen	Chattahoochee Judicial Circuit	October 23, 1995
Robert G. Johnston, III	Chattahoochee Judicial Circuit	October 23, 1995
Steve C. Jones	Western Judicial Circuit	November 17, 1995
S. Lark Ingram	Cobb Judicial Circuit	November 21, 1995
Jack Partain	Conasauga Judicial Circuit	November 22, 1995
William E. Woodrum, Jr.	Ogeechee Judicial Circuit	November 27, 1995
Kenneth O. Nix	Cobb Judicial Circuit	November 27, 1995
John Bailey, Jr.	Northern Judicial Circuit	December 15, 1995
Sammy Ozburn	Alcovy Judicial Circuit	December 20, 1995
Phil Brown	Macon Judicial Circuit	December 21, 1995
David Motes	Piedmont Judicial Circuit	December 21, 1995
Wendy Lee Shoob	Atlanta Judicial Circuit	March 4, 1996
Doris L. Downs	Atlanta Judicial Circuit	March 4, 1996
Constance C. Russell	Atlanta Judicial Circuit	March 4, 1996
Horace Frederick Mullis, Jr.	Oconee Judicial Circuit	March 29, 1996
Brenda S. Weaver	Appalachian Judicial Circuit	April 2, 1996
Edward D. Lukemire	Houston Judicial Circuit	September 3, 1996

(elected to take office January 1, 1997; appointed at the request of the chief judge of the circuit to serve the unexpired term of a judge who resigned.)

Ralph L. Van Pelt, Jr.	Lookout Mountain Judicial Circuit	September 20, 1996
Cynthia D. Wright	Atlanta Judicial Circuit	November 1, 1996
Melvin K. Westmoreland	Atlanta Judicial Circuit	September 24, 1997
Kathlene F. Gosselin	Northeastern Judicial Circuit	June 3, 1998
Melodie Snell Connor	Gwinnett Judicial Circuit	July 1, 1998
Hugh Wingfield	Ocmulgee Judicial Circuit	July 7, 1998
Don Howe	Douglas Judicial Circuit	July 8, 1998
Anne Workman	Stone Mountain Judicial Circuit	July 9, 1998
Jack Goger	Atlanta Judicial Circuit	August 5, 1998
Rowland Barnes	Atlanta Judicial Circuit	August 5, 1998
Michael Louis Murphy	Tallapoosa Circuit	December 3, 1998

<u>State Court</u>

S. Lark Ingram	Cobb County	May 16, 1991
Gail C, Flake	DeKalb County	June 6, 1991
John Jaye Ellington	Treutlen County	July 3, 1991
Robert W. Mock, Sr.	Gwinnett County	September 23, 1991
Grady K. Reddick	Screven County	January 9, 1992
Beverly M. Collins	Cobb County	January 9, 1992
Earl M. McRae, Jr.	Coffee County	February 17, 1992
Gail Tusan Joyner	Fulton County	July 6, 1992
Wendy Lee Shoob	Fulton County	July 6, 1992
John E. Morse, Jr.	Chatham County	July 30, 1992
Denise Majette	DeKalb County	June 8, 1992
Nathan Deaton	Jeff Davis County	September 29, 1993
Penny Haas	Chatham County	October 7, 1993
Daniel M. Mitchell, Jr.	Brooks County	October 11, 1993
Dale Jenkins	McIntosh County	October 11, 1993
Melodie Snell Connor	Gwinnett County	October 28, 1993
Andrew Prather, II	Muscogee County	January 21, 1994
H. Scott Allen	Presiding Judge, Civil and Magistrate Court, Richmond County	March 30, 1994
Lester M. Castellow	Colquitt County	July 13, 1994
Cynthia D. Wright	Fulton County	January 4, 1995
Harold Gregory Fowler	Chatham County	May 18, 1995
Ronald E. Ginsberg	Chatham County	May 18, 1995
John J. Goger	Fulton County	May 31, 1995
Thomas H. Baxley	Early County	November 6, 1995

Maureen Gottfried	Muscogee County	November 22, 1995
Robert Sullivan	Carroll County	December 20, 1995
Kelly D. Turner	Lowndes County	December 20, 1995
Linda Cowen	Clayton County	December 20, 1995
Russell Carlisle	Cobb County Division I	December 21, 1995
Irma Glover	Cobb County Division I	December 21, 1995
Toby Prodgers	Cobb County Division II	December 21, 1995
Patsy Y. Porter	Fulton County	March 8, 1996
John R. Mather	Fulton County	March 8, 1996
M. Gino Brogdon	Fulton County	March 8, 1996
Jerry C. Gray	Jackson County	July 15, 1996

(elected to take office January 1, 1997; appointed at the request of the chief judge of the circuit to serve the unexpired term of a judge who resigned.)

Yvette Miller	Fulton County	November 1, 1996
Jeffrey S. Bagley	Forsyth County	January 1, 1997
Barbara J. Nelson	Evans County	July 23, 1997
Richard A. Slaby	Richmond County Division I	July 23, 1997
David D. Watkins	Richmond County Division II	July 23, 1997
Susan Barker Forsling	Fulton County	October 17, 1997
Edward E. Carriere, Jr.	DeKalb County	January 5, 1998
John Herbert Cranford	Coweta County	May 27, 1998
Bonnie Chessher Oliver	Hall County	June 11, 1998
Wayne M. Purdom	DeKalb County	July 9, 1998
Brenda Cole	Fulton County	August 5, 1998
Henry Newkirk	Fulton County	August 5, 1998

District Attorneys

R. Joseph Martin, III	Ogeechee Judicial Circuit	July 16, 1991
Cheryl Fisher Custer	Rockdale Judicial Circuit	September 12, 1991
Peter John Skandalakis	Coweta Judicial Circuit	January 9, 1992
David Turk	Enotah Judicial Circuit	August 10, 1992
George C. Turner, Jr.	Tallapoosa Judicial Circuit	October 26, 1992
Lydia Jackson Sartain	Northeastern Judicial Circuit	September 13, 1993
Charles H. Weston	Macon Judicial Circuit	January 7, 1994
Richard E. Currie	Waycross Judicial Circuit	March 14, 1994
Timothy G. Vaughn	Oconee Judicial Circuit	April 20, 1994
Jim Cline	Ocmulgee Judicial Circuit	August 12, 1994
William T. McBroom	Griffin Judicial Circuit	September 29, 1995
John Gray Conger	Chattachoochee Judicial Circuit	January 17, 1996
Kermit N. McManus	Conasauga Judicial Circuit	February 7, 1996
Darrell Wilson	Enotah Judicial Circuit	January 7, 1998
Ben Smith	Cobb Judicial Circuit	March 3, 1998

Phillip Smith	Bell-Forsyth Judicial Circuit	July 1, 1998

<u>Solicitors</u>

Jerry Rylee	Hall County	March 13, 1991
B. Daniel Dubberly, III	Tattnall County	July 16, 1991
J. William Harvey	Wayne County	February 10, 1992
Hugh T. Hunter	Screven County	February 19, 1992
Maxine Blackwell	Baldwin County	October 26, 1992
Ralph C. Smith, Jr.	Decatur County	January 25, 1993
Kris Knox	Jeff Davis County	October 1, 1993
Adam Poppell	McIntosh County	October 11, 1993
Terry Turner	Appling County	January 10, 1994
Maureen Gottfried	Muscogee County	January 31, 1994
Ray C. Smith	Bryan County	August 15, 1994
Gates Peed	Bulloch County	March 15, 1994
James R. Coppage	McIntosh County	September 16, 1994
Timothy Lee Eidson	Worth County	August 21, 1995
Roger B. Lane, Sr.	McIntosh County	September 11, 1995
Roxann Gray Daniel	Muscogee County	February 16, 1996
Kevin Chason	Grady County	May 10, 1996
C. Deen Strickland	Ware County	May 31, 1995
John Willis Geiger	Houston County	July 12, 1996
Michael D. DeVane	Ware County	July 10, 1996
L. Clark Landrum	Worth County	July 10, 1996
Ben Kirbo	Decatur County	December 16, 1996
Channing Ruskell	Cherokee County	January 2, 1996
Barry Morgan	Cobb County	March 3, 1998
William Terry Turner	Jeff Davis County	March 27, 1998
James Thomas Irvin	Stephens County	July 2, 1998
Robert Stokely	Coweta County	August 14, 1998
Claire Willett	Mitchell County	August 26, 1998
Troy W. March, Jr.	Screven County	September 18, 1998

Merit System of Personnel Administration

When it was established over 50 years ago, we were in need of a professional workforce, free from patronage. But today, the Merit System hamstrings state government by slowing the hiring of essential employees and making it nearly impossible to fire bad employees. I want to create a modern system that makes state government more effective by recognizing and rewarding employee productivity.

Governor Zell Miller, February 1, 1996

When Governor Miller took office, he inherited a state government system of personnel administration that had been created in the 1940s and had seen little change over the ensuing decades. The state was saddled with outdated personnel practices and a byzantine maze of procedures for state agencies to follow, which kept agencies from pursuing innovations and improving their operations to better serve Georgia citizens.

The Governor's challenge was to remold the concept of state personnel administration from an inflexible, procedure driven, centralized bureaucracy dominated by a rigid encyclopedia of rules where seniority rather than performance was rewarded, and strict adherence to procedures, no matter how impractical, was valued over common sense. Governor Miller tackled this challenge on two fronts: pay for performance to reward employees on the caliber of their work instead of how long they had been on the state payroll, and Merit System reform which returned many personnel administration functions to the agencies, allowing them to address their personnel needs on their own timetable rather than the convoluted timetable of the old centralized system. These initiatives readied state government for the 21st century by creating a personnel administration system that equipped agencies with the tools and guidance to make timely and cost-effective decisions about hiring, paying, developing and motivating a high performing workforce.

Pay for performance

Throughout his two terms, Governor Miller strove to instill in state government the principle of "a day's pay for a day's work" or pay for performance, when evaluating and rewarding state employees' work. The outcome of the Governor's efforts was the implementation of the GeorgiaGain pay for performance management system for state government as recommended by the Governor's Commission on Effectiveness and Economy in Government (Williams Commission).

GeorgiaGain was created by a multi-agency taskforce, which the Governor appointed and charged to produce a sensible way of relating an employee's job performance to any salary increase that employee received. It was the first serious examination since the late 1970s of the employee evaluation and compensation process. Under GeorgiaGain, employees became eligible for pay for performance increases based on clearly defined performance standards, which were administered using a uniform system of managing and measuring employee performance. This pay-for-performance approach was the centerpiece of the Governor's strategy to elevate the performance of state employees, and in turn state agencies. It represented his unequivocal declaration to state employees and citizens that accountability and a conscientious work ethic in Georgia government would be the norm and not the exception.

Merit System reform

The Governor, grasping the long term advantage of having state government keep pace with modern business in coping with and competing for a changing workforce, won enactment of the Merit System Reform Act decentralizing the state's personnel functions. This decentralization, which incorporated elements of recommendations from the Williams Commission, allowed agencies more freedom in recruiting and managing personnel to better reflect each agency's own workforce needs and respond more effectively to the evolving labor market. Agencies could handle personnel situations thoughtfully and expediently without the burden of undue bureaucratic delays of weeks or months that had existed under the former centralized system and hindered the operation of state government.

Giving agencies the discretion to assume certain personnel selection, hiring and management duties from the Merit System led to a redefinition of personnel administrative roles and practices between agencies and the Merit System. The Merit System reshaped itself from being the central personnel administration authority for state agencies to being a flexible, sensitive and responsive resource to state agencies for consultation, training and technical support on personnel matters and issues.

The sweeping changes instituted through the Merit System Reform Act embodied Governor Miller's dynamic vision to ensure that state government had the most modern, accountable, effective long-term means of competing for, recruiting and hiring the best people possible to conduct the state's business. He left state government ably prepared to acquire the talents and skills needed as it entered the next millennium.

Department of Revenue

Our taxpayers expect us to be efficient and effective in what we do with their money. They also expect us to be efficient and effective in collecting their money and making sure all taxpayers pay their fair share.

Governor Zell Miller, January 16, 1997

The Department of Revenue's primary responsibility was to administer the state's tax laws. The department not only collected over $10 billion in tax revenues each year to keep state government running, but was also the state's most regular and direct point of contact with all of its citizens, businesses and local governments. These responsibilities made the Department of Revenue one of the state's most important agencies. Despite criticism, Governor Miller, a consistent champion of effectiveness and efficiency in government, did not shy away or back down from controversial decisions that were needed to overhaul and improve the department.

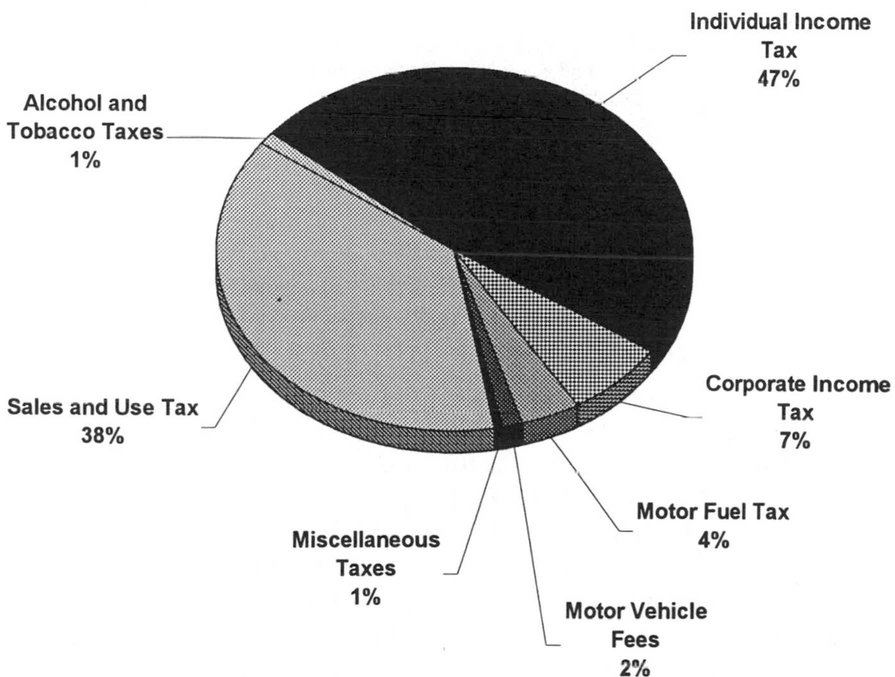

Upon taking office, Governor Miller took action rapidly to remedy problems resulting from the fact that most of the department's principal computer systems, dating back to the early 1970s, were mainframe systems designed to process limited specific objectives. The systems were flawed by their inability to expand and function beyond the original objectives. This situation was compounded by the practice of patching new, ill-documented, piecemeal measures onto the existing systems. These patchwork measures were originally intended to be temporary solutions to the mainframe systems' flaws, but instead were left in place as poor long-term answers to the systems' shortcomings. The result was feeble systems teetering on the brink of a massive failure, an accident waiting to happen. Governor Miller understood the significance of a system failure and consistently appropriated improvement funding to stabilize and upgrade system technology.

Fiscal Year	*Amount*	*Project Purpose*
1991	1,400,000	Continued development of Centralized Taxpayer Accounting
1991	700,000	Provide for entry to International Registration Plan
1992	1,000,000	CTA continued development
1993	3,693,812	Completion of CTA
1994	2,500,000	In-house development of GA Revenue Integrated Tax System
1994	170,000	Development of county online access to motor vehicle system
1995	1,000,000	Develop statewide integrated tag & title system
1995	850,000	Operating costs of county access to online MV system
1996	2,000,000	Continued development of statewide integrated tag & title system
1997	1,238,718	Implement imagining in tax processing areas
1997	578,000	Fund automatic collection systems at regional offices
1997	55,825	Automated cashiering for IRP
Total	$15,186,355	

These technology appropriations laid a firm foundation to prepare the department for the Governor's most ambitious plan. In August of 1996, Governor Miller created a steering committee of top government officials and high caliber business executives to develop a "Blueprint for Modernization" for the department. The committee was charged with designing long-term, comprehensive solutions for the future. Though anchored by Miller's leadership, the steering committee realized it would need exceptional professional management consultants. The committee hired KPMG Peat Marwick LLP, which spent four months investigating the department's structure, policies, procedures and systems; identifying opportunities for improvement; and developing the bold recommendations outlined in the "Blueprint for Modernization." The plan provided useful information for decision-makers to improve productivity and refine customer service.

KPMG proposed specific, targeted solutions with cost estimates and an implementation schedule that was spread over a five year period, 1997-2002. KPMG's proposed modernization plans were hailed as an investment that would pay for itself. The cost to the state was estimated to be $113.5 million over the five-year period, but KPMG reported that this investment would generate tens of millions of dollars in savings each and every year, thus making the investment one that Georgia could not pass by. An estimated total investment of $113.5 million over five years (1997-2002), was projected to realize revenue enhancements and cost-savings efficiencies totaling $210.1 million over the same time. The benefits to the state were projected to total more than the $96.6 million in cost savings and additional revenue collections.

Fiscal Year	Revenues	Expenditures	Savings
Amended 97 & 98	$23.8	$28.29	($4.5)
1999	$47.9	$32.6	$15.3
2000	$38.1	$29.3	$8.8
2001	$50.0	$12.9	$37.1
2002	$50.3	$10.4	$39.9
Total	$210.1	$113.5	$96.6

All dollar figures are in millions

Governor Miller immediately embraced the plan of action, funding the first phase of the project in the FY 1997 amended budget and having the needed legislation introduced in the 1997 legislative session. Funding continued in the FY 1998 and FY 1999 budgets.

Fiscal Year	Resources Committed
Fiscal Year 1997 Amended	$14,454,832
Fiscal Year 1998	$4,902,668
Fiscal Year 1998 Amended	$6,978,622
Fiscal Year 1999	$4,902,668
Total	$31,238,790

The KPMG program had strong support from Governor Miller during its first one and a half years. Completed, this reform program would become a legacy of the forward thinking and acting Miller Administration.

VIII. In Other's Words

"He has given citizens identifiable benefits....Miller's positive projects have touched nearly every family in the state." Bill Shipp, *Athens Daily News/Banner-Herald*, July 1, 1998

"Zell Miller is the toughest, most stubborn and just maybe, the best governor of my lifetime." Lee Walburn, Atlanta, October 1997

"...Miller has seen to it that the people's issue is his issue....Surely, this man has got to be one of Georgia's most effective leaders....Georgia's government is leaner, meaner, more privatized, professional and inclusive because of Miller's leadership. 'Redirection' of 4 percent of each department's budget toward items of top priority has produced a leaner government. Several straight years of teacher pay raises have lifted Georgia to one of the highest in terms of starting pay. And, of course, we're the only state in the union where 'B' students can go to college tuition-free. Lots of families are moving to Georgia for that reason alone. Who to thank? The man with the mountain twang." Jeff Dickerson, *The Atlanta Journal*, January 13, 1998

"...[Miller] is finishing his final term as one of our greatest governors. He loves Georgia, knows Georgia and has a vision of what he wants to do as its leader." Jim Minter, *The Atlanta Journal*, April 29, 1998

"Gov. Zell Miller has become such a master politician over the past 30 years, it seems wasteful to put his talent into retirement." Jim Wood, *Clayton Daily News*, January 23, 1998

"As governor of the '90s, Miller has presided over an era of unprecedented economic and political change in Georgia....So completely does Miller rule the political roost that it's hard to find a Democrat or Republican who'll criticize the governor....[President] Clinton has described Miller as a 'brilliant, brilliant governor.'" *The Atlanta Journal-Constitution*, January 11, 1998

"'...he has had many achievements and I think he has done some great things for the state of Georgia,' said Rep. Don Parsons, R-east Cobb.... 'no state in the nation is more pro-business, pro-education and pro-tax reduction than Georgia,' [Rep. Randy] Sauder said." *Marietta Daily Journal*, January 16, 1998

"Miller's legacy in most ways is clear: ...history will place him among Georgia's revered elite." *Columbus Ledger-Enquirer*, December 30, 1997

"As for Governor Miller, quite simply, he leaves the strongest treasury, the toughest and best prison system, a rapidly improving education system, a pre-kindergarten, the HOPE scholarships and achievements that will be very, very hard to duplicate....He has been courageous, firm, and right more than wrong." Mike Steed, *The Tallapoosa Journal*, January 19, 1998

"When Zell Miller was lieutenant governor, he wrote a book called "Great Georgians." Of course he did not include himself. If he expanded the book after his eight year tenure as governor, he still probably would not include himself. But most historians, political observers and the average Georgian would. Zell Miller has left a great legacy. He is still not finished....He is truly the state's education governor. The Young Harris mountain boy was an educator before he entered politics. Even in politics, Miller has continued his skills as an educator, explaining his vision to the people of Georgia and leading them in the right directions. Miller is a true leader. He gets things done because he has the backing of the people....Miller will be remembered for his deeds and will rightly gain a place as a great Georgian." *The Albany Herald*, February 4, 1998

"Zell Miller is a mountain man with a mountain man's twangy voice. He is an educator. He is an author. He is a leader. His second term as governor will earn him recognition as the best chief executive in Georgia's proud history. From one old Marine to another, Governor, you've stood tall. I respect you and I salute you. No doubt, I will even miss you." Charles Lockwood, *The Douglas Enterprise*, January 21, 1998

"Miller is almost revered for his service to the state....Miller's poll numbers remain high because he has given us something of value in return for our tax dollars. He has improved our lives. He has given us better schools and at least a slim chance of becoming lottery millionaires. He also has been a governor who has often made us proud and never embarrassed us." Bill Shipp, *Bill Shipp's Georgia*

"We, too, applaud Zell Miller for his service to the citizens of this state. While we have not always agreed with him on all matters, he has been a strong leader responsible for many programs which enrichen our lives. Zell Miller is a man of character, something that becomes more rare each day, especially in government. We thank him, and we will miss him. His shoes will be difficult to fill." *Americus Times*, January 16, 1998

"Gov. Zell Miller deserves a standing ovation from the citizens of the great state of Georgia.... Under leadership of men such as Zell Miller we, and our young, have opportunities unparalleled in this land or world." Jerry Smith, *Calhoun Times*, April 25, 1998

"...Miller kept his promises. And Georgia, during his time in office, has flourished beyond most of our dreams." Bill Shipp, *Athens Daily News/Banner-Herald*, July 15, 1998

"[Miller] restored optimism to state government. He showed that 'politician' could be on the list of honorable professions. Miller gave us a lottery, HOPE scholarships, day-care centers, computers for our kids and a stack of significant tax cuts." Bill Shipp, *Athens Daily News/ Banner-Herald*, July 22, 1998

"...look at the man's style, his character, his bent for leadership. He's a genuine leader....Miller is focused, and that has served him well. He chooses large themes (the lottery, education). He has discipline....He has been loyal to others, and others have stayed loyal to him. He isn't a policy wonk. He has guts. He doesn't think politics is the art of splitting the difference....I think Miller himself is one of the best and strongest personalities in today's parade." *The Atlanta Journal- Constitution*, August 2, 1998

"Miller...will leave behind him a very real legacy of accomplishments that have changed this state forever. He will be remembered, probably, as one of the best governors, especially of the modern age." *Athens Banner-Herald/Daily News*, January 18, 1998

"Republican pollster Whit Ayres... said, "Zell Miller is one of the very few politicians I've ever polled who polls as well with Republicans as he does with Democrats. He wants to be the governor for all the people, not just Democrats. He has done things many Republicans admire."

The Washington Post, October 16, 1998

"...in [Miller's] political stance is some common sense that other Democrats would do well to imitate." Lars-Erik Nelson, *The Charlotte Observer*, April 18, 1995

Efficient and Effective Government

Georgia Rebound

"To say that Governor Miller's 1992 legislative program, which he calls 'Georgia Rebound,' is ambitious—given the economy—is an understatement.

'Futuristic' might be a more accurate description." Billy Winn, *Columbus Ledger-Enquirer*, January 12, 1992

"Miller has touched on a source of revenue that could help support a staggering state economy on a continuing basis." Jeffrey L. Barnes, *Daily Sun* (Warner Robins), January 8, 1992

"We are glad the governor is looking to someone other than the property owner for more revenue....someone should have been doing this before now." *Ludowici News*, January 9, 1992

"The plan is innovative and bold....He has laid everything on the table for all Georgians to see and determine for themselves the worth of it." Max Lockwood, *Douglas Enterprise*, January 22, 1992

"'Georgia Rebound' seems to be a well-thought out plan to get our state moving once again." *Elberton Star*, January 15, 1992

"Governor Zell Miller's 'Georgia Rebound' program shows traces of excellence reflecting a long political career, and an experienced genius which has marked his life through thick and thin economic times." Jim Wood, *Clayton News Daily*, January 16, 1992

"'Georgia Rebound' ambitiously sets out to 'build Georgia's future' with a businesslike approach." *Cuthbert Times*, January 16, 1992

"...he has set the Starship Miller on Warp 4 and aimed it where no man has dared go before." David Nordan, *Daily News*, January 19, 1992

"His proposals show a far-sighted attitude that has not often been associated with Georgia state government....The proposals as outlined by Gov. Miller show a determination to improve Georgia in every significant way....it is obvious Zell Miller is thinking about the future of this state in the way a good governor must." *The Athens Observer*, January 9, 1992

"Many of Gov. Miller's proposals for 'Rebound Georgia' are progressive and long overdue." *The Daily Tribune News* (Cartersville), January 22, 1992

"...Gov. Zell Miller sees a parting of blue at the end of the economic horizon....With new revenue from higher user fees, and new construction pumping money and jobs into our economy, this package could help weather a recession. It might even help part the clouds." *The Atlanta Journal,* January 9, 1992

Tax cuts

"House Majority Leader Larry Walker, D-Perry, said Georgia's record of tax cuts over the past four years is unmatched nationally." *Athens Daily News,* January 29, 1998

Privatization

"Privatization gained momentum in Georgia because the governor, through his bipartisan commission, gave it emphasis." *The Atlanta Journal,* September 15, 1997

"While many government entities look to privatization as a way to increase efficiency and reduce costs, few have employed the approach as extensively as the state of Georgia. Last year, privatization activities saved Georgia millions of dollars, with long-term savings expected to approach $2 billion. Elected officials from both parties credit this accomplishment to the leadership of two-term governor, Zell Miller." *Solutions,* Spring 1998

"At precisely one minute after midnight, May 16, the state-run Lake Lanier Islands resort passed from public into private hands. Georgia will be better for it....when it comes to running hotels, bars and golf courses, the private sector can do a better job than government, saving taxpayers millions." *The Atlanta Journal-Constitution,* May 31, 1996

"Early indications are that the deal recently struck with U.S. Corrections Corp. is genuine privatization, and, for Georgia, unprecedented....That's a good deal for taxpayers." *The Atlanta Journal,* April 24, 1997

"Privatization is a win-win deal for the state. Fewer employees are on the public payroll, long-term costs are shifted off taxpayers and the state gets out of the business of directly competing with private industry." *The Atlanta Journal,* June 23, 1997

Education

"Georgia is on an upward swing of educational enhancement that ought to endure through the next century." Bill Shipp, *Bill Shipp's Georgia*

"[Miller] has proven himself to be Georgia's public education savior. He's funneled many funds into innovative school programs and lobbied hard to give Georgia teachers a livable salary....Governor Miller will be hard to replace. He's been Georgia's prime educator and we're in a better-educated state because of him. Thanks, Governor Miller!" Sandra Connell, *The Valdosta Daily Times*, January 25, 1998

"The governor focuses attention upon education and talks very specifically about what needs to be done. He defines who the people are who can make the proposals work and he spells out very clearly how the program is to be financed. This is a refreshing approach." Max Lockwood, *Douglas Enterprise*, January 22, 1992

"During his tenure as governor, Miller has fought vigorously to expand educational opportunities for Georgia students and to improve the status of the teaching profession." *The Associated Press*, July 6, 1998

"Governor Miller, with the HOPE Scholarship, with the pre-kindergarten program, with the commitment to hook up all your schools to the Internet, with all the other initiatives, has turned the lights on, and America is seeing the light." President Bill Clinton, February 5, 1997, WSB-TV Channel 2 Action News, *WAGA-TV Fox 5 Eyewitness News, WXIA-TV 11 News*

("Governor Miller, with the HOPE Scholarship...has turned the lights on, and America is seeing the light." President Bill Clinton, February 5, 1997, NBC Nightly News)

"Miller's support for the state's schools through his forceful push for sustained teacher pay hikes, lottery funding for pre-kindergarten programs, new technology, HOPE scholarships and other initiatives, have justly earned him the title of education governor." *Athens Daily News/Banner- Herald*, July 30, 1998

Prekindergarten

"Georgia's pre-kindergarten program recently won the prestigious, Innovations in American Government Award, an award funded by the Ford Foundation and administered by the John F. Kennedy School of Government at Harvard University." *Dawson County Advertiser & News*, November 13, 1997

"A recent study, comparing children who participated in one of Georgia's pre-kindergarten programs with those who did not showed the following: pre-k students scored more than three months higher than their peers on general academic skills as measured by the Developmental Profile II, a widely used standardized test; pre-k students scored higher than the national average on the Iowa Test of Basic Skills; and pre-k children had better attendance in school." *Forsyth County News*, October 17, 1997, et al.

"'To me one of the great strengths about this program is that it is family oriented,' said Dr. Sheila Hutchinson, who administers the [pre-k] program for the Camden County School System." *Tribune & Georgian*, October 17, 1997

"'In contrast to national studies, Georgia pre-k appears to be of consistently high quality,' said [Gary] Henry, [director of the Georgia State University-based Applied Research Center]." *The Atlanta Journal-Constitution*, November 17, 1997

"The words 'innovative' and 'Georgia' aren't usually found in the same sentence, but the state's acclaimed pre-kindergarten program is changing that. An independent evaluation of the 211 public and private pre-k classes across the state shows strong parent and teacher satisfaction with Gov. Zell Miller's groundbreaking program. Even more important, the field observations documented a consistently high quality of teaching....The pre-k program is often described as Miller's 'pet project.' But it may well end up being called his legacy." *The Atlanta Journal- Constitution*, November 20, 1997

"'I'm very satisfied with the [pre-k] program and, as an advocate for early childhood education, I can say it's one of the best they've offered,' [said pre-k teacher Debra Bostic]. 'This is the most critical period in a child's development. This sets the foundation for getting them ready for school.'" *Columbus Ledger-Enquirer*, November 18, 1997

"It's estimated that for every dollar spent now, preschool programs like Georgia's return more than seven dollars to society in the long term by reducing the amount spent on things like social programs, criminal justice and welfare." *CNN Parenting Today*, January 18, 1997

"Georgia's pre-kindergarten program, heralded as the most comprehensive in the nation, reaches a higher proportion of 4 year olds than in any other state." *Paulding Neighbor*, April 16, 1998

"After only four years, benefits of the prekindergarten program are evident. Teachers' ratings of children's skills in academic, social, communication, self-help and physical areas indicate that children who have had pre-kindergarten perform better in kindergarten than children who have not. Studies also indicate that children who participate in pre-kindergarten programs are more likely to attend school regularly and are less likely to drop out later in life." *The Harbor Sound*, June 17, 1997

"It's open enrollment time again for pre-kindergarten, an area where Georgia leads the nation. It's the only state with universal pre-k for 4-year-olds....Georgia's pre-k program is a matter of deserved pride." *The Atlanta Journal*, April 16, 1997

"Parents have toted lawn chairs and camped out before dawn at some child-care centers in metro Atlanta to be assured of a space in the [pre-k] program." *Atlanta Journal-Constitution*, April 10, 1997

"Prekindergarten is not just day care. The teachers must follow an actual curriculum, helping students become familiar with letters, numbers and the basic building blocks of their future, formal education." *The Daily Citizen-News*, April 18, 1997

"Child-care owners from around the country are lauding Georgia's lottery-funded pre-kindergarten program as a model of public-private initiative..." *The Atlanta Journal-Constitution*, March 9, 1996

"In the three years of the Georgia lottery, there are already dramatic results from children who have finished pre-kindergarten." *NBC Nightly News*, January 8, 1997

"...the pre-k graduates already are soaring past classmates who did not attend pre-k....What's even more encouraging to educators is that the pre-k graduates who are now excelling in elementary school were considered at-risk when they entered pre-k. They started farther back and leapfrogged past everyone else." *WXIA-TV 11 News*, August 16, 1997

"The preschool program, open to all four-year-olds, regardless of their families' income, is Governor Zell Miller's solution....Georgia's prekindergarten solution is starting to pay off. Recent studies show that these children have a better chance of succeeding even by the time they reach first grade. They scored above the national average on the Iowa Test of Basic Skills and significantly better in math, problem solving and reading comprehension....By paying for school a full year before kindergarten, Georgia's lottery has made winners out of parents,...taxpayers... and, most of all, children." *ABC World News Tonight*, October 15, 1996

"The state lottery in Georgia is paying off, and you don't even have to have a winning ticket.... the real windfall goes to children attending a new prekindergarten program in public schools....an impressive program to give youngsters a head start." *CNN Parenting Today*, January 18, 1997

HOPE

"...HOPE may motivate some students to strive for a college education that they could not normally afford. The program will help many more college-bound students attend the school of their choice..." *The Red and Black*, July 15, 1993

"A five point grant program to help outstanding pupils educationally (HOPE) will give Georgia families the opportunities they will need to succeed. The HOPE program enables every qualified graduate of a Georgia High School to receive a grant equal to the amount of freshman tuition at any Georgia public college or university." *Quitman Free Press*, June 23, 1993

"Ask almost any Georgian—particularly those with high school- or college-age children—and he or she will tell you that the jewel in Gov. Zell Miller's education crown is the HOPE scholarship program. So successful is this program that it has achieved national recognition, including a presidential proposal of the same name. With ringing endorsements from parents, teachers, students and elected officials, HOPE has achieved virtually universal approval in Georgia and has helped Gov. Miller achieve off-the-charts ratings in public opinion polls." *Bill Shipp's Georgia*, 1997

"...black enrollment at the state's institutions of higher learning has more than doubled in the past 10 years. The reason for the increase can be credited, in large part, to Gov. Zell Miller's innovative education initiatives, especially the HOPE scholarship program." *The Valdosta Daily Times*, September 5, 1997

"The governor's HOPE program has heightened the drive for education among Georgia's students, regardless of race....As Georgia's young people, many of whom are first-generation high school graduates, realize that the promise of prosperity is only a matter of maintaining a 'B' average, all of Georgia will become a symbol of the 'New South' and Miller's mark on this state will be indelible." *The Valdosta Daily Times*, September 5, 1997

"..it is the human stories behind the numbers that are most revealing about the impact of the HOPE program, brainchild of Georgia Gov. Zell Miller. Many Georgians who otherwise could not have afforded it have been able to go to college through HOPE scholarships. Some of these students are the first members of their families to go to college. Others are able to pursue dreams—becoming a physician, going to graduate school—that would once have strapped their families or piled up thousands of dollars in debt....The opportunity is there no matter what the socio-economic status of the individual. By any other name, that's a revolution." *Columbus Ledger-Enquirer*, September 30, 1997

"State officials say HOPE has given them a way, finally, to keep their best students from heading off to Virginia or Chapel Hill for college. Many public colleges in Georgia are admitting more students with good grades ands test scores. HOPE is also credited with helping to increase the number of black students on public campuses, which has doubled—to about 44,000—over the past decade....Above all, many observers believe, the principle beneficiary of HOPE has been the University of Georgia. Few state institutions have become so much more competitive so quickly....Almost all in-state freshmen have received a HOPE scholarship in recent years; they have made up 85 to 90 per cent of each year's entering class." *The Chronicle of Higher Education*, November 7, 1997

"The university said the HOPE scholarship has made the university much more attractive to achievement-oriented students who would otherwise have gone to Virginia, North Carolina, Duke, or Vanderbilt." *The Atlanta Journal-Constitution*, November 8, 1997

"Zell Miller campaigned for the governorship of Georgia, partly on a platform of passing a lottery law. He promised the voters he would use the profits from the lottery to educate (in the state's University System) the brightest and best of Georgia's high school graduates. And he did exactly what he promised. How about that?" William Penn Fallin, *Coffee County News*, June 20, 1997

"Georgia's HOPE scholarship, created four years ago to jump-start the state's education system, is having another, less-expected effect: It is shifting where people live in the Southeast. In a string of communities around the state's borders, families are moving into Georgia from neighboring states so their kids can get access to the 100 percent tuition grants, available to all students attending state colleges who maintain a 'B' average and aren't already receiving federal financial aid." *The Wall Street Journal*, July 30, 1997

"The phones at the HOPE office are ringing off the hook with inquiries from other states wanting to tap into this idea. It's an investment that stands to pay off in an increasingly skilled work force....As the Georgia plan is showing, offering free college tuition has a domino effect on grade school performance. The average grade point average and Scholastic Assessment Tests scores of freshmen entering Georgia's public university system have gone up. While HOPE is still too new to credit for long-term improvement, it seems logical that collegebound students would strive diligently for good grades if there was a free education at stake. And parents might take an even stronger interest in their child's studies." *The Hartford Courant*, January 30, 1998

"...Georgia's HOPE Scholarship program is running amazingly well....now, four years later, HOPE is credited with keeping many of Georgia's best and brightest students from going out of state." *Morning Edition*, NPR, February 5, 1997

"[HOPE] may be the only program in the country that pays full tuition for state residents going to state schools." *USA Today*, July 29, 1996

"Gov. Zell Miller's lottery-funded HOPE college scholarships are the crowning achievement not just of his education policy, but probably of his entire eight-year administration. HOPE has been cited as a model for educational progress in other states, and President Clinton has suggested adopting some version of it on a national level." *Columbus Ledger-Enquirer*, April 14, 1998

"'HOPE is one of the most successful education initiatives in Georgia history and has raised academic achievement standards throughout the state.'" GSFC executive director Glenn Newsome, qtd. in *Swainsboro Blade*, February 25, 1998

"More important is what lottery-funded HOPE is doing for Peach State students. It really does create hope by opening college doors each year to thousands of youngsters who otherwise would have them shut in their face....The governor, the University System Board of Regents and everyone else down the line associated with it get high grades for the work they're doing. Indeed, HOPE goes a long way toward giving Miller what he most covets—a legacy as the 'education governor.'" *The Augusta Chronicle*, January 10, 1998

"A study conducted by the Council for School Performance concludes the HOPE Scholarship has boosted academic expectations of college freshmen in Georgia. Borderline students stay in college longer, earn more credit hours and have slightly higher grades than students not receiving HOPE Scholarships." *The Harbor Sound*, June 17, 1997

"From that campaign plan came HOPE. In a state that measured its schools by its football teams, putting a premium on higher education was a breakthrough. It has set Georgia apart from its neighbors and its history as 26 states have come here to study the scholarship program." *Columbus Ledger-Enquirer*, June 8, 1997

"Georgia's best students are passing up some of the nation's most prestigious universities to take the money and go to school in Georgia." *The (Gainesville) Times*, May 5, 1997

"The HOPE Scholarship has given, and will continue to give, thousands of Georgia students the financial encouragement both to attend college and to persist and gain a degree. Students in Georgia know that if they work hard and do well academically, despite the rising cost of higher education, they will be provided the resources needed to further their education. Not only does the HOPE Scholarship reward those students who are willing to work hard with tuition money, but it also serves as incentive to keep Georgia's best and brightest in the great state of Georgia.... The Georgia HOPE Scholarship has been an overwhelming success and Georgians have been very fortunate to have reaped such a wealth of benefits from this innovative program." Senator Max Cleland, *Congressional Record*, May 8, 1997

"The most far-reaching state scholarship project in the nation, HOPE is funded entirely by lottery revenue." *Los Angeles Times*, April 5, 1994

"It's the kind of thing you look at half in amazement and half in anger, and wonder why your own bonehead state didn't think of it. Not only does it solve the college-expense problem for a lot of people, middle-class on down, but it gives students another reason to pay attention in school." Steve Lopez, *Philadelphia Inquirer*, June 9, 1996

"For a free ride, you better be on that midnight train to Georgia." *The Oregonian*, August 13, 1996

"Georgia's tuition (HOPE) Scholarship program, in its fourth year of funding with state lottery proceeds, has become the envy of states where lottery money has had a smaller impact on education." *The Dallas Morning News*, December 3, 1996

"In Georgia, the scholarship program Zell Miller proudly calls his 'baby' has been a dramatic success." *Newsweek*, February 3, 1997

"[In Georgia,] a special state lottery was set up to pay for the HOPE Scholarships for all state students, not only as an incentive to low-income residents, but to forestall the exodus of bright students overall." *The Washington Times*, November 22, 1996

"Another big prize coming out of the Georgia lottery is on college campuses. Two hundred thousand students, who must maintain a B average, have been on what are called Hope Scholarships. Many are the first in their families to go to college....The Hope scholarships have also changed attitudes in Georgia grade schools. With hard work college is attainable." *NBC Nightly News*, January 8, 1997

"State economic development officials say it's [HOPE] rapidly becoming a powerful incentive for businesses to locate in Georgia—a kind of compound interest on the state's highly popular experiment in funding public education." PBS, *The News Hour*, December 31, 1996

"The [HOPE] program has raised standards and aspirations and proven that educators, parents and students can win the lottery." *ABC World News Tonight*, June 4, 1996

Education technology

"Lottery money by the bucketful—$526 million—has been poured into technology to computerize the state's secondary school classrooms and to teach teachers how to use the technology. It also paid for an Internet-based program called 'Galileo,' which connects all the state's college libraries so students on any campus can tap the entire system's resources." *Marietta Daily Journal*, May 24, 1998

"Distance learning makes use of the latest technology to bring different classroom sites together for instruction. Classes at each site can communicate with each other, allowing students in one location to take advantage of classes in another without having to travel to the campus where it originates." *Valdosta Daily Times*, September 18, 1993

'...the satellite dish behind the school makes it possible for rural students to get the same educational opportunities as those in the big city." *The Macon Telegraph*, May 18, 1993

"...this 'telemedicine' system...will make specialized, state-of-the-art medical care as close as the telephone for health care facilities in rural Georgia." *The McDuffie Progress*, April 19, 1992

Lottery

"'Georgia is such an outstanding example of how successful a lottery can be,' said David Gale, executive director of the Cleveland, Ohio-based North American Association of State and Provincial Lotteries. 'I think a lot has to do with the types of programs Georgia lottery dollars support. The college scholarships, the preschool, are very important in today's society.'" *Savannah Morning News*, June 28, 1998

"If states wish to use lottery proceeds for education, then they should follow Georgia's example....Georgia's lottery is the only one that earmarks all proceeds for specific educational programs, such as the HOPE scholarship." Patrick Pierce and Don Miller, *The Washington Times*, December 27, 1997

"Of more than 30 states with a lottery, only Georgia and Texas have been able to beat the odds and increase sales each year." *Savannah Morning News*, June 28, 1997

"Now, Georgia's lottery for education is a model for other states to follow and Governor Miller has stuck by his guns and insisted that lottery monies be used only for educational purposes." *Barnesville Herald-Gazette*, June 24, 1997

"Because of its education funding and steady sales growth, the Georgia lottery is widely regarded as one of the nation's best." *The Atlanta Journal-Constitution*, July 13, 1997

"Measured by virtually any standard, Georgia's gamble on a lottery has paid off in a jackpot for new ventures in education....As the lottery marks its fifth anniversary on Monday, it sets another national record as the only lottery to record consecutive years of sales growth during its first five years....there's hardly a Georgian alive who doesn't know someone who has benefited from the HOPE scholarship, the pre-kindergarten program for 4-year-olds, or from special capital outlay projects..." *Columbus Ledger-Enquirer*, June 28, 1998

"What if a state seemed to promise lottery funds to education—and then stuck to it?...Georgia's over-and-above education spending seems to be catching on. Florida has a Georgialike proposal pending....Louisiana called this week for information. Zimbabwe is visiting." *The Richmond Times Dispatch*, February 21, 1997

"No where in this country is the lottery working as well as it is here in Georgia, where they have set the standard for the use of lottery profits. By earmarking those profits exclusively to enhance education, they are helping families from preschool all the way through college....Georgia is showing the way, earmarking the lottery money to enhance education, believing money spent now on its children is a wise investment." *NBC Nightly News*, January 8, 1997

"Is it possible for a state to create a lottery law that does guarantee extra money to a favored cause? Apparently, yes. Georgia seems to have done it. All the funds from the Georgia lottery are earmarked not just for education but for specific education programs that didn't exist before the lottery started up. The proceeds pay for three things—college scholarships, pre-kindergarten classes and technology for classrooms. It is illegal to use it for anything else." *Governing*, January 1998

"Georgia's discipline in dedicating lottery proceeds to programs like HOPE and pre-kindergarten has set this lottery apart from lotteries in other states. Lottery President Rebecca Paul agreed. 'If in 100 years someone tried to do a case study on state lotteries in the second half of the 20th century, Georgia would be that case study of how to do it right.'" *The Atlanta Journal-Constitution*, June 28, 1998

"When it comes to raising money for education, only Georgia's lottery has been widely regarded as a winner." *The Chronicle of Higher Education*, September 13, 1996

"Even those of us who were skeptical about the effectiveness, integrity and morality of a lottery as a means of funding schools are forced to concede that thus far, the state appears to be keeping faith with the voters and taxpayers who put education at the top of their priority list." *Columbus Ledger-Enquirer*, December 23, 1997

"...several politicians have been wrapping themselves in lotto colors, hoping to become known as the new champions of the Mother of All Good Causes. News Flash for them: Zell Miller won the title some time ago and has kept it so long the Lottery Hall of Fame (is there one?) Plans to retire his number." Don Farmer, *Bill Shipp's Georgia*

"The governor is right in his praiseworthy comments about the lottery. The promise has been kept. Education money has not been supplanted by lottery dollars. Lottery dollars have been added on top of the education spending in the state budget. And lottery dollars have been specifically earmarked for worthwhile programs—like HOPE scholarships, pre-kindergarten, technology and growth construction. The White House and others are drooling over our HOPE scholarship program. Thus, at the four year mark it seems the governor has birthed and nurtured a state lottery that is working." *Statesboro Herald*, June 7, 1997

"Unlike too many other states (such as Florida and California), Georgia's lottery proceeds are in addition to state tax funding for education; indeed, the lottery is icing on the cake and is responsible for putting Georgia in the front ranks of leaders in increased spending on its schools." *The (Gainesville) Times*, May 29, 1997

"Another factor that has helped sales climb is that the law that created the lottery allowed officials to run the game like a business instead of a governmental entity. That gives the lottery staff the ability to respond quickly to the demands of the market..." Associated Press, *South Georgia Sunday*, June 29, 1997

"If you've ever spent a dollar on a Georgia Lottery ticket, you probably didn't know you were educating a deserving young person. But because of a program developed by Gov. Zell Miller, America's 'Education Governor,' you're contributing to the higher education of Georgia's high school students." *Lotto World*, August 1996

Raising Teacher Salaries

"[Miller's] pledge to bring Georgia's teachers' salaries in line with the national average—by asking legislators for four 6 percent raises—is another example of his uncompromising approach." *Education Week*, May 14, 1997

Higher Education

"With professor Zell Miller running state government, the state's university system has been in fat city since 1991....Mr. Miller, who taught history and political science at three colleges earlier in his career, saw to it that faculty members were better paid, new buildings were built, classrooms bristled with new technology and high achievers could go to college for free.... 'We're not going to appreciate how good until he's gone,' said Hugh Hudson, a Georgia State University professor who is executive secretary of the American Association of University Professors in Georgia. 'I think Governor Miller has been perhaps the best governor in the entire country, perhaps in the entire century, for higher education.'" *The Augusta Chronicle*, October 5, 1997; *Savannah Morning News*, October 5, 1997

"Georgia gives high school graduates more than twice as much academic-based financial aid than any other state, a new national study has found." *The Atlanta Constitution*, April 30, 1998

"...few if any governors have done more for the University of Georgia, the University System and education in general than the state's current chief executive, Zell Miller." *Athens Daily News/Banner-Herald*, July 30, 1998

Human Services

Classical CDS for newborns

"What parent could possibly be opposed to bringing a child into the world of Mozzart [*sic*]? This is an idea John F. Kennedy would have suggested. Already secure as 'the education governor,' Miller can now ride off into the sunset as 'the arts governor.'" Charles Lockwood, *The Douglas Enterprise*, January 21, 1998

"A Mozart sonata might become the unofficial lullaby of Georgia babies. The response to Gov. Zell Miller's proposal to help stimulate a baby's brain development by introducing infants to classical music hit a high note...." *The Atlanta Journal-Constitution*, January 15, 1998

"For soothing fussy infants, 'Rocka-A-Bye Baby' is a parental favorite. But Gov. Zell Miller would rather they use Bach." *Los Angeles Times*, January 22, 1998

"The governor deserves praise for recognizing that concentrating on children when they are young makes more sense than spending money to incarcerate them as adults....If Gov. Miller's music proposal makes a difference for even some children it will be money well spent." *Waycross Journal Herald*, January 14, 1998

"Researchers say there is something inherently soothing about a concerto. Perhaps most importantly, kids who study the timeless beauty of the classics come to appreciate things that are bigger than us all....I, for one, say bravo maestro Miller." Clay Lambert, *The Times (Gainesville)*, January 17, 1998

"...research shows that classical music not only soothes infants and toddlers, but it also stimulates early brain development....[University of California-Irvine physicist Gordon] Shaw's group of Mozart-influenced preschoolers were more advanced in their ability to work mazes, draw geometric figures and copy patterns of two-color blocks than their counterparts....Playing classical music to babies from birth to age 3 is so important, researchers say, because brain development—which governs everything from emotional reaction to musical talent—is so critical during the first three years of life." *The Atlanta Journal-Constitution*, January 15, 1998

"National media seized the story, calling Miller a 'governor who gets it' on ABC's 'World News Tonight.' The British Broadcast Corp., 'Good Morning America' and other media outlets also featured Miller." *The Atlanta Journal-Constitution*, January 18, 1998

"'I'm not a classic man...but 'Ode to Joy'...will improve anybody's intellect,' said Sen. Minority Leader Chuck Clay of Marietta.... 'I support that for a small price to maybe make people think in new creative new ways to start infant development....I will support him all the way.'" *Marietta Daily Journal*, January 17, 1998

"Introduction to any music at an early age helps to improve performance in school and to make children become more patient and coordinated. At the very least, it would put music in homes where classical is the great unknown." Associated Press, *Athens Daily News/Banner-Herald*, January 16, 1998

"This is a wonderful idea. It's such a minor cost as compared to the cost of a child not having an opportunity, the cost of welfare, the cost of slow learning, the cost of clogging up the schools, teaching more and having math problems....The government is there to improve the lives of people, and this is the first start. The scientists stand behind the governor, and I applaud him for such a wonderful move." Don White, letter, *The Atlanta Journal-Constitution*, February 5, 1998

"There are theories that classical music helps some plants and flowers prosper and bloom; so why not children? Plus, this project has the added benefit of exposing parents to classical music, something that far too many folks consider 'high-brow.' Classical music can—and should—be enjoyed by everybody." *The Daily Citizen-News*, February 2, 1998

"Gov. Zell Miller is on the right track. I know that Mozart, Bach, Beethoven and all the other wonderful classical composers make children smarter." Elfriede H. Kristwald, letter, *The Atlanta Journal-Constitution*, July 1, 1998

"Years from now, if Georgia is a land of hyper-intelligent math prodigies, they can save a thank-you for Gov. Zell Miller." The Associated Press, June 25, 1998

"I applaud Georgia Gov. Zell Miller for having the courage to suggest distributing musical resources to every newborn—a revolutionary idea which I have dreamed about doing in the neighborhoods of our inner cities for children at risk." Cynthia Faisst, *The Orange County Register*, February 1, 1998

"...the great and captivating qualities of the music itself may ensure that the program accomplishes far more than Miller ever intended. And who knows, if enough legislators in Georgia—and everywhere—grow up listening to classical music, perhaps they'll realize one day that when they vote for high-quality, well-funded music education programs in the schools, they won't just be seeing to the care and feeding of zillions of little gray cells. They'll be helping to enrich beyond measure the lives of their children." Miles Hoffman, *The Washington Post*, July 5, 1998

"...with Zell Miller as governor, Georgia is jumping to the forefront by using music to help improve education. Thanks, Zell, for 'thinking outside the box' and benefiting Georgia with this vibrant and exciting new direction." Elliott Brack, *The Atlanta Journal-Constitution, Gwinnett Extra*, July 1, 1998

"Georgia is about to march off to a new beat." *NBC Nightly News*, June 24, 1998

"...we humbly suggest that Miller...[is] on the right track. Considering the glut of youthful outbursts of violence, exposure to the restful music of Mozart and Chopin might help defuse the need to open fire on classmates and teachers. And according to a number of detailed studies, listening to this music has been shown to make the little ones smarter." Marc Shulgold, *The Rocky Mountain News*, June 14, 1998

"...everybody wins: Babies get to hear Brahms' Lullaby in the original, music stores get to cultivate new customers, baby-shower guests get a new gift idea. And, for once, the taxpayers escape another shakedown. Sounds good to us." *Chattanooga Free Press*, January 25, 1998

"Finally, someone in a position of real power is doing something to promote the scientific fact that classical music is good for you....Studies linking classical music with intelligence and creativity aren't new. But Miller's plan to turn to Mozart to help Peach State citizens become smarter and more civilized most assuredly is. Just think. If the Miller proposal is successful, the next generation of Georgia-born Americans could have high grades in school, become creative individuals and understand what teamwork means. Classical music has been shown to stimulate numerous intellectual and developmental areas, especially in strengthening thinking skills of youngsters....Why didn't someone think of this before?...We can only hope that a political merchant in Georgia will triumph in selling his idea and spreading the sweet sounds the world so desperately needs." Donald Rosenberg, *The Plain Dealer*, January 25, 1998

"I think Georgia's Gov. Zell Miller has a great idea. The governor...wants to bring a little culture into the otherwise barren lives of our youngest citizens—that is, babies." George McEvoy, *The Palm Beach Post*, January 21, 1998

"The governor's proposal to use classical music to boost the brain power of newborns has struck a sweet chord." The Associated Press, *Chattanooga Free Press*, January 15, 1998

"...the governor who gets it. We've known for a long time that the governor of Georgia, Zell Miller, is committed to a better education for kids....Give a child music, and you get a better, brighter child." ABC News, *World News Tonight With Peter Jennings*, January 14, 1998

Welfare Reform

"Georgia, a state with a booming economy and relative prosperity, is in the process of radically changing how it assists its poorest citizens. If the process works, tens of thousands of Georgians will move into the labor force in the next four years....By passing Miller's package...state lawmakers have an opportunity to eradicate the welfare culture that has kept so many people in a cycle of poverty. It's an opportunity to enact a program that will help former welfare recipients become taxpaying workers." *The Atlanta Constitution*, March 12, 1997

"...there's no better time to try welfare-to-work than when the state's economy is strong and unemployment is low. For those who seek work, we think the jobs will be there." *The Atlanta Journal*, November 27, 1996

"The PEACH program, with training, education and child care, can make the idea of workfare a reality." *The Atlanta Journal*, January 29, 1993

"From the lottery to the way judges are chosen, Georgia has in Zell Miller an activist governor who had reform in mind when he impaneled a task force to study changes in the state's welfare laws." *The Atlanta Journal*, December 7, 1992

"It's the message, repeatedly emphasized, that is essential: Welfare is temporary assistance for needy families." Jim Wooten, *The Atlanta Journal*, November 20, 1996

"Miller calls his program 'Temporary Assistance for Needy Families.' Temporary is a message. So is a four-year time limit. That's good, too..." Jim Wooten, *The Atlanta Journal*, March 23, 1997

Deadbeat Parents

"Often the results of nice-sounding reforms fail to live up to their promise. Fortunately, that's not turning out to be true of Georgia's crackdown on deadbeat parents....These moves have helped cut 10,000 families off Georgia's welfare rolls. And...the state will get even tougher when it starts taking away the business or professional licenses of deadbeats who don't pay up. Collecting child support from non-custodial parents is one of the best ways to get families off the public dole. Not only does it save taxpayers big bucks, it also makes families more self-sufficient." *The Augusta Chronicle*, June 5, 1996

Infant Mortality

"With the 'Healthy Mothers: Babies Best Start' program, the community takes a significant step toward reducing the number of low-birth weight babies born each year. This effort will educate, encourage and empower all pregnant women throughout Georgia to obtain early and continuous prenatal care to ensure a healthier future for all mothers and their babies." *Decatur-DeKalb News Era*, August 5, 1993

Economic Development

"Georgia investors who feel burned by their brokers can take heart: The state has emerged as the nation's friendliest—and most rewarding—place for market players to bring a claim." *The Wall Street Journal*, July 24, 1996

"Miller's steering through the rocky economic times has won the admiration of many business leaders, who see him as a tough executive unafraid of difficult decisions." Associated Press, *The Florida Times-Union*, December 29, 1993

"Atlanta's economy is the strongest of any metro area in the nation..." *The Atlanta Constitution*, May 13, 1993

"...Georgia got an A in 'business vitality' in an annual study...comparing economic conditions across the country. It was a better mark than all but nine other states earned. Georgia also got A's in two other key categories, infrastructure and financial resources—also better than 40 or more other states. It got a B in the earnings/job quality area, better than 32 other states." *The Atlanta Constitution*, May 7, 1993

"New residents who arrived by the thousands via interstate highways and the birth canal made Georgia the fastest-growing state in the South and the 10th-fastest in the nation in 1992..." *The Atlanta Constitution*, December 30, 1992

"In 1996, the number of high-tech jobs in Georgia grew by 10,414, or 9.1%, the highest percentage gain among the top 15 states, according to the American Electronics Association, a Washington D.C. trade group." *The Wall Street Journal*, Southeast Journal, November 5, 1997

"...in 1995, for the fifth year, Georgia is the fastest growing state east of the Rocky Mountains and, for the seventh or eighth consecutive year, is among the leaders in new job creation in the United States." *Americus Times-Recorder*, May 22, 1996

"Metro Atlanta's economy will grow by almost 600,000 jobs—30 percent—between 1993 and 2005, pushing the 20-county metro population to 4 million, according to projections...by the U.S. Bureau of Economic Analysis....If current trends continue, by 2005 metro Atlanta would rank seventh nationally in total employment, up from ninth in 1993....Atlanta ranks among the nation's 15 fastest-growing large metropolitan areas in both the employment and population projections." *The Atlanta Journal-Constitution*, May 30, 1996

"...Georgia's continued growth, even through the 1991 recession, shows that the state has been doing the right things in economic development." *Catoosa County News*, June 9, 1993

Quick Start

"The [Quick Start] program gets high marks from employers who cite the quality of the workers, the content of the training programs and the effect on their bottom line." *The Atlanta Journal-Constitution*, October 20, 1992

"Georgia...has developed a program called Quick Start that not only provides technical training, but also modules on such skills as employee involvement, interpersonal relationships, and professional development....Led by Gov. Zell Miller, Georgia's programs are more comprehensive than those of most states, which often focus only on technical training." *Industry Week*, September 2, 1996

Georgia Research Alliance

"The Peach State is attempting to boost high-tech by investing strategically in the types of facilities that lure the best and brightest. Money is pouring into libraries, state-of-the-art laboratories and whatever else prized researchers demand....Since its inception five years ago, the not-for-profit Georgia Research Alliance has landed 26 researchers, with the public and private sectors raising $39 million to endow the positions." *Indianapolis Business Journal*, July 28, 1997

"Gov. Zell Miller has made investment in the Georgia Research Alliance a hallmark of his administration. Miller has included $42 million in GRA funding in his budget proposal—more than the consortium of research universities and business leaders has ever requested in one year." *The Atlanta Journal-Constitution*, January 8, 1998

"Atlanta is getting an incubator. And the infant biotech companies it nurtures there may someday turn into big business for the state." *The Atlanta Constitution*, August 14, 1998

International trade

"Business is booming on Georgia's international waterfronts..." *The Florida Times-Union*, July 29, 1993

"Atlanta...enjoys strong name recognition among foreign executives and is considered the best American city in which to locate new business facilities." *The Atlanta Constitution*, September 9, 1993

Rural Development

"The establishment of these [regional] service centers reflects Governor Zell Miller's long-standing commitment to regional and rural development and the General Assembly's interest in bringing state government closer to the people." *Perspective,* Summer 1998

Environment

Preservation 2000/RiverCare 2000

"Gov. Zell Miller has been good for the environment and has made the state an environmental leader in the Southeast....Of particular note have been Miller's Preservation 2000 initiative, under which the state bought 100,000 acres to preserve as natural habitat, and River Care 2000, a similar program aimed at protecting Georgia's river corridors." *The Macon Telegraph,* November 1, 1997

"Miller's Preservation 2000 and RiverCare 2000 programs have protected about 120,000 acres of natural, historic and recreational lands in the past eight years." *Savannah Morning News,* April 21, 1998

"Georgians in the next century will be able to enjoy an unspoiled environment on two coastal islands..." *The Atlanta Constitution,* October 24, 1991

"Parcel by parcel, tract by tract the state is bringing more endangered lands and scenic lands under government protection in a program that could open new opportunities for outdoor recreation enthusiasts." Associated Press, *The Courier Herald* (Dublin), December 21, 1992

"A gorge here, swamp there, island somewhere else, Georgia's special places are being saved from development and opened for outdoor recreation under the 'Preservation 2000' program." Associated Press, *Americus Times-Recorder,* December 21, 1992

"Gov. Zell Miller's plan to purchase 100,000 acres of public land promises to be a windfall for anyone who likes to hunt deer, catch fish or hug trees." Stuart Leavenworth, *The Macon Telegraph,* January 11, 1992

"Those interested in protecting our area's rivers, as well as those who see them as neglected but potentially powerful assets for community revitalization, should rejoice at news of a $1.5 million state grant for Athens earlier this week....The awarding of the RiverCare grant and the investment from the sales tax referendum give Athens the opportunity to restore its rivers to the vital role they played in the early days of our community's development." *Athens Daily News/Banner- Herald*, November 19, 1997

"Miller created the Rivercare 2000 conservation program in 1995 to protect and conserve Georgia's 70,000 miles of rivers and streams, most of which originate in the state. 'Georgia has a unique opportunity to determine the future of its own rivers, from their headwaters all the way downstream,' says [Harvey] Young [of the Georgia Department of Natural Resources]." *The Atlanta Constitution*, November 15, 1997

Wildlife vehicle tags

"Georgians have given wildlife a $7.4 million chance. So far this year, state residents have bought more than five times as many conservation license plates as officials anticipated. Some 10 percent of Georgia cars now sport the plates..." *The Macon Telegraph*, October 17, 1997

Coastal Zone Management

"Environmentalists see a good Coastal Zone Management Program as salvation for the barrier islands and wetlands." *The Florida Times-Union*, March 1, 1994

Hazardous Waste

"...when Gov. Zell Miller and the Legislature depoliticized and reorganized the [Georgia Hazardous Waste Management Authority] last year, the responsibility for significantly reducing hazardous waste generation was given priority." Elliott Levitas, *The Atlanta Journal- Constitution*, August 16, 1992

Law Enforcement

"Last month, the board [of Pardons and Paroles] trumpeted the fact that more lifers died in prison in the past year than were released: 21 to 19....Meanwhile, the count of lifers being paroled has declined dramatically since 1991—the year Miller took office—when 205 were released." *The Florida Times-Union*, June 13, 1998

"Two strikes"

"Georgia may be the toughest state in the union on crime. For example, its 'two strikes and you're out' policy mandates that anyone convicted twice of a violent crime spends the rest of his life in prison—no parole, no exceptions." *The Atlanta Journal-Constitution*, February 10, 1998

Boot camp

"The positive change is amazing. The same inmates that were initially terrified and resentful are actually speaking of positive things they are getting out of boot camp....judging from the reactions of both the probation and parole inmates, boot camp does seem to be having a positive affect with non-violent criminals." *Prison Life*, November 19, 1993

"...President Clinton focused on the 10-year-old boot camp program as being one of the answers to shielding young, first-time, nonviolent offenders from the violent felons in the general prison population and still deal out stiff punishment with hopes of rehabilitation....Besides being cheaper, these new prisons save nearby communities and the state thousands of dollars by the work they do on roads, irrigation ditches, municipal projects like school repair and dozens of other community service projects. They also have a somewhat better record of preventing graduates from returning to general prisons, than do the general prisons themselves." *The Brunswick News*, April 17, 1993

"A key element of Georgia's new comprehensive boot camp program is something that was lacking in the states's previous boot camp program: meaningful substance abuse treatment and counseling....As Georgia further enhances and expands its boot camp prison programs in the years ahead, it is likely that the behavior management techniques proven successful in the boot camp concept will find their way into virtually every level of offender life." *Corrections Today*, October 1991

Appointments

"'Like Paul Bunyan, Gov. Miller took a sledge hammer and broke through the glass ceiling in the judiciary, with the appointment of Justice Leah Sears to the Supreme Court of Georgia—making her the first female ever to serve that August body,' [said Stacy Davis Steed, treasurer of the Atlanta Urban League Board of Directors].... 'He has appointed more women, more African-Americans and more Republicans...to state positions than all previous Georgia governors combined.'" Atlanta Daily World, November 27, 1997

"What was that landmark political happening? It was the announcement last week by Governor-Elect Zell Miller of his plans to name Former State Senator, Al Scott of Savannah as State Labor Commissioner....The Scott appointment is a signal...that color and competence are now welcome at the Capitol." Ron Sailor, December 6, 1990

Miller Administration Legislative Agenda

1991 Miller Bills Passed

HR 7 Placed on the 1992 ballot a constitutional amendment authorizing the General Assembly to establish a state lottery whose net proceeds would be dedicated to education programs. House passed 126-51. Senate passed 47-9.

HB 263 Provided an income tax credit to employers who provided literacy training to their employees of $150 per full-time student or one-third of the training cost per full-time student. House passed 154-0. Senate passed 39-0.

HB 284 Supplemental appropriations bill, FY 1991. House adopted conference committee report 161-3. Senate adopted conference committee report 51-0.

HB 285 General appropriations bill, FY 1992. House adopted conference committee report 173-3. Senate adopted conference committee report 49-1.

HR 288 Placed constitutional amendment on the 1992 ballot requiring all local school superintendents to be appointed and all local school boards to be elected. House passed 141-29. Senate passed 47-3.

HB 589 Removed teacher certification from the Department of Education and placed it in a newly created, separate, smaller agency, the Professional Standards Commission. House passed 158-0. Senate passed 53-0.

SB 328 Set up a program of tests for students in grades 3, 5, 8, and 11 to be compared to national scores. The 11th grade test was the high school exit exam. A writing assessment was to be given in each of the above grades. House passed 164-0. Senate passed 53-0.

HB 792 Allowed local school systems to pledge state funds as security for local school bond issues to get a better bond credit rating. House passed 148-2. Senate passed 51-1.

SB 217 Added middle school counselors to the funding part of the QBE formula. House passed 142-13. Senate passed 47-3.

SB 72 Strengthened Georgia's bribery statute. House passed 160-9. Senate passed 51-1.

HB 72 Allowed law enforcement officials to seize and sell the real property of those convicted of drug trafficking. House passed 163-3. Senate passed 46-1.

SB 177 Raised the upper age limit for eligibility for placement in a boot camp from 25 to 30. House passed 167-0. Senate passed 50-0.

SB 110 Comprehensive reform of auto insurance regulation included 15 percent rate rollback, prior approval of rate increases, arbitration to settle disputed property claims, stronger regulations against companies non-renewing and canceling policies for small claims, tougher penalties for committing insurance fraud, and elimination of mandatory no-fault. House passed 149-25. Senate passed 52-1.

HB 274 Separated the positions of Commissioner of Natural Resources and Director of the Environmental Protection Division to eliminate any conflicts, and specified that the director of the EPD reported to the Board of Natural Resources. House passed 148-0. Senate passed 39-0.

HB 643 Required protection of mountains and rivers to be included as part of land-use planning under the Growth Strategies planning process. House passed 167-0. Senate passed 46-2.

SB 97 Required state agencies to prepare reports on the environmental effects of their projects before they began them. House passed 152-2. Senate passed 54-0.

HB 709 Toughened penalties for violating the Air Quality Act and levied fees against industries for specific levels of emissions for certain types of pollutants. House passed 100-0. Senate passed 49-0.

HR 110 Requested the US Fish & Wildlife Service to conduct a study of Georgia's rivers to determine which, if any, were in need of additional protection. House passed 157-0. Senate passed 46-0.

HB 66 Provided for the automatic forfeiture of the automobiles of habitual violators on the 4th offense. House passed 159-5. Senate passed 43-2.

HB 63 Comprehensive revision of DUI laws including .06 tolerance for and elimination of a nolo plea for drivers under 18 years old, publication of the photograph on the third DUI conviction, .08 BAC presumptive and .10 BAC per se for adults. Increased fine from $1,000 to $2,500 for driving without a license. House passed 168-0. Senate passed 49-4.

HB 1 Created an income tax credit for food and other purchases for low and middle income families. Total tax relief was $30 million. House passed 171-0. Senate passed 50-0.

SB 95 Reconstituted the Georgia Residential Finance Authority as the Georgia Housing and Finance Authority and allowed it to issue bonds for economic development purposes in addition to housing. Designed to assist in attracting businesses to rural areas. House passed 153-2. Senate passed 48-1.

HB 268 Required state employees who work with the legislature during the session to register as lobbyists. House passed 147-0. Senate passed 51-0.

HB 261 Authorized the issuance of an Olympic commemorative license plate. House passed 162-0. Senate passed 51-0.

HR 402 Established a commission to propose an appropriate tribute to former President Carter. House passed 139-6. Senate passed 46-1.

SR 72 Established the Children and Youth Study Committee to examine the delivery of programs and services to children and youth. House passed 104-1. Senate passed 52-0.

SB 101 Extended the life of the Consumers' Utility Counsel to April 1, 1995. House passed 148-0. Senate passed 50-0.

SB 100 Added two members to the World Congress Center Authority. House passed 101- 1. Senate passed 46-0.

SB 99 Added two members to the Lake Lanier Islands Authority. House passed 114-1. Senate passed 50-0.

SB 98 Added two members to the Stone Mountain Memorial Association. House passed 150-0. Senate passed 49-1.

SB 94 Change Composition- Changed the composition of the Georgia Hazardous Waste Management Authority, provided for an executive director of the authority, and provided that priority in state hazardous waste programs be given to source reduction. House passed 105-1. Senate passed 51-0.

SB 96 Changed the qualifications for membership on the Georgia Environmental Facilities Authority. House passed 97-1. Senate passed 50-0.

SB 167 Added one member to the Georgia Education Authority-Universities and authorized financing of equipment. House passed 117-2. Senate passed 46-0.

HB 1EX Special session general appropriations bill. House adopted conference committee report 158-9. Senate adopted conference committee report 51-1.

1991 Miller Bills That Did Not Pass

HB 64 Zero blood alcohol tolerance for drivers under 21. Assigned to Motor Vehicles Committee, no further action taken in House. No action in Senate

HB 65 Suspended license for implied consent violations or DUI presumption. Removed temporary permit provisions and provided for immediate suspension of driver's license for implied consent violations, or if testing of blood alcohol content indicated a presumption of DUI. Assigned to Motor Vehicles Committee, no further action taken in House. No action in Senate

HB 260 Established a $25 annual renewal fee for special and prestige license plates, established manufacturing fees for certain plates. Assigned to Motor Vehicles Committee, no further action taken in House. No action in Senate.

HB 509 Provided that the offense of insurance fraud is a felony offense. Authorized insurers to notify law enforcement agencies upon knowledge of a fraudulent insurance act which has not been reported to a law enforcement agency. Amends motor vehicle insurance provisions. Assigned to Insurance Committee, no further action taken. No action in Senate.

HR 10 Proposed a constitutional amendment to reduce the rate of state sales and use taxation on food for off-premises human consumption by 1 percent per year until such food was completely exempt. Assigned to Ways and Means Committee, no further action taken in House. No action in Senate.

HR 384 Proposed a constitutional amendment authorizing guaranteed revenue debt to be incurred to finance revenue-producing educational facilities or the renovation of such facilities of the Board of Regents of the University of Georgia. Assigned to Appropriations, no further action taken in House. No action in Senate.

HR 385 Proposed an amendment to the Constitution to authorize guaranteed revenue debt to be incurred to finance loans to, and the acquisition of loans made by others to businesses to encourage economic development in the state. Appropriations Committee, no further action taken in House. No action in Senate.

SB 73 Expanded the items subject to forfeiture for controlled substances to include all property traceable to an exchange of controlled substances, changes forfeiture procedures. Senate passed 51-0. Assigned to House Public Safety Committee, no further action.

SB 74 Created a new Department of Public Safety consisting of the divisions of the Georgia State Patrol, the GBI, the Georgia Police Academy, the Georgia Public Safety Training Center, and the Georgia Fire Academy. Created an executive director of the new Department. Senate passed 50-3. Assigned to House Public Safety Committee, no further action.

SB 417 Amended the QBE law to provide high school credit for courses at eligible institutions. Senate passed 50-3. Assigned to House Education Committee, no further action.

SR 70 Proposed an amendment to the Constitution to authorize the Supreme Court to designate, on a case-by-case basis, special trial districts upon the petition of the Attorney General or an affected District Attorney for purposes of the investigation and prosecution of criminal offenses against public administration, involving controlled substances, or offenses involving racketeer influenced and corruption organizations. Special investigative grand juries might also be empaneled. Senate passed by substitute 47-0. Assigned to House Judiciary Committee, no further action.

SR 200 Proposed an amendment to the Constitution so as to include the director of the Office of Planning and Budget as a member of the Georgia State Financing and Investment Commission. Senate passed 51-1. Assigned to House Judiciary Committee, no further action.

1992 Miller Bills Passed

HB 1262 Supplemental appropriations bill. House adopted conference committee report 150-10. Senate adopted conference committee report 47-3.

HB 1261 General appropriations bill. House adopted conference committee report 131-39. Senate adopted conference committee report 45-10.

HB 196 Changed the date of the presidential preference primary in Georgia to the first Tuesday in March. House agreed to Senate changes 121-43. Senate passed 35-12.

HB 1145 Established a title transfer fee for vehicles previously titled outside of Georgia and changed certain fees. House passed 116-55. Senate passed 40-14.

HB 1146 Limited amount of compensation allowed to vendors for collecting certain sales and use taxes and the second motor fuel tax. Vendors would be allowed to collect a maximum of 3 percent of the first $3,000 of taxes due and 0.5 percent of the amount over $3,000. House passed 127-36. Senate passed 35-11.

HB 1276 Allowed for automatic payroll deduction for accident and sickness insurance as part of child support collections. House passed 97-16. Senate passed 47-0.

HB 1277 Established such a putative father registry with the Department of Human Resources, made information provided to the registry admissible, and allowed such information to be used by governmental entities to establish or enforce a child support obligation. House passed 106-5. Senate passed 42-0.

HB 1387 Establish- Authorized the establishment and operation of a program of volunteer services in the Department of Natural Resources to facilitate, amplify, or supplement the objectives and functions of the department. House passed 108-2. Senate passed 47-0.

HB 1389 Clarified and strengthened regulations for coastal marshlands. House passed 102- 0. Senate passed 52-0.

HB 1388 Broadened definition of conservation easement, as well as those who may hold such an easement. Created a third-party right of enforcement. Intended to preserve the historical, cultural, and aesthetic heritage of Georgia. House passed 110-28. Senate passed 44-0.

HB 1390 Outlawed houseboats and live-aboard boats on the state's rivers. Authorized the commissioner of Department of Natural Resources to order the removal of vessels. House passed 166-6. Senate passed 42-6.

HB 1391 Authorized the Georgia Environmental Facilities Authority to use certain funds for solid waste loan purposes. House passed 159-0. Senate passed 44-0.

HB 1392 Increased fees for licenses, tags, and for registering boats to fund Preservation 2000 to increase the amount of protected public lands by 100,000 acres by the end of the Miller Administration. House passed 136-13. Senate passed 45-9.

HB 1394 Created the Georgia Superfund, funded by fees paid by water generators and transporters, to clean up hazardous waste sites not covered by the federal program. Funds to be used to identify, investigate, and clean up sites that pose a threat to human health or to the environment. House passed 163-4. Senate passed 48-0.

HB 1395 Authorized the payment of taxes by electronic funds transfer by those owing more than $10,000 in conjunction with any return, report, or other document required to be filed with the Department of Revenue. House passed 121-28. Senate passed 45-0.

HB 1396 Fines and forfeitures collected pursuant to enforcement of vehicle load limitations shall be paid into the fine and forfeiture fund of county treasury where collected. House passed 102-5. Senate passed 47-1.

HB 1397 Reduced the time period in which certain unclaimed property is assumed to be abandoned. Also reduced the other record keeping and procedural time periods involving unclaimed property. Reduced from 7 to 5 years on July 1, 1992, and 5 to 3 years on July 1, 1994. House passed 154-5. Senate passed 48-1.

HB 1399 Changed the annual job income tax credit from $1,000 to $2,000 per new full-time job for businesses in the lowest 40 counties ranked as less developed areas. Provided a $1,000 job tax credit per new full-time job for businesses in the next lowest 40 counties ranked as less developed areas. House passed 156-0. Senate passed 46-0.

HB 1400 Required the State Depository Board to prescribe cash management policies and required state agencies to employ them. Policies and procedures must be designed to maximize the efficient and effective utilization of a state's cash resources for the state as a whole. House passed 105-0. Senate passed 48-0.

HB 1405 Established a one-time tax amnesty program to be completed by the end of calendar year 1992, allowing businesses and individuals who owed back taxes to pay the taxes and interest owed without facing monetary and civil penalties or criminal prosecution. House passed 162-4. Senate passed 46-0.

HB 1401 If the father acknowledged paternity at the time of birth, his social security number was required to be placed on the child's birth certificate. House passed 113-4. Senate passed 41-0.

HB 1412 Required the Department of Education to develop environmental education and recycling programs in public schools. Also created the Environmental Education Council to award grants to schools for programs that enhance awareness of environmental issues. House passed 120-0. Senate passed 49-0.

HB 1541 Enabling legislation for the lottery, created the Georgia Lottery Corporation. Specified that lottery money would be used for educational purposes only, and briefly defined those programs. House passed 127-32. Senate passed 46-7.

HB 1549 Created the Department of Children and Youth Services to improve the visibility of children's issues, especially in the area of juvenile justice, and to strengthen support services for children. Recommendation of the Joint Study Committee on Children and Youth. House passed 168-1. Senate passed 46-0.

HB 1680 Prohibited employees of Regional Development Centers who were compensated by the RDC from also serving as a board member, officer, or paid employee of an entity contracting with an RDC. Required disclosures of certain transactions. House passed 122-0. Senate passed 48-0.

HB 1779 Created a new criminal offense of manufacturing, distributing, dispensing, or possessing with intent to distribute, a controlled substance in, on, or within 1000 feet of any real property dedicated and set apart by a county or municipal governing authority as a park, playground, or recreation center or in, on, or within 1,000 feet of any real property or any publicly owned or publicly operated housing project. House passed 163-0. Senate passed 46-0.

HR 732 Proposed a constitutional amendment to allow general obligation debt to be incurred by the state for the Georgia Environmental Facilities Authority to make loans to counties, municipal corporations, political subdivisions, local authorities, and other local governmental entities for solid waste recycling and other solid waste facilities or systems. House passed 165-0. Senate passed 46-0.

HR 840 Proposed an amendment to the Constitution to authorize the General Assembly to provide by general law for the dedication and deposit of revenues raised from specified sources for the purpose of the fund into the Indigent Care Trust Fund. House passed 142-0. Senate passed 46-0.

SB 144 Created the Distance Learning and Telemedicine Governing Board to direct the implementation of a consolidated, integrated, statewide shared use distance learning and telemedicine network. Authorized DOAS to be sole administrator of the Universal Services Fund. House passed 139-4. Senate passed 49-0.

SB 417 Authorized access to postsecondary programs in colleges and technical institutes to high school juniors and seniors at no cost to the student for credit both for college and high school graduation. House passed 124-1. Senate passed 50-3.

SB 486 Established as a criterion that the candidate for state court have been a resident of the state for three years. House passed 99-8. Senate passed 52-1.

SB 487 Created the offense of habitual impaired driving, meaning driving after three or more DUI convictions in a five-year period. Prohibited habitual violators from operating a motor vehicle in Georgia. Established the crime of endangering a child by driving under the influence of alcohol or drugs with the child in the vehicle. House passed 142-0. Senate passed 53-0.

SB 488 Authorized and directed the State Board of Education to devise and implement a pay-for-performance program to reward local schools. Established a performance evaluation system to determine the level of performance achieved, and those schools judged exemplary would receive an award. House passed 104-5. Senate passed 51-0.

SB 489 Suspended driver's license for second and subsequent offenses, suspended the driver's license upon a chemical test indicating that the driver was in per se violation of the prohibition against driving under the influence of alcohol. House passed 171-1. Senate passed 53-1.

SB 590 Changed the composition of the Governor's Development Council by increasing from 6 to 9 the number of private sector members. House passed 98-1. Senate passed 52-0.

SB 593 Made it a felony to hire, solicit, engage, or use an individual under age 17 in any manner to manufacture, distribute, or dispense, on behalf of the solicitor, any controlled substance. House passed 96-0. Senate passed 51-0.

SB 594 Required blood samples to be taken for DNA analysis upon conviction of certain sex offenses, to be performed by the Division of Forensic Services of GBI. DNA data bank to be maintained by GBI. House passed 155-0. Senate passed 53-0.

SB 595 Created the Georgia Emergency Management Agency as a separate agency and successor to the Emergency Management Division, Department of Defense. Established a director of emergency management to be appointed by the Governor. House passed 159-0. Senate passed 50-0.

SB 679 Increased the membership of the Ports Authority from seven to nine members. House passed 152-1. Senate passed 51-0.

1992 Miller Bills That Did Not Pass

HR 385 Proposed to amend the Constitution to authorize guaranteed revenue debt to be incurred to finance revenue-producing educational facilities or the renovation of such facilities of the Board of Regents of the University of Georgia. Assigned to House Appropriations Committee, no further action.

HR 384 Proposed to amend the Constitution so as to authorize guaranteed revenue debt to be incurred to finance loans to, and the acquisition of loans made by others to, businesses to encourage economic development in the state as provided by general law. Assigned to Appropriations Committee, no further action.

HB 1148 Increased the special fee paid by public service corporations and utilities subject to the jurisdiction of the Public Service Commission. Assigned to Industry Committee, no further action.

SR 70 Established special judicial circuits to be composed of each multi-county judicial circuit, or, if a single-county judicial circuit, that circuit plus each county immediately adjacent to that circuit. Senate passed in 1991 47-0. House took no action.

SR 200 Proposed an amendment to the Constitution to provide that the Office of Planning and Budget director be a member of the Georgia State Financing and Investment Commission. Senate passed 51-1 in 1991; took no action in 1992. House Appropriations Committee gave do pass recommendation.

SB 541 Prohibited state agencies from expending any public funds for personal services rendered or to be rendered by or under the direct supervision of any retired employee during a period of two calendar years immediately following such employee's retirement. Senate passed 48-0. Assigned to House Rules Committee, no further action.

SB 600 Required the Georgia Housing and Finance Authority to foster and promote the provision of adequate markets for borrowing money for local governments for the financing of their public improvements and health facilities at reasonable interest rates. Authorized the purchase or refund of local government bonds. Senate passed 48-6. Assigned to House Appropriations Committee, no further action.

1993 Miller Bills Passed

HB 121 Supplemental appropriations bill. House adopted conference committee report 146-27. Senate adopted conference committee report 53-1.

SB 30 Authorized comprehensive cooperative agreements regarding services and facilities in defense matters among federal, state, and local governments and authorities. Authorized the Department of Defense and other state agencies to compete and contract with the United States for the establishment of a Defense Finance and Accounting Services Facility. House passed 161-8. Senate passed 52-0.

HB 86 Authorized general obligation debt for facilities of the Department of Defense, specifically the Defense Financing and Accounting Services Site. House passed 148-24. Senate passed 53-0.

HB 87 Required Department of Revenue to set clear standards of courtesy and responsiveness in its dealings with taxpayers; required plain English in explaining protest and appeal procedures. House passed 111-0. Senate passed 53-0.

HB 90 Created rebuttable presumption of paternity if probability is 97 percent or higher that person is father based on scientific testing. Welfare Reform Task Force recommendation. House passed 169-2. Senate passed 46-0.

HR 180 Established a study committee to examine recommendations for the certification and licensure of lead-based paint inspectors and contractors, financial assistance for abatement, risk assessment and inspection, and other related matters. House passed 106-0. Senate passed 44-0.

SB 210 Authorized the Insurance Commissioner to permit the coverage of certain children covered by Medicaid in a plan developed by the Commissioner to cover the basic health needs of children when such participation is approved by the Secretary of the United States Department of Health & Human Services. House passed 100-6. Senate passed 48-1.

SB 74 Encouraged innovation in education by freeing certain schools from state and local system regulation. Charter schools must sign an agreement with the State Board of Education agreeing to work toward national educational goals using school-created strategies that include performance and accountability measures. House passed 171-3. Senate passed 46-5.

HB 350 Defined "computer software" and identified criteria for establishing its value for ad valorem tax purposes. As a result, computer software would be taxed at the intangible tax rate (.1 mills) instead of at a county's regular tax rate (ranging in 1994 from 10.64 mills to 47.54 mills). House passed 167-5. Senate passed 48-5.

HB 485 Permitted the judge or jury to impose a sentence of life without parole if aggravating circumstances were present. Judge could impose life without parole if jury finds aggravating circumstance but cannot unanimously agree on imposition of death penalty. Judge could also impose life without parole if no jury trial is requested provided the judge finds aggravating circumstances present. House passed by substitute 101-60. Senate passed 52-2.

HB 536 Provided a job tax credit of $2,000 annually for each new full-time employee job for five years for those business enterprises in areas designated by the commissioner of community affairs for less developed areas. House passed 152-1. Senate passed 51-0.

HB 486 Authorized the use of victim impact statements in capital felony cases. House passed 130-37. Senate passed 49-6.

SB 269 Required certain employers to report their hires within five days to the Department of Human Resources to enforce child support collections. House passed 110-56. Senate passed 50-0.

SB 162 Created the Office of Treasury and Fiscal Services by separating the fiscal division and its fiscal activities from the Department of Administrative Services and attaching it to DOAS only for administrative purposes. House passed 99-0. Senate passed 46-1.

SB 192 Underscored the state's commitment to making environmentally sound purchasing decisions by taking into account life cycle costs as well as acquisition costs when purchasing items. House passed 168-0. Senate passed 54-0.

SB 200 Transferred voluntary waste minimization, pollution prevention and hazardous waste source reduction programs to Office of Pollution Prevention Assistance. Put focus on source reduction. Separated command and control regulatory programs administered by the Environmental Protection Division from voluntary efforts administered by Office of Pollution Prevention Assistance. House passed 161-0. Senate passed by substitute 47-7.

SB 29 Made all positions within the Office of Planning and Budget unclassified, and required OPB to institute a pay-for-performance system. House passed 153-0. Senate passed 50-4.

SB 234 Strengthened and changed the focus of the Child Fatality Review Panel and renamed it the Statewide Child Abuse Prevention Panel. Moved the panel from DHR to the Criminal Justice Coordinating Council and charged it with recommending changes to make the Division of Family and Children Services more responsive and efficient. The panel charged to review the specific circumstances of high-profile child fatalities, and recommend steps to make sure that counties submit fatality reports to the panel. House passed 157-1. Senate passed 48-0.

SB 73 Established the Council on School Performance as an independent watchdog over local schools and school systems. Council was not affiliated with DOE. It was to evaluate schools and school systems using uniform standards and issue reports of its findings. House passed 119-39. Senate passed 47-2.

SB 335 Changed the budget process by making accountability, efficiency, and the attainment of agreed-upon directions which were outlined in a comprehensive state strategic plan the driving forces behind budget decisions. Mandated an ongoing review of agency continuation budgets and a more detailed review of expenditures at the individual program level. Encouraged systems to implement cost-saving measures through a system of monetary incentives that allowed them to retain a portion of any savings for internal agency use. House passed 172-0. Senate passed 51-0.

SB 26 Provided a family cap on welfare so that there will be no incremental increase in benefits for children born while on welfare. Required never-married teen mothers under 18 to live with parent, adult guardian or in some other supervised setting rather than allowing the teen mother to move out of the home and qualify for AFDC. Cut off welfare benefits to any able-bodied adult who refused to accept employment at minimum wage; with exceptions. Required the Department of Labor to periodically station people in DFACS offices to inform others about training and employment opportunities. House passed 174-1. Senate passed 43-0.

SB 28 Authorized judges to require ignition interlock devices for repeat DUI offenders as a condition of probation under certain circumstances. House passed 134-38. Senate passed 54-0.

HB 259 General appropriations bill. House adopted conference committee report 142-34. Senate adopted conference committee report 50-6.

1993 Miller Bills That Did Not Pass

HB 587 Created a tax credit for certain investments in real and personal property for use in the construction or expansion of a recycling or manufacturing facility. Credit ranged from 4 percent to 12.5 percent of the cost incurred. Assigned to Ways and Means Committee, do pass recommendation. No further action.

SB 71 Returned the state flag to pre-1956 design. Senate passed 38-18. Assigned to
House Rules Committee, no further action taken.

HB 260 Allowed employees who became members of the Employees' Retirement System on or after July 1, 1982 to receive creditable service for forfeited sick and annual leave toward retirement date. Reduced abuse of sick and annual leave. Assigned to Retirement Committee, no further action.

SB 72 Extended compulsory school attendance age to 17 for 1993-1994 school year; then to 18 for 1994-1995 school year. Senate passed 40-14. Assigned to House Education Committee, no further action.

SB 226 Established Georgia Reform Insurance Plan for health insurance to increase the availability of affordable health insurance; required managed care with cost containment features, and access to health care services through guaranteed issue insurance. Created state-wide or service area insurance pools to reduce insurance administrative costs, and required rating methods that served the broadest cross-section of the general community. Prohibited individual or group health-insurance policies from being issued unless they were community rated, complied with all chapter requirements, were guaranteed renewable, and the underwriting involved no more than the imposition of a preexisting condition limitation. Established portability provisions. Senate passed 48-8. Assigned to House Insurance Committee, no further action.

HB 351 Changed state mileage reimbursement rate to 22.5 cents per mile, and included legislators. Costs to be absorbed through agencies' budgets. House passed 84-62. Assigned to Senate Appropriations Committee, no further action.

SB 27 Required immediate suspension of a first-time DUI offender's driver's license for 120 days if at a per se level of blood alcohol content of .10 or higher. Senate passed 48-8. Assigned to House Judiciary Committee, do pass recommendation.

1994 Miller Bills Passed

HB 1296 Supplemental appropriations bill. House adopted conference committee report 146-28. Senate adopted conference committee report 47-8.

HB 1375 General appropriations bill. House adopted conference committee report 143-25. Senate adopted conference committee report 42-8.

HB 1383 Authorized the Board of Trustees of the Teachers' Retirement System to establish the percentage of a member's salary to be paid as the employee's contribution, with the stipulation that the percentage cannot be less than five percent or greater than the current six percent rate. House passed 161-0. Senate passed 51-0.

SB 415 Authorized the Department of Industry, Trade, and Tourism to acquire, construct, and operate a convention and the Savannah Maritime Convention Center in Chatham County, and to contract with the City of Savannah, and local authorities for its construction and operation. House passed 154-0. Senate passed 51-0.

HB 1527 Known as Georgia Business Expansion Support Act (BEST), stimulated businesses and Georgia industries by using income tax credits and sales tax exemptions to lower the effective costs of hiring additional workers, adding to investment property, retraining employees, offering child care, upgrading manufacturing machinery, and equipping new or expanded warehouse or distribution facilities. Credits and exemptions would be so categorized that those in counties with the weakest economic performance, in counties linked by a joint development authority, would feel the strongest stimuli. House passed 165-0. Senate passed 52-0.

HB 596 Increased dependent exemption and retirement income exclusion, providing $100 million in tax relief for families with dependents and senior citizens. Dependent exemption increased by $1,000 from $1,500 to $2,500. Annual retirement income exclusion rose from $10,000 to $12,000. Most families with two children saved $120 per year. House passed 174-0. Senate passed 51-0.

SB 440 Required every public school to develop a school safety plan with input from students, teachers, community leaders and law enforcement officials. Created violence-free zones, areas in which penalties are increased for possession of weapons and for assaults on students and teachers. Persons under 18 are also prohibited from possessing a handgun except in limited circumstances. Juveniles who commit certain violent crimes must be tried and sentenced as adults, with time to be served in a designated youth unit operated by the Department of Corrections. House passed 155-14. Senate passed 54-0.

SR 395 Proposed constitutional amendment to provide minimum mandatory sentences of ten years without possibility of parole for those convicted of murder, armed robbery, kidnaping, aggravated child molestation, rape, aggravated sodomy and aggravated sexual battery. Anyone convicted of one of the offenses for a second time must be sentenced to life without parole. Also doubled from 7 to 14 years the minimum sentence which must be served before those under life sentences can even be considered for parole. House passed 165-0. Senate passed 50-0.

SB 441 Enabling Legislation for SR 395. House passed 166-7. Senate passed 53-0.

SB 464 Required 20 hours of community service each month from those who have received welfare for 24 out of the last 36 months. House passed 115-58. Senate passed 55-0.

SB 418 Administrative license suspension expanded to include first-time DUI offenders, nolo contendere pleas eliminated for those testing above .15 BAC. Stronger penalties were provided, including mandatory minimum jail terms for second and third-time offenders and mandating community service for first, second, and third-time offenders. House passed 164-1. Senate passed 53-0.

1994- Miller Bills That Did Not Pass

HB 1764 Allowed a business located anywhere within the jurisdiction of a joint development authority to qualify for the highest job credit available among the included counties. Also provided a supplemental job tax credit of $500. House passed 97-0. Assigned to Senate Finance and Public Utilities Committee, no further action.

HB 1315 Changed habitual violator provisions to apply to those with three prior DUI convictions in any time period, not merely the last five years. All prior DUI convictions and pleas of nolo contendere would be counted in imposing penalties, driving restrictions, and license suspensions regardless of when such pleas or convictions were obtained. Changed the penalties for driving under the influence of alcohol or drugs. Established mandatory jail time for DUIs. Eliminates the nolo plea. Assigned to Judiciary Committee, no further action.

1995 Miller Bills Passed

HB 201 Supplemental appropriations bill. House adopted conference committee report 141-25. Senate adopted conference committee report 50-4.

HB 202 General appropriations bill. House adopted conference committee report 116-53. Senate adopted conference committee report 48-8.

SB 47 Permitted private colleges to participate in the Postsecondary Options program for high school students who live more than 25 miles from a public college. House passed 110-0. Senate passed 53-0.

SB 54 Changed the period of the charter for charter schools from an initial three years to a period of up to five years, removed the requirement for a two-thirds vote of faculty and parents and changed the requirement to a simple majority. House passed 152-7. Senate passed 50-1.

SB 81 Included aggravated sexual battery on the list of offenses bailable only before a Superior Court judge. Created a rebuttable presumption against granting of bail if the accused has a conviction of a serious violent felony and is currently charged with a serious violent felony. House passed 100-1. Senate passed 53-0.

SB 113 Required that death penalty habeas corpus petitions state with specificity which claims were raised at trial or on direct appeal with citations to the record. Required that the petition include which claims were previously raised in the case of prior habeas corpus proceedings. Required the Council of Superior Court Judges to establish appropriate time periods and schedules challenging for the first time state court proceedings resulting in a death sentence. Limited discovery in habeas proceedings. House passed 101-61. Senate passed 45-5.

SB 239 Created the Governor's Council on Developmental Disabilities to serve as the designated state agency and state planning council for purposes of carrying out certain federal provisions. House passed 161-0. Senate passed 50-0.

SB 256 Created the Georgia Policy Council for Children and Families to develop and implement a state plan for improving issues involving children such as teen pregnancy, child abuse and neglect, juvenile crime, low birth weight babies, and poor school performance. House passed 102-66. Senate passed 43-10.

HB 90 Provided a refund procedure and refunds of certain income taxes to certain federal employees. House passed 168-0. Senate passed 56-0.

HB 128 Issued a warranty affirming the quality and appropriateness of a student's education. If a student, after graduation, was determined to be deficient in reading, writing, or mathematics by an employee after three months of employment, the individual would be able to enroll at no cost in any technical and adult education school. House passed 112-55. Senate passed 44-7.

HB 129 Required that any lottery funds appropriated for purposes of new capital construction be placed in a Construction Reserve Trust Fund to be maintained by the appropriate fiscal officers of state government. Established method of appropriation. Changed program weights allotted to state authorized instructional programs for purposes of the Quality Basic Education formula, and changes program weights to reflect funds for salaries of superintendents, administrative, personnel, and visiting teachers. House passed 163-0. Senate passed 51-1.

HB 170 Increased the maximum amount of compensation payable to and on behalf of victims of crime. Established the "Crime Victims' Bill of Rights" which required that victims be notified of the accused's arrest, possibility of pretrial release of the accused, the victim's role in the criminal justice process, the availability of victim compensation; and the availability of community based victim service programs. Required the Criminal Justice Coordinating Council to be the coordinating entity between various law enforcement agencies, the courts, and social service delivery agencies. Also required that the victim be offered the opportunity to express his/her opinion on the disposition of an accused's case, including parole or any other form of executive clemency action. House passed 169-0. Senate passed 48-0.

HB 174 Increased fine for the crime of littering on public or private property or waters from $300 to $1,000. House passed 124-6. Senate passed 50-0.

HB 178 Increased the duties of District Attorneys to require that they assist victims and witnesses of crimes through the complexities of the criminal justice system. Included in the duties of assistant district attorneys the protection of the rights of victims. House passed 165-1. Senate passed 47-0.

HB 332 Created the Consumers' Utility Counsel division of the Governor's Office of Consumer Affairs. House passed 146-0. Senate passed 47-8.

HB 336 Authorized the Commissioner of Community Affairs to include in the tier 1 BEST designation any tier 2 county which underwent a sudden and severe period of economic distress caused by the closing of one or more business enterprises located in such county. Provided tax credits for qualified investment property purchases under certain circumstances. Exempted certain products from sales and use taxes. House passed 163-2. Senate passed 54-0.

HB 435 Established a community service pilot project of five judicial circuits in which community service was a condition of probation. Provided exceptions for certain offenders. Expanded the scope of the County Probation Advisory Council to include municipal probation systems. Revised provisions for private probation contracts. House passed 115-6. Senate passed 41-11.

1995 Miller Bills That Did Not Pass

SB 220 Intended to promote the availability of health insurance coverage to small employers regardless of their employees' health status or claims experience, to require disclosure of rating practices to purchasers, to establish rules regarding renewability of coverage, to establish limitations on the use of preexisting condition exclusions, to provide for development of basic and standard health benefit plans to be offered to all small employers and to improve the overall fairness and efficiency of the small group health insurance market. Created a Health Benefit Plan Committee. Assigned to Insurance and Labor Committee.

HB 528 Created a separate Department of Public Health, along with a Board of Public Health to establish the general policy of the department, to carry out all powers and functions of the Division of Public Health of DHR. House passed 162-7. Assigned to Senate Health and Human Services Committee, no further action.

HB 89 Defined term state purpose tax for purposes of any constitutional restrictions on or procedures for increases in state purpose taxation as any tax imposed by general law where tax applied to same class of subjects on a state-wide basis and the revenues collected accrued for the benefit of the state general treasury. Assigned to Ways and Means Committee, no further action.

HB 265 Reduced the state's sales and use tax rate applicable to purchase of food for off- the-premises consumption from its current 4 percent to 3, 2, 1, and 0 percent on July 1, 1996, July 1, 1997, July 1, 1998, and July 1, 1999 respectively. Assigned to House Ways and Means Committee, no further action taken.

HB 487 Provided for staggered motor vehicle registration over a 4-month or 12-month period. Changed certain licensing and registration deadlines. Assigned to Motor Vehicles Committee, no further action taken.

HB 488 Created the Department of Motor Vehicles and a commissioner of motor vehicles. Transferred certain functions from the Department of Revenue to the Department of Motor Vehicles. Assigned to Motor Vehicles Committee, no further action.

HB 678 Provided a 5 percent rate increase in state salary and reimbursement for participation in the national certification program for certain Georgia public schools' teachers who have received national certification. House passed 154-1. Senate passed 47-0. House failed to vote on Senate Floor Amendment in 1995.

HR 29 Proposed to amend the Constitution to govern introductions or increases of any "state purpose tax." In one case, change in general taxes would have to be approved before implementation by a majority of electors voting in a referendum in a general election. Under a second approach, increases or introductions of state purpose taxes could become effective through a two-thirds vote in each house of the General Assembly. Assigned to Ways and Means committee, no further action.

SB 79 Impounded license plates of habitual violators, and provided for the issuance of special license plates. Established a driving curfew for those under 18. Established a minimum mandatory term of imprisonment for persons convicted of DUI; zero tolerance for those under 21; eliminated nolo plea; required the use of seatbelts by all passengers if the driver is under 18. Senate passed 54-0. Assigned to House Special Judiciary, do pass recommendation, no further action.

SB 227 Denied renewal or initial application of professional licenses for certain individuals in arrears in child support. Senate passed 52-0. Assigned to House Judiciary Committee, no further action.

SB 387 Enacted the Southern Regional Emergency Management Compact (SREMC). Provided for mutual assistance among the states in managing any emergency or disaster that is declared by the Governor of the affected state. Senate passed 48-3. House took no action.

1996 Miller Bills Passed

HB 1186 Supplemental appropriations bill. House adopted conference committee report 145-27. Senate adopted conference committee report 47-4.

HB 1265 General appropriations bill. House adopted conference committee report 162-17. Senate adopted conference committee report 52-3.

HB 265 Provided for phased-in exemption of state sales tax on food over a three-year period. State tax was reduced to 2 percent after October 1, 1996, 1 percent after October 1, 1997, and was completely eliminated on October 1, 1998. Total tax savings of $500 million. Largest tax cut in state history. Exempted from state sales taxes the sale of "eligible food and beverages" for off-premises consumption and use. "Eligible food and beverages" as defined in federal food stamp law. House passed 171-2. Senate passed 51-1.

SB 550 Increased minimum dollar amounts required for noncompetitive bidding, competitive sealed bidding, and for other purchases and contracts, and would increase the maximum amounts state entities may be authorized to expend on their behalf. Authorized the Department of Administrative Services to permit agencies to use procurement cards for certain purchases, and to permit medical facilities under the Board of Regents to purchase medical equipment and supplies necessary for medical teaching purposes and to enter into agreements with other states. House passed 165-0. Senate passed 52-0.

HB 1316 Increased sentences for those over 21 convicted of statutory rape from 1 to 20 years to 10 to 20 years. House passed 160-10. Senate passed 52-0.

HB 1299 Granted juvenile court judges additional authority in imposing sanctions against family members or custodians who do not appear at proceedings involving their children. Judges may impose restitution directly, fines, reimbursing the state for the costs of detention, treatment, or rehabilitation, community service, or requiring the parent, guardian, or custodian to enter into a contract to provide for the supervision and control of the child. House passed 163-0. Senate passed 48-0.

SB 387 Provided for mutual assistance between the states in managing any emergency or disaster that is declared by the Governor of the affected state. House passed 146-23. Senate passed 48-3.

SB 227 Provided judicial and administrative authority to suspend or deny the applications or renewals of occupational licenses, as well as the drivers' licenses, of those who are over 60 days in arrears in child support obligations. House passed 175-3. Senate passed 52-0.

HB 1419 Reorganized the Georgia Housing Finance Authority into the Department of Community Affairs, abolishing both boards and creating a single new Board of Directors for both. GHFA became DCA's housing division. DCA would administer GHFA's programs under contract. House passed 151-6. Senate passed 47-0.

HB 1443 Authorized the Department of Revenue to use funds received as collection fees paid by delinquent contractors in any one fiscal year to pay private contractors to collect previously uncollected delinquent taxes. House passed 151-6. Senate passed 47-0.

SB 635 Reformed the Georgia Merit System by providing that all positions filled on or after July 1, 1996 either by new hires or as a result of voluntary transfer, promotions, or other voluntary movements of classified employees to management positions or advanced professional positions shall be included in the unclassified status. House passed 141-35. Senate passed 39-9.

HB 1501 Enhanced BEST by lowering the number of jobs required to claim the jobs tax credit depending on the type of county, lowered the job threshold for the census tract program. Extended by two years, until the end of 1998, the time within which the jobs and investment tax credit could both be taken in tier 1 counties and reduced the number of jobs which must be created in order to claim the credits. Increases the retraining tax credits. Equalized the amount of the exemption for the sale of electricity used directly in the manufacture of a product for new and existing manufacturers, lowered the threshold for the exemption on sales tax for the sale of material handling equipment for major warehouse and distribution projects. Added an exemption to the sales and use tax for sales of machinery used directly in the remanufacture of aircraft engines or parts or components in such a facility. Added a phased-in exemption to the sales and use tax for sales of certain overhead materials by a government defense contractor. House passed 163-0. Senate passed 51-0.

SB 750 Added one judge to Court of Appeals. House passed 151-11. Senate passed 49- 0.

SB 675 Authorized the commissioner of the Department of Corrections to make and execute any contract for the design, construction, operation, maintenance, use, lease, or management of a state correctional institution, or for services pertaining to the custody, care, and control of inmates. House passed 129-40. Senate passed 49-0.

HB 1569 Eliminated filing fees, sheriff's service fee, and any other fees assessed by magistrate's court which had been assessed against victims of domestic violence. House passed 165-0. Senate passed 43-0.

SB 709 Created the Office of School Readiness for the prekindergarten and related programs, to be attached to the Department of Education for administrative purposes only. Transferred the oversight of county and regional libraries from the Department of Education to the Department of Technical and Adult Education. Granted additional hiring, firing, and contractual authority to the State School Superintendent. House passed 160-4. Senate passed 49-4.

HB 1785 Provided a 5 percent rate increase in state salary and reimbursement for the participation fee in a national certification program for certain Georgia public schools teachers who receive national certification. House passed 160-4. Senate passed 49-4.

1996 Miller Bills That Did Not Pass

SB 568 Allowed zero tolerance for drivers under 21, mandatory jail time for DUI first offenders and increased time for second offense. Eliminated the nolo contendere plea. Required the surrender of license plates for habitual violators. Senate passed 56-0. House Special Judiciary, no further action.

1997 Miller Bills Passed

HB 34 Supplemental appropriations bill. House adopted conference committee report 148-22. Senate adopted conference committee report 48-5.

HB 204 General appropriations bill. House adopted conference committee report 157-17. Senate adopted conference committee report 48-5.

HB 148 Established an interstate water compact among Georgia, Alabama, and the United States. Created the Alabama-Coosa-Tallapoosa Basin Commission to establish and modify an allocation formula for apportionment among the states. House passed 164-7. Senate passed 53-2.

HB 149 Established an interstate water compact among Georgia, Florida, Alabama and the United States for the purpose of long-term management of the waters of the three-river basin. Created an Apalachicola-Chattahoochee-Flint River Basin Commission to establish and modify an allocation formula for apportionment among the states. House passed 162-8. Senate passed 50-2.

HB 167 Provided Georgia the authority to participate as a member of the federal program as outlined in the Coastal Management Act of 1972. Georgia will receive technical assistance, funding, and authority to review and approve federal activities which might impact Georgia's natural resources. Required all state agencies to coordinate and cooperate along the coast. House passed 154-8. Senate passed 54-0.

HB 284 Made extensive changes to child support enforcement requirements based on the federal Personal Responsibility and Work Opportunity Act of 1996, including enacting the Uniform Interstate Family Support Act (UIFSA) to replace URESA, establishing faster procedures for seizing assets from delinquent parents, and loosening paternity laws to make it easier to establish paternity. House passed 159-7. Senate passed 47-0.

HB 377 Provided a legal mechanism for the seizure and forfeiture to the state of property and proceeds obtained through acts of fraud committed to obtain medical assistance benefits or payments. House passed 170-0. Senate passed 55-0.

HB 428 Added telecommunications to the group of industries qualifying for the present incentives of the Georgia Business Support and Expansion Act of 1994. Added a tax credit for expanded outlays on research and a special credit for fast-growing smaller companies. The coverage of telecommunications would apply to tax years starting on or after January 1, 1997; the new research and growth industries would go into effect on January 1, 1998. House passed 165-0. Senate passed 47-0.

HB 438 Transferred Eastman Youth Development Facility from the Department of Corrections to the Department of Children and Youth Services. House passed 119-0. Senate passed 49-0.

HB 479 Authorized the commissioner of the Revenue Department to settle and compromise tax assessments by abolishing the Settlement and

Compromise Board. Authorized commissioner to adopt rules setting forth procedures for satisfying signature requirements for returns by electronic or voice signature. Authorized commissioner to transmit an execution for the collection of any tax, penalty, or interest to sheriffs via electronic means. Authorized the commissioner to develop standards to administratively discharge any debt or obligation barred by the state of limitations. Permitted additional electronic filings. House passed 157-14. Senate passed 51-1.

HB 487 Pursuant to the Peat Marwick Report, this bill authorized the commissioner of the Revenue Department to adopt rules to delegate to a county tag agent custodial responsibility for receiving, processing, issuing, and sorting motor vehicle titles and registrations. Authorized the commissioner to enter into contracts with private parties for the sale of prestige license plates when they are authorized by the General Assembly. Provided that license plates issued for government vehicles shall be permanent plates for the vehicle rather than reissued every five years. Authorized commissioner to delegate additional responsibilities. House passed 160-0. Senate passed 49-0.

HB 681 Nolo contendere plea will be treated as a conviction for all DUIs. Required substance treatment program for second time DUI violators if a clinical evaluation determines that a problem is indicated. Required license tag seizure for violators who are convicted of DUI and whose drivers' licenses are suspended as a habitual violator. Established zero tolerance for blood alcohol in drivers under age 21. Required mandatory jail time for all DUI violators with a blood alcohol content of .08 or more upon conviction for 24 hours. Established a graduated licensing system for teenage drivers, so that 16-year-olds may only receive an intermediate permit which prohibits driving between 1 am until 5 am except under limited circumstances, and limits the number of passengers under 21. Prior to receiving a full driver's license, the valid intermediate permit cannot have been suspended, and, for a period of not less than 12 consecutive months prior to application for a full license, the person cannot have a conviction of certain moving traffic incidents. Provided special revocation provisions for drivers under 21 if they are convicted of certain offenses. Drivers licenses for persons under 18 will be suspended for school attendance problems. House passed 171-6. Senate passed 53-0.

HR 249 Created a Graduate Medical Education Study Commission to undertake a study of the Graduate Medical Education Trust Fund. To stand abolished on January 1, 1998. Created because the changing market and health care environment required a change in the way medical education is reimbursed. House passed 163-0. Senate passed 53-0.

SB 15 Because a 1996 law mistakenly removed the ten year minimum mandatory sentence for those convicted of rape and aggravated sodomy, simply returned that minimum mandatory sentence for those crimes. House passed 171-0. Senate passed 55-0.

SB 80 Provided a civil remedy to allow people in the community who are harmed by illegal drugs to sue drug dealers for damages caused by the illegal drug use. Persons who are adversely affected by an individual abuser's use who can file such an action include the parent, spouse, or child of the abuser; a child whose mother was an abuser when the child was in utero; the abuser's employer; or medical facilities that provide treatment for the abuser. The abuser could not sue. House passed 154-6. Senate passed 53-0.

SB 90 Permitted residents of Georgia who were victims of international terrorism or mass violence while outside the United States to be eligible for victims compensation. Extended the time within which claims by victims may be filed. Permitted award of victims compensation even if it has been received from another state so long as it is less than what the victim would be entitled to in Georgia. House passed 166-0. Senate passed 49-0.

SB 104 Replaced the Aid to Families with Dependent Children (AFDC) program with the Temporary Assistance for Needy Families Program (TANF). TANF focused on helping families become self-sufficient through work. Receipt of benefits required fulfillment of certain personal responsibilities and work requirements. Recipients were required to participate in work activities as soon as possible, but no later than 24 months after first receiving assistance. Cash assistance was limited to 48 months. Required the Department of Human Resources to establish a social assistance register, to develop a plan to provide incentives for employers to hire recipients; establish procedures to address domestic violence; and to establish a pilot LEARNFARE program. Eliminated the tax incentive for the Jobs First Program. House passed 156-11. Senate passed 54-1.

SB 81 Amended rulemaking requirements of the Administrative Procedures Act by providing that an agency, when making rules, shall choose an alternative that does not impose excessive regulatory costs on any person which costs could be reduced by a less expensive alternative that accomplished the objectives of the law upon which the proposed rule is based. Also authorized agencies subject to the APA to grant variances or waivers to certain rules upon petition showing substantial hardship if the current rule were applied as written. House passed 155-5. Senate passed 45-8.

SB 105 Made technical changes to the Sexual Offender Registration Law so that it would come into compliance with the federal "Megan's Law" and the federal Crime Control Act. House passed 146-12. Senate passed 51-0.

1997 Miller Bills That Did Not Pass

HB 163 Provided federal law enforcement officers with the same authority, privileges, and immunities as a peace officer of this state when making an arrest or rendering assistance to local officers under certain circumstances. Assigned to Public Safety Committee, do pass recommendation, no further action.

HB 482 Provided that the Governor determine the salary of the revenue commissioner, rather than the General Assembly, since the commissioner is an appointee of the Governor. Assigned to Appropriations Committee, no further action.

HB 863 Changed program weights allotted to state authorized instructional programs for purposes of the Quality Basic Education formula. Assigned to Education Committee, no further action.

SB 67 Created the offense of family violence simple battery, family violence assault, family violence aggravated assault, and family violence aggravated battery. Established minimum mandatory jail times which would not be suspended, stayed, probated, deferred, or withheld. Also established that it would be a high and aggravated misdemeanor to commit the offenses of assault and battery on persons over 65. Senate passed 52-0. Assigned to House Special Judiciary Committee, do pass recommendation. Recommitted to Special Judiciary Committee.

SB 292 Made several changes to the Georgia Education Authority to allow it to be more appropriately structured, including eliminating certain members and adding the director of the investment division of the Georgia State Finance and Investment Commission. Limited the total amount of bonds that could be issued and shortened the maturity of bonds, required the approval of projects by the Board of Regents, the Governor, and the General Assembly before they are considered for financing. Added parking decks and student centers to the type of facilities that could be financed. Senate passed 42-9. Assigned to House University System of Georgia Committee, no further action.

1998 Miller Bills Passed

HB 1167 Supplemental appropriations bill. House adopted conference committee report 145-20. Senate adopted conference committee report 46-5.

HB 1250 General appropriations bill. House adopted conference committee report 151-23. Senate adopted conference committee report 49-7.

HB 1162 Increased personal income tax exemption from $1,500 to $2,700 for each taxpayer and dependent for all taxable years beginning in January, 1998. Increased deduction in lieu of personal exemption for an estate and a trust. Increased deductions for senior citizen taxpayers age 65 or older, as well as all blind taxpayers from $700 to $1,300. Increased withholding exemption allowable to track personal exemption increases. Total fiscal impact was $205 million and was the second largest tax cut in Georgia history. House passed 175-0. Senate passed 54-0.

HB 1161 Provided a $1,500 tax credit for the purchase or lease of a new low-emission vehicle registered in a "covered area." Provided a tax credit for the conversion of a conventionally fueled to an alternative fuel vehicle for the amount of the conversion up to $1,500. House passed 156-0. Senate passed 53-0.

HB 1163 Provided a method of privatization of all publicly owned wastewater treatment facilities with average monthly flow limits of 20 or more million gallons of water a day that have certain permits. Privatization required if certain provisions of the permit have been violated, or if it has three major treatment facility bypasses during a 12-month period. Established a State Wastewater Privatization Oversight Committee to review and approve privatization plans. Provided penalties for failure to comply. House passed 172-0. Senate passed 46-2.

HB 1164 Clarified that first-offender statute shall not apply to the ten-year mandatory minimum requirement for murder, armed robbery, kidnaping, aggravated child molestation, aggravated sodomy, or aggravated sexual battery. House passed 170-0. Senate passed 55-0.

HB 1165 Required a judge to order an adult offender to make restitution to any victim as a condition of any relief upon conviction of a crime dealing with damage to or intrusion upon property or theft. House passed 161-0. Senate passed 55-0.

SB 410 Created the Children's Health Insurance Program (PeachCare) to provide low-cost health insurance for children from birth through 18 years of age who are not eligible for assistance under Medicaid and who live in families with family incomes below 200 percent of the federal poverty level. Required the payment of modest premiums for children six or over. Program to be run by the Department of Medical Assistance. House passed 159-17. Senate passed 37-15.

SB 409 Provided that $3 per month of any supervision fee collected by any entity authorized to supervise probationers be forwarded to the Crime Victims Emergency Fund. That fund provided a source of monies for violent crime victims who were otherwise uncompensated for injuries and damages from other sources. House passed 152-2. Senate passed 55-0.

SB 421 Required that the fingerprints and photographs of juveniles be taken whenever they were charged with an act that would be a felony if committed by an adult. Required the Georgia Crime Information Center to be the central state repository for juvenile fingerprints and photographs. Juvenile information contained in the GCIC may only be retrieved for criminal justice purposes. House passed 153-1. Senate passed 46-0.

SB 535 Repealed Professional Practices Commission and merged its duties into the Professional Standards Commission. House passed 152-0. Senate passed 50-0.

HB 1419 Merged the duties of the Georgia Sports Hall of Fame Board with the Sports Hall of Fame Authority, so that the Sports Hall of Fame Authority is responsible for all functions related to the Sports Hall of Fame. House passed 169-0. Senate passed 51-0.

1998 Miller Bills That Did Not Pass

SR 463 Proposed a constitutional amendment to abolish the authority of the Board of Pardons and Paroles to grant reprieves, pardons, and paroles, to commute penalties, to remove disabilities by law, and to remit any part of a sentence after conviction for all persons convicted on or after July 1, 1999 of crimes as defined by the General Assembly. House passed 141-30. Senate passed 55-0. No agreement in conference committee.

SR 477 Created a bipartisan Joint Commission on Parole Abolition and Sentencing Reform to make recommendations to the Governor and the General Assembly on all matters related to the abolition of parole and the adoption and implementation of a truth in sentencing system for the State of Georgia. House passed 167-0. Senate passed 55-0. No agreement in conference committee.

HB 1396 Authorized the Governor to determine the salary of the commissioner of banks and banking, the state revenue commissioner, and the commissioner of administrative services, rather than setting these salaries by statute. Authorized the board of corrections to determine the salary of the commissioner of corrections subject to approval by the Governor. Authorized the Legislative Services Committee to determine the salary of the state auditor. Assigned to Appropriations Committee, no further action.

Bills introduced 1991-1998: 205
Bills that became law 1991- 1998: 173

Miller Administration Floor Leaders

HOUSE	SENATE
1991-1992	
DuBose Porter, Floor Leader	Hal Dawkins, Floor Leader
Jeanette Jamieson, Ass. Floor Leader	Pete Robinson, Ass. Floor Leader
Thurbert Baker, Ass. Floor Leader	Mark Taylor, Ass. Floor Leader
1993	
Thurbert Baker, Floor Leader	Hal Dawkins, Floor Leader
Nan Grogan Orrock, Ass. Floor Leader	Steve Henson, Ass. Floor Leader
Tom Bordeaux, Ass. Floor Leader	Mark Taylor, Ass. Floor Leader
1994-1998	
*Thurbert Baker, Floor Leader	**Mark Taylor, Floor Leader
Nan Grogan Orrock, Ass. Floor Leader	Robert Brown, Ass. Floor Leader
Tom Bordeaux, Ass. Floor Leader	***Guy Middleton, Ass. Floor Leader

* Thurbert Baker resigned his seat in the House of Representatives May 31, 1997 when he was appointed Attorney General of the State of Georgia.

** Mark Taylor resigned as Floor Leader in May, 1997 to pursue a campaign for Lieutenant Governor.

***Guy Middleton resigned as Assistant Floor Leader in the beginning of the 1998 legislative session to become chair of the Senate's Health and Human Services Committee.

Agency Heads During the Miller Administration

Office of State Administrative Hearings

Mark Cohen	April 1, 1995 - August 1995
Vicki Snow	August 1995 - October 31, 1996
Mark Dickerson	November 1, 1996 -

Department of Administrative Services

Larry Clark	December 1983 - July 31, 1991
Dave Evans	August 1, 1991 - May 31, 1996
Dotty Roach	June 1, 1996 -

Agricultural Exposition Authority

Wilson T. Sparks	July 1, 1987 - June 30, 1992
Michael Froelich	July 1, 1992 -

Department of Agriculture

Tommy Irvin	January 22, 1969 -

Agrirama Development Authority

Judy Neal	January 1, 1991 - October 22, 1993
Teresa Veazey	December 13, 1993 -

Georgia Council for the Arts

Frank Ratka	July 3, 1978 - March 29, 1991
Elizabeth Weltner	January 17, 1991 - December 31, 1992
Caroline Ballard Leake	December 16, 1993 -

Department of Audits

G. W. Hogan	1985 - November 1992
Claude Vickers	November 1992 -

Department of Banking and Finance

Edward Dunn	January 2, 1972 - July 31, 1997
Stephen Bridges	August 1, 1997 - September 30, 1997
	(Acting) October 1, 1997 -

Georgia Building Authority	
Luther Lewis	March 1990 - June 4, 1995 (Acting)
	June 5, 1995 -
Children and Youth Coordinating Council	
Lydia Jackson Sartain	February 1, 1991 - September 12, 1993
Judy Neal	October 25, 1993 -
Department of Community Affairs	
Jim Higdon	June 1980 -
Office of Consumer Affairs	
Barry Reid	June 1, 1982 -
Department of Corrections	
Bobby Whitworth	January 1, 1990 - June 15, 1993
Allen Ault	June 16, 1993 - December 7, 1995
J. Wayne Garner	December 7, 1995 -
Criminal Justice Coordinating Council	
Minuard McGuire	January 14, 1991 - January 31, 1992
Sid Miles	February 17, 1992 - April 15, 1993
Terry Norris	April 16, 1993 - November 15, 1995
Pat Jarvis	November 16, 1995 - January 31, 1996
Martha Gilland	March 1, 1996 -
Department of Defense	
Jerry Sanders	January 14, 1991 - April 16, 1991
William Bland, Jr.	April 17, 1991 -
Georgia Development Authority	
David Skinner	March 18, 1985 -
Department of Education	
Werner Rogers	1986 - January 1995
Linda Schrenko	January 1995 -
Georgia Emergency Management Agency	
Billy Clack	June 16, 1987 - March 8, 1991
Gary McConnell	July 1, 1992 -

Employees' Retirement System

Rudolph Johnson	June 1, 1988 -

Environmental Facilities Authority

Leamon Scott	June 1987 - February 31, 1991
Lace Futch	March 1, 1991 - October 31, 1991
Mike Jones	November 1, 1991 - April 30, 1992
Steven McCoy	May 1, 1992 - July 15, 1993
Paul Burks	July 16, 1994 -

Commission on Equal Opportunity

Carla Ford	January 14, 1991 - March 31, 1992
Mustafa Aziz	March 31, 1993 -

State Ethics Commission

Theodore Lee	1990 -

Joint Board of Family Practice

Michael Ashe	1989 - February 28, 1993
John E. Brown	March 1, 1993 - May 31, 1996
C. Dee Hanson	June 1, 1996 -

Georgia State Financing and Investment Commission

Financing and Investment Division:

Weyman Smith	August 1, 1987 -

Construction Division:

Bill Roberts	January 31, 1979 - November 30, 1994
John Butler	November 30, 1994 - (Acting)

Georgia Fire Academy

Harold Thompson (Superintendent)	January 1, 1991 - December 31, 1991
C. David Saye	January 1, 1992 - (Superintendent)

Georgia Firefighter Standards and Training Council

George Hope	August 1, 1975 - April 1, 1994
Jim Hansford	April 1, 1994 -

Forestry Commission

John Mixon	January 1983 - July 31, 1995
David Westmoreland	August 1, 1995 - October 31, 1997
Fred Allen	November 1, 1997 -

State Health Planning Agency	
Dotty W. Roach	June 1989 - August 1996
Pamela S. Stephenson	August 1996 -
Herty Foundation	
Michael J. Kocurek	May 1986 - January 31, 1997
Karl M. Counts	February 1, 1997 -
Georgia State Games Commission	
Nick Gailey	September 24, 1990 - Present
Office of Highway Safety	
Minuard McGuire	- January 31, 1991
Thomas Coleman	January 22, 1991 - January 31, 1995
Betty Cook	July 1, 1995 - December 21, 1996
Timothy Jones, Sr.	January 1, 1997 -
Human Relations Commission	
Joy Berry	January 16, 1988 -
Department of Human Resources	
James G. Ledbetter	June 1982 - December 31, 1994
Tommy Olmstead	January 1, 1995 -
Georgia Council for the Humanities	
Ronald E. Benson	June 1, 1980 - August 31, 1997
Jamil S. Zainaldin	October 20, 1997 -
Information Technology Policy Council	
Mike Hale	July 1, 1995 -
Department of Industry, Trade and Tourism	
Randolph B. Cardoza	April 1990 -
Office of the Commissioner of Insurance	
Tim Ryles	January 14, 1991 - January 8, 1995
John Oxendine	January 9 -
Georgia Bureau of Investigation	
J. Robert Hamrick	September 1, 1985 - August 1, 1993
Milton Nix, Jr.	August 1, 1993 -

Jekyll Island Authority

George Chambliss	January 1984 - January 1995
James A. Bradley	January 1995 - August 30, 1997
Bill Donohue	September 1, 1997 -

Department of Juvenile Justice (became separate department in July 1992)

George Napper, Jr.	July 16, 1992 - September 16, 1994
Garfield Hammonds, Jr.	October 3, 1994 - January 8, 1995
Eugene T. Walker	January 9, 1995 -

Department of Labor

Ray Hollingsworth	November 1990 - January 1991
Al Scott	January 1991 - January 1993
David Poythress	January 1993 - January 1998
Martha Fullerton	January 1998 -

Lake Lanier Islands Development Authority

R. L. Burson	November 1, 1976 - July 15, 1996
Lee Smith	July 16, 1996 -

Department of Law

Michael Bowers	August 1, 1981 - May 31, 1997
Thurbert Baker	June 1, 1997 -

Department of Medical Assistance

Russell Toal	January 16, 1991 - December 31, 1993
Marjorie Smith	January 1, 1994 - November 30, 1997
William Taylor	December 1, 1997 -

State Medical Education Board

Joseph Lawley	1984 -

Merit System of Personnel Administration

Charles Storm	January 1, 1997 - June 30, 1992
Bobbie Jean Bennett	July 1, 1992 - December 31, 1996
Dana Russell	January 1, 1997 - April 15, 1997 (Acting)
W. Daniel Ebersole	April 16, 1997 - November 30, 1997
Dana Russell	December 1, 1997 -

Department of Natural Resources

Joe D. Tanner	January 1991 - May 1995
Lonice Barrett	May 1995 -

Georgia Net Authority	
Tom Bostick	June 15, 1996 -

Nonpublic Postsecondary Education Commission	
William Mangum	July 1, 1991 - December 31, 1995
Randy Powers	June 1, 1996 -

State Board of Pardons and Paroles - Chairman	
Wayne Snow, Jr.	July 1, 1985 - May 1, 1993
James Morris	May 1, 1993 - October 1, 1994
J. Wayne Garner	October 1, 1994 - December 6, 1995
Garfield Hammonds	January 2, 1996 - October 31, 1996
Walter Ray	November 1, 1996 -

Georgia Peace officer Training and Standards Council	
Frankie Lovvorn	October 1988 - August 1995
Michael F. Vollmer	August 1995 - February 1996 (Acting)
Pat Jarvis	February 1996 - May 1996
Steve Black	May 1996 - May 1997
C. Richard Darby	June 1997 -

Office of Planning and Budget	
Henry Huckaby	February 1, 1991 - July 31, 1995
Tim Burgess	August 1, 1995 -

Georgia Police Academy	
Ben Jordan	1968 - October 1991
C. David Saye	January 1, 1992 -

Georgia Ports Authority	
George J. Nichols	1976 - December 1994
Doug J. Marchand	January, 1995 - present

Professional Practices Commission (placed under Professional Standards Commission in 1998)

Hans J. Schacht	July 1, 1973 - June 30, 1991
James J. Carter	July 1, 1991 - June 30, 1998

Professional Standards Commission	
Robert R Hill	July 1, 1991 - June 30, 1996
Margaret Torrey	July 1, 1996 -

<u>State Properties Commission</u>	
Ray Crawford	September 26, 1985 -
<u>Department of Public Safety</u>	
Curtis Earp	October 3, 1986 - January 31, 1991
Ronald Bowman	February 1, 1991 - April 1, 1993
Sid Miles	April 1, 1993 -
<u>Georgia Public Safety Training Center</u>	
C. David Saye	April 1, 1981
<u>Public Service Commission - Chairman</u>	
Bob Durden	March 1, 1991 - May 5, 1992
Bobby Rowan	May 8, 1992 - January 18, 1993
Mac Barber	January 19, 1993 - January 17, 1994
Robert Baker	January 18, 1994 - January 16, 1995
Bob Durden	January 17, 1995 - January 15, 1996
Dave Baker	January 16, 1996 - January 20, 1997
Stan Wise	January 21, 1997 - January 20, 1998
Mac Barber	January 21, 1998 - May 1, 1998
Robert Baker	May 5, 1998 -
<u>Georgia Public Telecommunications Commission</u>	
Richard Ottinger	July 1, 1981 - November 30, 1994
Frank Bugg	December 1, 1994 - January 8, 1995
Werner Rogers	January 8, 1995 -
<u>Georgia Rail Passenger Authority</u>	
Arthur A. Vaughn	August 1996 - present
<u>Georgia Real Estate Commission</u>	
Charles Clark	September 1976 -
<u>Board of Regents, University System of Georgia</u>	
H. Dean Propst	July 1, 1985 - December 31, 1993
Harry Downs	January 1, 1994 - June 30, 1994 (Acting)
Stephen R. Portch	July 1, 1994 -
<u>Department of Revenue</u>	
Marcus Collins, Sr.	September 1, 1983 - August 31, 1996
T. Jerry Jackson	September 1, 1996 - April 14, 1997 (Acting)
	April 14, 1997 -

Office of School Readiness	
Michael F. Vollmer	1996 - June 30, 1997
Celeste Osborne	July 1, 1997 - August 15, 1997 (Acting)
	August 15, 1997 -
Secretary of State	
Max Cleland	January 11, 1983 - January 7, 1995
Lewis Massey	January 8, 1996 -
State Soil and Water Conservation Commission	
F. Graham Liles, Jr.	November 1979 - present
Stone Mountain Memorial Association	
Larry Allen	October 1983 - May 1994
Curtis Branscombe	July 1994 -
Georgia Student Finance Commission	
Stephen Dougherty	1987 - 1996
Glen Newsome	1996 -
Teachers' Retirement System/Public School Employees' Retirement System	
Gerald Gilbert	March 1981 -
Department of Technical and Adult Education	
Kenneth H. Breeden	July 1, 1988 - present
Department of Transportation	
Hal Rives	May 1, 1987 - October 31, 1991
Wayne Shackleford	November 1, 1991 - present
Office of Treasury and Fiscal Services	
Steven McCoy	July 1, 1993 - November 30, 1997
W. Daniel Ebersole	December 1, 1997 -
Department of Veterans Services	
Peter Wheeler	June 1954 -
Georgia Commission on Women	
Rita Samuels	August 1, 1992 - July 31, 1994
Nellie Dunaway Duke	August 1, 1994 -

State Board of Workers Compensation

James W. Oxendine	October 1, 1986 - December 17, 1992
Harrill L. Dawkins	December 18, 1992 -

Georgia World Congress Center

Daniel A. Graveline	June 1976 - present

Governor Miller's Staff During his Administration

Name:	Hire Date	Termination Date
Governor: Miller, Zell B.	Jan 91	Jan 99
Support Staff:		
Brown, Toni W.	Jan 91	Jan 99
Beazley, Mary	Jan 91	Mar 98
Moore, Charmaine M.	Aug 93	Jan 95
Lucas, Kimberly	Aug 93	Jan 96
Sanders, Carletha	Jan 91	Jan 99
Jones, Judy H.	Dec 94	Jan 99
Whitworth, Morene	Jan 93	Jan 99
Kirkland, Michelle	Jan 91	May 98
Assistant to the First Lady:		
Messer, Beverly T.	Jan 91	Jan 99
Executive Secretary:		
Cohen, Mark H.	July 98	
Wrigley, Steve W.	Nov 94	Jun 98
Ebersole, W. Daniel	May 94	Nov 94
Wrigley, Steve W.	May 93	May 94
Mason, Keith	Jan 91	Jun 93
Support Staff:		
McMillan, Tammy D.	Feb 97	
Dosie, Lisa K.	Nov 94	Feb 97
Cantrell, Betty	May 94	Nov 94
Dosie, Lisa K.	Jan 91	May 94
Shartar, Bettye	May 91	Jan 99
Bennett, Christy	Jan 91	Oct 91
Lucas, Kimberly	Jan 91	Apr 91
Executive Counsel:		
Joslyn-Gaul, Jacqueline Danette	Jul 98	

Name:	Hire Date	Termination Date
Cohen, Mark H.	Jan 95	Jun 98
Snow, Vickie	Dec 94	Aug 95
Wright, Cynthia	Jan 91	Jan 95
Support Staff:		
Johnson, Amy	Jul 98	
Bennett, Christy	Oct 91	Jun 98
Thomas, Barbara	Jan 91	Jun 91
Assistant Executive Counsel:		
Joslyn-Gaul, Jacqueline Danette	Sep 95	Jun 98
Caffarelli, Stephen J.	Oct 91	Mar 95
Phelps, Sarah Catherine	Jan 94	Jan 95
Love, Debra H.	Jan 91	Jun 91
Support Staff:		
Johnson, Amy	Nov 96	Jun 98
Roark, Kelly	Nov 93	Nov 96
Powell, Cyd	Feb 91	Nov 93
Dabbagh, Cherine	Mar 97	May 97
Ledvinka, Christine	Mar 97	May 97
Senior Executive Assistant:		
Wade, Thomas E.	Apr 97	Jan 99
Ebersole, W. Daniel	Nov 94	Apr 97
Watts, David	May 94	Dec 94
Ebersole, W. Daniel	Jan 93	May 94
Wrigley, Steve W.	Jan 91	Nov 92
Support Staff:		
Cantrell, Bettye B.	Aug 93	Jan 99
Dosie, Lisa K.	Jan 91	Nov 92
Executive Assistant:		
Fullerton, Martha	Apr 97	Jan 98
Support Staff:		
Snow, Stacey	Aug 97	Jan 98
Executive Assistant:		
Mangum, William C. Jr.	Jan 91	Apr 91

Name:	**Hire Date**	**Termination Date**
Support Staff:		
Adams, Kristi	Jan 91	Apr 91
Director of Communications:		
Bentley, Tim E.	May 98	Jan 99
Dent, Richard	Sep 93	May 98
Reece, Charles C.	May 91	Sep 93
Stephens, William	Jan 91	May 91
Deputy Director of Communications:		
Lagana, Susan P.	Jul 98	Jan 99
Carvell, Candice K.	Jan 96	May 98
Tompkins, Stephen G.	Jan 95	Sep 97
Rickles, Robert G.	Jan 95	Dec 94
Moody, Peggy A.	Aug 92	Feb 94
Support Staff:		
Begina, Courtney A.	Aug 98	Jan 99
Roberson, Timothy R.	Apr 96	Oct 97
George, Tangelia N.	Aug 94	Sep 94
Bingham, Pamela	Jan 91	May 91
Blackburn, William H.	Jun 91	Sep 91
Braselton, Kim	Jan 91	May 91
Robey, Denise S.	Dec 94	Aug 95
Bufford, Joe E.	Dec 91	May 91
Cain, Kimberly R.	Dec 97	Aug 98
Cline, Darin R.	Jan 95	Jan 96
Evans, Mary Ann K.	Aug 93	Jan 96
Floyd, Pam Kendall	Sep 92	Nov 95
Fitzgerald, Hattie Elaine	Jan 91	Jan 99
Garmany-Ylla, Judy	Oct 93	Dec 97
Hamilton, Amanda Nolen	Oct 97	Jun 98
Hudgins, Kimberly A.	Jan 98	Jan 99
Rudnik, Stephanie A.	Jan 91	Apr 91
Koppel, Tara	Mar 95	Mar 96
Layson, Jean A.	Feb 92	Mar 96
Lee, Peter M.	May 91	Jan 93
Moore, Charmaine M.	Aug 92	Apr 93
Lucas, Kimberly	Apr 91	Aug 93

Name:	Hire Date	Termination Date
Speech Writer		
Eby-Ebersole, Sarah	Jan 91	Jan 99
Director of Community Affairs:		
Bates, Frank	Jan 91	Jun 97
Support Staff:		
Sims, Deborah A.	Nov 92	Jun 97
Graham, Linda J.	Jan 91	Jan 93
Director, Intergovernmental Relations:		
Kilgore, Kenneth E.	Sept. 92	Dec. 94
Mead, Howard	Jan 91	Dec 93
Support Staff:		
McMillan, Tammy D.	Jun 96	Feb 97
Cherry, Monica	Jan 95	Apr 96
Executive Assistant, Education & Health:		
Vollmer, Michael	Jan 91	Dec 93
Support Staff:		
Hayes, Brenda	Aug 92	Dec 93
Moore, Charmaine M.	Apr 93	Aug 93
English, Ronda L.	Jan 91	Jul 93
Assistant for Legal Affairs:		
Hicks, Marvin	Jan 91	Aug 94
Special Projects Coordinator:		
Gilland, Martha	Nov 94	Feb 96
Jones, Judy	Apr 94	Nov 94
Gilland, Martha	Jan 91	Apr 94
Director, Constituent Services:		
Shartar, Bettye	Jun 93	Jan 99
Preston, Rosemary D.	Jan 91	Nov 93
Support Staff:		
Bevelle, Deborah K.	Jan 91	Jan 99
Hudson, Ethelyn	Feb 91	Jan 99
Mulligan, Patricia A.	Aug 94	Jan 99
Butler, Terria R.	Jan 91	Jan 99
Knight, Gwendolyn R.	Jul 91	Jan 99

Name:	**Hire Date**	**Termination Date**
Brooks, Jan	Oct 93	Jan 99
Hall, Gwen	Mar 98	Jan 99
Hunnicutt, Pam Mitchell	Aug 92	Jan 99
Perkins, Amy R.	Jun 97	Jan 99
Fillingame, Lasonya	Jan 94	Mar 98
Suggs, Gayle B.	Jan 91	May 97
Sheheane, Dene H.	Jan 93	Jul 94
Jarrett, Carolyn P.	Jan 91	Dec 93
Sanders, Tracy L.	Oct 93	Jul 98
Director, Case Work:		
Dobson, Ann Y.	Jan 93	Dec 94
McCord, Jeffrey L.	Jun 93	Dec 96
Intern Director:		
Manry, Theresa B.	May 91	Jan 99
Cooper, Kenneth	Jan 91	May 91
Support Staff:		
Usher, Michelle S.	Jan 91	Jan 99
Butts, Laura, A.	Apr 98	Jan 99
Tucker, Richard L. Jr.	Jan 95	Jan 99
Reid, Thomas	Jul 91	Jul 93
Manry, Theresa B.	Jan 91	May 91
Conway, Brendan	Feb 94	Apr 95
Long, Scott	Jan 91	Nov 92
Chopin, Alexandra	Jun 94	Sep 94
Director of Appointments:		
McCord, Jeffrey L.	Dec 96	Jan 99
Driskill, Linda	Jan 91	Jun 96
Support Staff:		
McMahon, Susan F.	Aug 98	Jan 99
Phillips, Jennifer A.	Jan 97	Aug 98
Swingley, Kari M.	Sep 92	Feb 94
Carr, Mitzi	Jan 91	Jul 96
Special Assistant:		
Key, John W.	Dec 94	Feb 98
Wise, Brittley C.	Dec 96	May 97
Meeks, Kevin G.	Jun 93	May 96

Name:	**Hire Date**	**Termination Date**
Butler, Joselyn H.	Jan 95	Nov 95
Hall, Thad	Jan 91	Jul 93
Part-Time Assistant:		
Patel, Sima	Sep 98	Jan 99
Wachter, Eric M.	May 98	Aug 98
Newsome, Lauren L.	Jun 98	Jun 98
Disantis, Denise A.	Jan 96	Aug 96
Mitchell, Zak A.	Sep 96	Dec 96
Floor Leaders Support Staff:		
Ewing, Susan C.	Nov 93	Jan 99
Howell, Linda Tirado	Jun 97	Jan 99
Chapman, Arline	Aug 91	May 97
Norman, Barbara	Jan 93	Nov 93
Orchard, Barbara	Jan 91	Jan 91
Strawhand, Jane S.	Aug 91	Dec 92
Harkins, Marvin	Feb 98	Mar 98
Photographer:		
Heath, Laura C.	Aug 95	Jan 99
Kandul, Phyllis B.	Jan 91	Jun 95
Computer Support:		
Anderson, Larry	Jan 95	Jan 99
Porter:		
Bruce Phyllis	Jun 96	Jan 99
Scott, Clifford	Jan 91	Feb 94
Grimes, Luther	Jan 91	Jun 93

Index